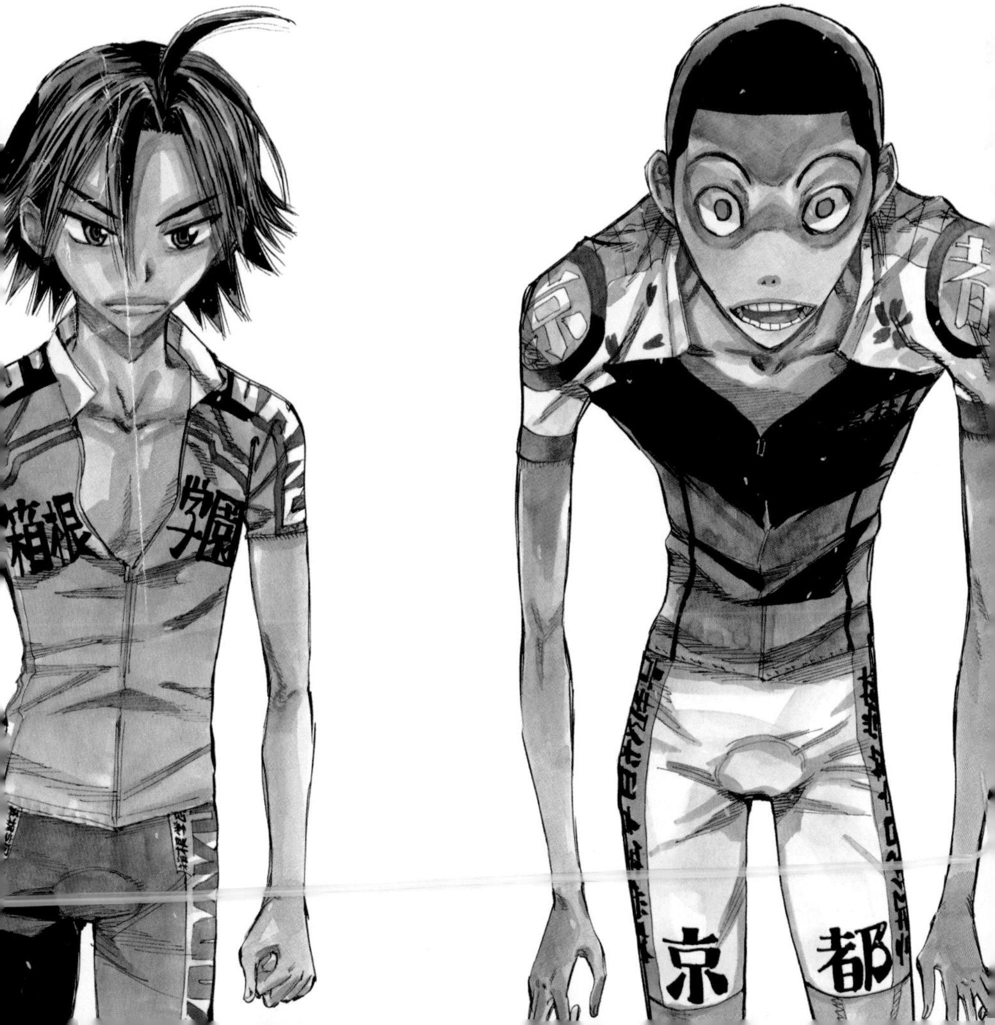
箱根
学園
京 都

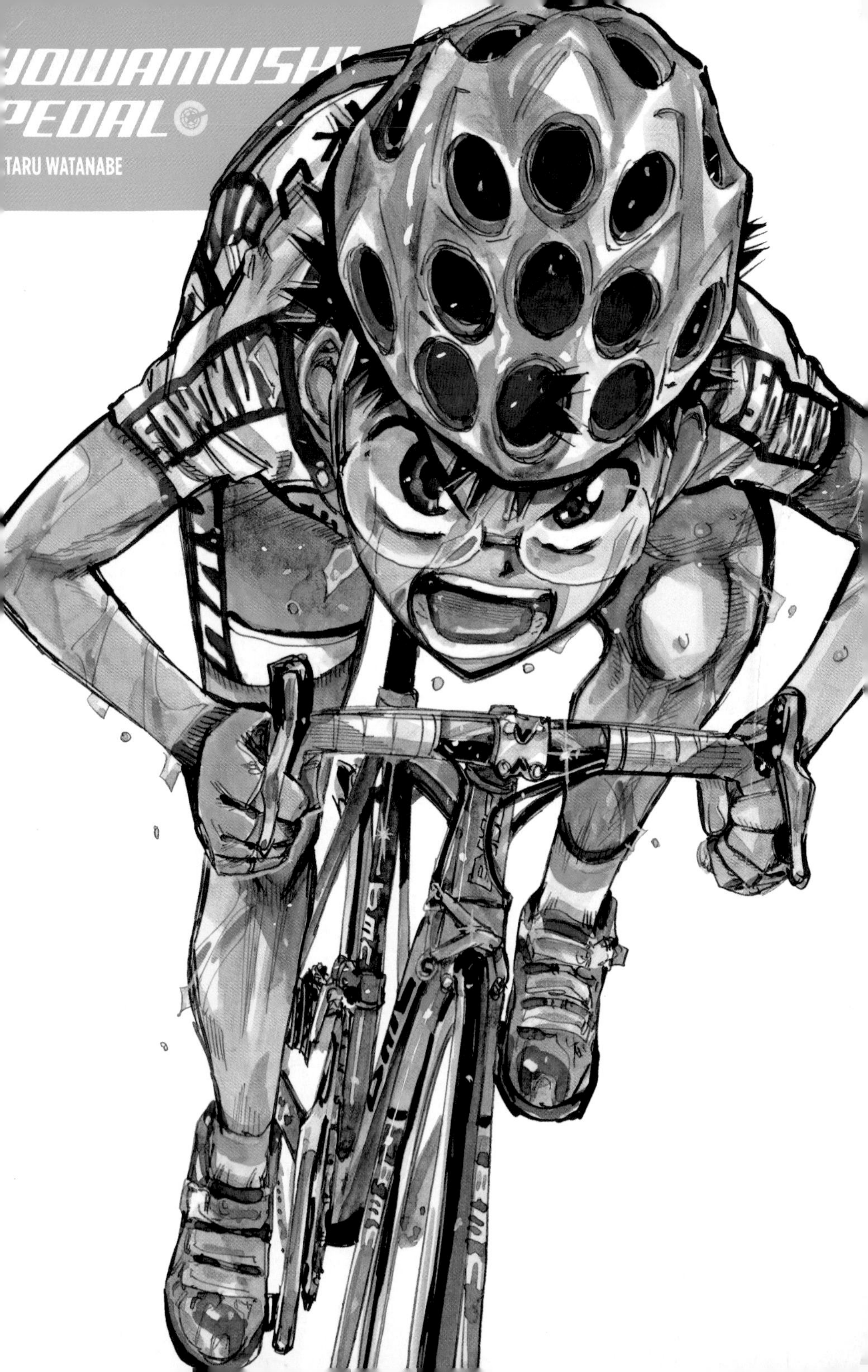
YOWAMUSHI
PEDAL
TARU WATANABE

YOWAMUSHI PEDAL

12

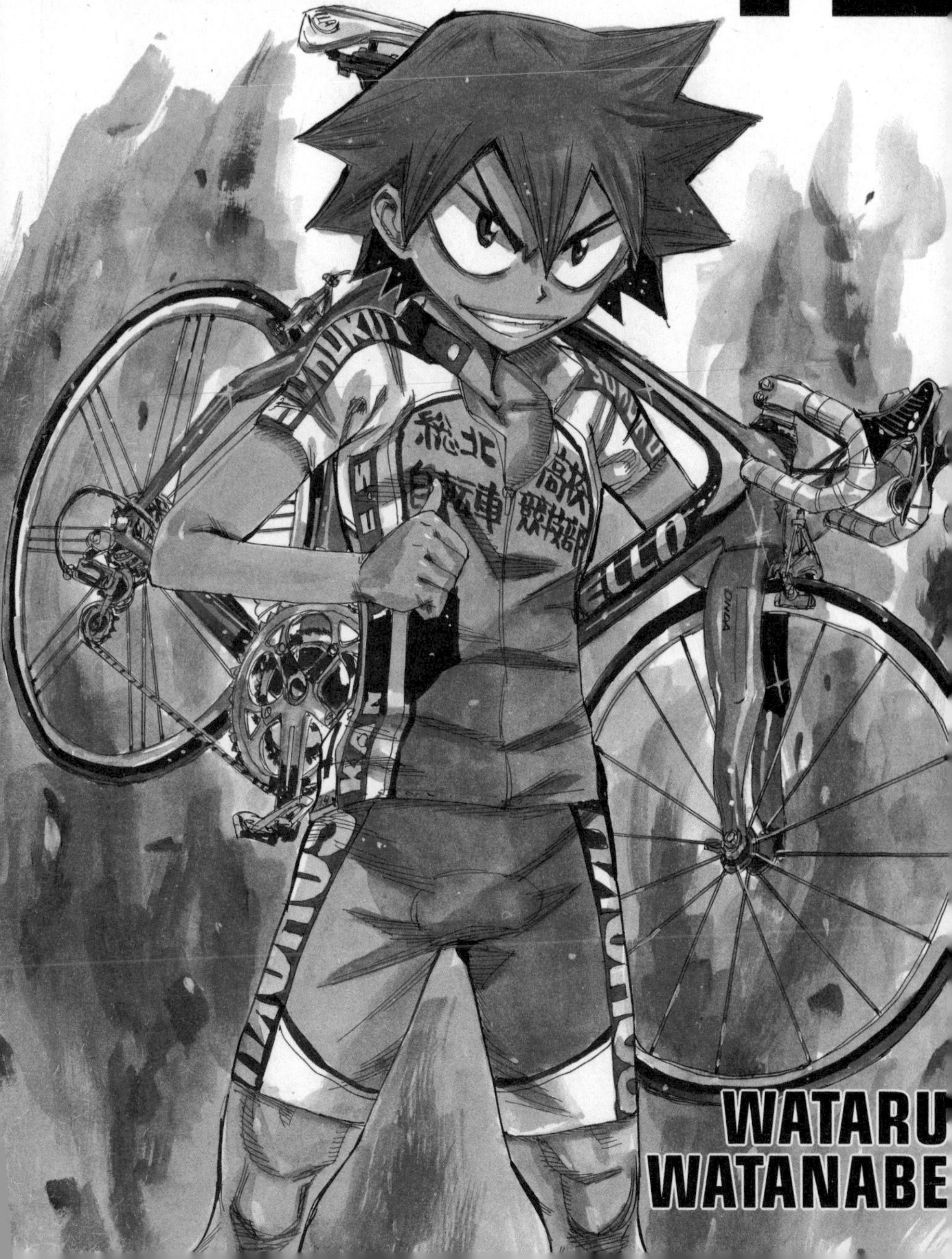
総北
高校
自転車競技部

WATARU WATANABE

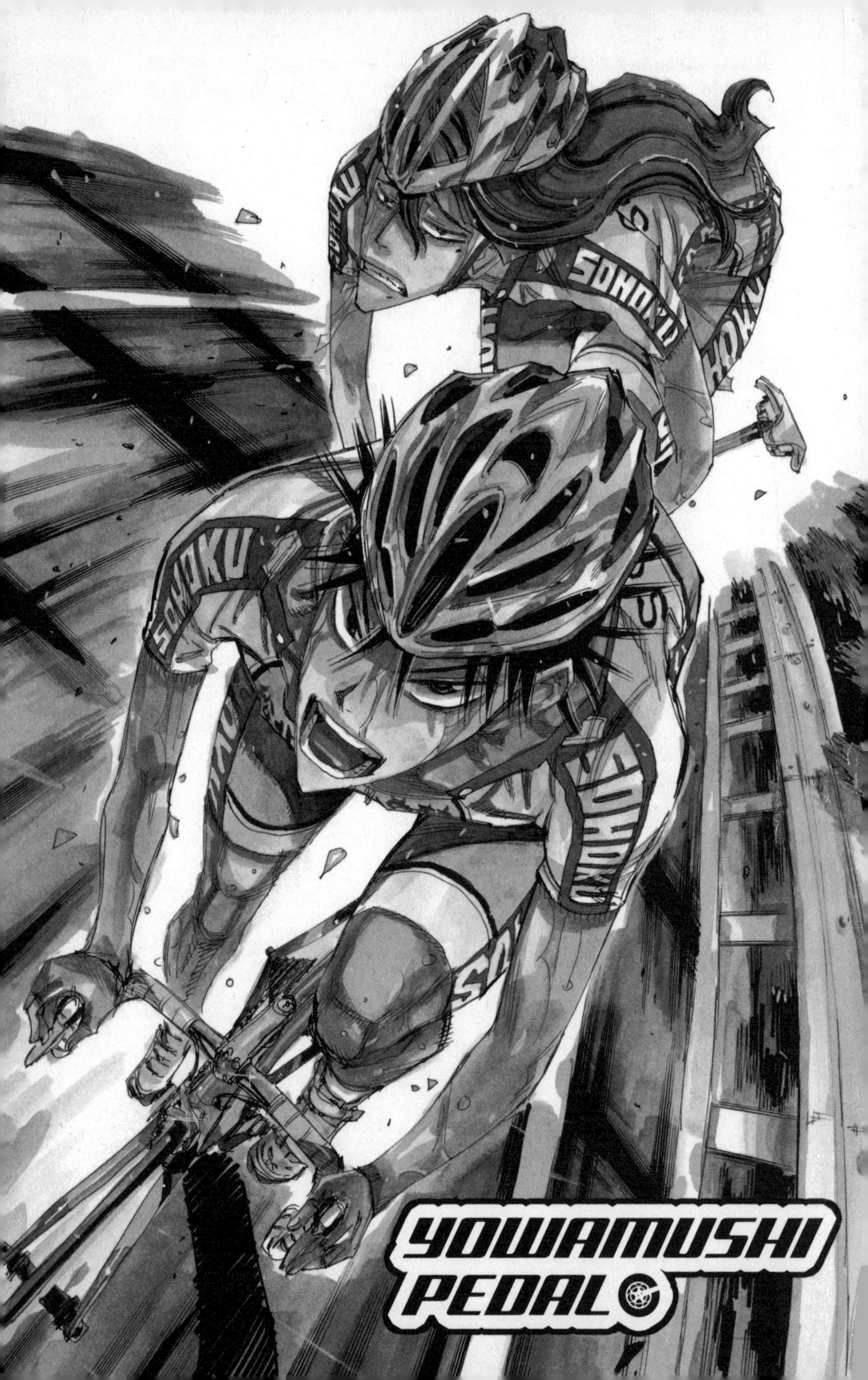
YOWAMUSHI
PEDAL

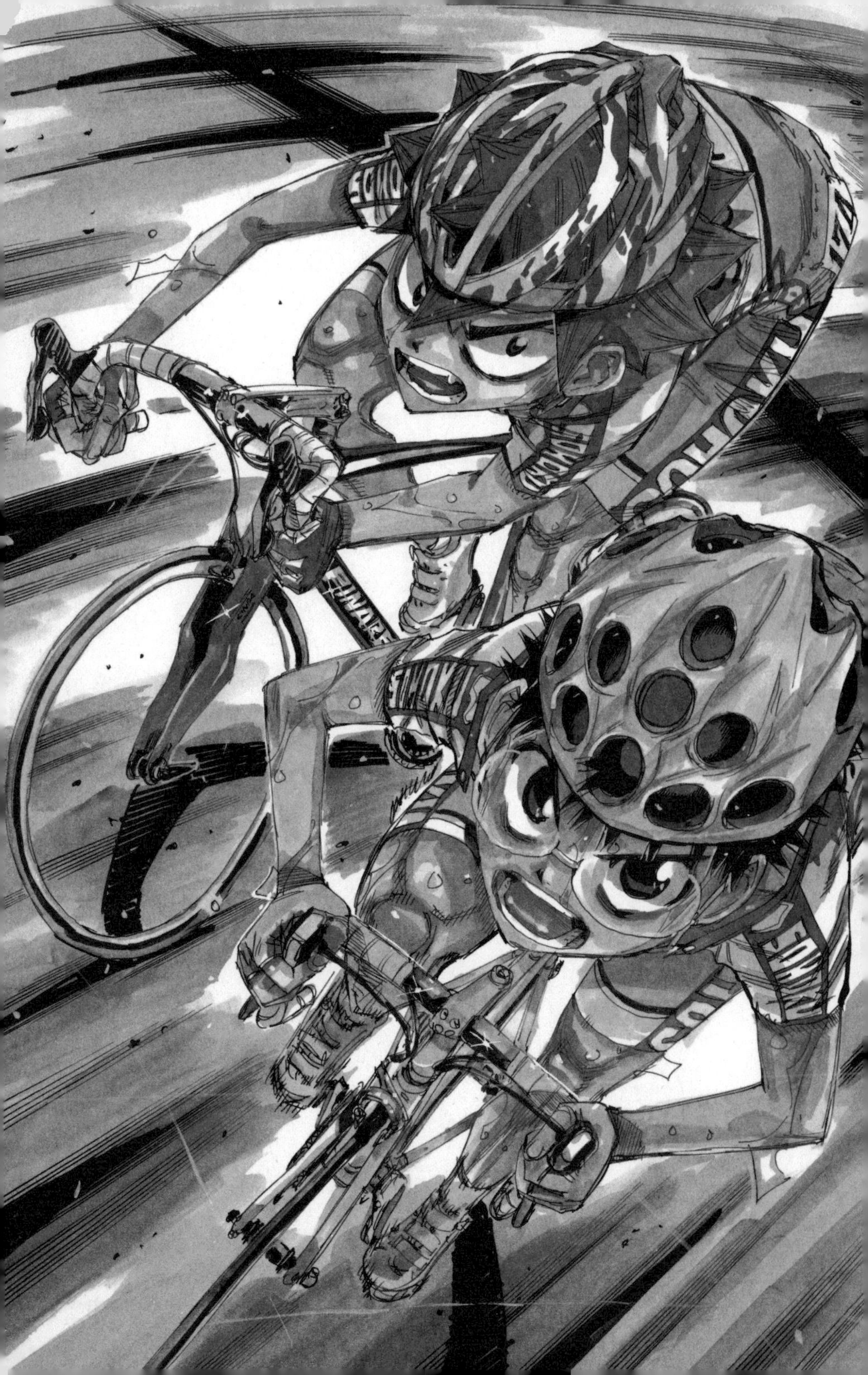

YOWAMUSHI PEDAL

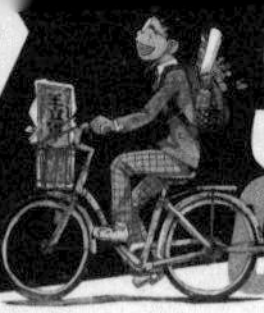

STORY & CHARACTER

INTRODUCTION

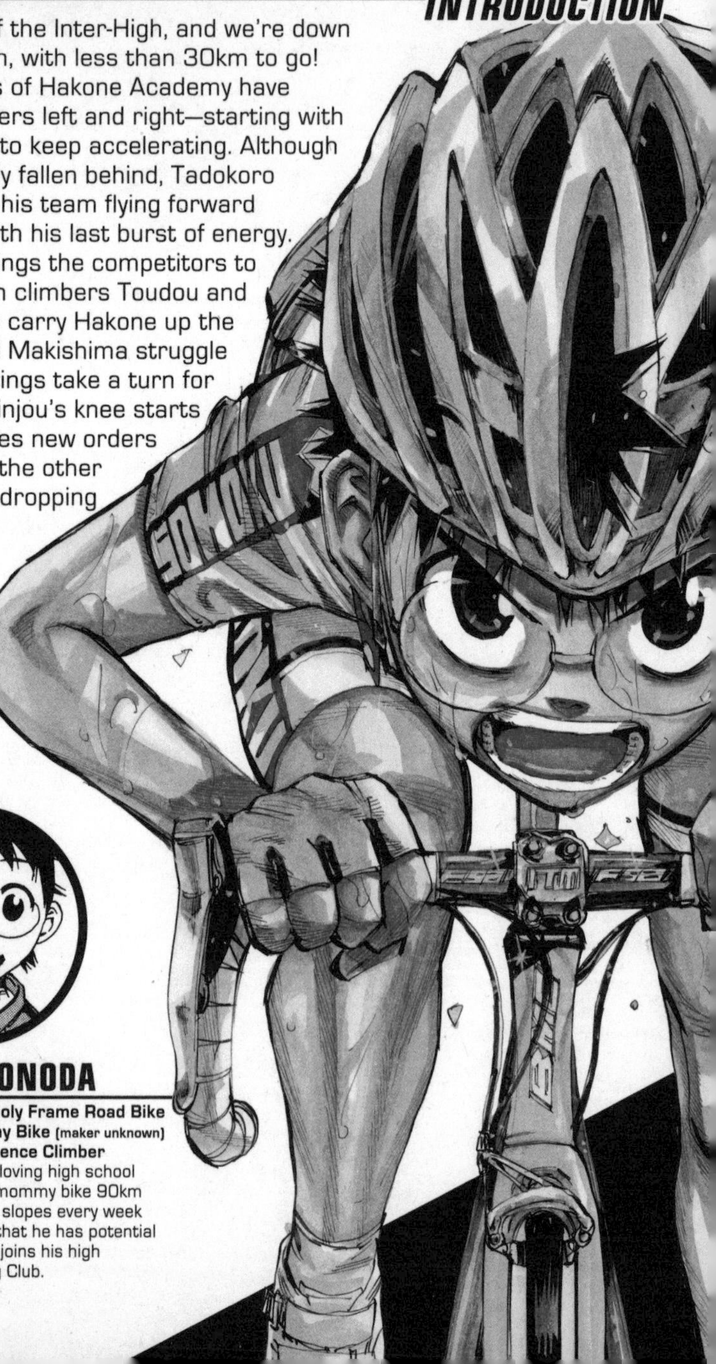

SOHOKU

It's the final day of the Inter-High, and we're down to the final stretch, with less than 30km to go! The reigning kings of Hakone Academy have been dropping riders left and right—starting with Izumida—in order to keep accelerating. Although Sohoku had initially fallen behind, Tadokoro manages to send his team flying forward toward Hakone with his last burst of energy. The final stage brings the competitors to the mountain, with climbers Toudou and Manami poised to carry Hakone up the slopes. Kinjou and Makishima struggle to keep up, and things take a turn for the worst when Kinjou's knee starts to give out. He gives new orders to Sakamichi and the other first-years before dropping out. With Kinjou's will driving them, Makishima and the first-years have their sights set on Hakone and the mountain that looms ahead!!

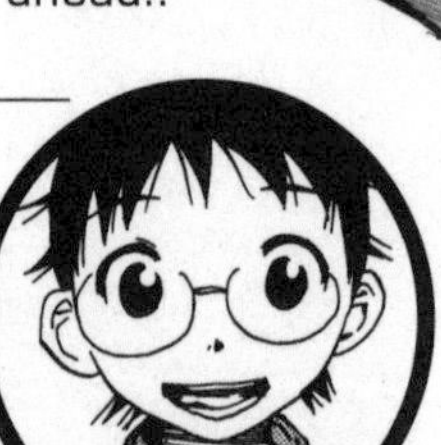

SAKAMICHI ONODA

Preferred Bike: **Chromoly Frame Road Bike**
Mommy Bike (maker unknown)
Cycling Style: **High Cadence Climber**
Sakamichi is an anime-loving high school student who rides his mommy bike 90km round- trip up extreme slopes every week to visit Akiba. Hearing that he has potential as a cyclist, Sakamichi joins his high school's Bicycle Racing Club.

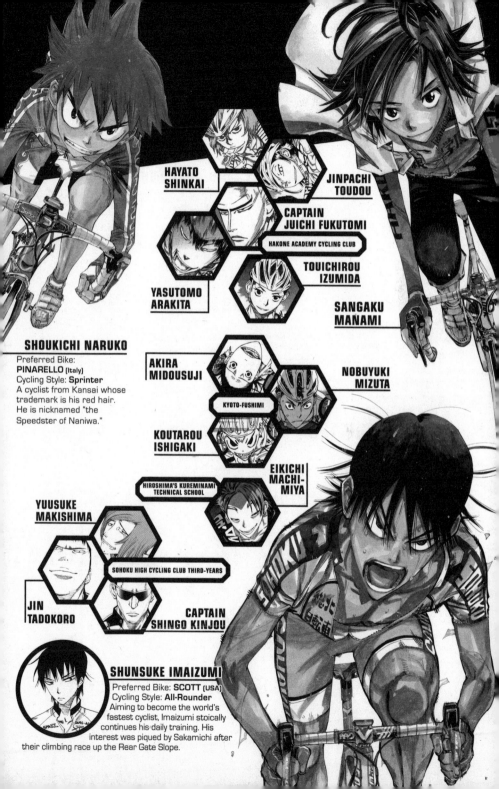

HAYATO
SHINKAI

JINPACHI
TOUDOU

CAPTAIN
JUICHI FUKUTOMI

HAKONE ACADEMY CYCLING CLUB

TOUICHIROU
IZUMIDA

YASUTOMO
ARAKITA

SANGAKU
MANAMI

SHOUKICHI NARUKO
Preferred Bike:
PINARELLO (Italy)
Cycling Style: **Sprinter**
A cyclist from Kansai whose
trademark is his red hair.
He is nicknamed "the
Speedster of Naniwa."

AKIRA
MIDOUSUJI

NOBUYUKI
MIZUTA

KYOTO-FUSHIMI

KOUTAROU
ISHIGAKI

EIKICHI
MACHI-
MIYA

HIROSHIMA'S KUREMINAMI
TECHNICAL SCHOOL

YUUSUKE
MAKISHIMA

SOHOKU HIGH CYCLING CLUB THIRD-YEARS

JIN
TADOKORO

CAPTAIN
SHINGO KINJOU

SHUNSUKE IMAIZUMI
Preferred Bike: SCOTT (USA)
Cycling Style: **All-Rounder**
Aiming to become the world's
fastest cyclist, Imaizumi stoically
continues his daily training. His
interest was piqued by Sakamichi after
their climbing race up the Rear Gate Slope.

VOL.12

YOWAMUSHI PEDAL
CONTENTS

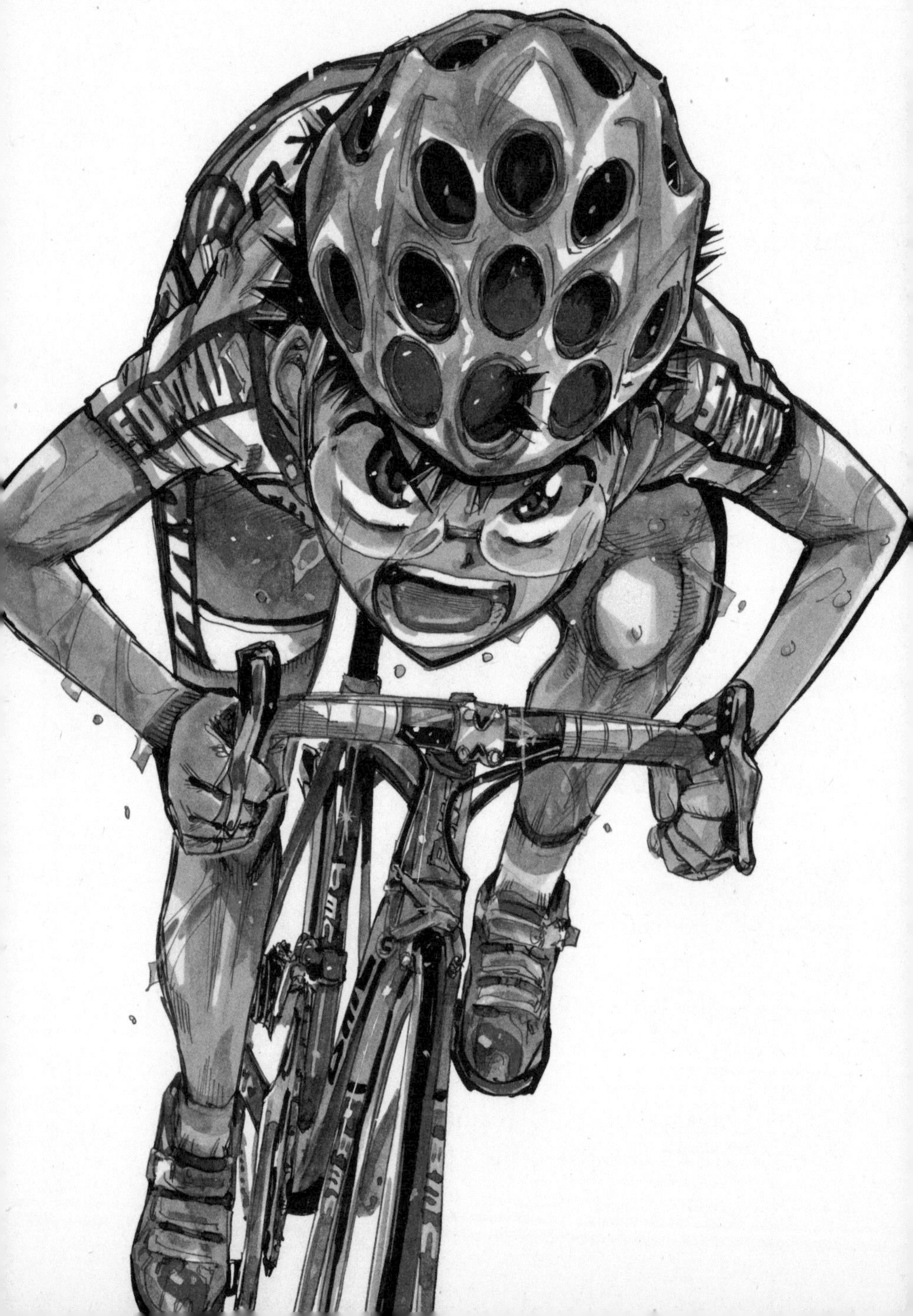

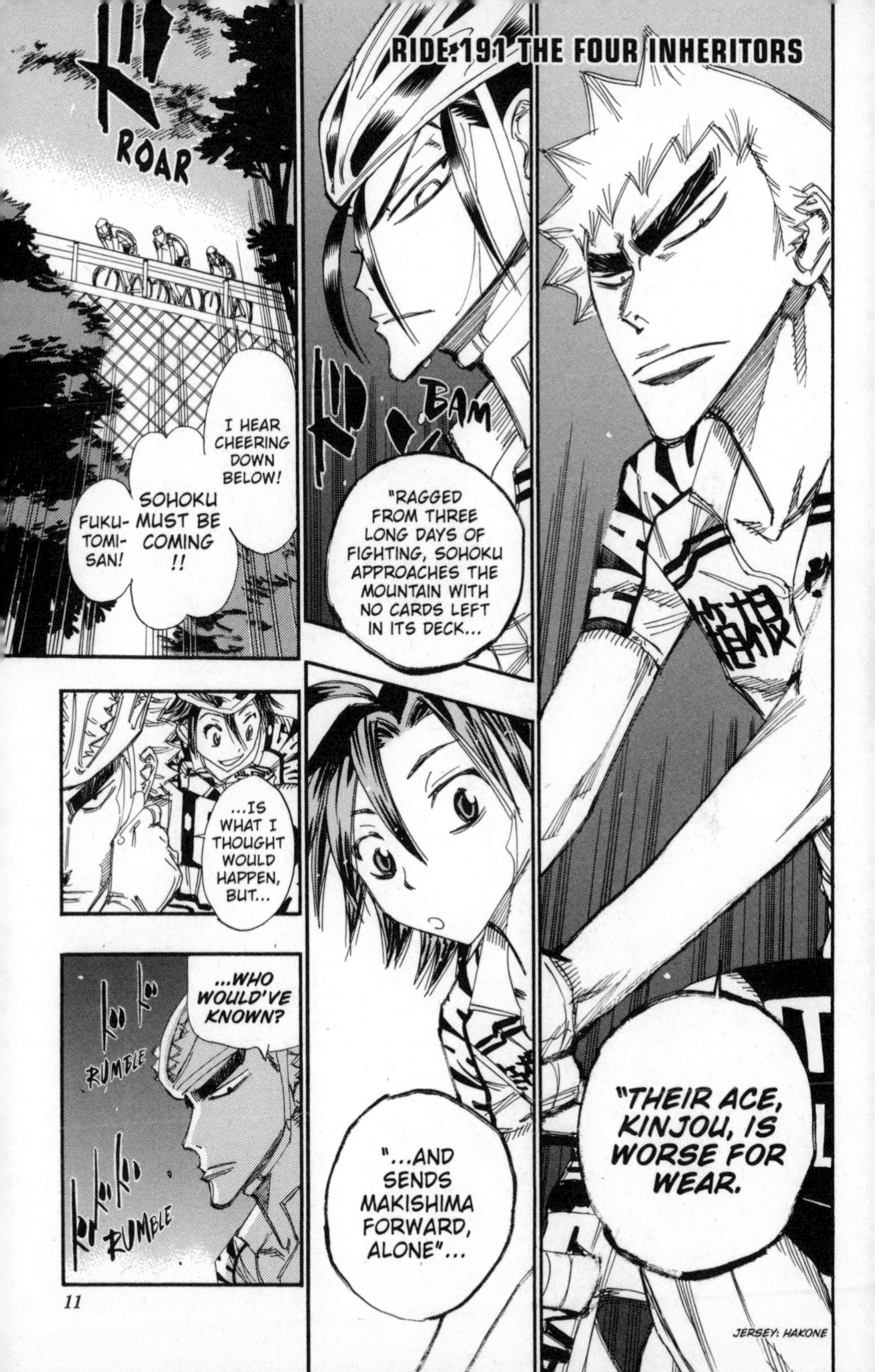
RIDE:191 THE FOUR INHERITORS
"THEIR ACE, KINJOU, IS WORSE FOR WEAR.
JERSEY: HAKONE
BAM
"RAGGED FROM THREE LONG DAYS OF FIGHTING, SOHOKU APPROACHES THE MOUNTAIN WITH NO CARDS LEFT IN ITS DECK...
ROAR
I HEAR CHEERING DOWN BELOW!
SOHOKU MUST BE COMING!!
FUKU-TOMI-SAN!
"...AND SENDS MAKISHIMA FORWARD, ALONE"...
...IS WHAT I THOUGHT WOULD HAPPEN, BUT...
...WHO WOULD'VE KNOWN?
RUMBLE
RUMBLE

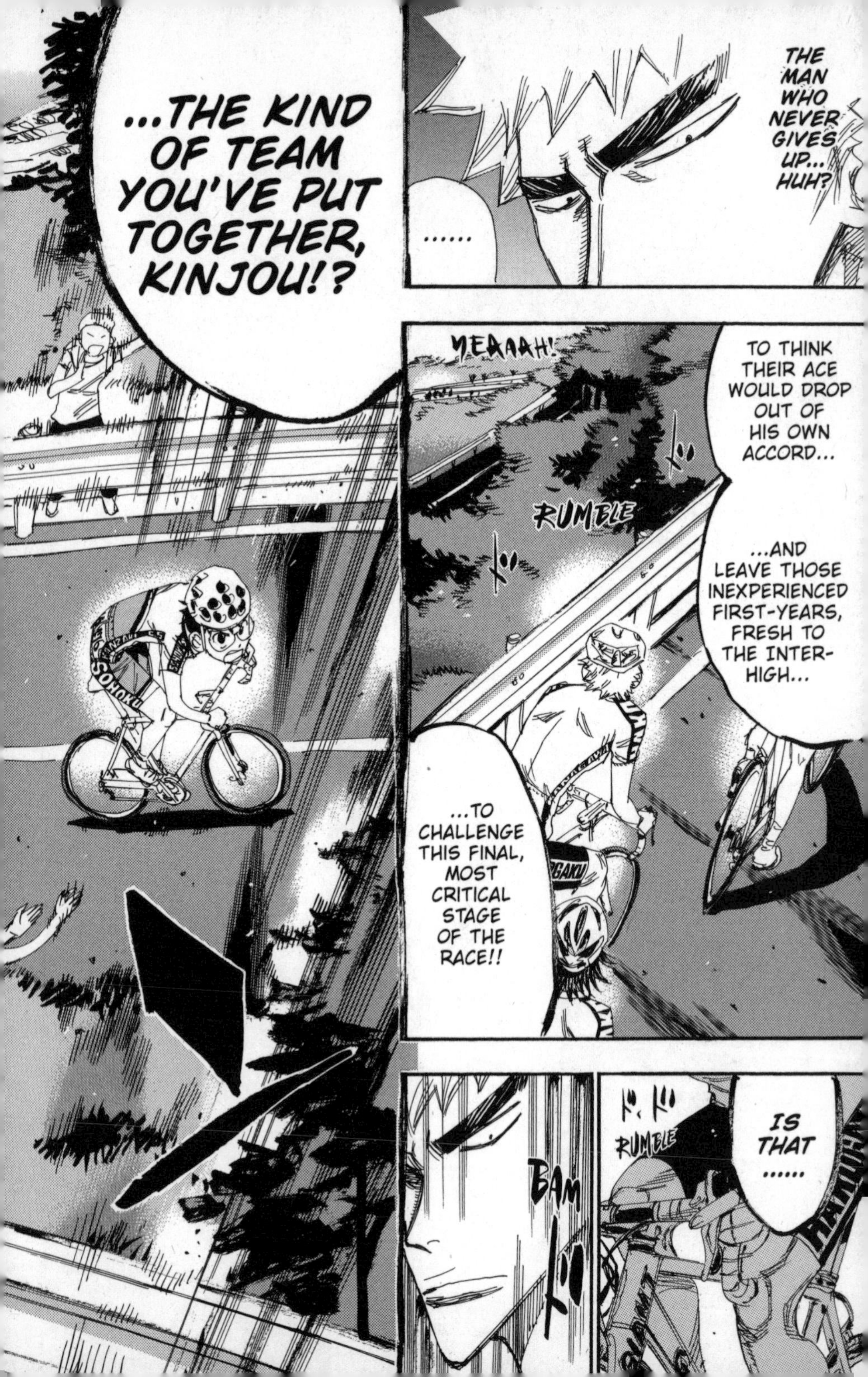
THE MAN WHO NEVER GIVES UP... HUH?
......
YEAAAH!
TO THINK THEIR ACE WOULD DROP OUT OF HIS OWN ACCORD...
RUMBLE
...AND LEAVE THOSE INEXPERIENCED FIRST-YEARS, FRESH TO THE INTER-HIGH...
...TO CHALLENGE THIS FINAL, MOST CRITICAL STAGE OF THE RACE!!
RUMBLE
IS THAT ......
BAM
...THE KIND OF TEAM YOU'VE PUT TOGETHER, KINJOU!?

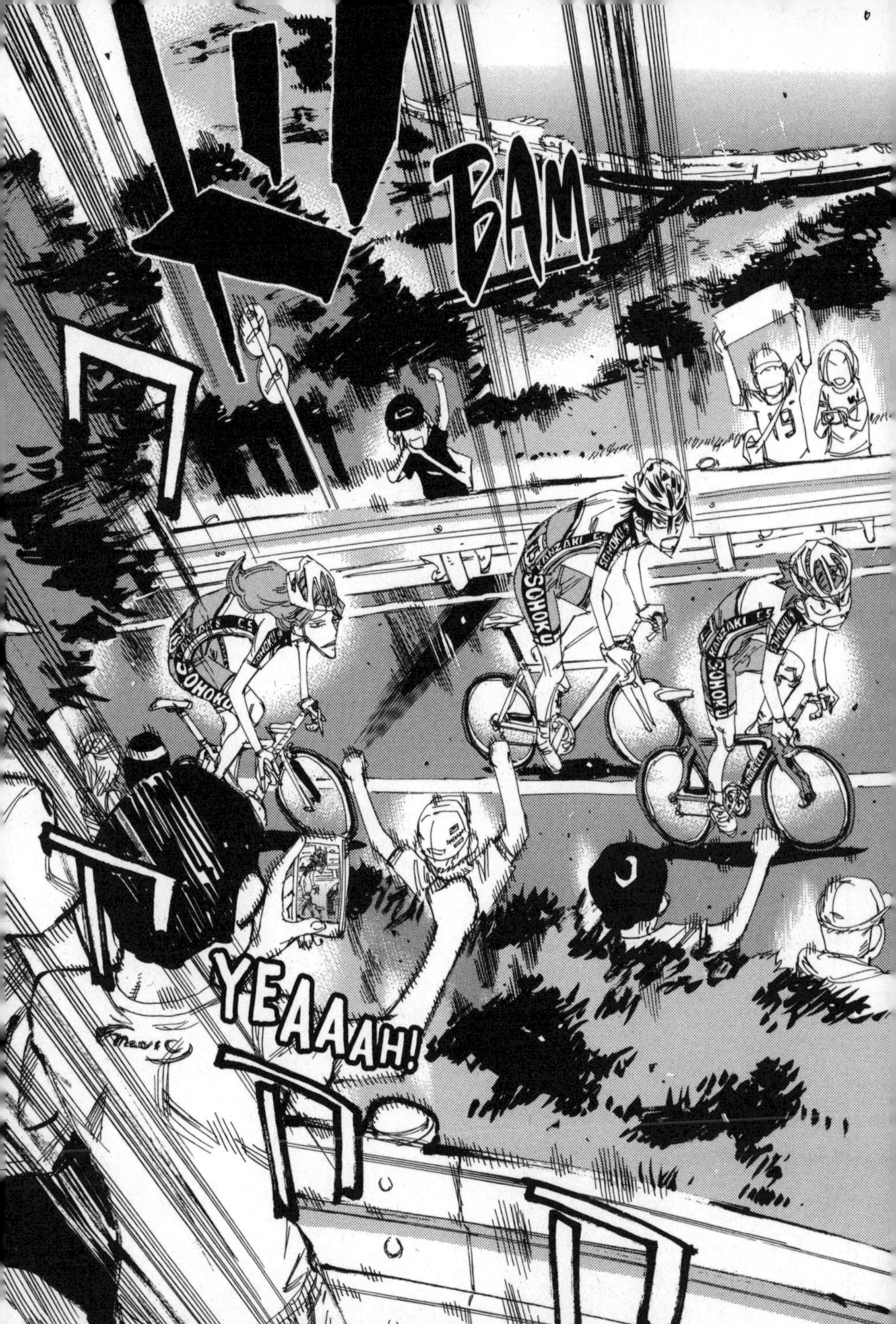
BAM
YEAAAAH!

RIDE.191 THE FOUR INHERITORS

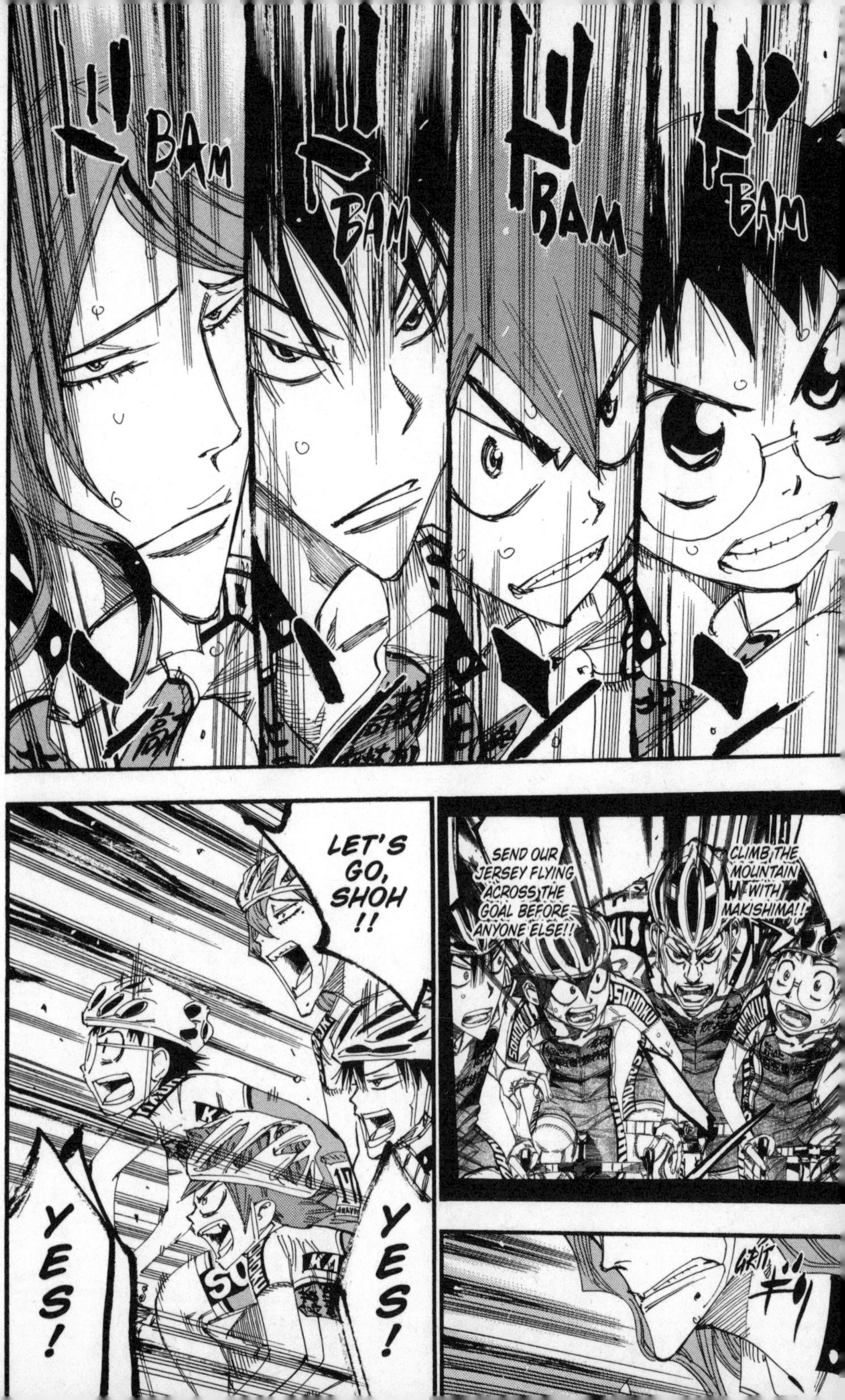
BAM
BAM
BAM
BAM
CLIMB THE MOUNTAIN WITH MAKISHIMA!!
SEND OUR JERSEY FLYING ACROSS THE GOAL BEFORE ANYONE ELSE!!
GRIT
LET'S GO, SHOH!!
YES!
YES!

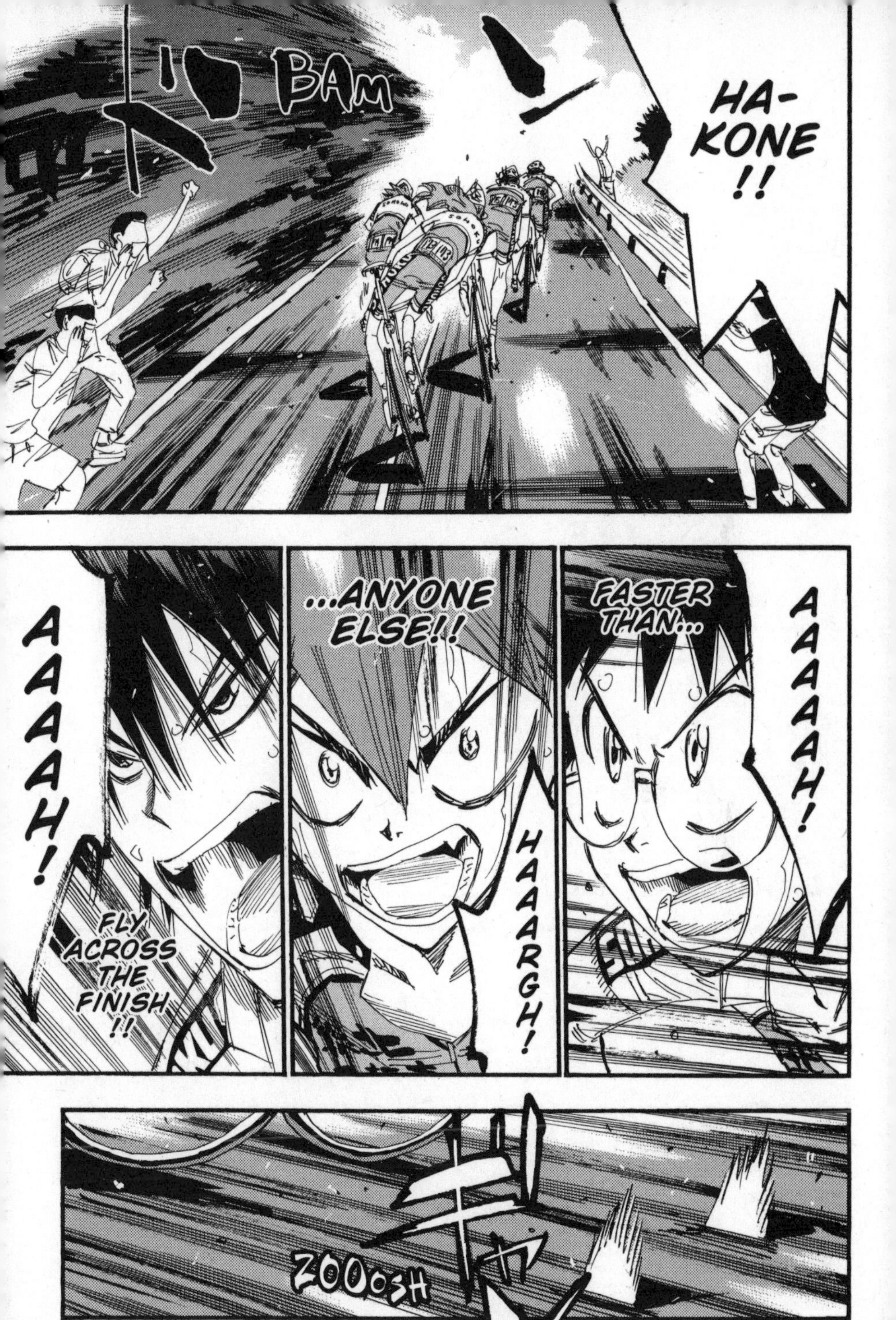
HA-
KONE
!!
BAM
FASTER THAN...
AAAAAAH!
...ANYONE ELSE!!
HAAAARGH!
AAAAAH!
FLY ACROSS THE FINISH!!
ZOOOSH

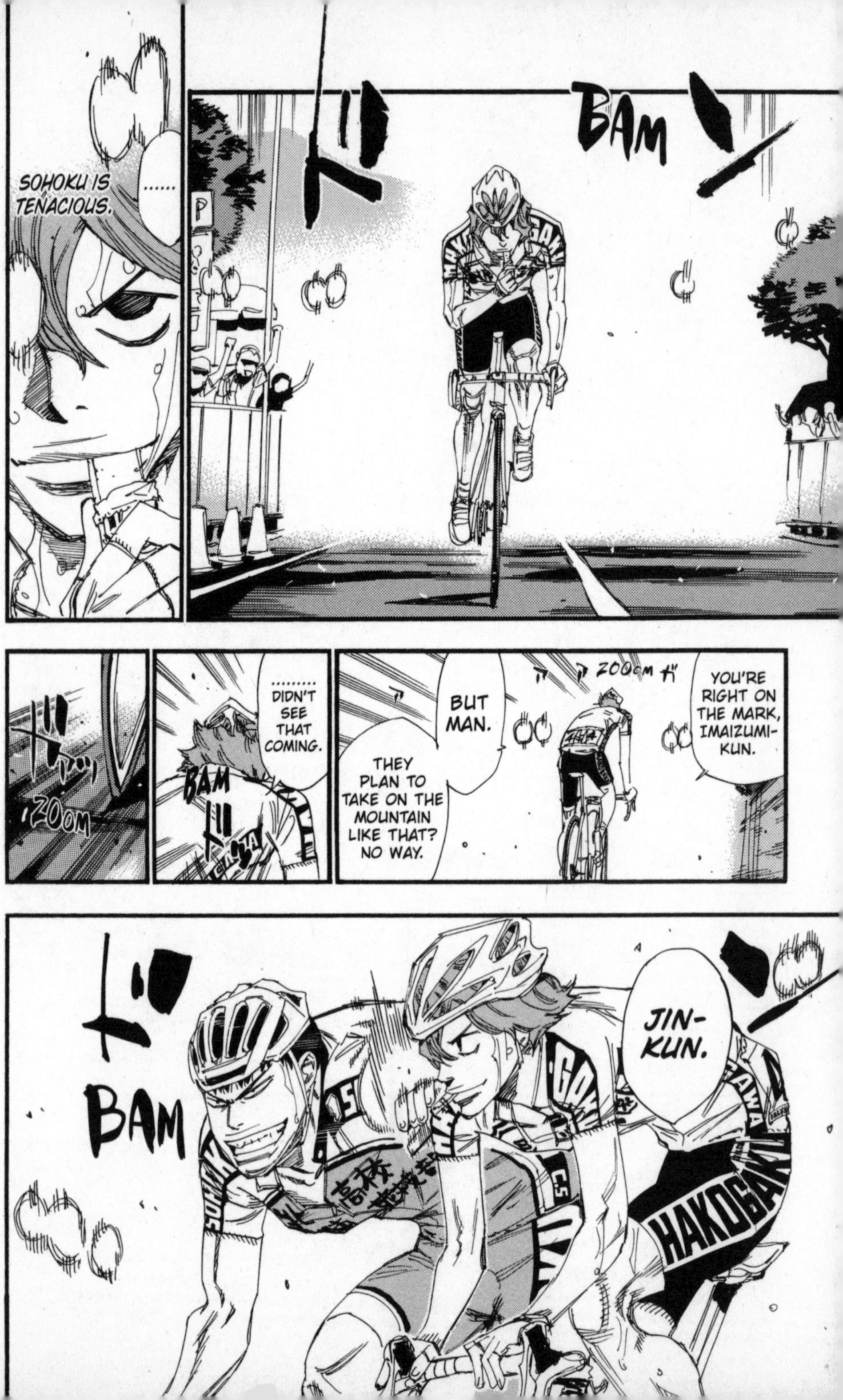
BAM
SOHOKU IS TENACIOUS.
......
ZOOOM
YOU'RE RIGHT ON THE MARK, IMAIZUMI-KUN.
BUT MAN.
THEY PLAN TO TAKE ON THE MOUNTAIN LIKE THAT? NO WAY.
....
DIDN'T SEE THAT COMING.
BAM
ZOOM
JIN-KUN.
BAM

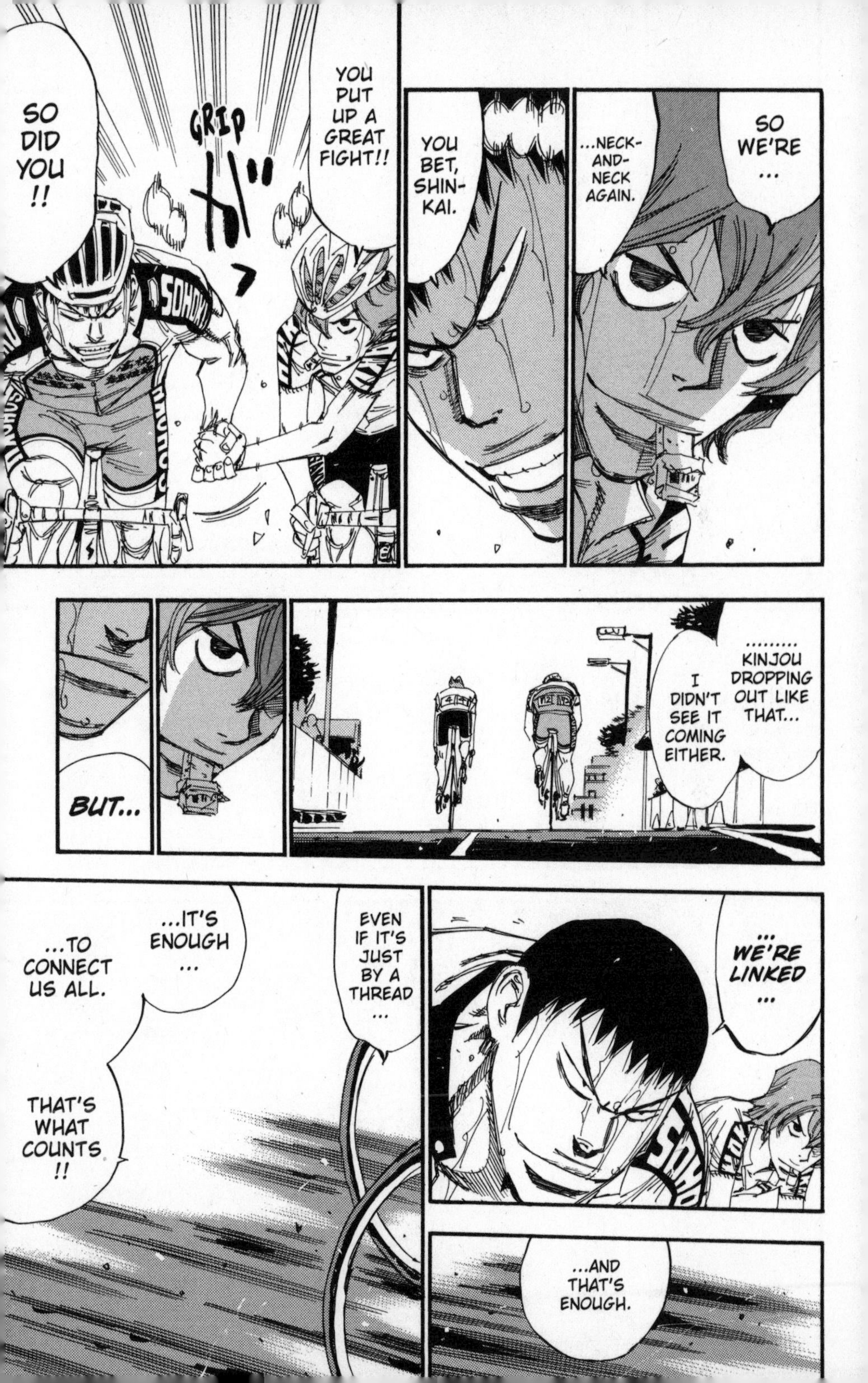
SO WE'RE ...
...NECK-AND-NECK AGAIN.
YOU BET, SHINKAI.
YOU PUT UP A GREAT FIGHT!!
GRIP
SO DID YOU !!
.... KINJOU DROPPING OUT LIKE THAT...
I DIDN'T SEE IT COMING EITHER.
BUT...
... WE'RE LINKED ...
...AND THAT'S ENOUGH.
EVEN IF IT'S JUST BY A THREAD ...
...IT'S ENOUGH ...
...TO CONNECT US ALL.
THAT'S WHAT COUNTS !!

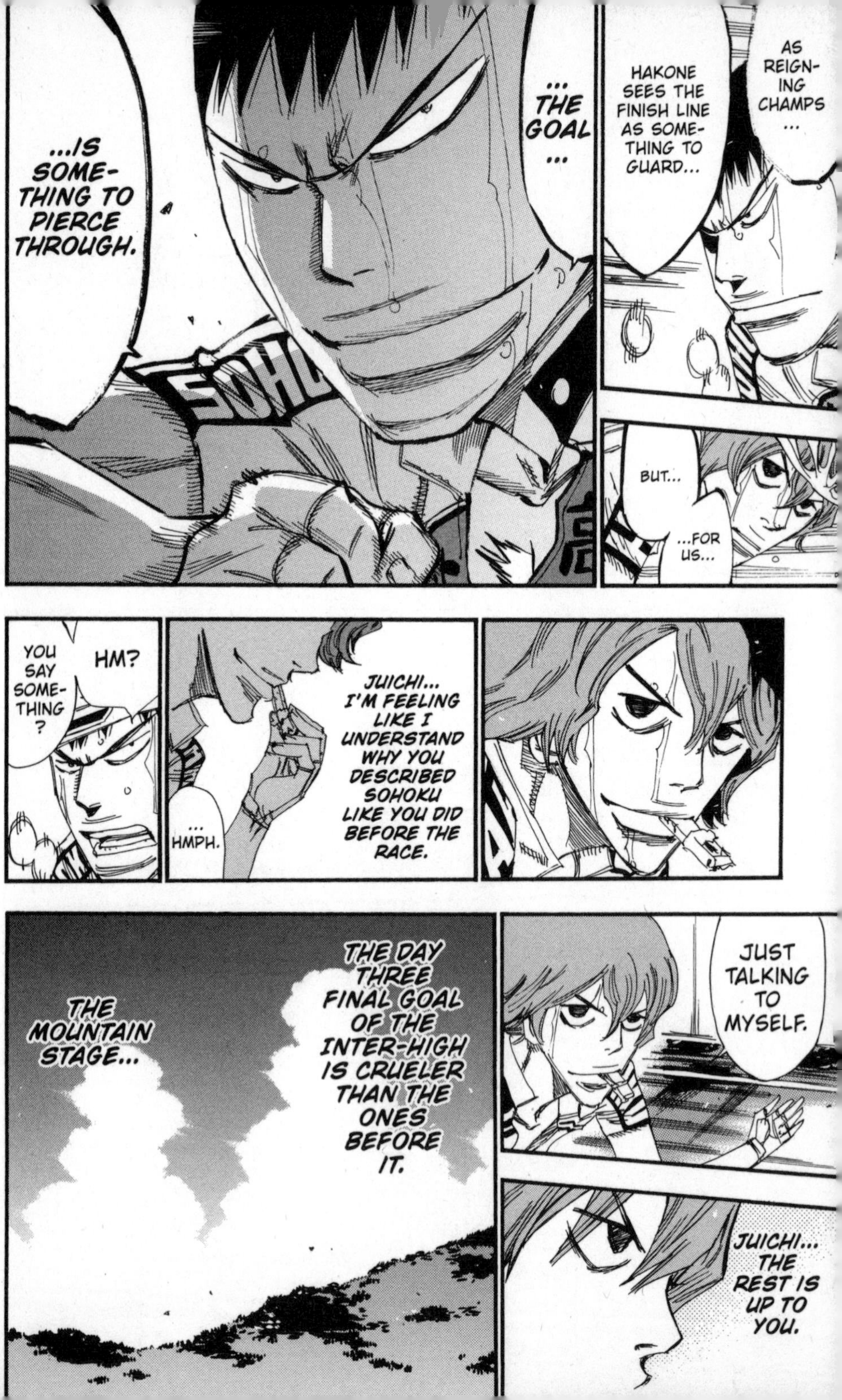
AS REIGNING CHAMPS...
HAKONE SEES THE FINISH LINE AS SOMETHING TO GUARD...
BUT...
...FOR US...
...THE GOAL...
...IS SOMETHING TO PIERCE THROUGH.
JUICHI... I'M FEELING LIKE I UNDERSTAND WHY YOU DESCRIBED SOHOKU LIKE YOU DID BEFORE THE RACE.
...HMPH.
HM?
YOU SAY SOMETHING?
JUST TALKING TO MYSELF.
JUICHI... THE REST IS UP TO YOU.
THE DAY THREE FINAL GOAL OF THE INTER-HIGH IS CRUELER THAN THE ONES BEFORE IT.
THE MOUNTAIN STAGE...

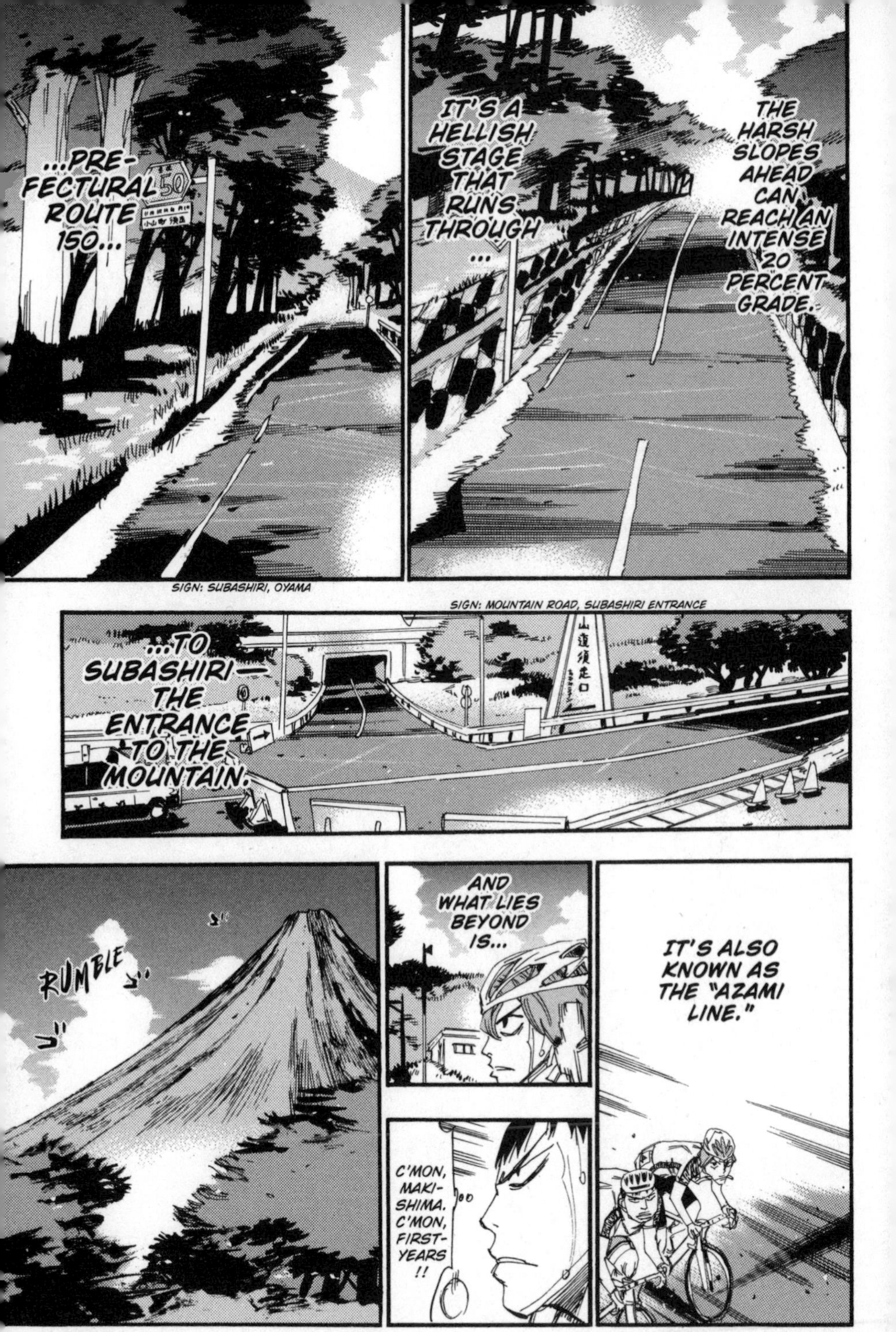
THE HARSH SLOPES AHEAD CAN REACH AN INTENSE 20 PERCENT GRADE.
IT'S A HELLISH STAGE THAT RUNS THROUGH...
...PRE-FECTURAL ROUTE 150...
SIGN: SUBASHIRI, OYAMA
SIGN: MOUNTAIN ROAD, SUBASHIRI ENTRANCE
...TO SUBASHIRI—THE ENTRANCE TO THE MOUNTAIN.
IT'S ALSO KNOWN AS THE "AZAMI LINE."
AND WHAT LIES BEYOND IS...
C'MON, MAKI-SHIMA. C'MON, FIRST-YEARS!!
RUMBLE

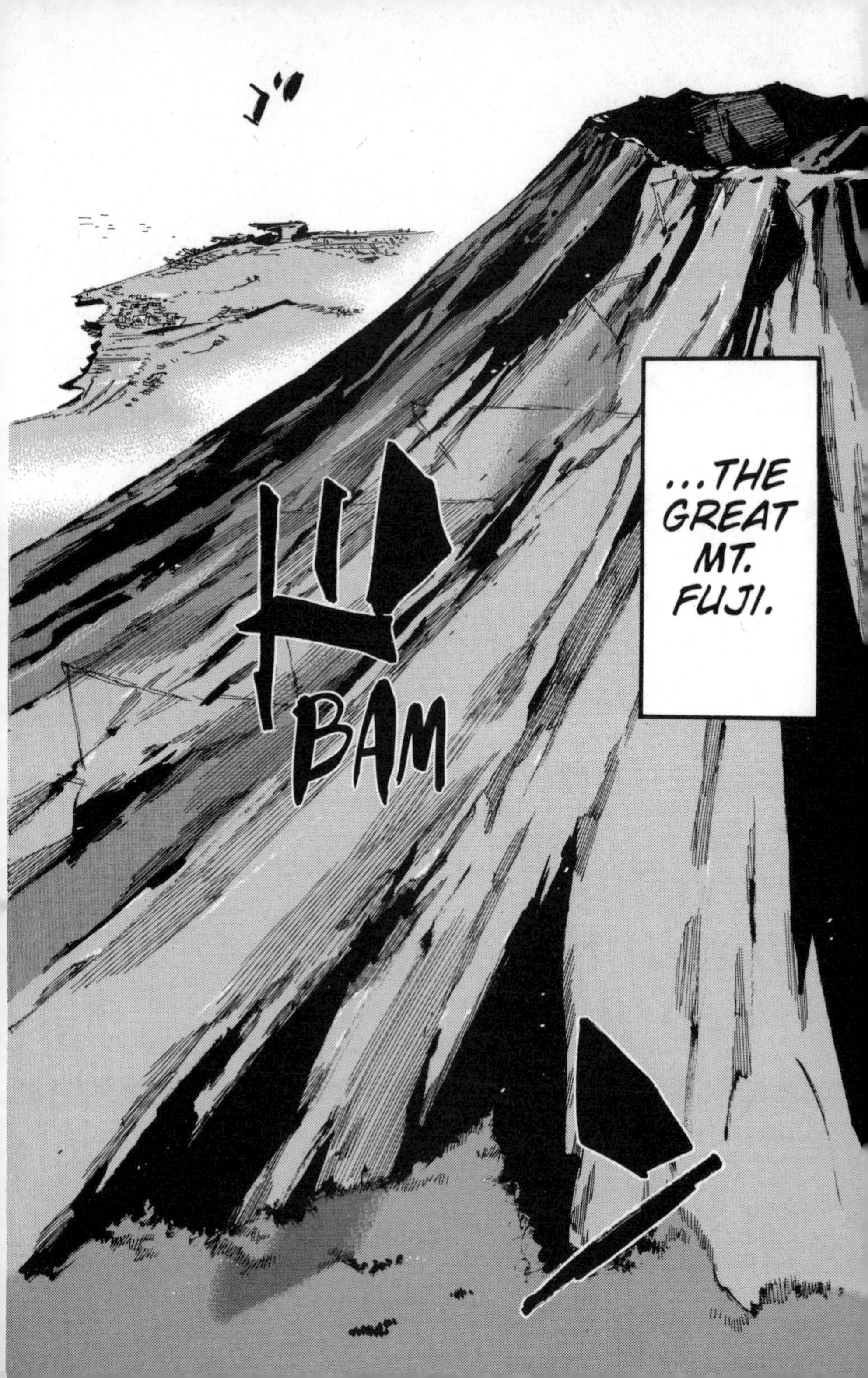
...THE GREAT MT. FUJI.
BAM

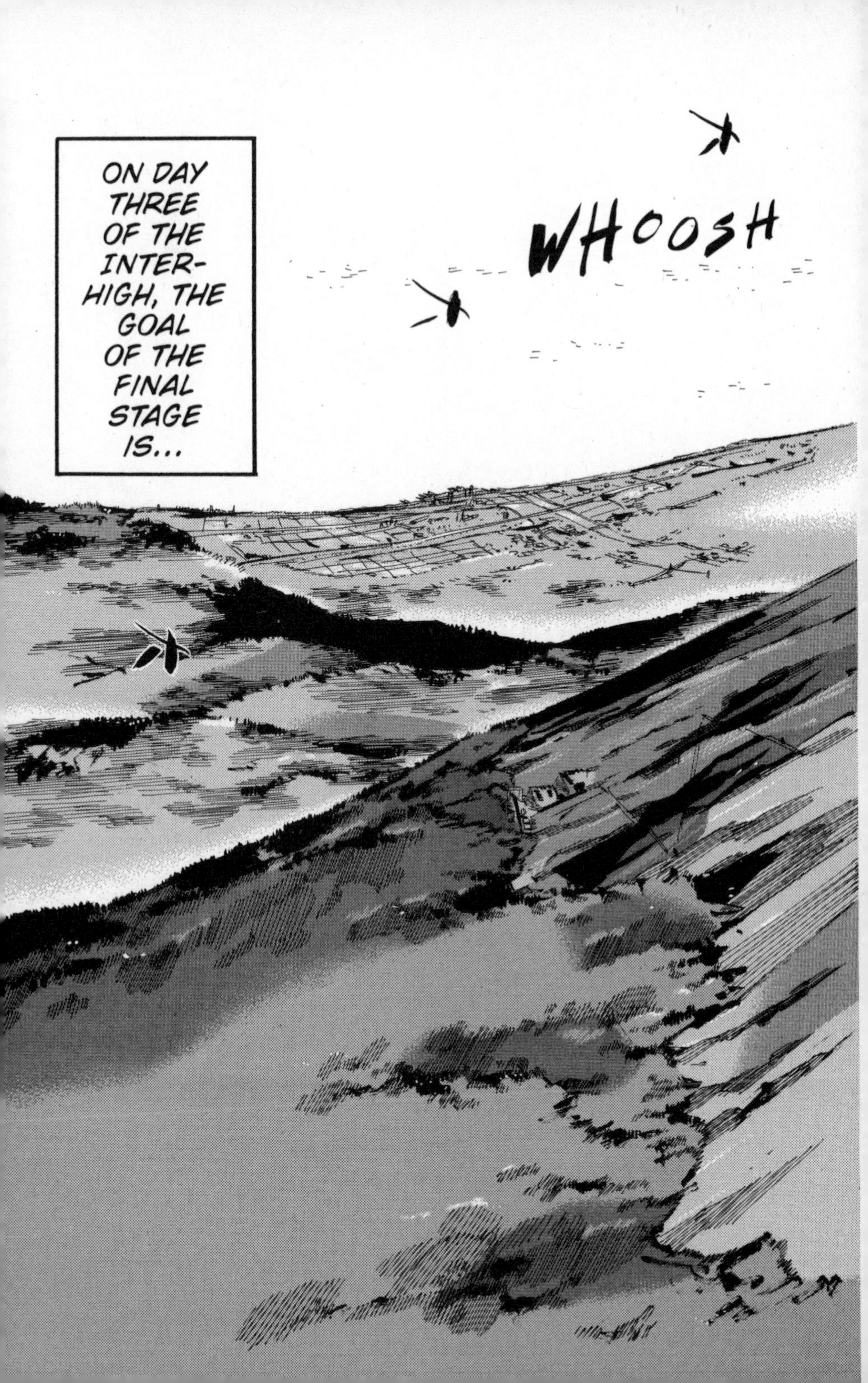
ON DAY THREE OF THE INTER-HIGH, THE GOAL OF THE FINAL STAGE IS...
WHOOSH

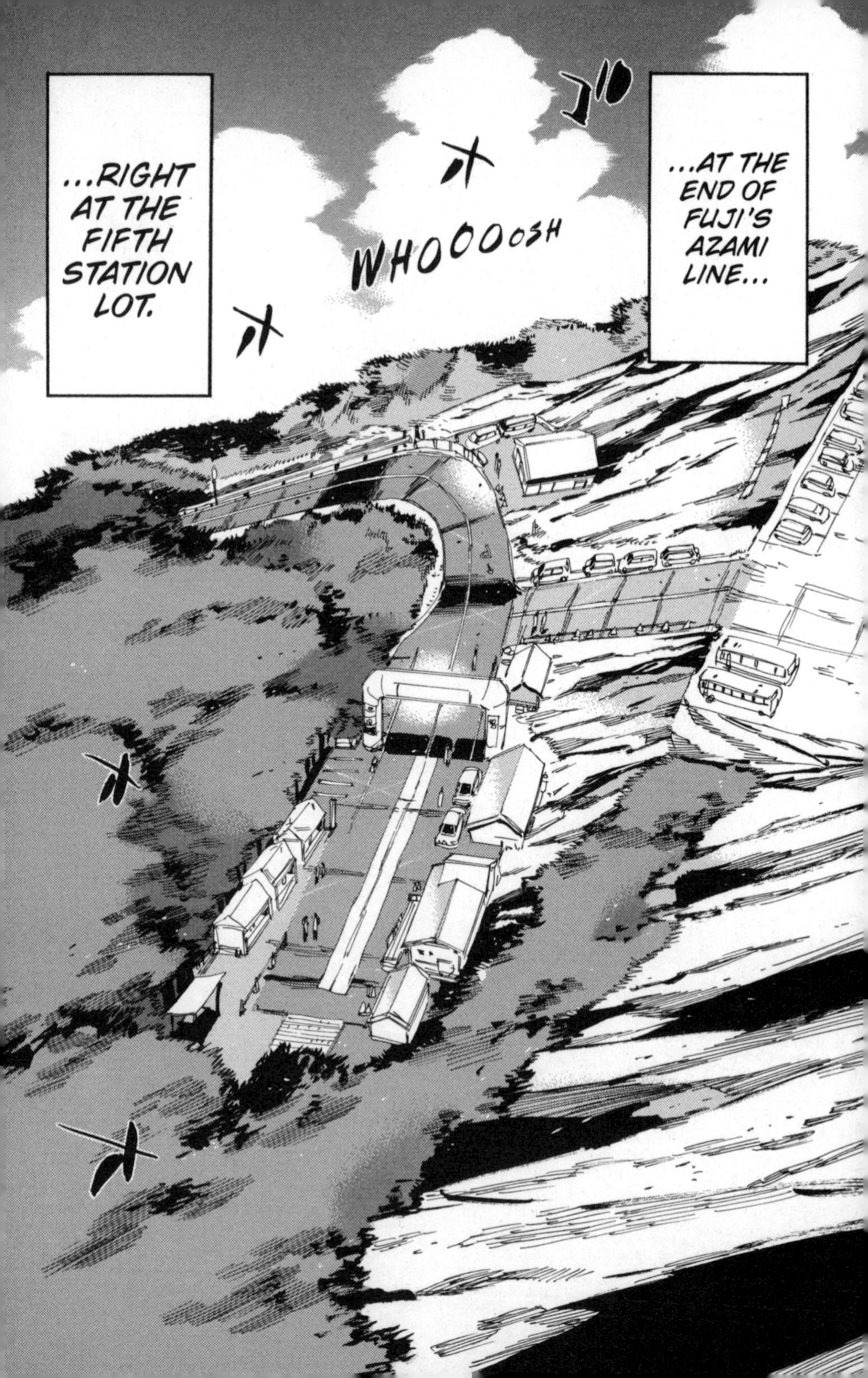
...AT THE END OF FUJI'S AZAMI LINE...
WHOOOOOSH
...RIGHT AT THE FIFTH STATION LOT.

PILLAR: MT. FUJI SUBASHIRI ENTRANCE, FIFTH STATION LOT

SIGN: DEAD END AHEAD

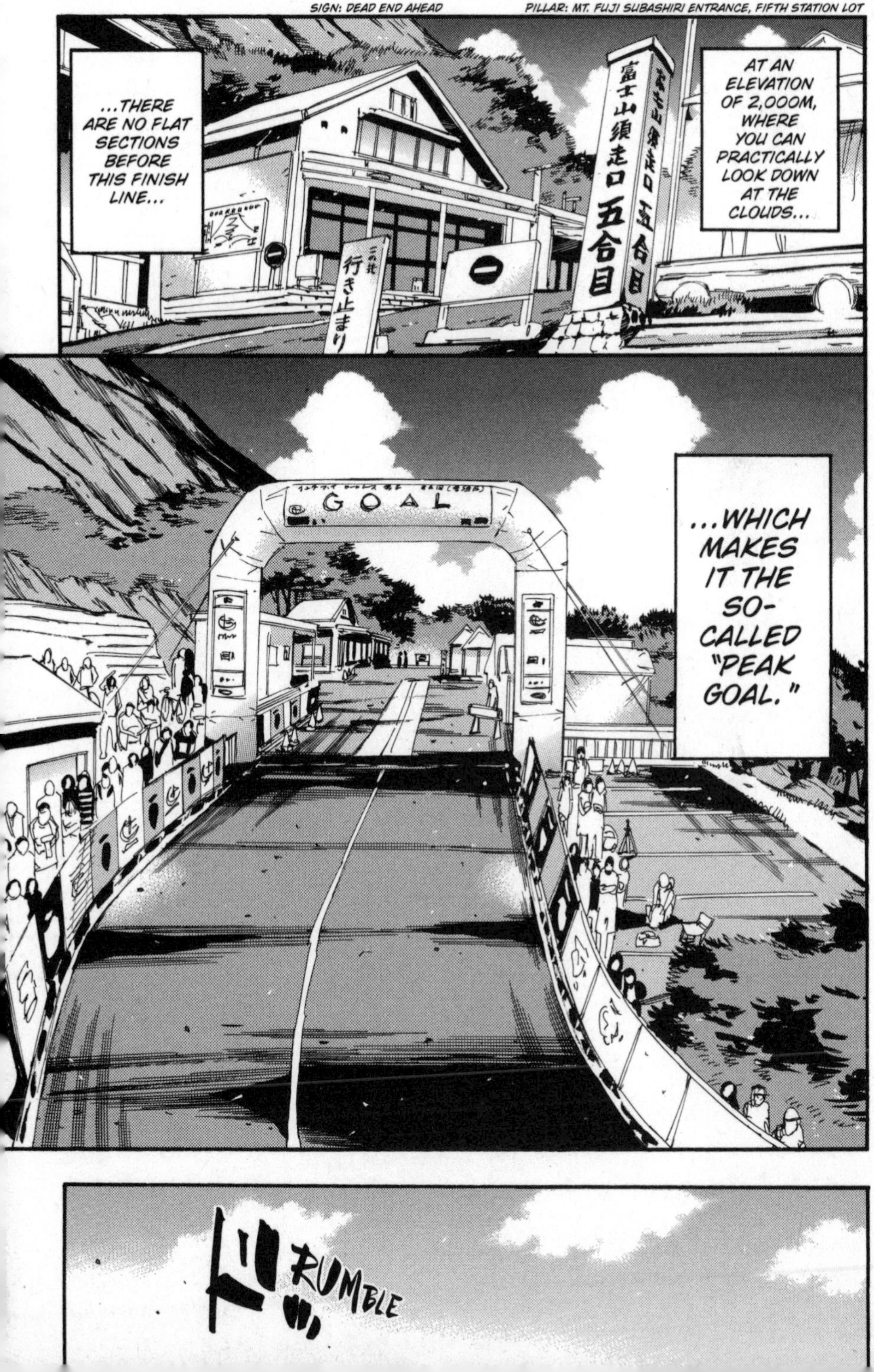
富士山須走口 五合目
AT AN ELEVATION OF 2,000M, WHERE YOU CAN PRACTICALLY LOOK DOWN AT THE CLOUDS...
行き止まり
...THERE ARE NO FLAT SECTIONS BEFORE THIS FINISH LINE...
GOAL
...WHICH MAKES IT THE SO-CALLED "PEAK GOAL."
RUMBLE

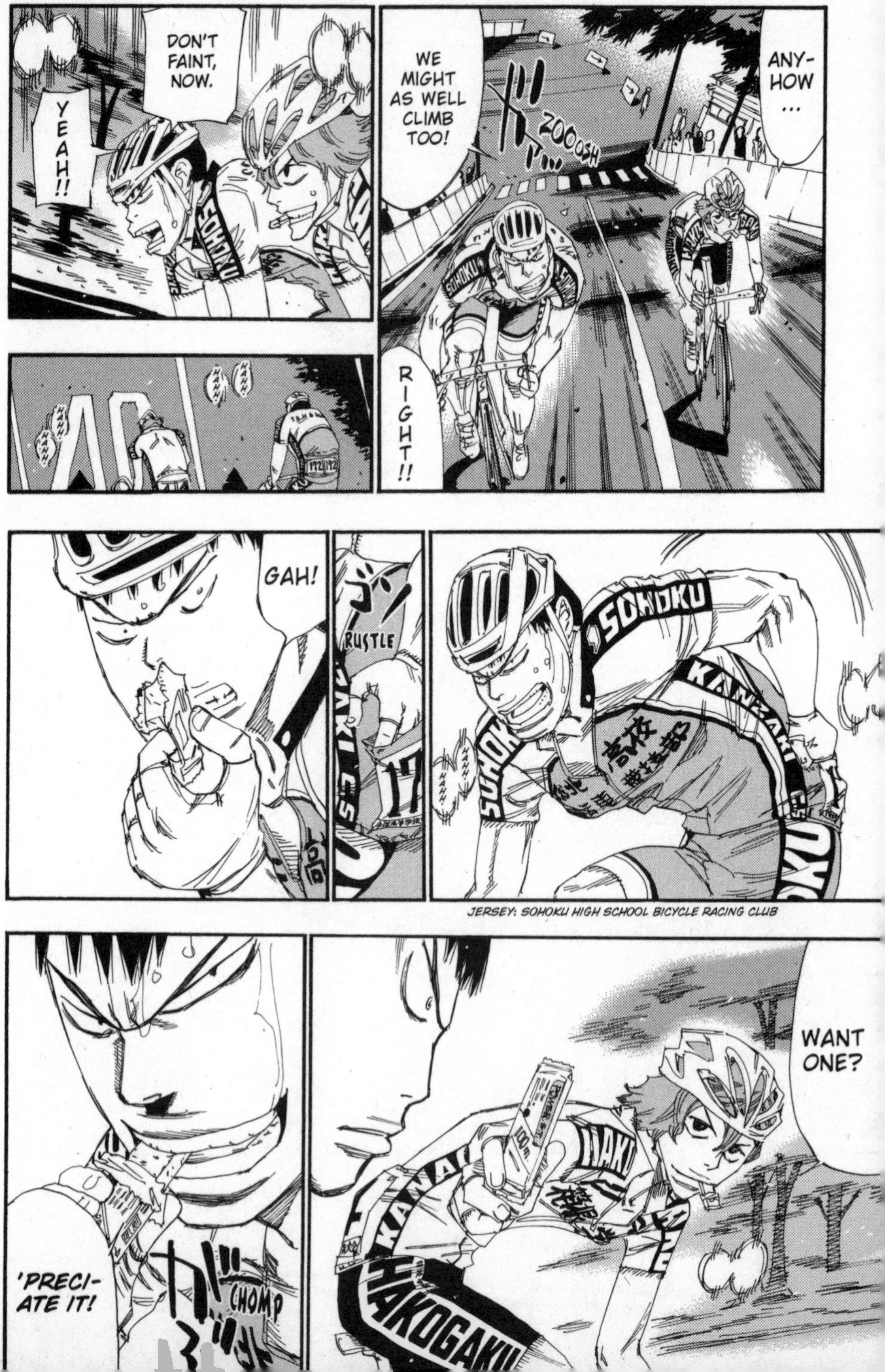
ANY-HOW ...
WE MIGHT AS WELL CLIMB TOO!
ZOOOSH
RIGHT!!
DON'T FAINT, NOW.
YEAH!!
RUSTLE
GAH!
JERSEY: SOHOKU HIGH SCHOOL BICYCLE RACING CLUB
WANT ONE?
CHOMP
'PRECI-ATE IT!

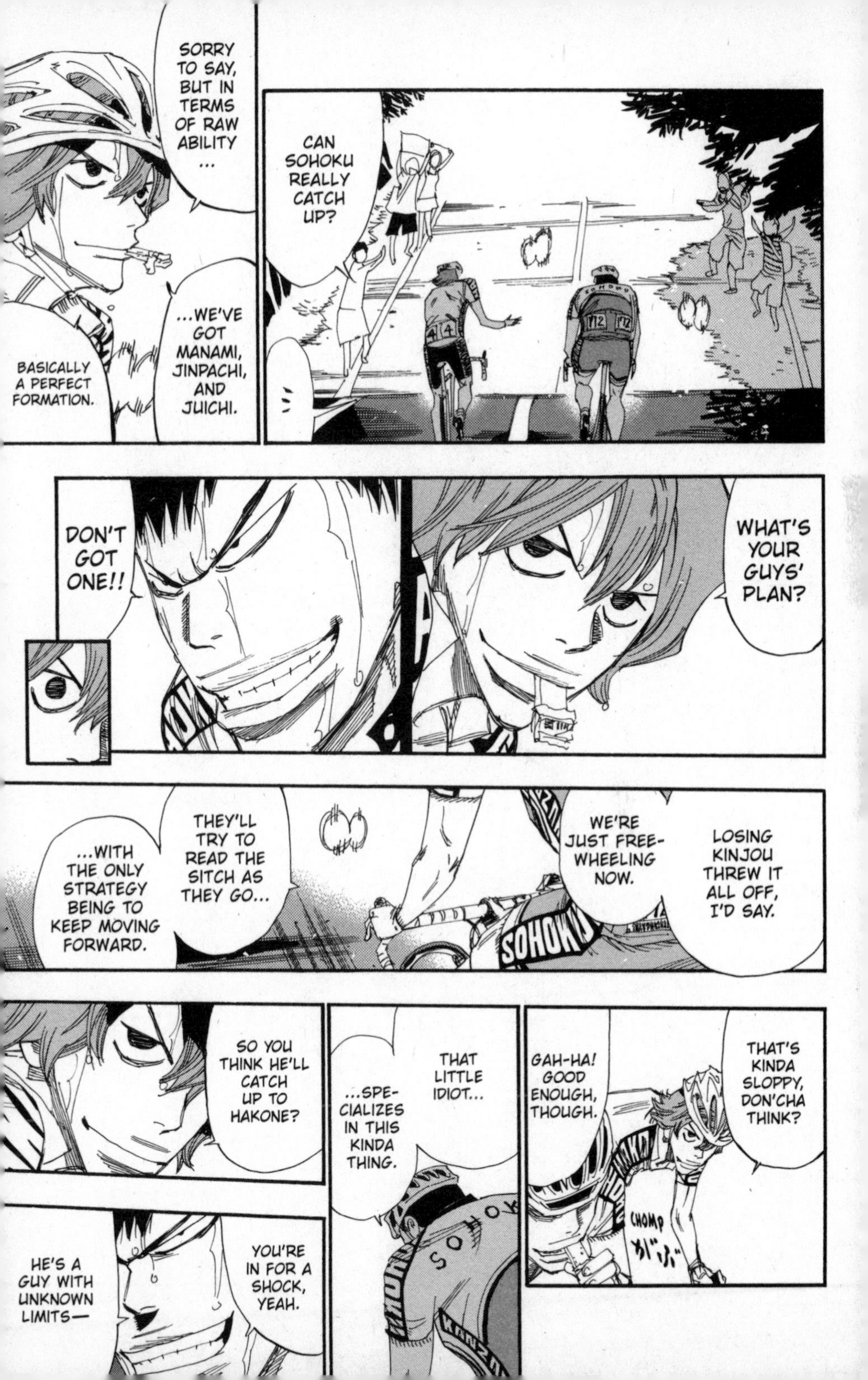
CAN SOHOKU REALLY CATCH UP?
SORRY TO SAY, BUT IN TERMS OF RAW ABILITY ...
...WE'VE GOT MANAMI, JINPACHI, AND JUICHI.
BASICALLY A PERFECT FORMATION.
WHAT'S YOUR GUYS' PLAN?
DON'T GOT ONE!!
LOSING KINJOU THREW IT ALL OFF, I'D SAY.
WE'RE JUST FREE-WHEELING NOW.
THEY'LL TRY TO READ THE SITCH AS THEY GO...
...WITH THE ONLY STRATEGY BEING TO KEEP MOVING FORWARD.
THAT'S KINDA SLOPPY, DON'CHA THINK?
GAH-HA! GOOD ENOUGH, THOUGH.
CHOMP
THAT LITTLE IDIOT...
...SPE-CIALIZES IN THIS KINDA THING.
SO YOU THINK HE'LL CATCH UP TO HAKONE?
YOU'RE IN FOR A SHOCK, YEAH.
HE'S A GUY WITH UNKNOWN LIMITS—

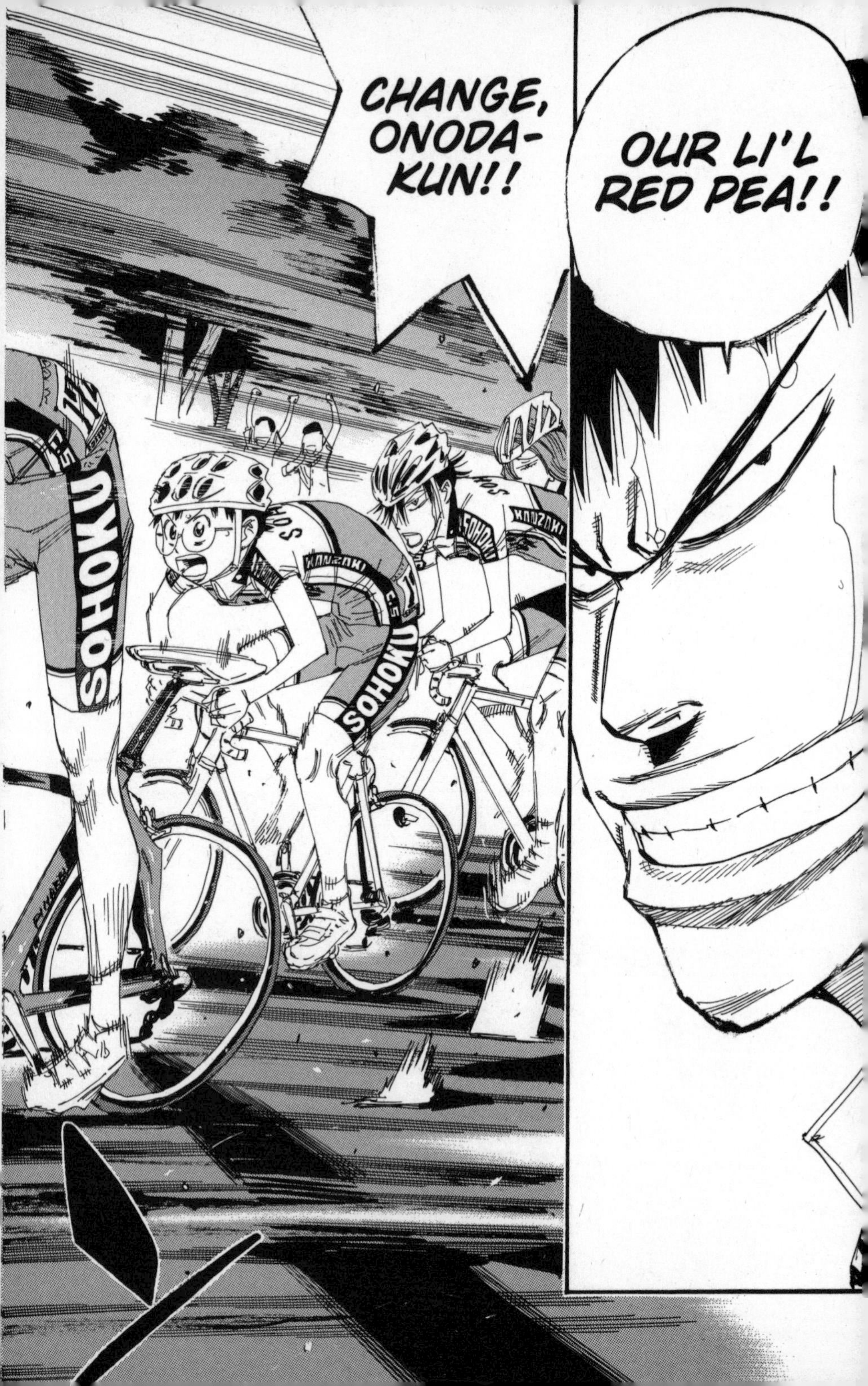
OUR LI'L RED PEA!!
CHANGE, ONODA-KUN!!

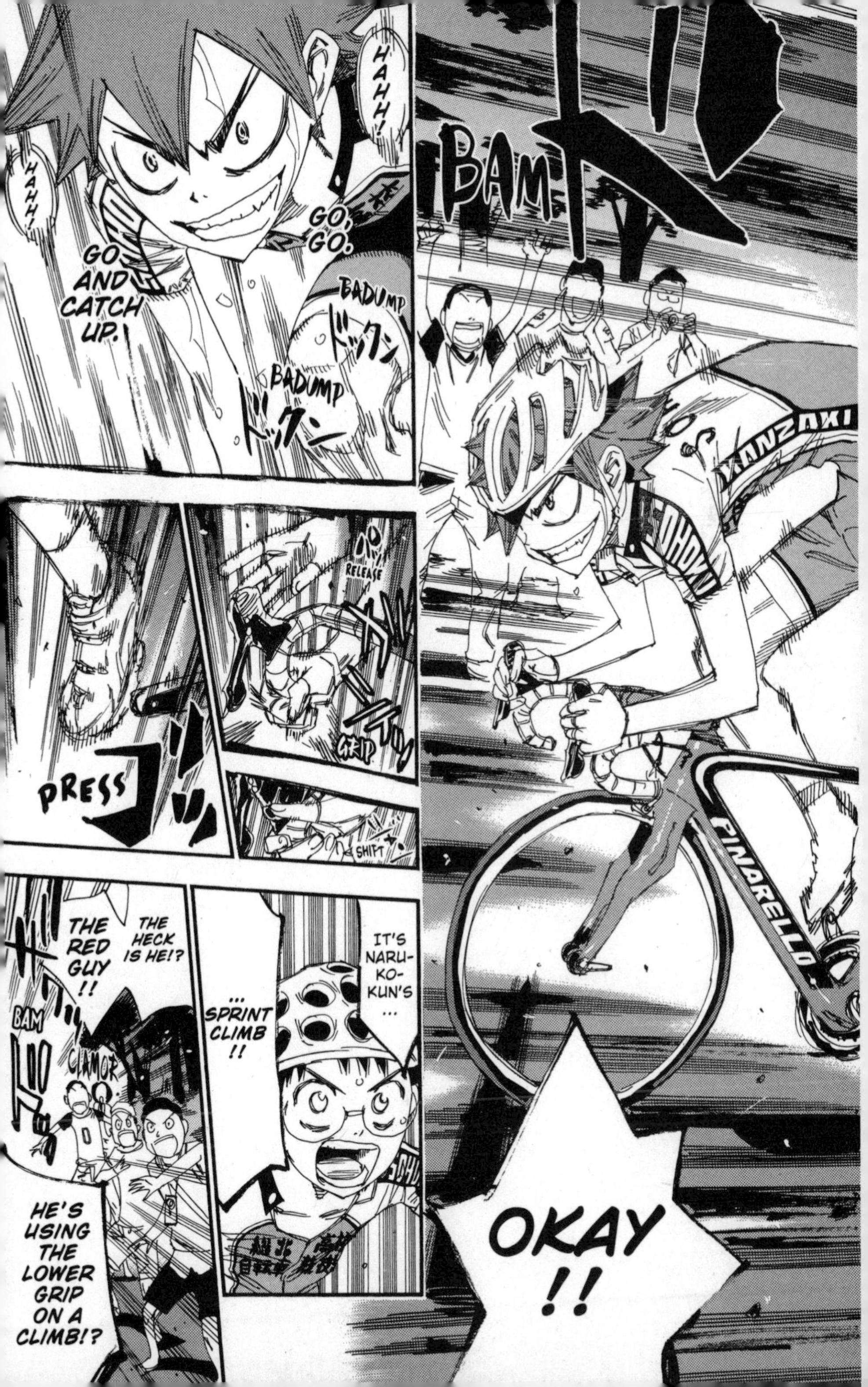
BAM
OKAY!!
HAHH!
GO, GO.
HAHH!
GO AND CATCH UP.
BADUMP
BADUMP
RELEASE
GRIP
SHIFT
PRESS
IT'S NARUKO-KUN'S...
...SPRINT CLIMB!!
THE HECK IS HE!?
THE RED GUY!!
BAM
CLAMOR
HE'S USING THE LOWER GRIP ON A CLIMB!?

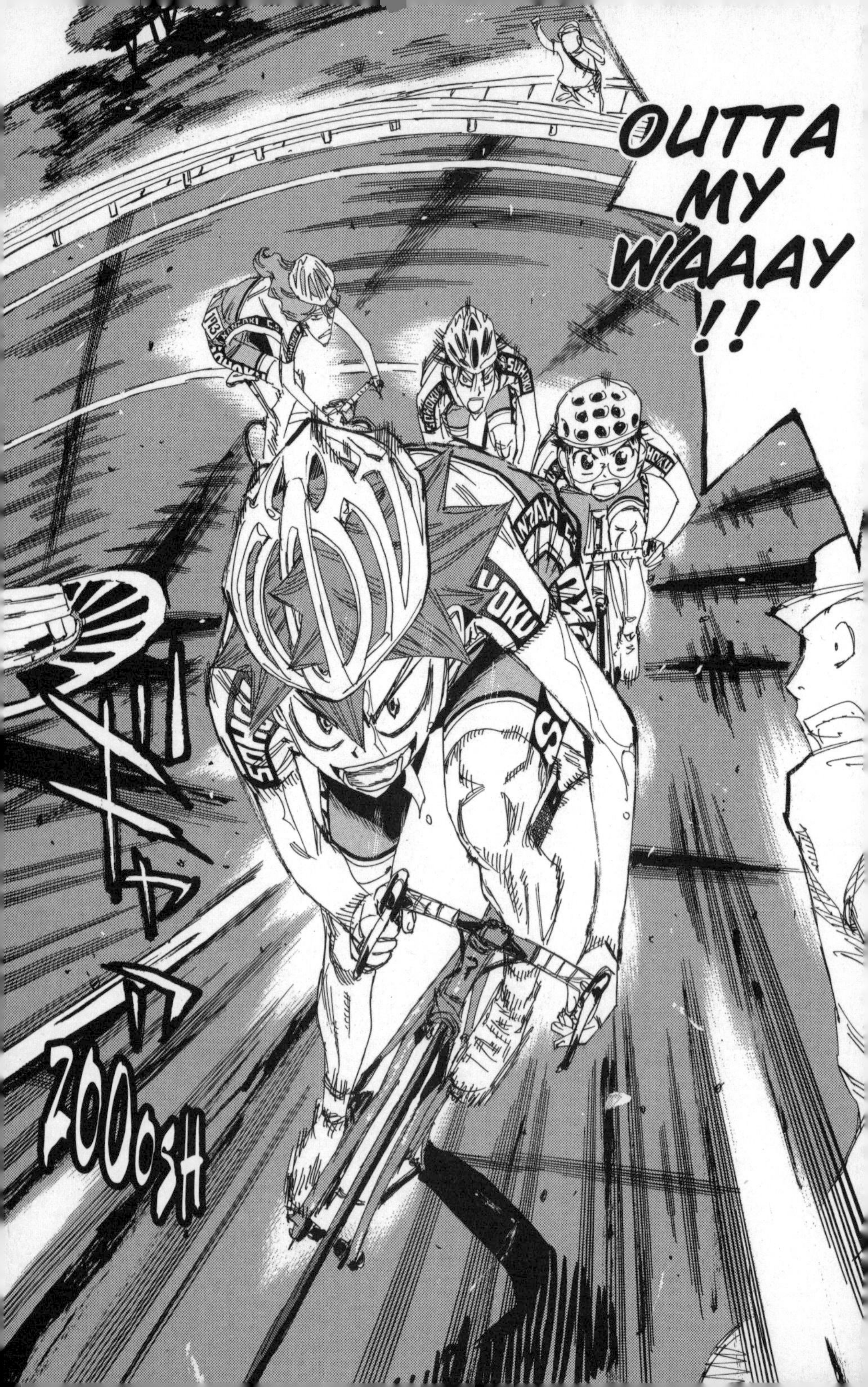
OUTTA MY WAAAY!!
ZOOOSH

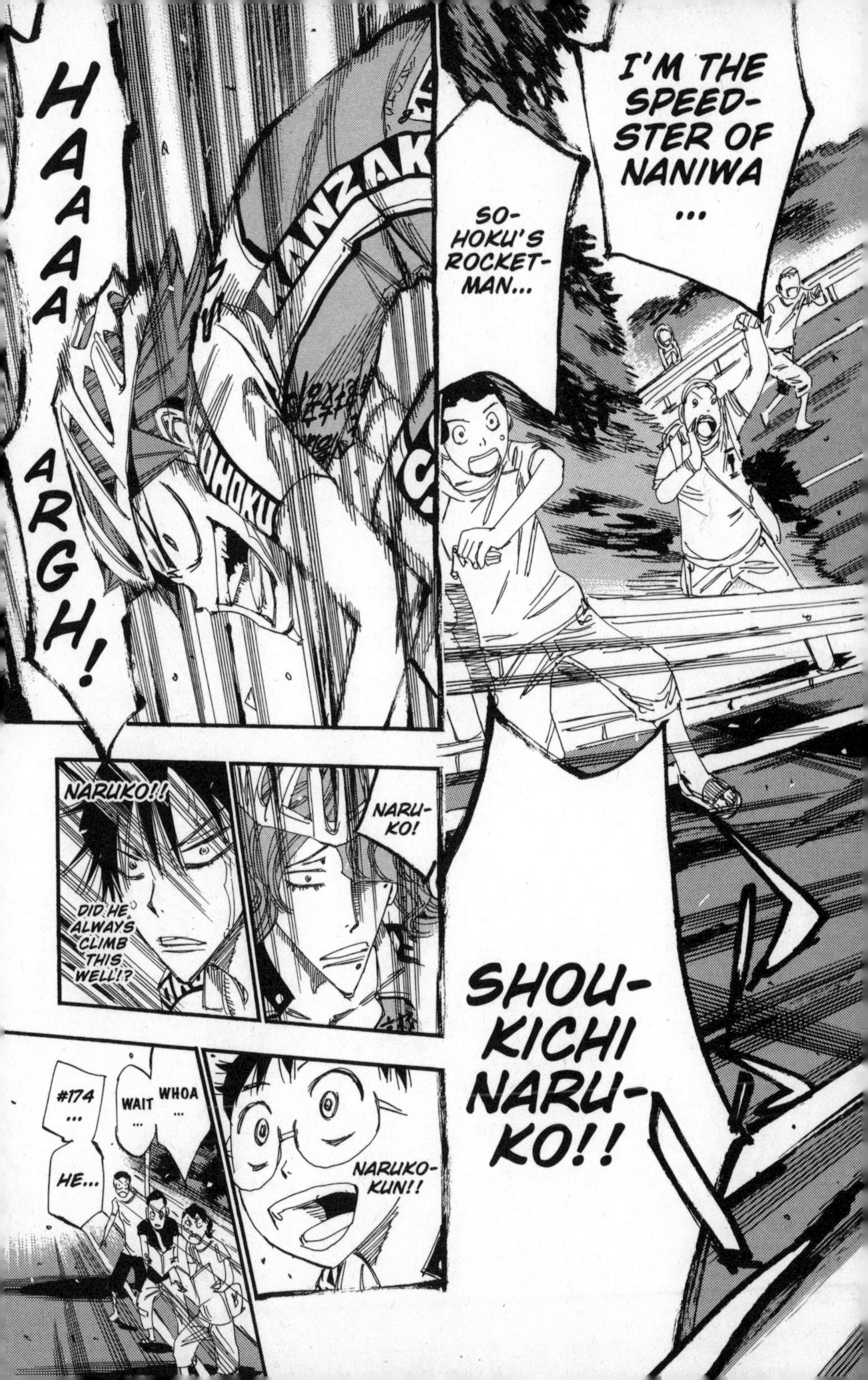
I'M THE SPEEDSTER OF NANIWA ...
SOHOKU'S ROCKETMAN...
SHOUKICHI NARUKO!!
HAAAAA ARGH!
NARUKO!
NARUKO!!
DID HE ALWAYS CLIMB THIS WELL!?
NARUKO-KUN!!
WHOA ...
WAIT ...
#174 ...
HE...

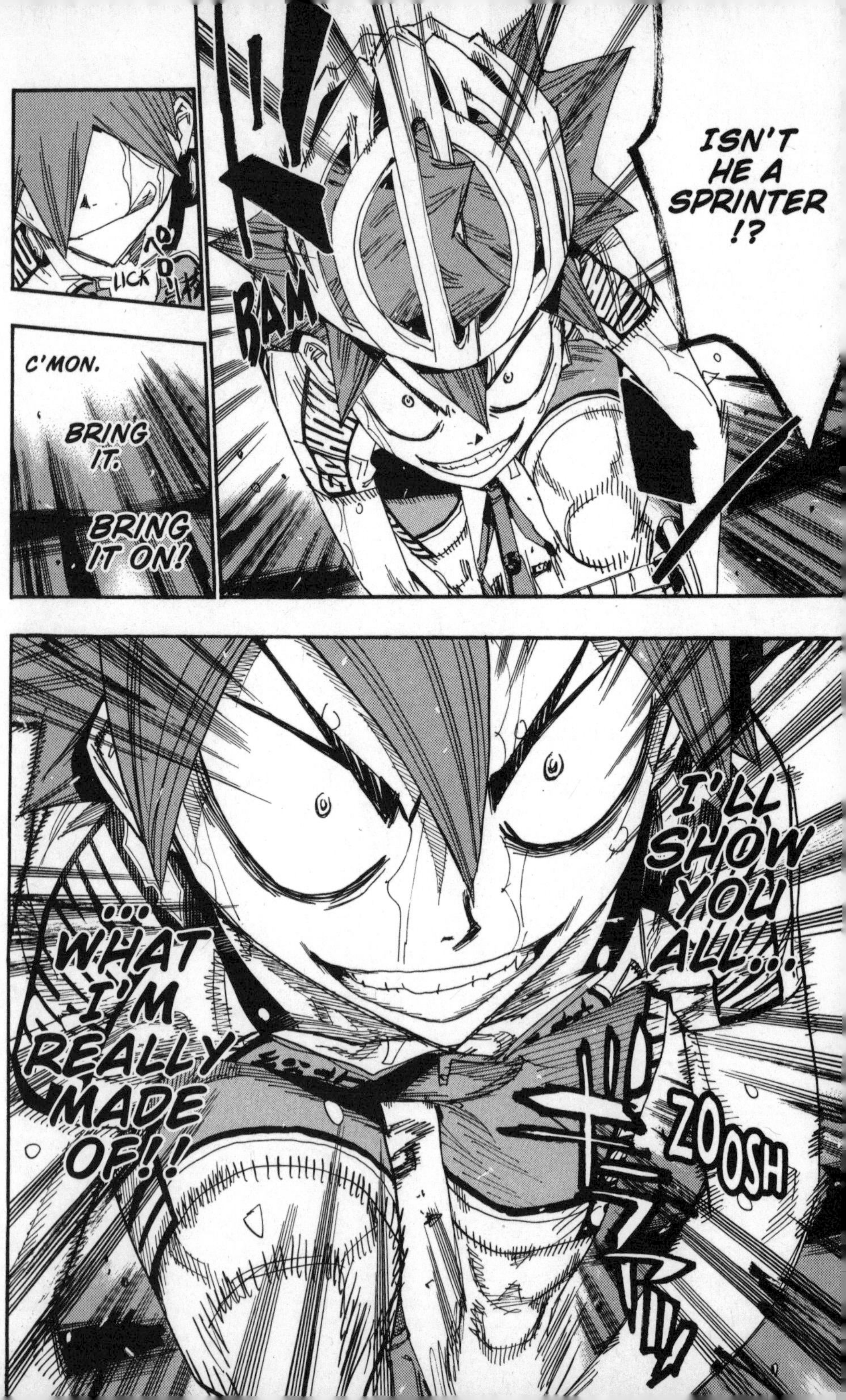
ISN'T HE A SPRINTER !?
BAM
LICK
C'MON.
BRING IT.
BRING IT ON!
I'LL SHOW YOU ALL...
...WHAT I'M REALLY MADE OF!!
ZOOSH

RIDE.192 NARUKO'S TRUE WORTH!!

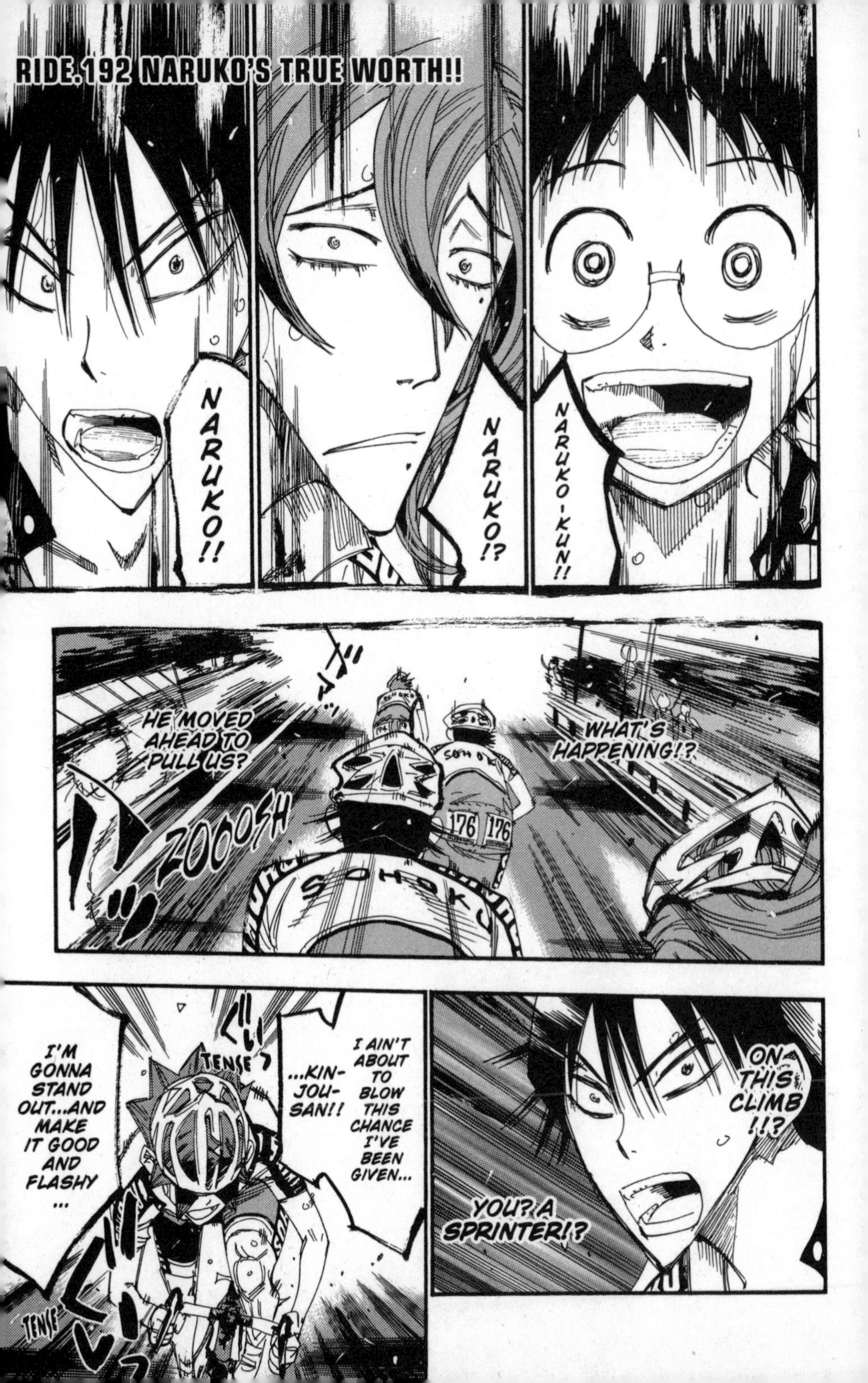
NARUKO-KUN!!
NARUKO!?
NARUKO!!
WHAT'S HAPPENING!?
HE MOVED AHEAD TO PULL US?
ZOOOSH
ON THIS CLIMB!!?
YOU? A SPRINTER!?
I AIN'T ABOUT TO BLOW THIS CHANCE I'VE BEEN GIVEN...
...KIN-JOU-SAN!!
TENSE
I'M GONNA STAND OUT...AND MAKE IT GOOD AND FLASHY...
TENSE

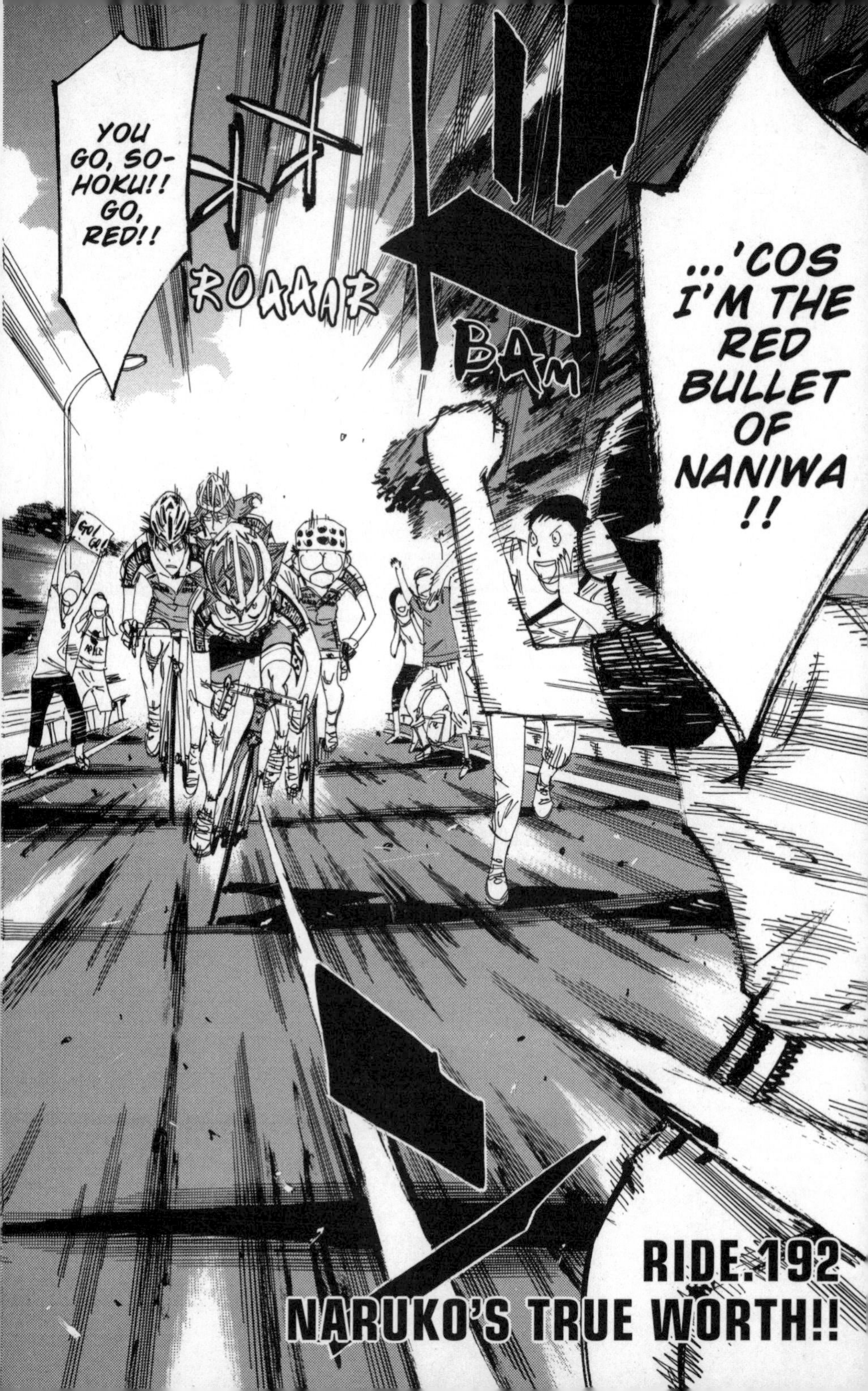
...'COS I'M THE RED BULLET OF NANIWA!!
BAM
ROAAAR
YOU GO, SO-HOKU!! GO, RED!!
GO! GO!
RIDE.192
NARUKO'S TRUE WORTH!!

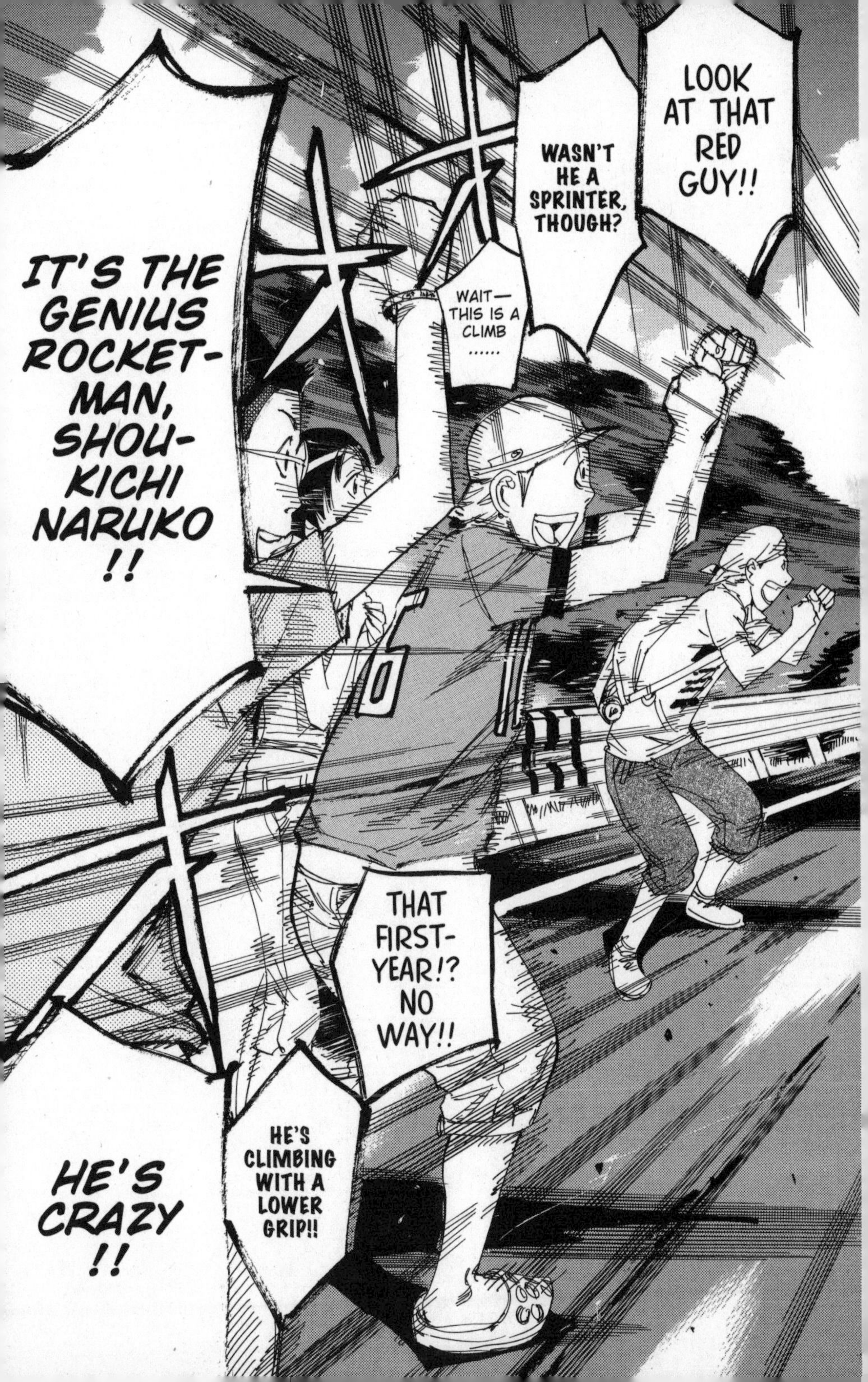
LOOK AT THAT RED GUY!!
WASN'T HE A SPRINTER, THOUGH?
WAIT— THIS IS A CLIMB ......
IT'S THE GENIUS ROCKET-MAN, SHOU-KICHI NARUKO !!
THAT FIRST-YEAR!? NO WAY!!
HE'S CLIMBING WITH A LOWER GRIP!!
HE'S CRAZY !!

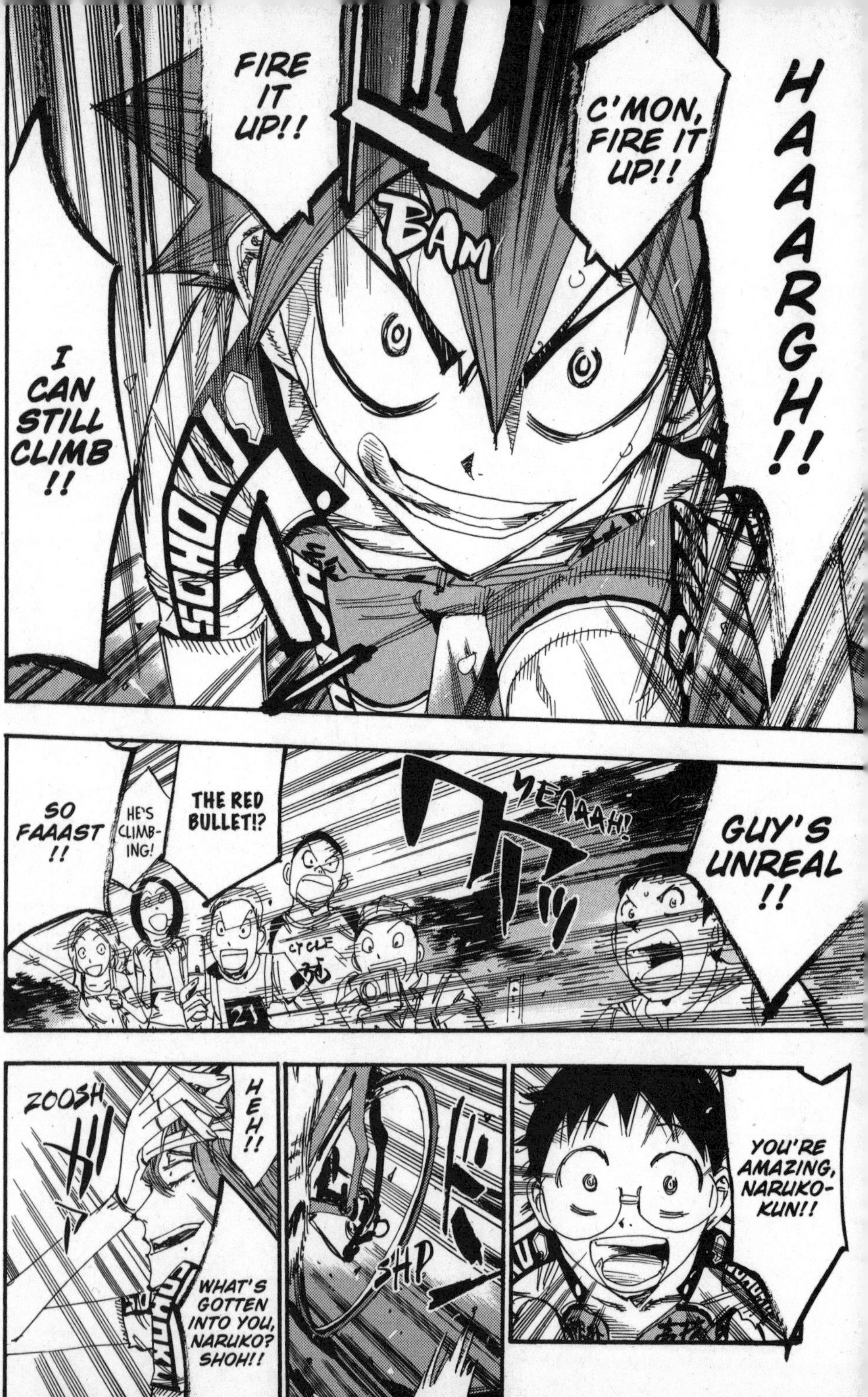
HAAARGH!!
C'MON, FIRE IT UP!!
BAM
FIRE IT UP!!
I CAN STILL CLIMB!!
GUY'S UNREAL!!
YEAAAAH!
THE RED BULLET!?
HE'S CLIMBING!
SO FAAAST!!
YOU'RE AMAZING, NARUKO-KUN!!
SHP
HEH!!
ZOOSH
WHAT'S GOTTEN INTO YOU, NARUKO? SHOH!!

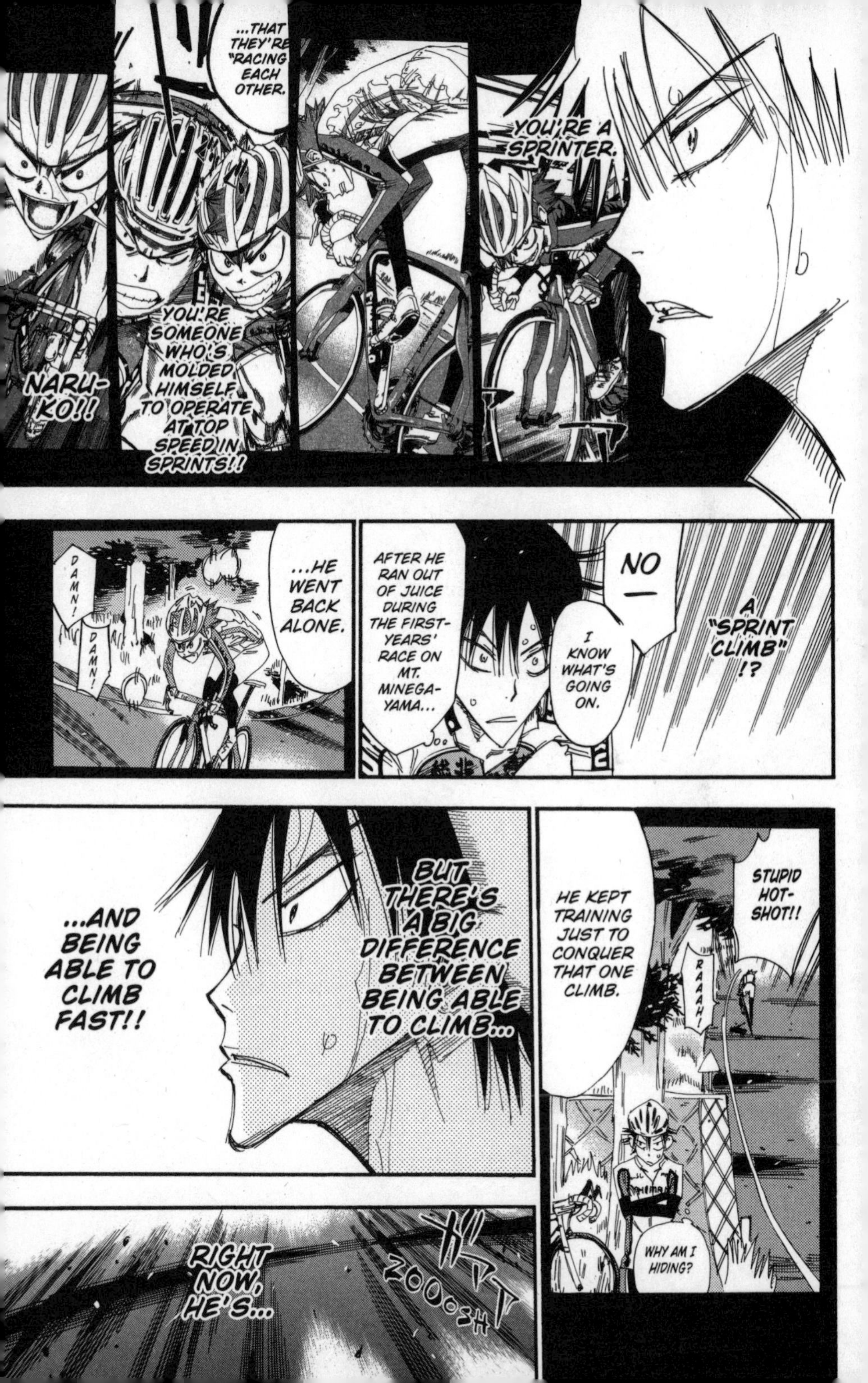
YOU'RE A SPRINTER.
...THAT THEY'RE "RACING EACH OTHER."
YOU'RE SOMEONE WHO'S MOLDED HIMSELF TO OPERATE AT TOP SPEED IN SPRINTS!!
NARU-KO!!
A "SPRINT CLIMB"!?
NO —
I KNOW WHAT'S GOING ON.
AFTER HE RAN OUT OF JUICE DURING THE FIRST-YEARS' RACE ON MT. MINEGA-YAMA...
...HE WENT BACK ALONE.
DAMN!
DAMN!
STUPID HOT-SHOT!!
HE KEPT TRAINING JUST TO CONQUER THAT ONE CLIMB.
RAAAH!
WHY AM I HIDING?
BUT THERE'S A BIG DIFFERENCE BETWEEN BEING ABLE TO CLIMB...
...AND BEING ABLE TO CLIMB FAST!!
ZOOOSH
RIGHT NOW, HE'S...

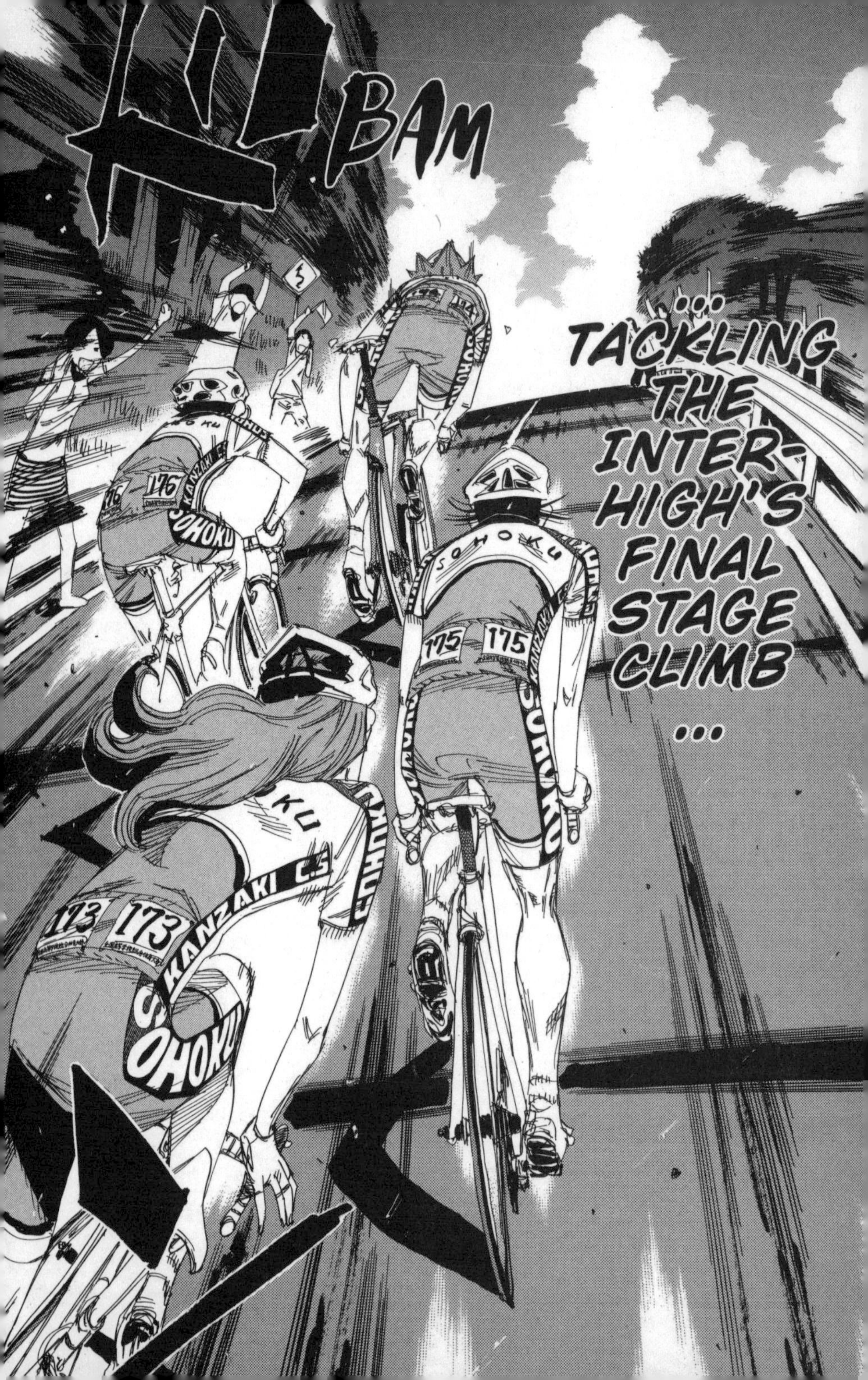
BAM
...TACKLING THE INTER-HIGH'S FINAL STAGE CLIMB...

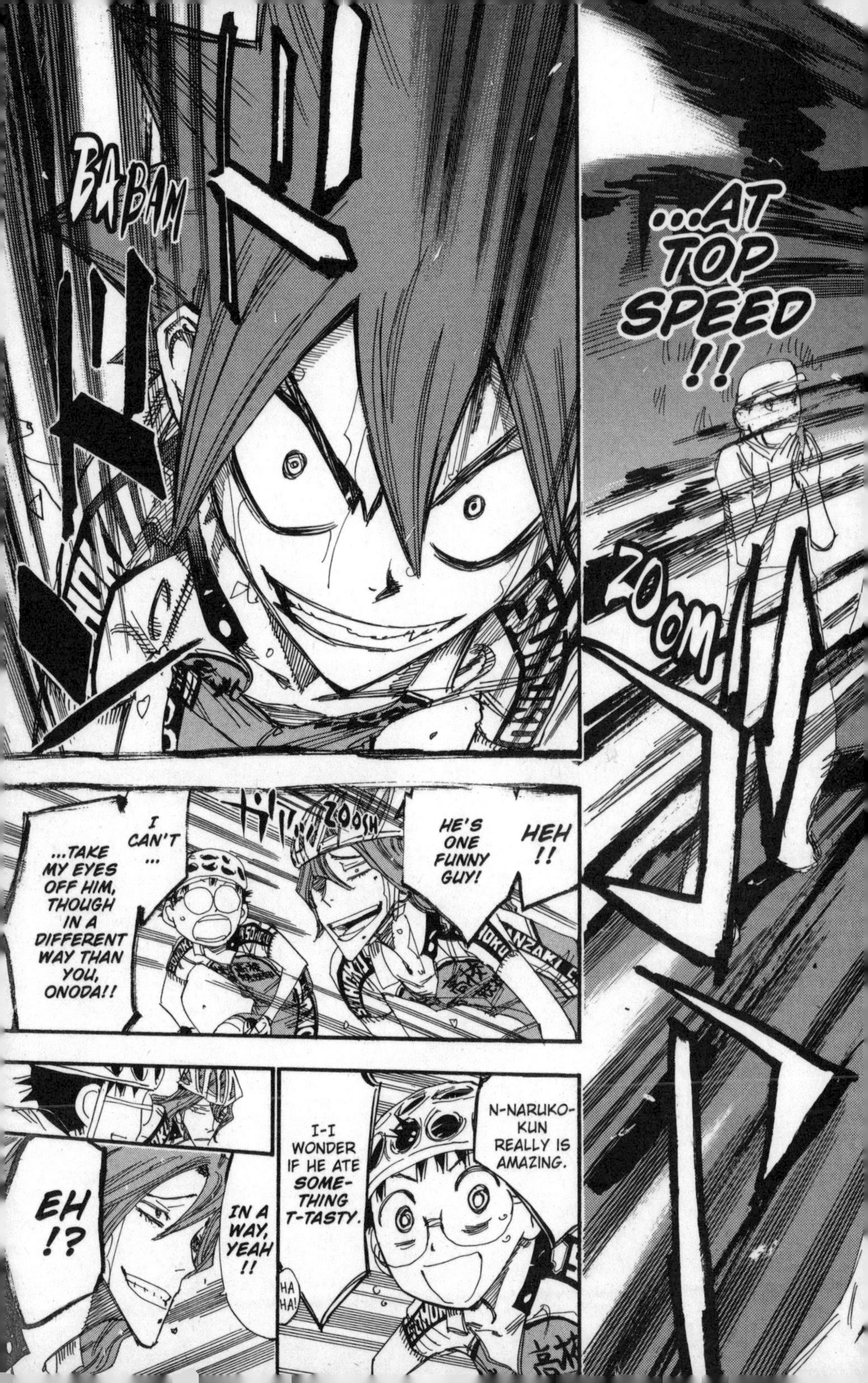

...AT TOP SPEED!!
ZOOM
BABAM
HEH!!
HE'S ONE FUNNY GUY!
ZOOSH
I CAN'T...
...TAKE MY EYES OFF HIM, THOUGH IN A DIFFERENT WAY THAN YOU, ONODA!!
N-NARUKO-KUN REALLY IS AMAZING.
I-I WONDER IF HE ATE SOMETHING T-TASTY.
HA HA!
IN A WAY, YEAH!!
EH!?

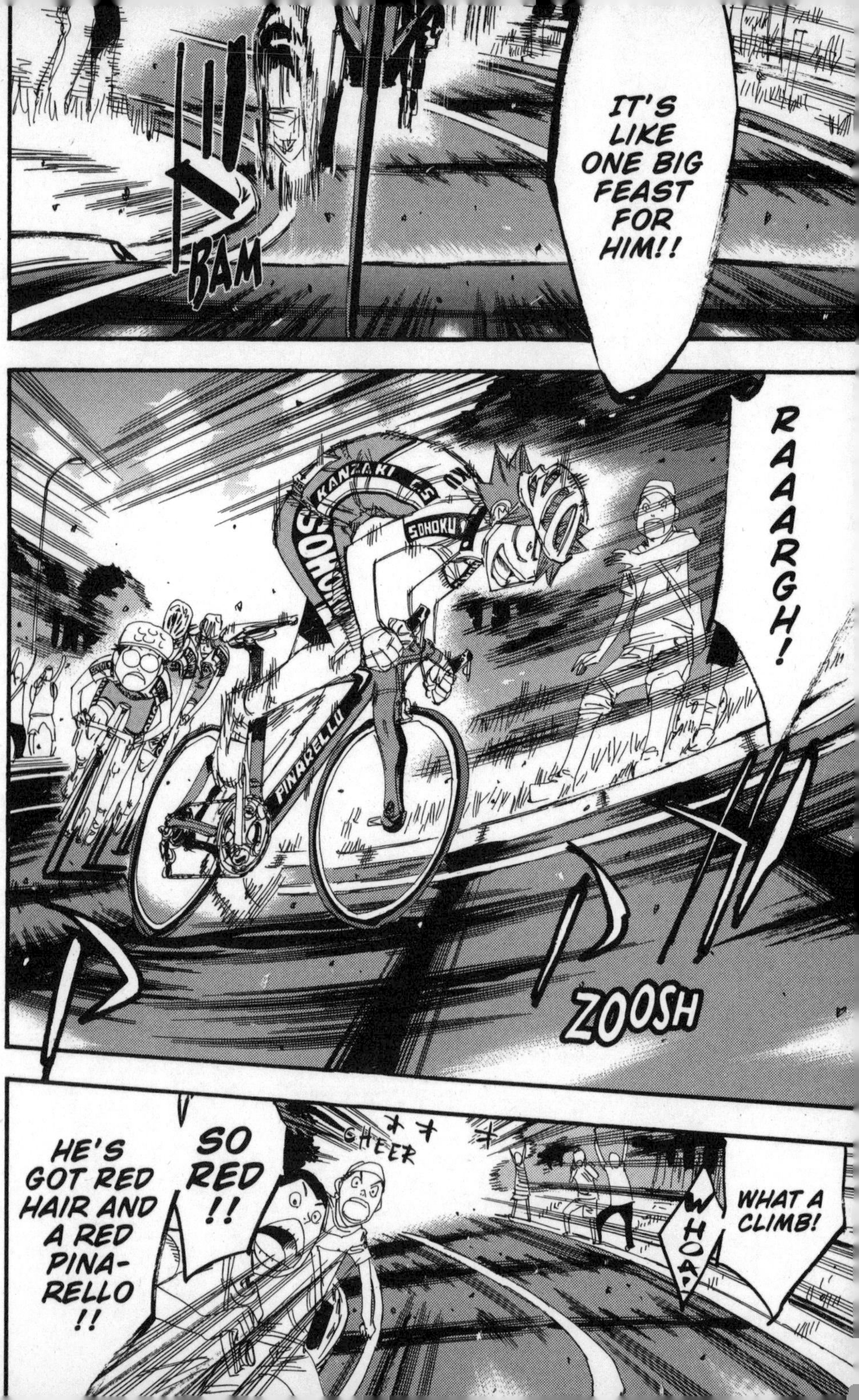
IT'S LIKE ONE BIG FEAST FOR HIM!!
BAM
RAAAARGH!
KANZAKI
SOHOKU
SOHOKU
PINARELLO
ZOOSH
WHAT A CLIMB!
WHOA!
CHEER
SO RED!!
HE'S GOT RED HAIR AND A RED PINA-RELLO!!

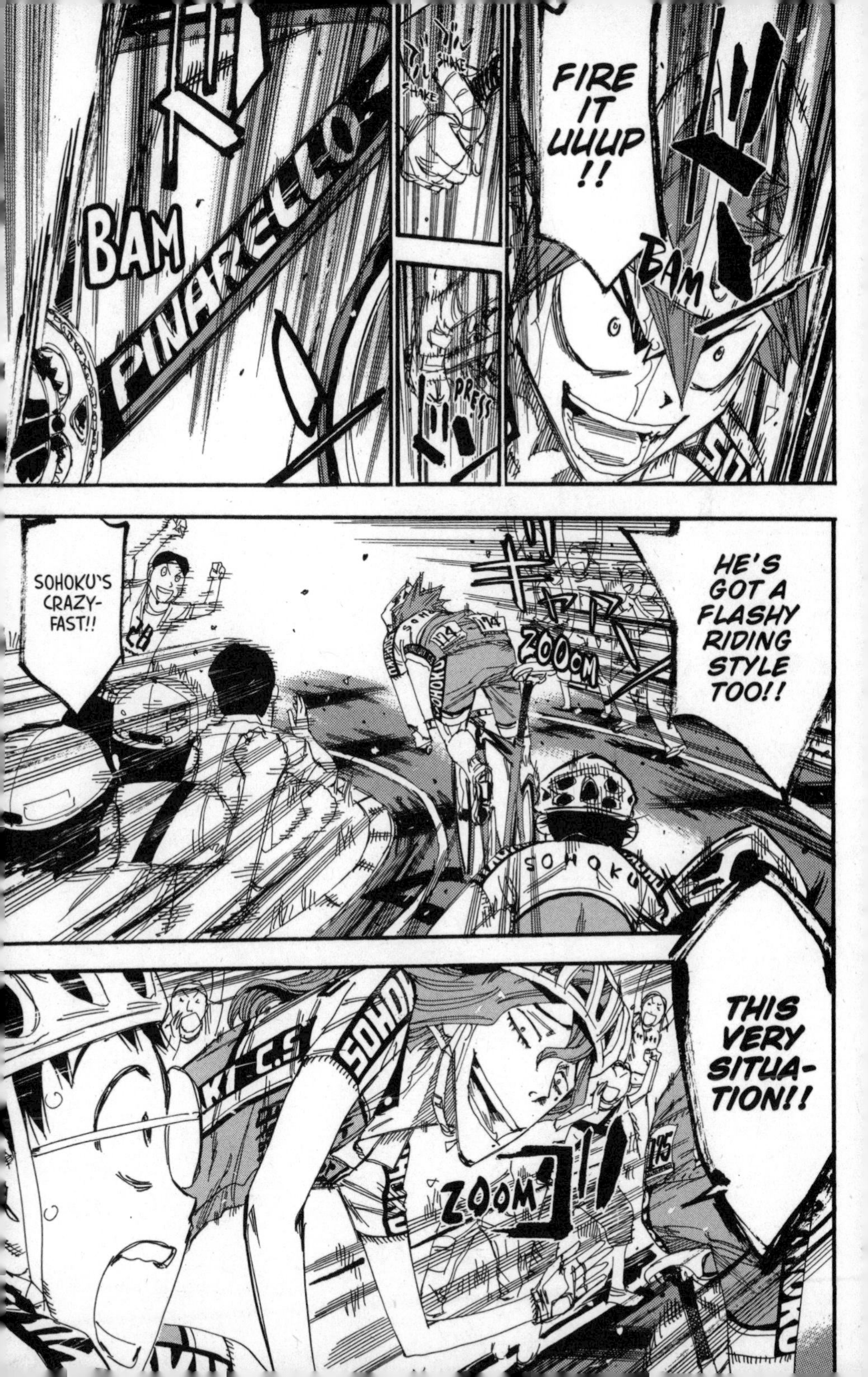
FIRE IT UUUP!!
BAM
SHAKE
SHAKE
PRESS
BAM
PINARELLO
HE'S GOT A FLASHY RIDING STYLE TOO!!
ZOOOM
SOHOKU'S CRAZY-FAST!!
SOHOKU
THIS VERY SITUATION!!
ZOOM
SOHOKU

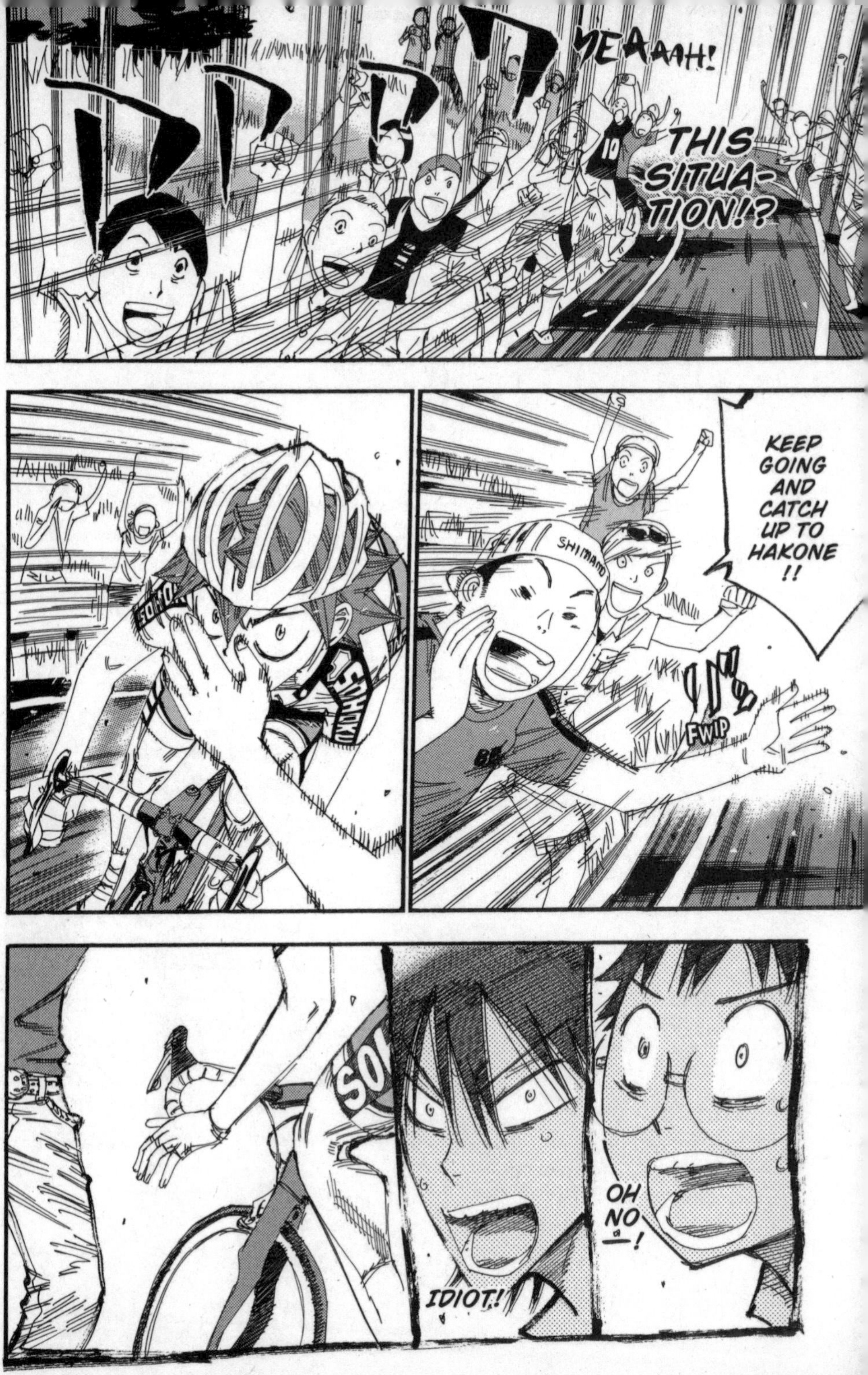
YEAAAH!
THIS SITUATION!?
KEEP GOING AND CATCH UP TO HAKONE!!
FWIP
OH NO!
IDIOT!

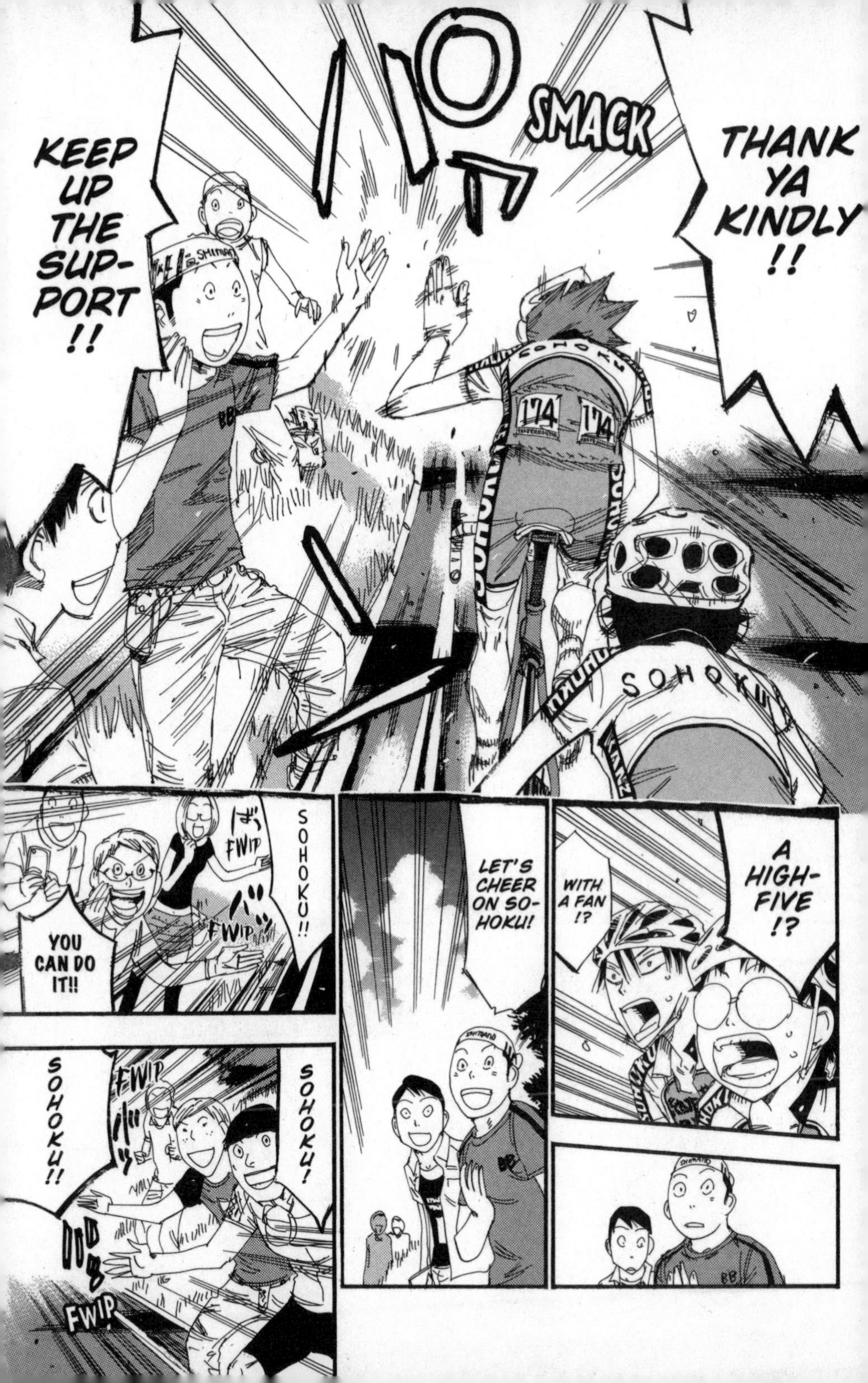
THANK YA KINDLY!!
SMACK
KEEP UP THE SUP-PORT!!
A HIGH-FIVE!?
WITH A FAN!?
LET'S CHEER ON SO-HOKU!
SOHOKU!!
ぱっ
FWIP
バッ
FWIP
YOU CAN DO IT!!
SOHOKU!
SOHOKU!!
FWIP
FWIP

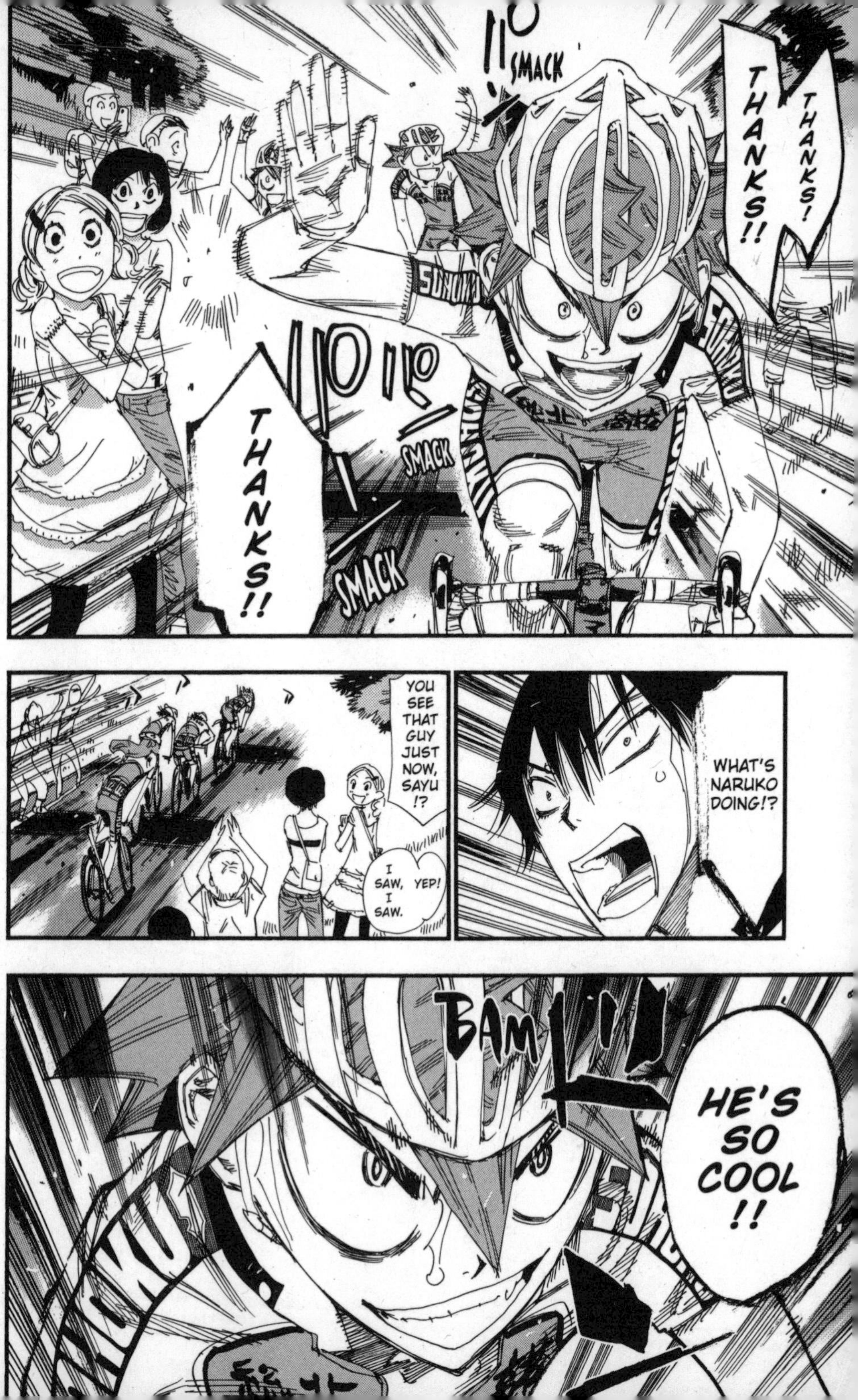
SMACK
THANKS! THANKS!!
THANKS!!
SMACK
SMACK
WHAT'S NARUKO DOING!?
YOU SEE THAT GUY JUST NOW, SAYU!?
I SAW, YEP! I SAW.
BAM
HE'S SO COOL!!

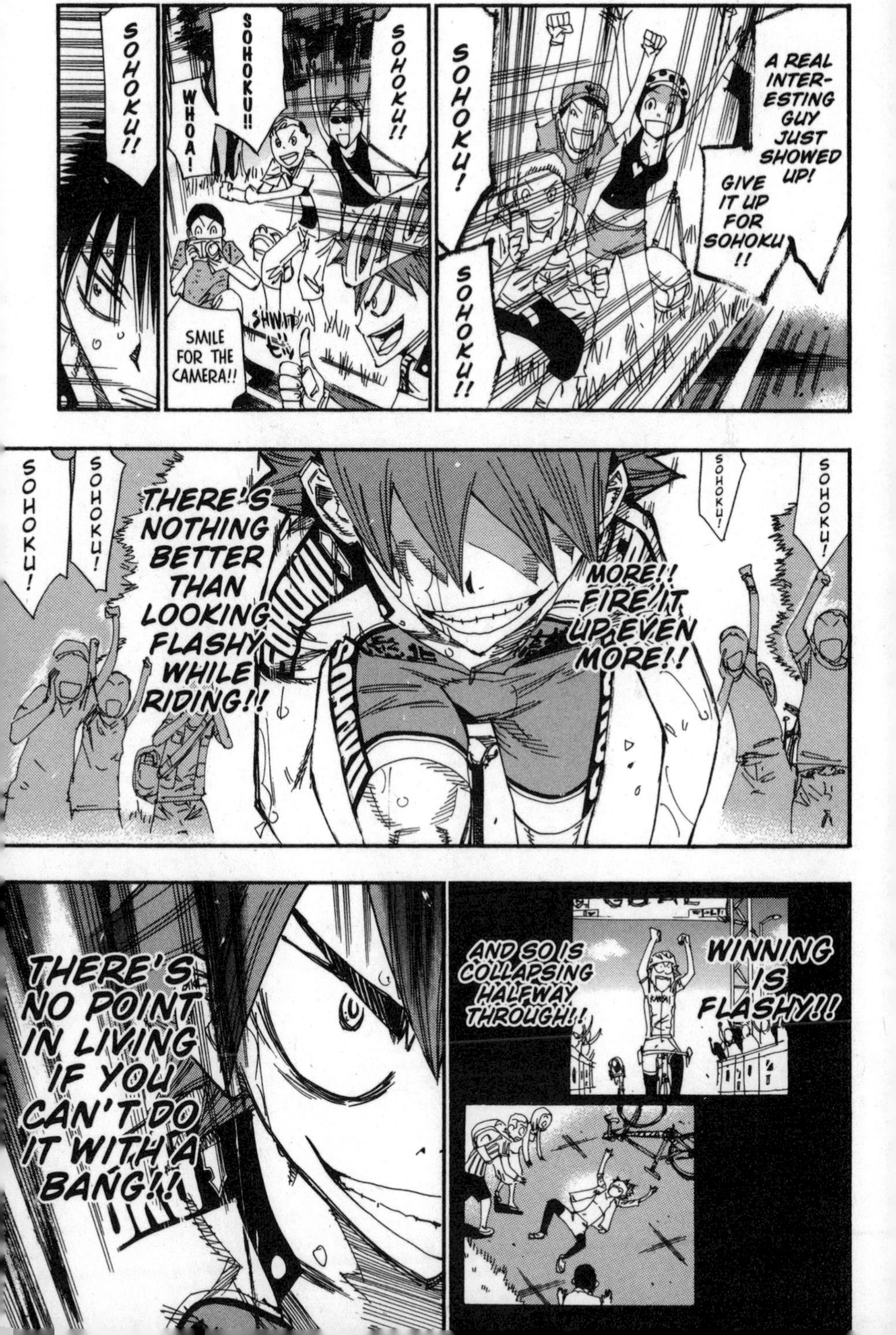
A REAL INTERESTING GUY JUST SHOWED UP!
GIVE IT UP FOR SOHOKU!!
SOHOKU!
SOHOKU!!
SOHOKU!!
SOHOKU!!
WHOA!
SMILE FOR THE CAMERA!!
SOHOKU!!
SOHOKU!
SOHOKU!
MORE!! FIRE IT UP EVEN MORE!!
THERE'S NOTHING BETTER THAN LOOKING FLASHY WHILE RIDING!!
SOHOKU!
SOHOKU!
WINNING IS FLASHY!!
AND SO IS COLLAPSING HALFWAY THROUGH!!
THERE'S NO POINT IN LIVING IF YOU CAN'T DO IT WITH A BANG!!

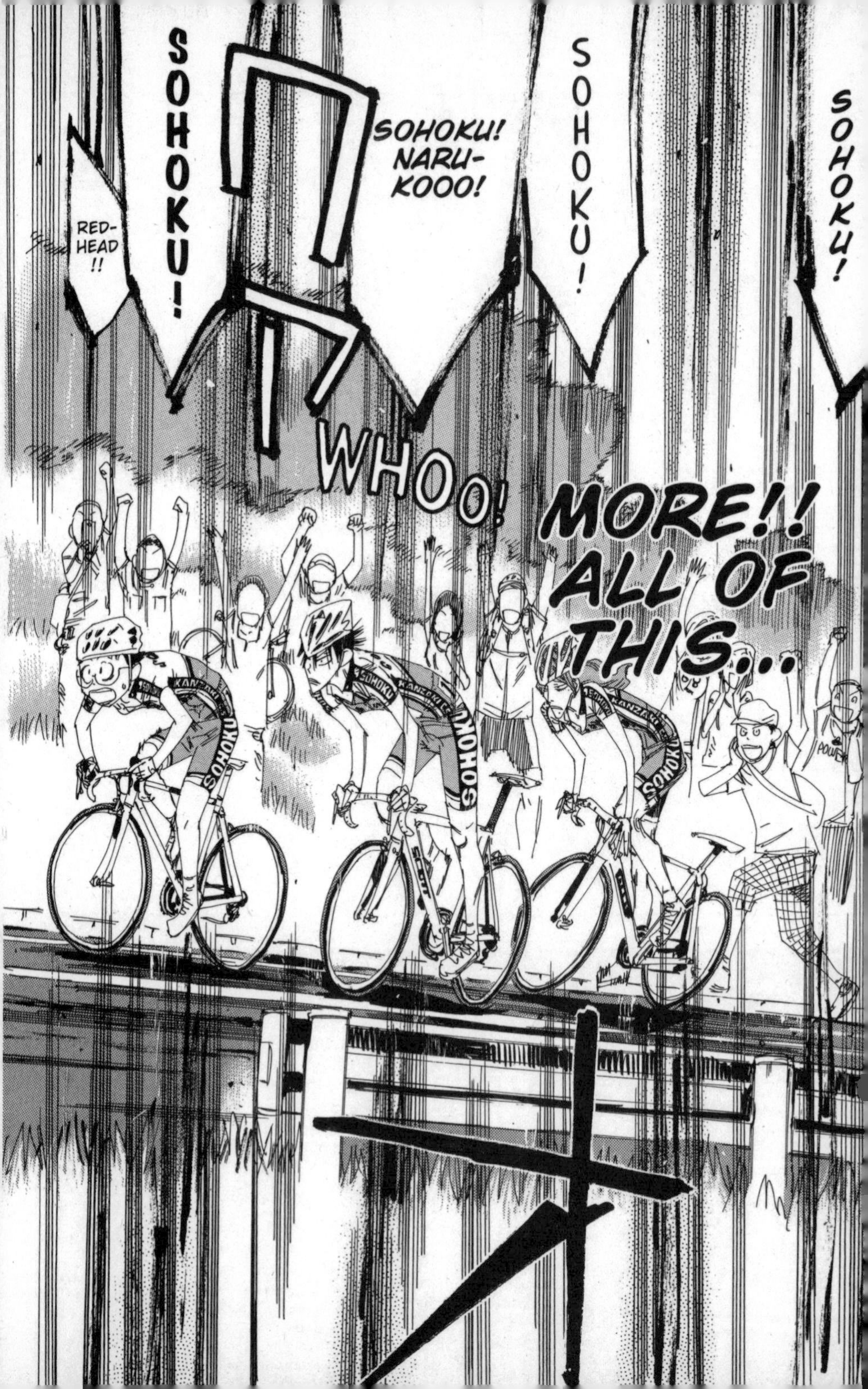
SOHOKU!
SOHOKU!
SOHOKU! NARU-KOOO!
SOHOKU!
RED-HEAD!!
WHOO!
MORE!! ALL OF THIS...

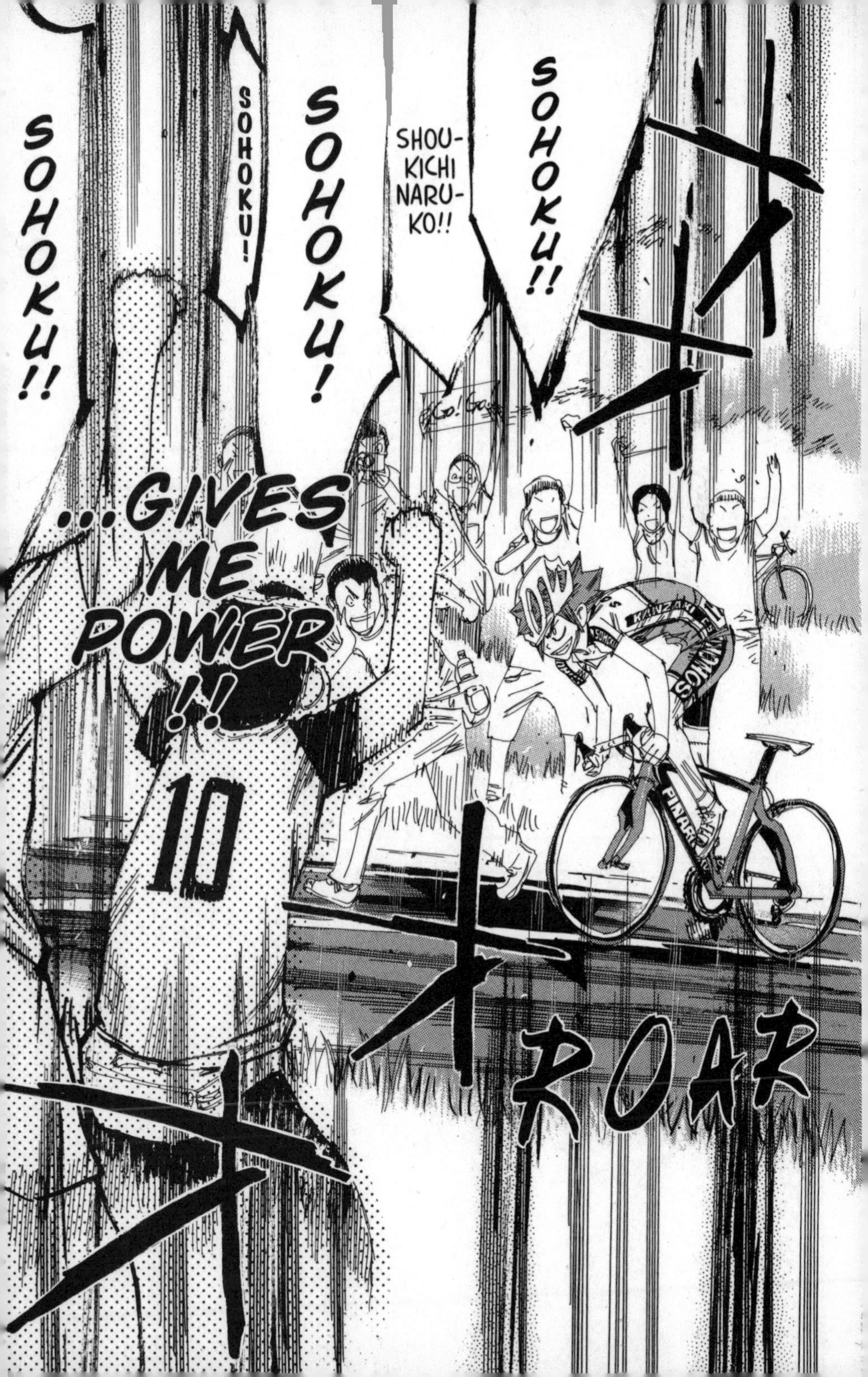
SOHOKU!!
SHOU-KICHI NARU-KO!!
Go! Go!
SOHOKU!
SOHOKU!
SOHOKU!!
...GIVES ME POWER!!
ROAR

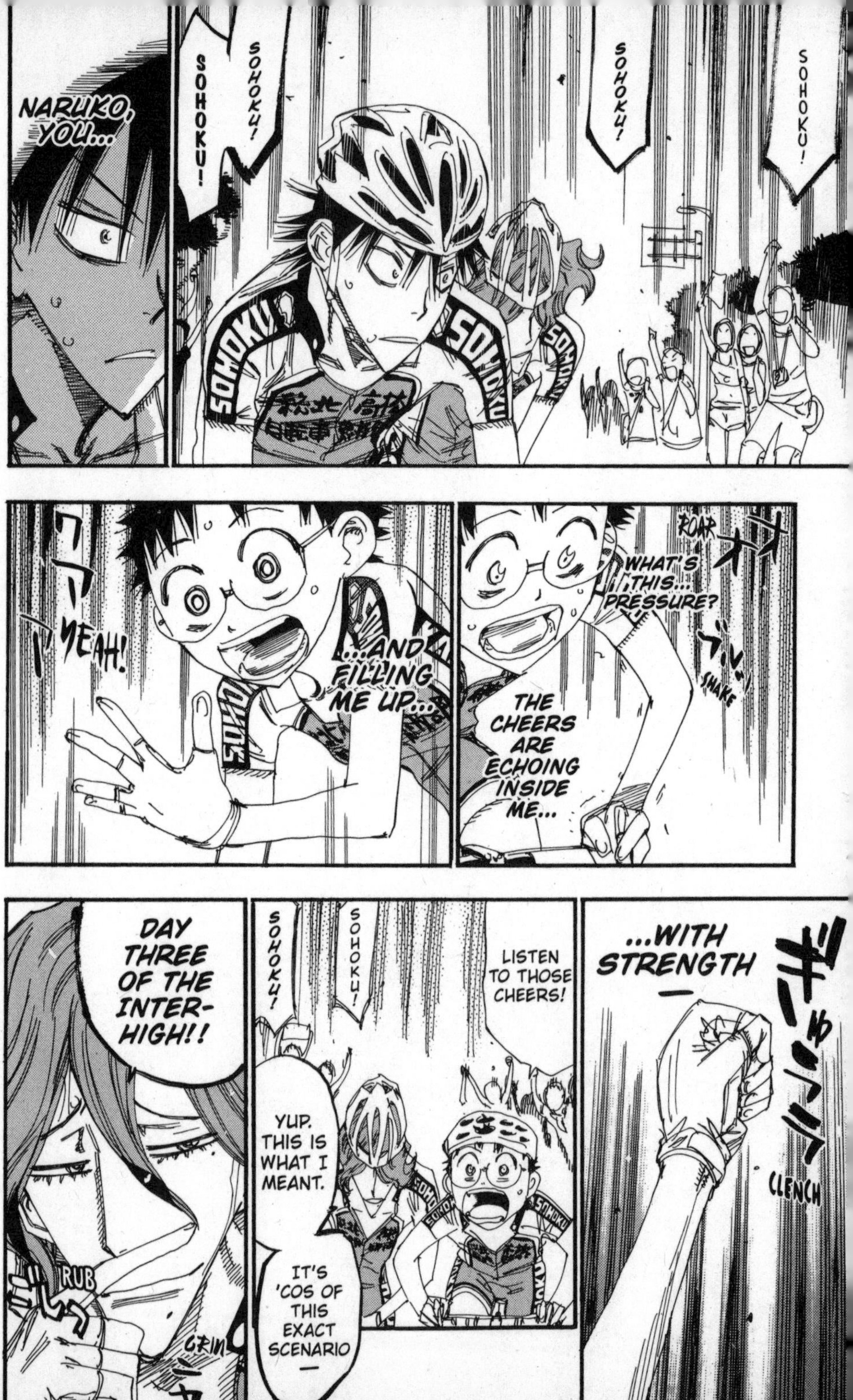
SOHOKU!
SOHOKU!
SOHOKU!
SOHOKU!
NARUKO, YOU...
ROAR
WHAT'S THIS... PRESSURE?
SHAKE
THE CHEERS ARE ECHOING INSIDE ME...
YEAH!
...AND FILLING ME UP...
...WITH STRENGTH—
CLENCH
SOHOKU!
SOHOKU!
LISTEN TO THOSE CHEERS!
YUP. THIS IS WHAT I MEANT.
IT'S 'COS OF THIS EXACT SCENARIO—
DAY THREE OF THE INTER-HIGH!!
RUB
GRIN

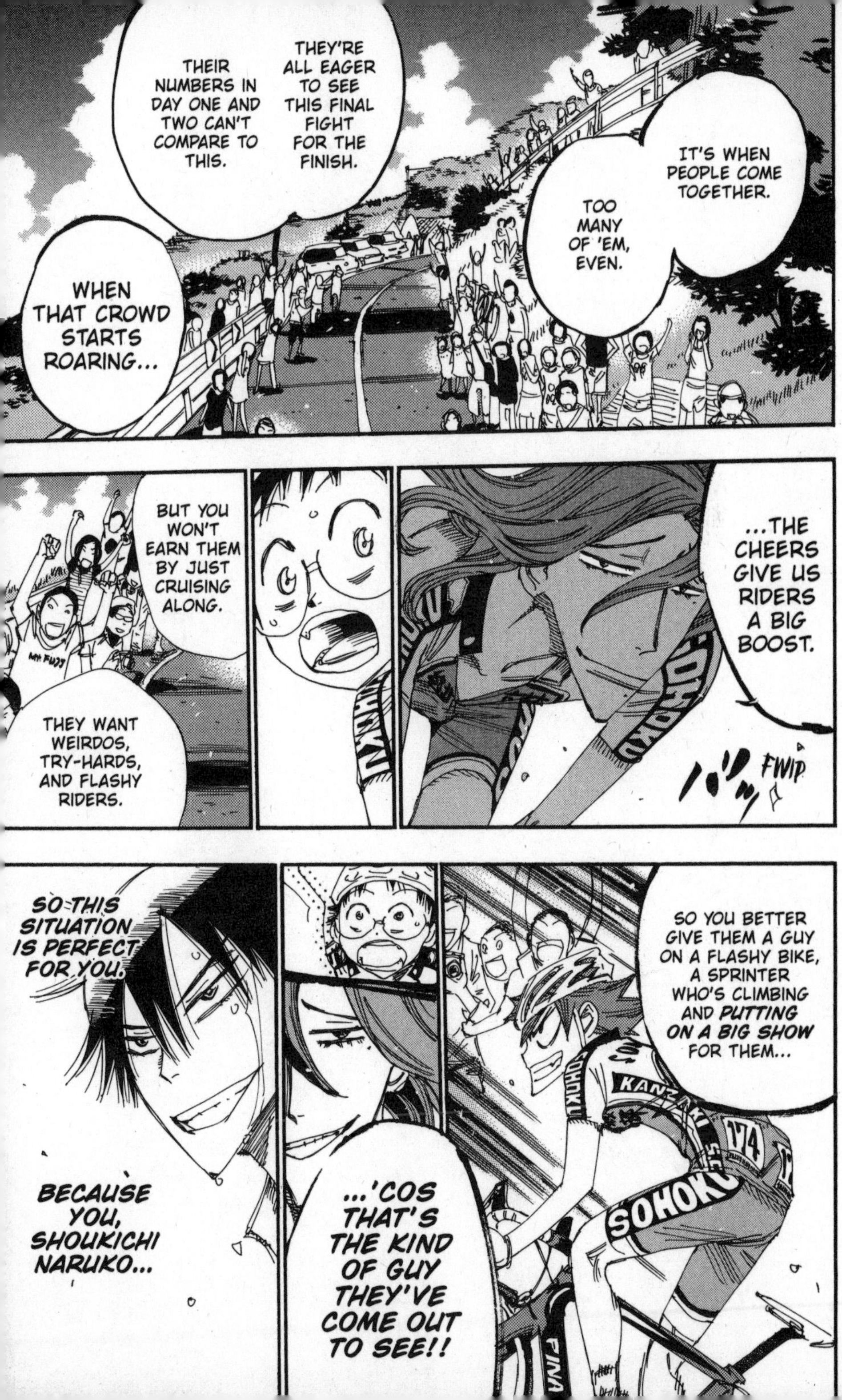
IT'S WHEN PEOPLE COME TOGETHER.
TOO MANY OF 'EM, EVEN.
THEY'RE ALL EAGER TO SEE THIS FINAL FIGHT FOR THE FINISH.
THEIR NUMBERS IN DAY ONE AND TWO CAN'T COMPARE TO THIS.
WHEN THAT CROWD STARTS ROARING...
...THE CHEERS GIVE US RIDERS A BIG BOOST.
FWIP
BUT YOU WON'T EARN THEM BY JUST CRUISING ALONG.
THEY WANT WEIRDOS, TRY-HARDS, AND FLASHY RIDERS.
SO YOU BETTER GIVE THEM A GUY ON A FLASHY BIKE, A SPRINTER WHO'S CLIMBING AND PUTTING ON A BIG SHOW FOR THEM...
...'COS THAT'S THE KIND OF GUY THEY'VE COME OUT TO SEE!!
SO THIS SITUATION IS PERFECT FOR YOU.
BECAUSE YOU, SHOUKICHI NARUKO...

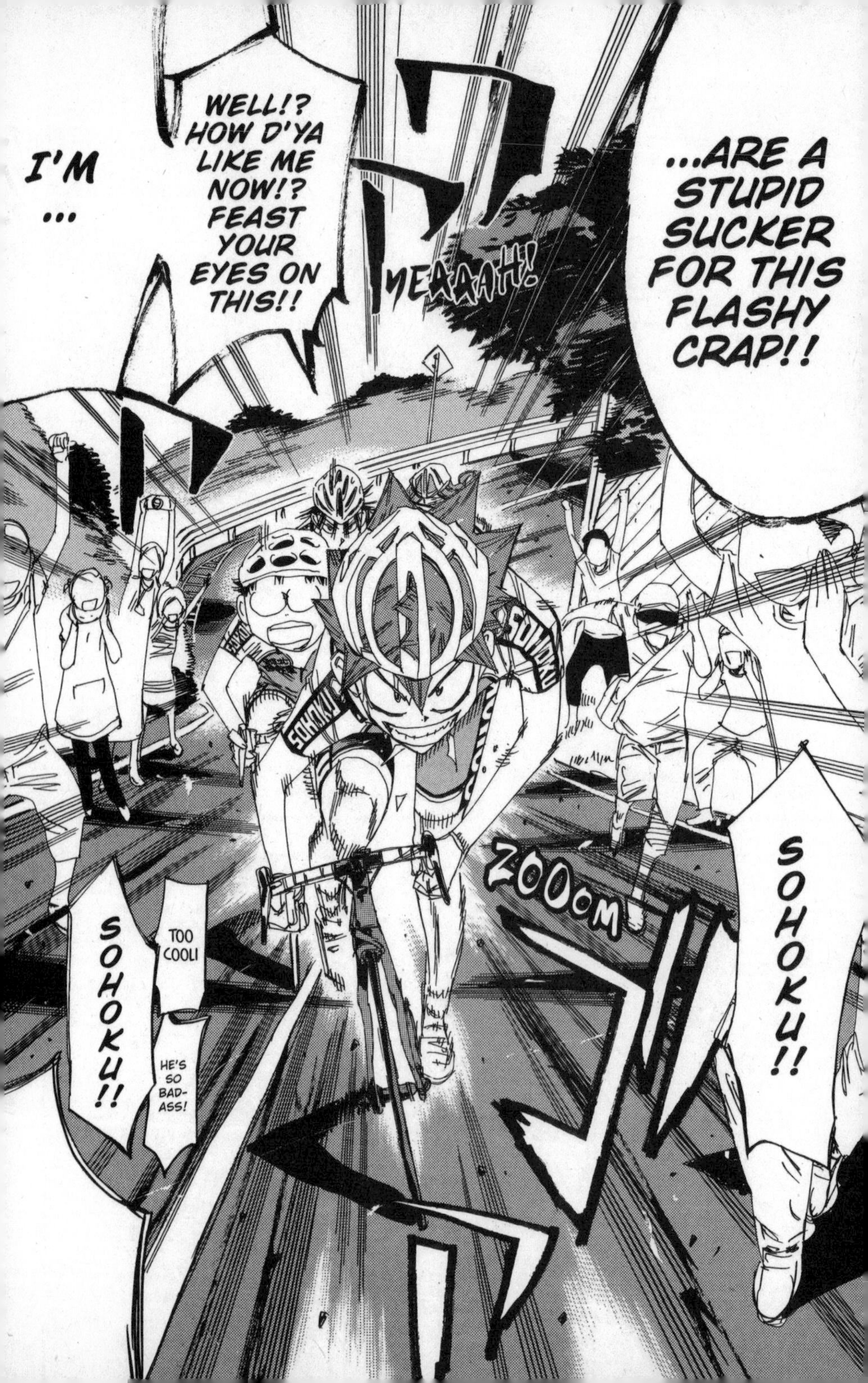
...ARE A STUPID SUCKER FOR THIS FLASHY CRAP!!
YEAAAH!
WELL!? HOW D'YA LIKE ME NOW!? FEAST YOUR EYES ON THIS!!
I'M ...
SOHOKU!!
ZOOOM
TOO COOL!
HE'S SO BAD-ASS!
SOHOKU!!

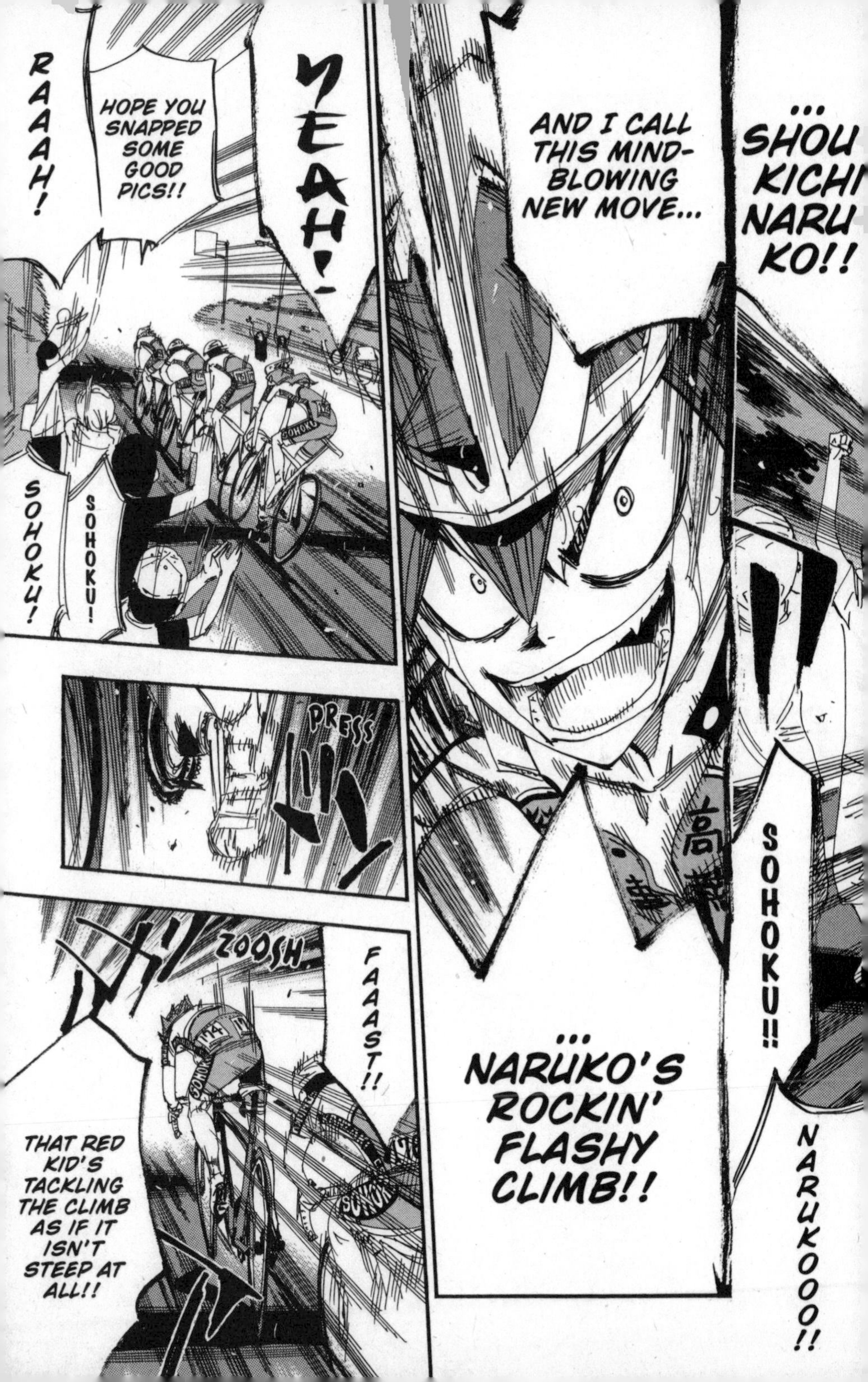

...SHOU KICHI NARU KO!!
AND I CALL THIS MIND-BLOWING NEW MOVE...
SOHOKU!!
...NARUKO'S ROCKIN' FLASHY CLIMB!!
NARUKOOO!!
YEAH!
HOPE YOU SNAPPED SOME GOOD PICS!!
RAAAAH!
SOHOKU!
SOHOKU!
PRESS
ZOOSH
FAAAAST!!
THAT RED KID'S TACKLING THE CLIMB AS IF IT ISN'T STEEP AT ALL!!

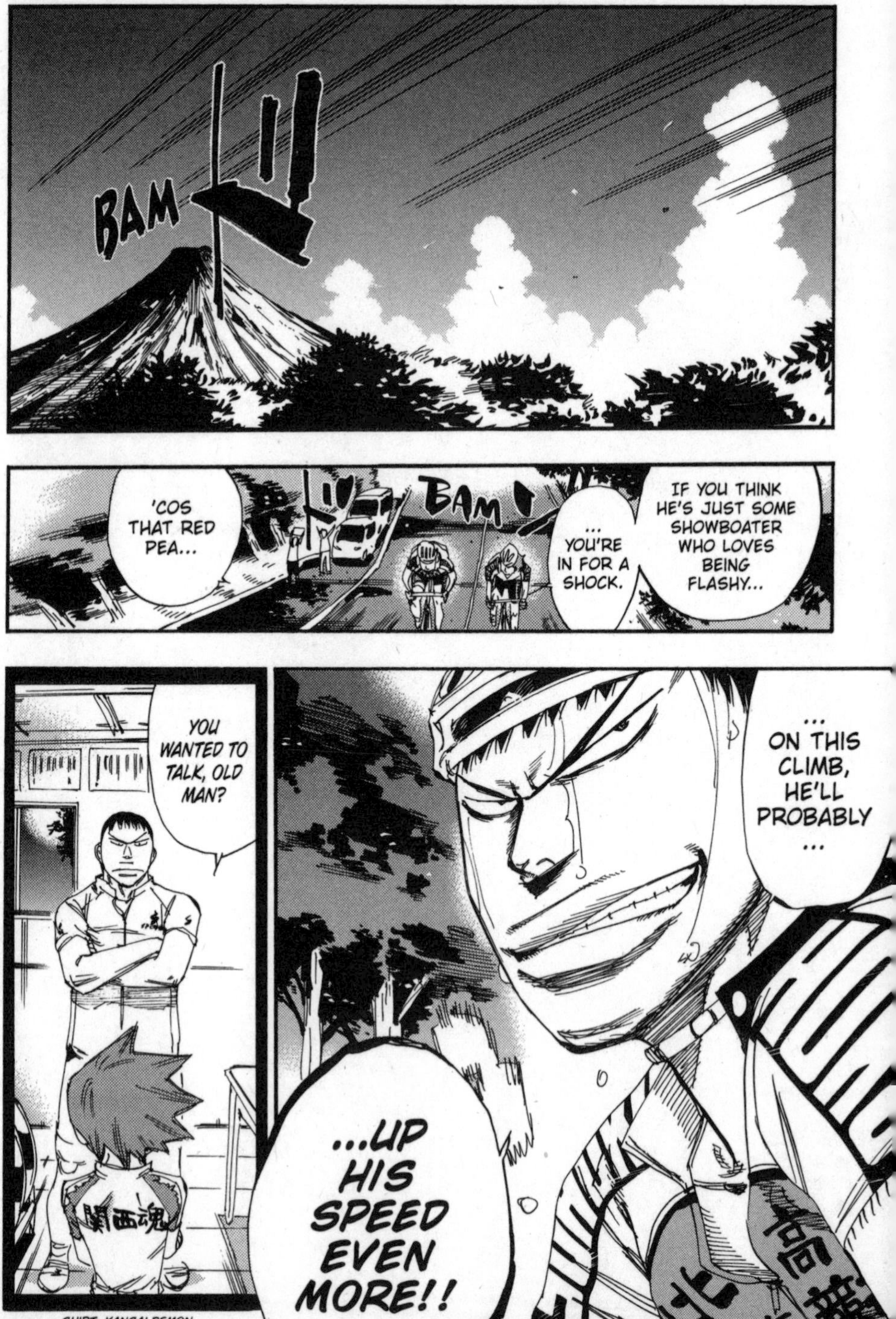
BAM
IF YOU THINK HE'S JUST SOME SHOWBOATER WHO LOVES BEING FLASHY...
...YOU'RE IN FOR A SHOCK.
BAM
'COS THAT RED PEA...
...ON THIS CLIMB, HE'LL PROBABLY...
...UP HIS SPEED EVEN MORE!!
YOU WANTED TO TALK, OLD MAN?
関西魂
SHIRT: KANSAI DEMON

RIDE.193 THE UNVEILING!!

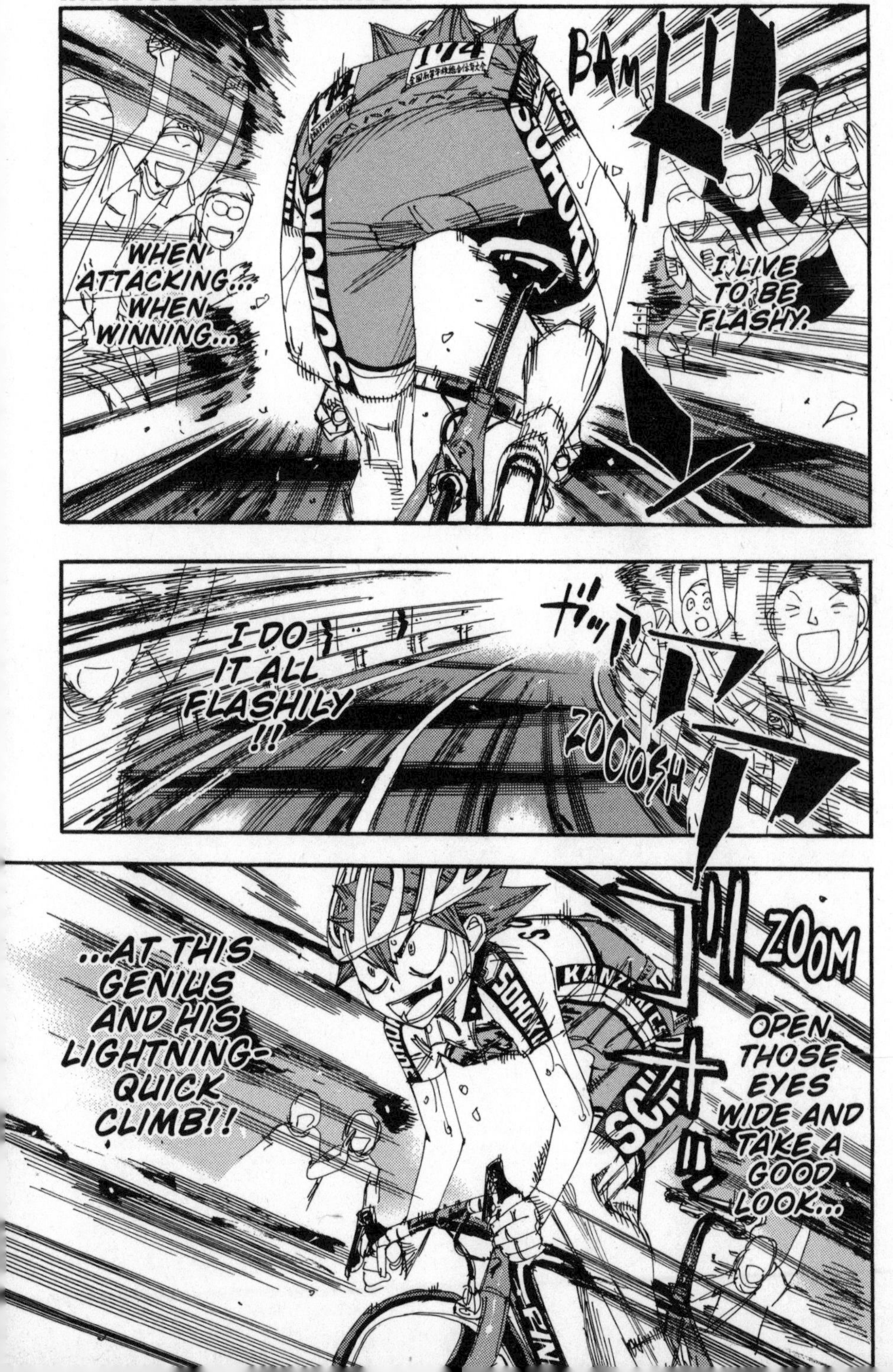

BAM
I LIVE TO BE FLASHY.
WHEN ATTACKING... WHEN WINNING...
ZOOOOSH
I DO IT ALL FLASHILY!!
ZOOM
OPEN THOSE EYES WIDE AND TAKE A GOOD LOOK...
...AT THIS GENIUS AND HIS LIGHTNING-QUICK CLIMB!!

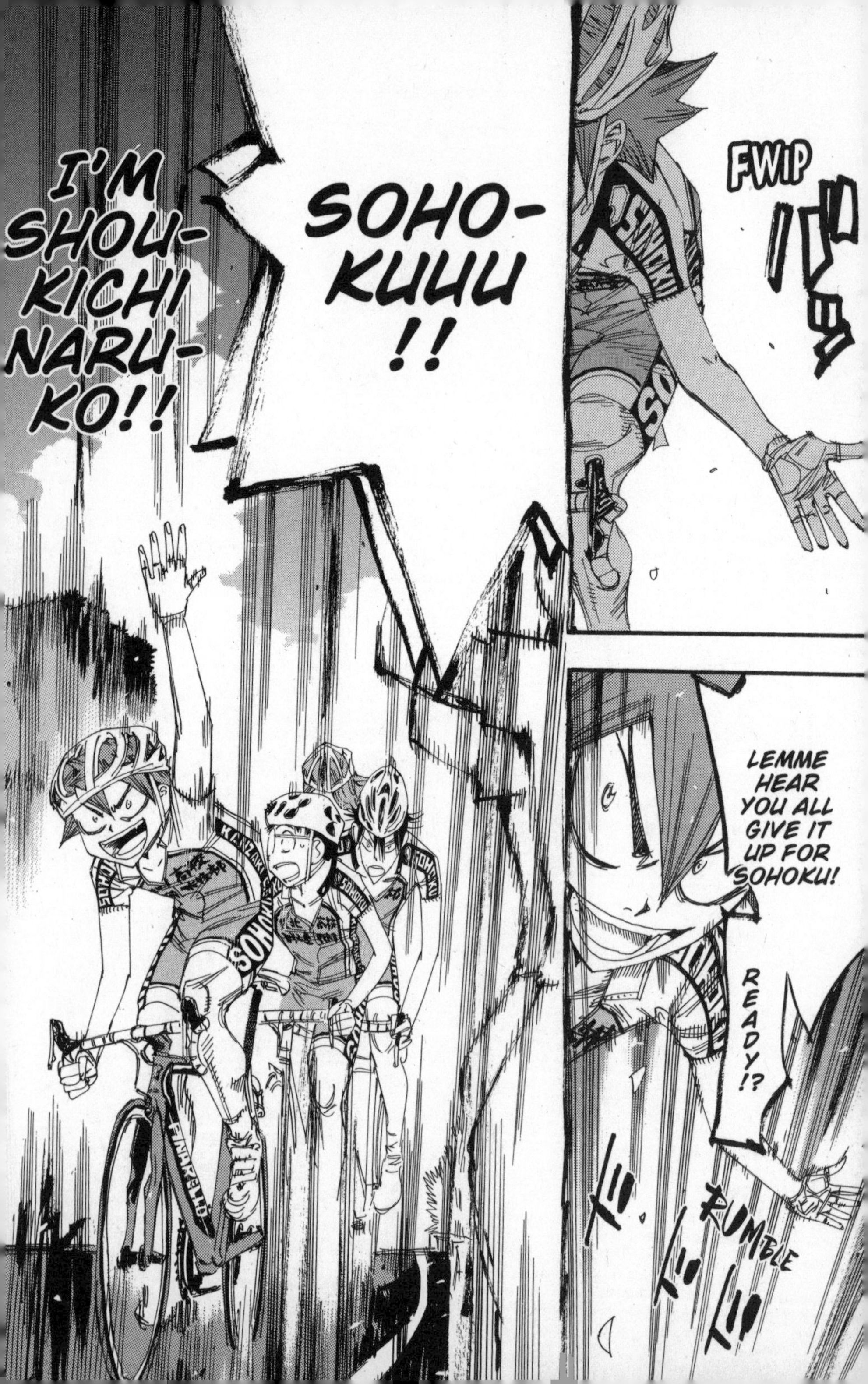
FWIP
LEMME HEAR YOU ALL GIVE IT UP FOR SOHOKU!
READY!?
RUMBLE
SOHO-KUUU!!
I'M SHOU-KICHI NARU-KO!!

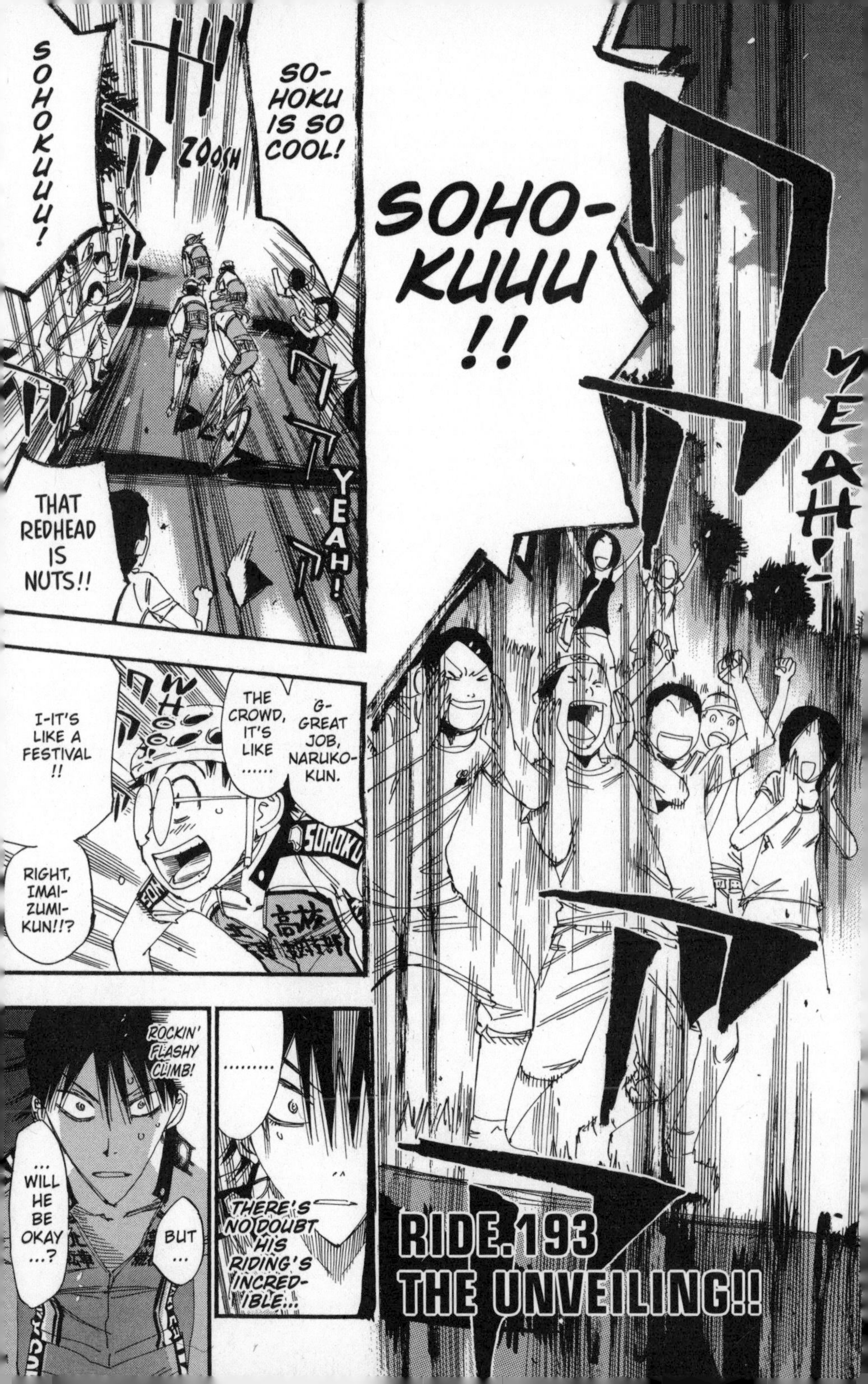
SOHO-KUUU!!
YEAH!
RIDE.193 THE UNVEILING!!
SO-HOKU IS SO COOL!
ZOOSH
SOHOKUUUU!
YEAH!
THAT REDHEAD IS NUTS!!
G-GREAT JOB, NARUKO-KUN.
THE CROWD, IT'S LIKE ......
I-IT'S LIKE A FESTIVAL!!
RIGHT, IMAIZUMI-KUN!!?
....
THERE'S NO DOUBT HIS RIDING'S INCREDIBLE...
ROCKIN' FLASHY CLIMB!
BUT ...
... WILL HE BE OKAY ...?

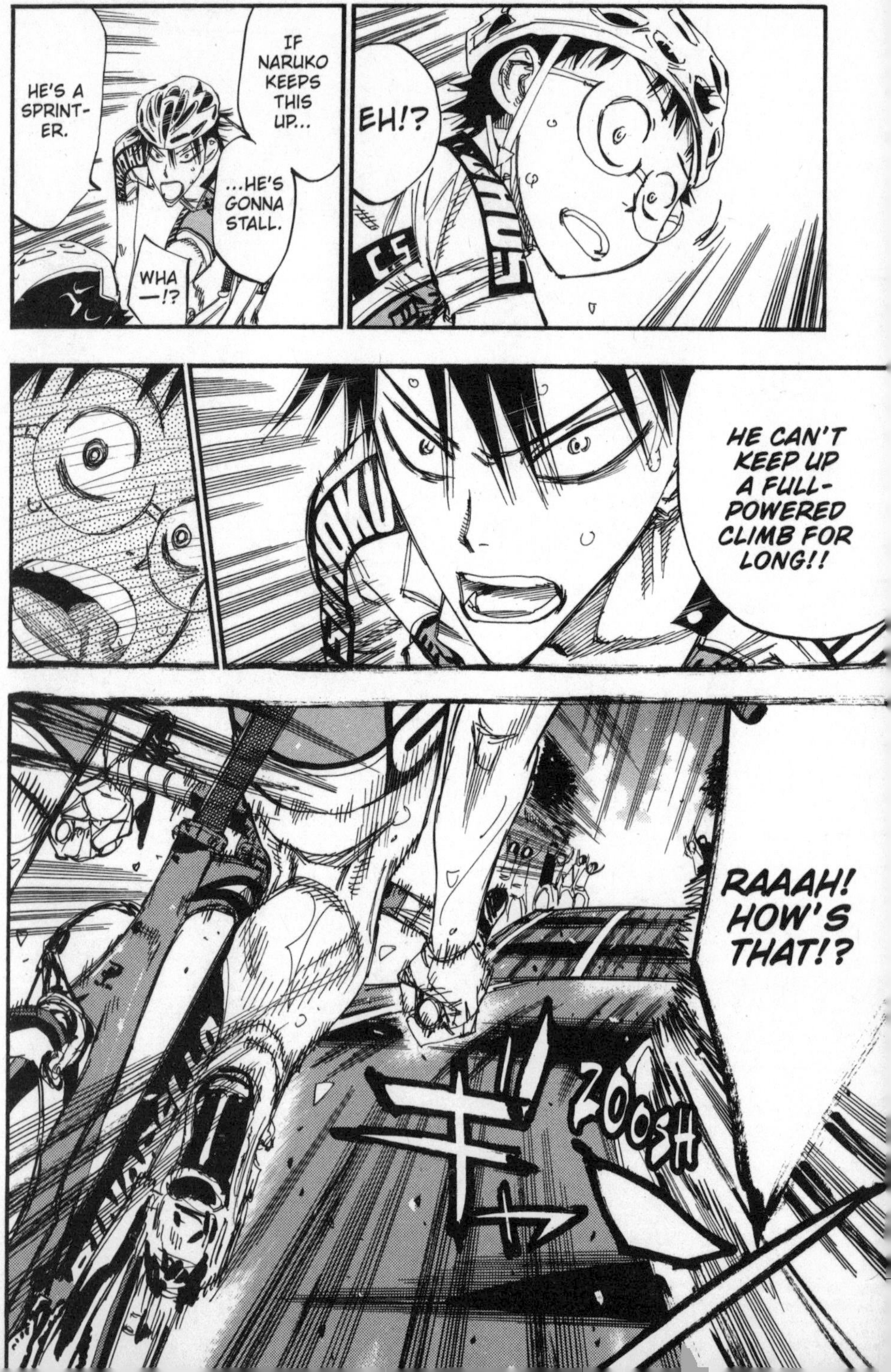
EH!?
IF NARUKO KEEPS THIS UP...
HE'S A SPRINT-ER.
...HE'S GONNA STALL.
WHA—!?
HE CAN'T KEEP UP A FULL-POWERED CLIMB FOR LONG!!
RAAAH! HOW'S THAT!?
ZOOSH

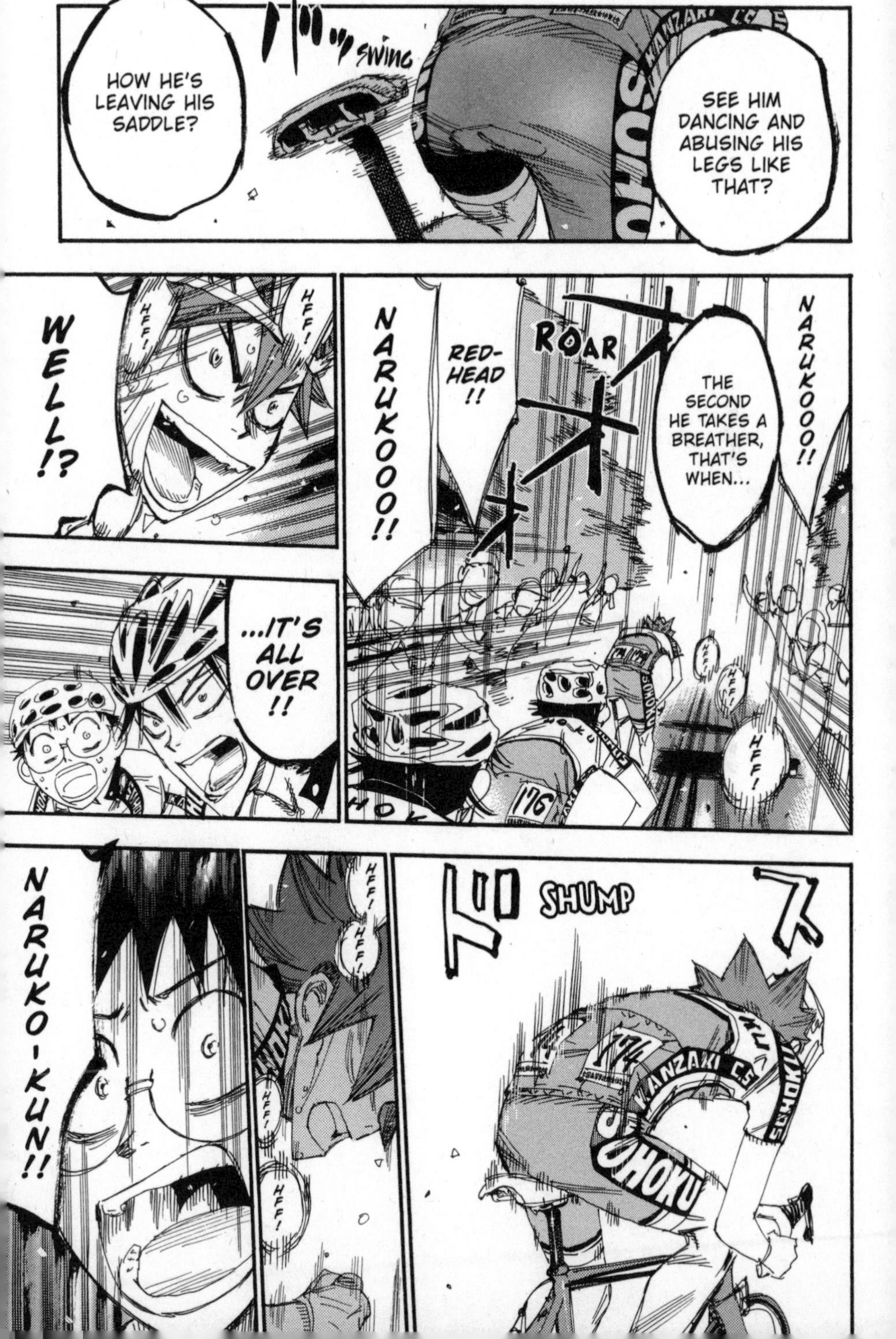
SEE HIM DANCING AND ABUSING HIS LEGS LIKE THAT?
SWING
HOW HE'S LEAVING HIS SADDLE?
NARUKOOOO!!
THE SECOND HE TAKES A BREATHER, THAT'S WHEN...
ROAR
RED-HEAD!!
NARUKOOOO!!
HFF!
HFF!
HFF!
HFF!
HFF!
WELL!?
...IT'S ALL OVER!!
SHUMP
HFF!
HFF!
HFF!
HFF!
NARUKO-KUN!!

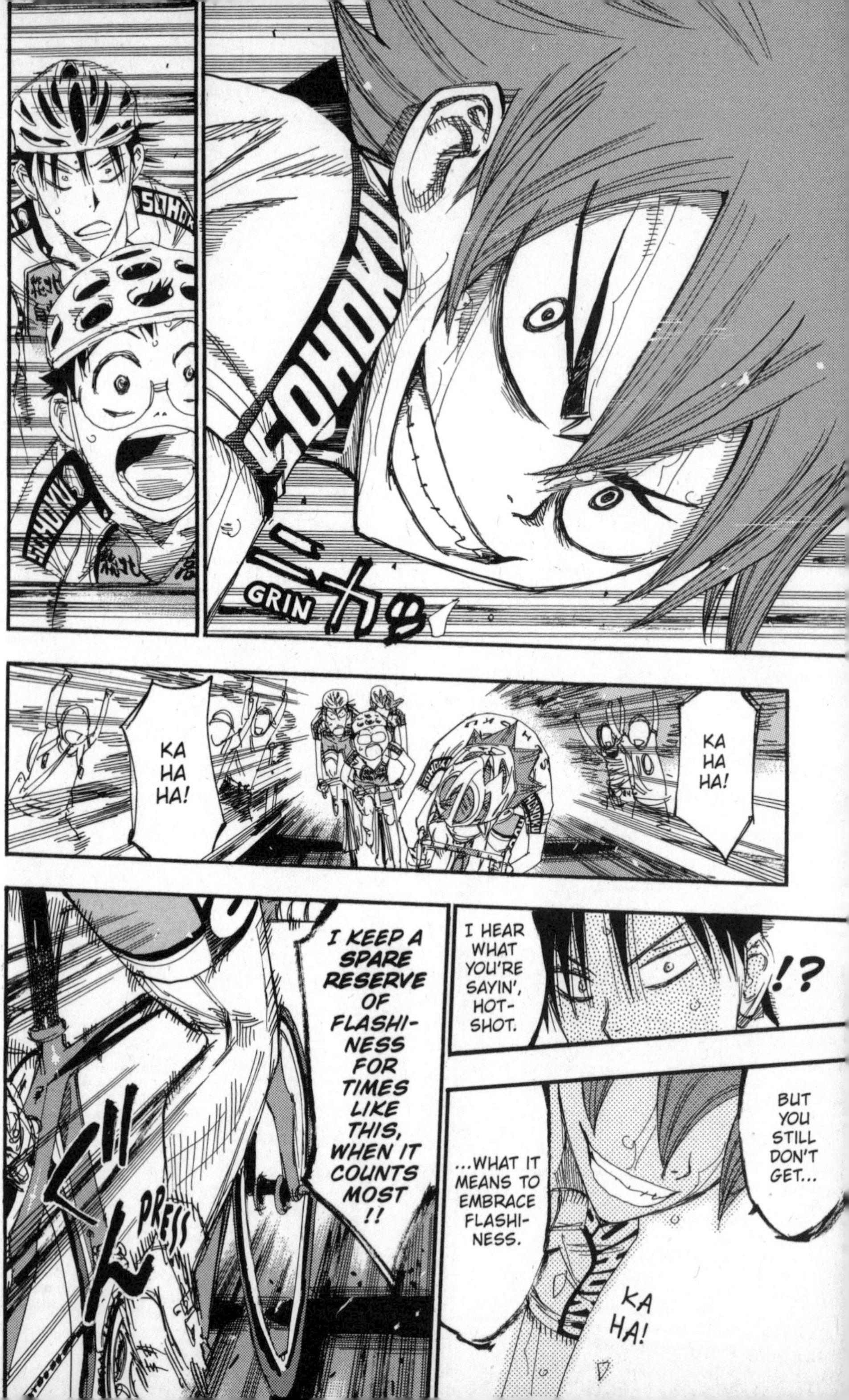
GRIN
KA HA HA!
KA HA HA!
I HEAR WHAT YOU'RE SAYIN', HOT-SHOT.
!?
BUT YOU STILL DON'T GET...
...WHAT IT MEANS TO EMBRACE FLASHI-NESS.
KA HA!
I KEEP A SPARE RESERVE OF FLASHI-NESS FOR TIMES LIKE THIS, WHEN IT COUNTS MOST!!
PRESS

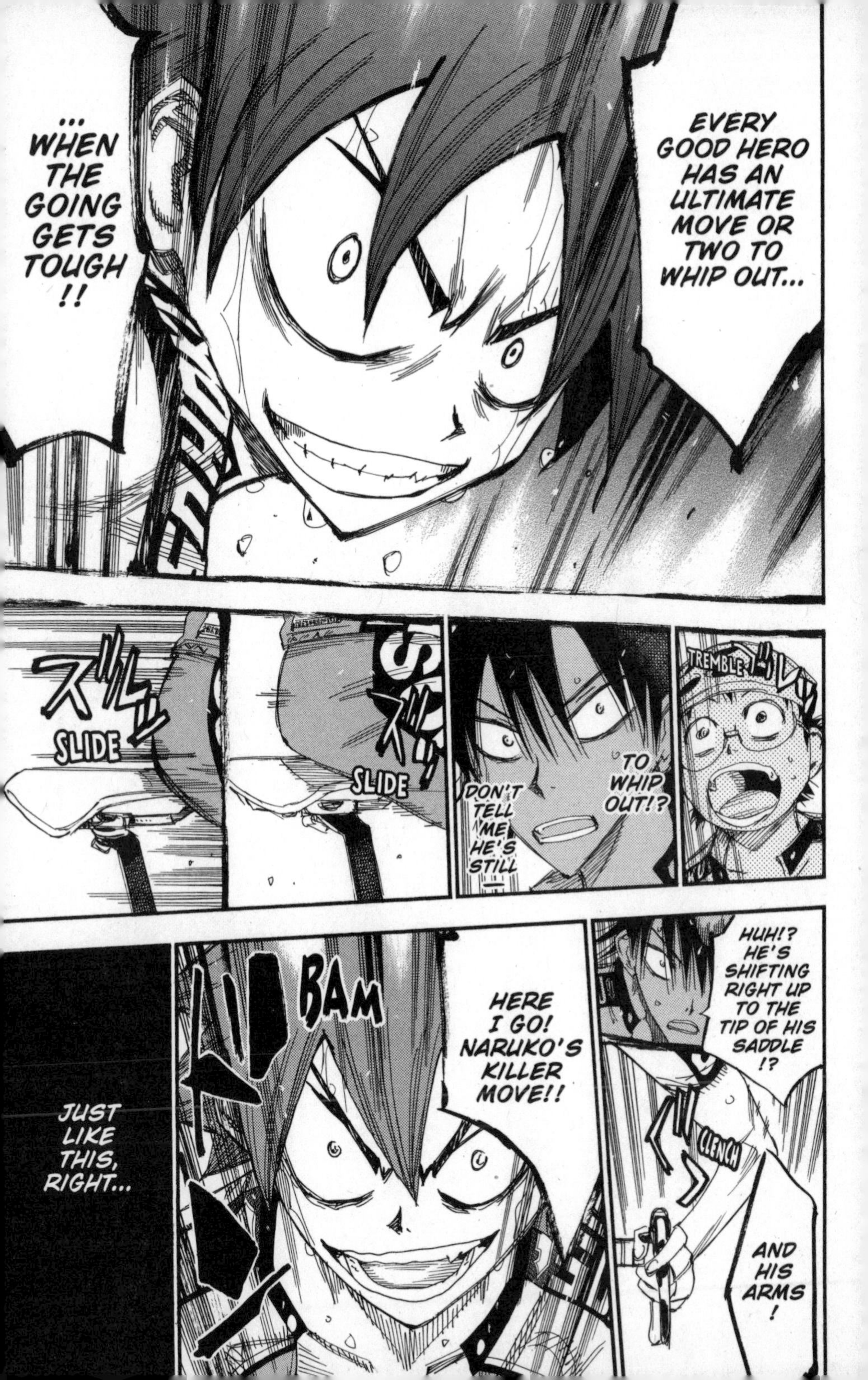
EVERY GOOD HERO HAS AN ULTIMATE MOVE OR TWO TO WHIP OUT...
...WHEN THE GOING GETS TOUGH!!
TREMBLE
TO WHIP OUT!?
DON'T TELL ME HE'S STILL
SLIDE
SLIDE
HUH!? HE'S SHIFTING RIGHT UP TO THE TIP OF HIS SADDLE!?
CLENCH
AND HIS ARMS!
BAM
HERE I GO! NARUKO'S KILLER MOVE!!
JUST LIKE THIS, RIGHT...

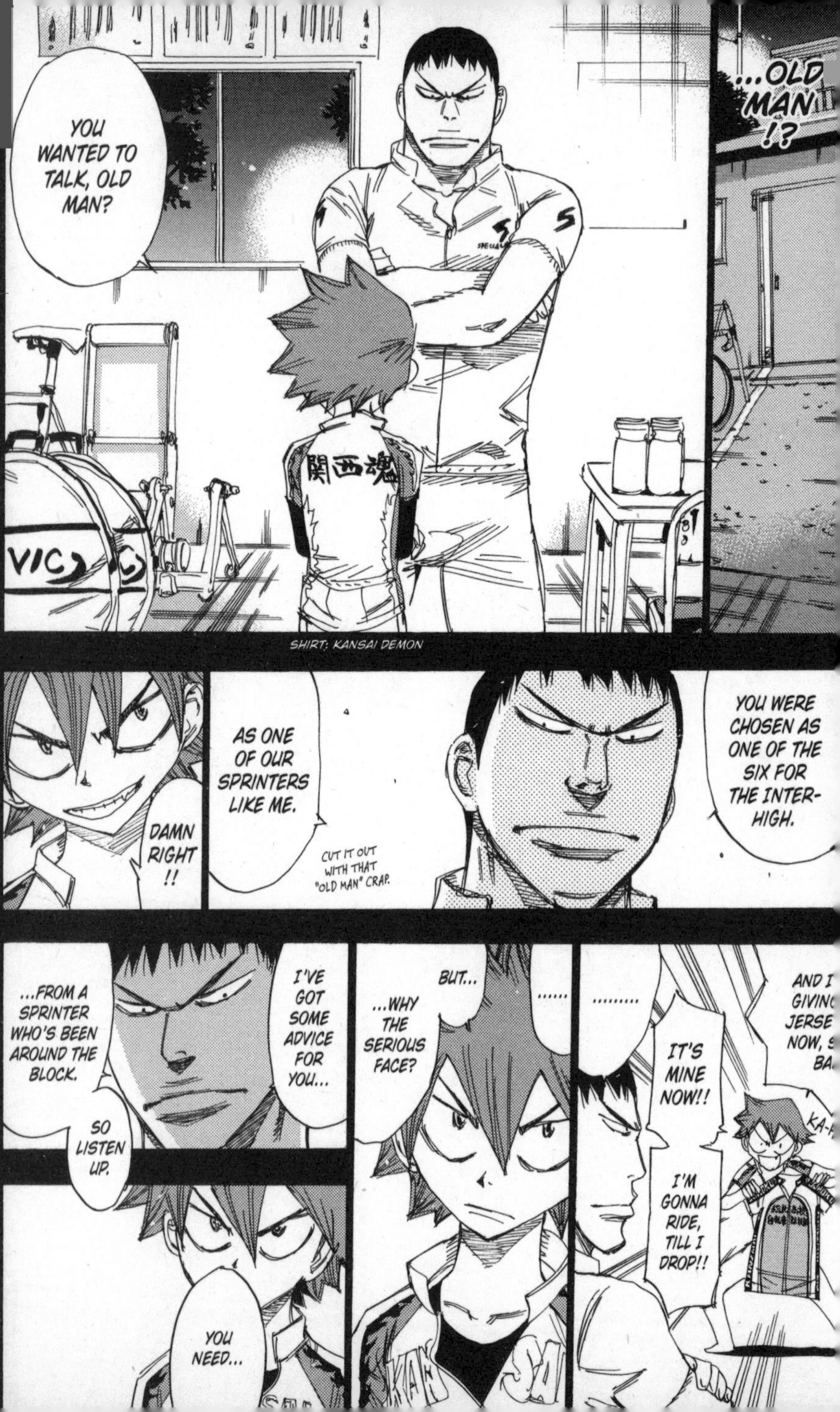
...OLD MAN !?
YOU WANTED TO TALK, OLD MAN?
SHIRT: KANSAI DEMON
YOU WERE CHOSEN AS ONE OF THE SIX FOR THE INTER-HIGH.
AS ONE OF OUR SPRINTERS LIKE ME.
CUT IT OUT WITH THAT "OLD MAN" CRAP.
DAMN RIGHT !!
IT'S MINE NOW!!
I'M GONNA RIDE, TILL I DROP!!
....
......
BUT...
...WHY THE SERIOUS FACE?
I'VE GOT SOME ADVICE FOR YOU...
...FROM A SPRINTER WHO'S BEEN AROUND THE BLOCK.
SO LISTEN UP.
YOU NEED...

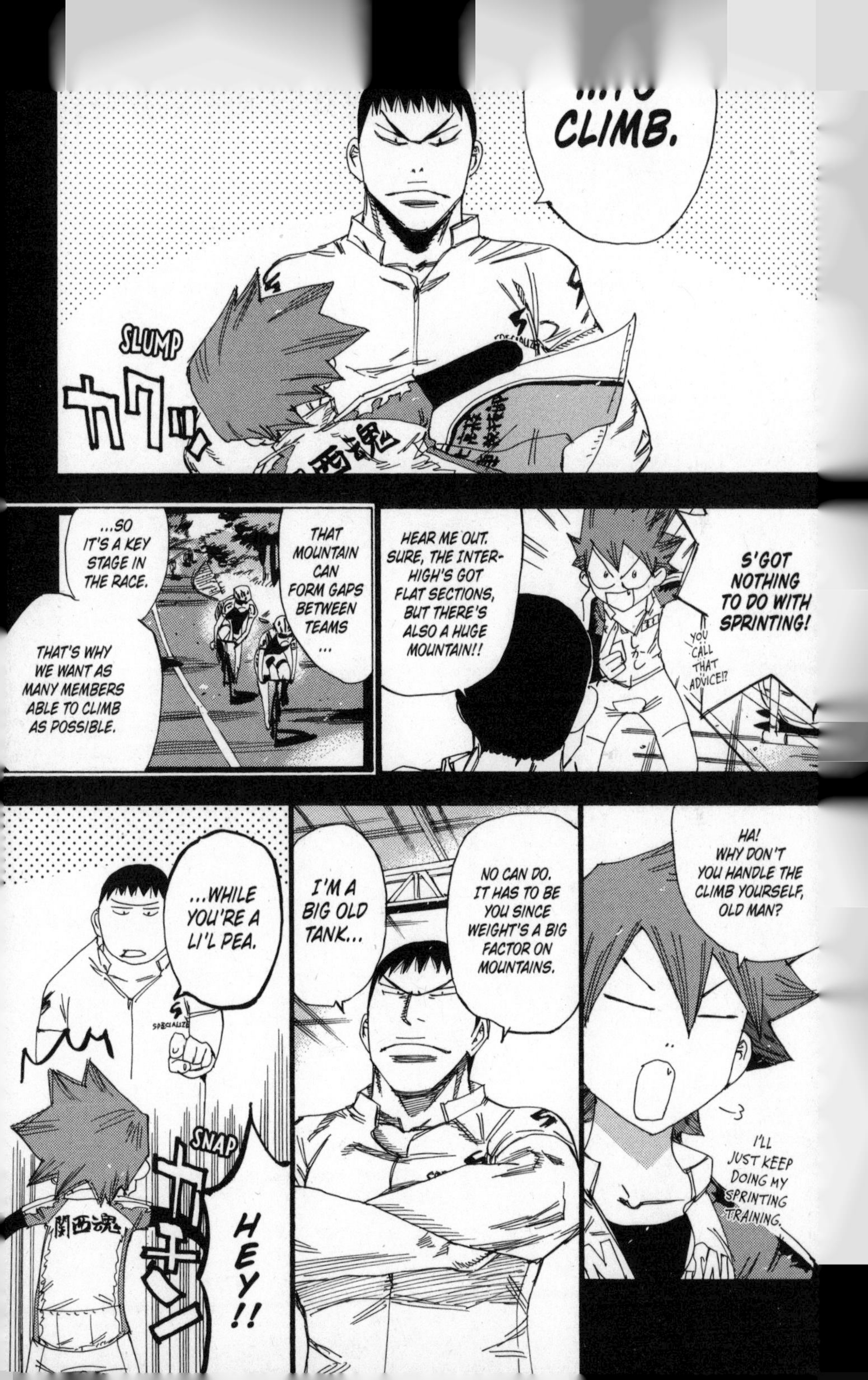
CLIMB.
SLUMP
S'GOT NOTHING TO DO WITH SPRINTING!
YOU CALL THAT ADVICE!?
HEAR ME OUT. SURE, THE INTER-HIGH'S GOT FLAT SECTIONS, BUT THERE'S ALSO A HUGE MOUNTAIN!!
THAT MOUNTAIN CAN FORM GAPS BETWEEN TEAMS ...
...SO IT'S A KEY STAGE IN THE RACE.
THAT'S WHY WE WANT AS MANY MEMBERS ABLE TO CLIMB AS POSSIBLE.
HA! WHY DON'T YOU HANDLE THE CLIMB YOURSELF, OLD MAN?
I'LL JUST KEEP DOING MY SPRINTING TRAINING.
NO CAN DO. IT HAS TO BE YOU SINCE WEIGHT'S A BIG FACTOR ON MOUNTAINS.
I'M A BIG OLD TANK...
...WHILE YOU'RE A LI'L PEA.
SNAP
HEY!!

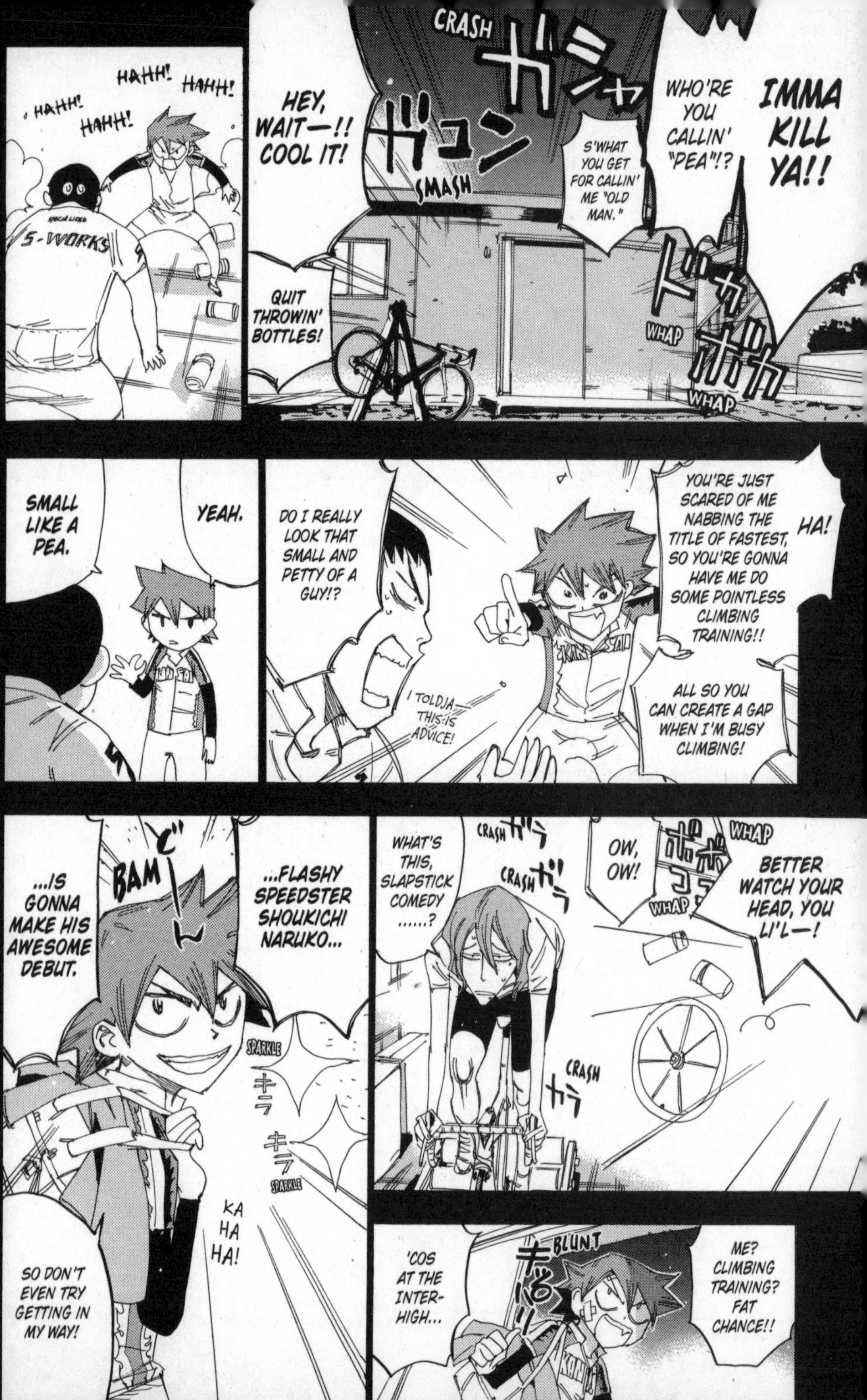
IMMA KILL YA!!
WHO'RE YOU CALLIN' "PEA"!?
CRASH
S'WHAT YOU GET FOR CALLIN' ME "OLD MAN."
HEY, WAIT—!! COOL IT!
SMASH
WHAP
WHAP
QUIT THROWIN' BOTTLES!
HAHH! HAHH!
HAHH! HAHH!
HA!
YOU'RE JUST SCARED OF ME NABBING THE TITLE OF FASTEST, SO YOU'RE GONNA HAVE ME DO SOME POINTLESS CLIMBING TRAINING!!
DO I REALLY LOOK THAT SMALL AND PETTY OF A GUY!?
ALL SO YOU CAN CREATE A GAP WHEN I'M BUSY CLIMBING!
I TOLDJA THIS IS ADVICE!
YEAH.
SMALL LIKE A PEA.
BETTER WATCH YOUR HEAD, YOU LI'L—!
WHAP
OW, OW!
WHAP
WHAT'S THIS, SLAPSTICK COMEDY......?
CRASH
CRASH
CRASH
ME? CLIMBING TRAINING? FAT CHANCE!!
BLUNT
'COS AT THE INTER-HIGH...
...FLASHY SPEEDSTER SHOUKICHI NARUKO...
BAM
...IS GONNA MAKE HIS AWESOME DEBUT.
SPARKLE
SPARKLE
KA HA HA!
SO DON'T EVEN TRY GETTING IN MY WAY!

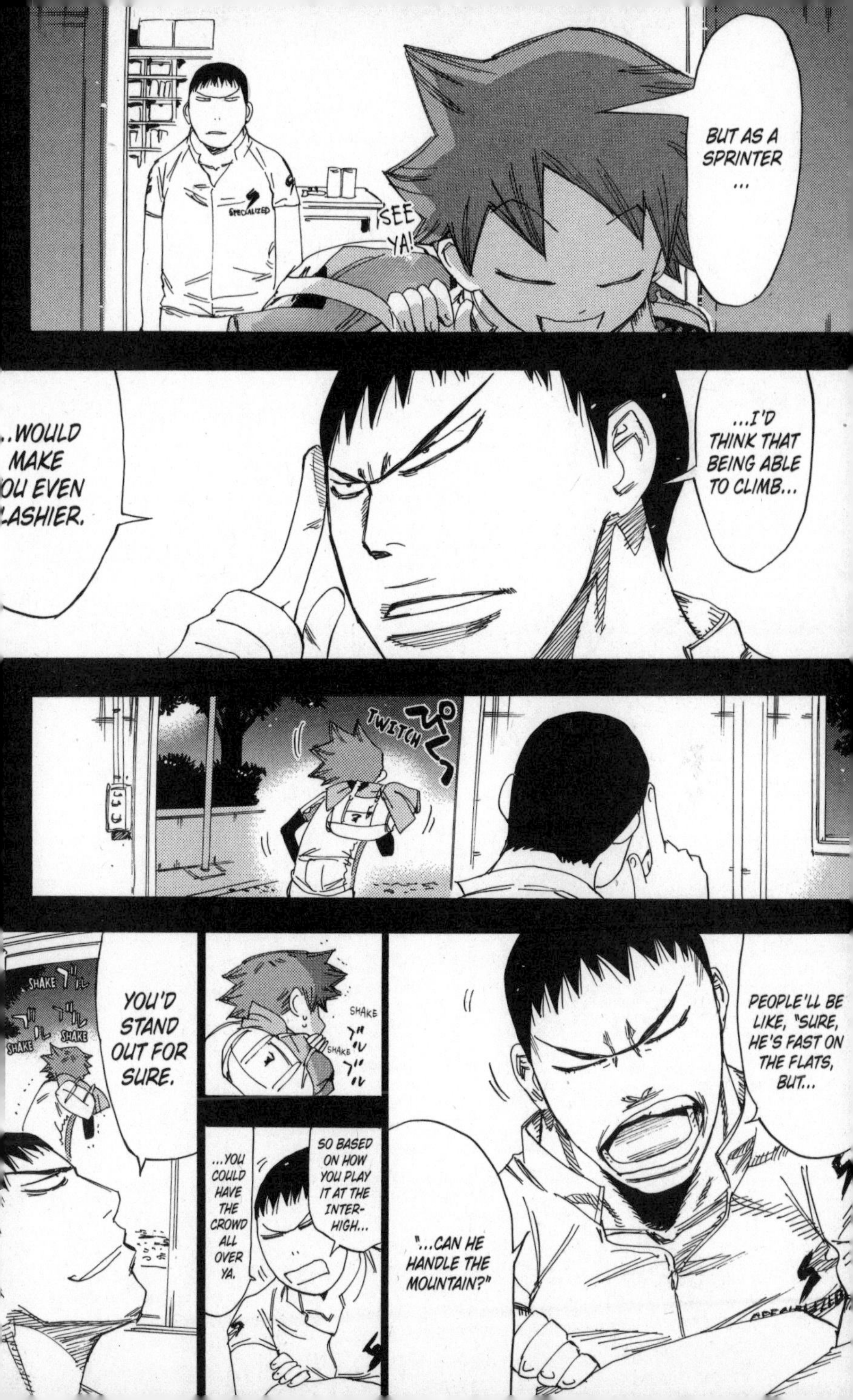

BUT AS A SPRINTER ...
SEE YA!
SPECIALIZED
...I'D THINK THAT BEING ABLE TO CLIMB...
..WOULD MAKE OU EVEN LASHIER.
TWITCH
PEOPLE'LL BE LIKE, "SURE, HE'S FAST ON THE FLATS, BUT...
"...CAN HE HANDLE THE MOUNTAIN?"
SHAKE
SHAKE
SO BASED ON HOW YOU PLAY IT AT THE INTER-HIGH...
...YOU COULD HAVE THE CROWD ALL OVER YA.
YOU'D STAND OUT FOR SURE.
SHAKE
SHAKE
SHAKE

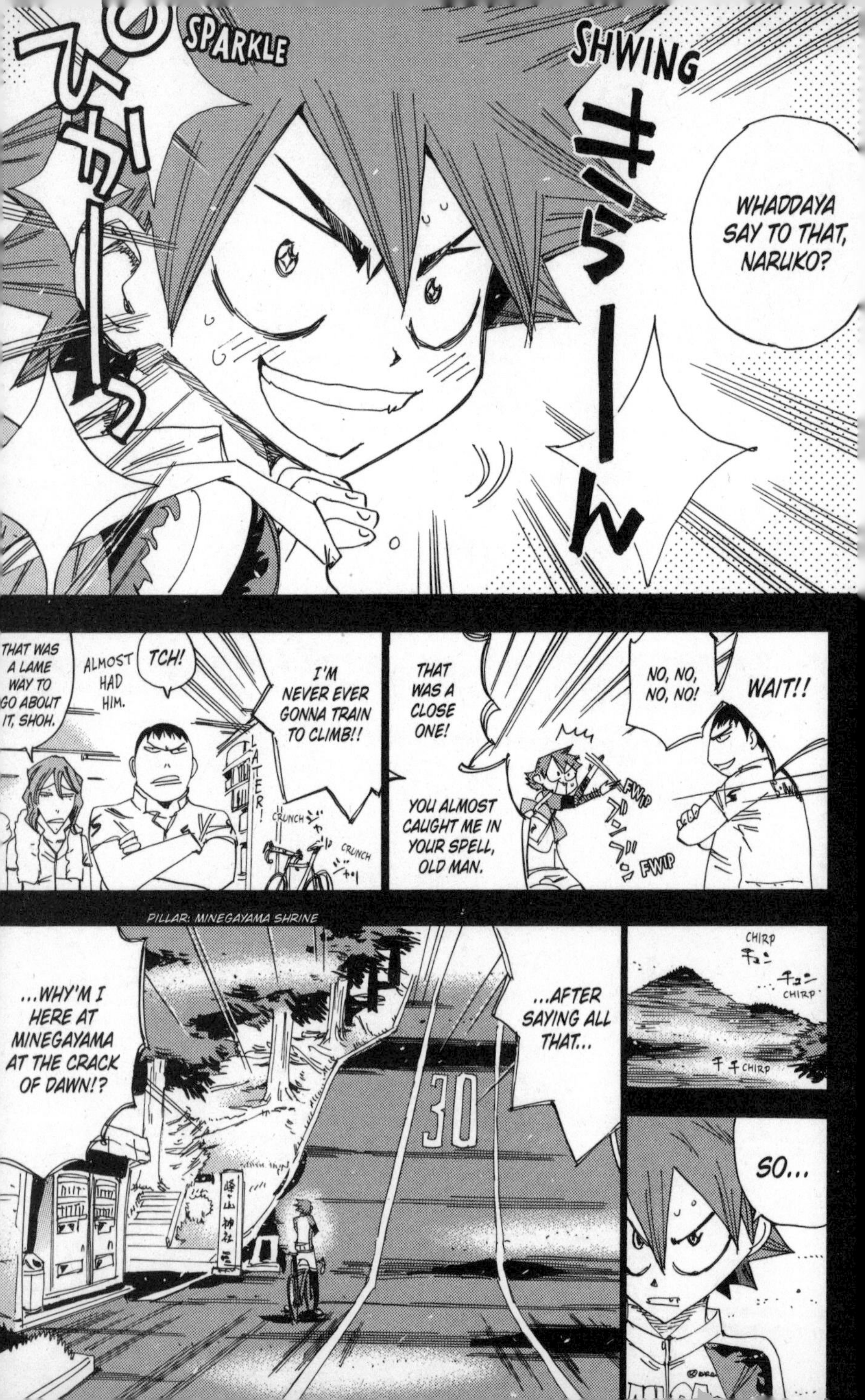
SHWING
WHADDAYA SAY TO THAT, NARUKO?
SPARKLE
WAIT!!
NO, NO, NO, NO!
THAT WAS A CLOSE ONE!
YOU ALMOST CAUGHT ME IN YOUR SPELL, OLD MAN.
FWIP
FWIP
I'M NEVER EVER GONNA TRAIN TO CLIMB!!
LATER!
TCH!
ALMOST HAD HIM.
THAT WAS A LAME WAY TO GO ABOUT IT, SHOH.
CRUNCH
CRUNCH
CHIRP
CHIRP
CHIRP
SO...
...AFTER SAYING ALL THAT...
...WHY'M I HERE AT MINEGAYAMA AT THE CRACK OF DAWN!?
PILLAR: MINEGAYAMA SHRINE
30

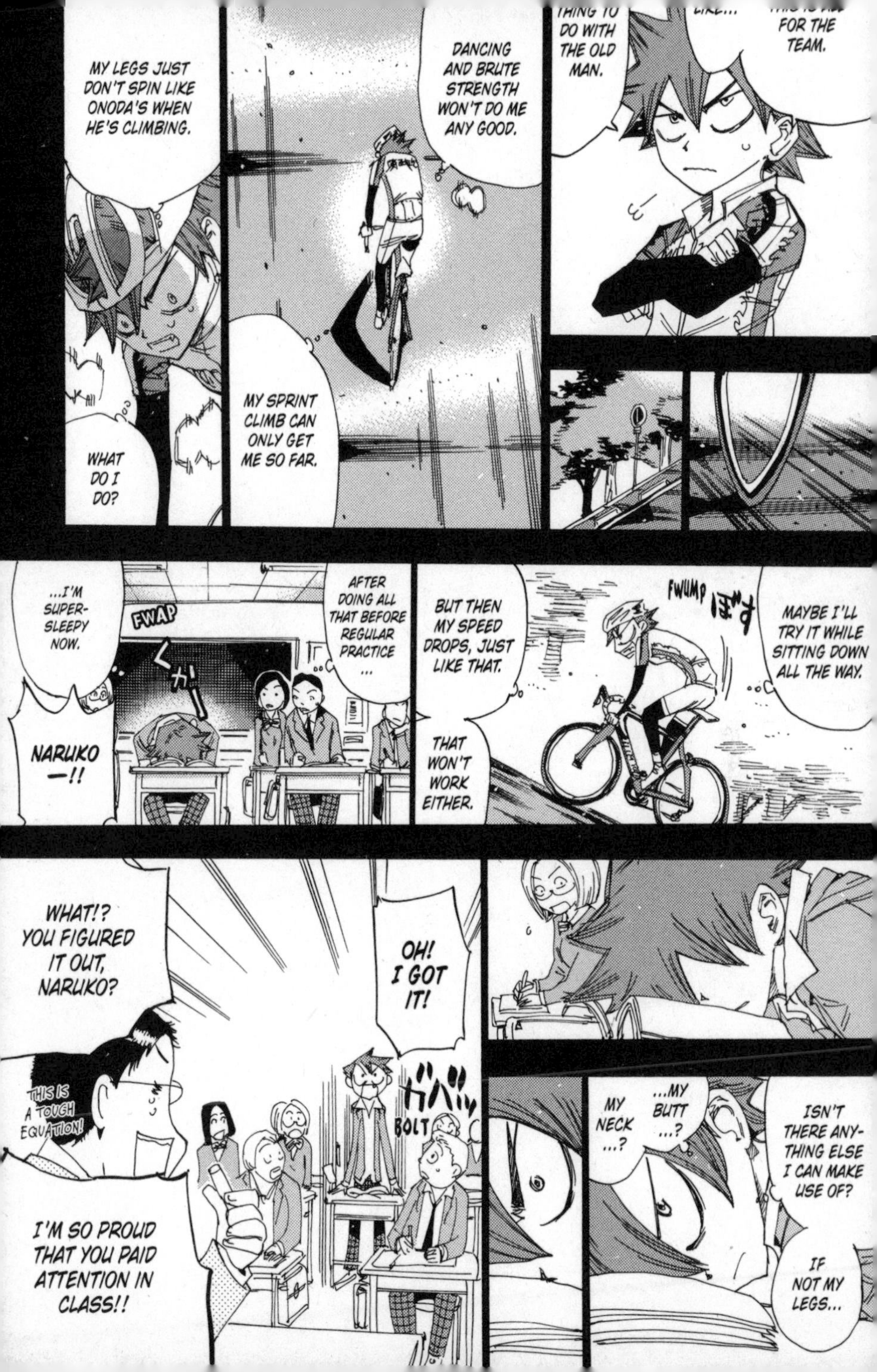
FOR THE TEAM.
LIKE...
THING TO DO WITH THE OLD MAN.
DANCING AND BRUTE STRENGTH WON'T DO ME ANY GOOD.
MY SPRINT CLIMB CAN ONLY GET ME SO FAR.
MY LEGS JUST DON'T SPIN LIKE ONODA'S WHEN HE'S CLIMBING.
WHAT DO I DO?
FWUMP
MAYBE I'LL TRY IT WHILE SITTING DOWN ALL THE WAY.
BUT THEN MY SPEED DROPS, JUST LIKE THAT.
THAT WON'T WORK EITHER.
AFTER DOING ALL THAT BEFORE REGULAR PRACTICE ...
...I'M SUPER-SLEEPY NOW.
FWAP
NARUKO—!!
ISN'T THERE ANYTHING ELSE I CAN MAKE USE OF?
IF NOT MY LEGS...
...MY BUTT ...?
MY NECK ...?
OH! I GOT IT!
BOLT
WHAT!? YOU FIGURED IT OUT, NARUKO?
THIS IS A TOUGH EQUATION!
I'M SO PROUD THAT YOU PAID ATTENTION IN CLASS!!

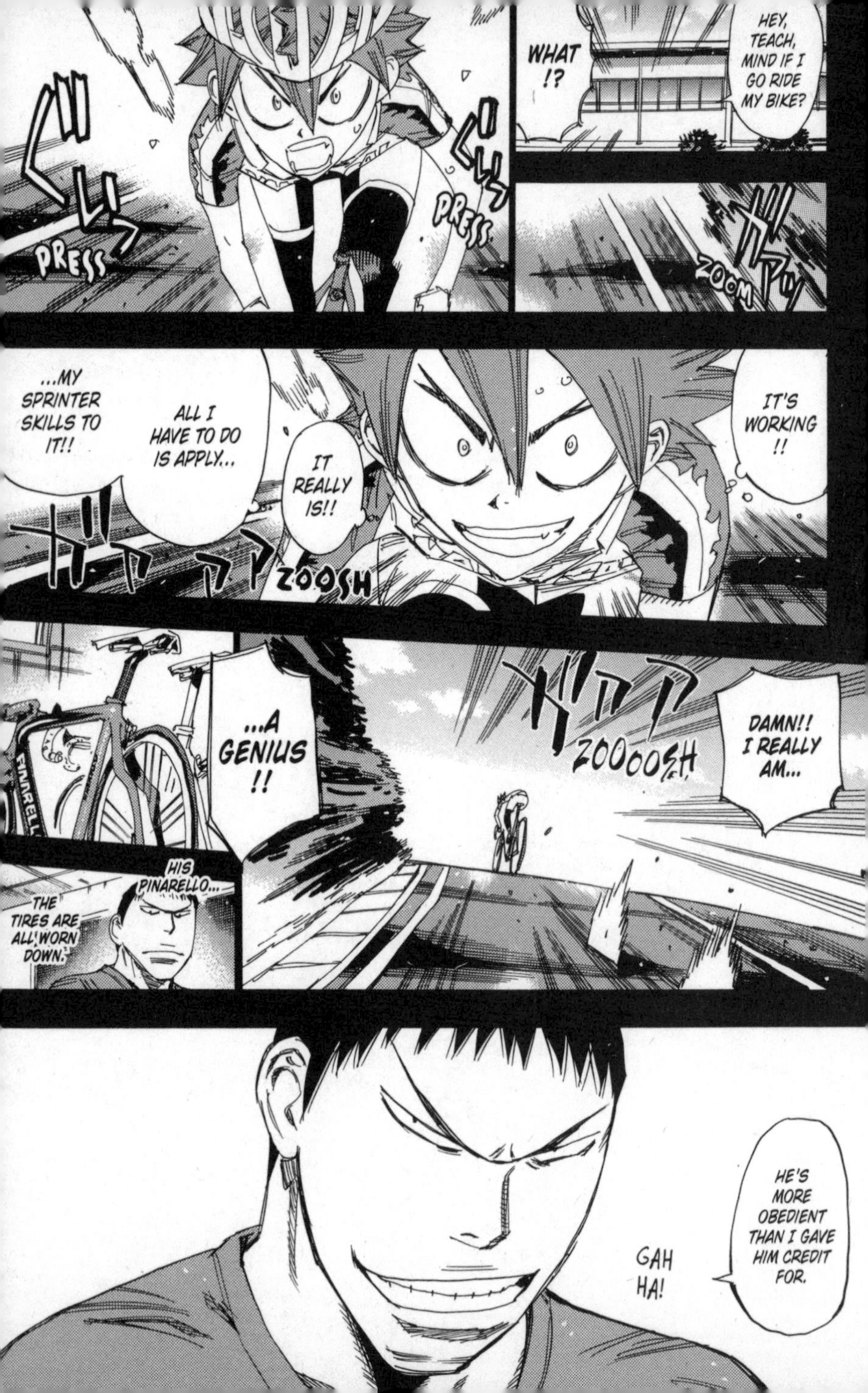
HEY, TEACH, MIND IF I GO RIDE MY BIKE?
WHAT !?
ZOOM
PRESS
PRESS
IT'S WORKING !!
IT REALLY IS!!
ALL I HAVE TO DO IS APPLY...
...MY SPRINTER SKILLS TO IT!!
ZOOSH
DAMN!! I REALLY AM...
ZOOOOSH
...A GENIUS !!
HIS PINARELLO...
THE TIRES ARE ALL WORN DOWN.
HE'S MORE OBEDIENT THAN I GAVE HIM CREDIT FOR.
GAH HA!

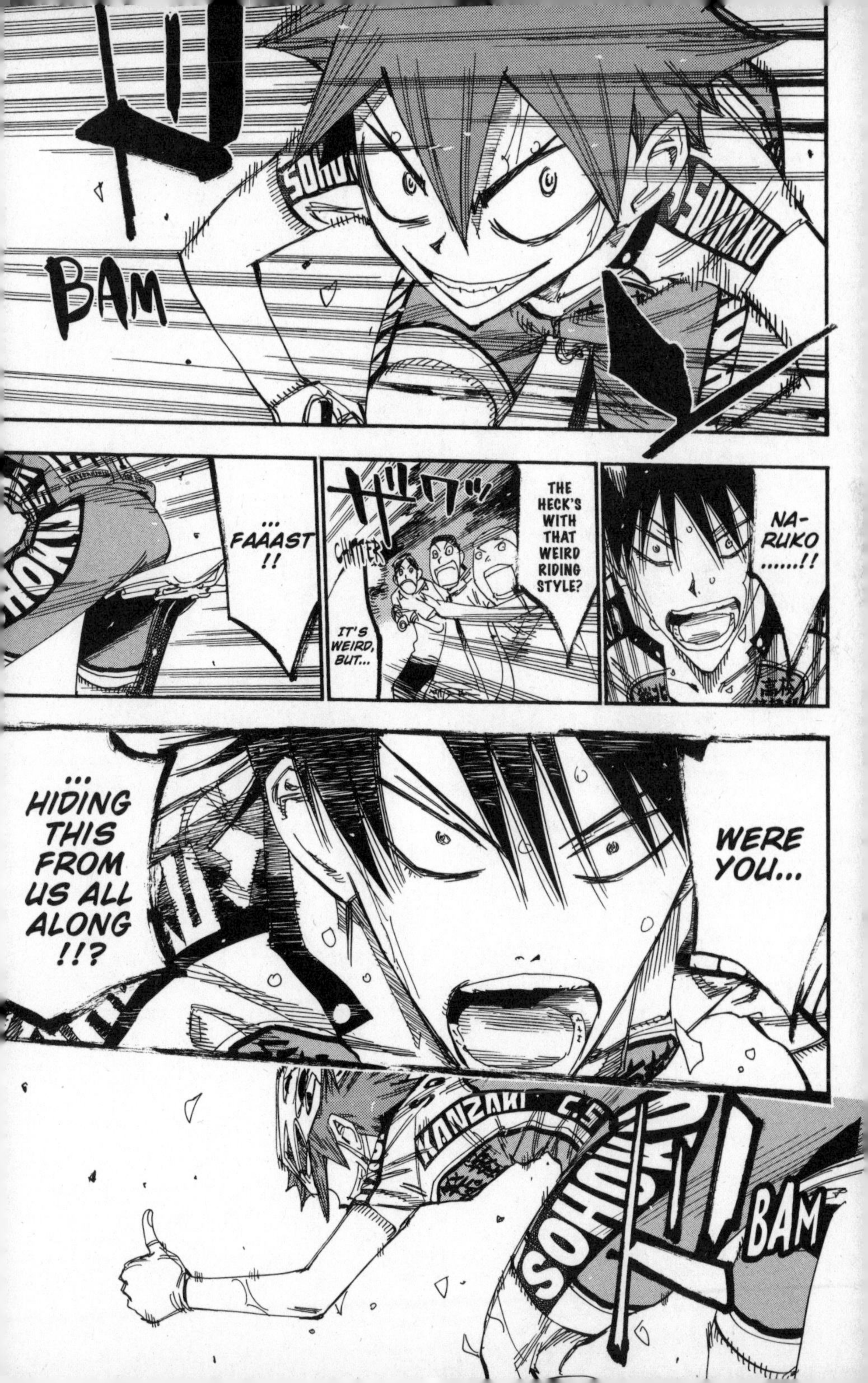
BAM
NA-RUKO ......!!
THE HECK'S WITH THAT WEIRD RIDING STYLE?
CHATTER
IT'S WEIRD, BUT...
... FAAAST !!
WERE YOU...
... HIDING THIS FROM US ALL ALONG !!?
BAM

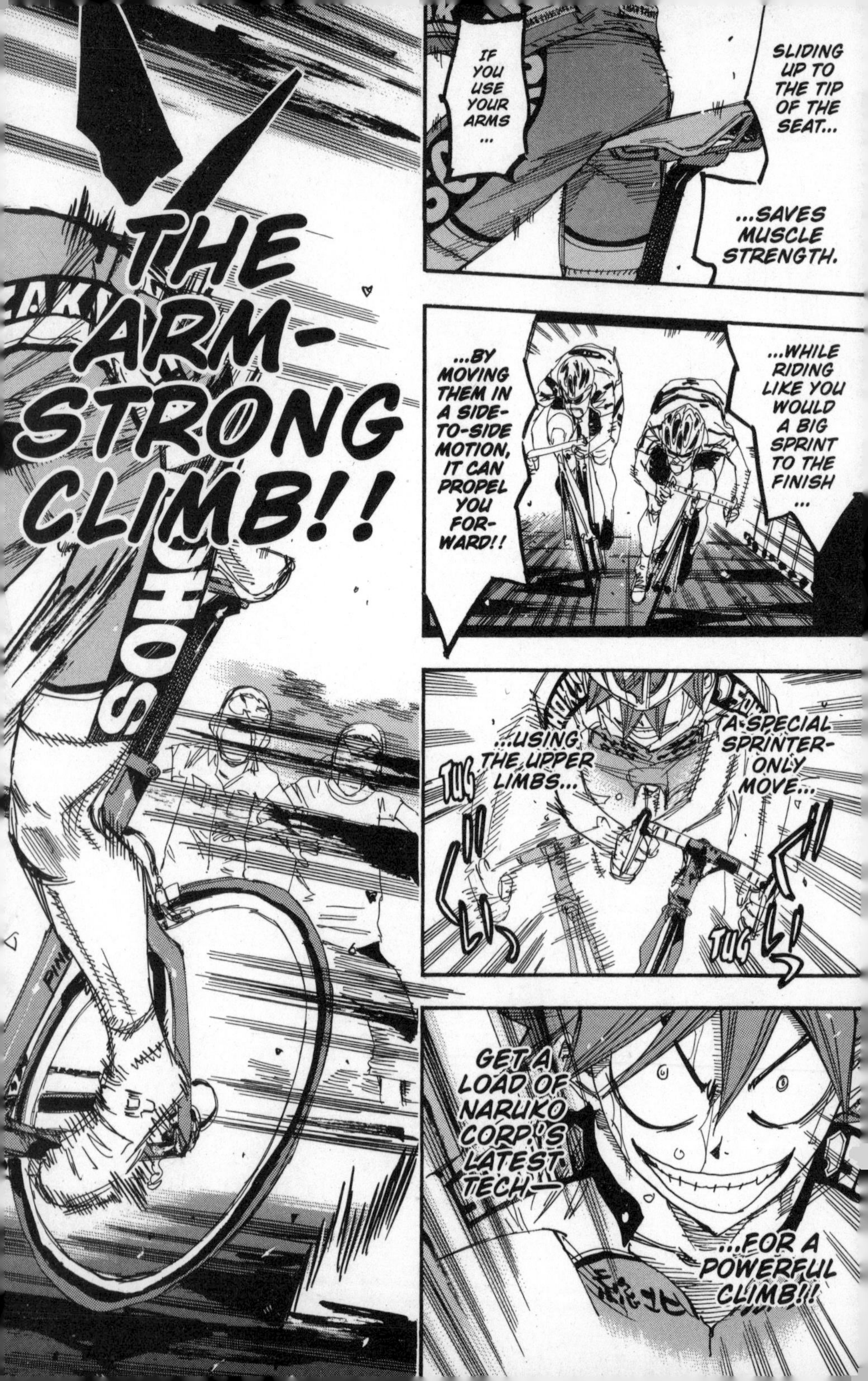
SLIDING UP TO THE TIP OF THE SEAT...
IF YOU USE YOUR ARMS ...
...SAVES MUSCLE STRENGTH.
...WHILE RIDING LIKE YOU WOULD A BIG SPRINT TO THE FINISH ...
...BY MOVING THEM IN A SIDE-TO-SIDE MOTION, IT CAN PROPEL YOU FOR-WARD!!
A SPECIAL SPRINTER-ONLY MOVE...
...USING THE UPPER LIMBS...
TUG
TUG
GET A LOAD OF NARUKO CORP.'S LATEST TECH—
...FOR A POWERFUL CLIMB!!
THE ARM-STRONG CLIMB!!

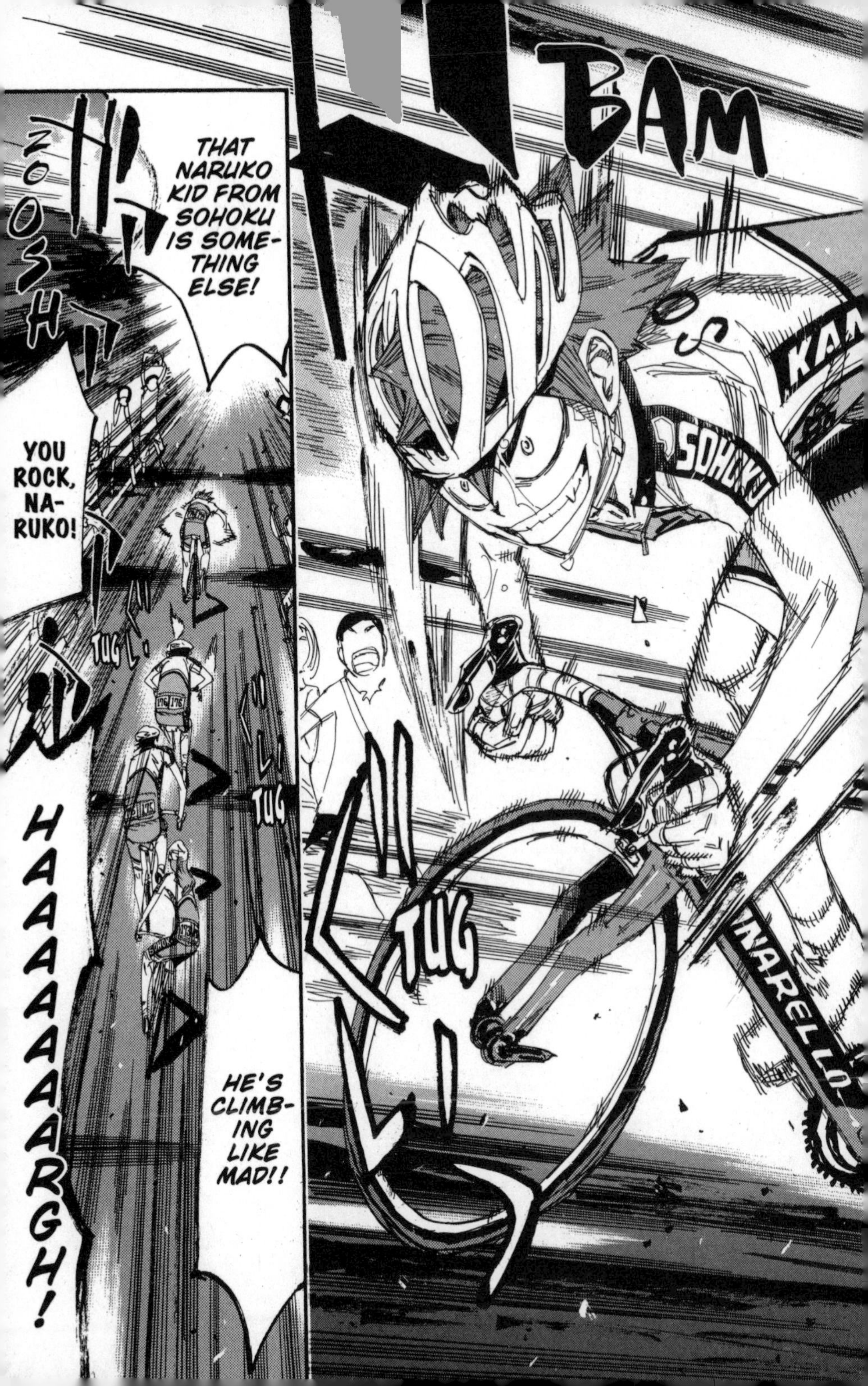
BAM
SOHOKU
TUG
THAT NARUKO KID FROM SOHOKU IS SOMETHING ELSE!
ZOOSH
YOU ROCK, NARUKO!
TUG
TUG
HAAAAAAARGH!
HE'S CLIMBING LIKE MAD!!

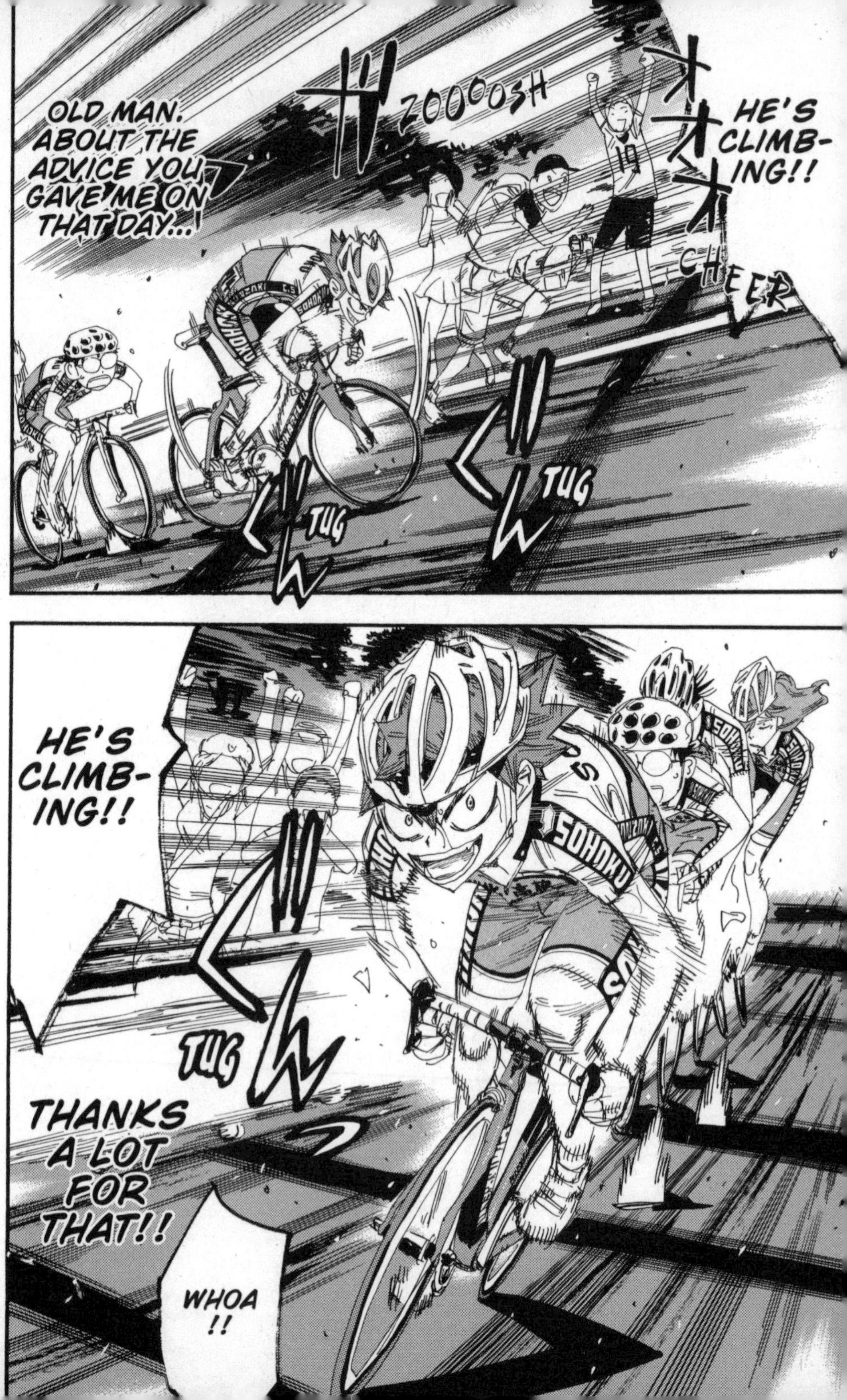
HE'S CLIMB-ING!!
CHEER
ZOOOOOSH
OLD MAN. ABOUT THE ADVICE YOU GAVE ME ON THAT DAY...
TUG
TUG
HE'S CLIMB-ING!!
TUG
THANKS A LOT FOR THAT!!
WHOA!!

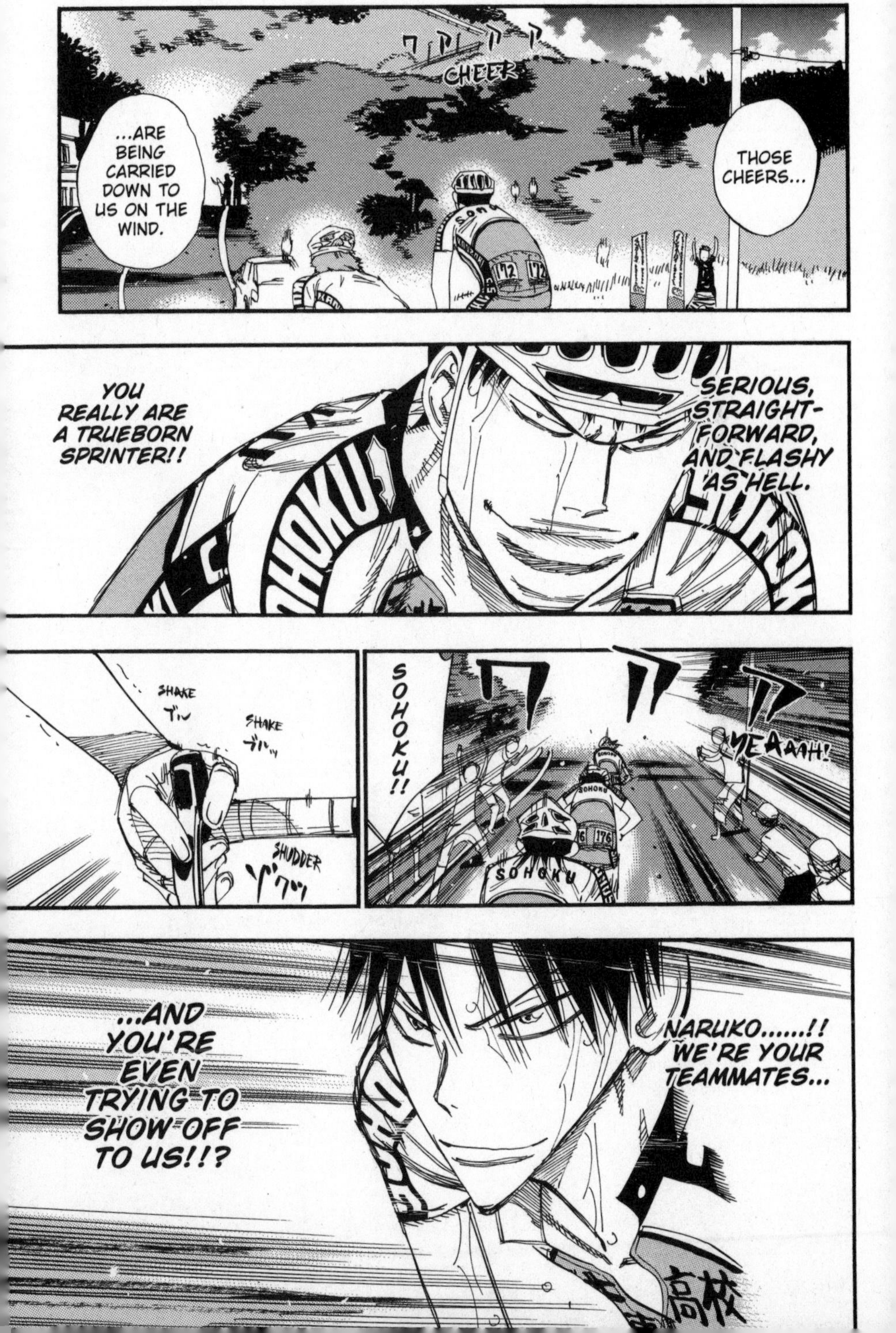
CHEER
THOSE CHEERS...
...ARE BEING CARRIED DOWN TO US ON THE WIND.
SERIOUS, STRAIGHT-FORWARD, AND FLASHY AS HELL.
YOU REALLY ARE A TRUEBORN SPRINTER!!
SOHOKU!!
YEAAAH!
SHAKE
SHAKE
SHUDDER
NARUKO......!! WE'RE YOUR TEAMMATES...
...AND YOU'RE EVEN TRYING TO SHOW OFF TO US!!?
高校

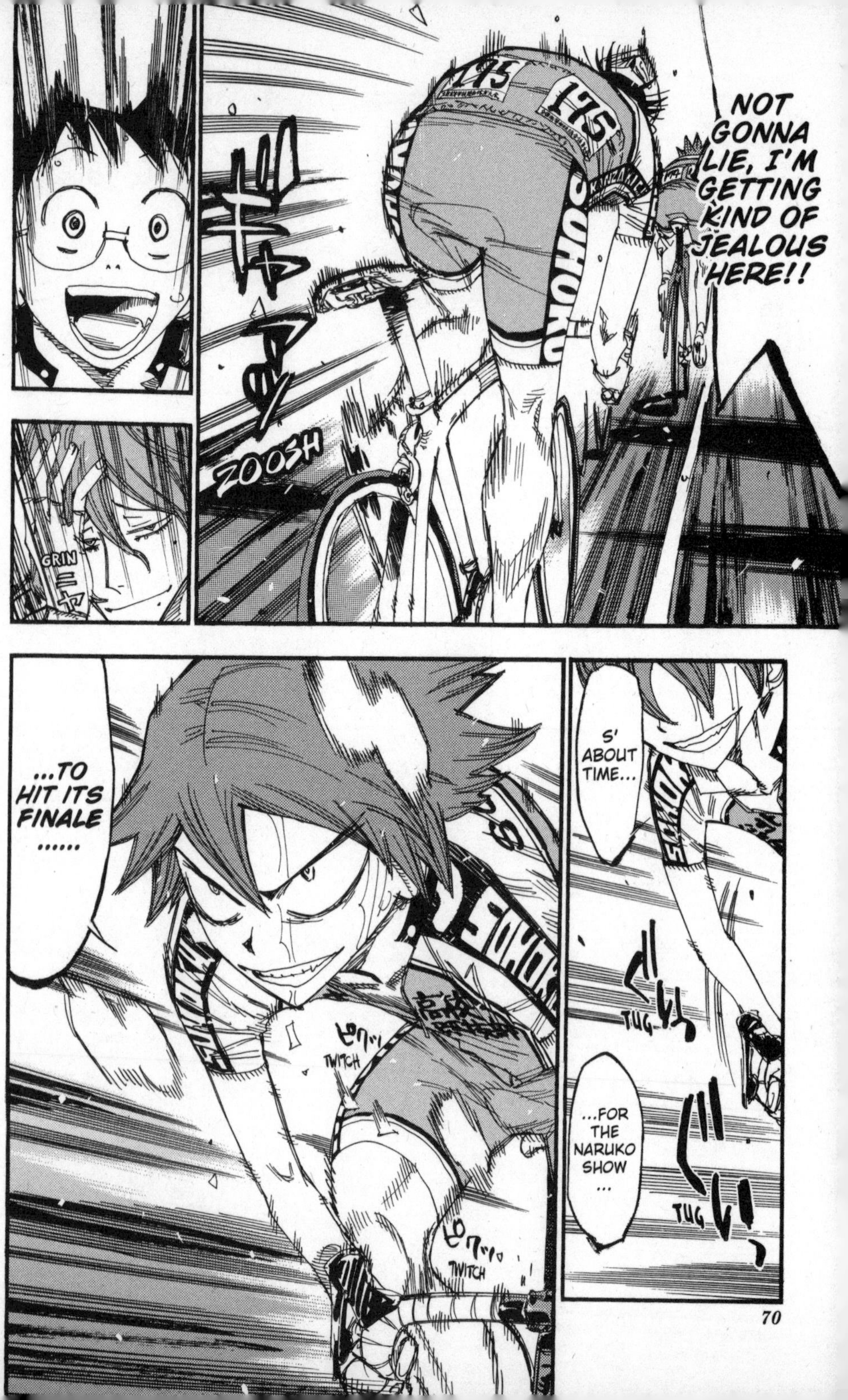
NOT GONNA LIE, I'M GETTING KIND OF JEALOUS HERE!!
ZOOSH
GRIN
S' ABOUT TIME...
TUG
...FOR THE NARUKO SHOW...
TUG
...TO HIT ITS FINALE......
TWITCH
TWITCH

RIDE.194 STUBBORN WILL

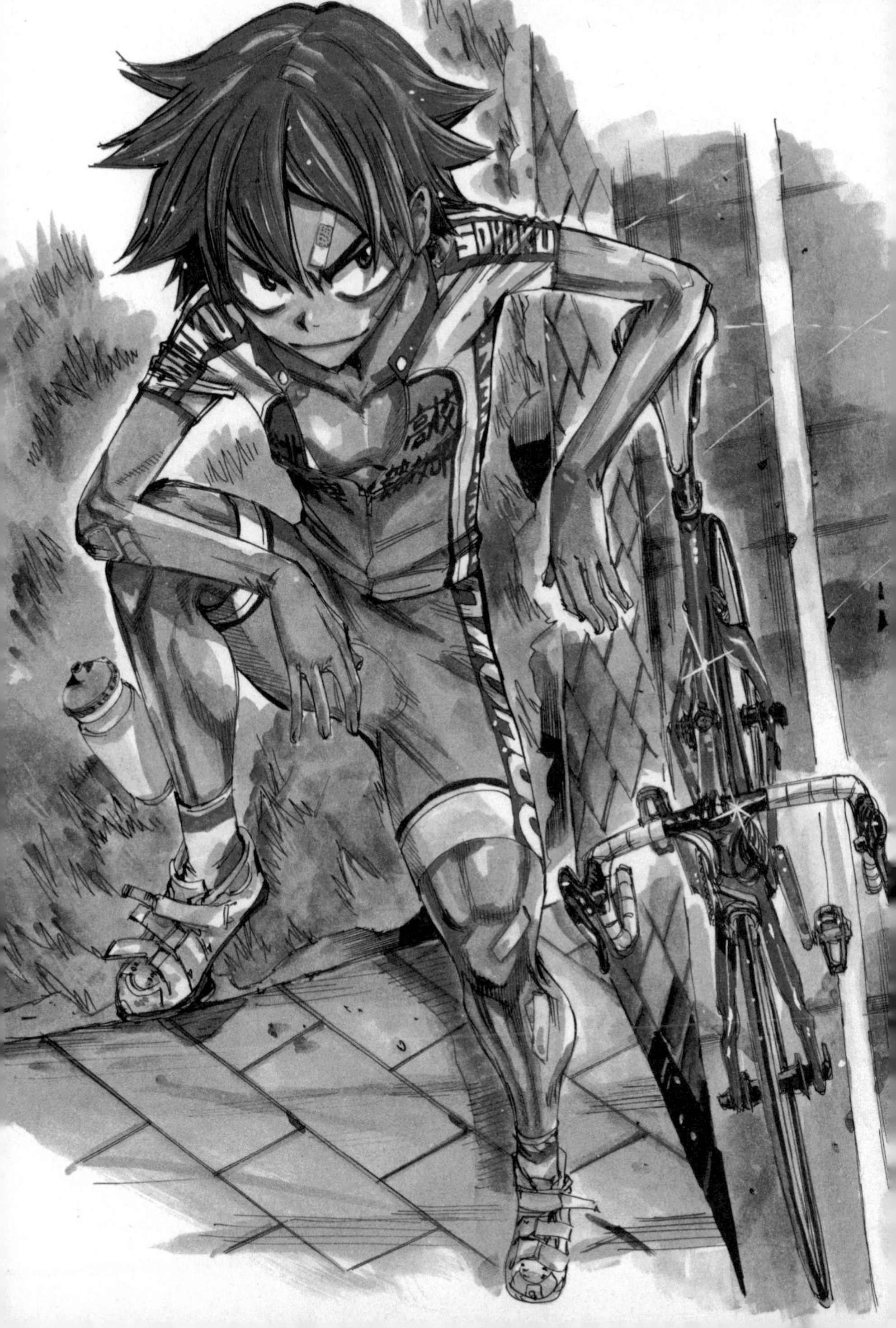

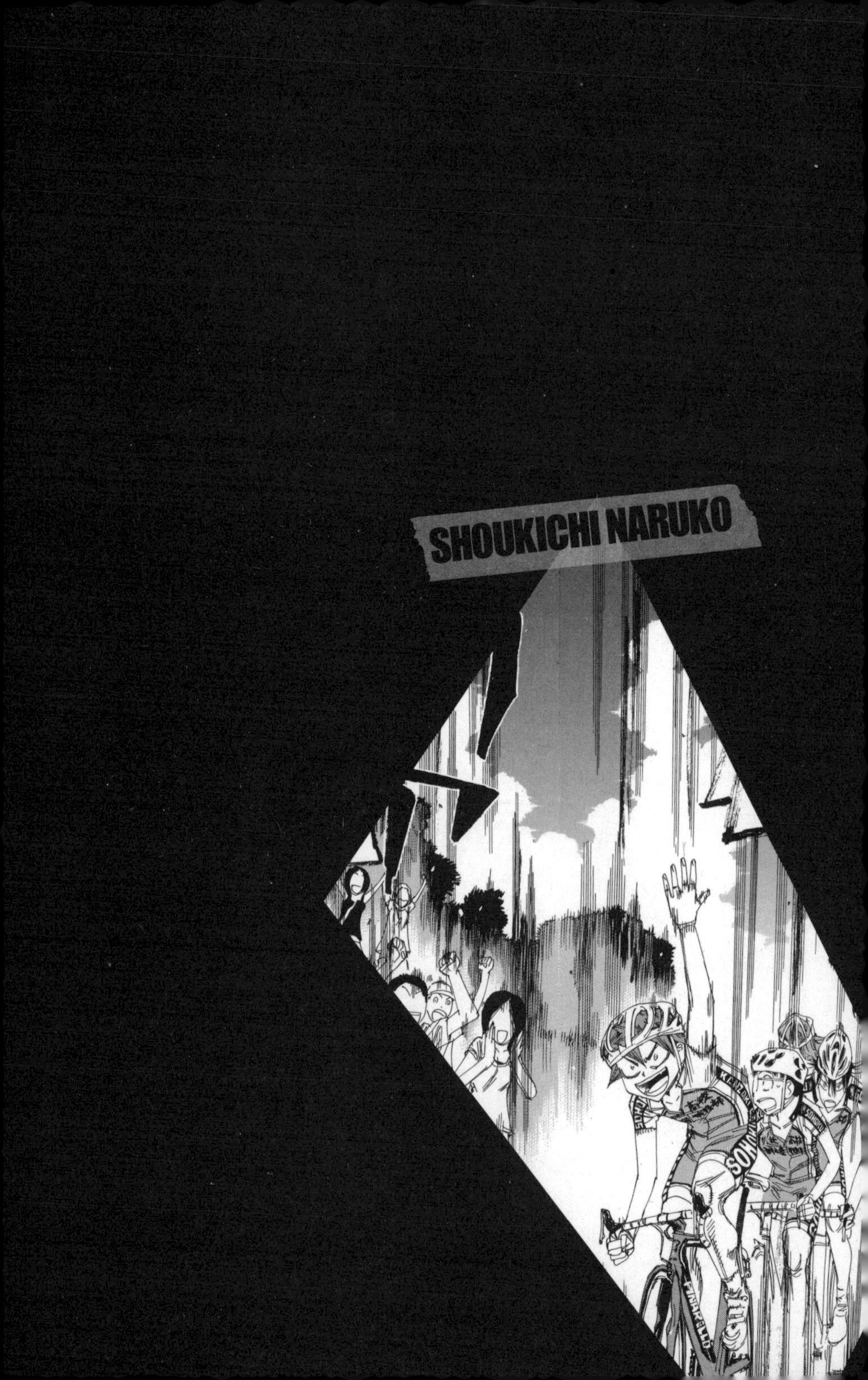
SHOUKICHI NARUKO

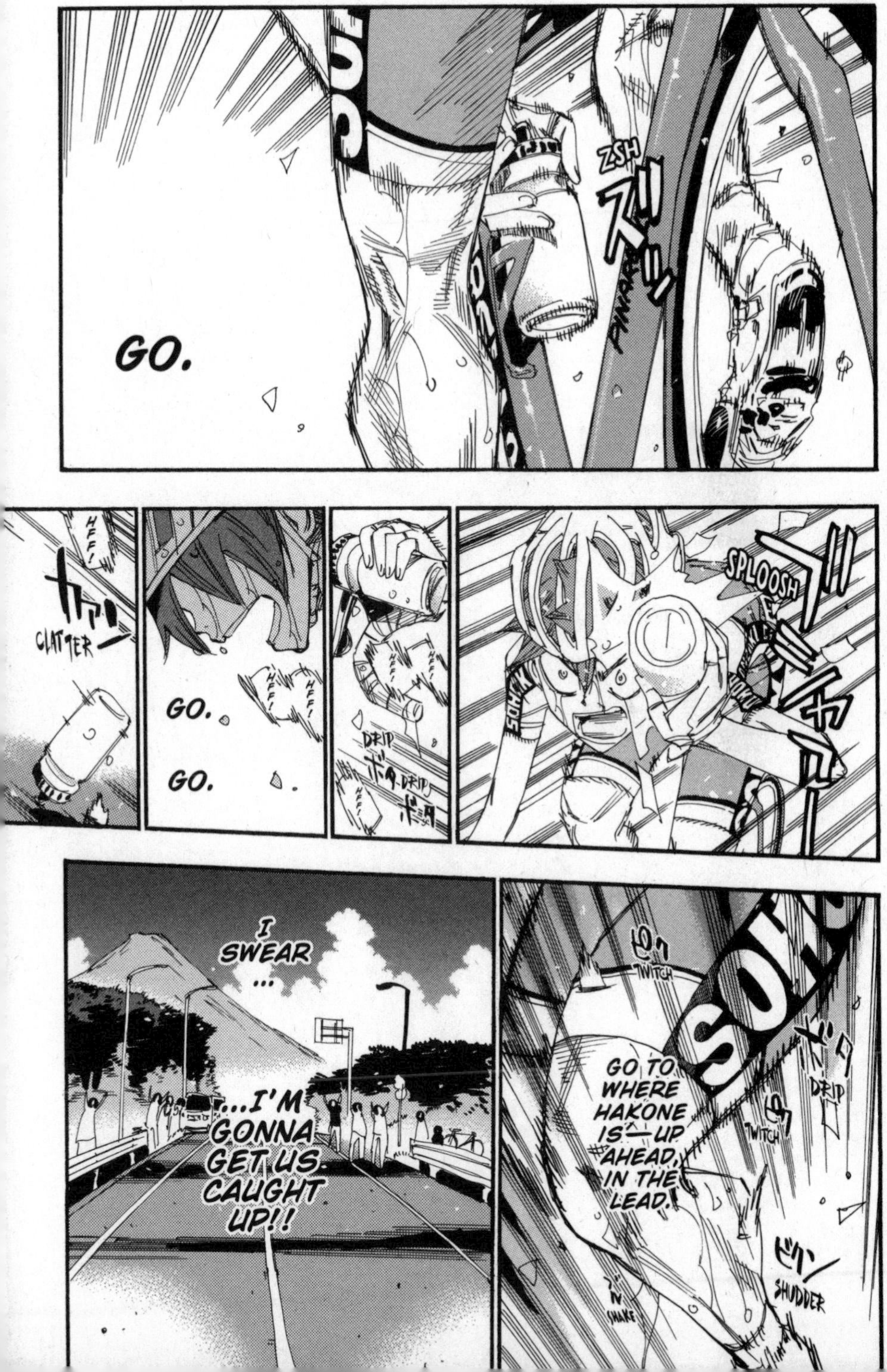
ZSH
GO.
SPLOOSH
HFF!
DRIP
DRIP
HFF!
GO.
GO.
HFF!
HFF!
HFF!
CLATTER
TWITCH
GO TO WHERE HAKONE IS—UP AHEAD, IN THE LEAD!
DRIP
TWITCH
SHUDDER
SHAKE
I SWEAR ...
...I'M GONNA GET US CAUGHT UP!!

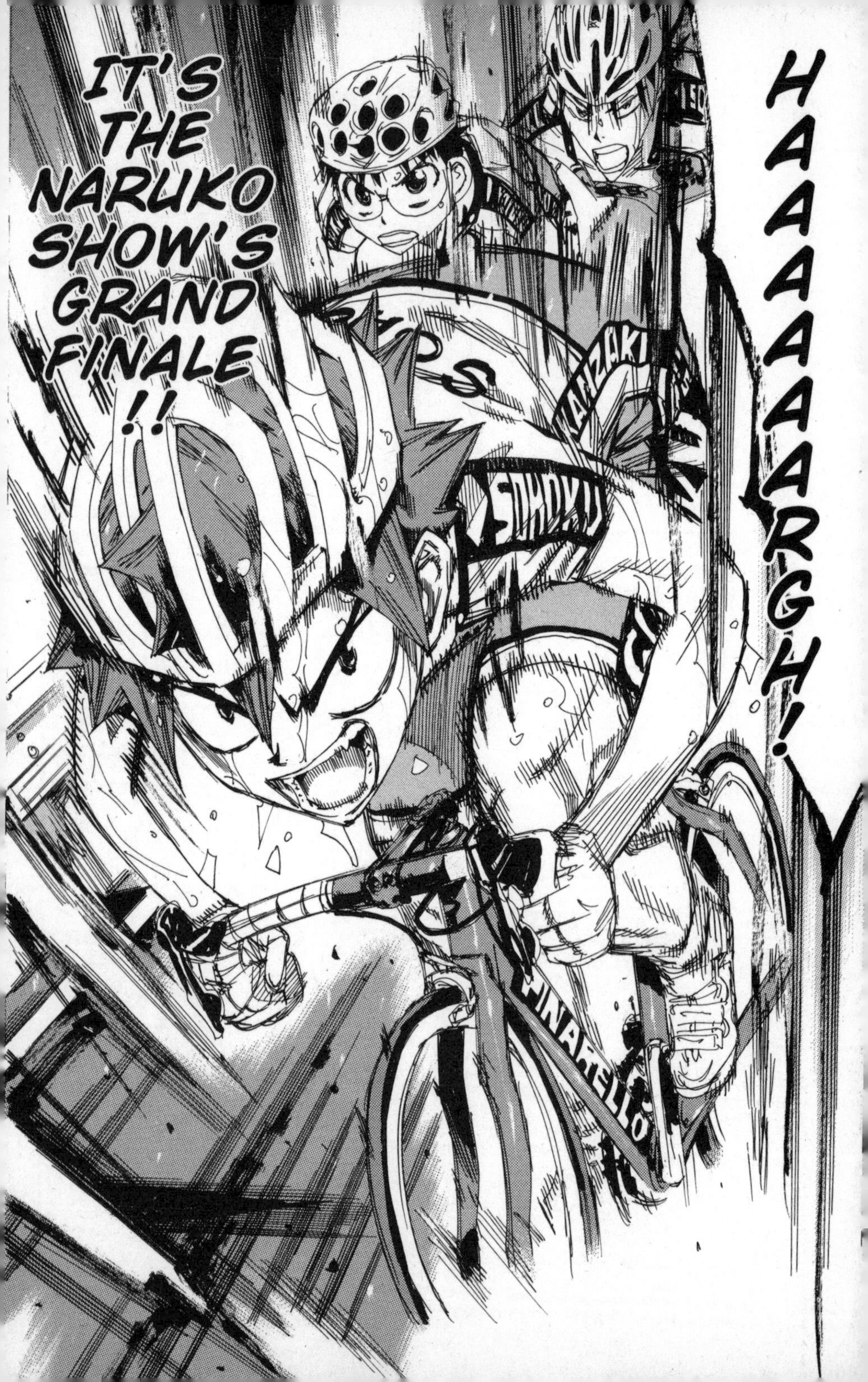
HAAAAAARGH!
IT'S THE NARUKO SHOW'S GRAND FINALE!!

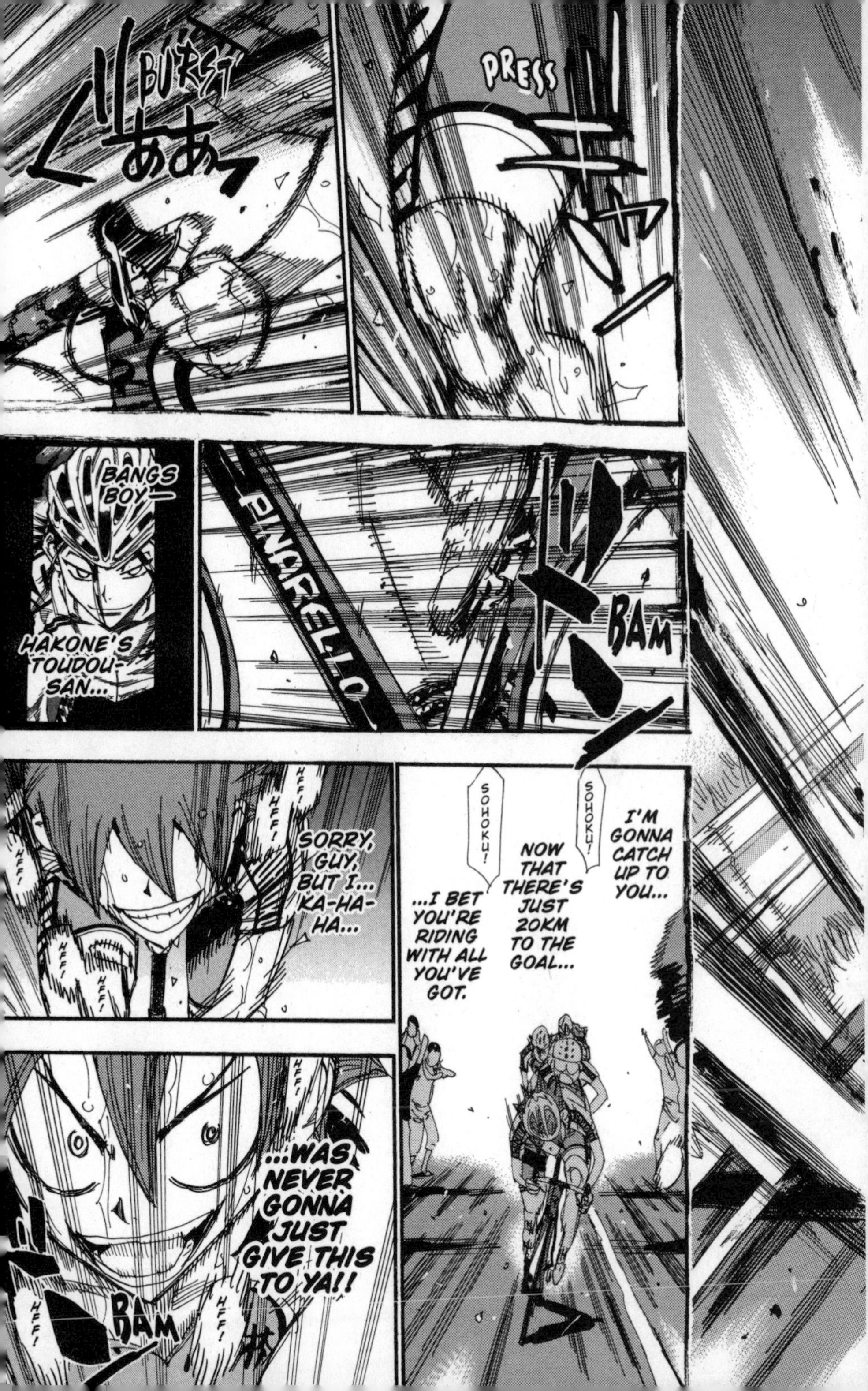
PRESS
BURST
BAM
BANGS BOY—
HAKONE'S TOUDOU-SAN...
I'M GONNA CATCH UP TO YOU...
SOHOKU!
NOW THAT THERE'S JUST 20KM TO THE GOAL...
SOHOKU!
...I BET YOU'RE RIDING WITH ALL YOU'VE GOT.
HFF!
HFF!
SORRY, GUY, BUT I... KA-HA-HA...
HFF!
HFF!
HFF!
...WAS NEVER GONNA JUST GIVE THIS TO YA!!
HFF!
BAM
HFF!

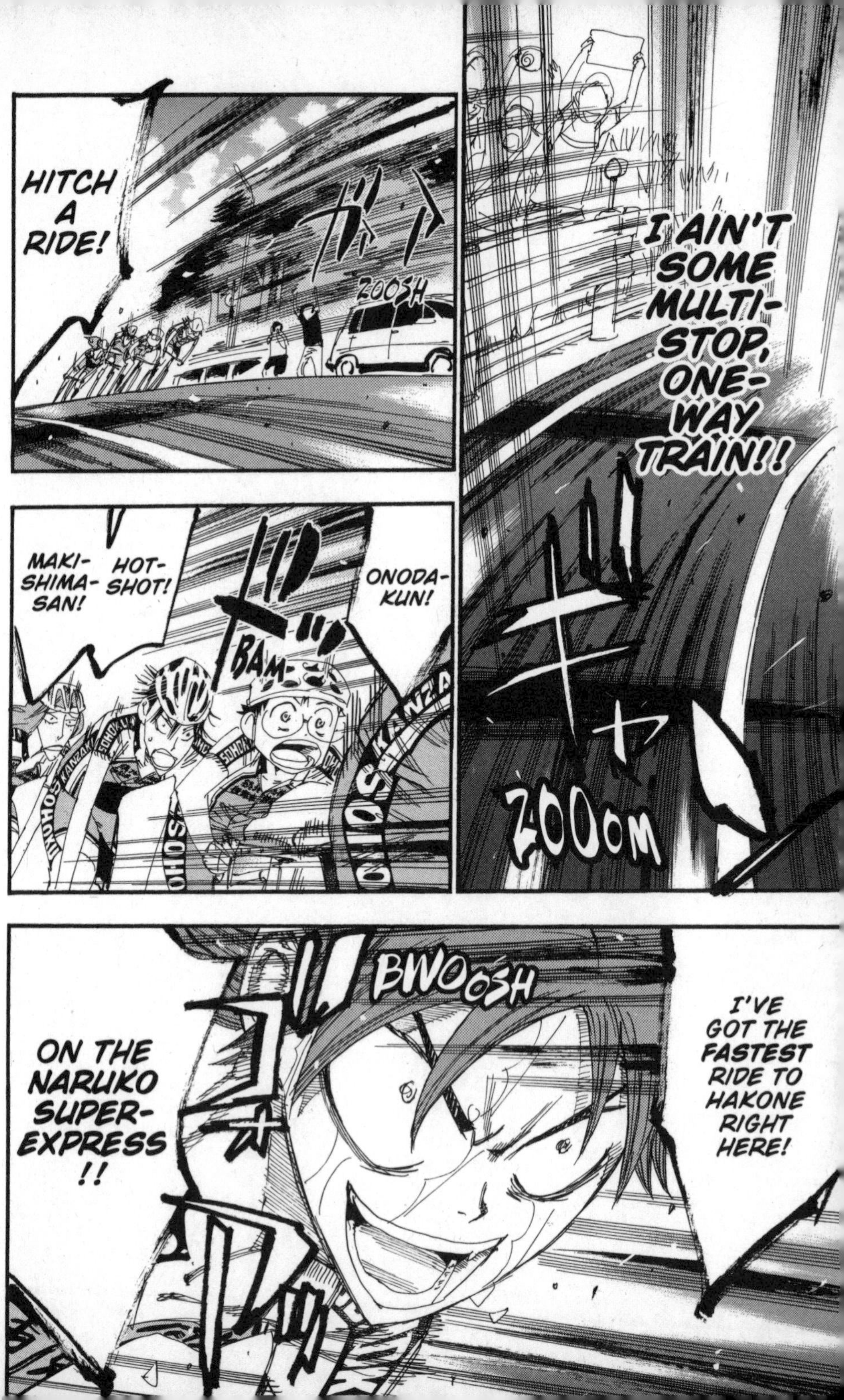
I AIN'T SOME MULTI-STOP, ONE-WAY TRAIN!!
ZOOOM
HITCH A RIDE!
ZOOSH
ONODA-KUN!
BAM
HOT-SHOT!
MAKI-SHIMA-SAN!
I'VE GOT THE FASTEST RIDE TO HAKONE RIGHT HERE!
BWOOSH
ON THE NARUKO SUPER-EXPRESS!!

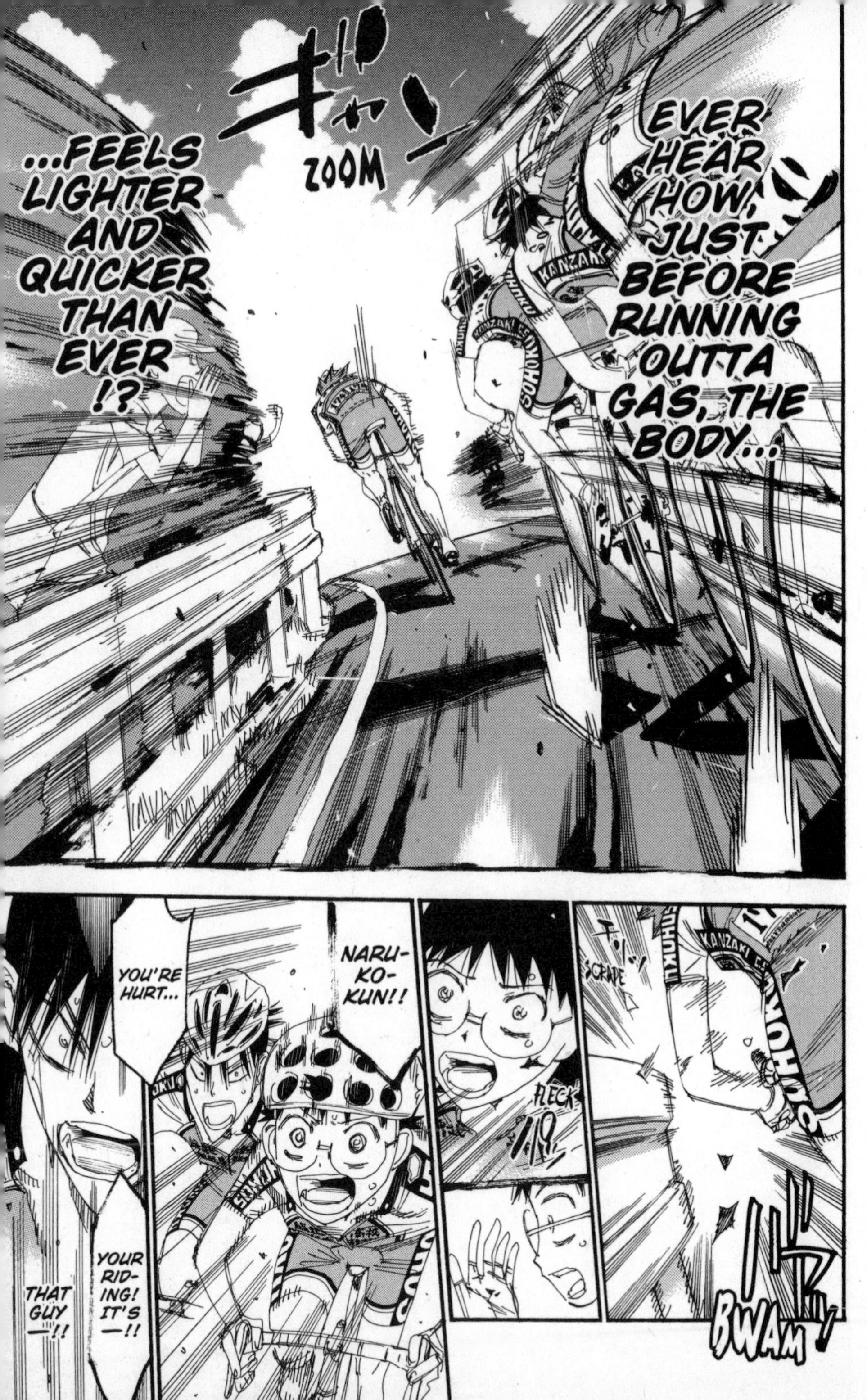

EVER HEAR HOW, JUST BEFORE RUNNING OUTTA GAS, THE BODY...
ZOOM
...FEELS LIGHTER AND QUICKER THAN EVER!?
SCRAPE
BWAM!
FLECK
NARU-KO-KUN!!
YOU'RE HURT...
YOUR RIDING! IT'S—!!
THAT GUY—!!

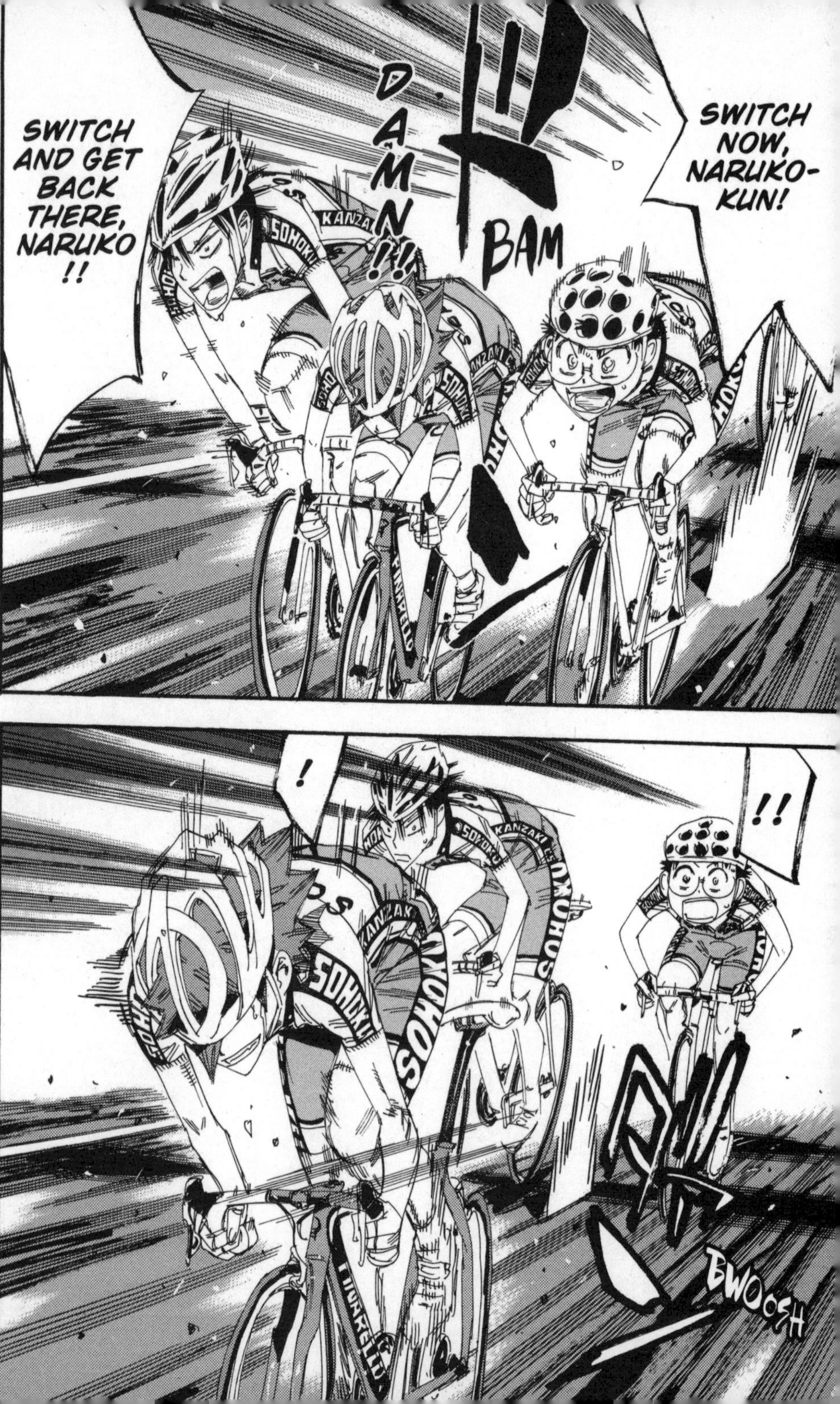
SWITCH NOW, NARUKO-KUN!
DAMN!!
BAM
SWITCH AND GET BACK THERE, NARUKO!!
!!
!
BWOOSH

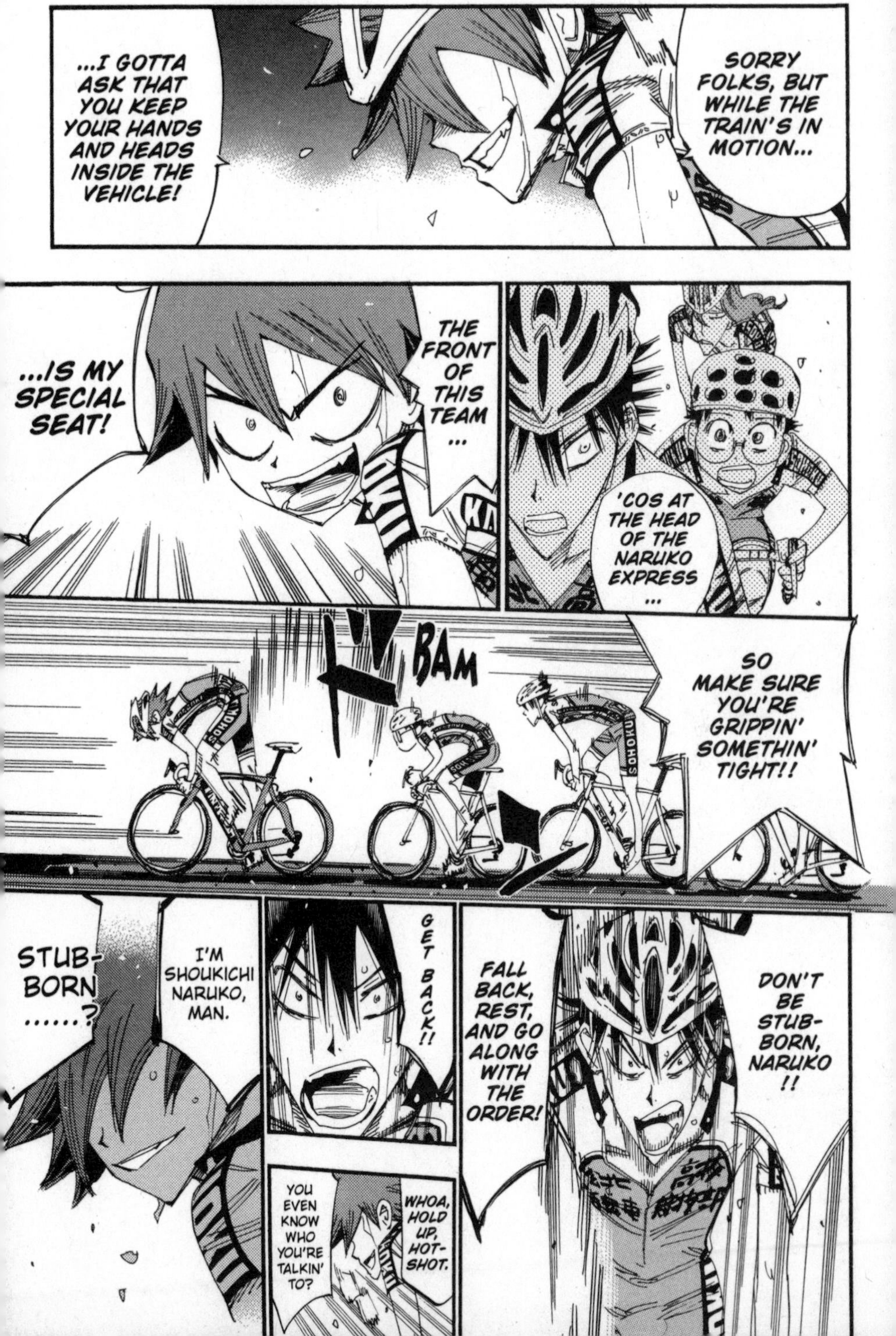
SORRY FOLKS, BUT WHILE THE TRAIN'S IN MOTION...
...I GOTTA ASK THAT YOU KEEP YOUR HANDS AND HEADS INSIDE THE VEHICLE!
'COS AT THE HEAD OF THE NARUKO EXPRESS ...
THE FRONT OF THIS TEAM ...
...IS MY SPECIAL SEAT!
SO MAKE SURE YOU'RE GRIPPIN' SOMETHIN' TIGHT!!
BAM
DON'T BE STUB-BORN, NARUKO !!
FALL BACK, REST, AND GO ALONG WITH THE ORDER!
GET BACK!!
WHOA, HOLD UP, HOT-SHOT.
YOU EVEN KNOW WHO YOU'RE TALKIN' TO?
STUB-BORN ......?
I'M SHOUKICHI NARUKO, MAN.

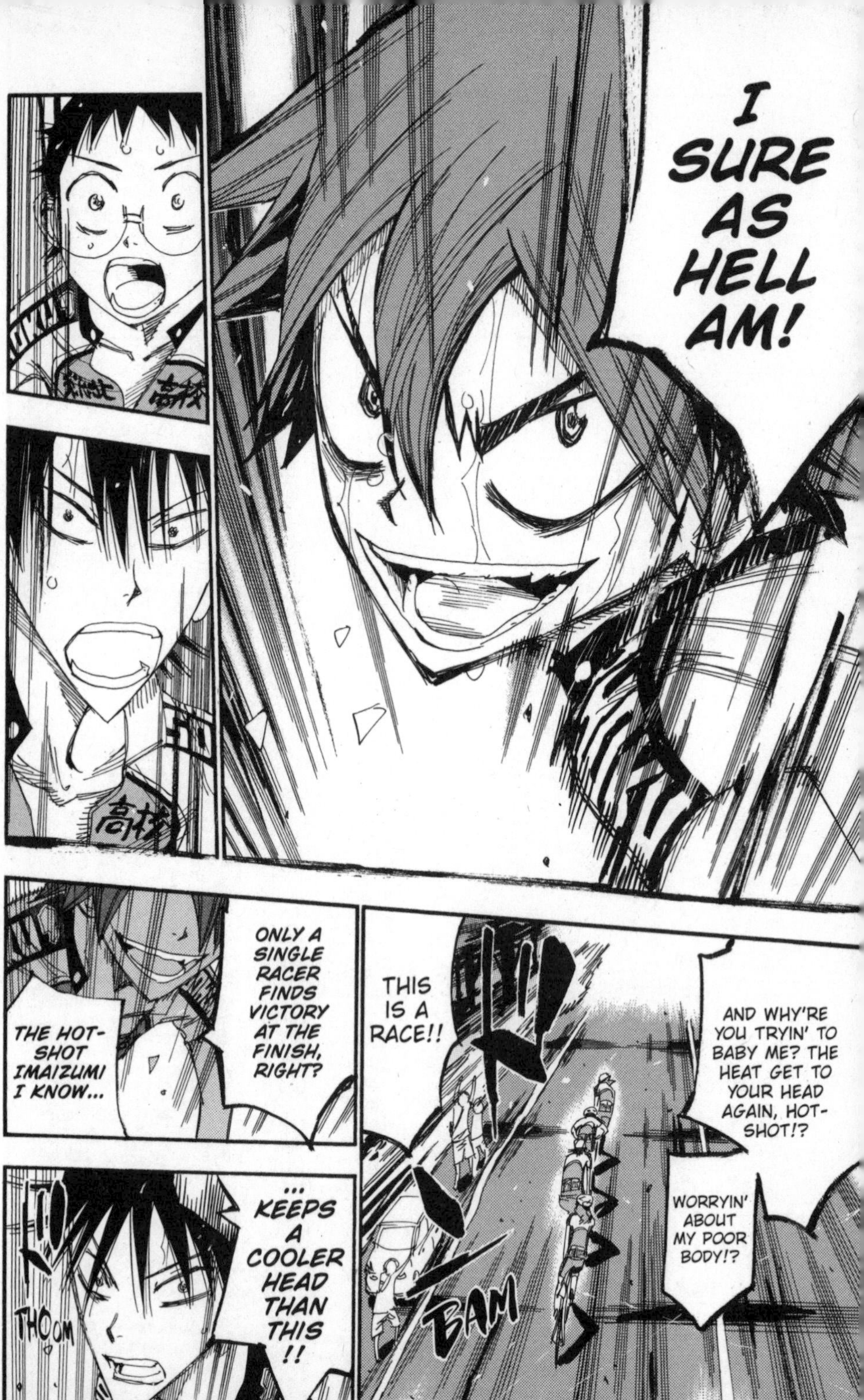
I SURE AS HELL AM!
AND WHY'RE YOU TRYIN' TO BABY ME? THE HEAT GET TO YOUR HEAD AGAIN, HOT-SHOT!?
WORRYIN' ABOUT MY POOR BODY!?
THIS IS A RACE!!
BAM
ONLY A SINGLE RACER FINDS VICTORY AT THE FINISH, RIGHT?
THE HOT-SHOT IMAIZUMI I KNOW...
!!
THOOM
...KEEPS A COOLER HEAD THAN THIS!!

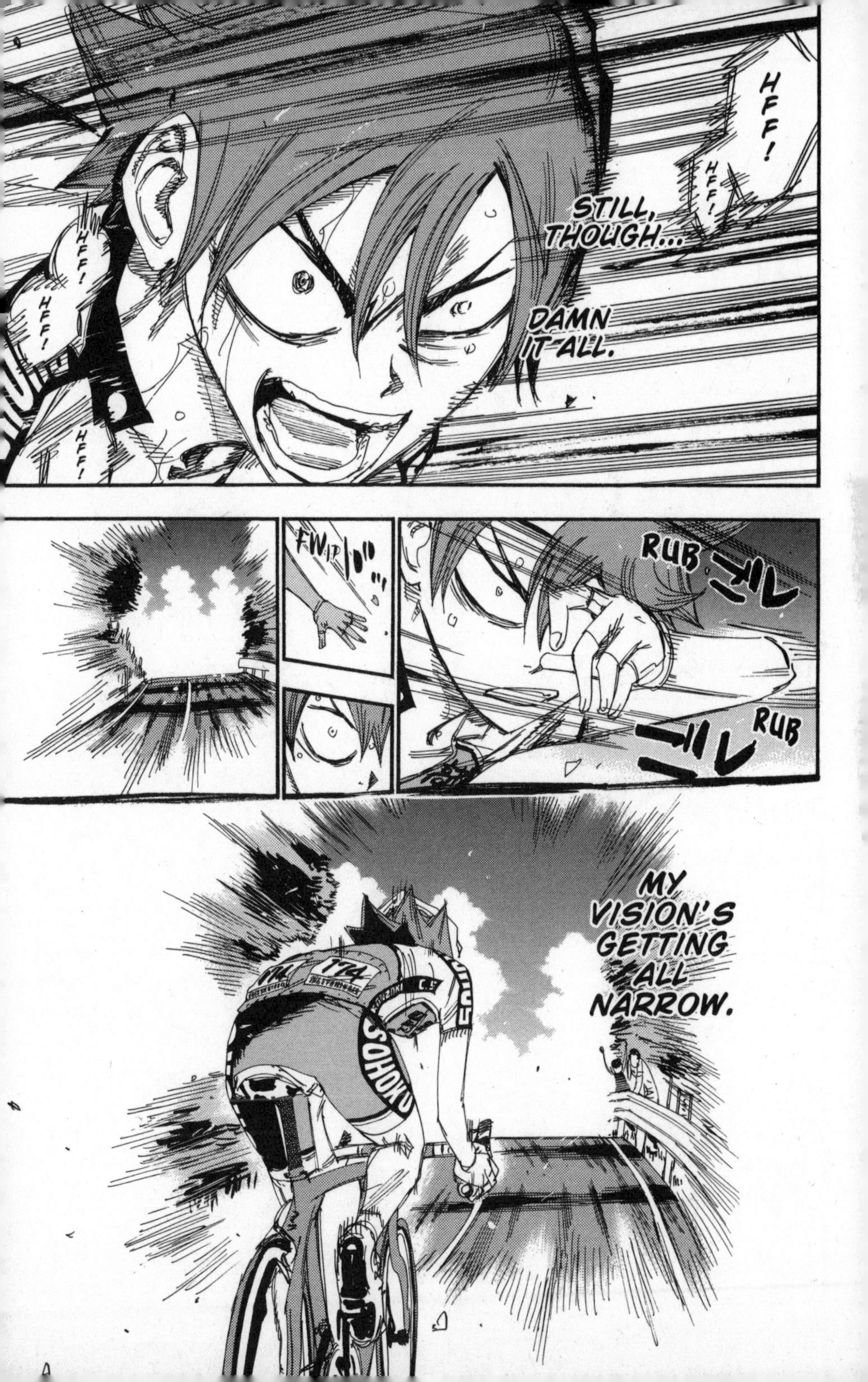
HFF!
HFF!
STILL, THOUGH...
DAMN IT ALL.
HFF!
HFF!
HFF!
RUB
RUB
FWIP
MY VISION'S GETTING ALL NARROW.

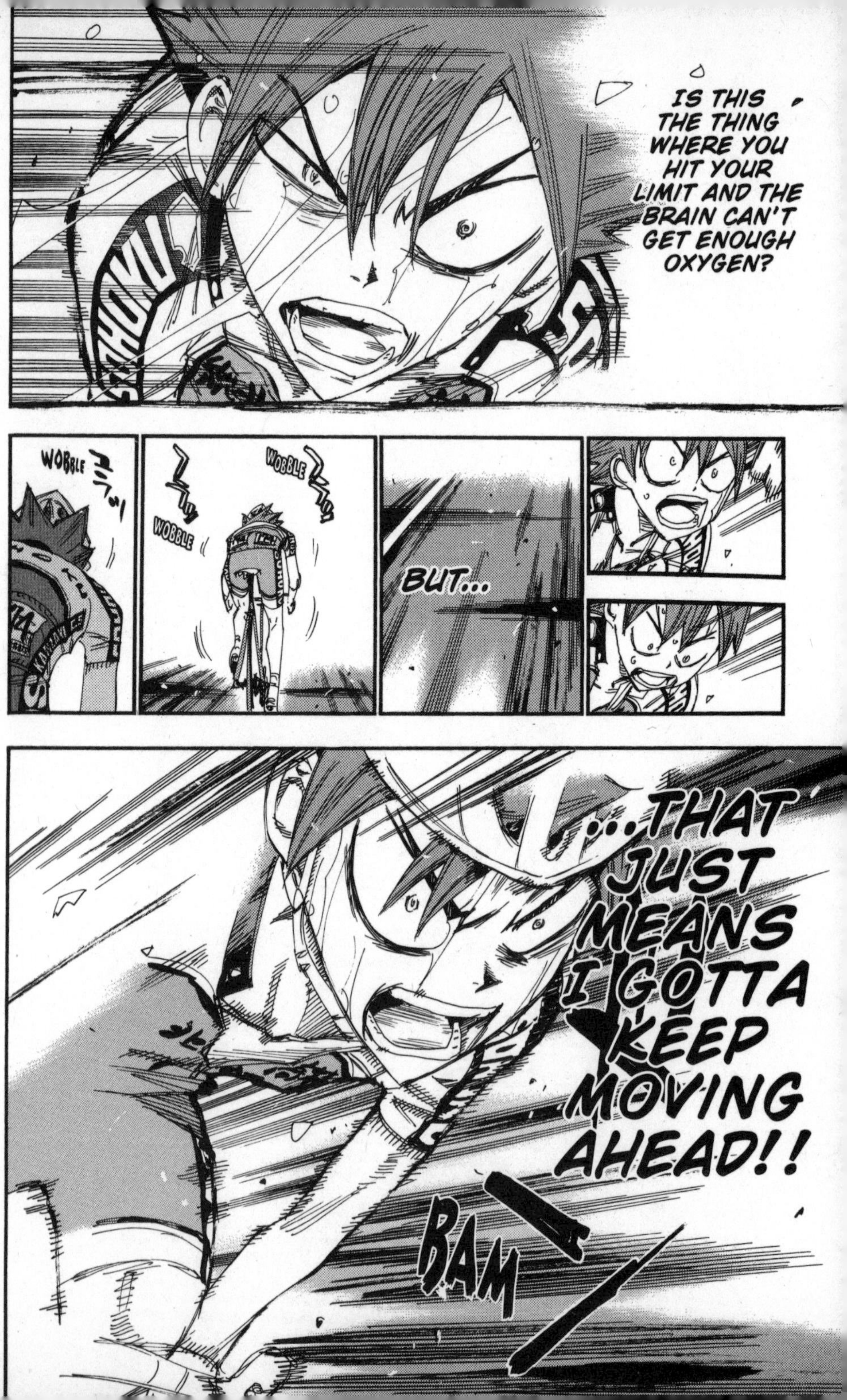
IS THIS THE THING WHERE YOU HIT YOUR LIMIT AND THE BRAIN CAN'T GET ENOUGH OXYGEN?
BUT...
WOBBLE
WOBBLE
WOBBLE
...THAT JUST MEANS I GOTTA KEEP MOVING AHEAD!!
BAM

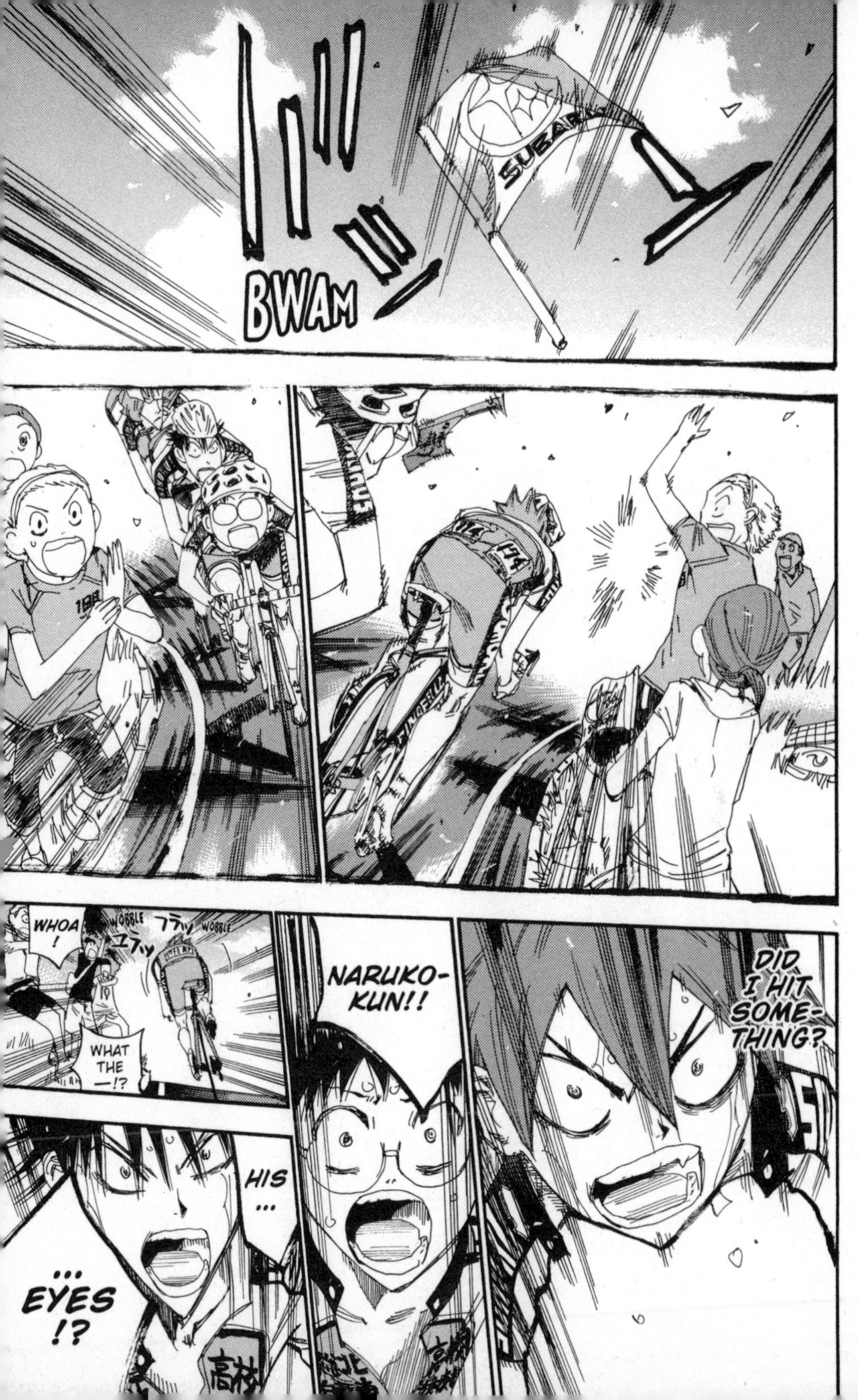
BWAM
DID I HIT SOME-THING?
NARUKO-KUN!!
WOBBLE
フラッ
ユラッ
WOBBLE
WHOA!
WHAT THE—!?
HIS...
...EYES!?

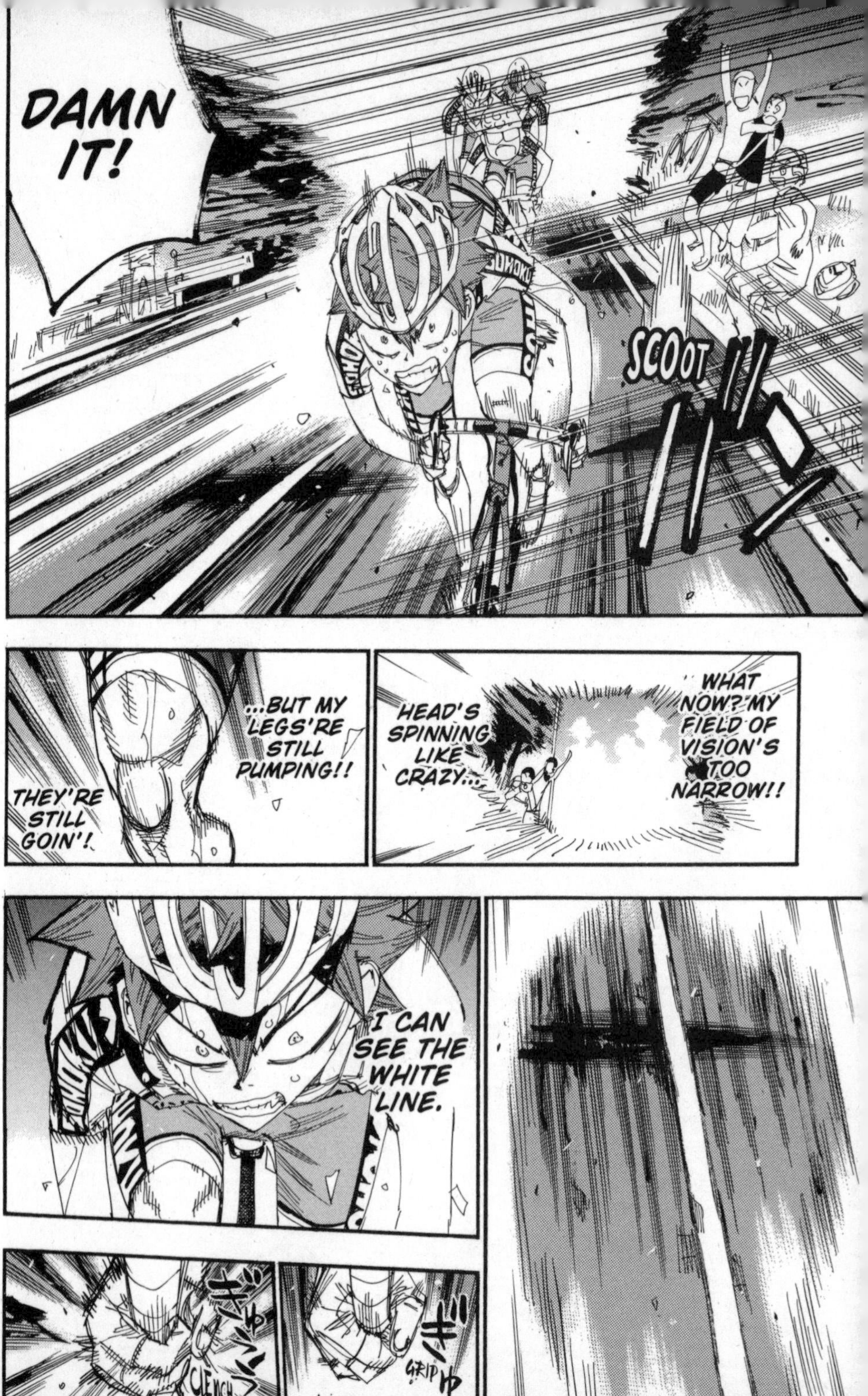

DAMN IT!
SCOOT
WHAT NOW? MY FIELD OF VISION'S TOO NARROW!!
HEAD'S SPINNING LIKE CRAZY...
...BUT MY LEGS'RE STILL PUMPING!!
THEY'RE STILL GOIN'!.
I CAN SEE THE WHITE LINE.
GRIP
CLENCH

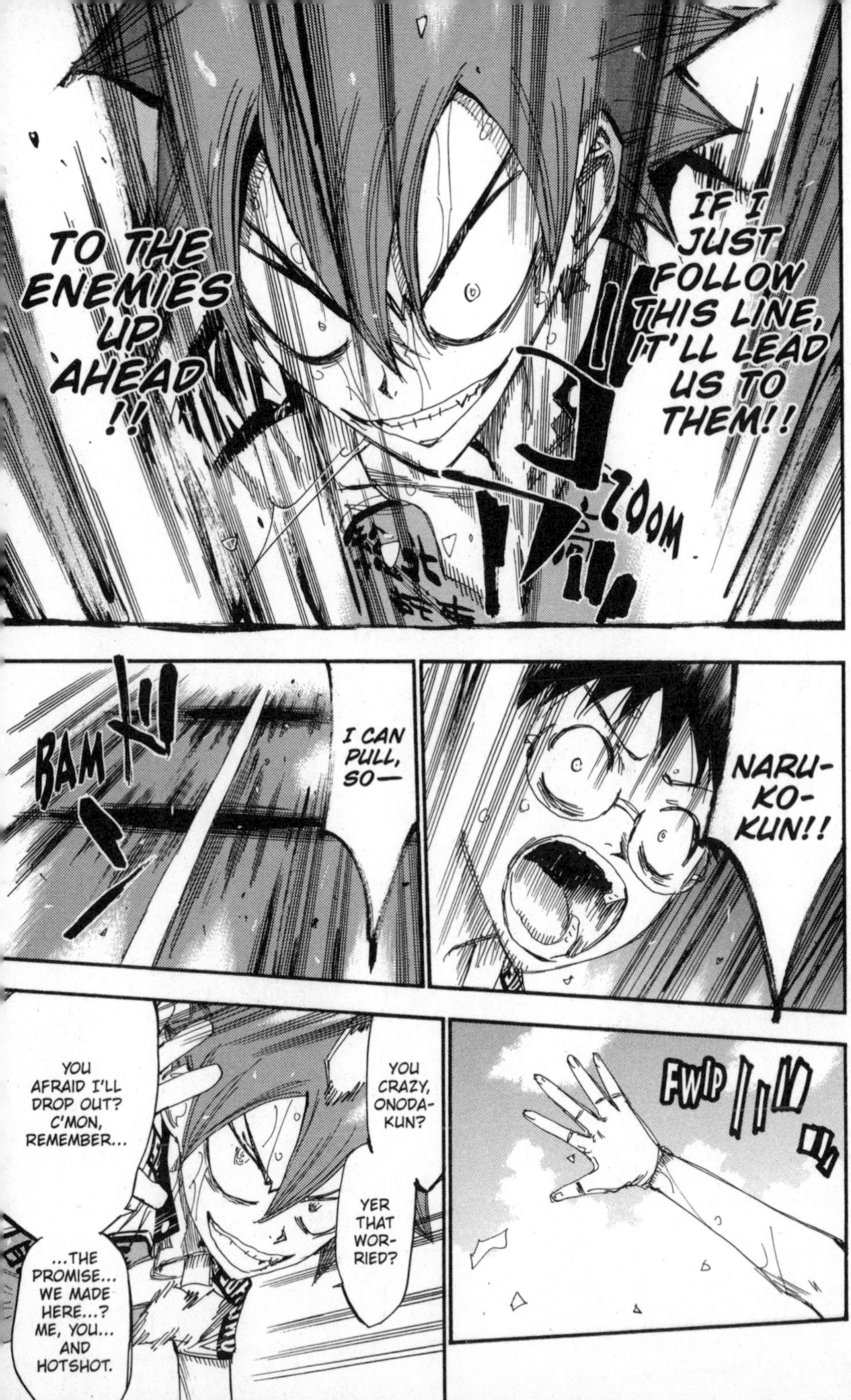
IF I JUST FOLLOW THIS LINE, IT'LL LEAD US TO THEM!!
ZOOM
TO THE ENEMIES UP AHEAD!!
NARU-KO-KUN!!
I CAN PULL, SO—
BAM
FWIP
YOU CRAZY, ONODA-KUN?
YER THAT WOR-RIED?
YOU AFRAID I'LL DROP OUT? C'MON, REMEMBER...
...THE PROMISE... WE MADE HERE...? ME, YOU... AND HOTSHOT.

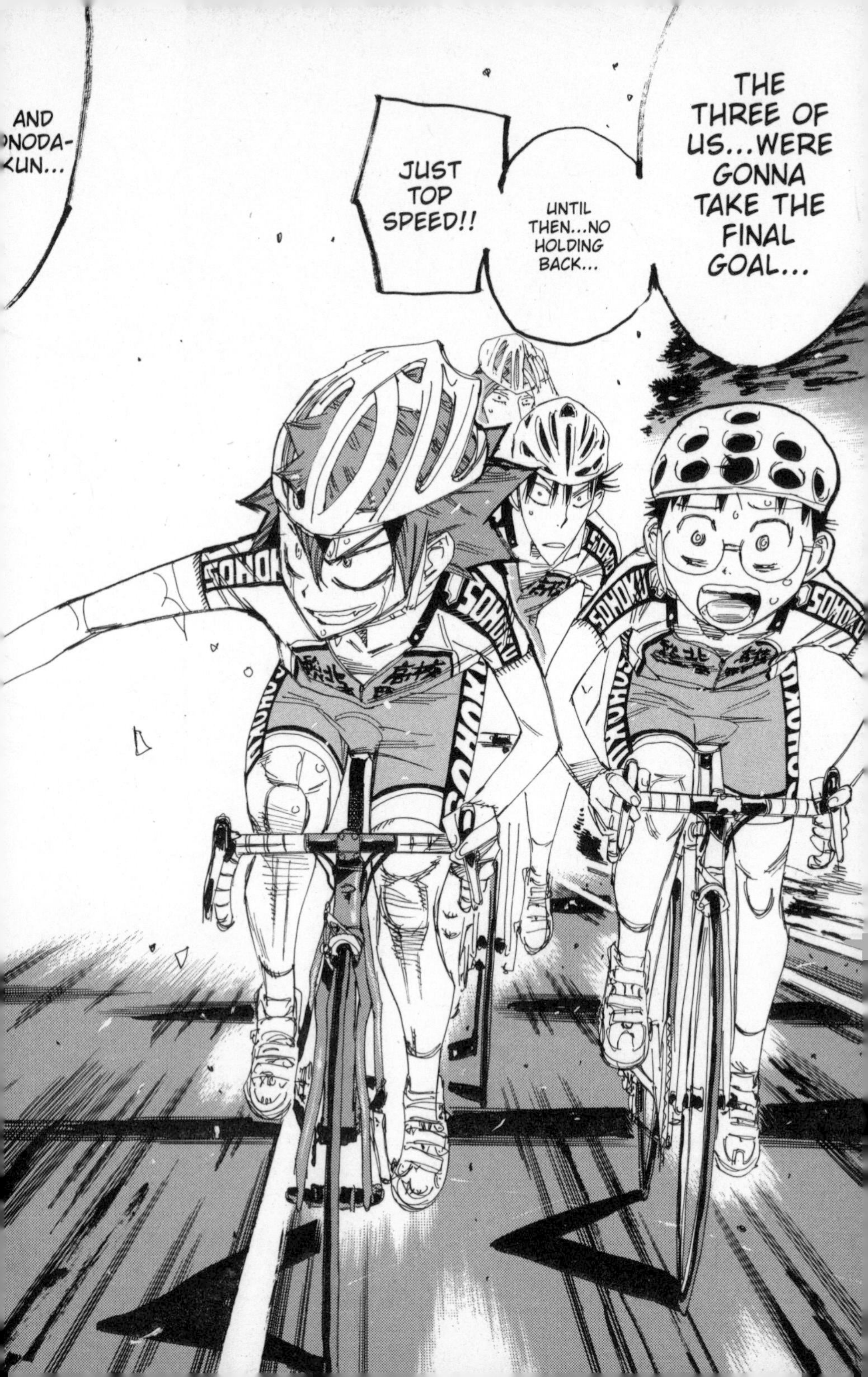
THE THREE OF US...WERE GONNA TAKE THE FINAL GOAL...
UNTIL THEN...NO HOLDING BACK...
JUST TOP SPEED!!
AND NODA- KUN...

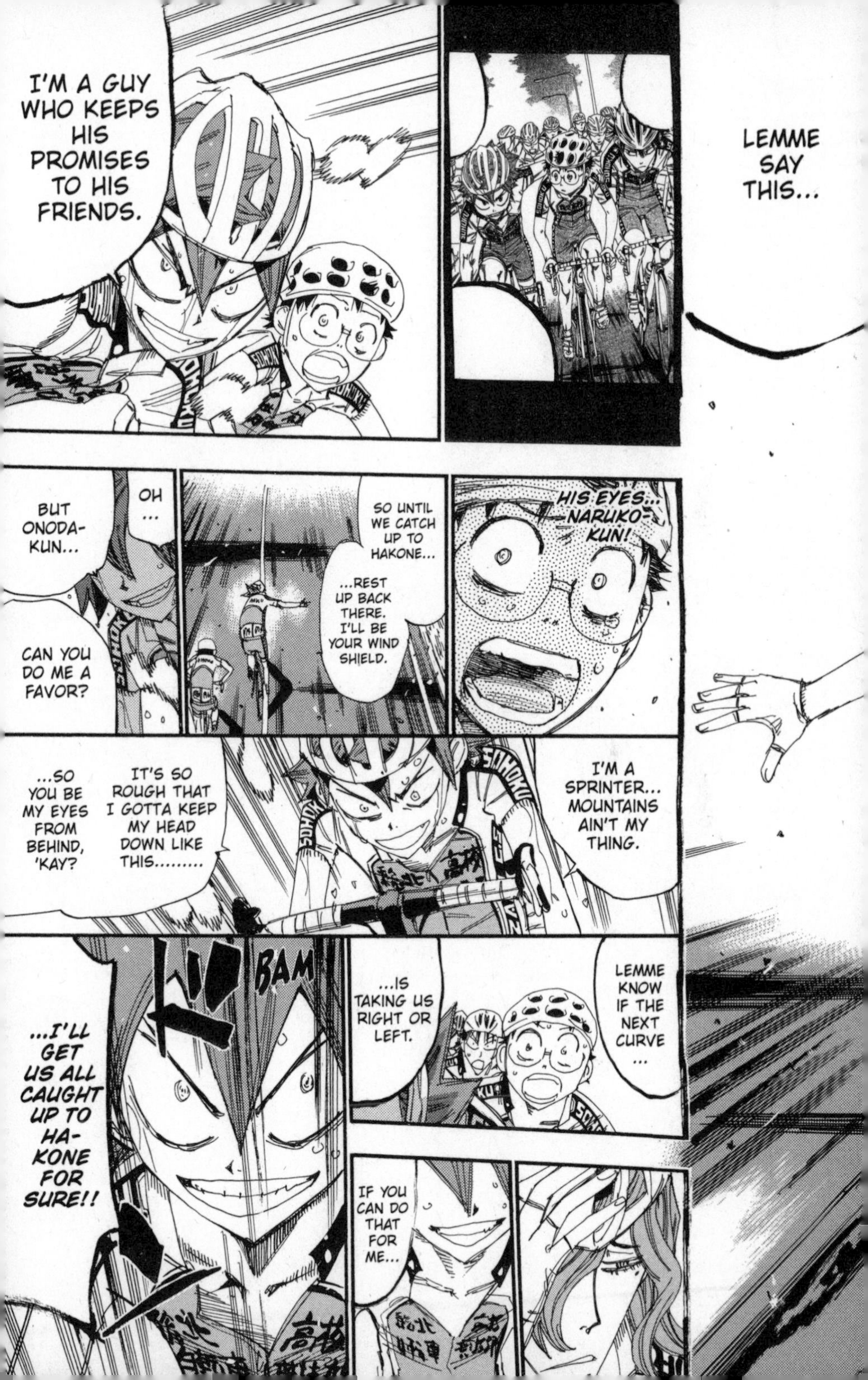
LEMME SAY THIS...
I'M A GUY WHO KEEPS HIS PROMISES TO HIS FRIENDS.
HIS EYES... NARUKO-KUN!
SO UNTIL WE CATCH UP TO HAKONE...
...REST UP BACK THERE. I'LL BE YOUR WIND SHIELD.
OH ...
BUT ONODA-KUN...
CAN YOU DO ME A FAVOR?
I'M A SPRINTER... MOUNTAINS AIN'T MY THING.
IT'S SO ROUGH THAT I GOTTA KEEP MY HEAD DOWN LIKE THIS.........
...SO YOU BE MY EYES FROM BEHIND, 'KAY?
LEMME KNOW IF THE NEXT CURVE ...
...IS TAKING US RIGHT OR LEFT.
IF YOU CAN DO THAT FOR ME...
BAM
...I'LL GET US ALL CAUGHT UP TO HA-KONE FOR SURE!!

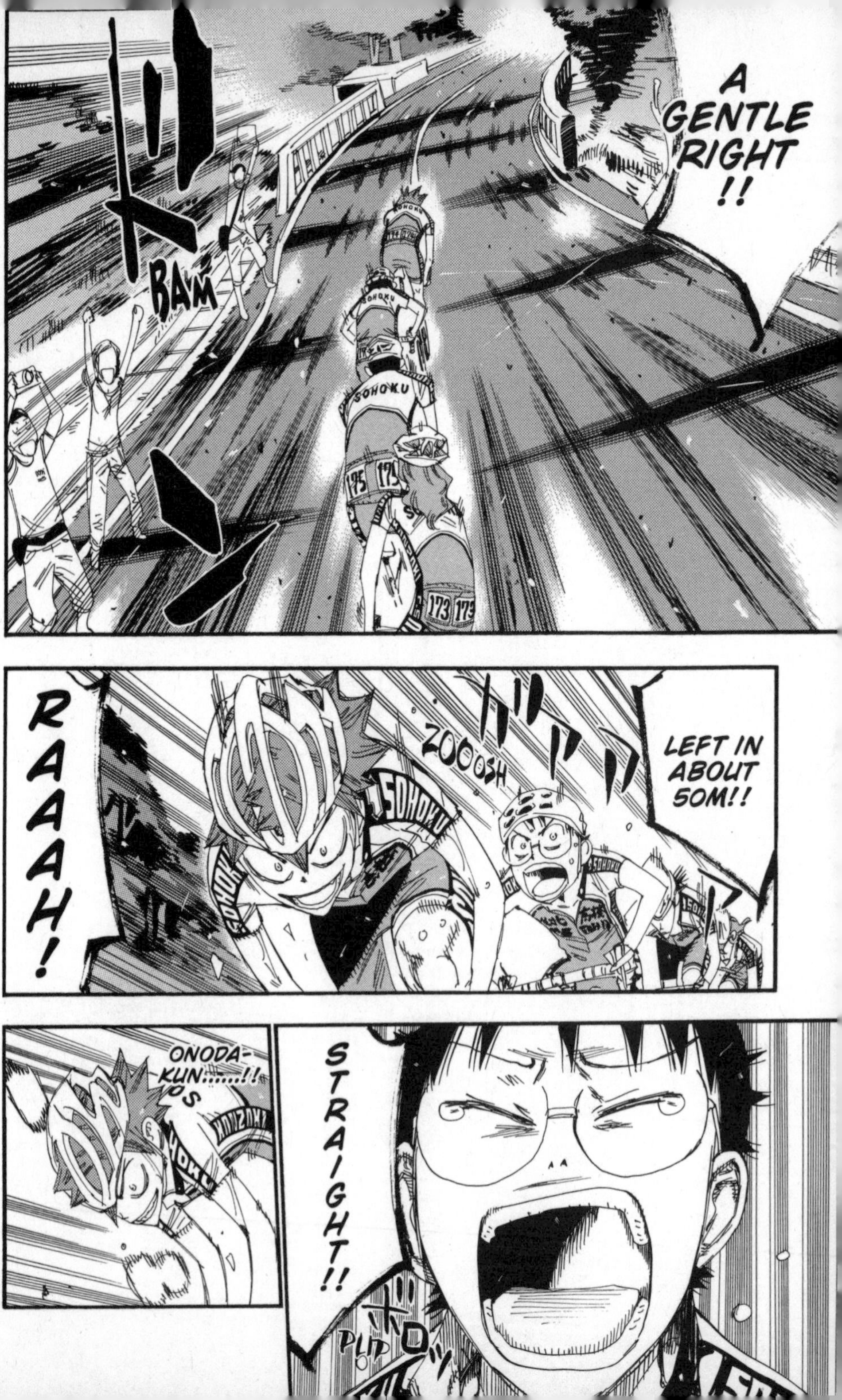
A GENTLE RIGHT !!
BAM
LEFT IN ABOUT 50M!!
ZOOOSH
RAAAAH!
STRAIGHT!!
PLIP
ONODA-KUN......!!

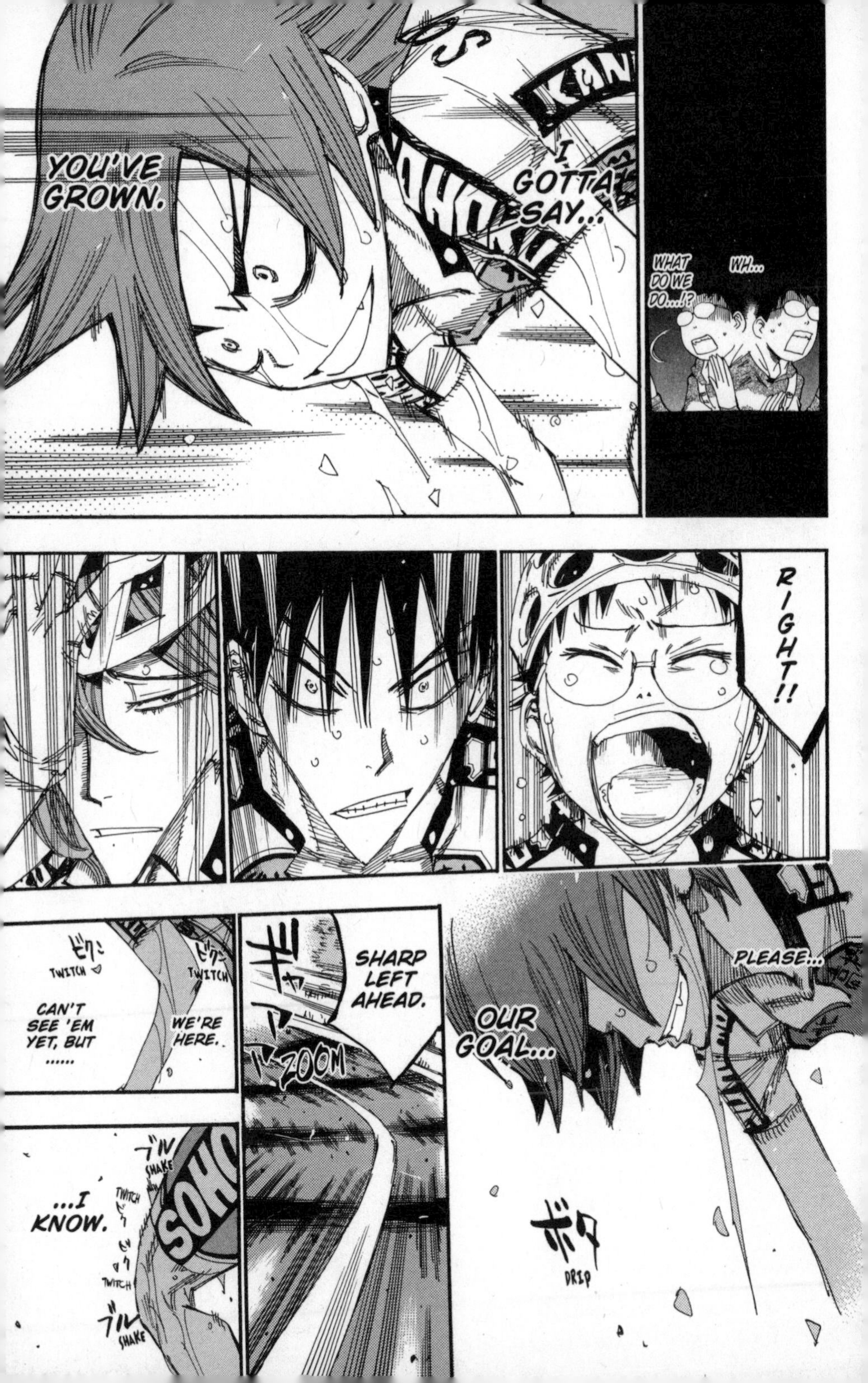
WH...
WHAT DO WE DO...!?
I GOTTA SAY...
YOU'VE GROWN.
RIGHT!!
PLEASE...
OUR GOAL...
DRIP
SHARP LEFT AHEAD.
ZOOM
TWITCH
WE'RE HERE.
TWITCH
CAN'T SEE 'EM YET, BUT ......
SHAKE
TWITCH
...I KNOW.
TWITCH
SHAKE

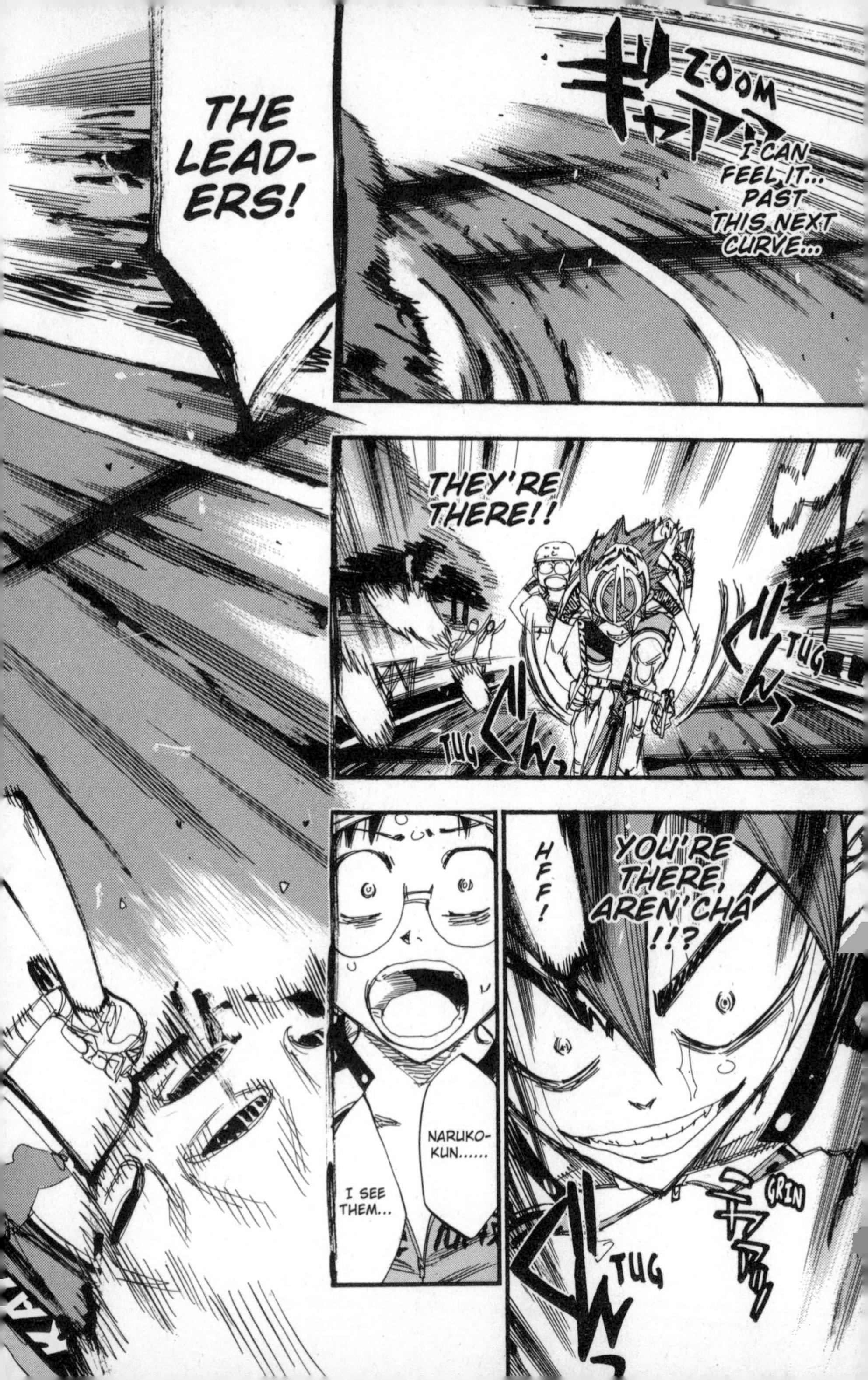
ZOOM
I CAN FEEL IT... PAST THIS NEXT CURVE...
THEY'RE THERE!!
TUG
TUG
YOU'RE THERE, AREN'CHA!!?
HFF!
GRIN
TUG
NARUKO-KUN......
I SEE THEM...
THE LEADERS!

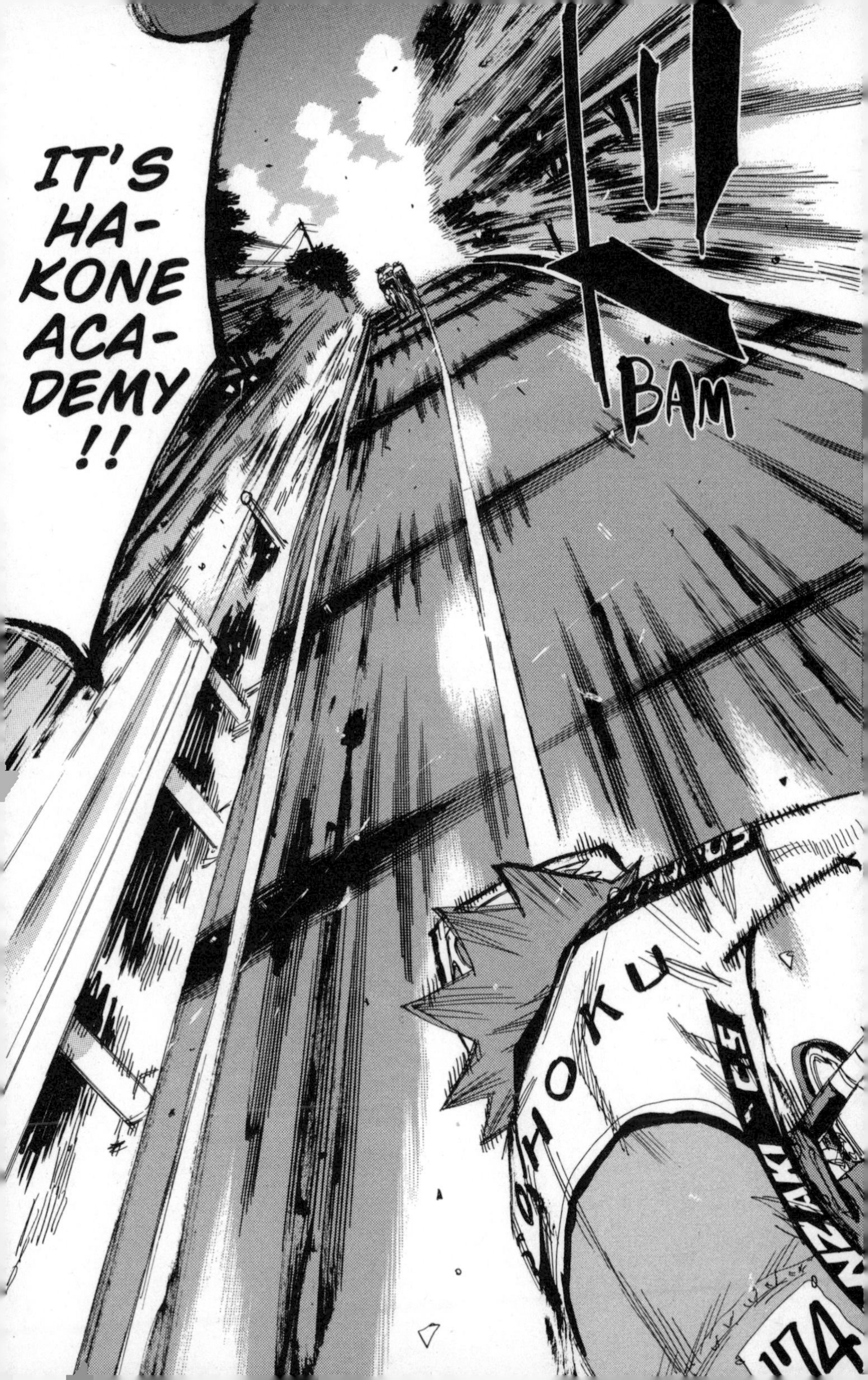
BAM
IT'S HA-KONE ACA-DEMY!!

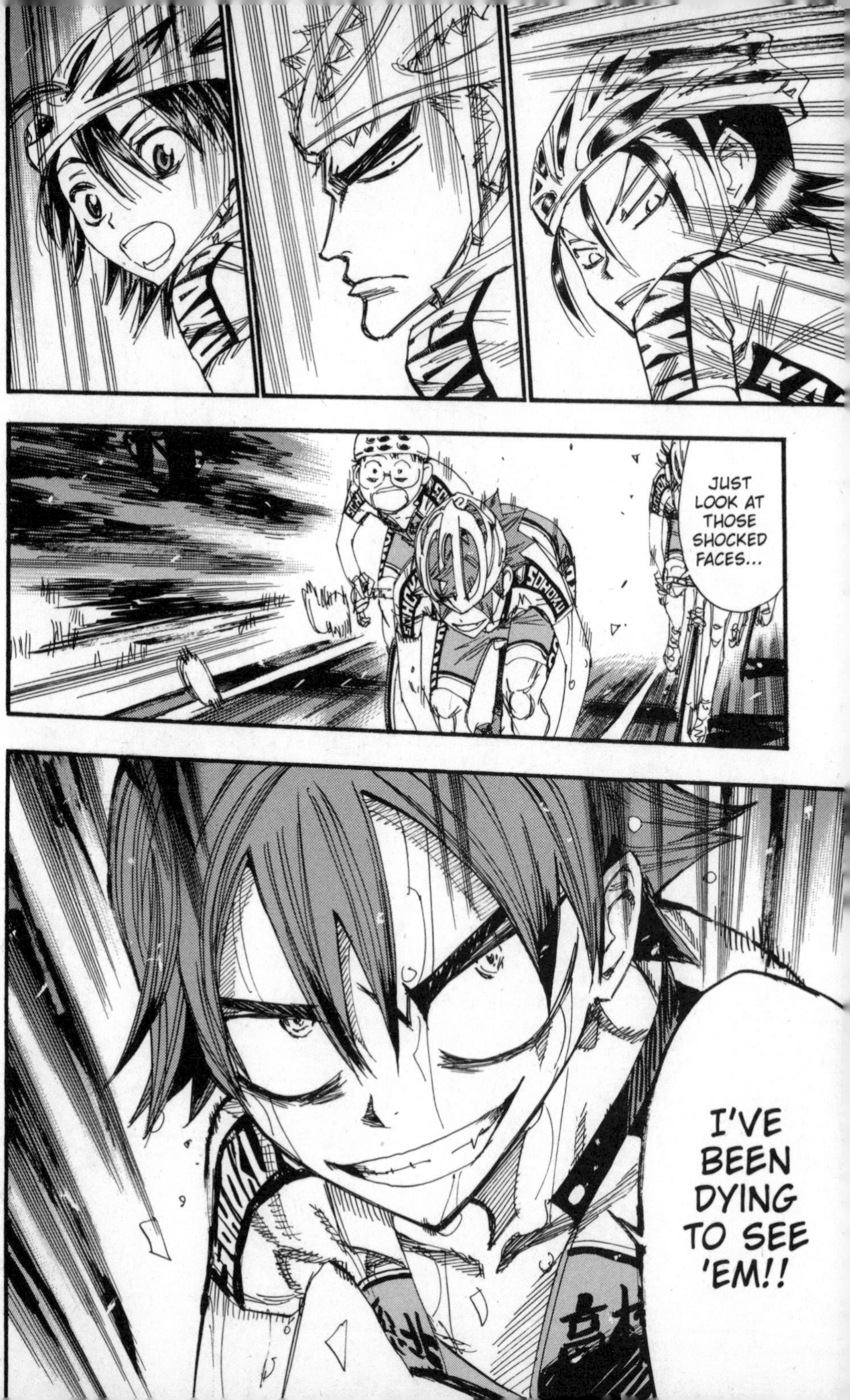
JUST LOOK AT THOSE SHOCKED FACES...
I'VE BEEN DYING TO SEE 'EM!!

RIDE.195 THE MAN WHO SAW IT THROUGH

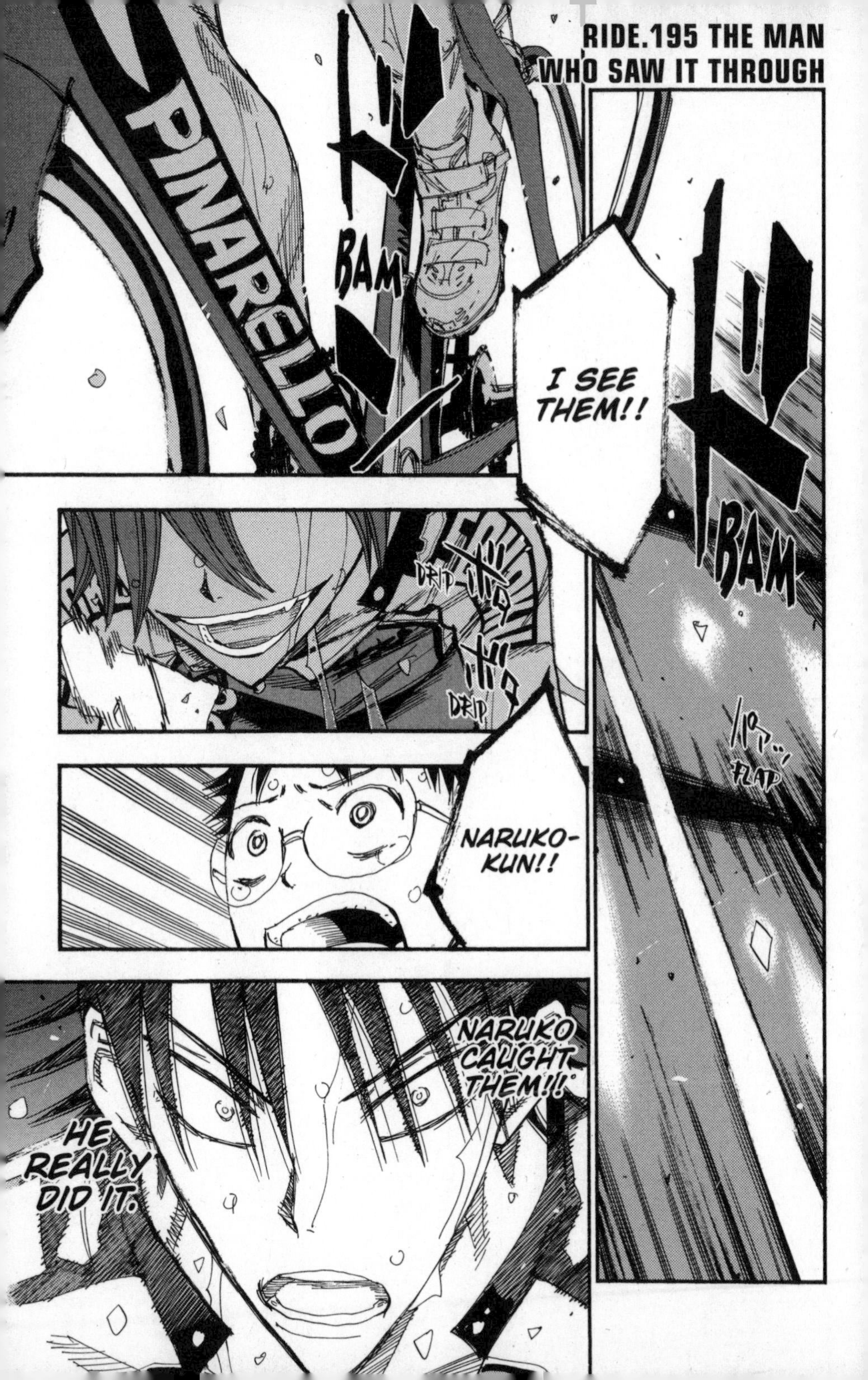
I SEE THEM!!
BAM
FLAP
PINARELLO
BAM
DRIP
DRIP
NARUKO-KUN!!
NARUKO CAUGHT THEM!!
HE REALLY DID IT.

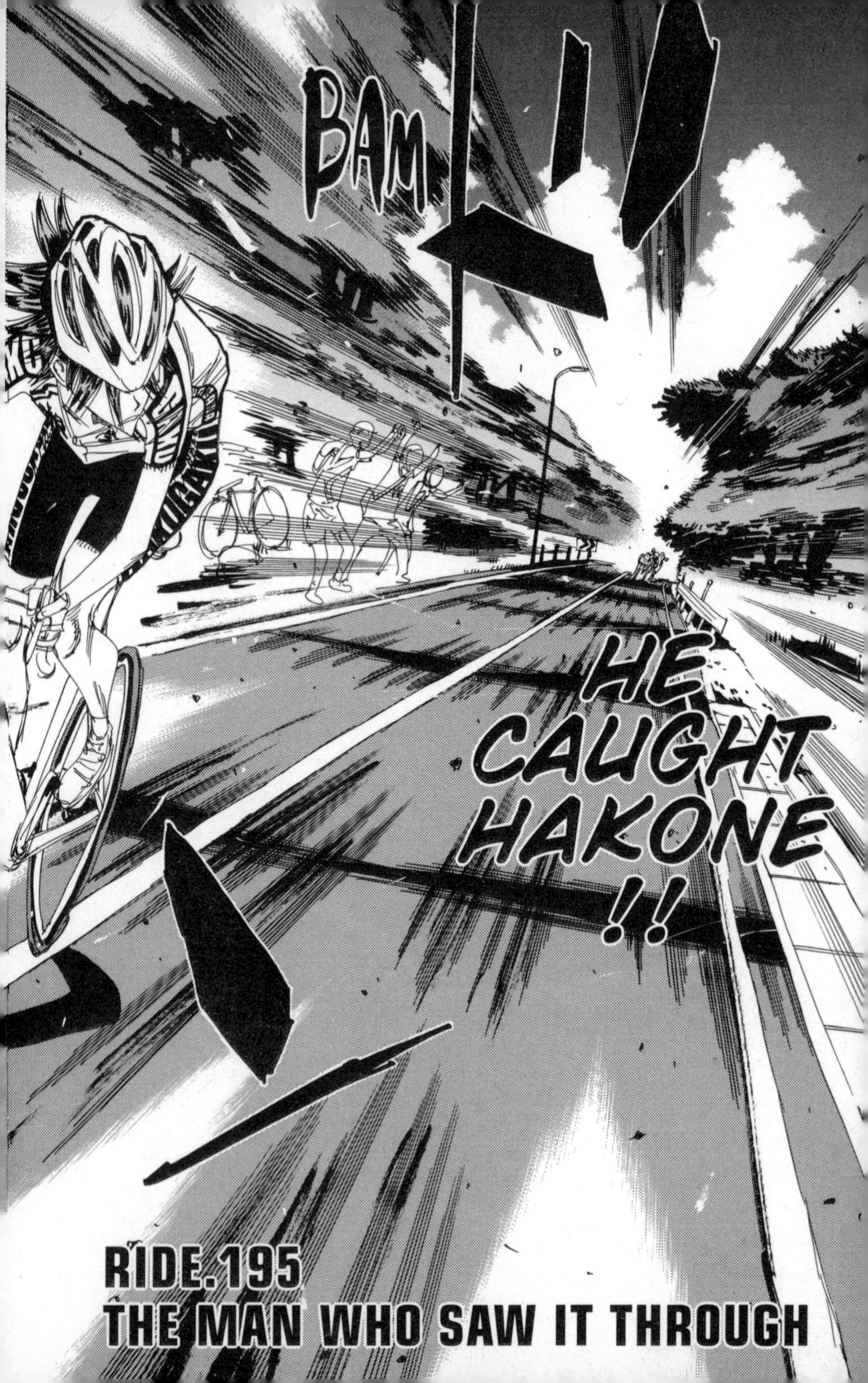
BAM
HE CAUGHT HAKONE!!

RIDE.195
THE MAN WHO SAW IT THROUGH

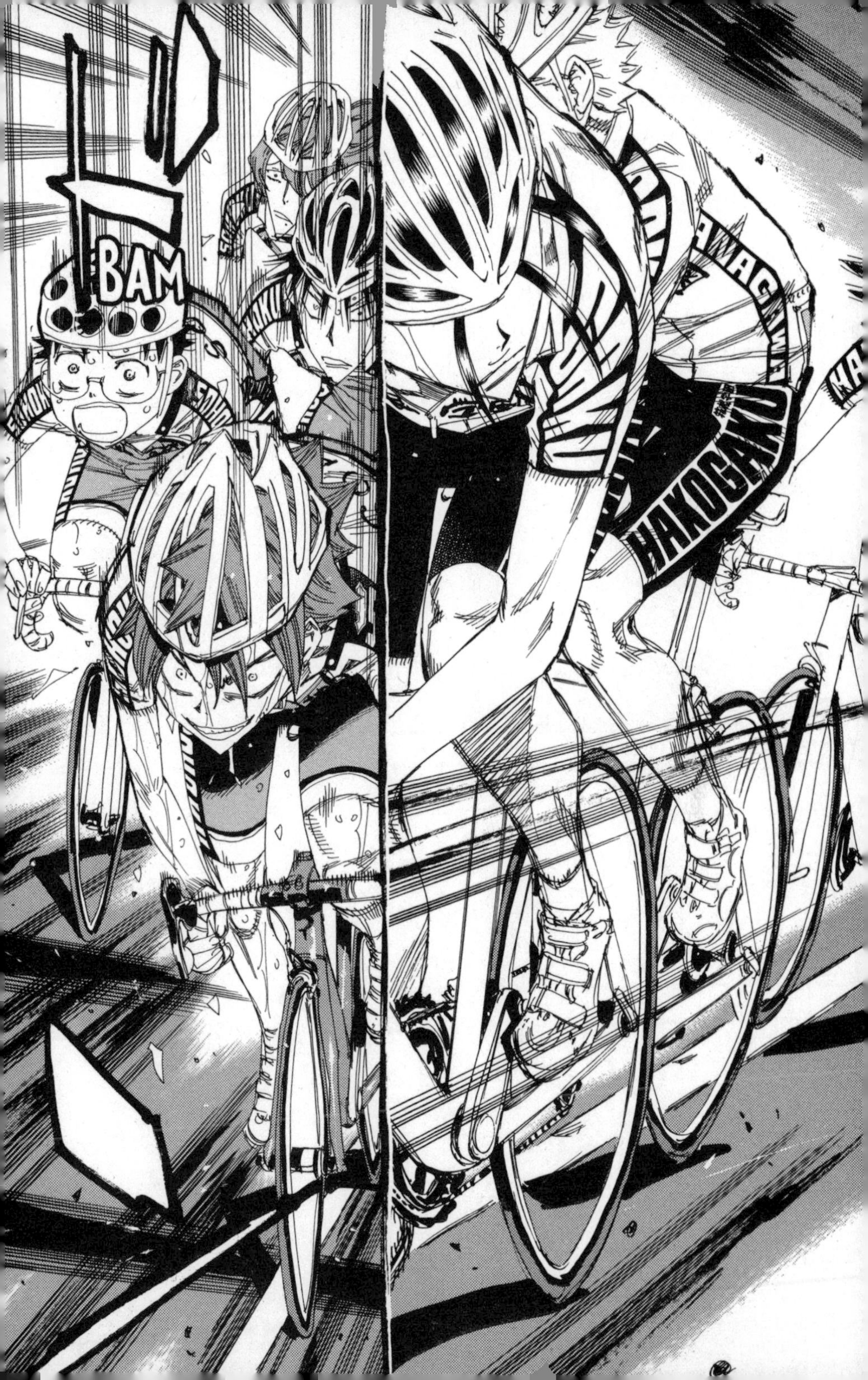
BAM

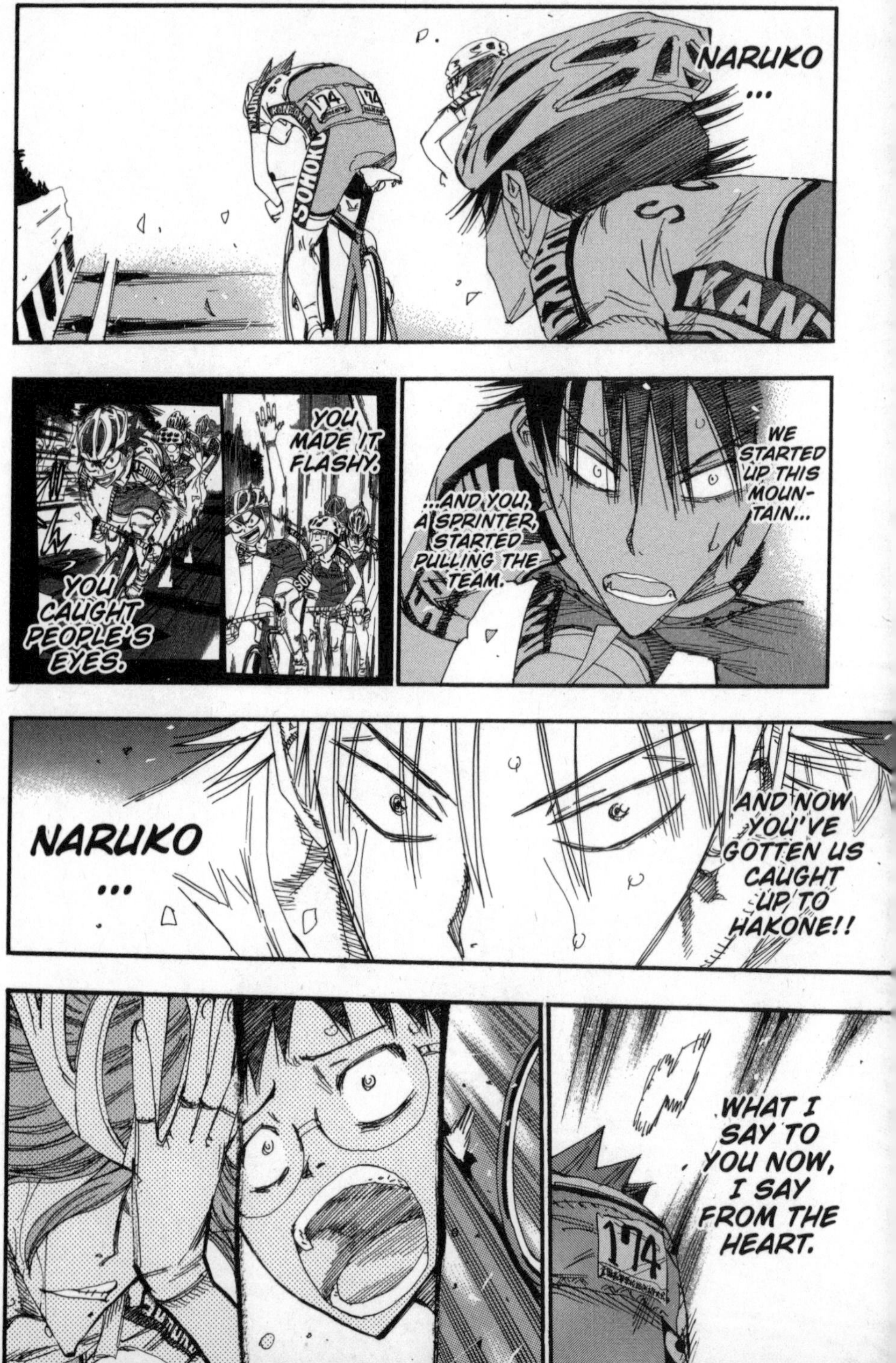
NARUKO ...
WE STARTED UP THIS MOUN-TAIN...
...AND YOU, A SPRINTER, STARTED PULLING THE TEAM.
YOU MADE IT FLASHY.
YOU CAUGHT PEOPLE'S EYES.
AND NOW YOU'VE GOTTEN US CAUGHT UP TO HAKONE!!
NARUKO ...
WHAT I SAY TO YOU NOW, I SAY FROM THE HEART.

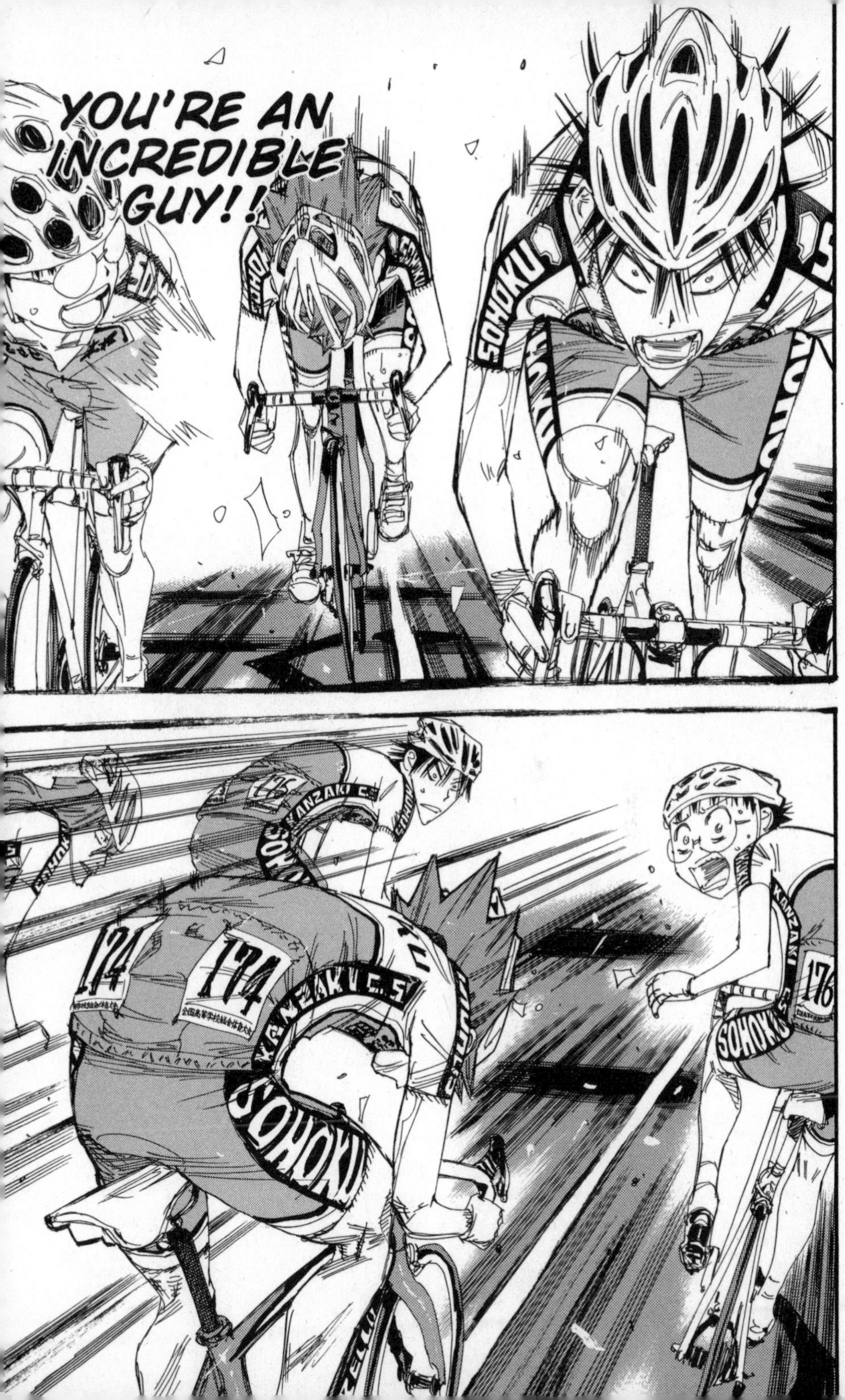
YOU'RE AN INCREDIBLE GUY!!

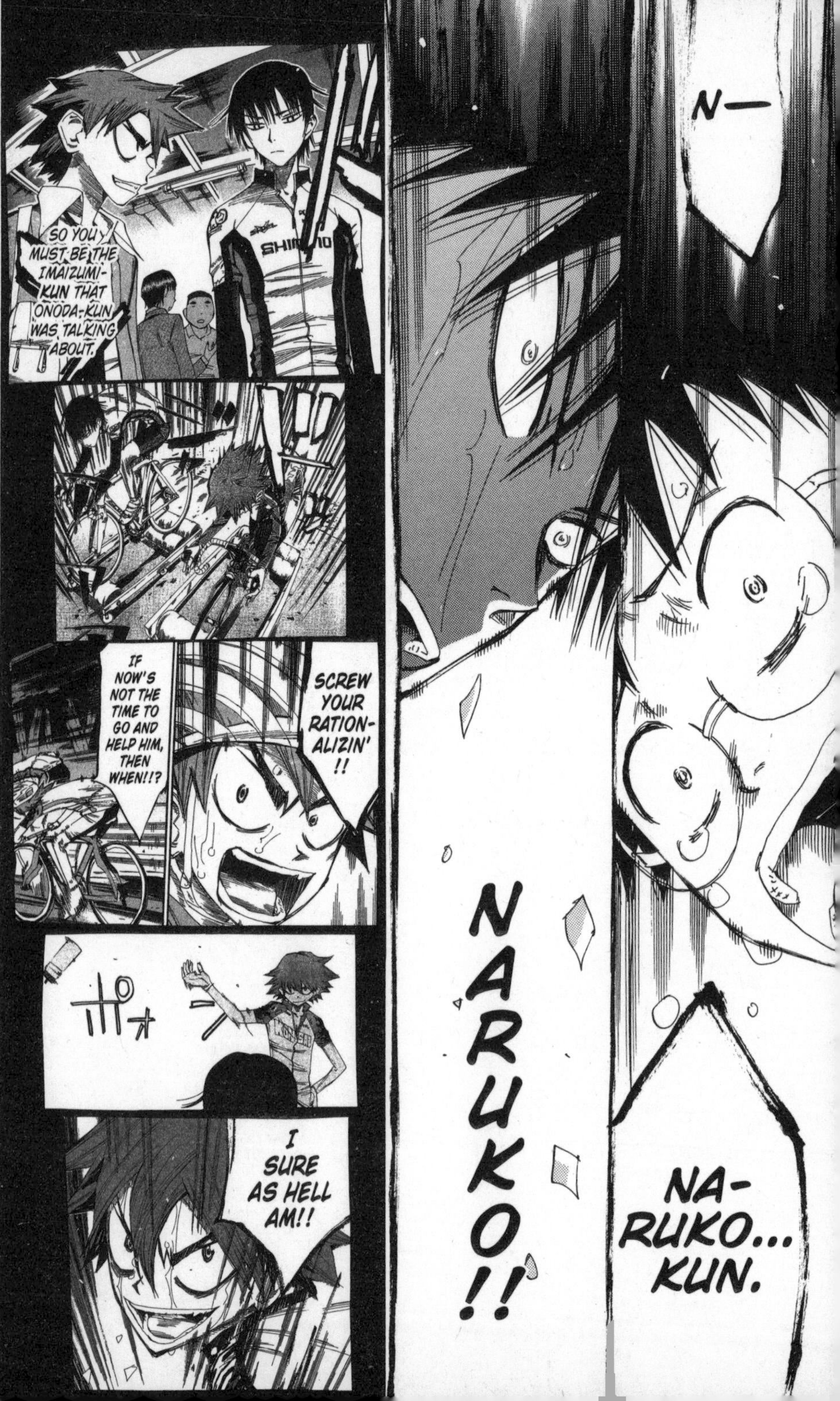
N—
NA-RUKO... KUN.
NARUKO!!
SO YOU MUST BE THE IMAIZUMI-KUN THAT ONODA-KUN WAS TALKING ABOUT.
SCREW YOUR RATION-ALIZIN'!!
IF NOW'S NOT THE TIME TO GO AND HELP HIM, THEN WHEN!!?
I SURE AS HELL AM!!

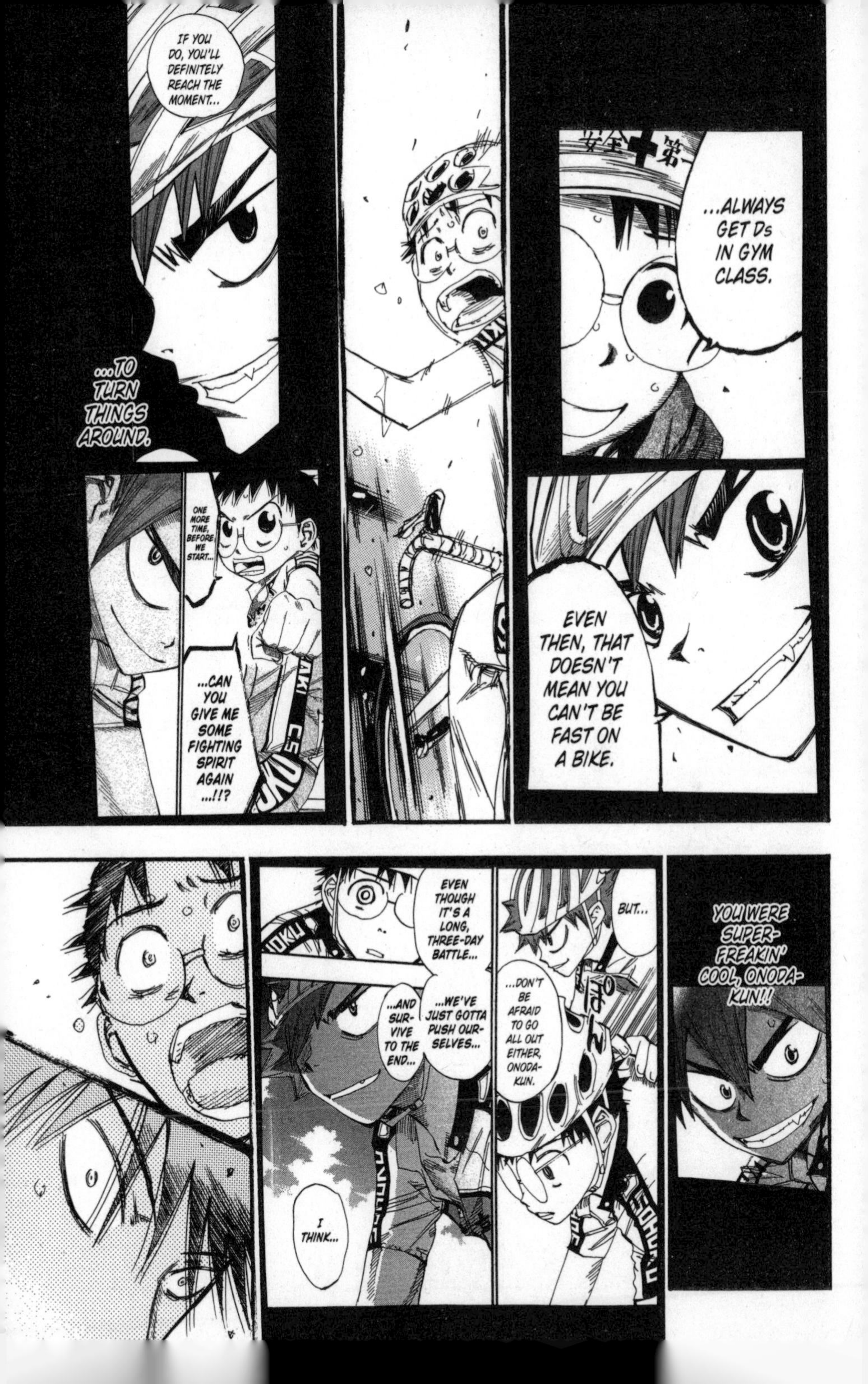
...ALWAYS GET Ds IN GYM CLASS.
EVEN THEN, THAT DOESN'T MEAN YOU CAN'T BE FAST ON A BIKE.
IF YOU DO, YOU'LL DEFINITELY REACH THE MOMENT...
...TO TURN THINGS AROUND.
ONE MORE TIME, BEFORE WE START...
...CAN YOU GIVE ME SOME FIGHTING SPIRIT AGAIN ...!!?
YOU WERE SUPER-FREAKIN' COOL, ONODA-KUN!!
BUT...
...DON'T BE AFRAID TO GO ALL OUT EITHER, ONODA-KUN.
EVEN THOUGH IT'S A LONG, THREE-DAY BATTLE...
...WE'VE JUST GOTTA PUSH OURSELVES...
...AND SURVIVE TO THE END...
I THINK...

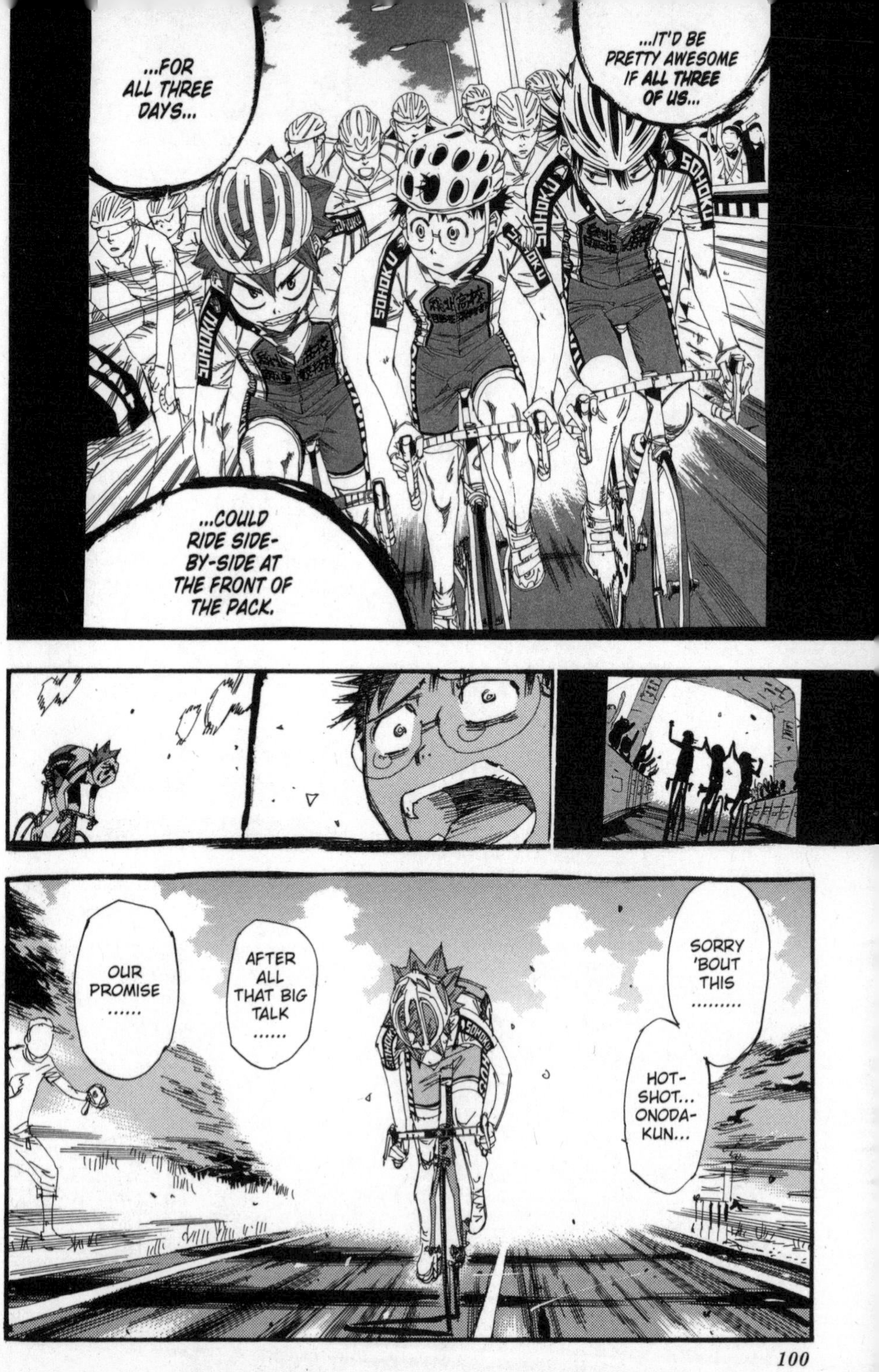
...IT'D BE PRETTY AWESOME IF ALL THREE OF US...
...FOR ALL THREE DAYS...
...COULD RIDE SIDE-BY-SIDE AT THE FRONT OF THE PACK.
SORRY 'BOUT THIS ....
HOT-SHOT... ONODA-KUN...
AFTER ALL THAT BIG TALK ......
OUR PROMISE ......

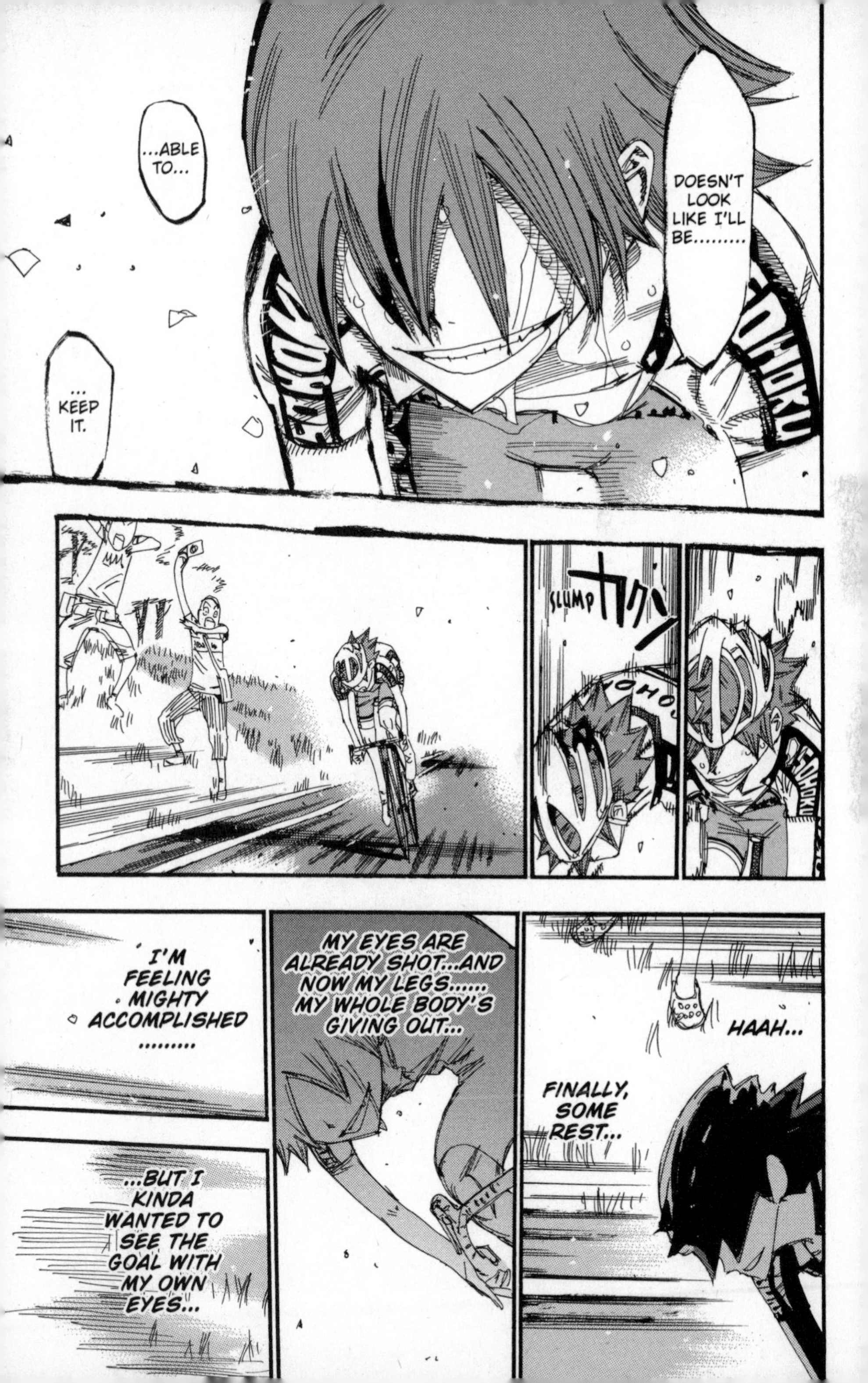
DOESN'T LOOK LIKE I'LL BE.........
...ABLE TO...
...KEEP IT.
SLUMP カクン
HAAH...
FINALLY, SOME REST...
MY EYES ARE ALREADY SHOT...AND NOW MY LEGS...... MY WHOLE BODY'S GIVING OUT...
I'M FEELING MIGHTY ACCOMPLISHED ....
...BUT I KINDA WANTED TO SEE THE GOAL WITH MY OWN EYES...

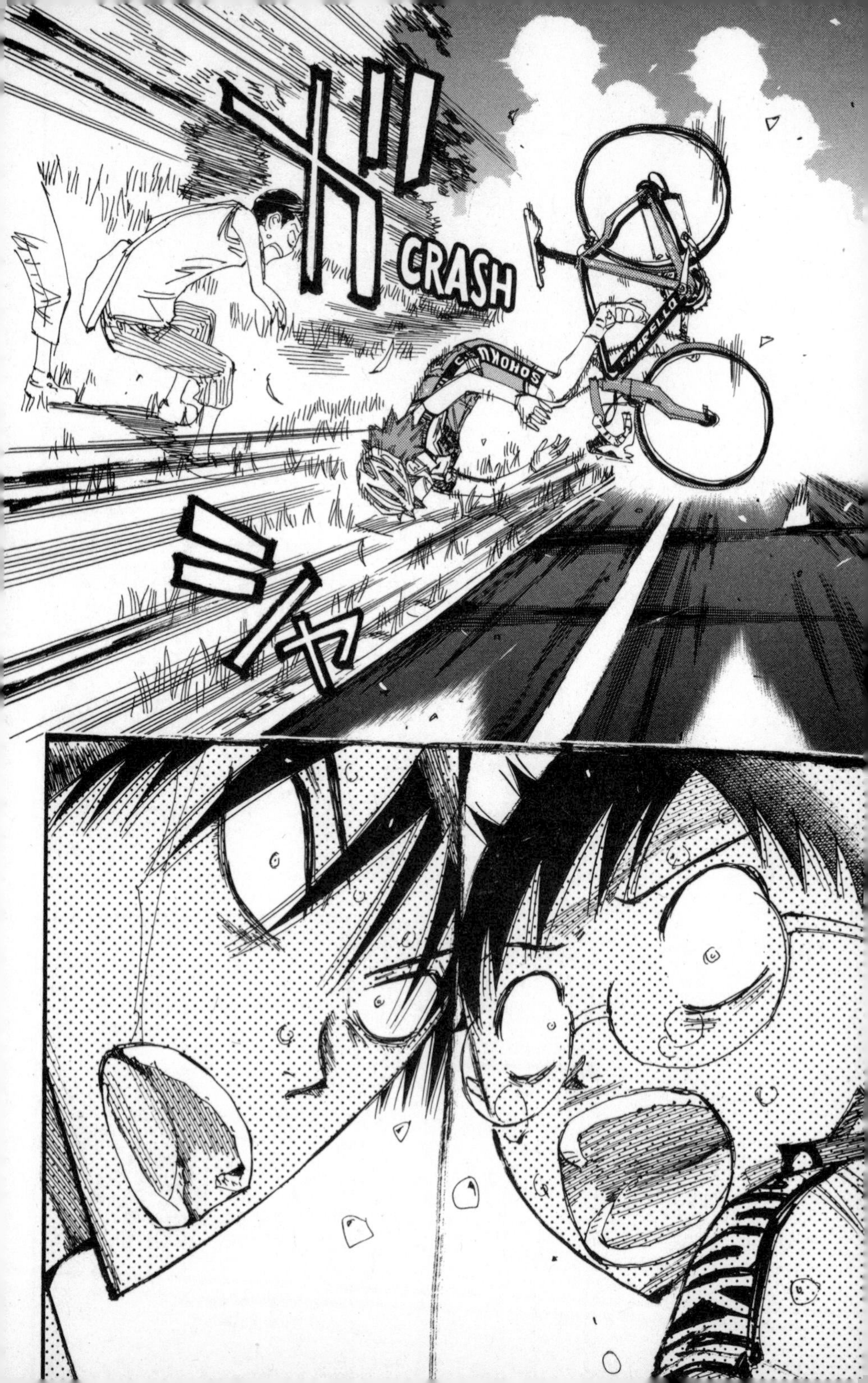
CRASH

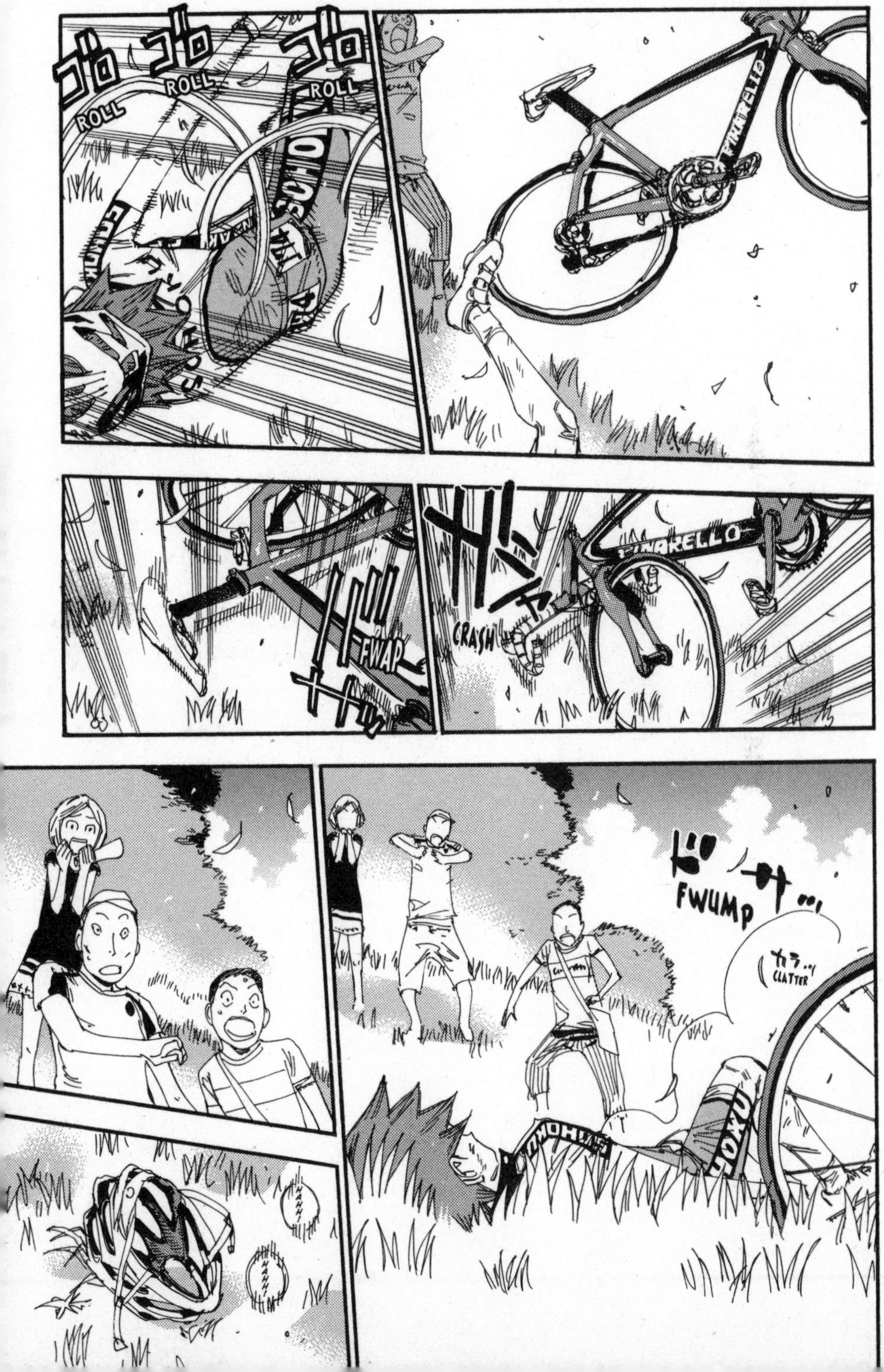
PINARELLO
ROLL
ROLL
ROLL
PINARELLO
CRASH
FWAP
FWUMP
CLATTER
HAHH!
HAHH!

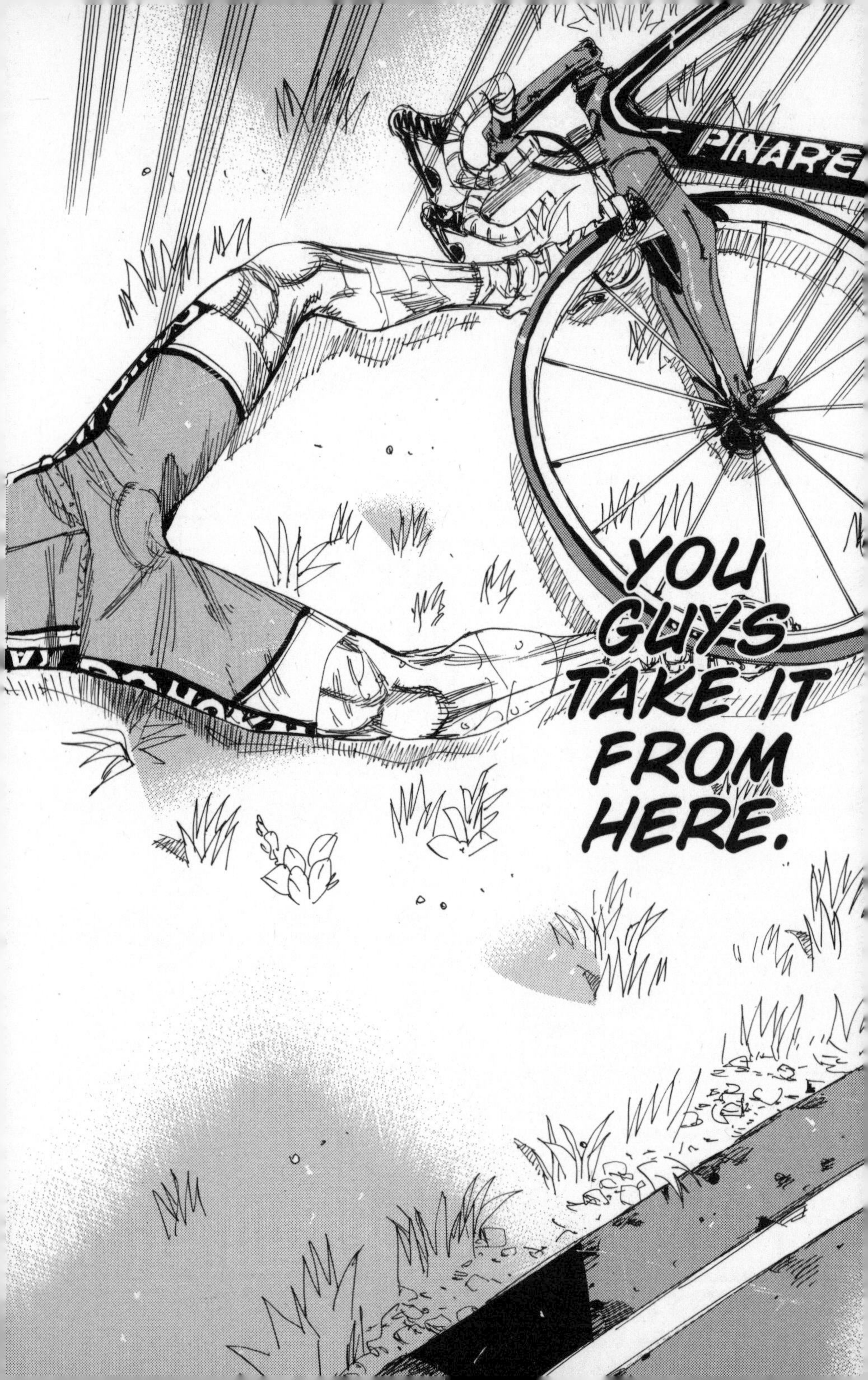
YOU GUYS TAKE IT FROM HERE.

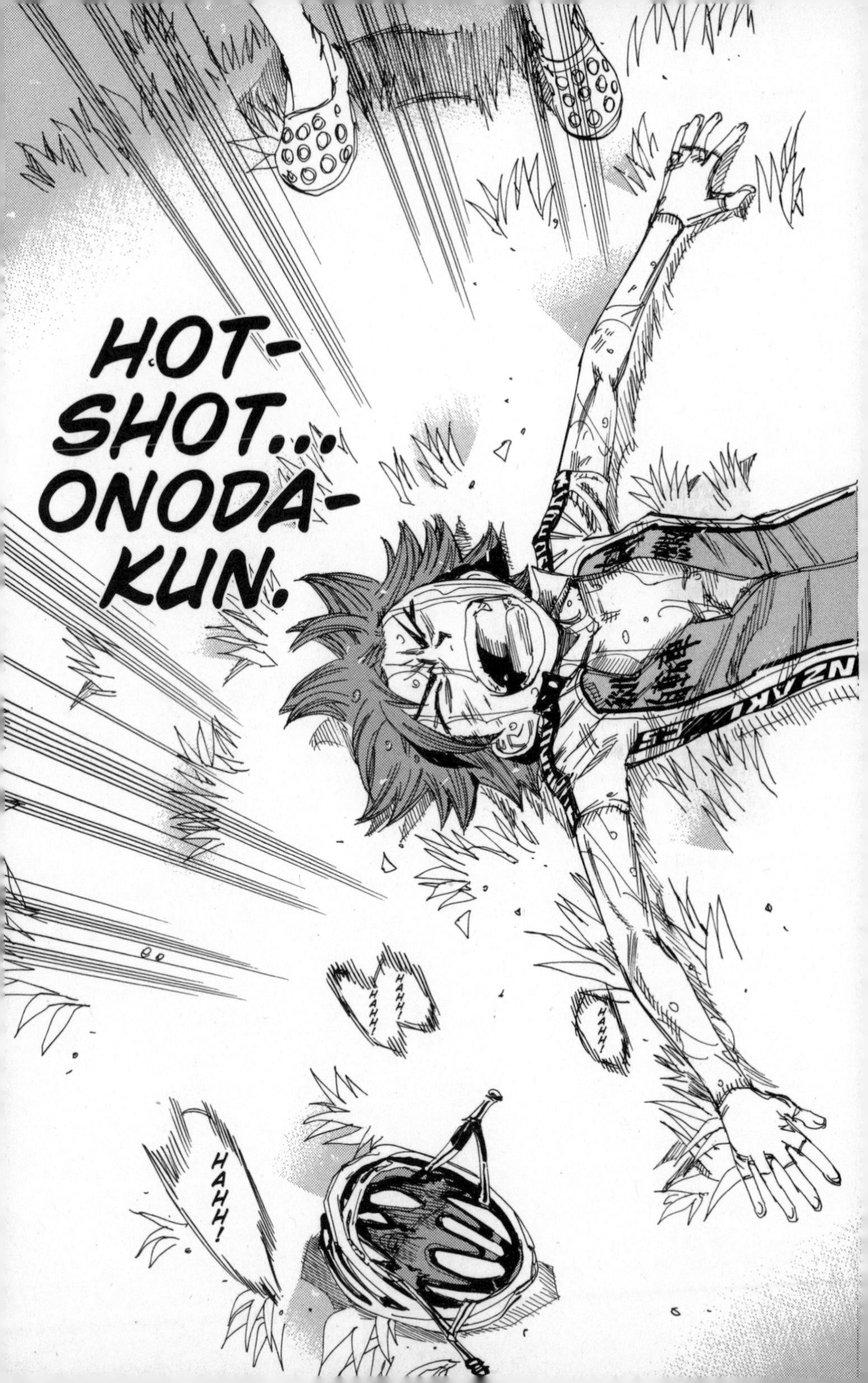
HOT-
SHOT...
ONODA-
KUN.
HAHH!
HAHH!
HAHH!
HAHH!

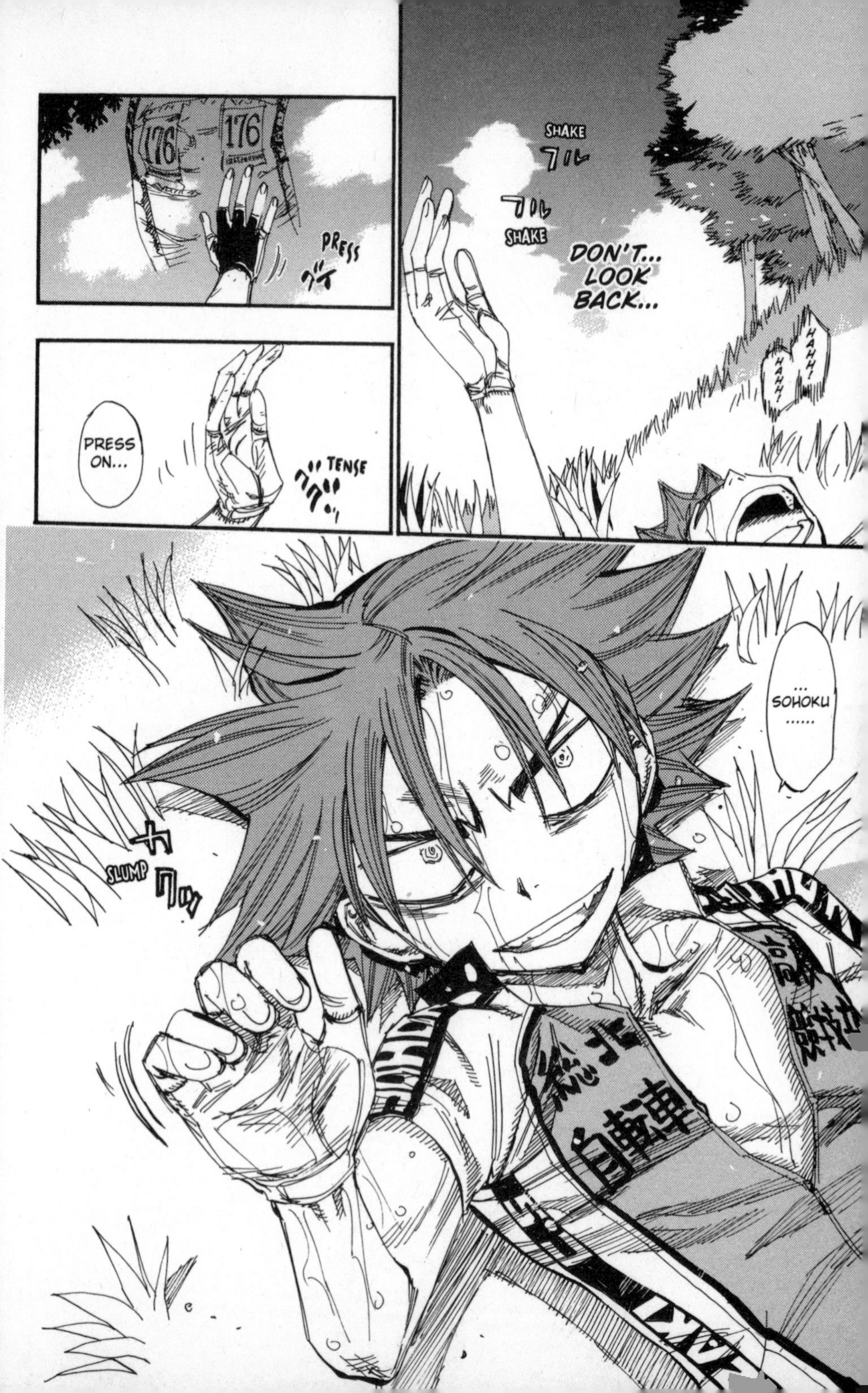
SHAKE
フル
フル
SHAKE
DON'T... LOOK BACK...
HAHH! HAHH!
176
176
PRESS
グイ
PRESS ON...
TENSE
...SOHOKU......
SLUMP

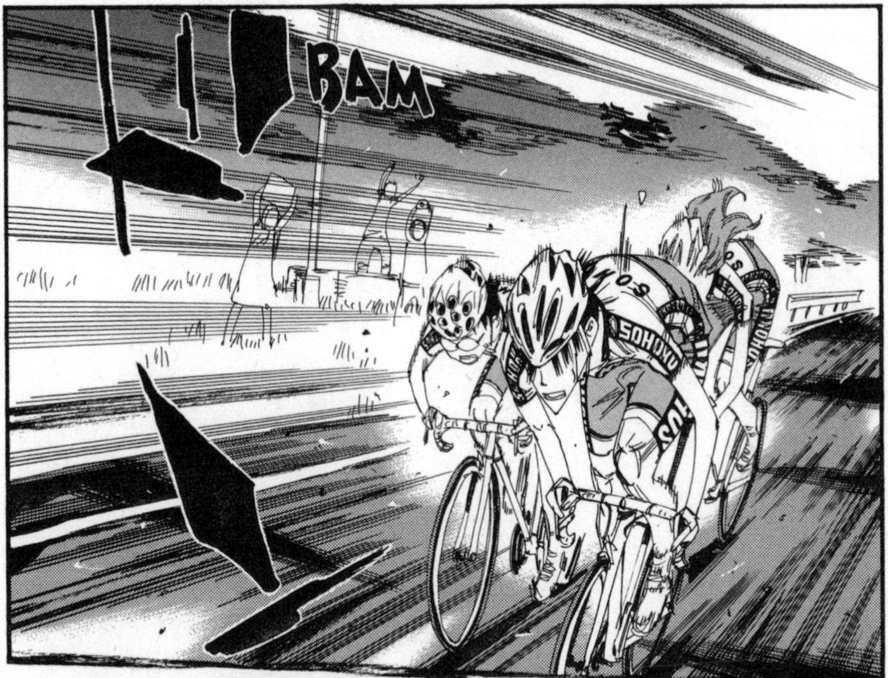
BAM
SOHOKU
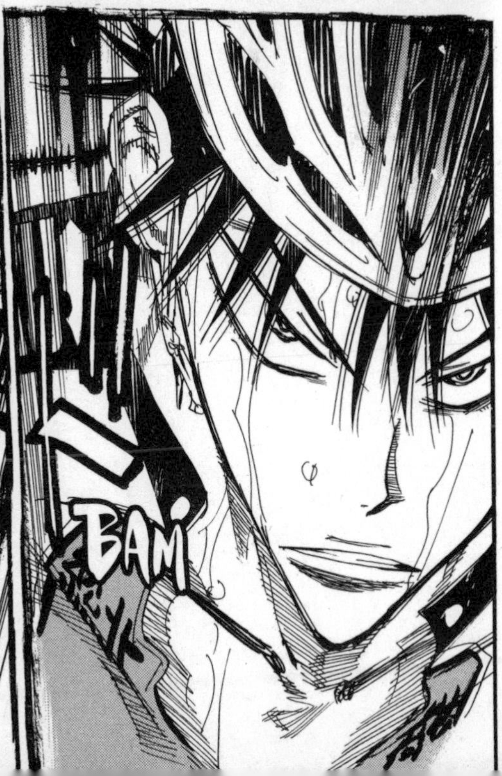
BAM
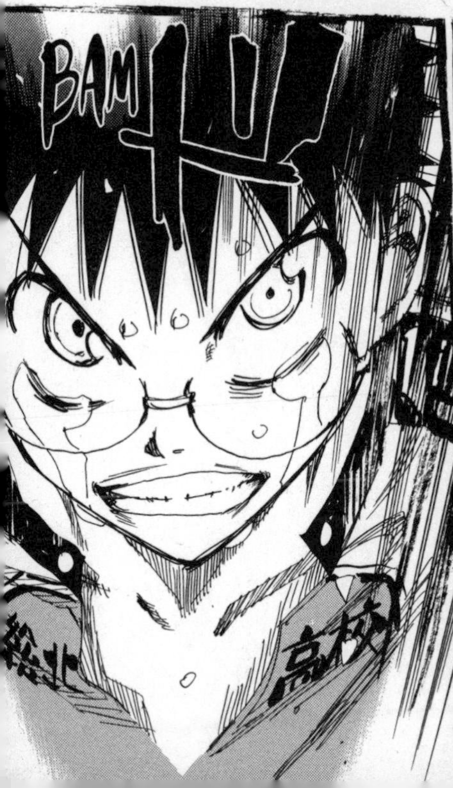
BAM
総北
高校

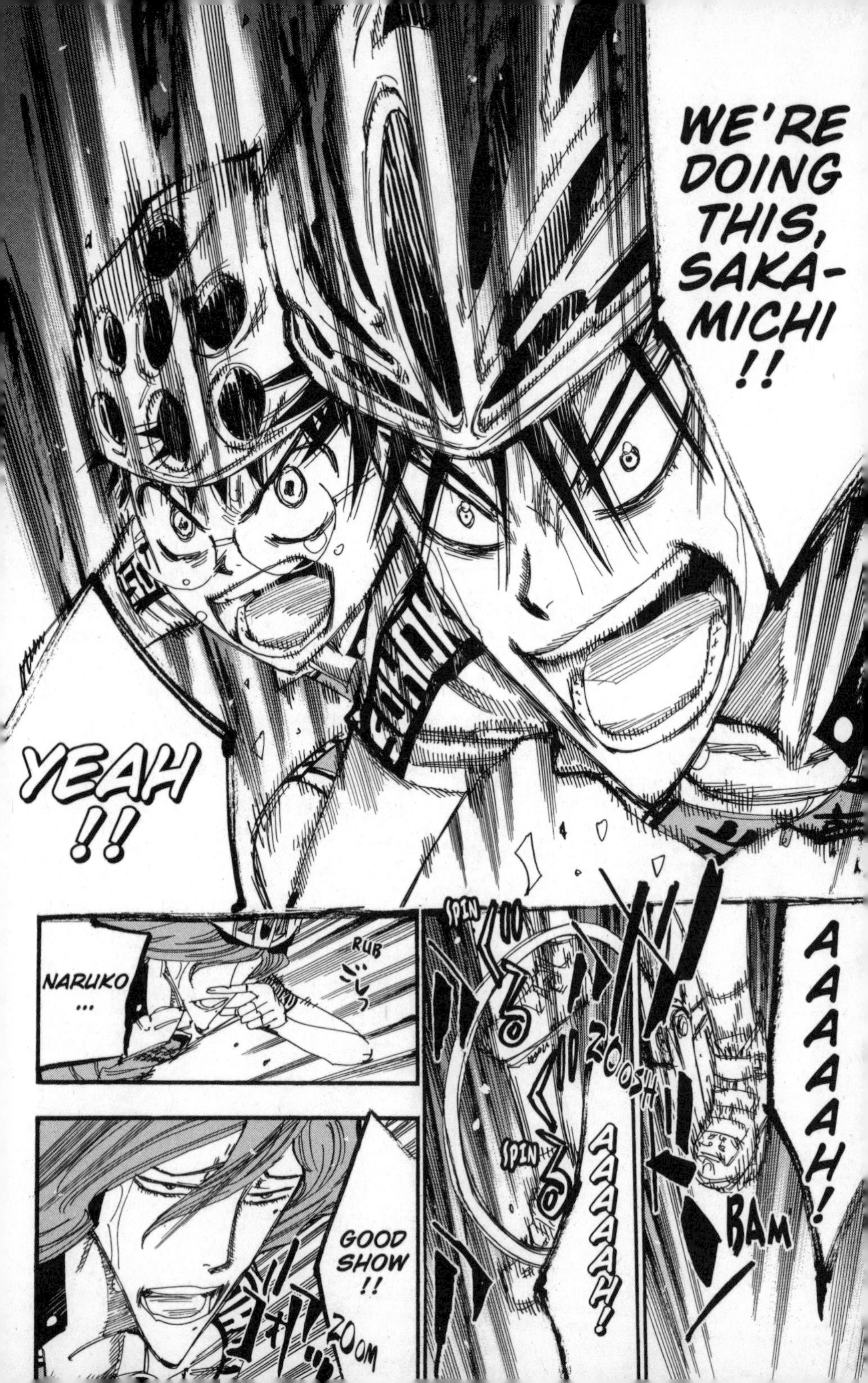
WE'RE DOING THIS, SAKAMICHI!!
YEAH!!
AAAAAAH!
SPIN
ZOOSH
BAM
SPIN
AAAAAAH!
RUB
NARUKO...
GOOD SHOW!!
ZOOM

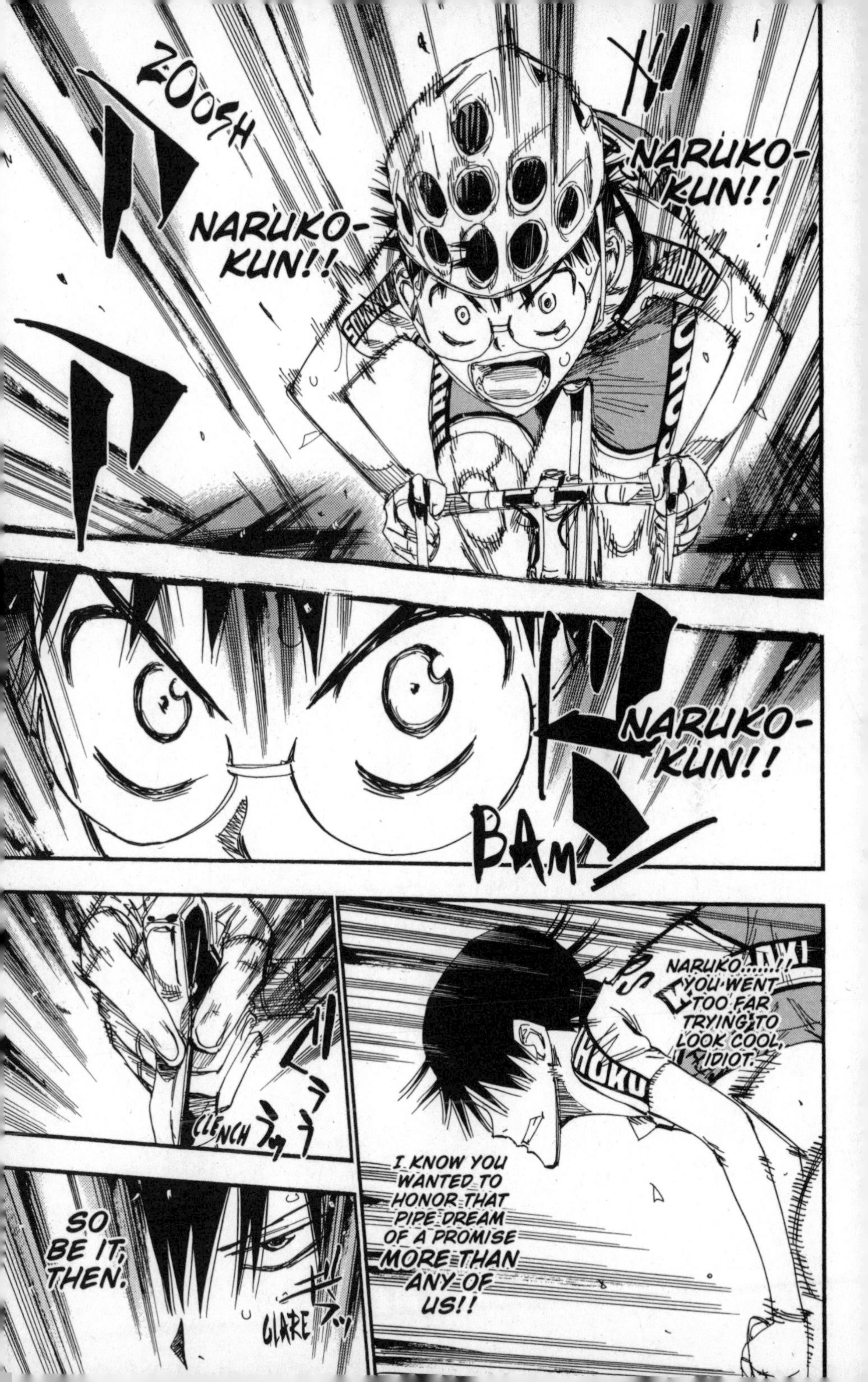
NARUKO-KUN!!
ZOOSH
NARUKO-KUN!!
NARUKO-KUN!!
BAM
NARUKO......!!
YOU WENT TOO FAR TRYING TO LOOK COOL, IDIOT.
CLENCH
I KNOW YOU WANTED TO HONOR THAT PIPE DREAM OF A PROMISE MORE THAN ANY OF US!!
SO BE IT, THEN.
GLARE

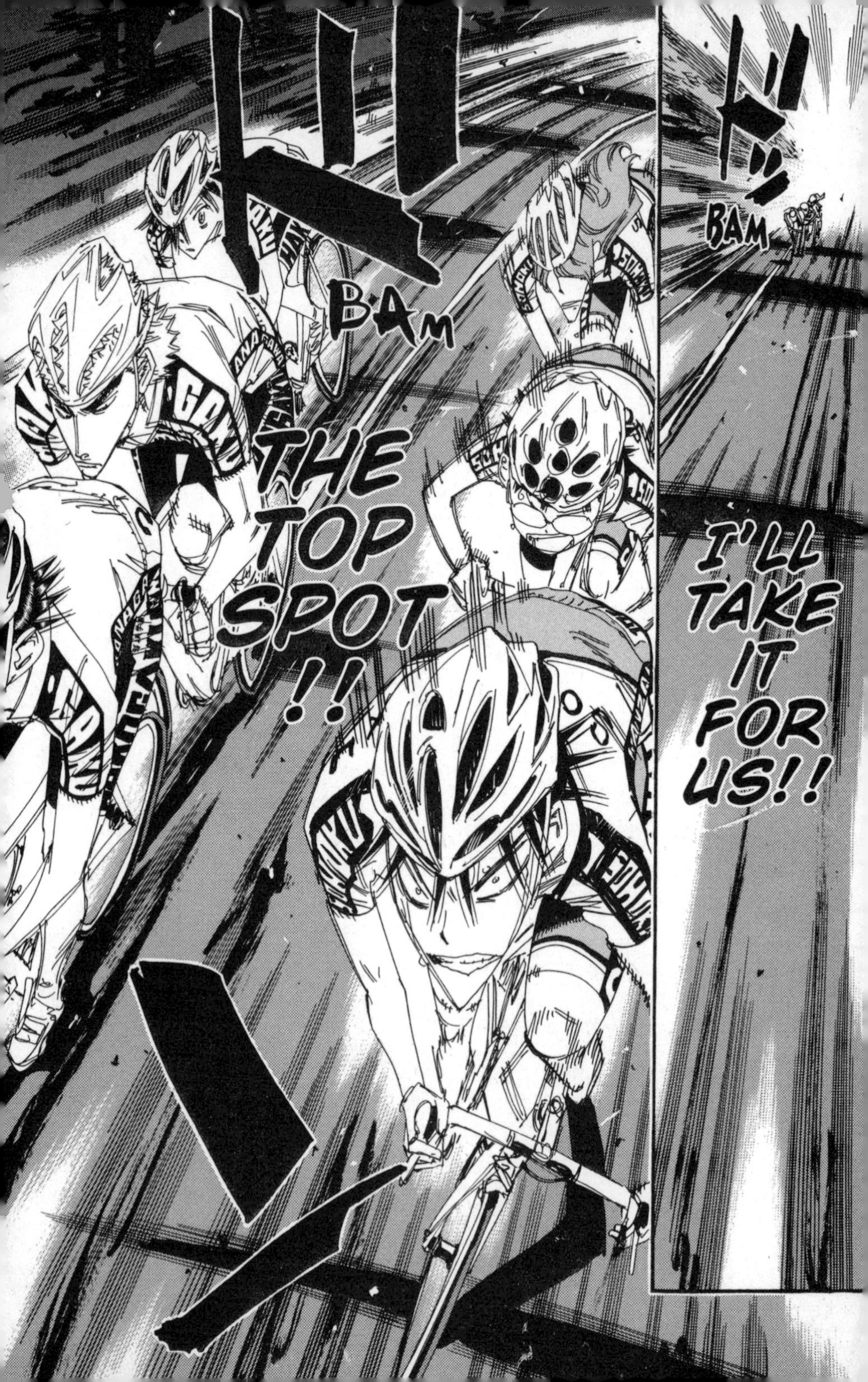
BAM
I'LL TAKE IT FOR US!!
BAM
THE TOP SPOT!!

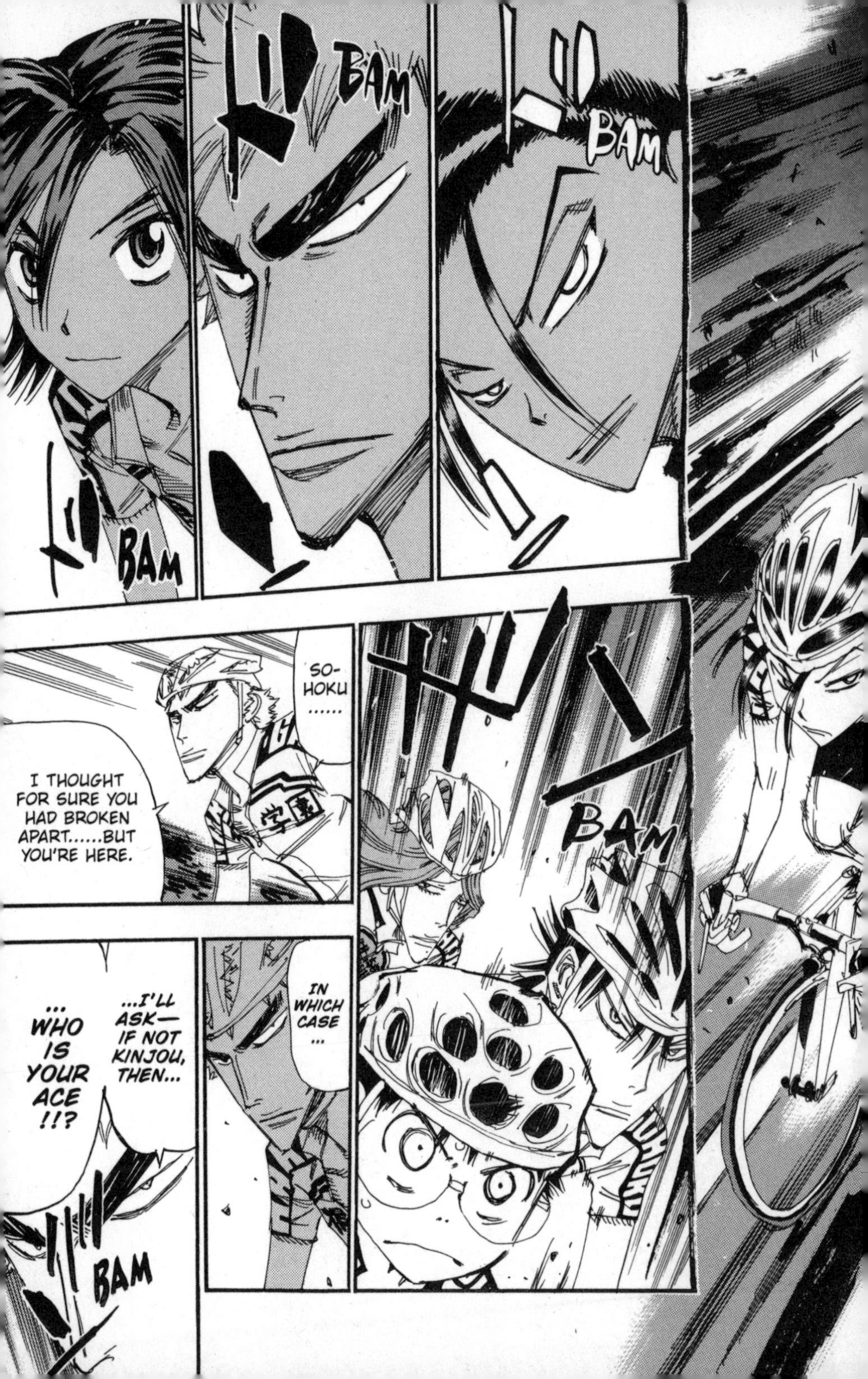
BAM
BAM
BAM
BAM
SO-HOKU......
I THOUGHT FOR SURE YOU HAD BROKEN APART......BUT YOU'RE HERE.
IN WHICH CASE...
...I'LL ASK— IF NOT KINJOU, THEN...
...WHO IS YOUR ACE!!?
BAM

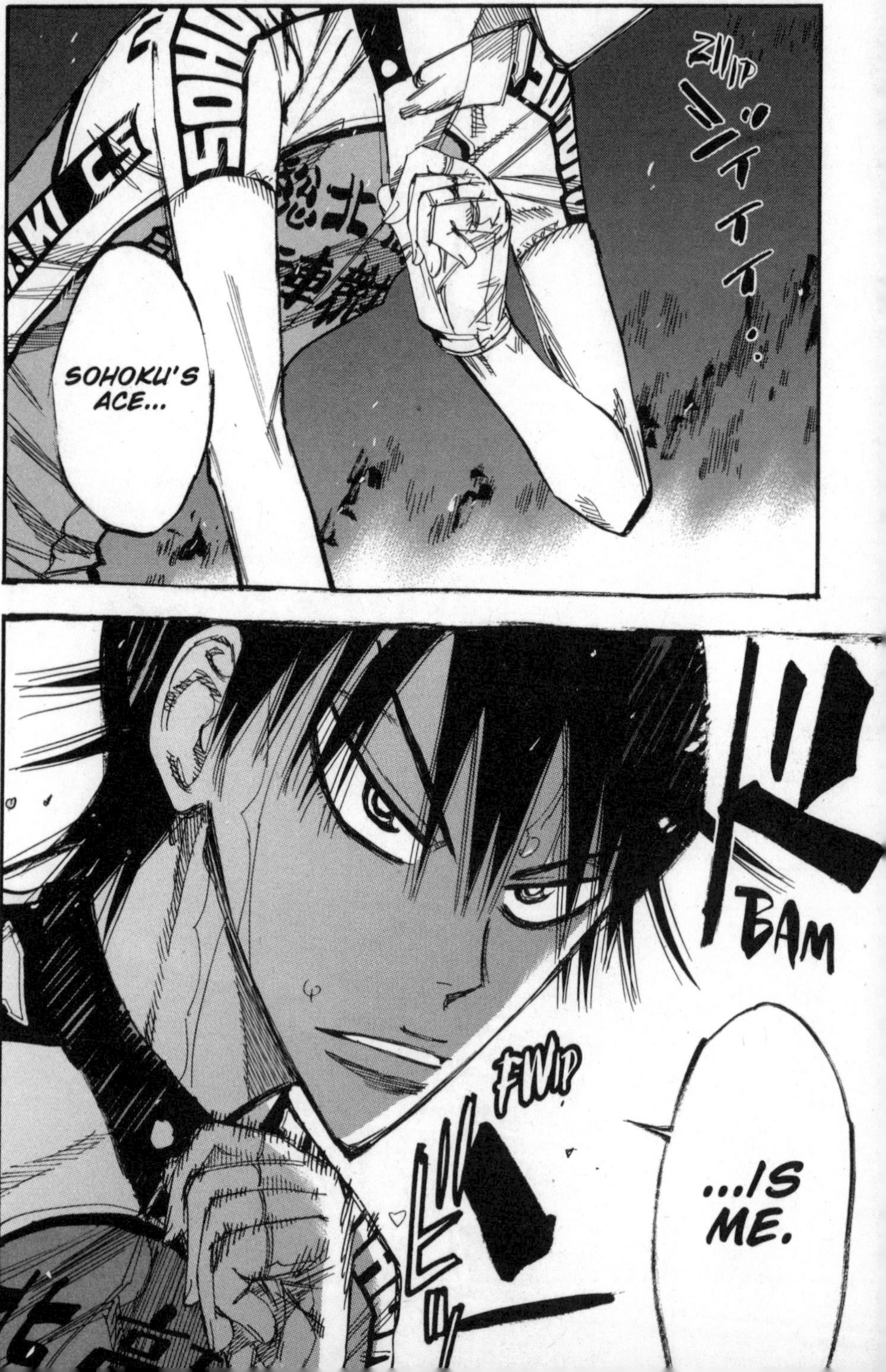
ZIIIP
SOHOKU'S ACE...
BAM
...IS ME.
FWIP

RIDE.196 IMAIZUMI, THE ACE!

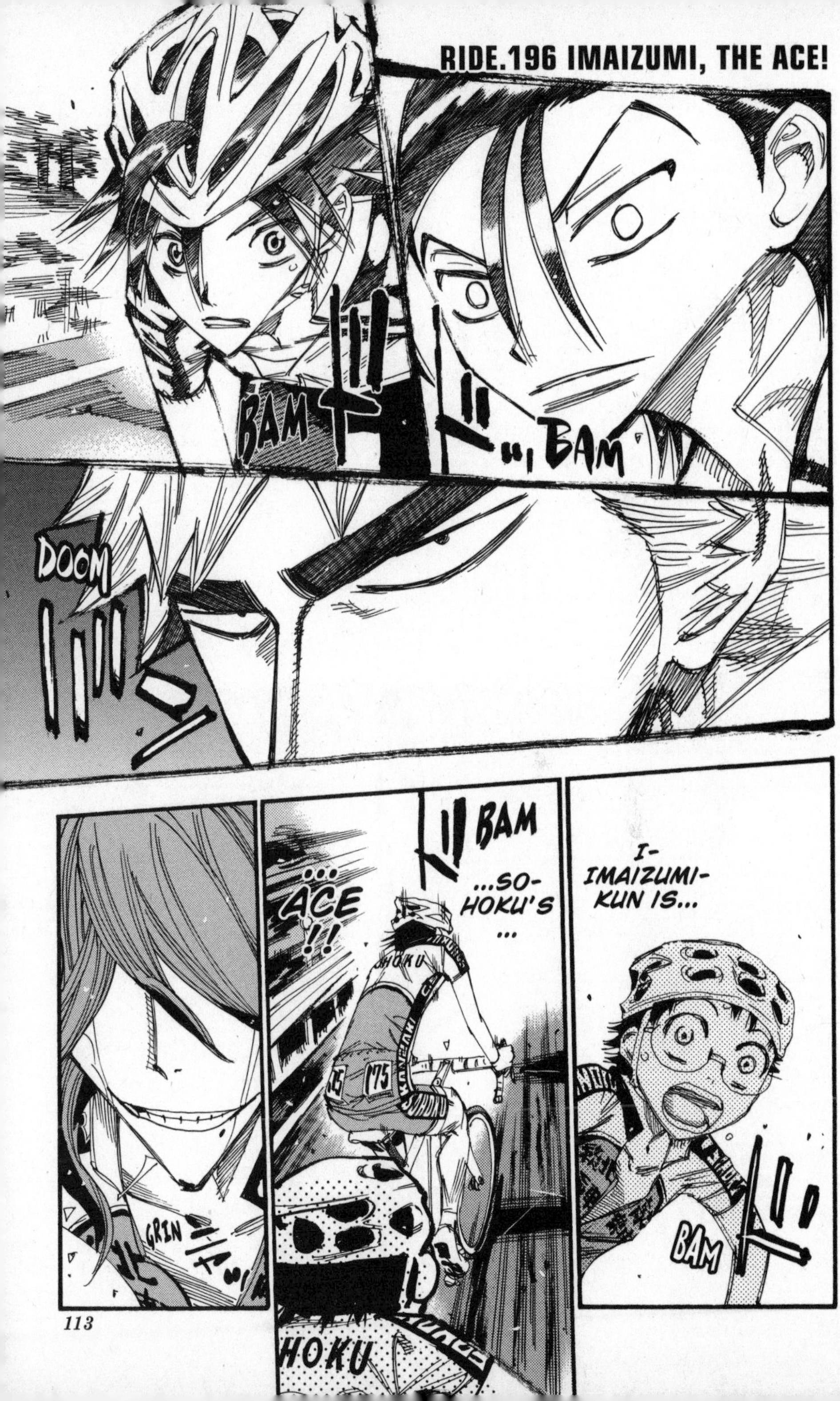
BAM
BAM
DOOM
I-
IMAIZUMI-
KUN IS...
BAM
...SO-
HOKU'S
...
BAM
...ACE
!!
HOKU
GRIN

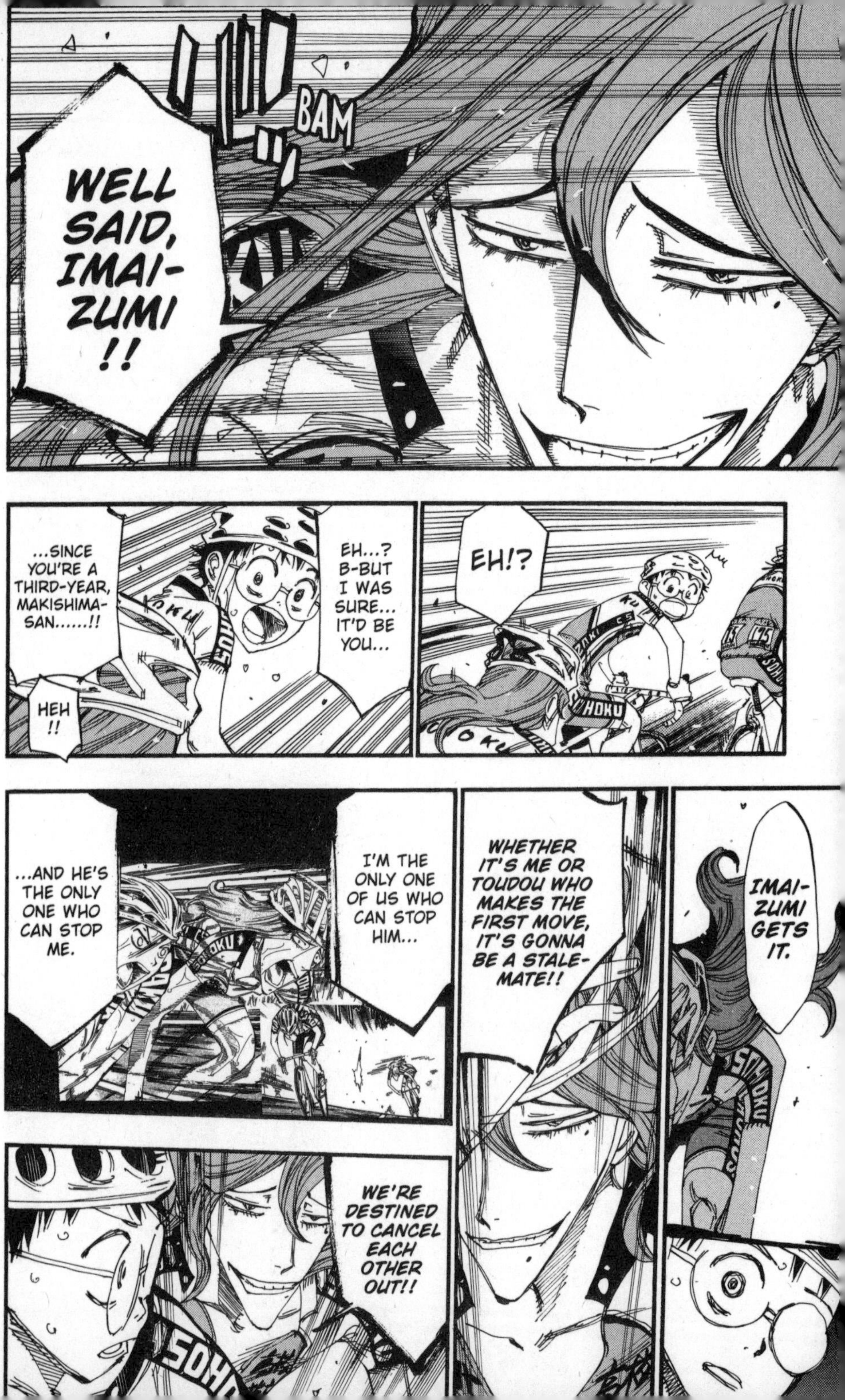
BAM
WELL SAID, IMAIZUMI!!
EH!?
EH...? B-BUT I WAS SURE... IT'D BE YOU...
...SINCE YOU'RE A THIRD-YEAR, MAKISHIMA-SAN......!!
HEH!!
IMAIZUMI GETS IT.
WHETHER IT'S ME OR TOUDOU WHO MAKES THE FIRST MOVE, IT'S GONNA BE A STALEMATE!!
I'M THE ONLY ONE OF US WHO CAN STOP HIM...
...AND HE'S THE ONLY ONE WHO CAN STOP ME.
WE'RE DESTINED TO CANCEL EACH OTHER OUT!!

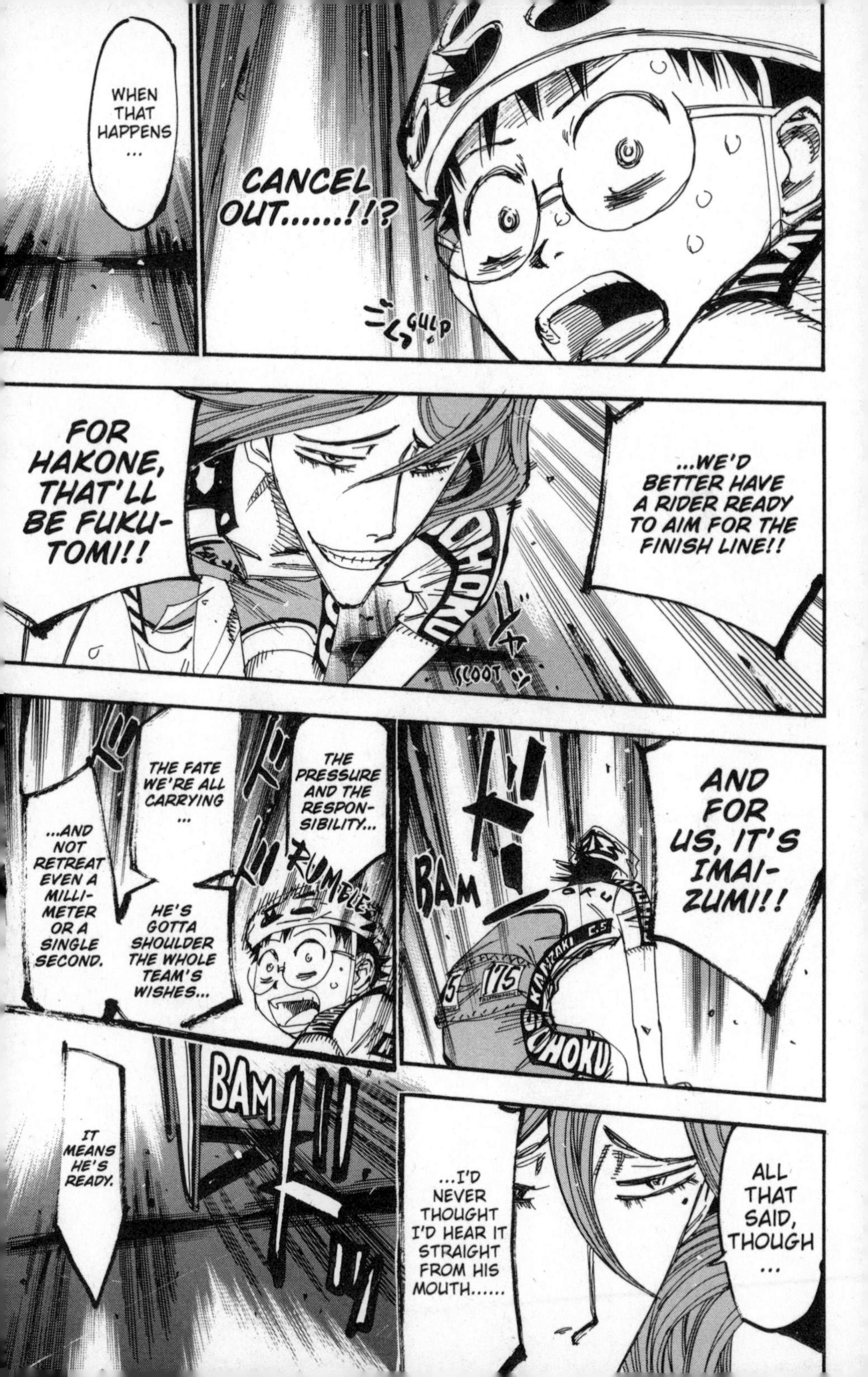
CANCEL OUT......!!?
GULP
WHEN THAT HAPPENS ...
...WE'D BETTER HAVE A RIDER READY TO AIM FOR THE FINISH LINE!!
FOR HAKONE, THAT'LL BE FUKU-TOMI!!
SCOOT
AND FOR US, IT'S IMAI-ZUMI!!
BAM
THE PRESSURE AND THE RESPON-SIBILITY...
THE FATE WE'RE ALL CARRYING ...
HE'S GOTTA SHOULDER THE WHOLE TEAM'S WISHES...
...AND NOT RETREAT EVEN A MILLI-METER OR A SINGLE SECOND.
RUMBLE
ALL THAT SAID, THOUGH ...
...I'D NEVER THOUGHT I'D HEAR IT STRAIGHT FROM HIS MOUTH......
BAM
IT MEANS HE'S READY.

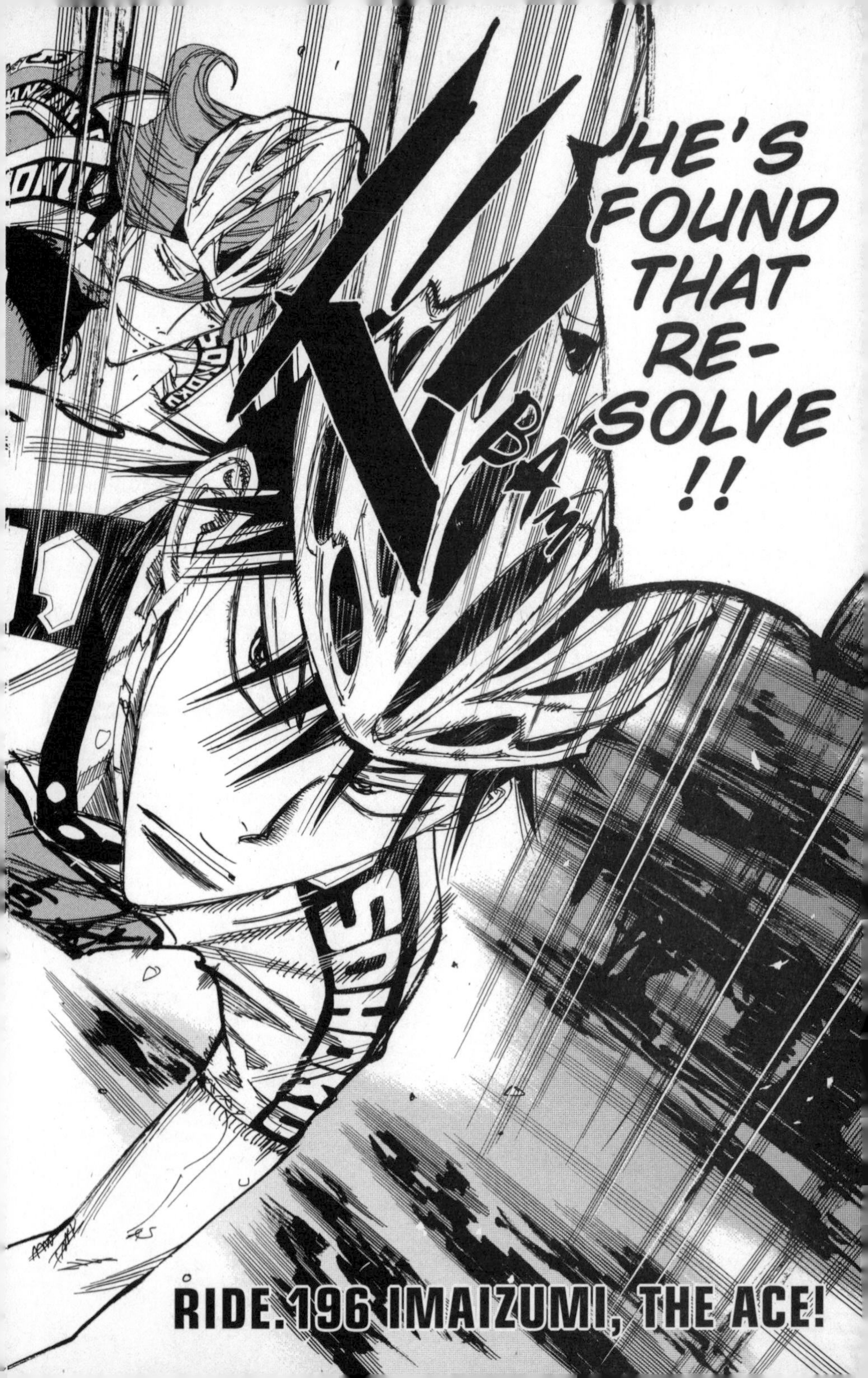
HE'S FOUND THAT RE- SOLVE !!
BAM

RIDE. 196 IMAIZUMI, THE ACE!

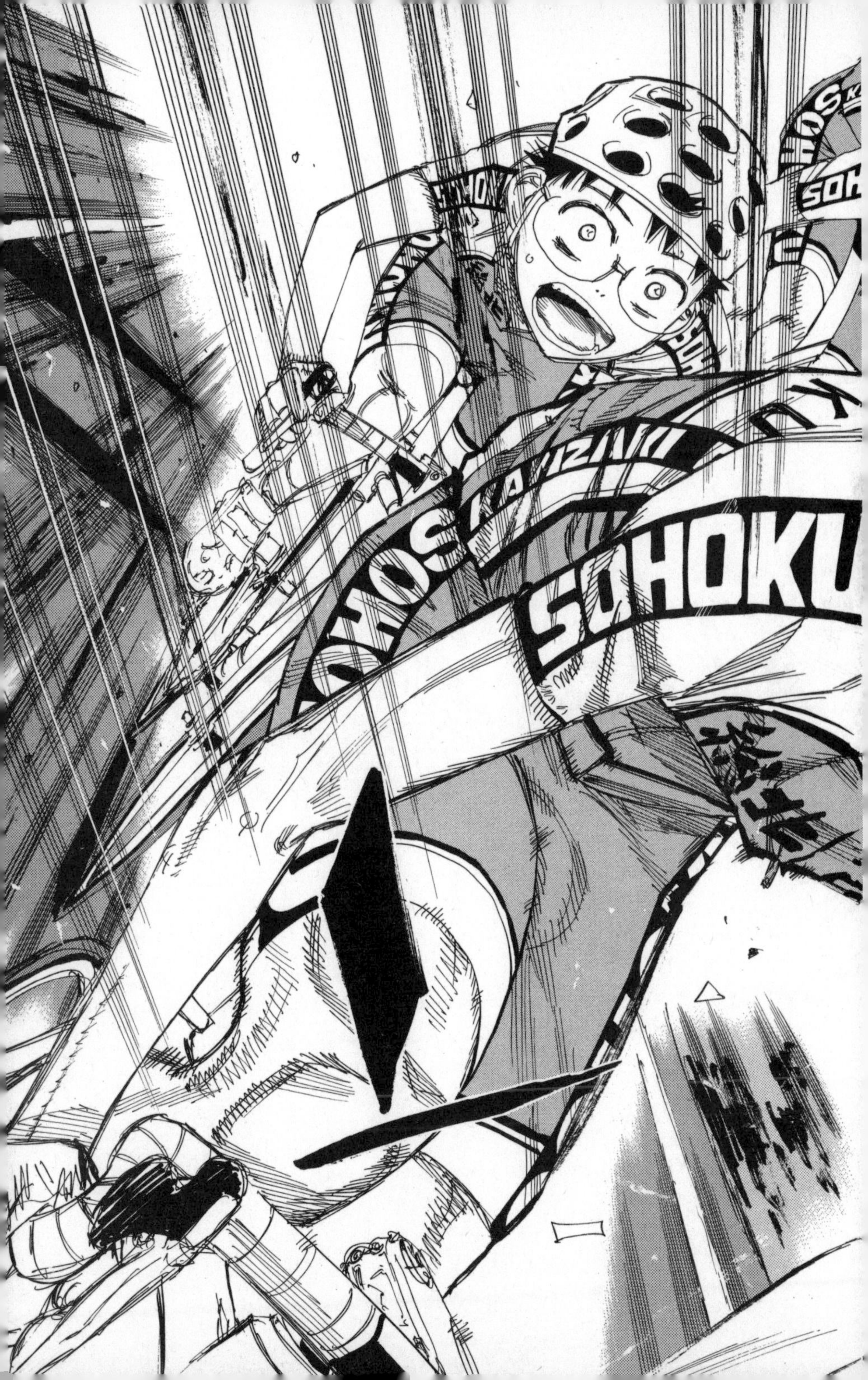
SOHOKU

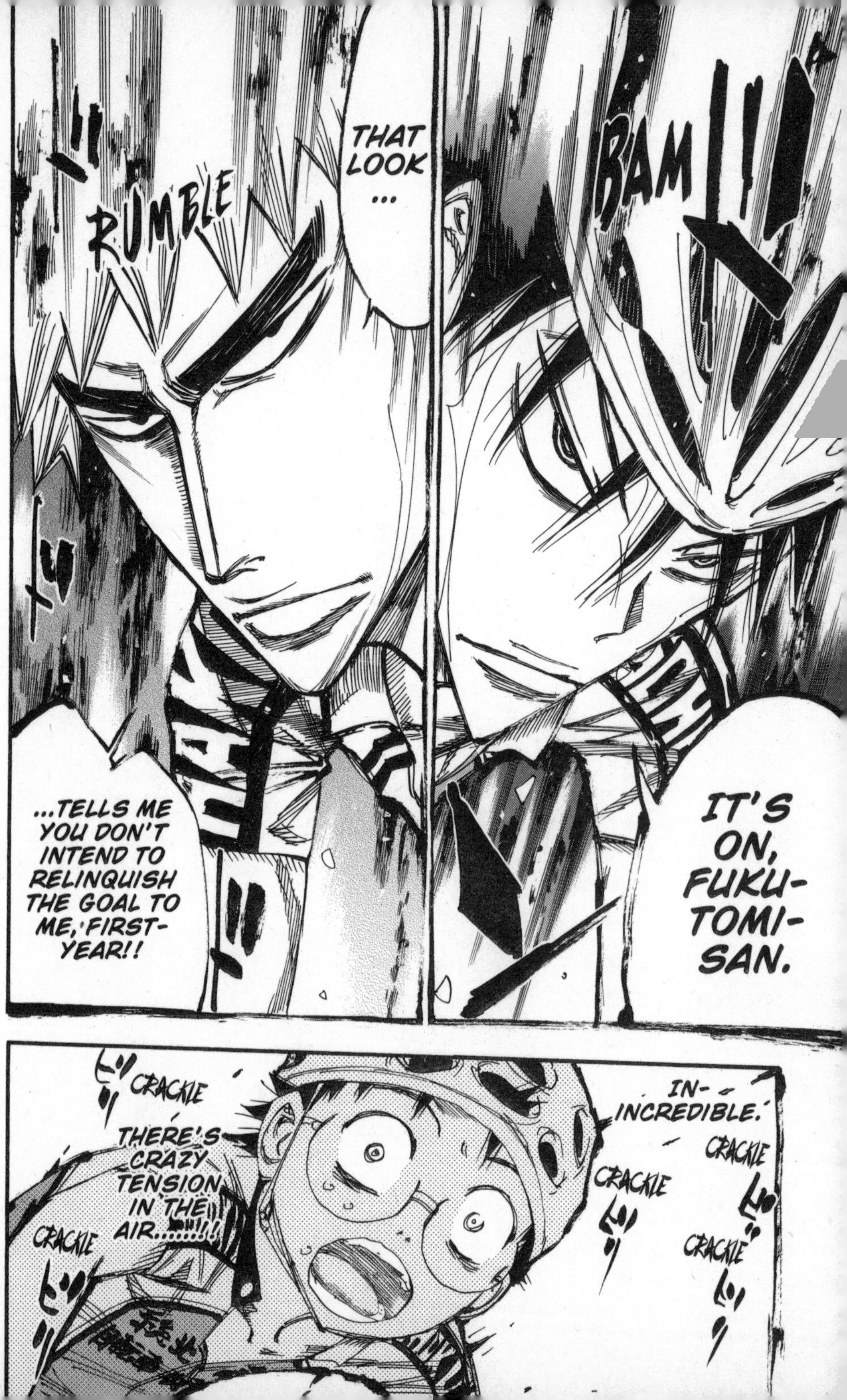
BAM!!
IT'S ON, FUKUTOMI-SAN.
THAT LOOK...
RUMBLE
...TELLS ME YOU DON'T INTEND TO RELINQUISH THE GOAL TO ME, FIRST-YEAR!!
IN-INCREDIBLE.
CRACKLE
CRACKLE
CRACKLE
CRACKLE
THERE'S CRAZY TENSION IN THE AIR...!!
CRACKLE

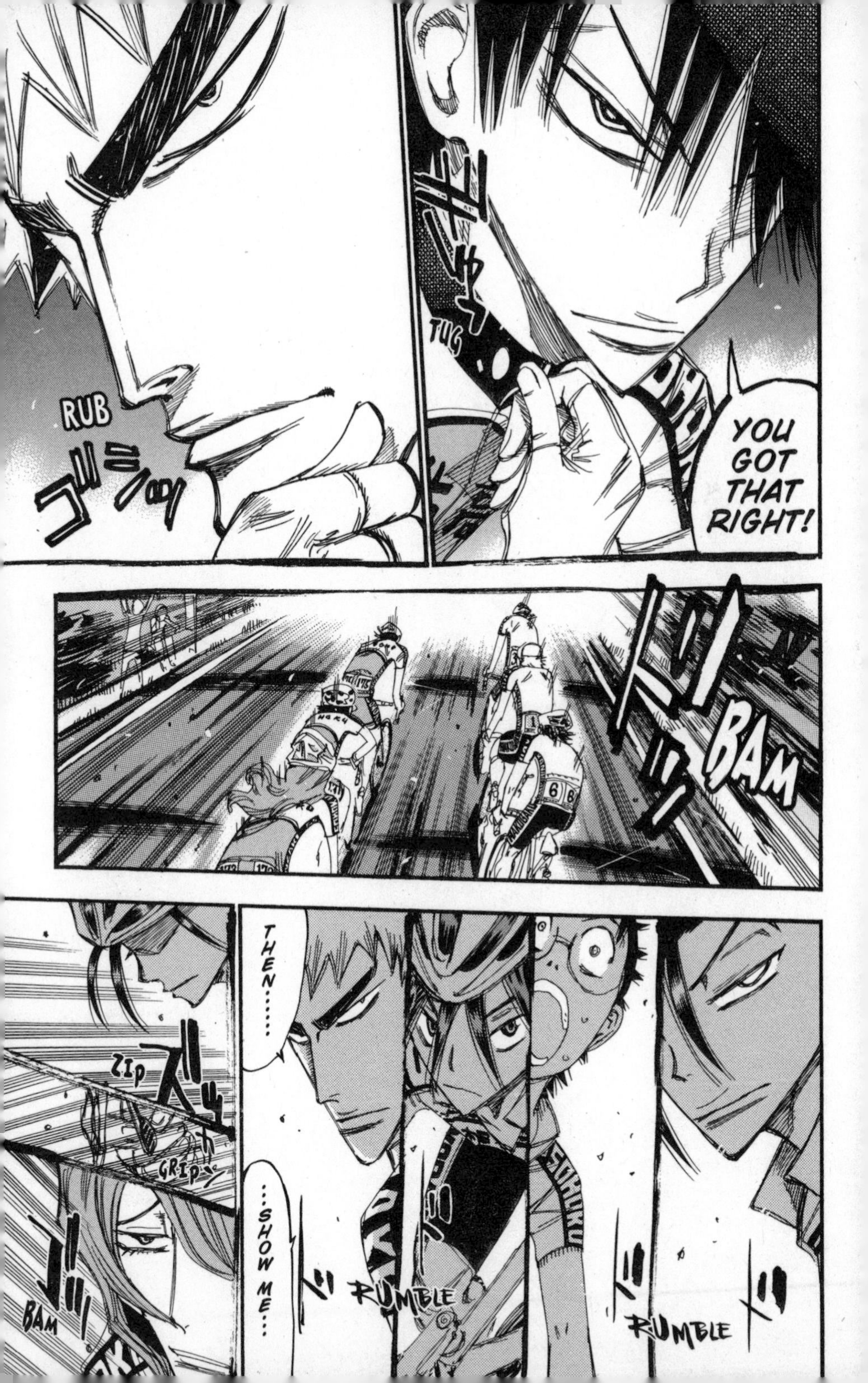
TUG
YOU GOT THAT RIGHT!
RUB
BAM
THEN......
...SHOW ME...
RUMBLE
RUMBLE
ZIP
GRIP
BAM

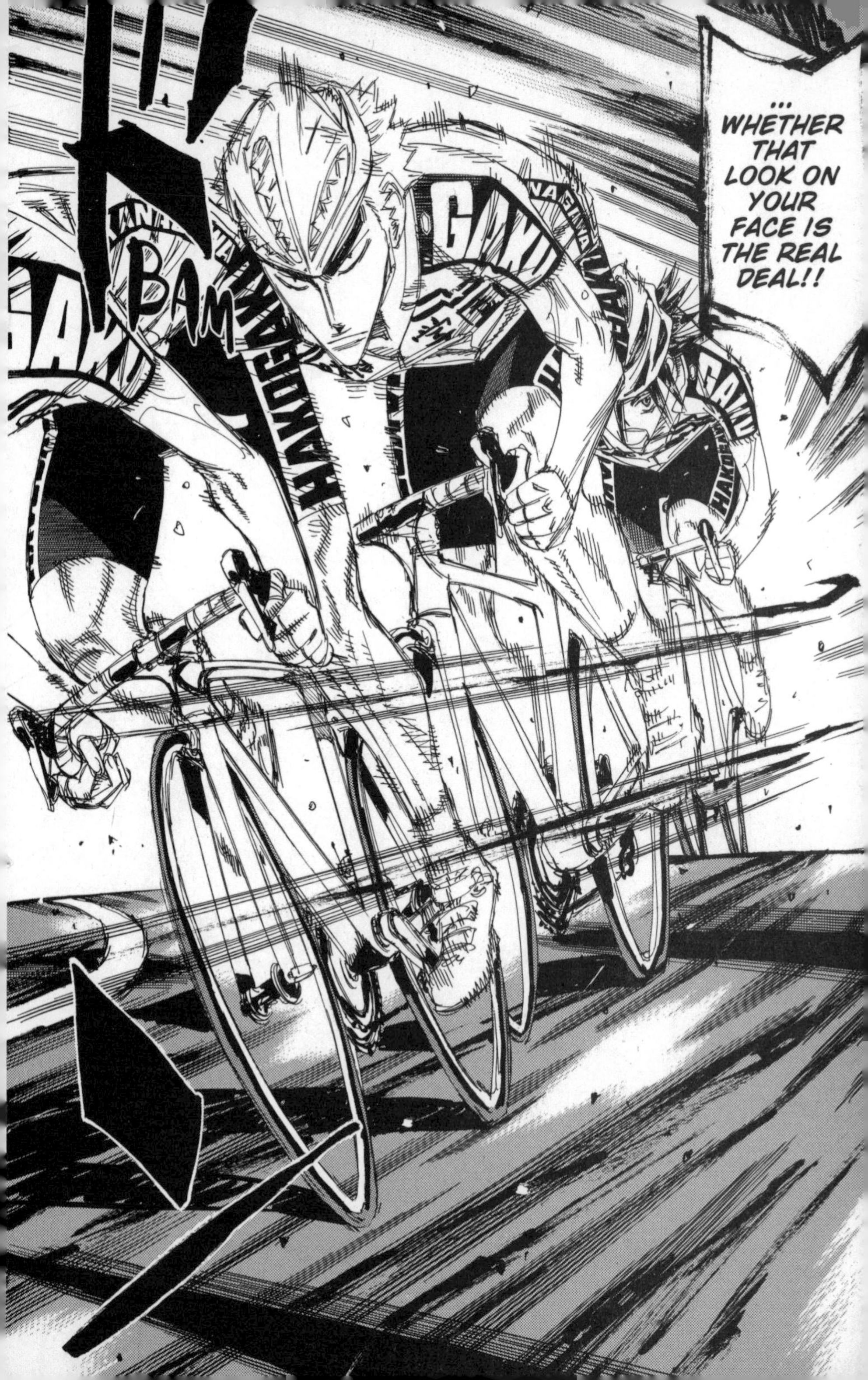
... WHETHER THAT LOOK ON YOUR FACE IS THE REAL DEAL!!
!!
BAM

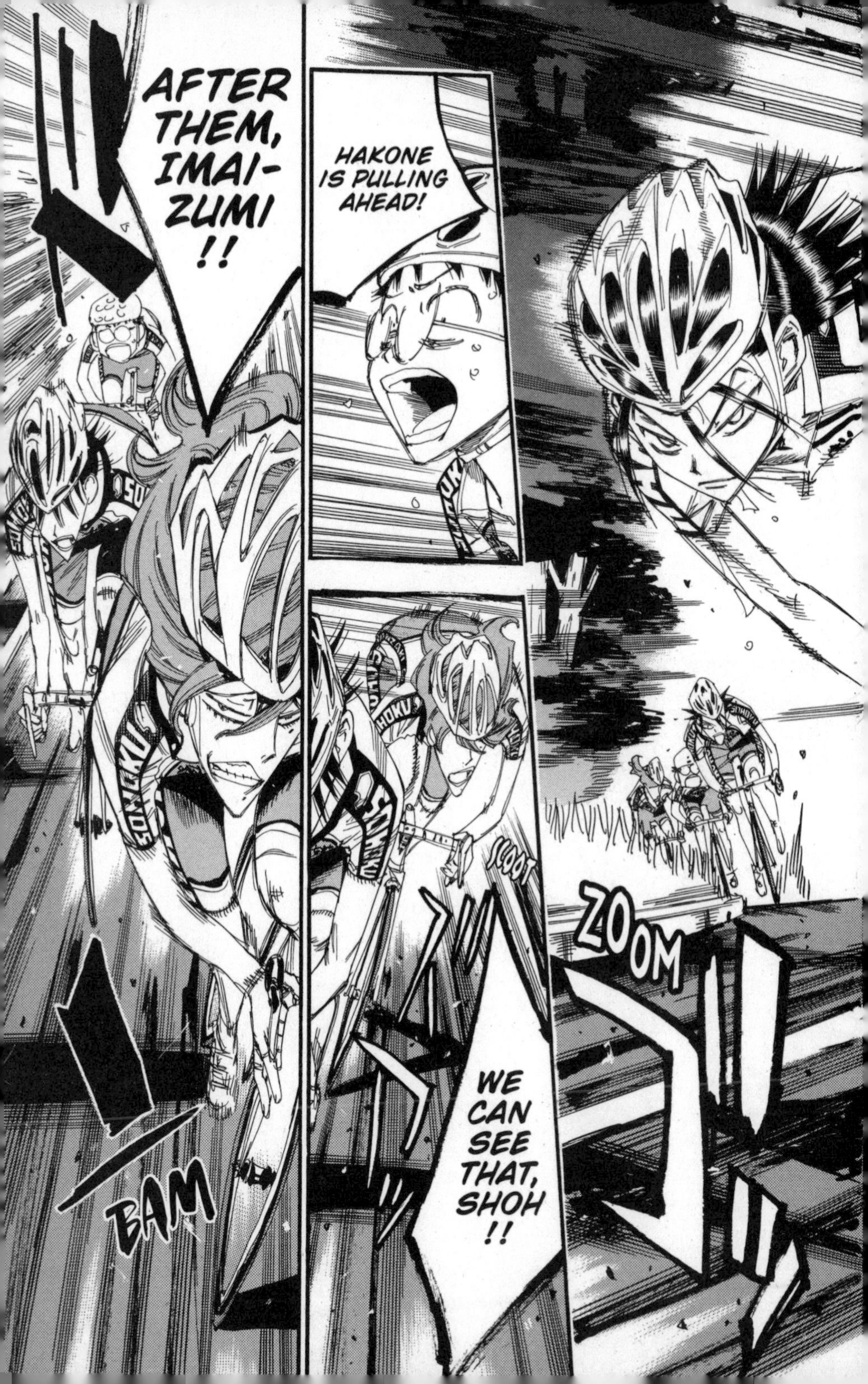
HAKONE IS PULLING AHEAD!
ZOOM
SCOOT
WE CAN SEE THAT, SHOH!!
AFTER THEM, IMAI-ZUMI!!
BAM

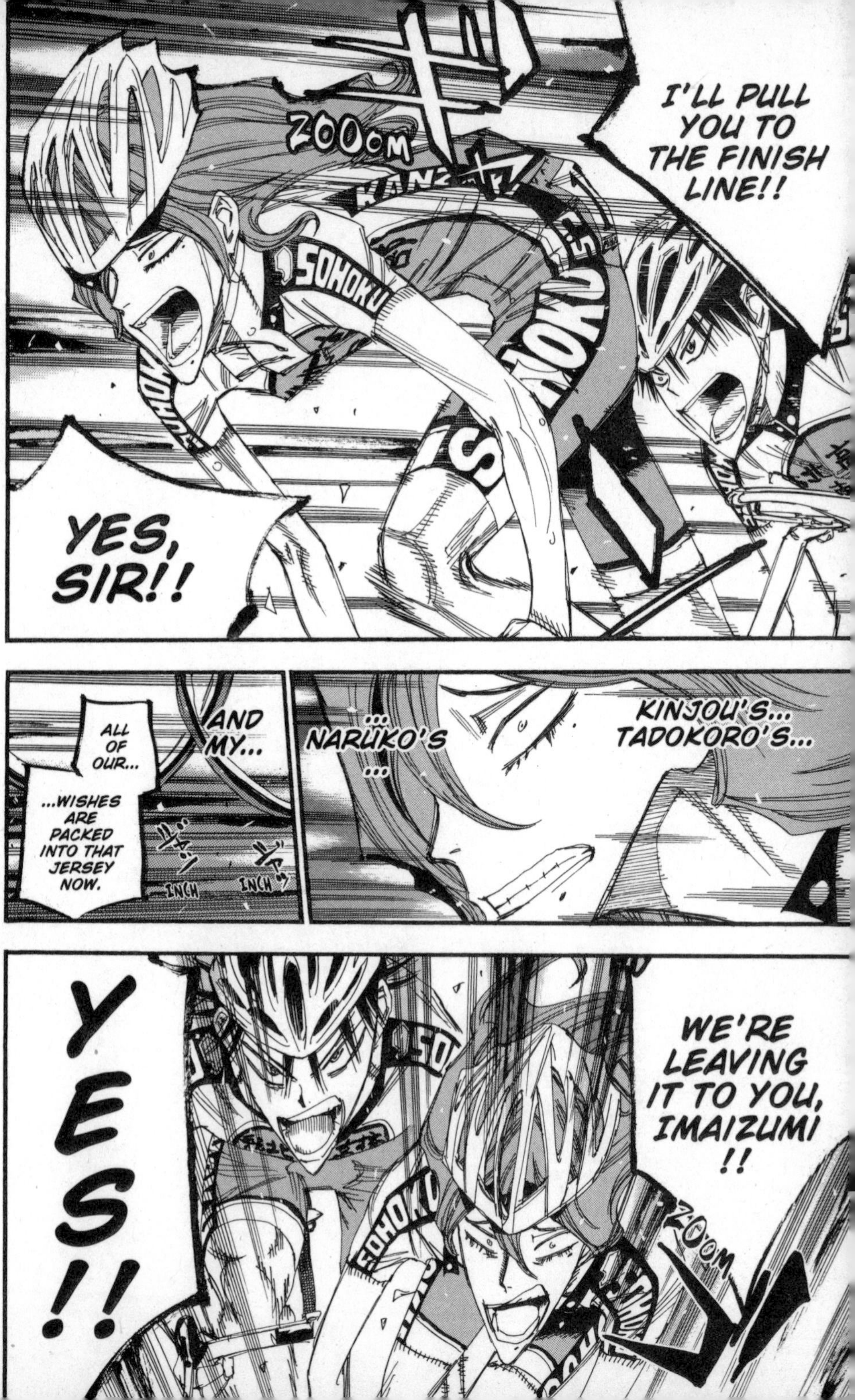
I'LL PULL YOU TO THE FINISH LINE!!
ZOOOM
YES, SIR!!
KINJOU'S... TADOKORO'S...
...NARUKO'S...
AND MY...
ALL OF OUR...
...WISHES ARE PACKED INTO THAT JERSEY NOW.
INCH
INCH
WE'RE LEAVING IT TO YOU, IMAIZUMI!!
ZOOOM
YES!!

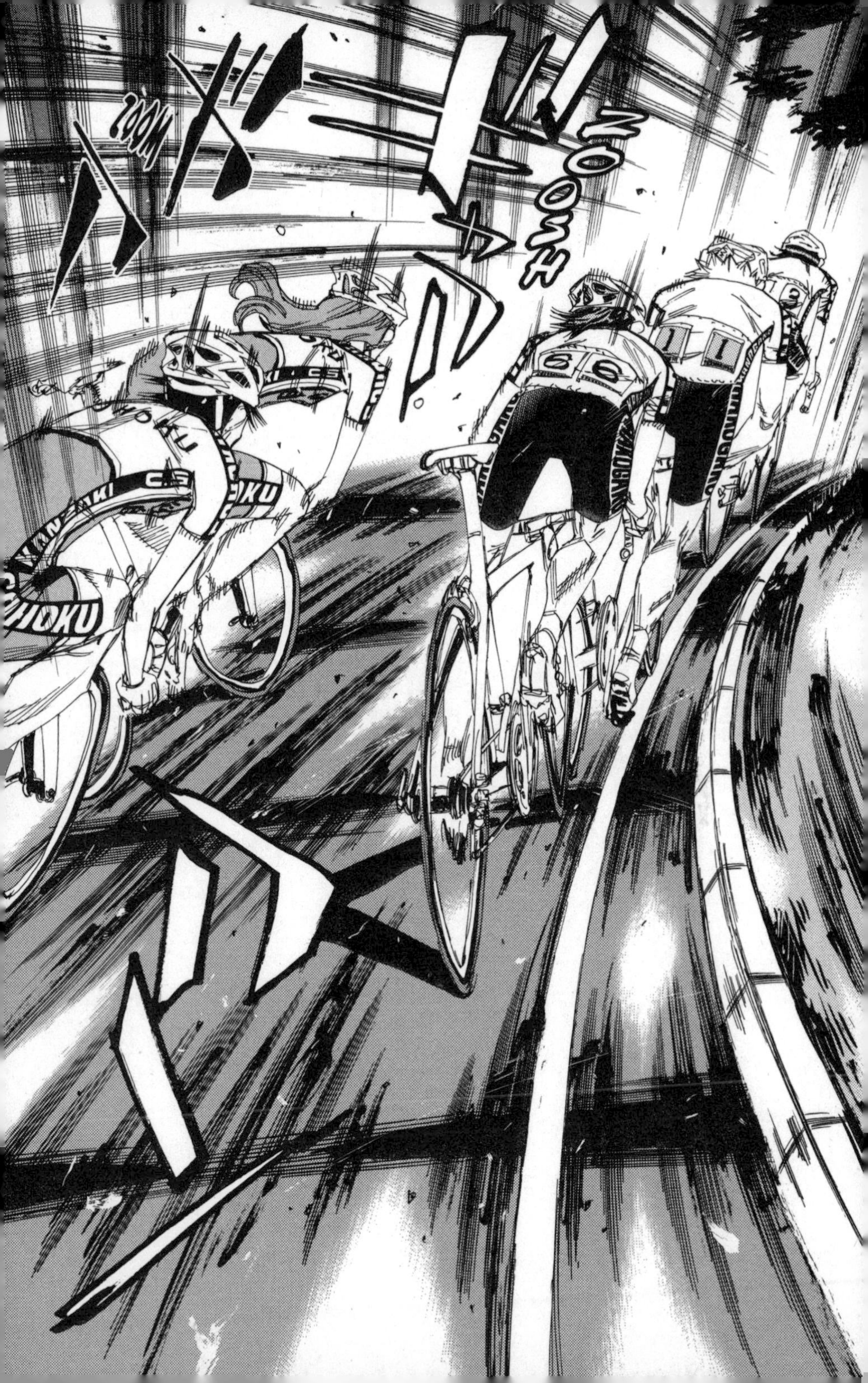
WHOOOOM
ZOOM

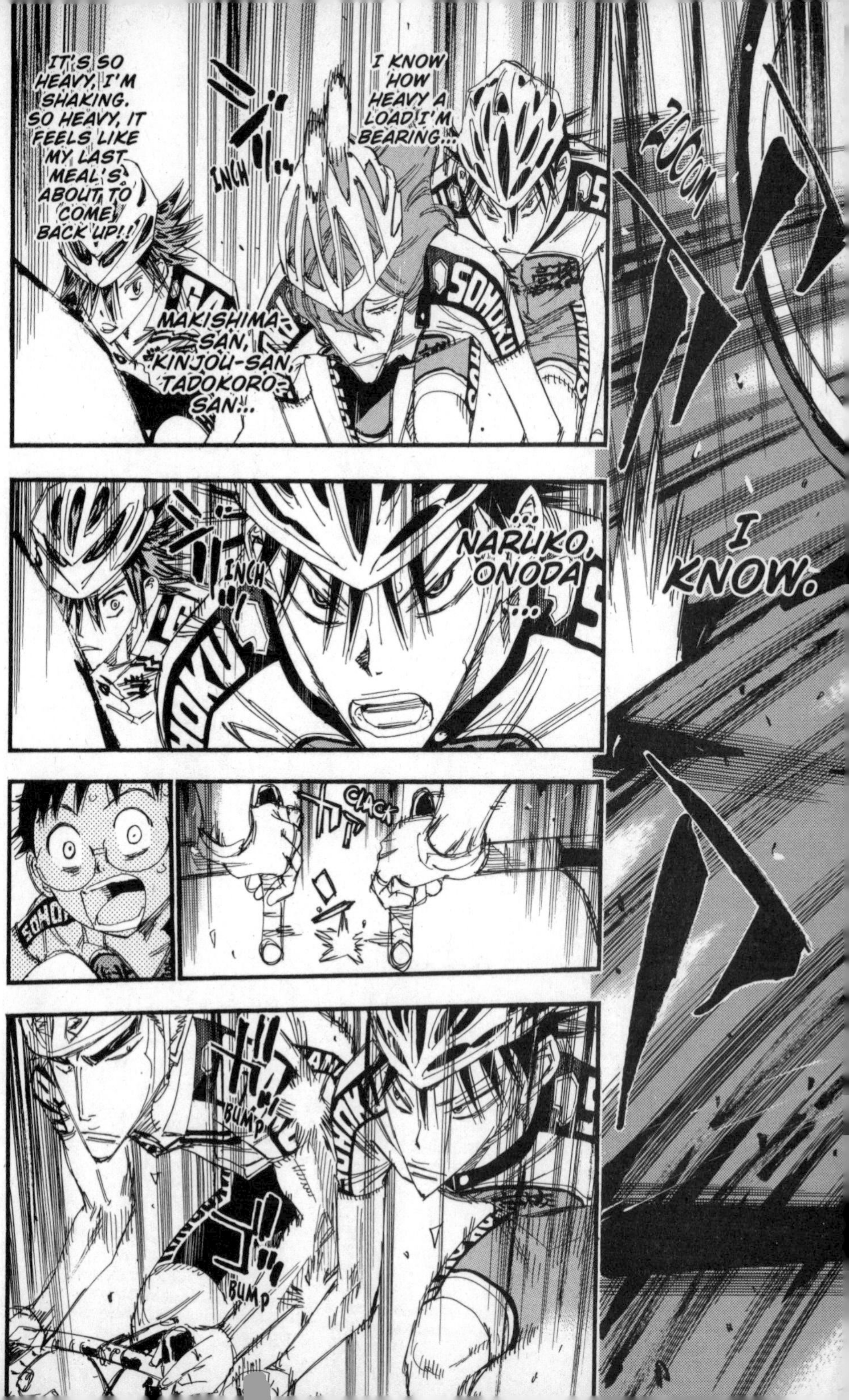
ZOOM
I KNOW.
I KNOW HOW HEAVY A LOAD I'M BEARING...
INCH
IT'S SO HEAVY, I'M SHAKING. SO HEAVY, IT FEELS LIKE MY LAST MEAL'S ABOUT TO COME BACK UP!!
MAKISHIMA-SAN, KINJOU-SAN, TADOKORO-SAN...
NARUKO, ONODA...
INCH
CLACK
BUMP
BUMP

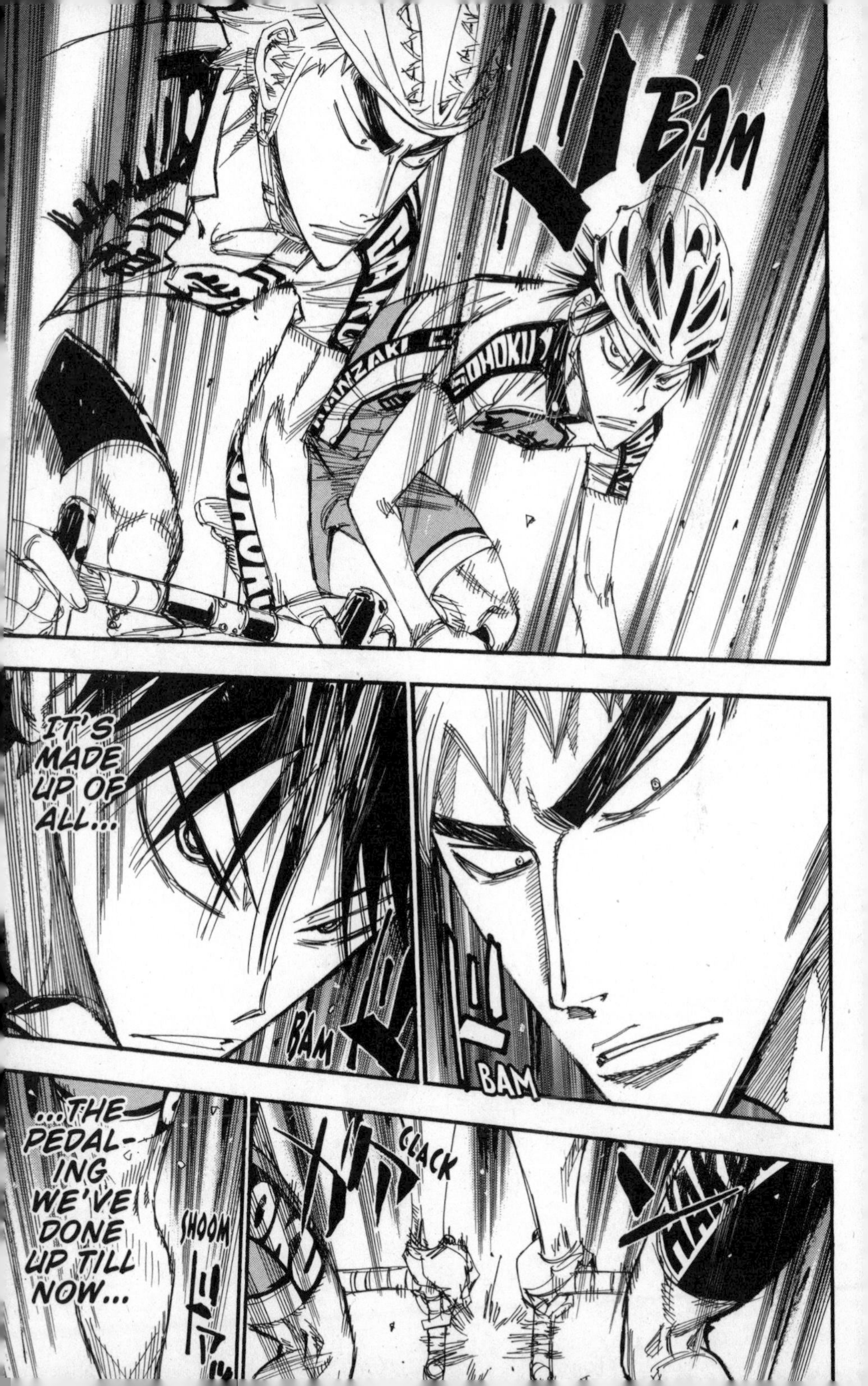
BAM
IT'S MADE UP OF ALL...
BAM
BAM
...THE PEDALING WE'VE DONE UP TILL NOW...
CLACK
SHOOM

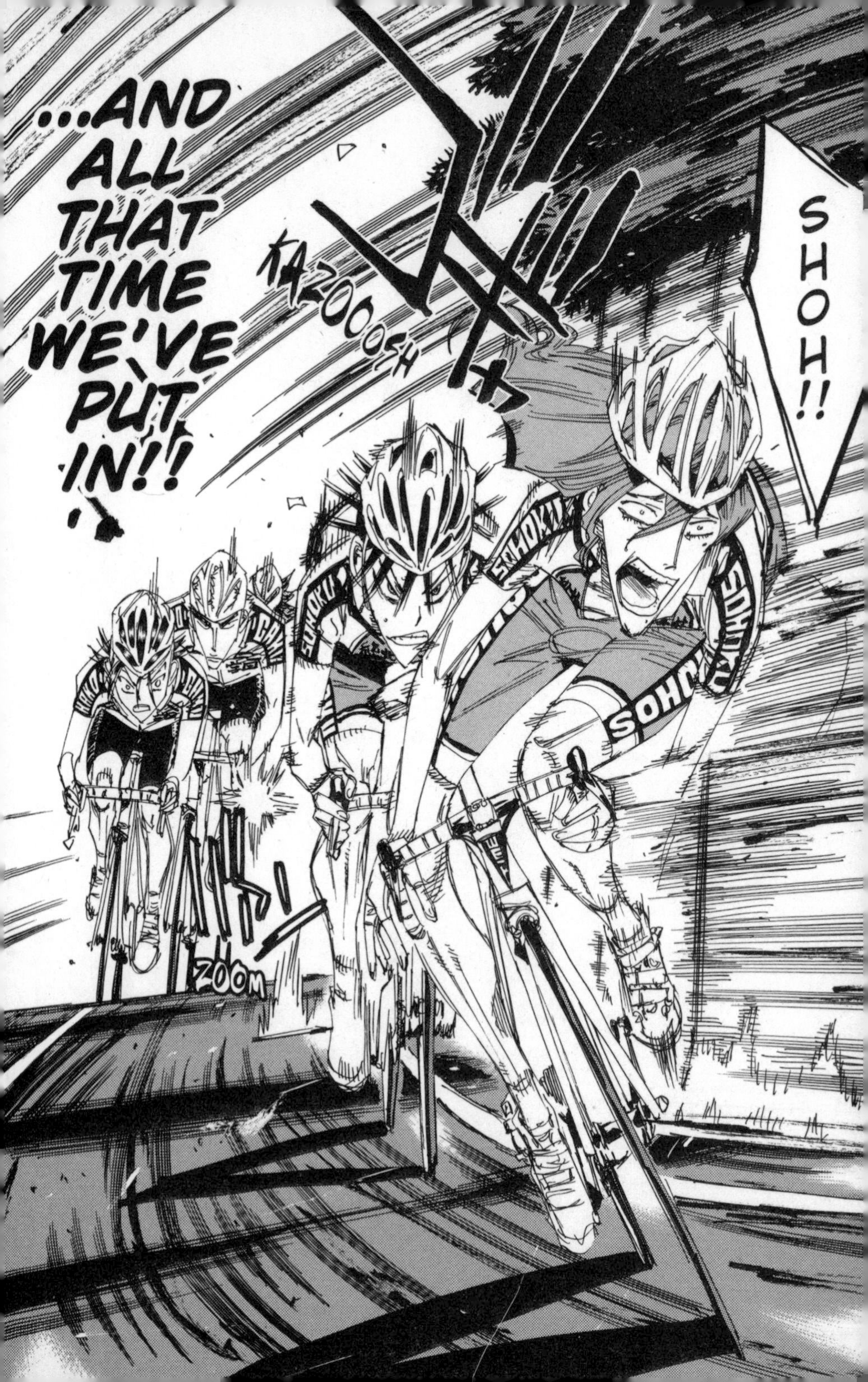
SHOH!!
KAZOOOSH
...AND ALL THAT TIME WE'VE PUT IN!!
ZOOM

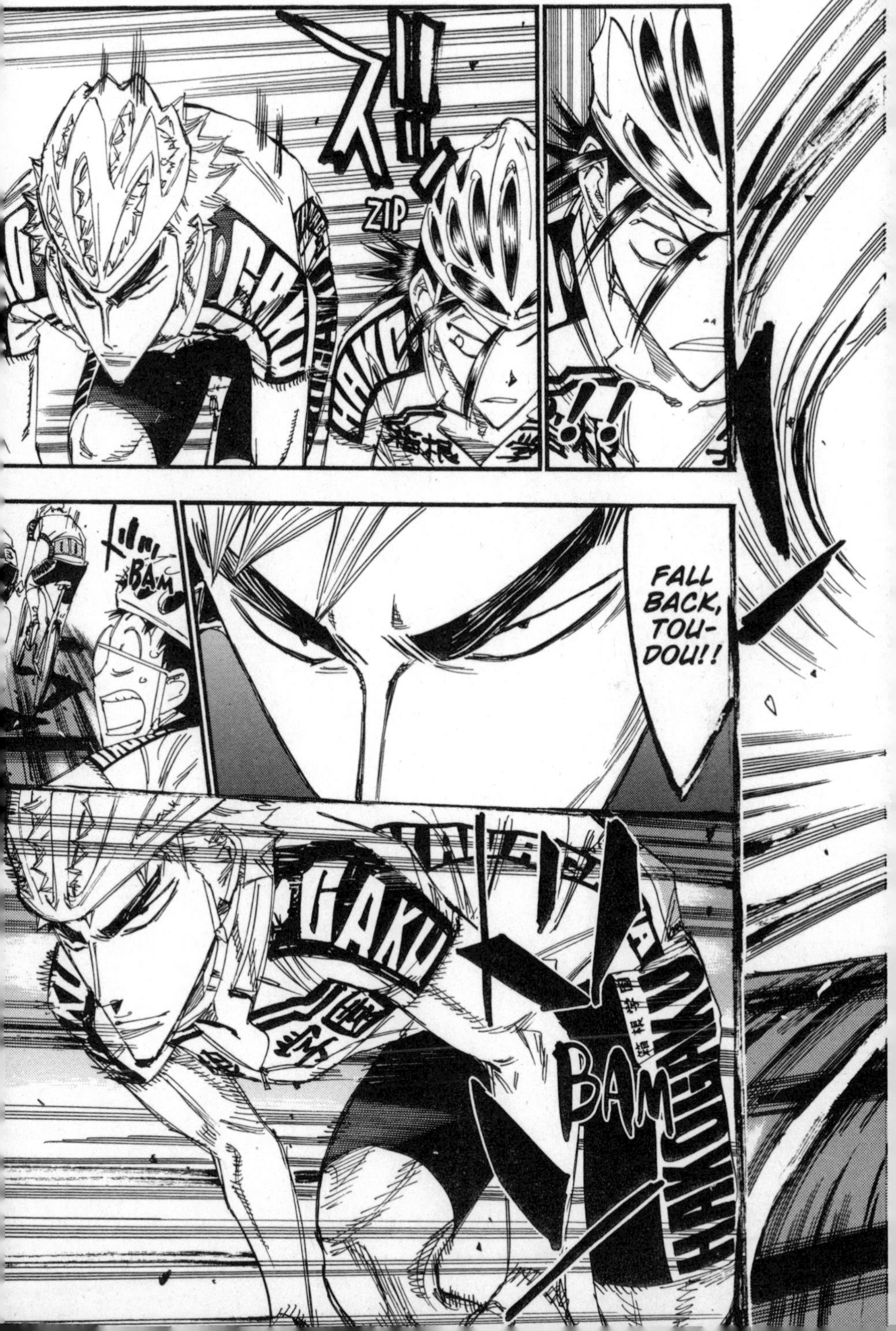
ZIP
FALL BACK, TOU-DOU!!
BAM
BAM

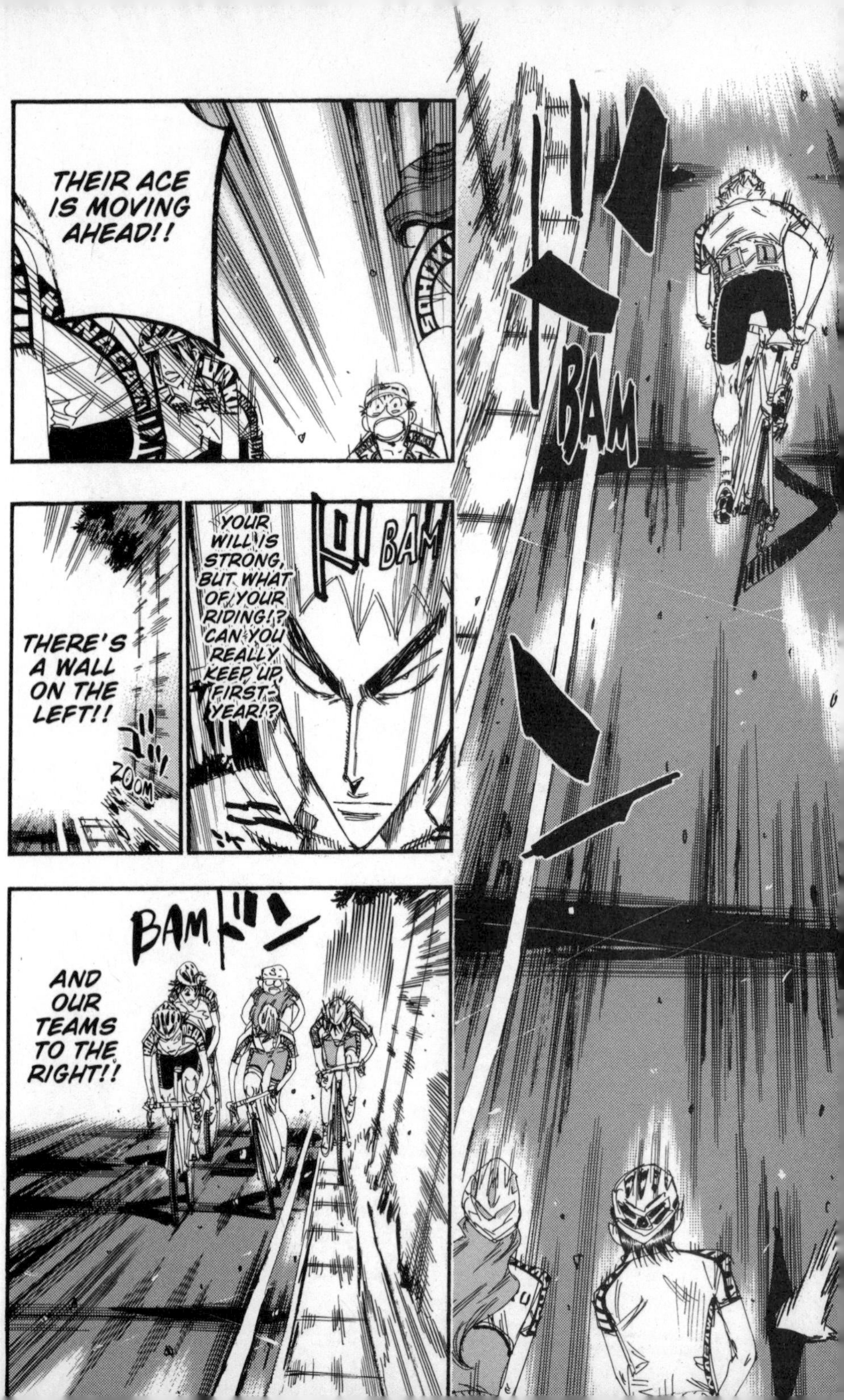
BAM
THEIR ACE IS MOVING AHEAD!!
BAM
YOUR WILL IS STRONG, BUT WHAT OF YOUR RIDING!? CAN YOU REALLY KEEP UP, FIRST-YEAR!?
THERE'S A WALL ON THE LEFT!!
ZOOM
BAM
AND OUR TEAMS TO THE RIGHT!!

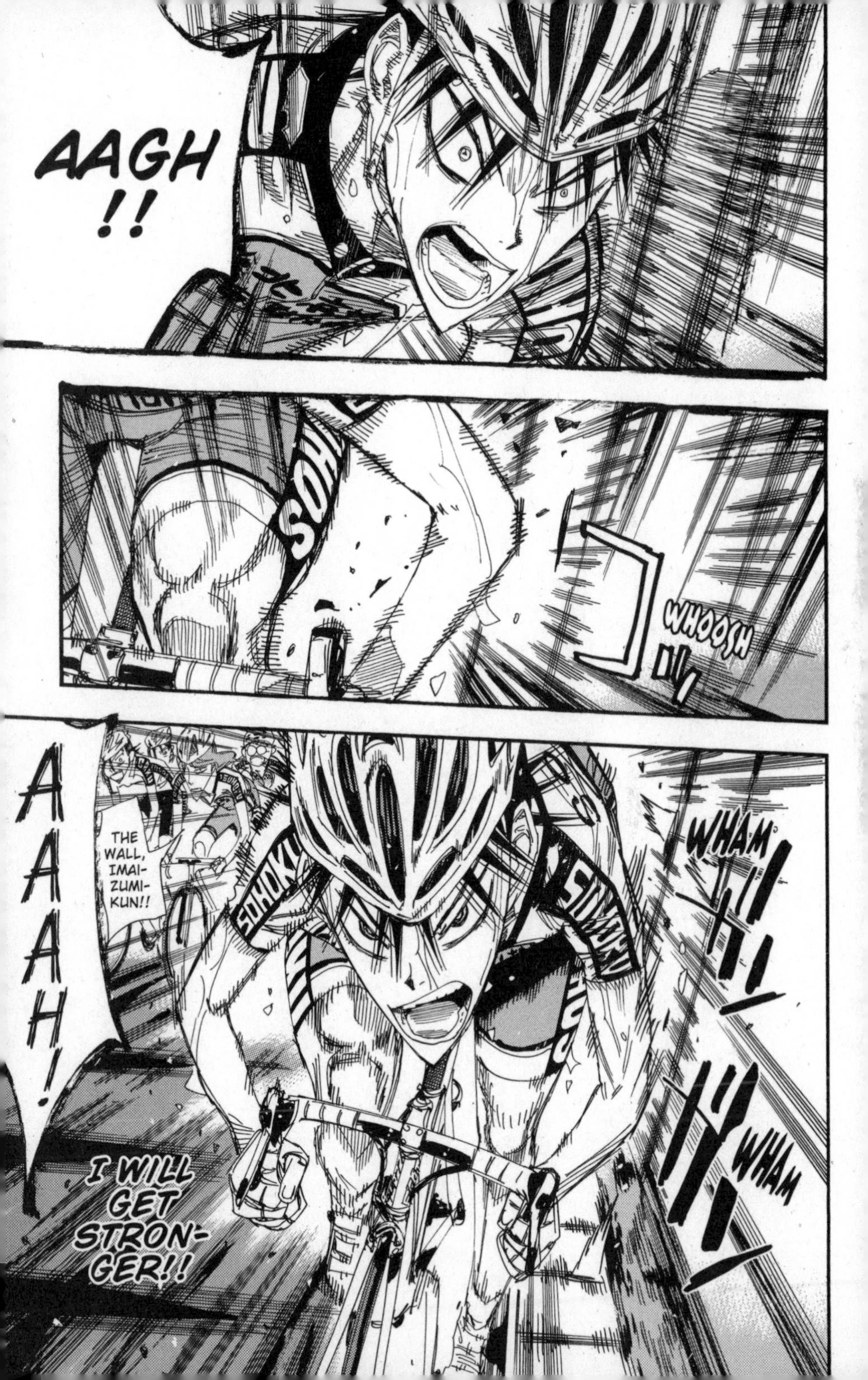
AAGH!!
WHOOSH
WHAM
THE WALL, IMAIZUMI-KUN!!
AAAAH!
WHAM
I WILL GET STRONGER!!

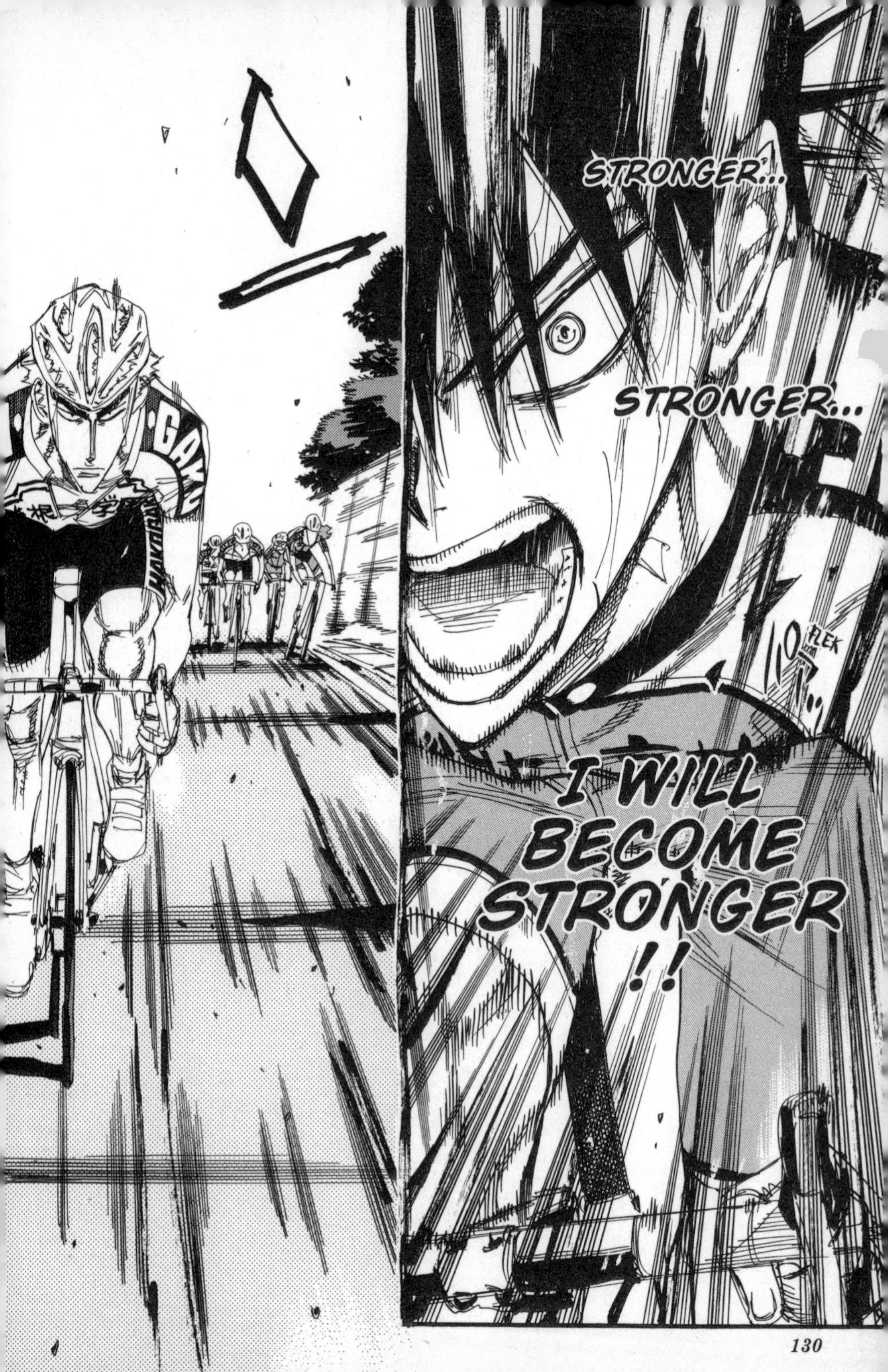
STRONGER...
STRONGER...
FLEK
I WILL BECOME STRONGER !!

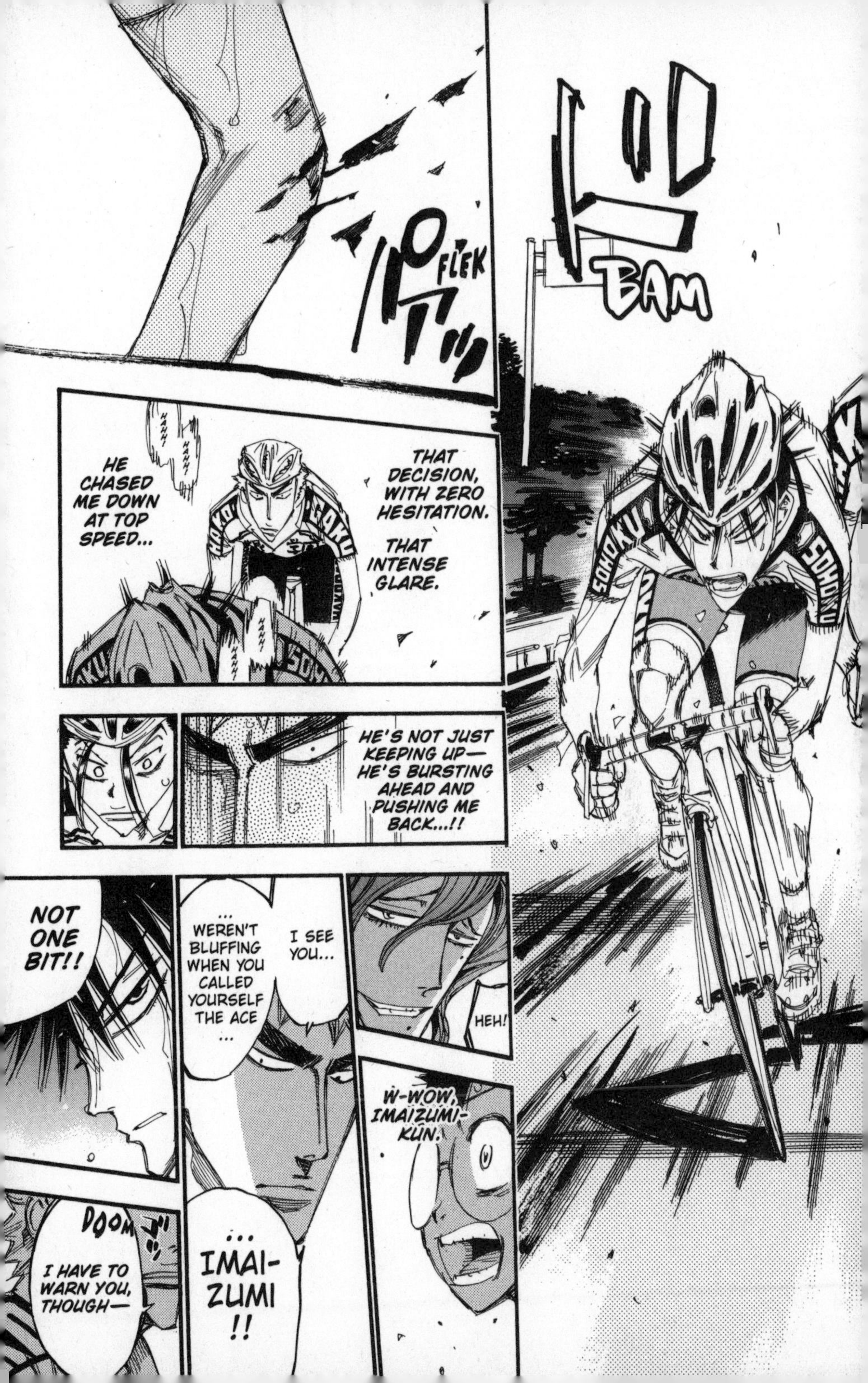
BAM
FLEK
THAT DECISION, WITH ZERO HESITATION.
THAT INTENSE GLARE.
HE CHASED ME DOWN AT TOP SPEED...
HE'S NOT JUST KEEPING UP— HE'S BURSTING AHEAD AND PUSHING ME BACK...!!
HEH!
I SEE YOU...
...WEREN'T BLUFFING WHEN YOU CALLED YOURSELF THE ACE...
NOT ONE BIT!!
W-WOW, IMAIZUMI-KUN.
...IMAIZUMI!!
DOOM
I HAVE TO WARN YOU, THOUGH—

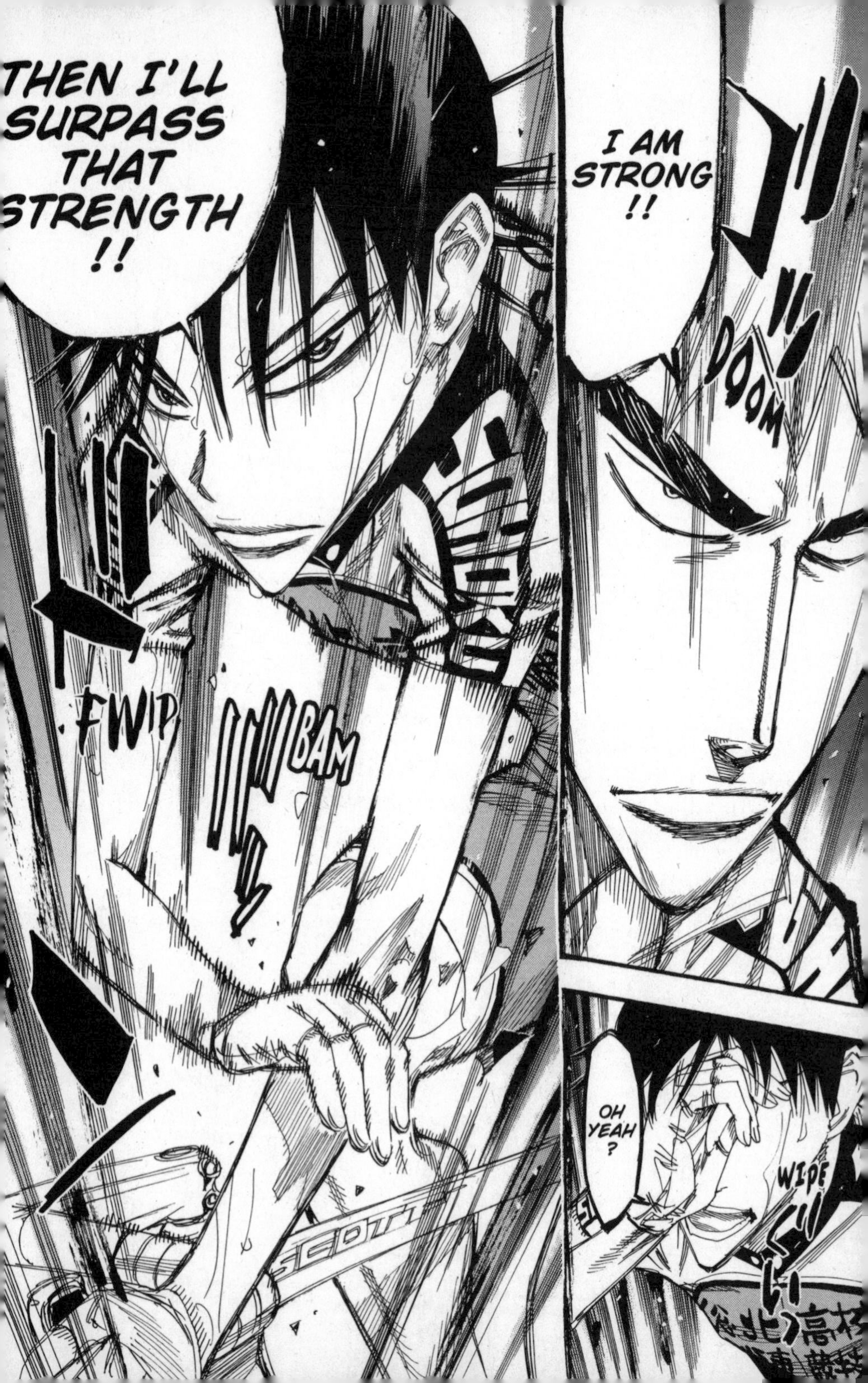
I AM STRONG !!
DOOM
OH YEAH ?
WIPE
THEN I'LL SURPASS THAT STRENGTH !!
FWIP
BAM
SCOTT

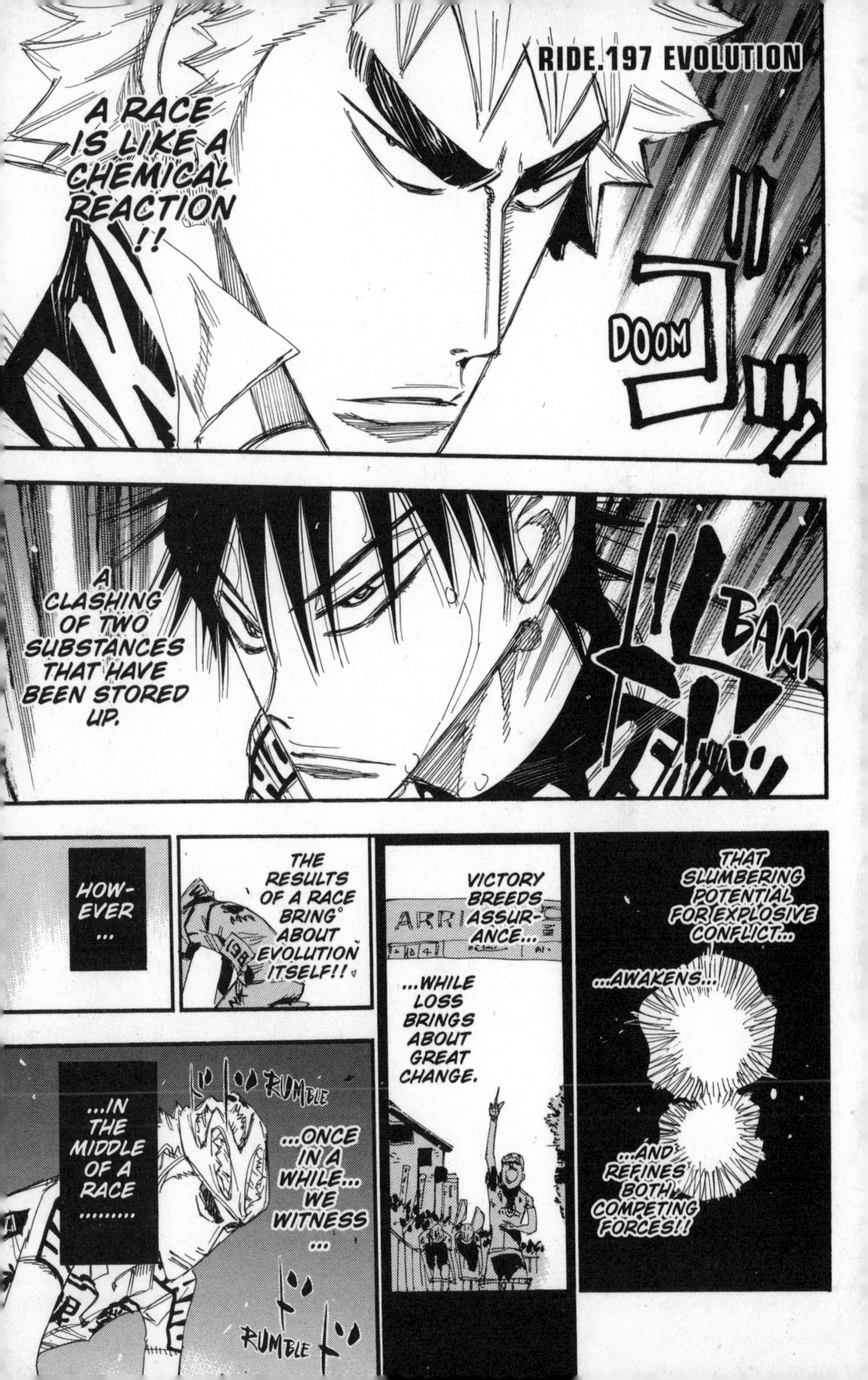
RIDE.197 EVOLUTION
A RACE IS LIKE A CHEMICAL REACTION!!
DOOM
BAM
A CLASHING OF TWO SUBSTANCES THAT HAVE BEEN STORED UP.
THAT SLUMBERING POTENTIAL FOR EXPLOSIVE CONFLICT...
...AWAKENS...
...AND REFINES BOTH COMPETING FORCES!!
VICTORY BREEDS ASSURANCE...
...WHILE LOSS BRINGS ABOUT GREAT CHANGE.
ARRI
THE RESULTS OF A RACE BRING ABOUT EVOLUTION ITSELF!!
HOWEVER...
RUMBLE
...IN THE MIDDLE OF A RACE.........
...ONCE IN A WHILE... WE WITNESS...
RUMBLE

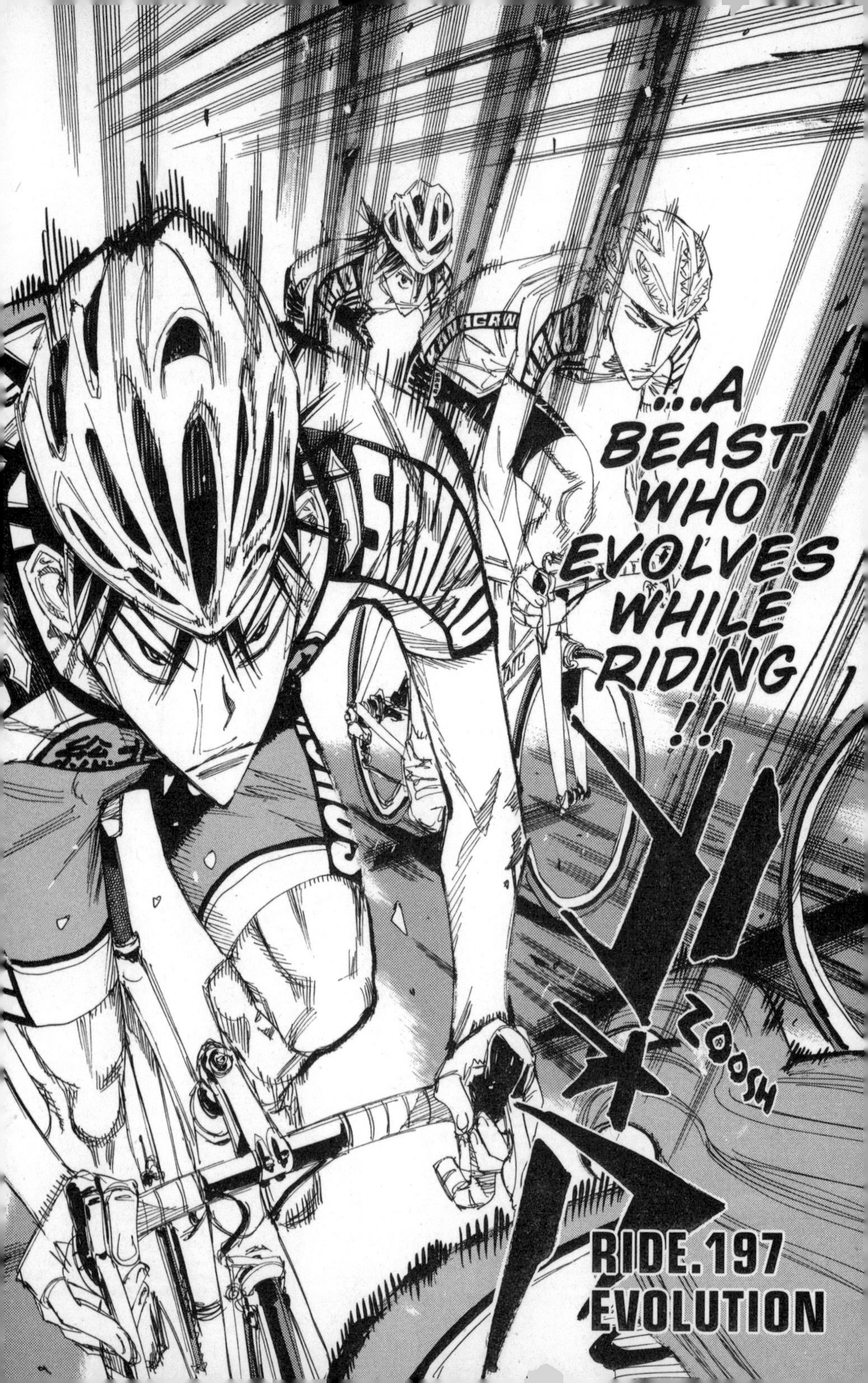
...A BEAST WHO EVOLVES WHILE RIDING!!
ZOOSH
RIDE.197 EVOLUTION

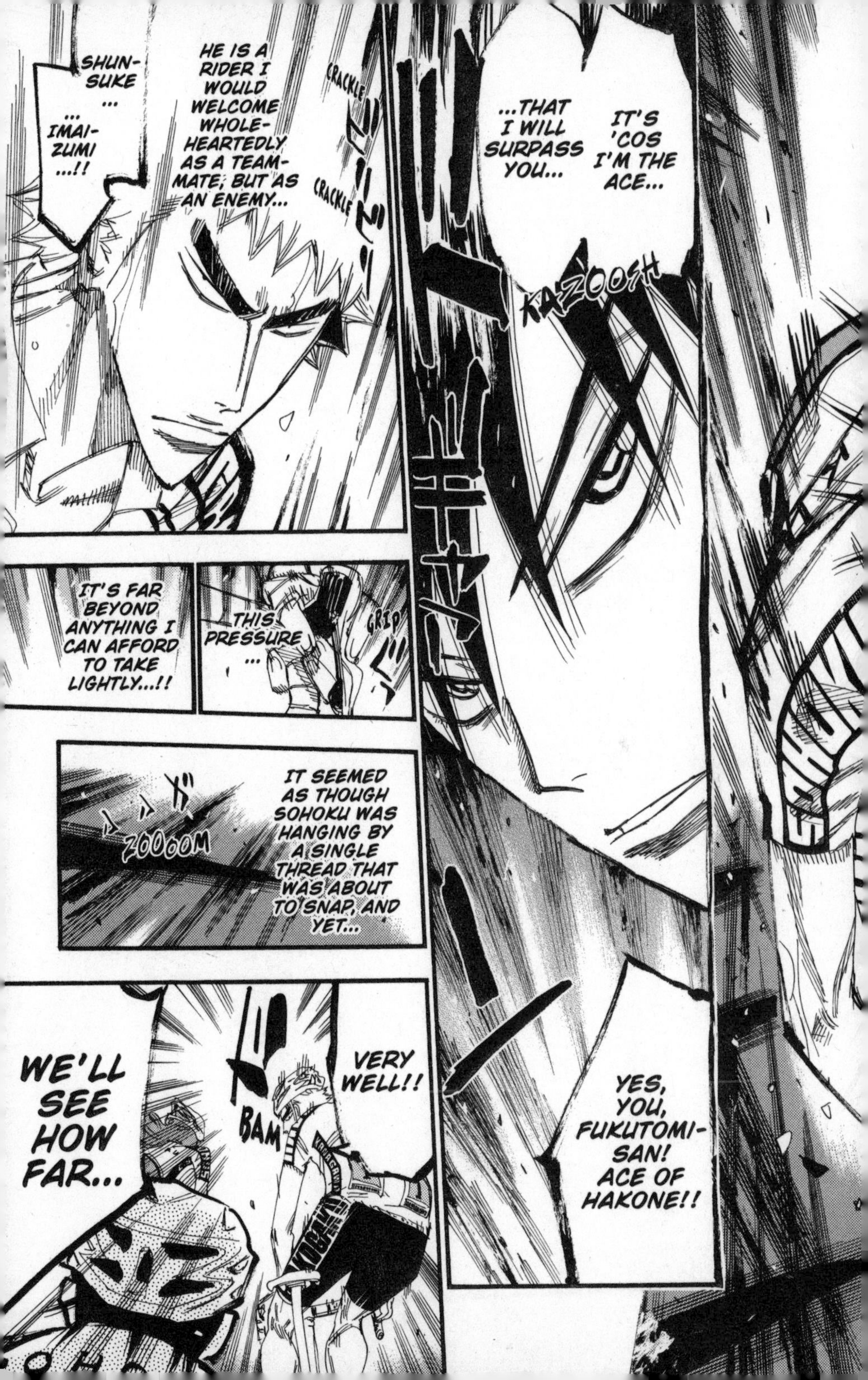
IT'S 'COS I'M THE ACE...
...THAT I WILL SURPASS YOU...
KA-ZOOSH
YES, YOU, FUKUTOMI-SAN! ACE OF HAKONE!!
CRACKLE
CRACKLE
HE IS A RIDER I WOULD WELCOME WHOLE-HEARTEDLY AS A TEAM-MATE, BUT AS AN ENEMY...
SHUN-SUKE ... ... IMAI-ZUMI ...!!
GRIP
THIS PRESSURE ...
IT'S FAR BEYOND ANYTHING I CAN AFFORD TO TAKE LIGHTLY...!!
IT SEEMED AS THOUGH SOHOKU WAS HANGING BY A SINGLE THREAD THAT WAS ABOUT TO SNAP, AND YET...
ZOOOOM
VERY WELL!!
BAM
WE'LL SEE HOW FAR...

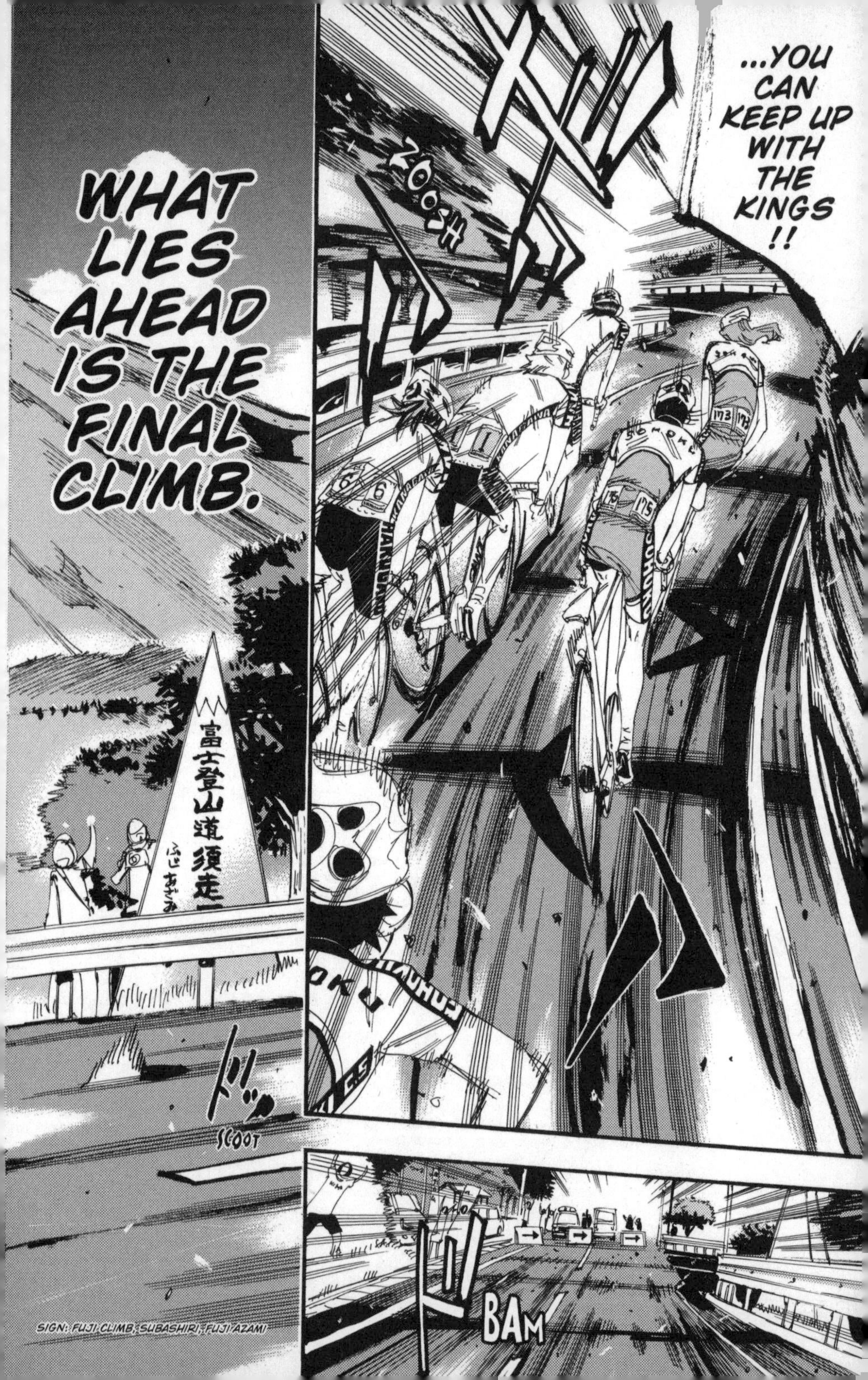
...YOU CAN KEEP UP WITH THE KINGS!!
ZOOSH
BAM
WHAT LIES AHEAD IS THE FINAL CLIMB.
富士登山道 須走
ふじあざみ
SCOOT
SIGN: FUJI CLIMB, SUBASHIRI, FUJI AZAMI

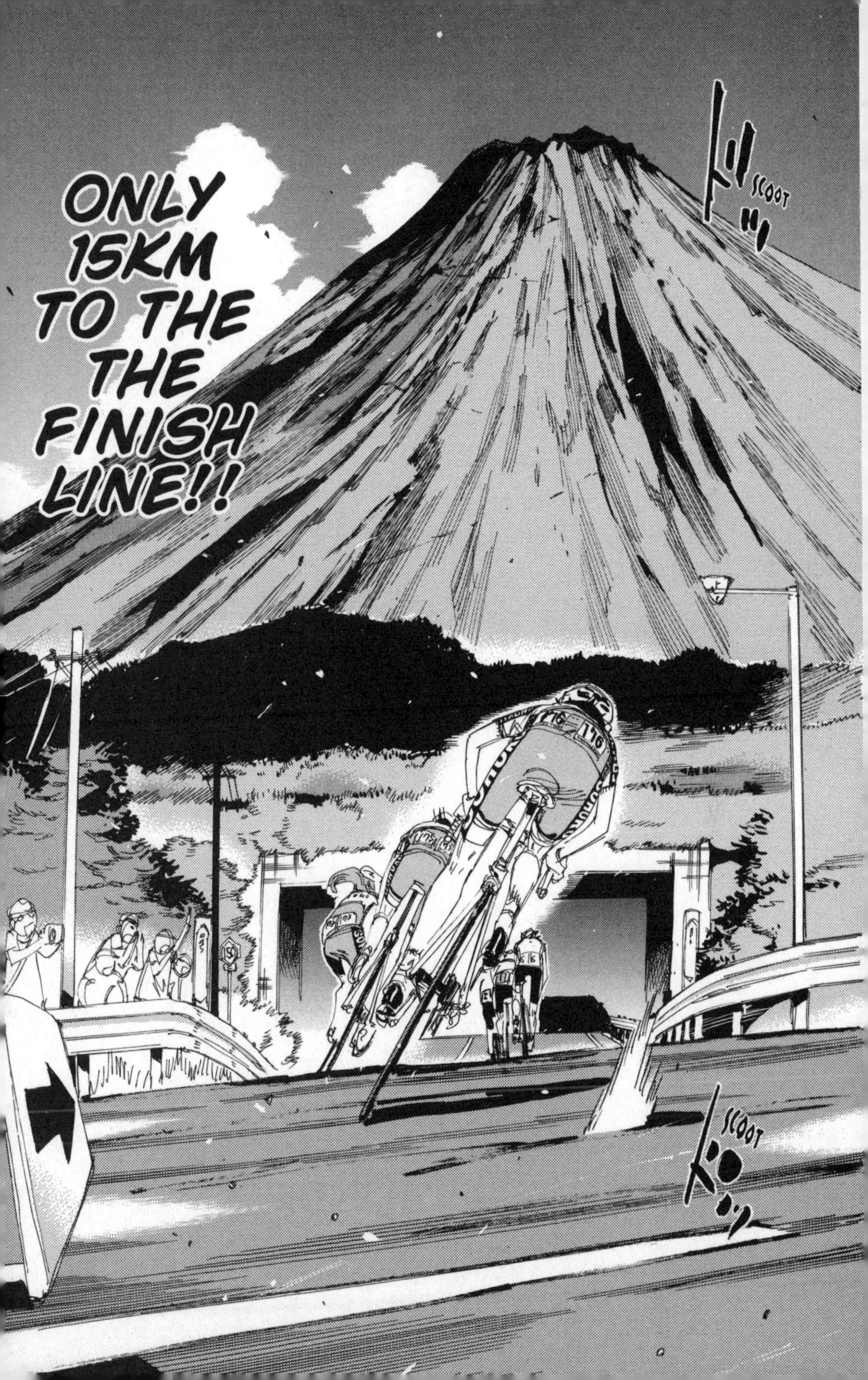
SCOOT
ONLY 15KM TO THE THE FINISH LINE!!
SCOOT

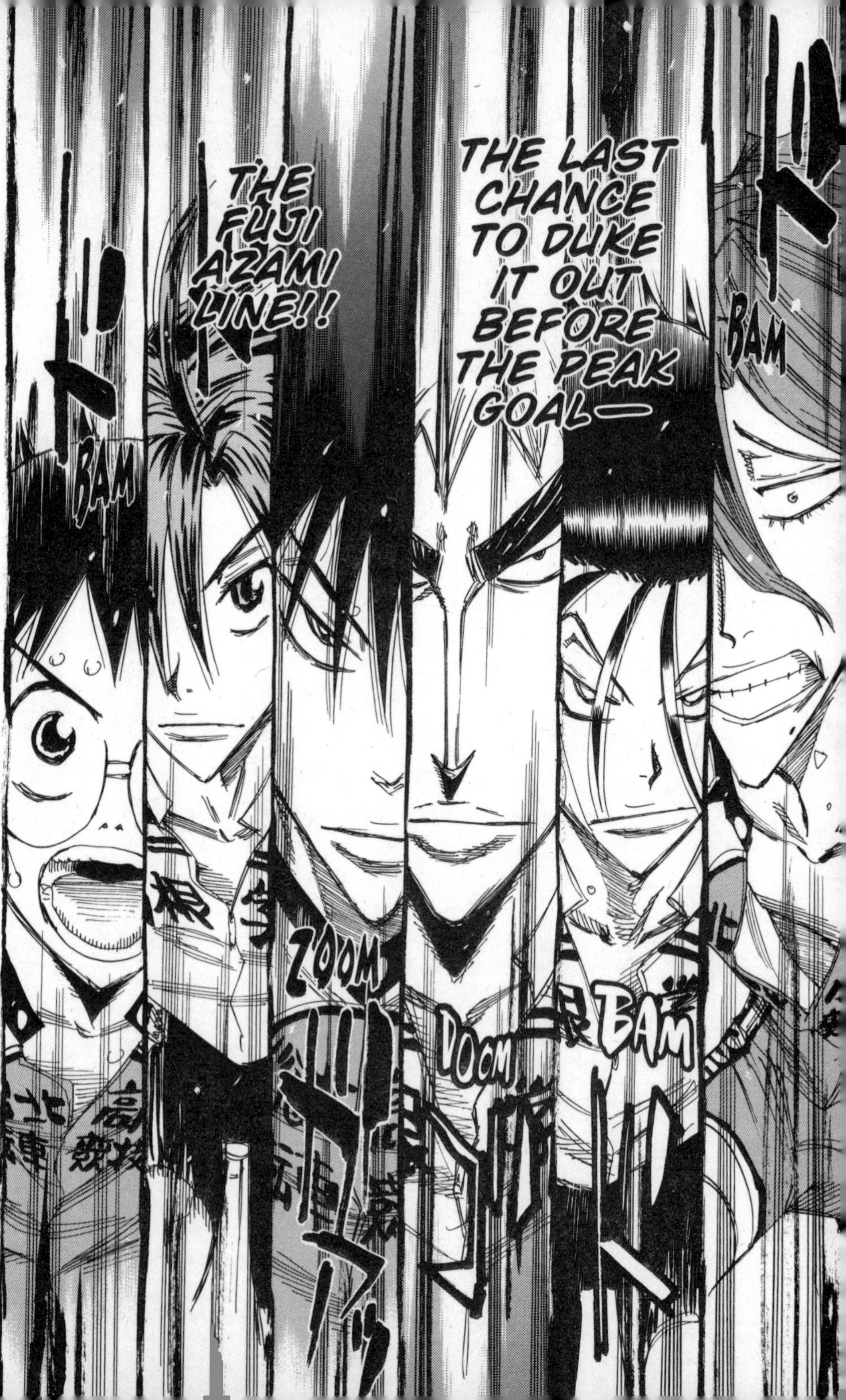
BAM
THE LAST CHANCE TO DUKE IT OUT BEFORE THE PEAK GOAL—
THE FUJI AZAMI LINE!!
BAM
BAM
DOOM
ZOOM

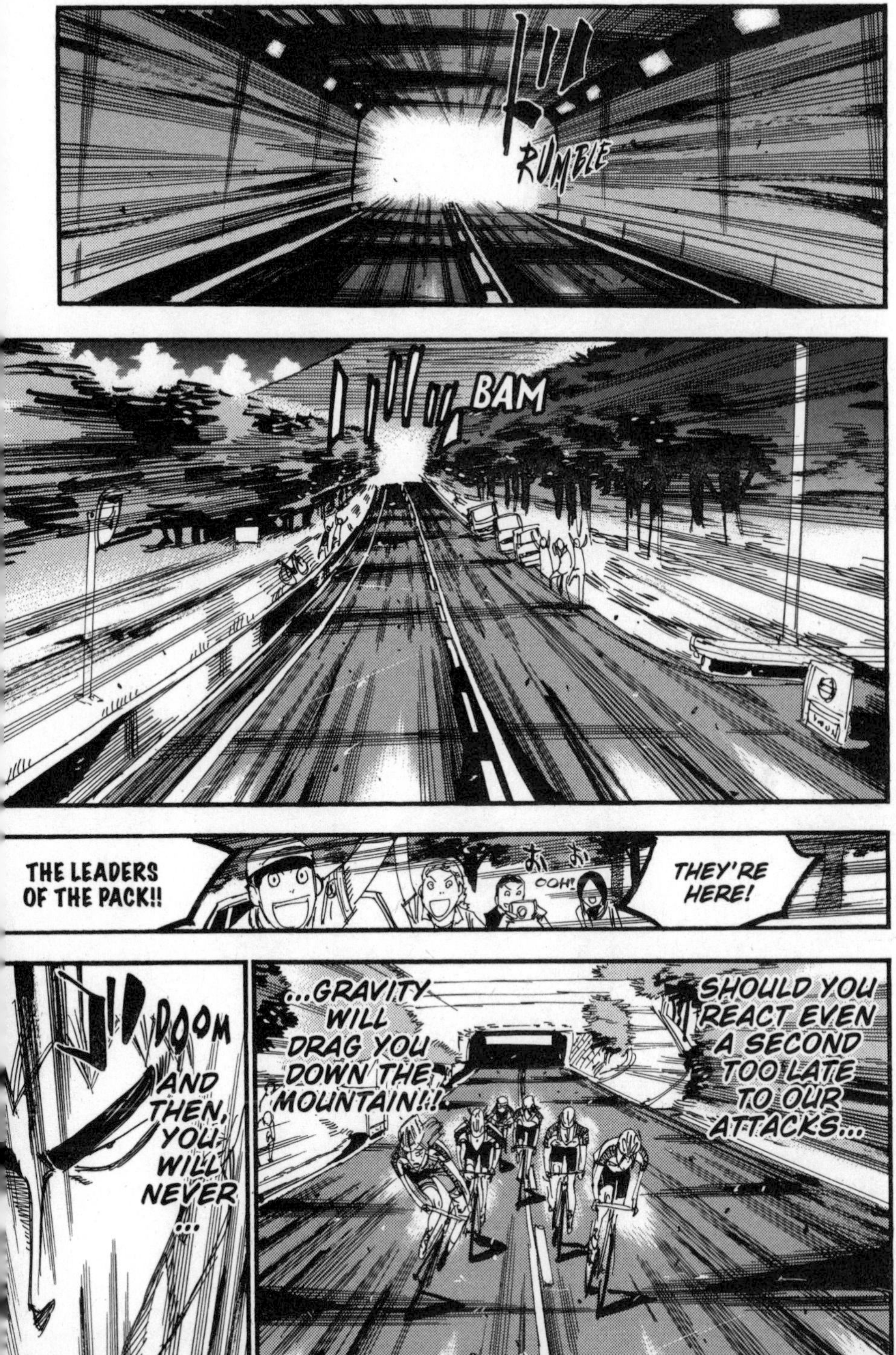
RUMBLE
BAM
THEY'RE HERE!
OOH!
THE LEADERS OF THE PACK!!
SHOULD YOU REACT EVEN A SECOND TOO LATE TO OUR ATTACKS...
...GRAVITY WILL DRAG YOU DOWN THE MOUNTAIN!!
DOOM
AND THEN, YOU WILL NEVER...

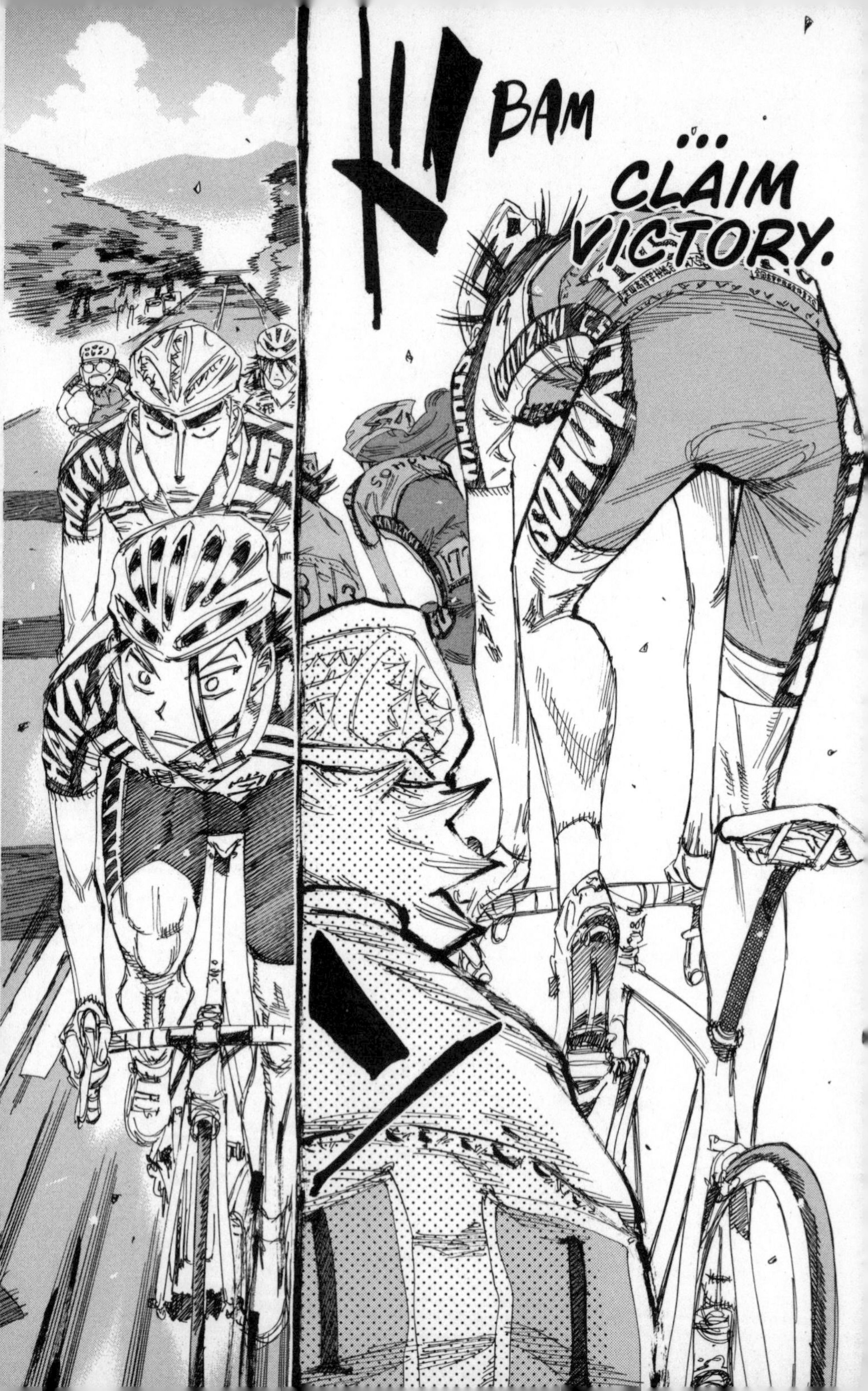
BAM
... CLAIM VICTORY.

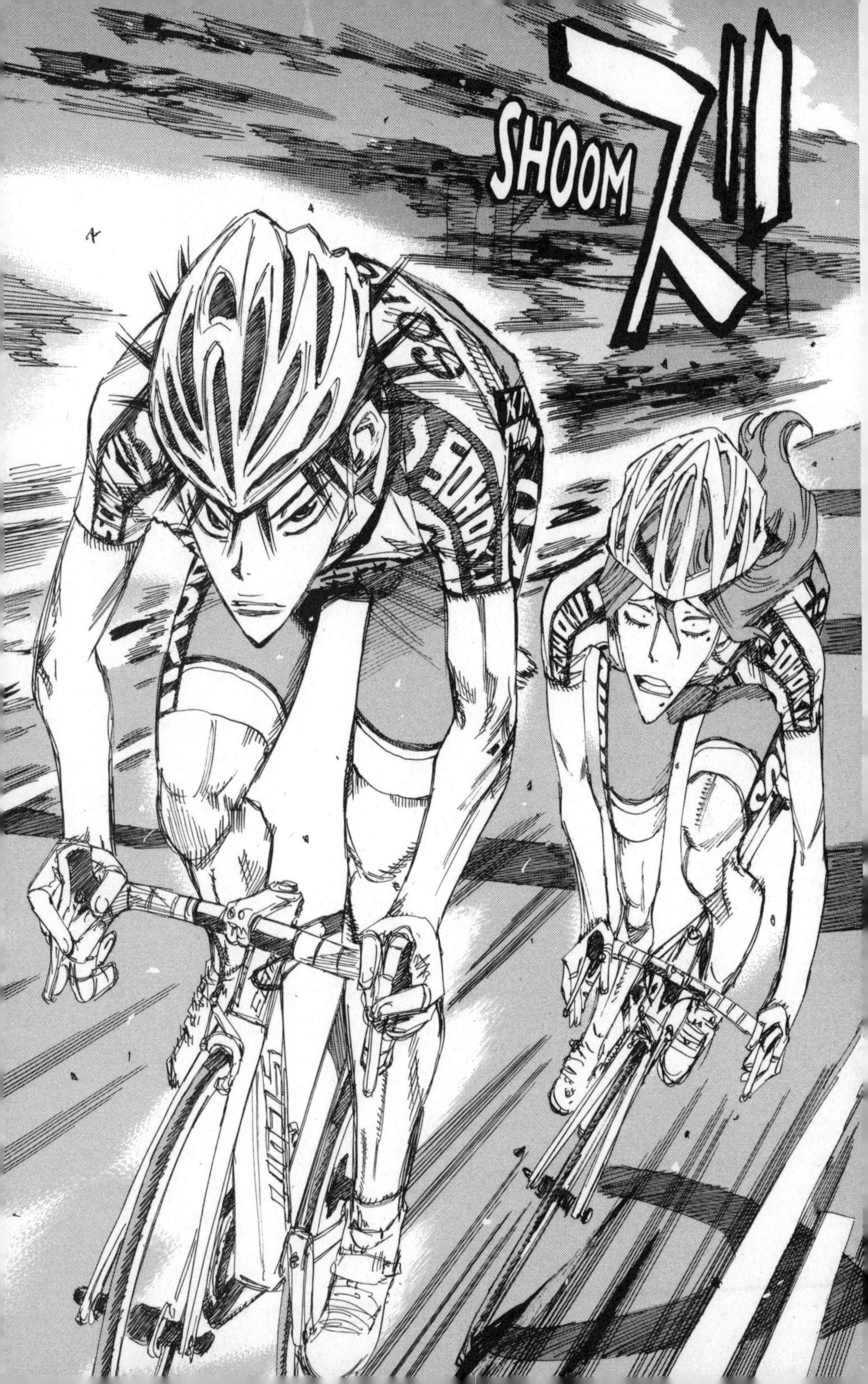
SHOOM

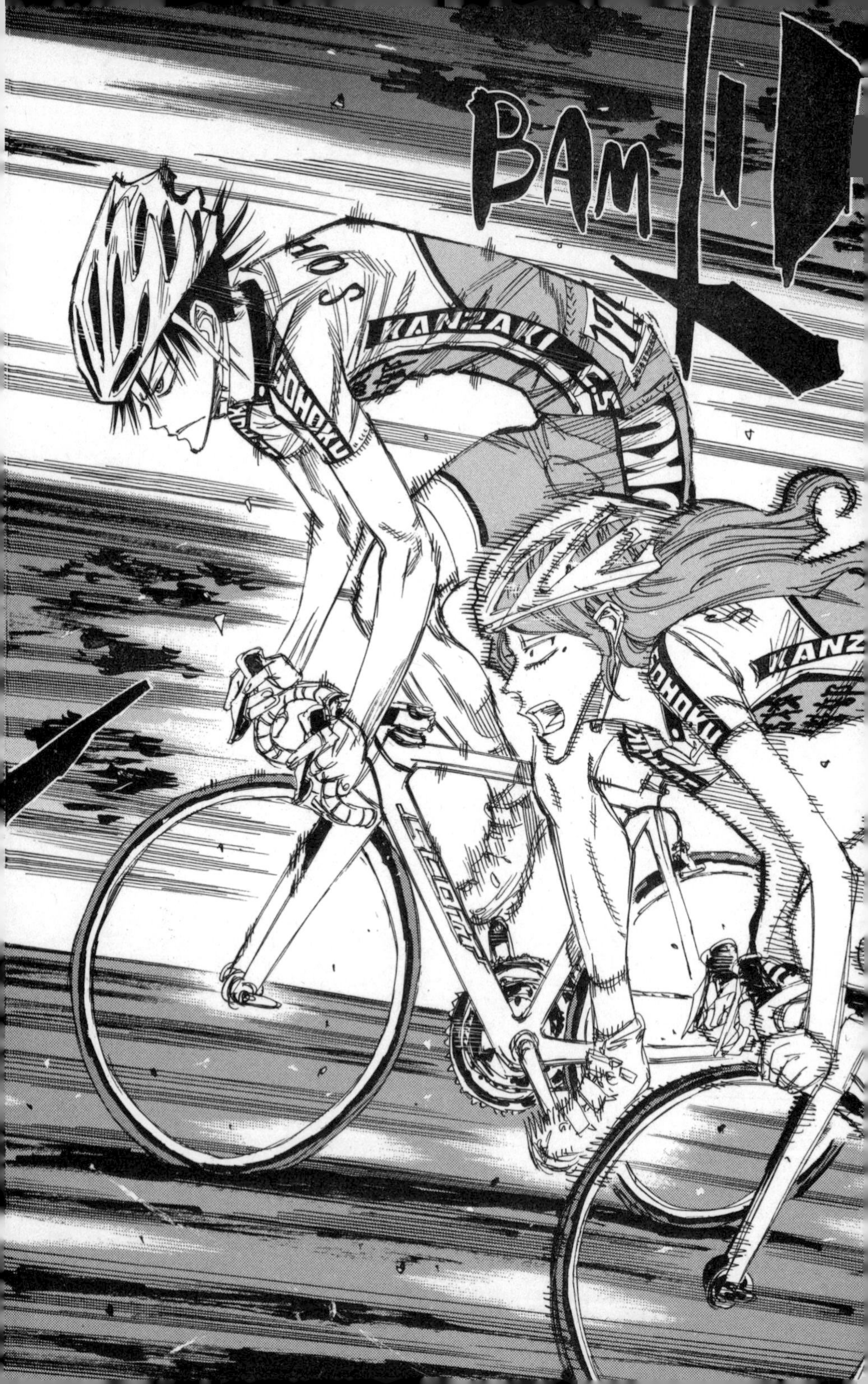
BAM!!
KANZAKI
SOHOKU

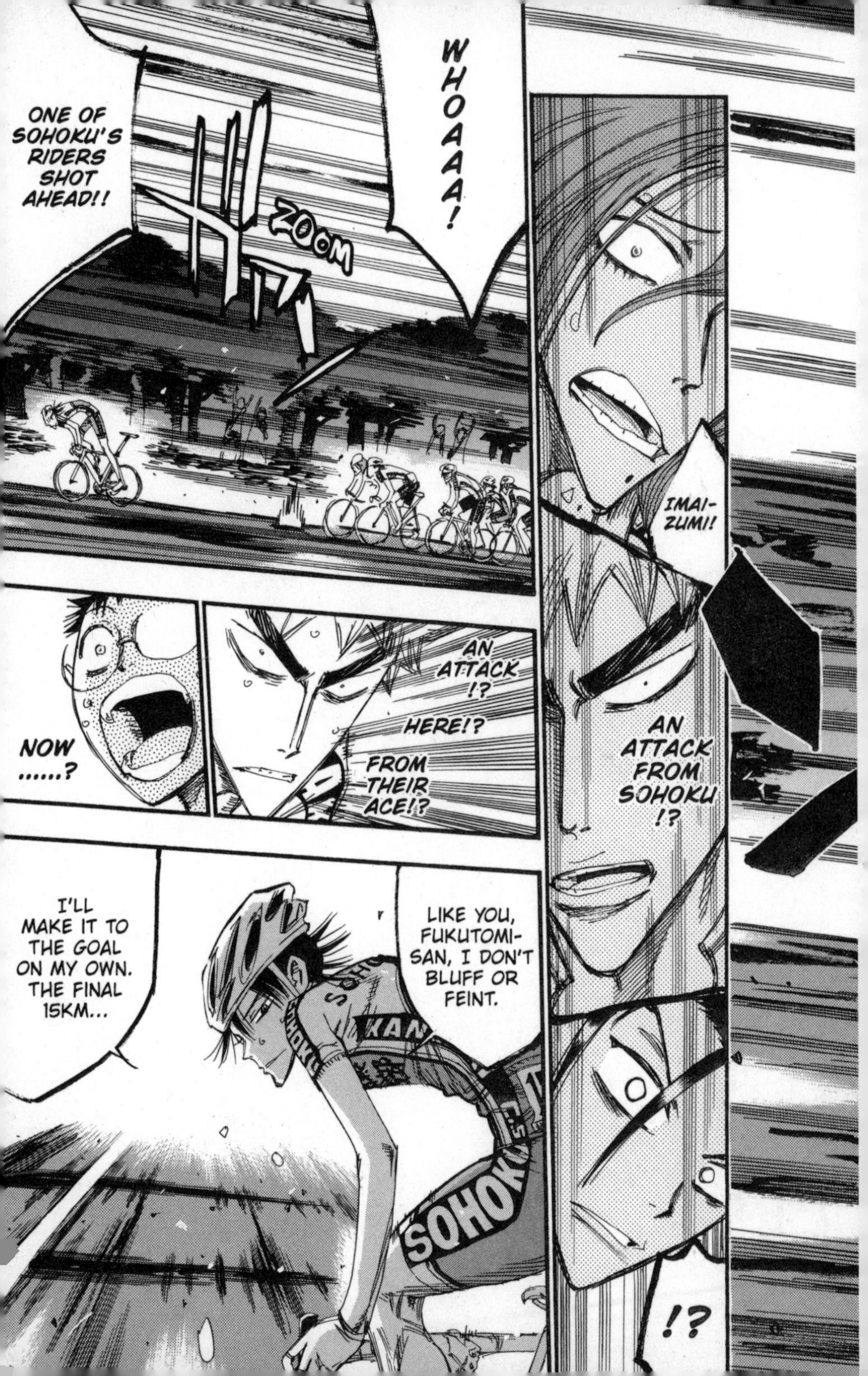
ONE OF SOHOKU'S RIDERS SHOT AHEAD!!
WHOAAAA!
ZOOM
IMAI-ZUMI!
AN ATTACK FROM SOHOKU!?
!?
AN ATTACK!?
HERE!?
FROM THEIR ACE!?
NOW ......?
LIKE YOU, FUKUTOMI-SAN, I DON'T BLUFF OR FEINT.
I'LL MAKE IT TO THE GOAL ON MY OWN. THE FINAL 15KM...

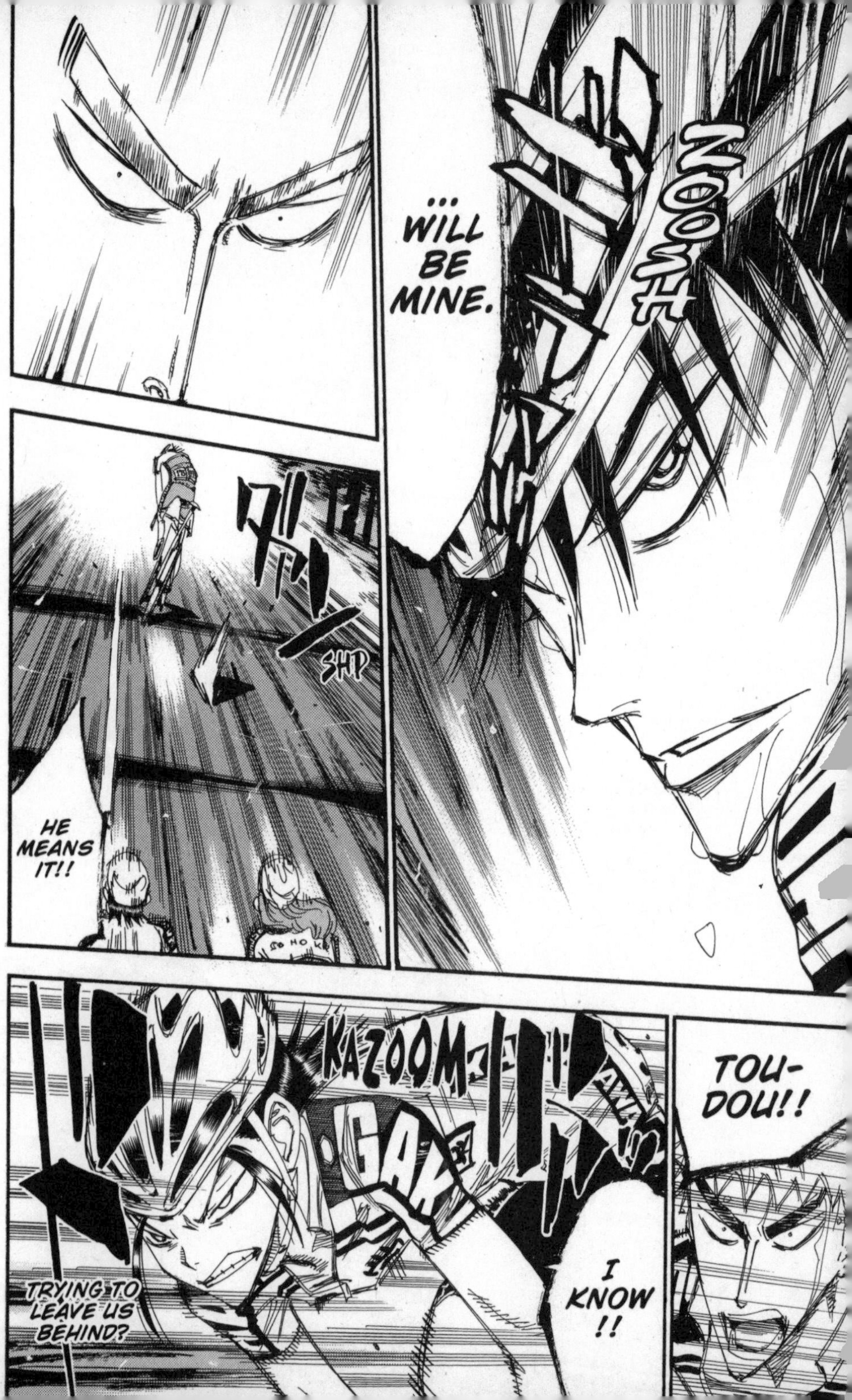
WOOSH
...WILL BE MINE.
SHP
HE MEANS IT!!
TOU-DOU!!
KAZOOM
GAK
I KNOW!!
TRYING TO LEAVE US BEHIND?

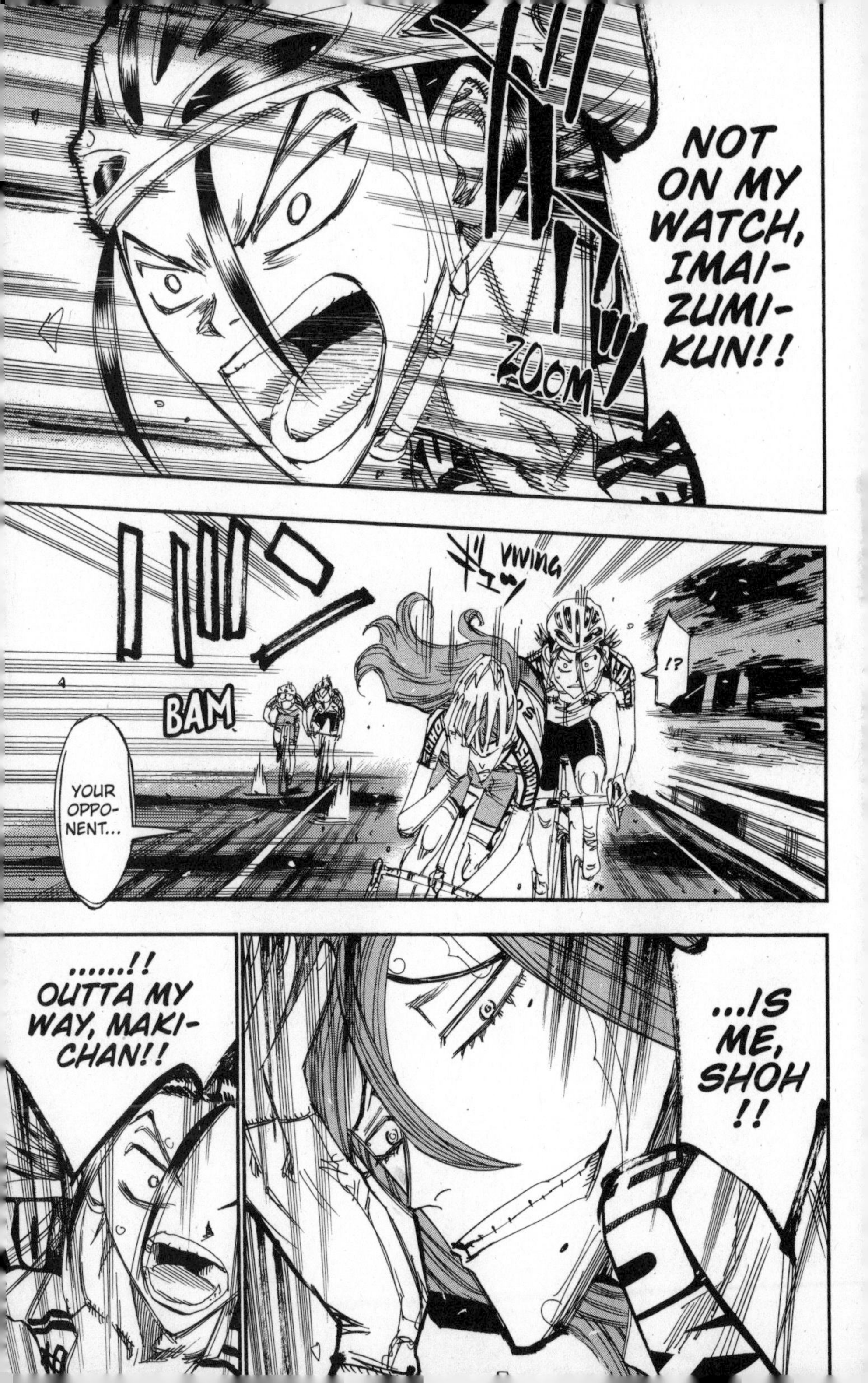
NOT ON MY WATCH, IMAIZUMI-KUN!!
ZOOM
VWING
!?
BAM
YOUR OPPONENT...
...IS ME, SHOH!!
......!! OUTTA MY WAY, MAKI-CHAN!!

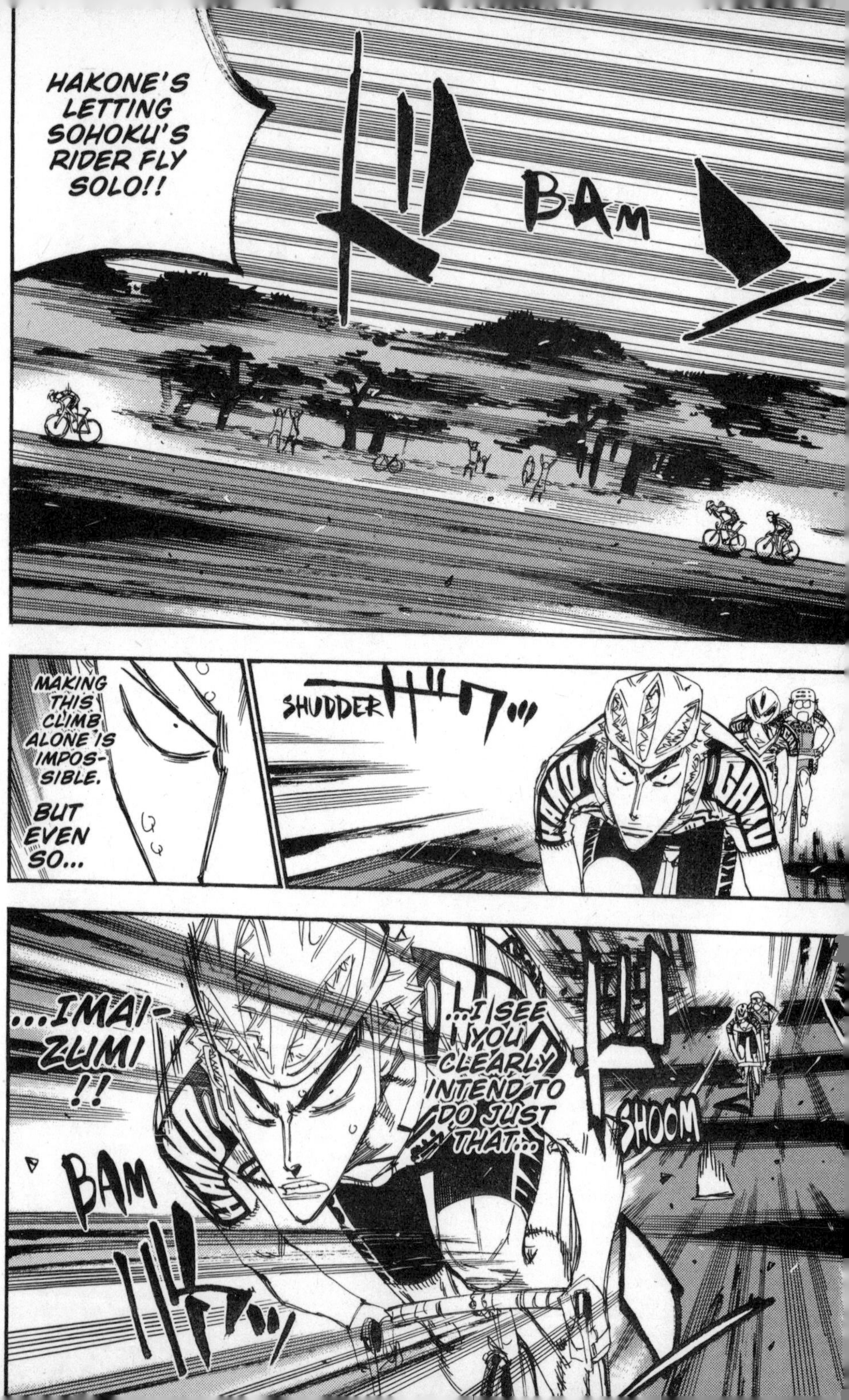

HAKONE'S LETTING SOHOKU'S RIDER FLY SOLO!!
BAM
SHUDDER
MAKING THIS CLIMB ALONE IS IMPOSSIBLE.
BUT EVEN SO...
...I SEE YOU CLEARLY INTEND TO DO JUST THAT...
SHOOM
...IMAI-ZUMI!!
BAM

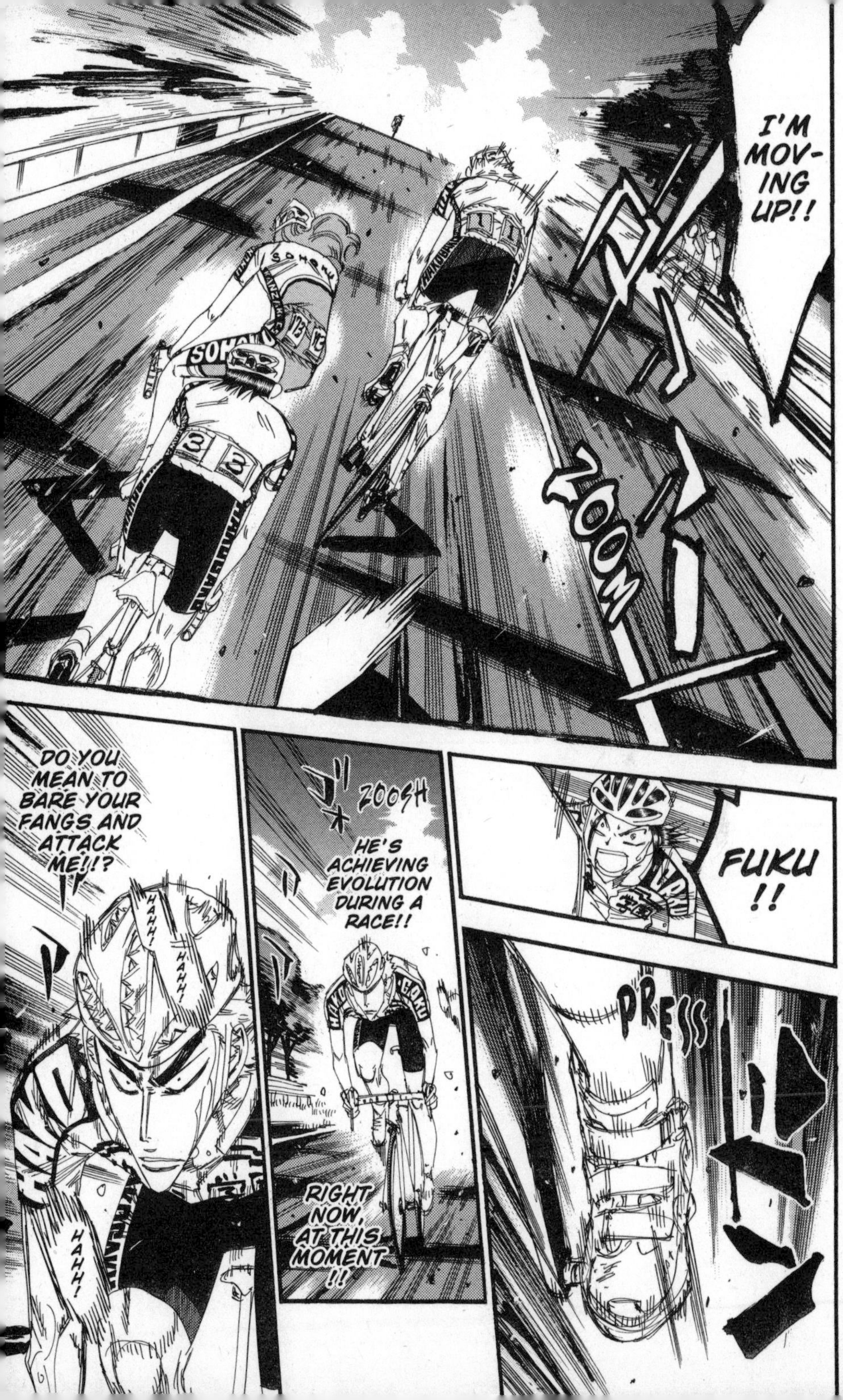
I'M MOV-ING UP!!
ZOOM
FUKU !!
PRESS
ZOOSH
HE'S ACHIEVING EVOLUTION DURING A RACE!!
RIGHT NOW, AT THIS MOMENT !!
DO YOU MEAN TO BARE YOUR FANGS AND ATTACK ME!!?
HAHH!
HAHH!
HAHH!

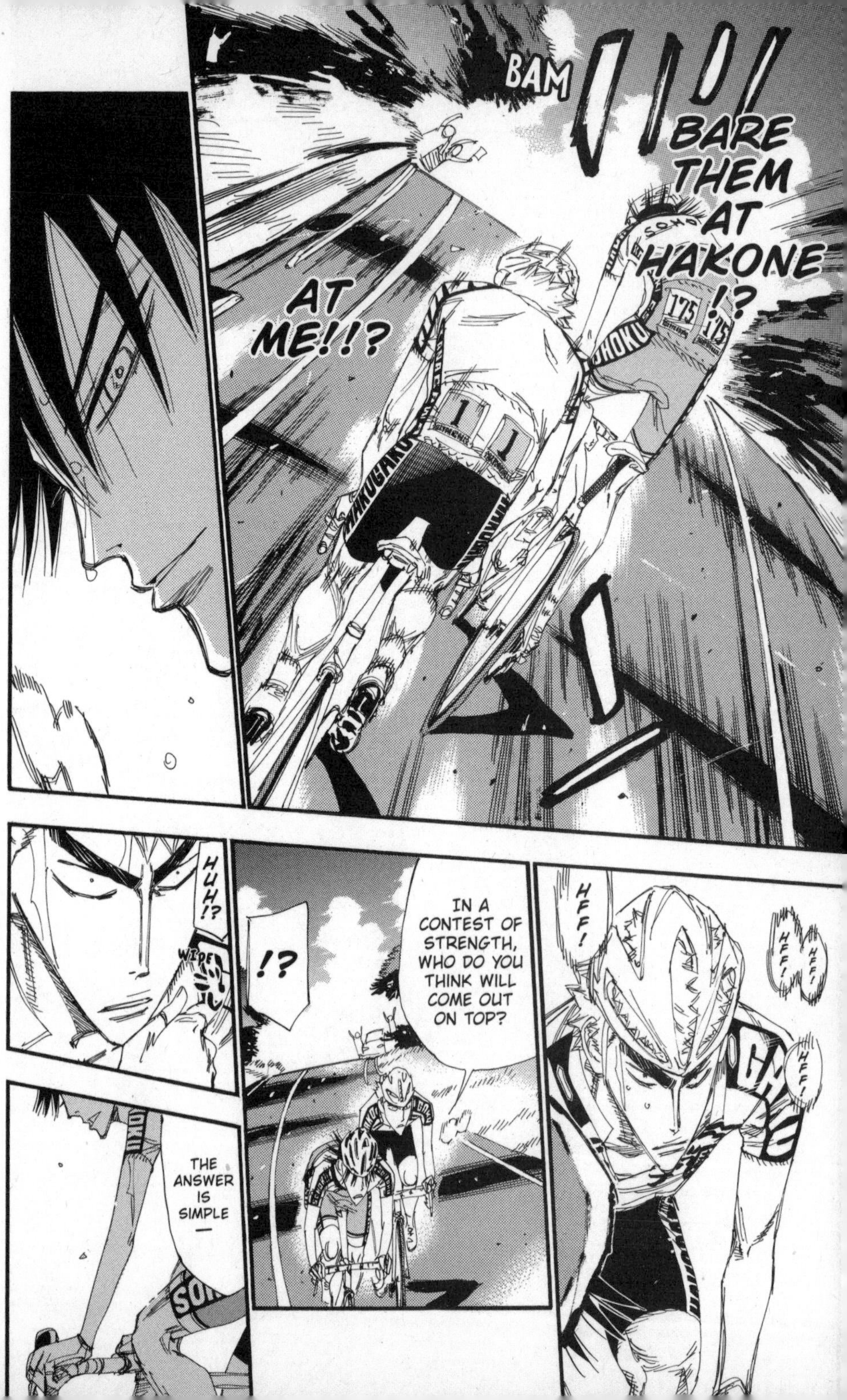
BAM
BARE THEM AT HAKONE!?
AT ME!!?
HFF!
HFF!
HFF!
HFF!
IN A CONTEST OF STRENGTH, WHO DO YOU THINK WILL COME OUT ON TOP?
!?
HUH!?
WIPE
THE ANSWER IS SIMPLE—

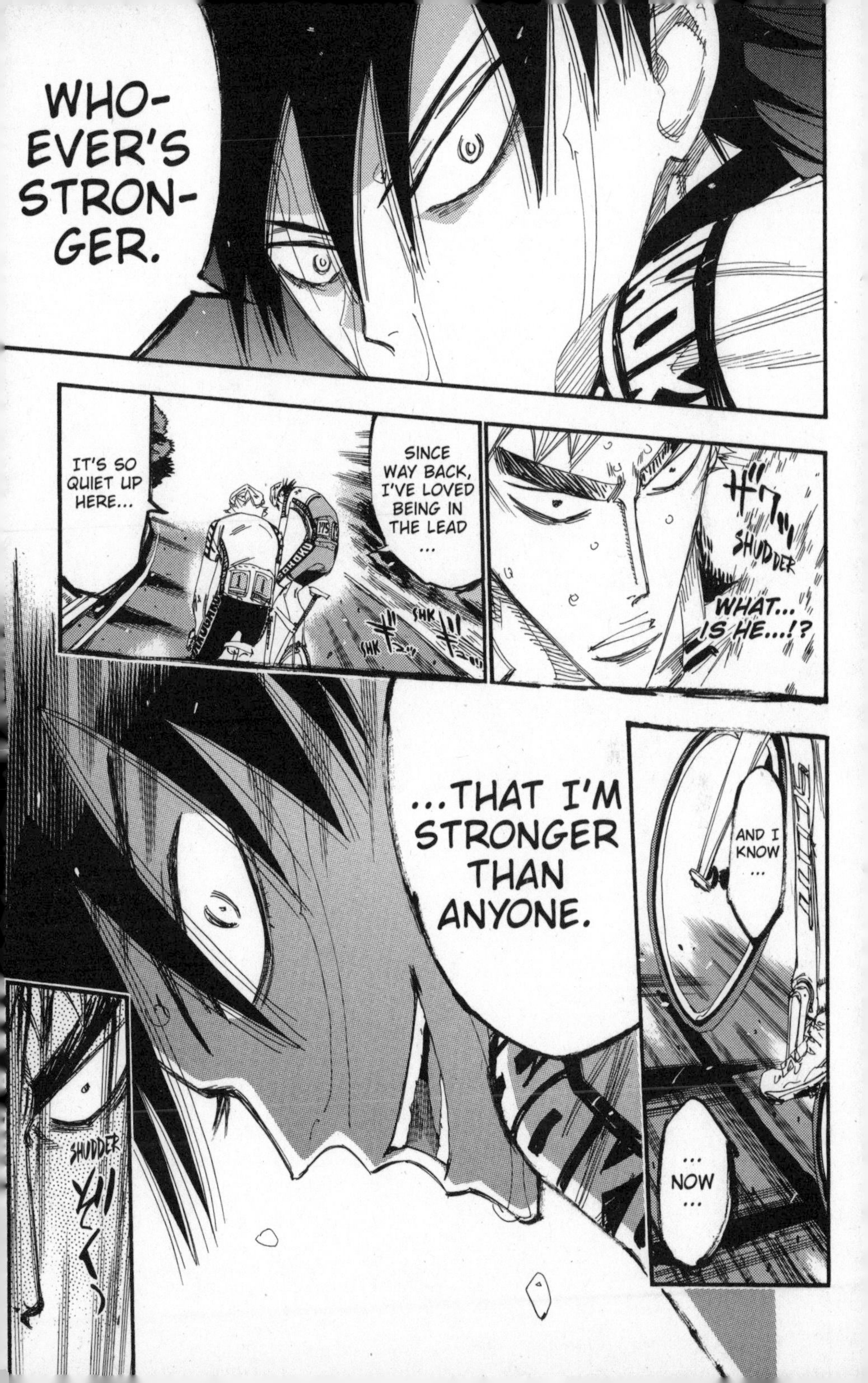
WHO-EVER'S STRON-GER.
SHUDDER
WHAT... IS HE...!?
SINCE WAY BACK, I'VE LOVED BEING IN THE LEAD ...
IT'S SO QUIET UP HERE...
SHK
SHK
AND I KNOW ...
...THAT I'M STRONGER THAN ANYONE.
... NOW ...
SHUDDER

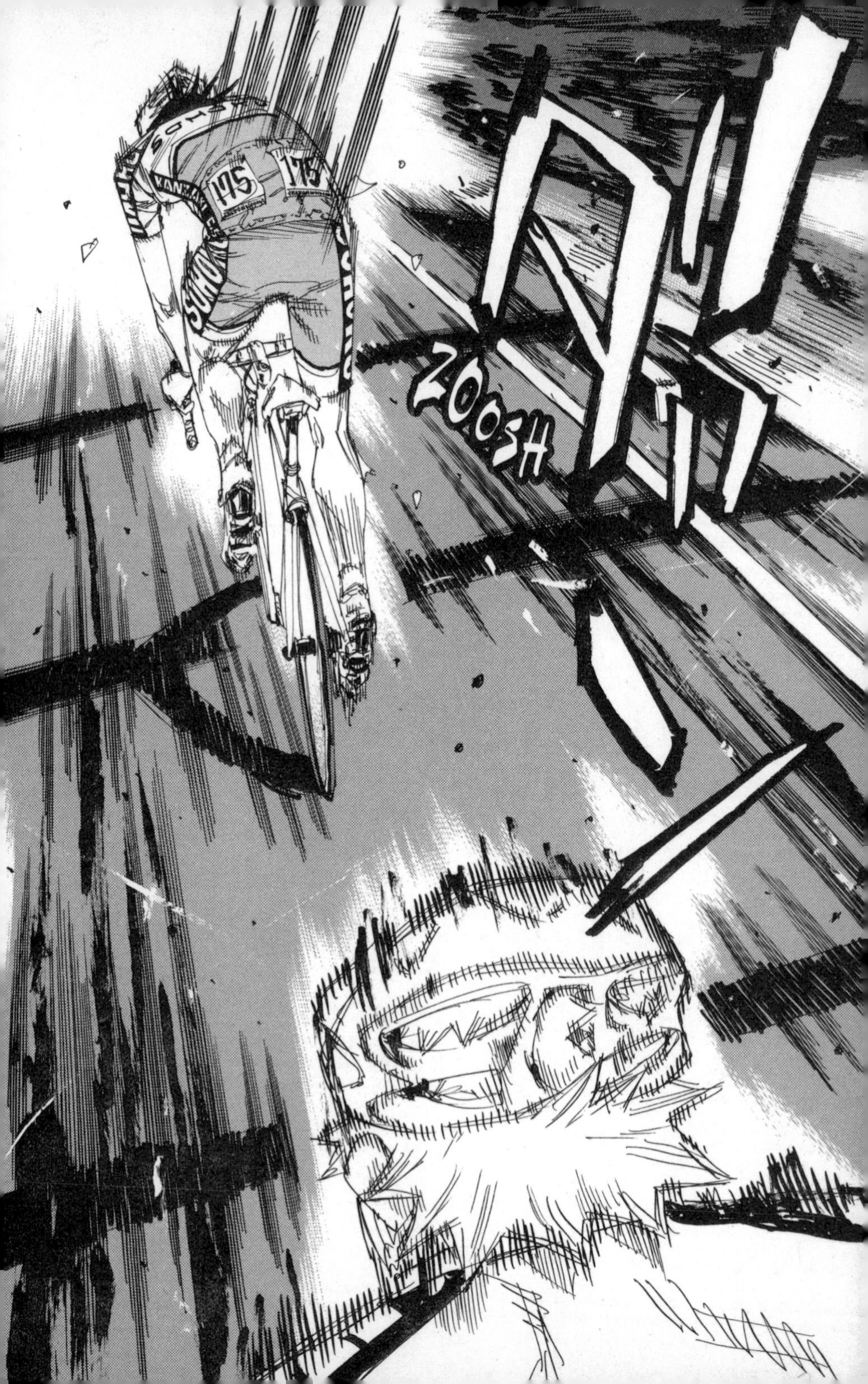
ZOOSH

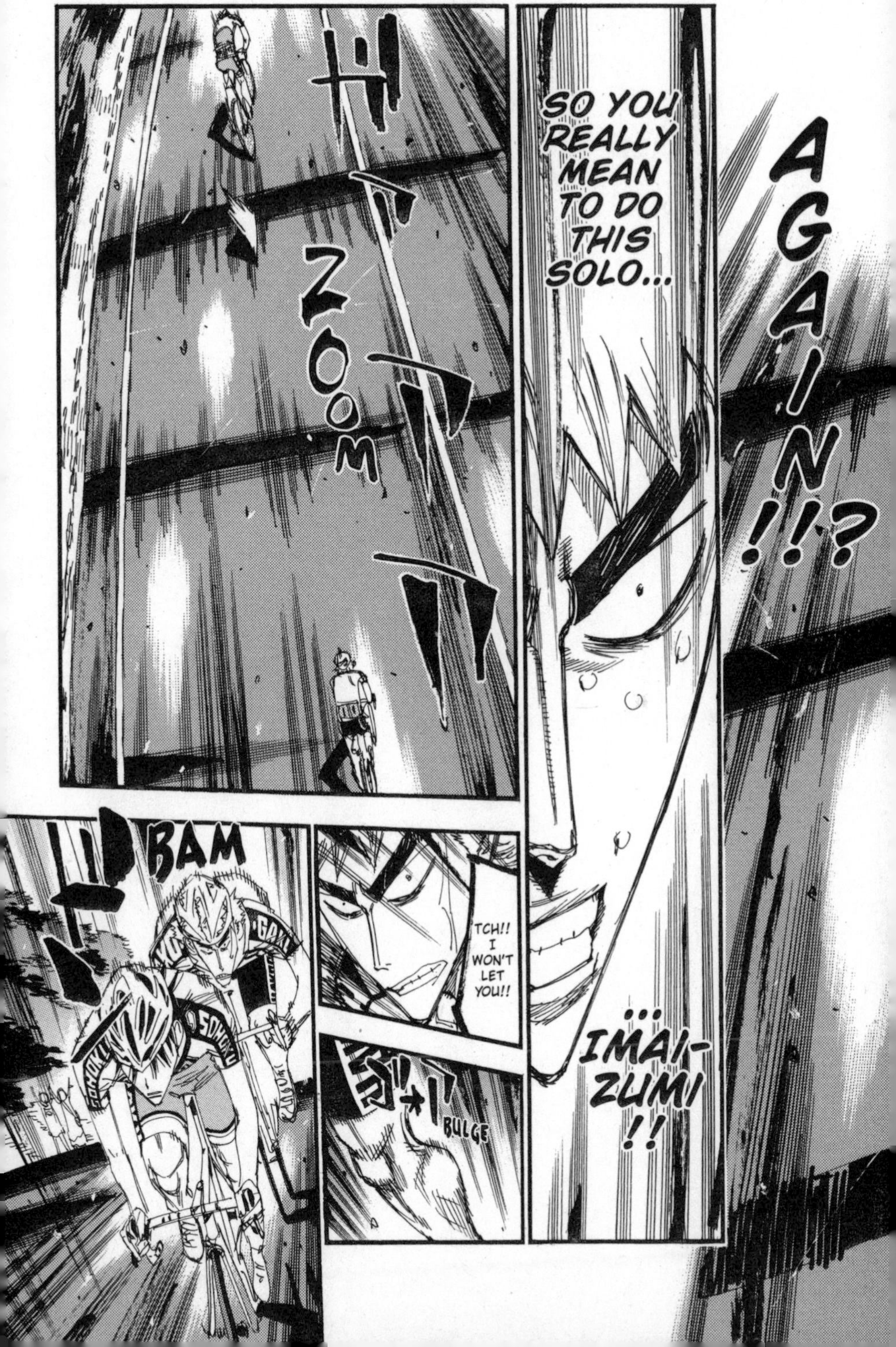
SO YOU REALLY MEAN TO DO THIS SOLO...
AGAIN!!?
...IMAI-ZUMI!!
ZOOM
TCH!! I WON'T LET YOU!!
BULGE
BAM

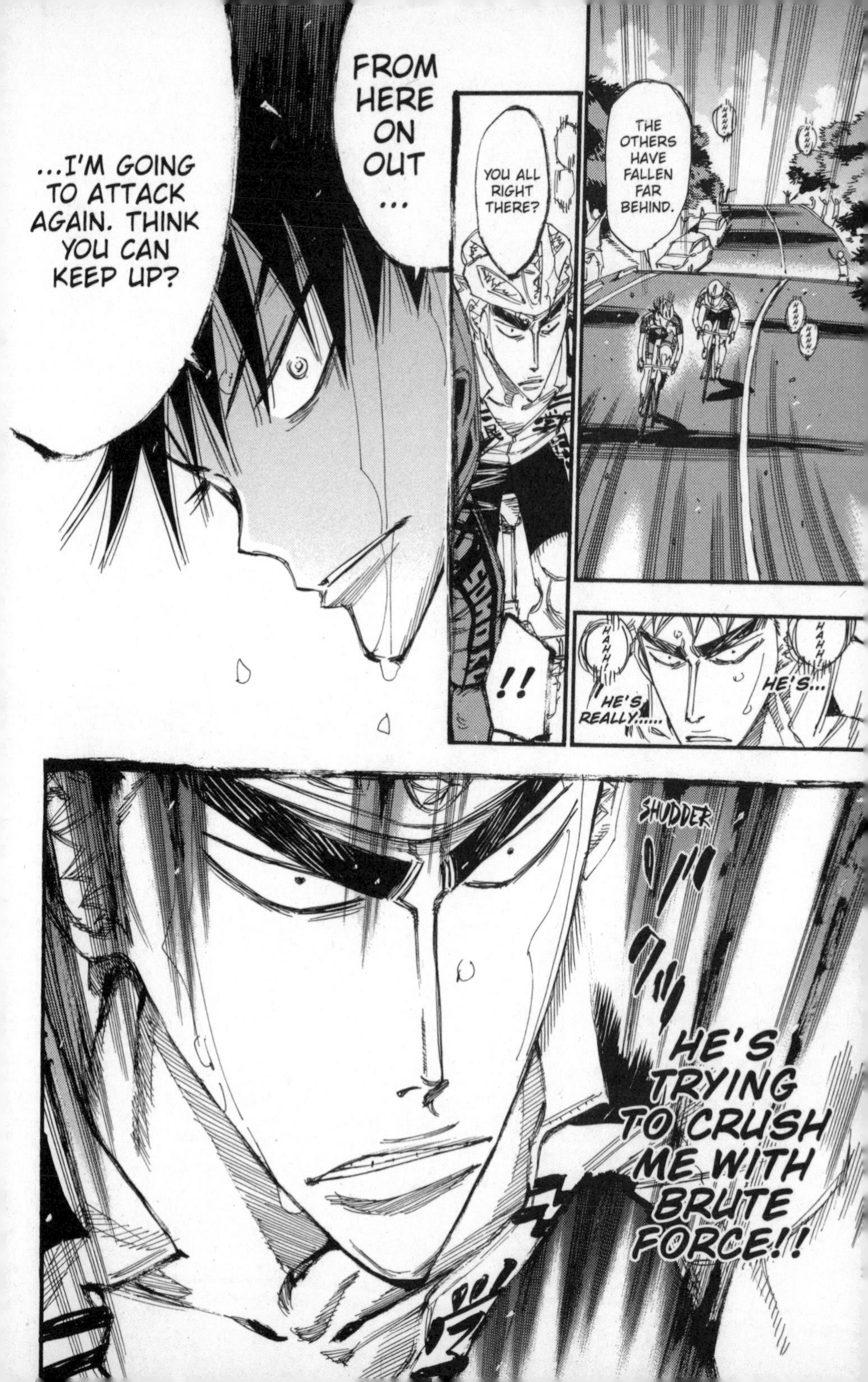
THE OTHERS HAVE FALLEN FAR BEHIND.
HE'S...
HE'S REALLY......
YOU ALL RIGHT THERE?
!!
FROM HERE ON OUT ...
...I'M GOING TO ATTACK AGAIN. THINK YOU CAN KEEP UP?
SHUDDER
HE'S TRYING TO CRUSH ME WITH BRUTE FORCE!!

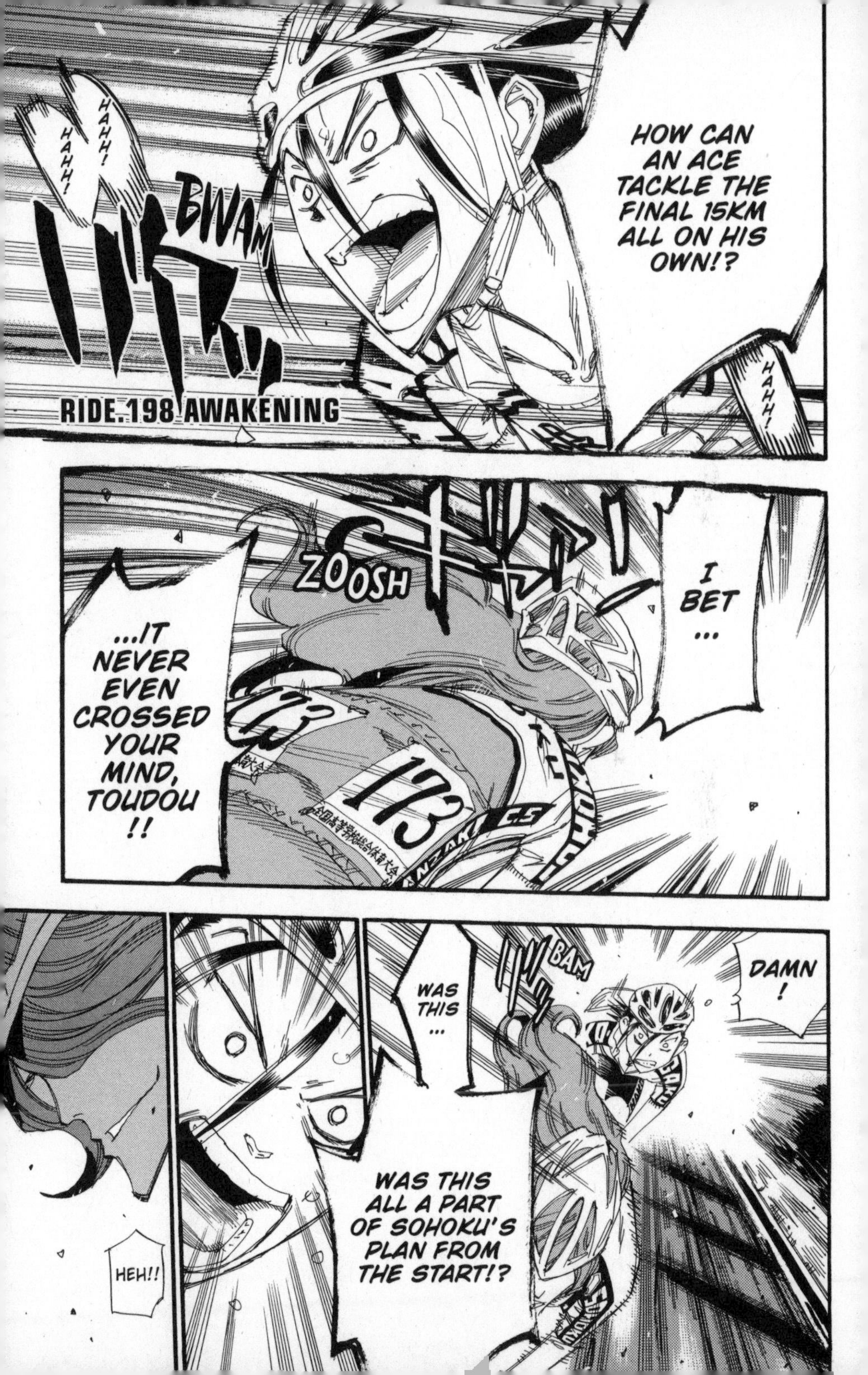
HOW CAN AN ACE TACKLE THE FINAL 15KM ALL ON HIS OWN!?
HAHH!
BWAM
HAHH! HAHH!
RIDE. 198 AWAKENING
I BET...
ZOOSH
...IT NEVER EVEN CROSSED YOUR MIND, TOUDOU!!
173
DAMN!
BAM
WAS THIS...
WAS THIS ALL A PART OF SOHOKU'S PLAN FROM THE START!?
HEH!!

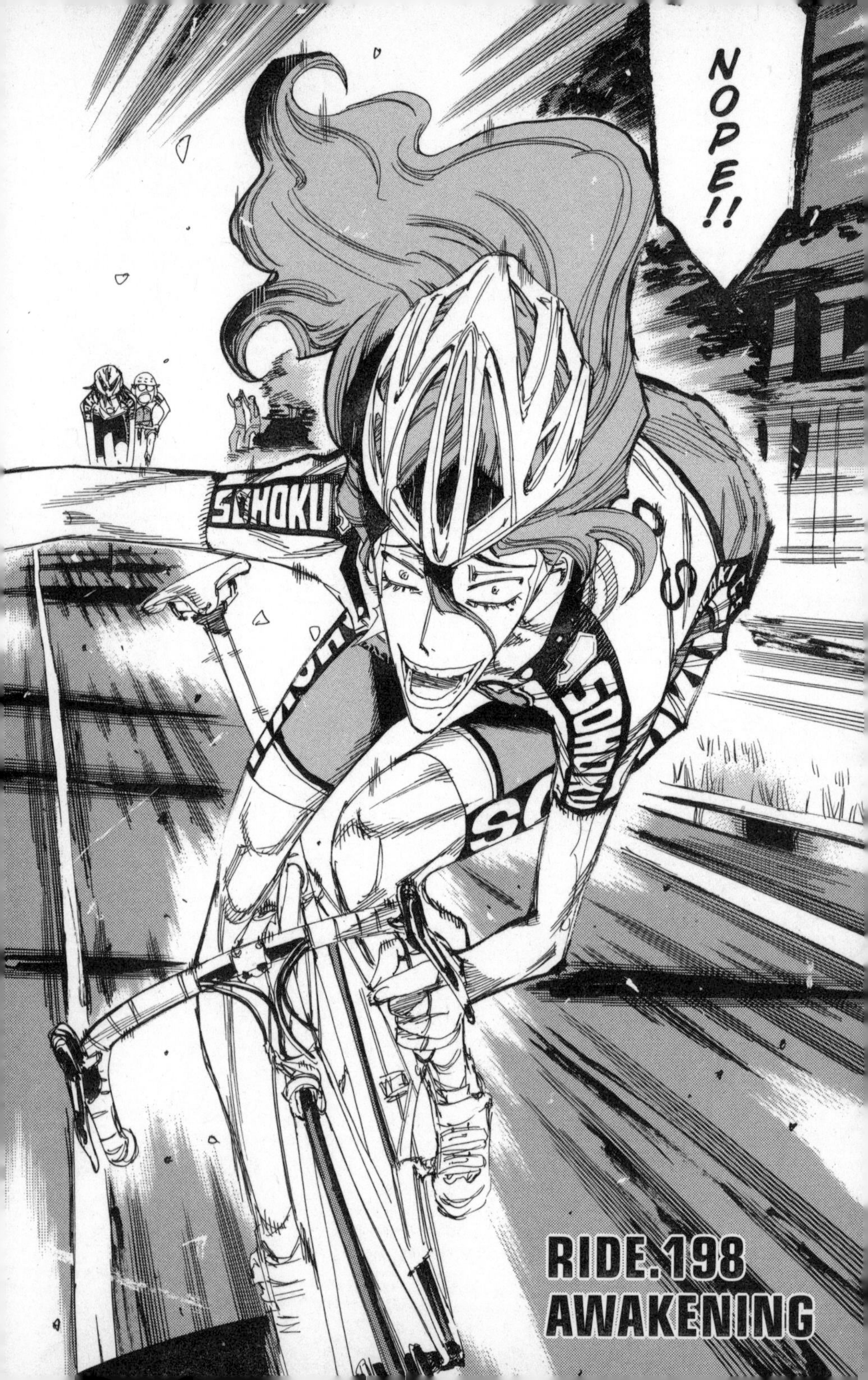
NOPE!!
SOHOKU
RIDE.198
AWAKENING

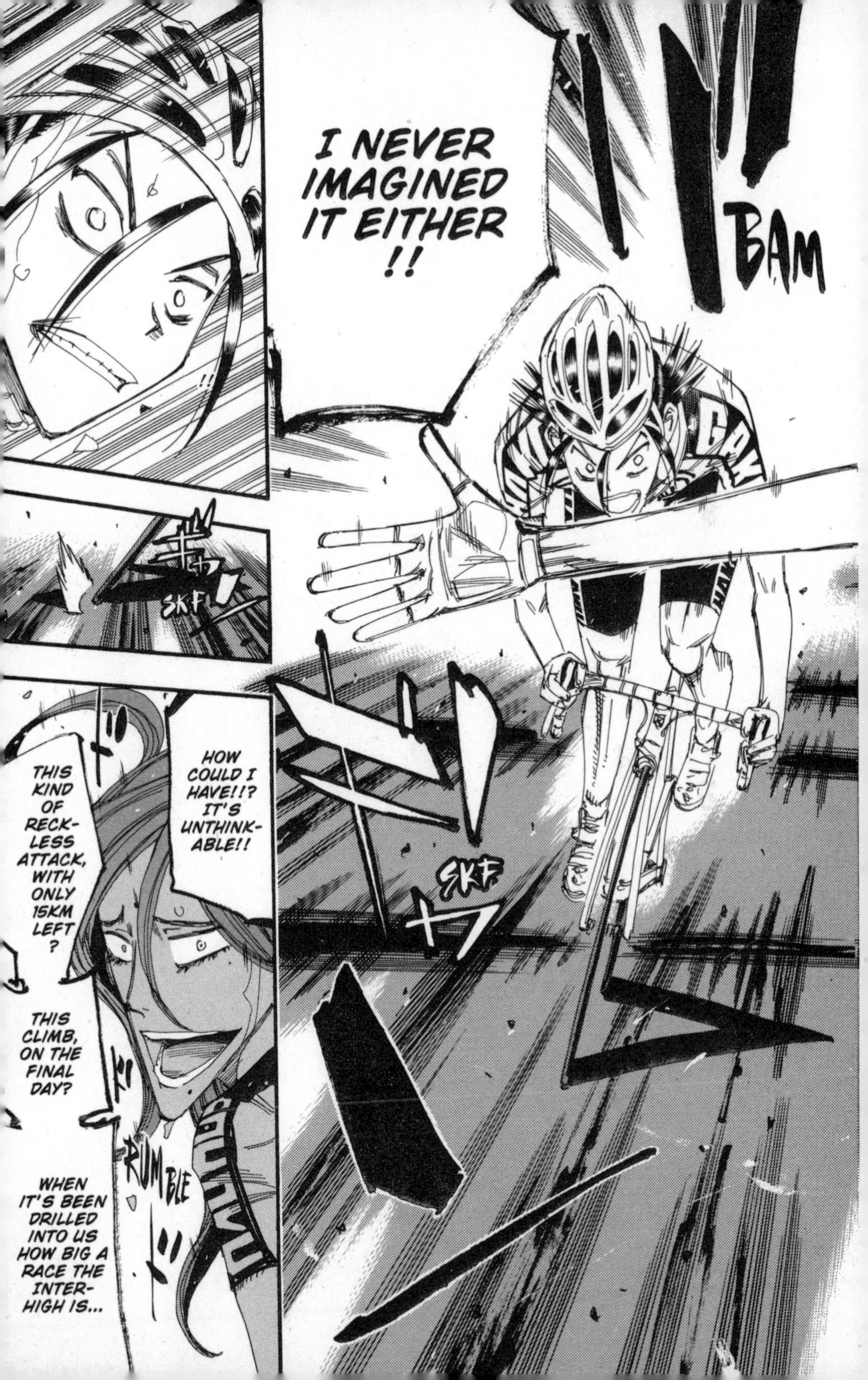
I NEVER IMAGINED IT EITHER!!
BAM
SKF
SKF
HOW COULD I HAVE!!? IT'S UNTHINKABLE!!
THIS KIND OF RECKLESS ATTACK, WITH ONLY 15KM LEFT?
THIS CLIMB, ON THE FINAL DAY?
WHEN IT'S BEEN DRILLED INTO US HOW BIG A RACE THE INTER-HIGH IS...
RUMBLE

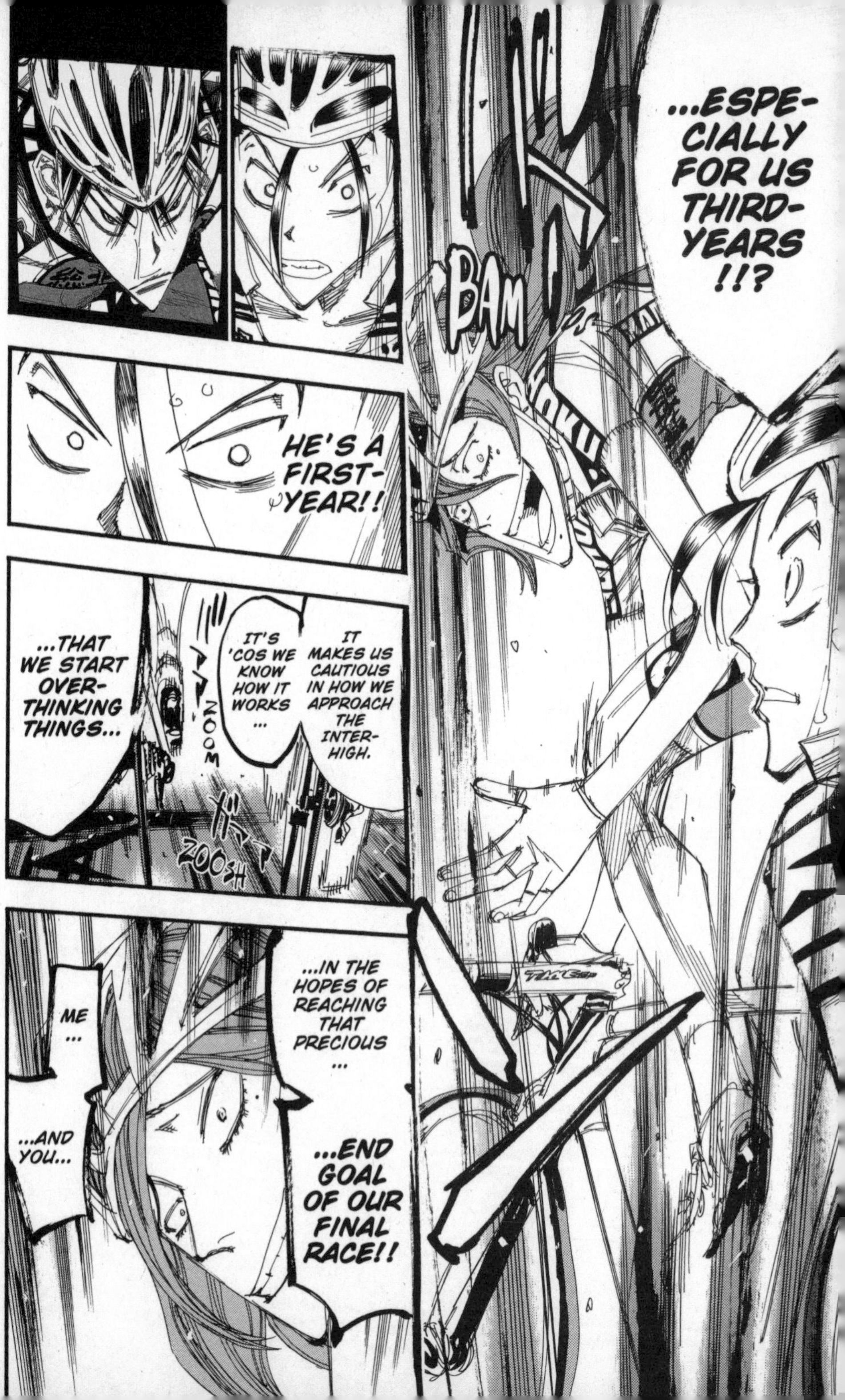
...ESPE-CIALLY FOR US THIRD-YEARS!!?
BAM
HE'S A FIRST-YEAR!!
IT MAKES US CAUTIOUS IN HOW WE APPROACH THE INTER-HIGH.
IT'S 'COS WE KNOW HOW IT WORKS...
...THAT WE START OVER-THINKING THINGS...
ZOOM
ZOOSH
...IN THE HOPES OF REACHING THAT PRECIOUS...
...END GOAL OF OUR FINAL RACE!!
ME...
...AND YOU...

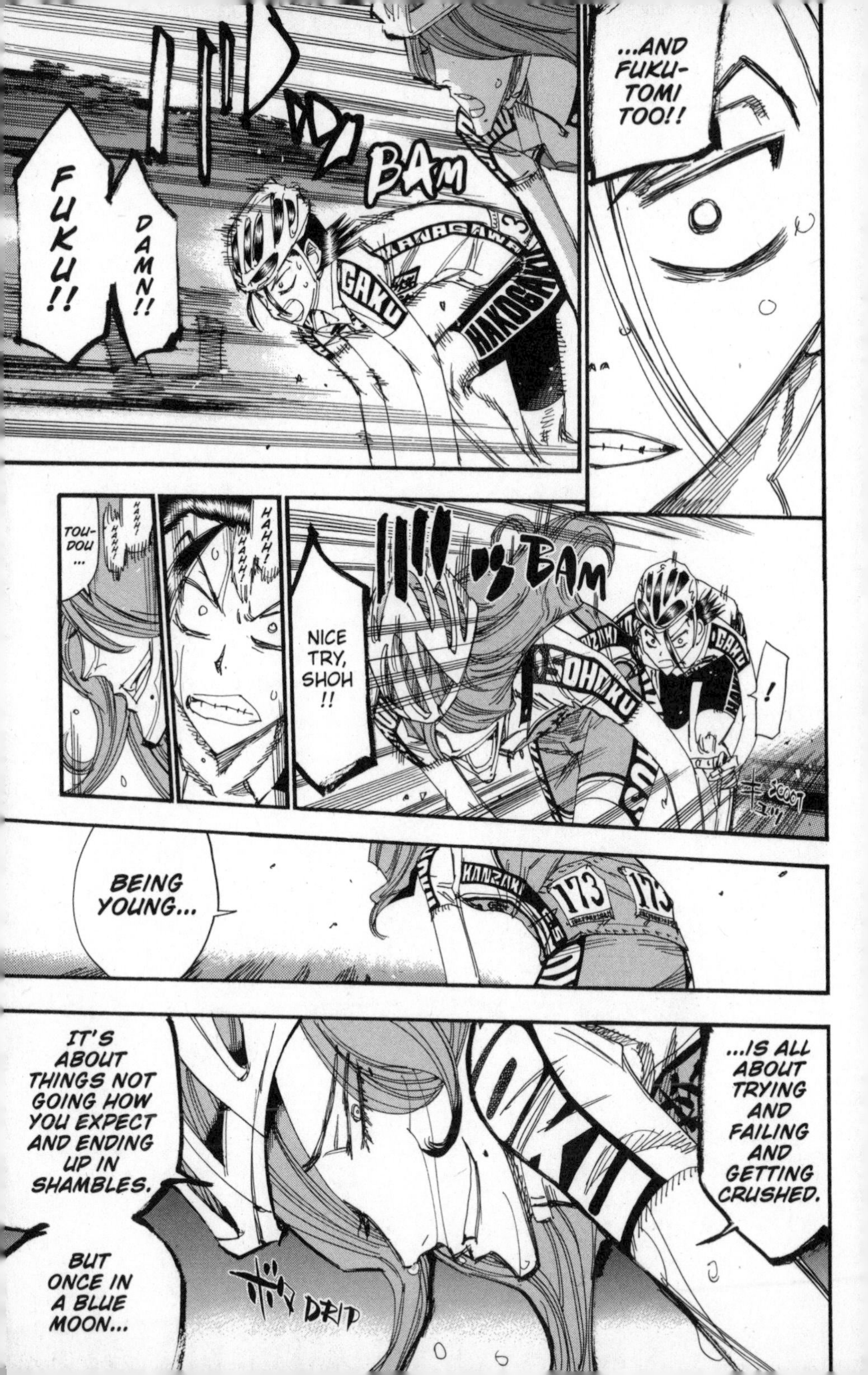
...AND FUKU-TOMI TOO!!
BAM
DAMN!!
FUKU!!
BAM
!
NICE TRY, SHOH!!
HAHH! HAHH!
HAHH! HAHH!
TOU-DOU...
BEING YOUNG...
...IS ALL ABOUT TRYING AND FAILING AND GETTING CRUSHED.
IT'S ABOUT THINGS NOT GOING HOW YOU EXPECT AND ENDING UP IN SHAMBLES.
BUT ONCE IN A BLUE MOON...
DRIP

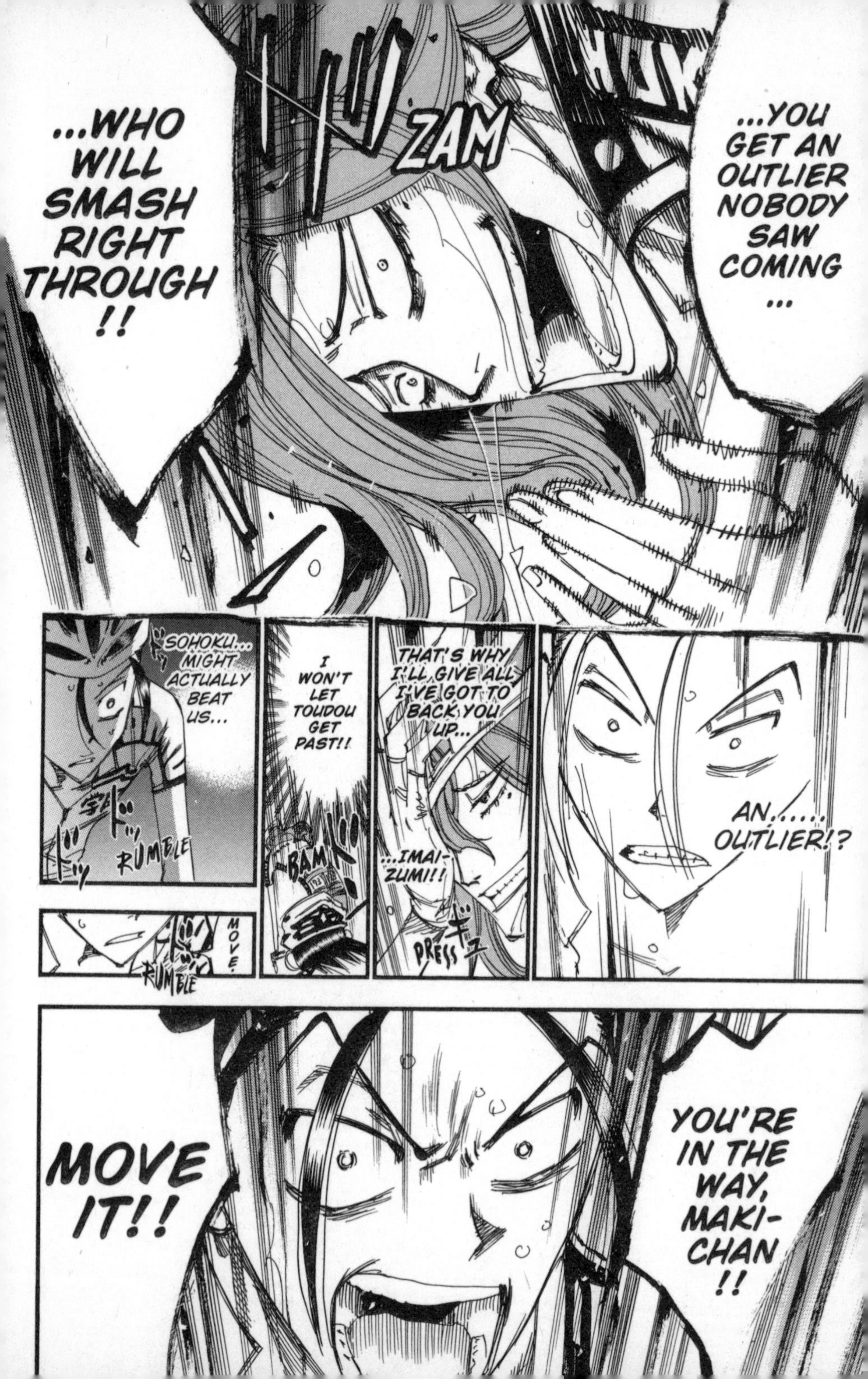
...YOU GET AN OUTLIER NOBODY SAW COMING ...
ZAM
...WHO WILL SMASH RIGHT THROUGH !!
AN...... OUTLIER!?
THAT'S WHY I'LL GIVE ALL I'VE GOT TO BACK YOU UP...
...IMAI-ZUMI!!
PRESS
I WON'T LET TOUDOU GET PAST!!
BAM
SOHOKU... MIGHT ACTUALLY BEAT US...
RUMBLE
MOVE.
RUMBLE
YOU'RE IN THE WAY, MAKI-CHAN !!
MOVE IT!!

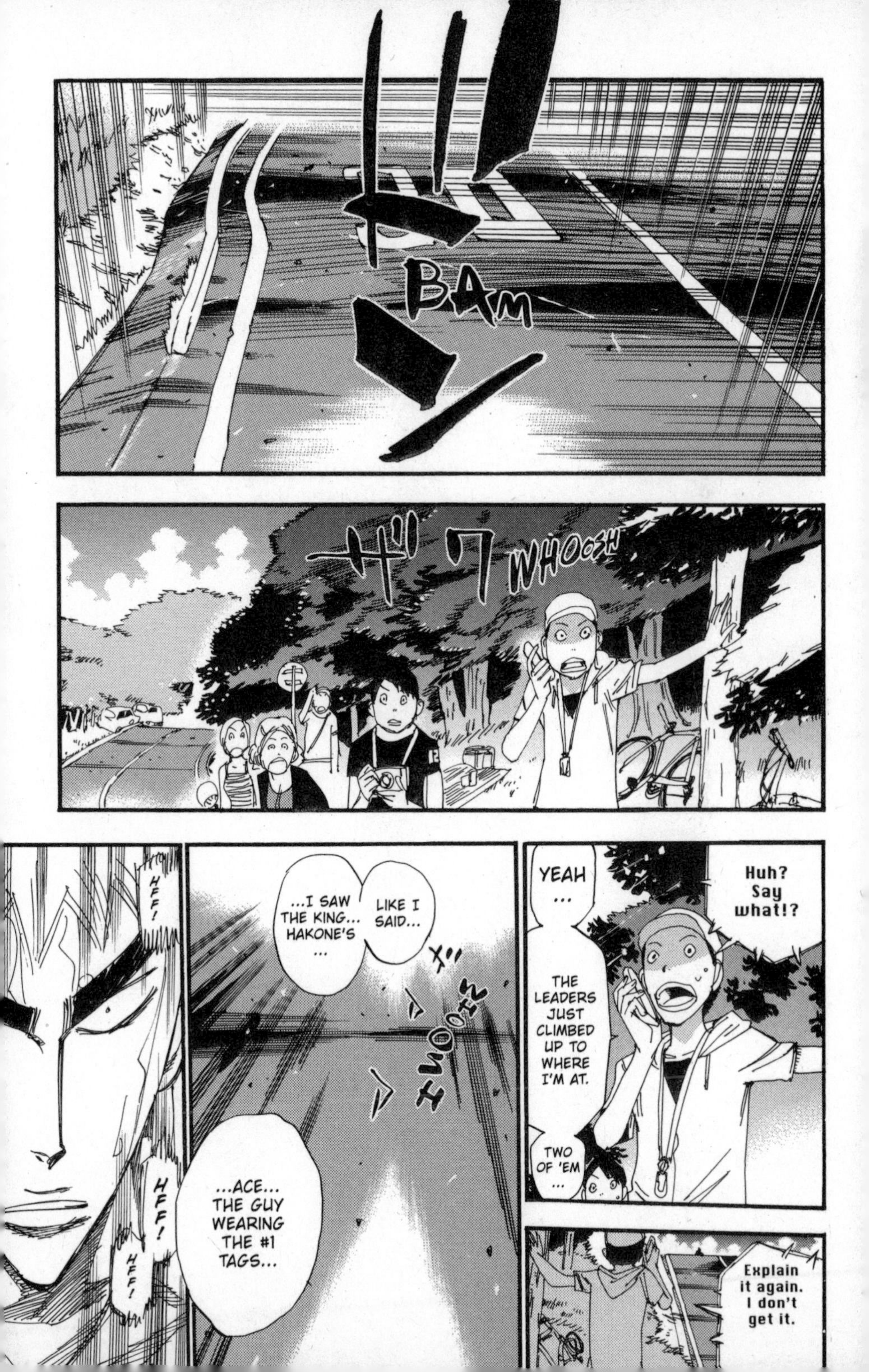
BAM
WHOOSH
Huh? Say what!?
YEAH ...
THE LEADERS JUST CLIMBED UP TO WHERE I'M AT.
TWO OF 'EM ...
Explain it again. I don't get it.
LIKE I SAID...
...I SAW THE KING... HAKONE'S ...
WHOOSH
...ACE... THE GUY WEARING THE #1 TAGS...
HFF!
HFF!
HFF!

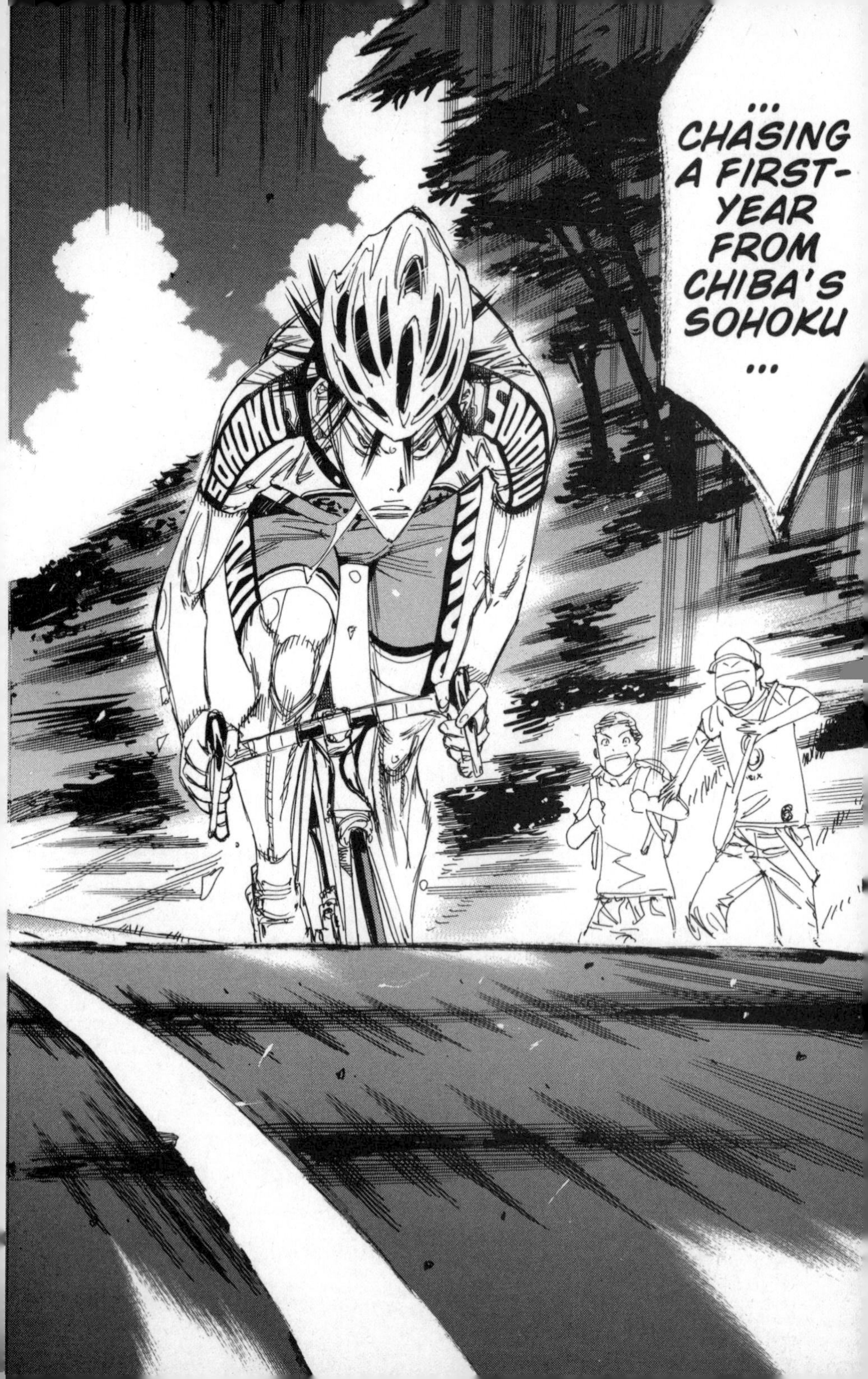
...CHASING A FIRST-YEAR FROM CHIBA'S SOHOKU...
SOHOKU

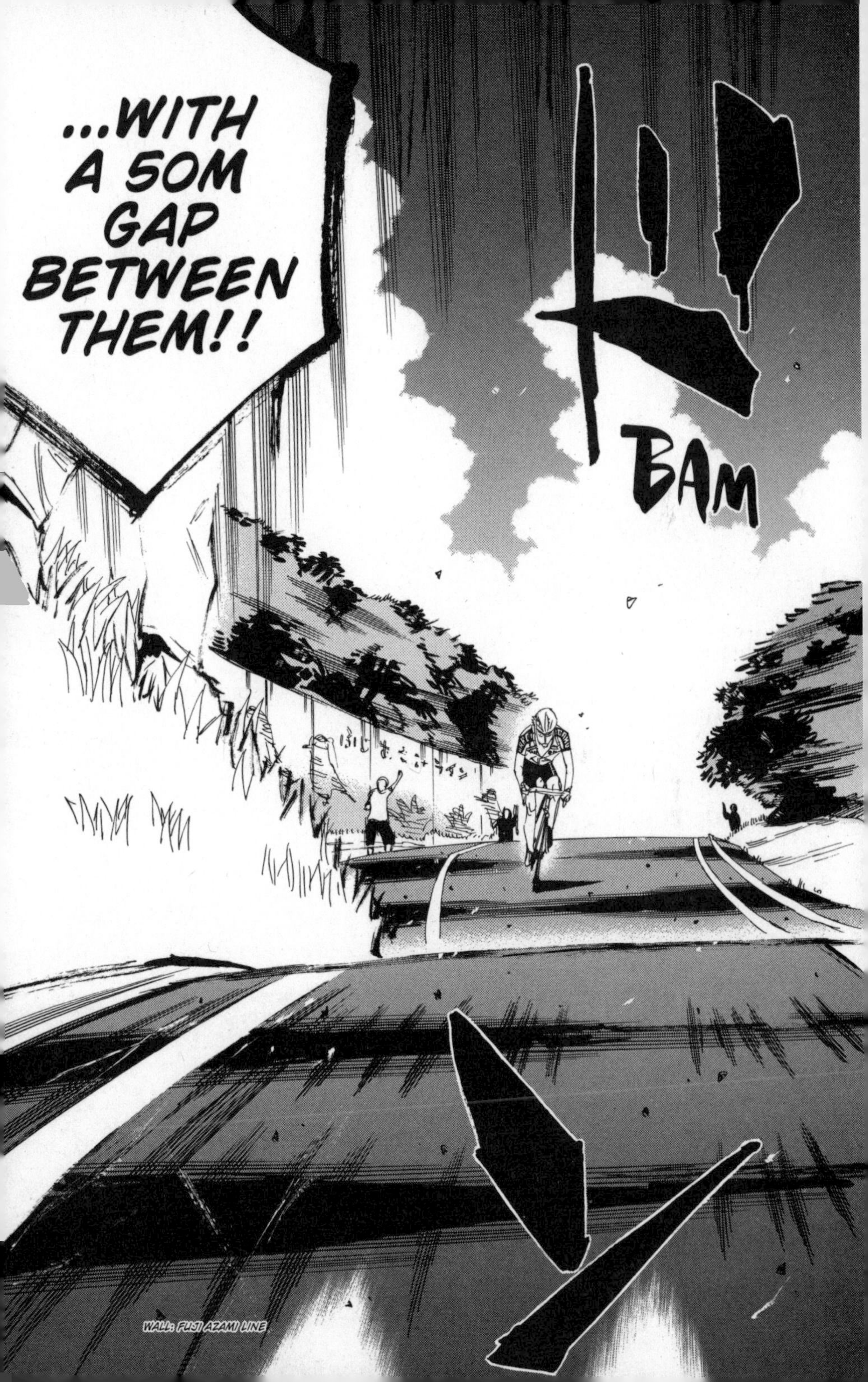
...WITH A 50M GAP BETWEEN THEM!!
BAM
WALL: FUJI AZAMI LINE

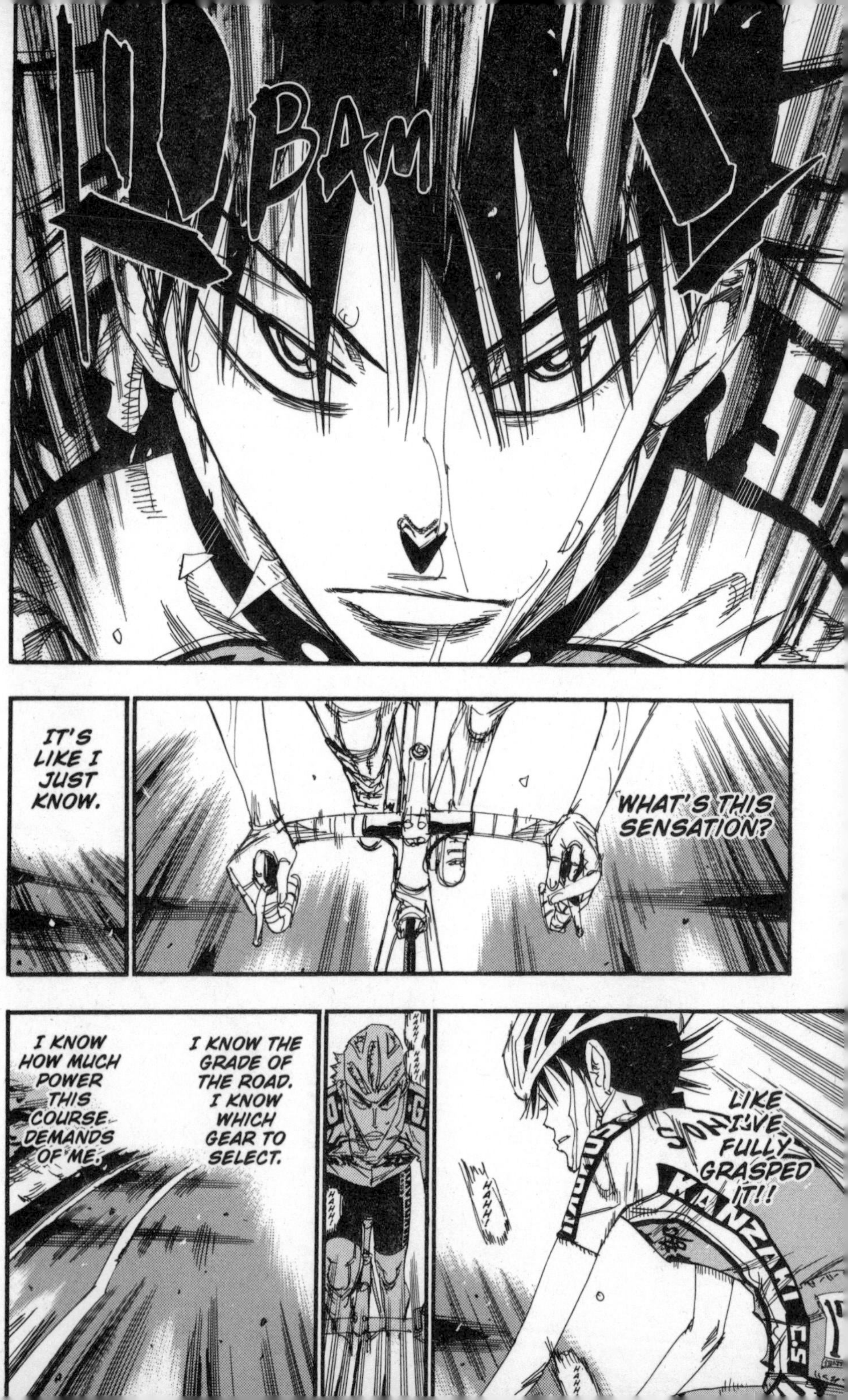
BAM
WHAT'S THIS SENSATION?
IT'S LIKE I JUST KNOW.
LIKE I'VE FULLY GRASPED IT!!
I KNOW THE GRADE OF THE ROAD. I KNOW WHICH GEAR TO SELECT.
I KNOW HOW MUCH POWER THIS COURSE DEMANDS OF ME.

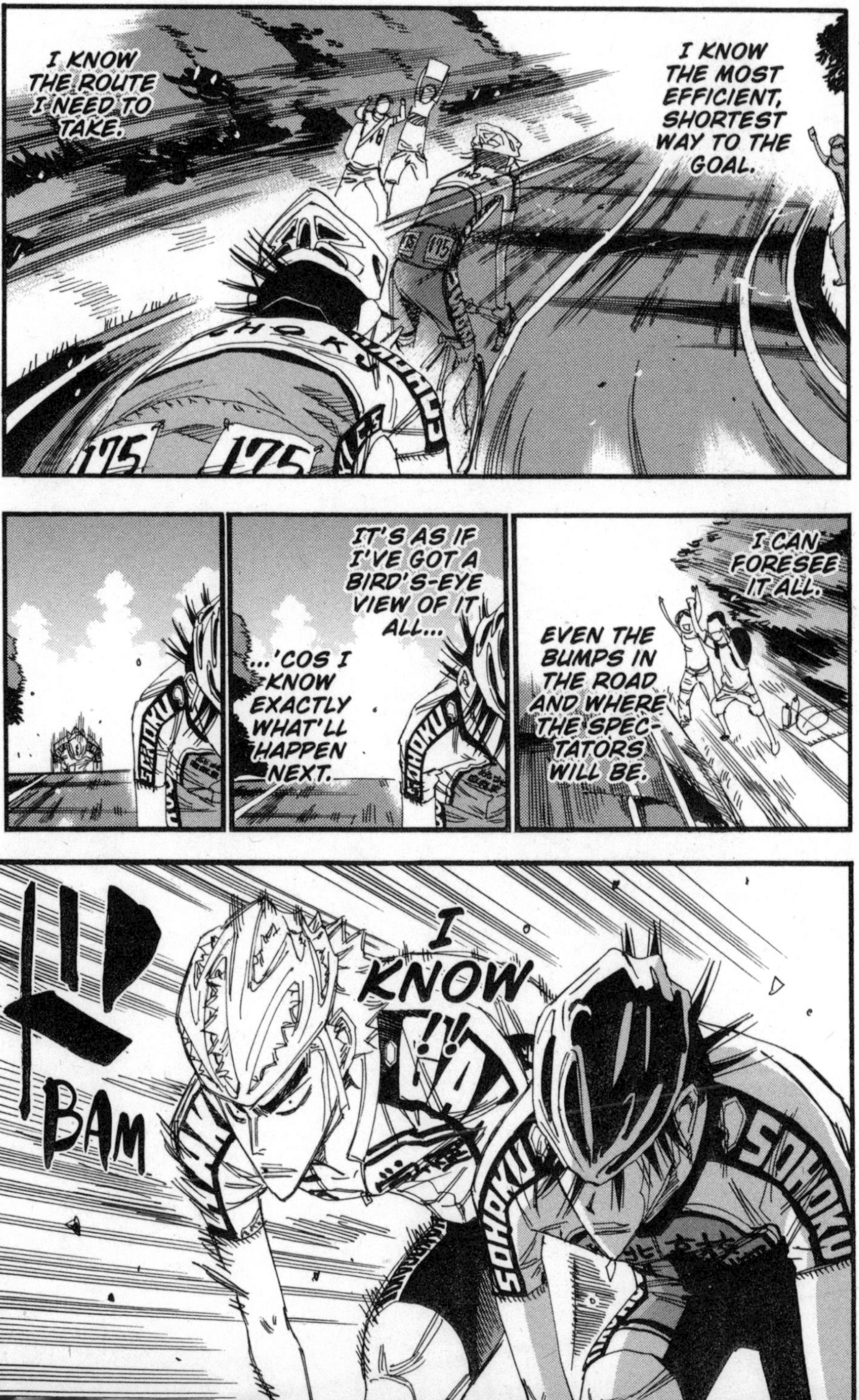
I KNOW THE MOST EFFICIENT, SHORTEST WAY TO THE GOAL.
I KNOW THE ROUTE I NEED TO TAKE.
I CAN FORESEE IT ALL.
EVEN THE BUMPS IN THE ROAD AND WHERE THE SPEC-TATORS WILL BE.
IT'S AS IF I'VE GOT A BIRD'S-EYE VIEW OF IT ALL...
...'COS I KNOW EXACTLY WHAT'LL HAPPEN NEXT.
I KNOW!!
BAM

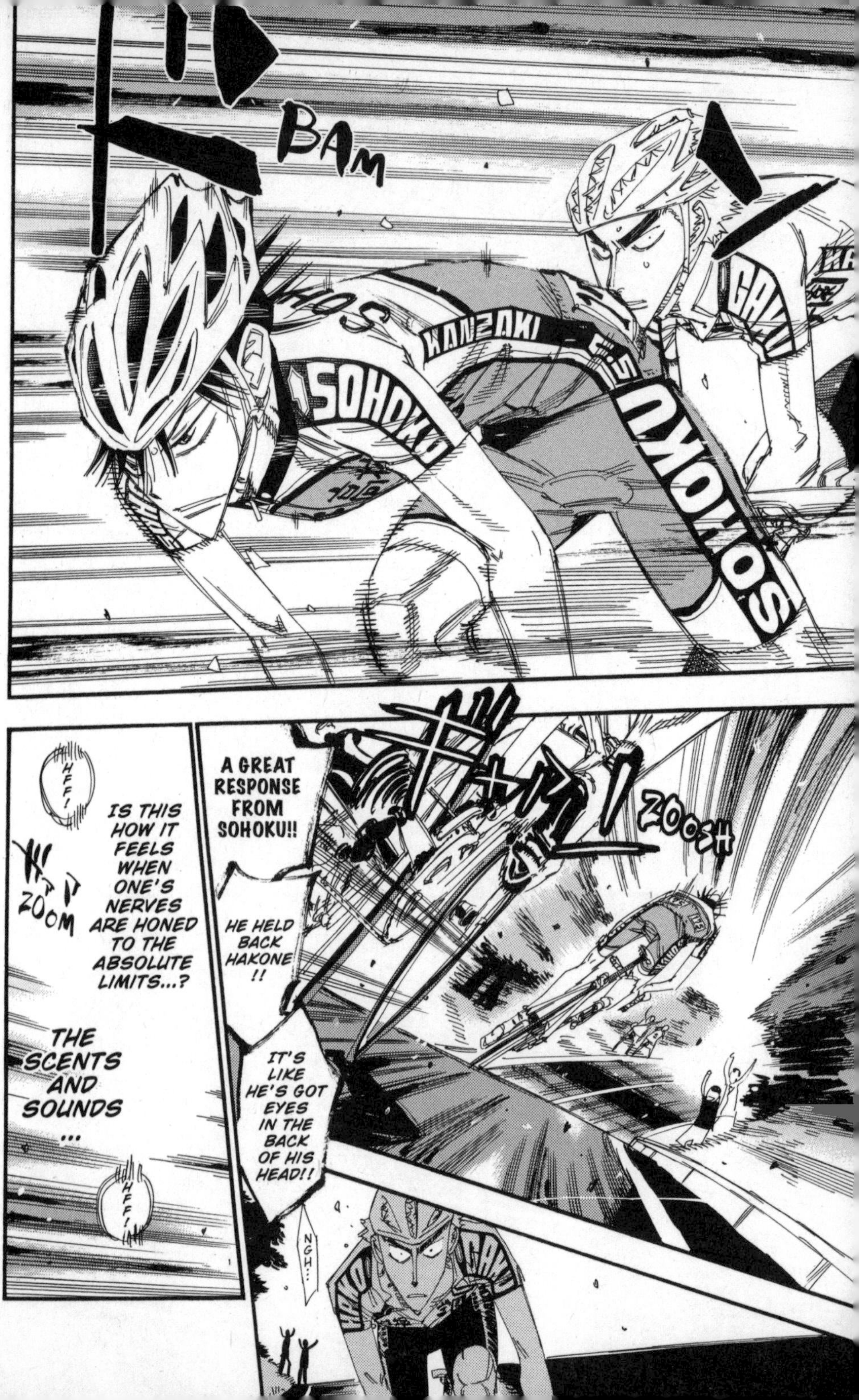
BAM
ZOOSH
A GREAT RESPONSE FROM SOHOKU!!
HE HELD BACK HAKONE!!
IT'S LIKE HE'S GOT EYES IN THE BACK OF HIS HEAD!!
NGH...
HFF!
IS THIS HOW IT FEELS WHEN ONE'S NERVES ARE HONED TO THE ABSOLUTE LIMITS...?
ZOOM
THE SCENTS AND SOUNDS...
HFF!

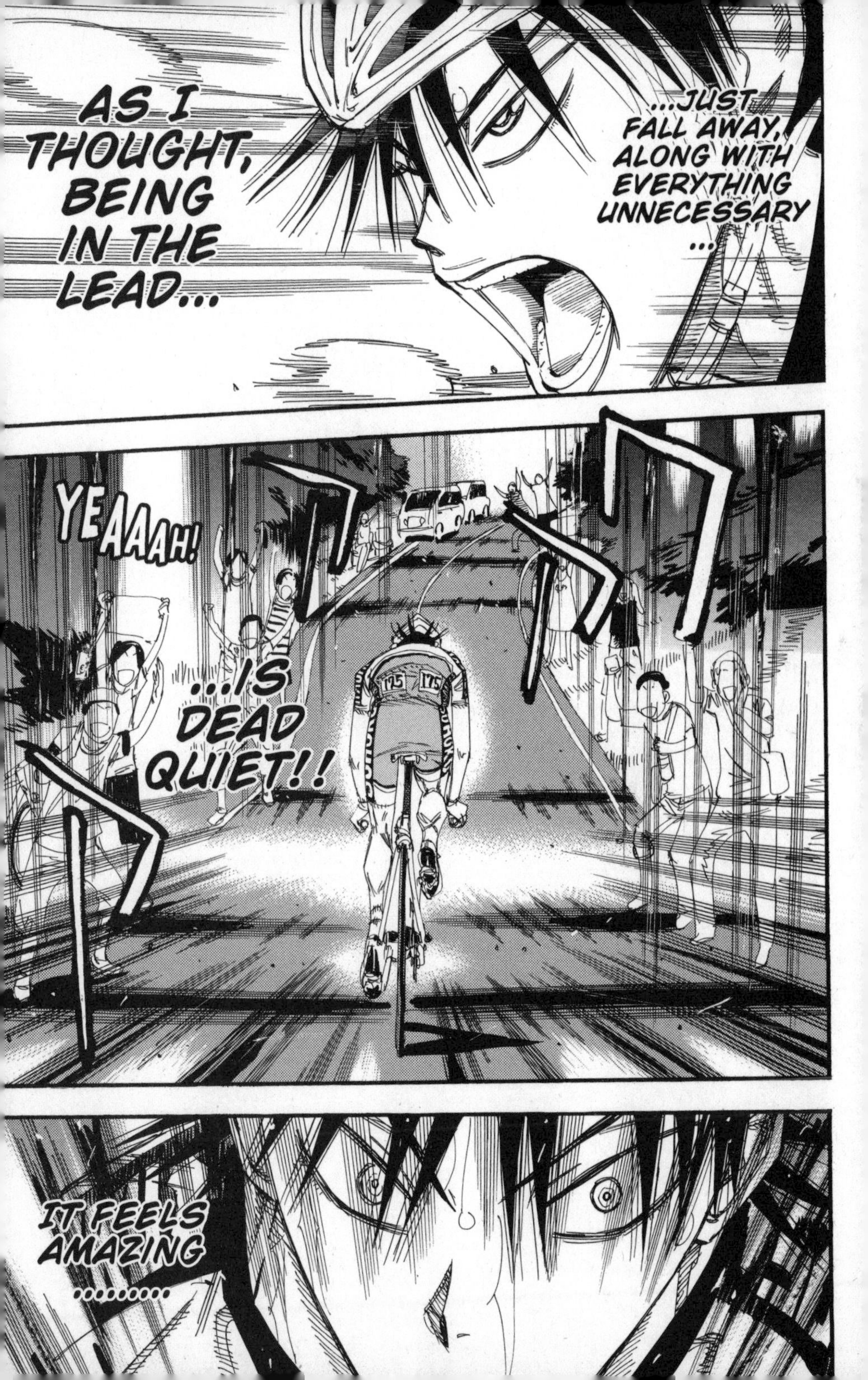
...JUST FALL AWAY, ALONG WITH EVERYTHING UNNECESSARY ...
AS I THOUGHT, BEING IN THE LEAD...
YEAAAH!
...IS DEAD QUIET!!
IT FEELS AMAZING ....

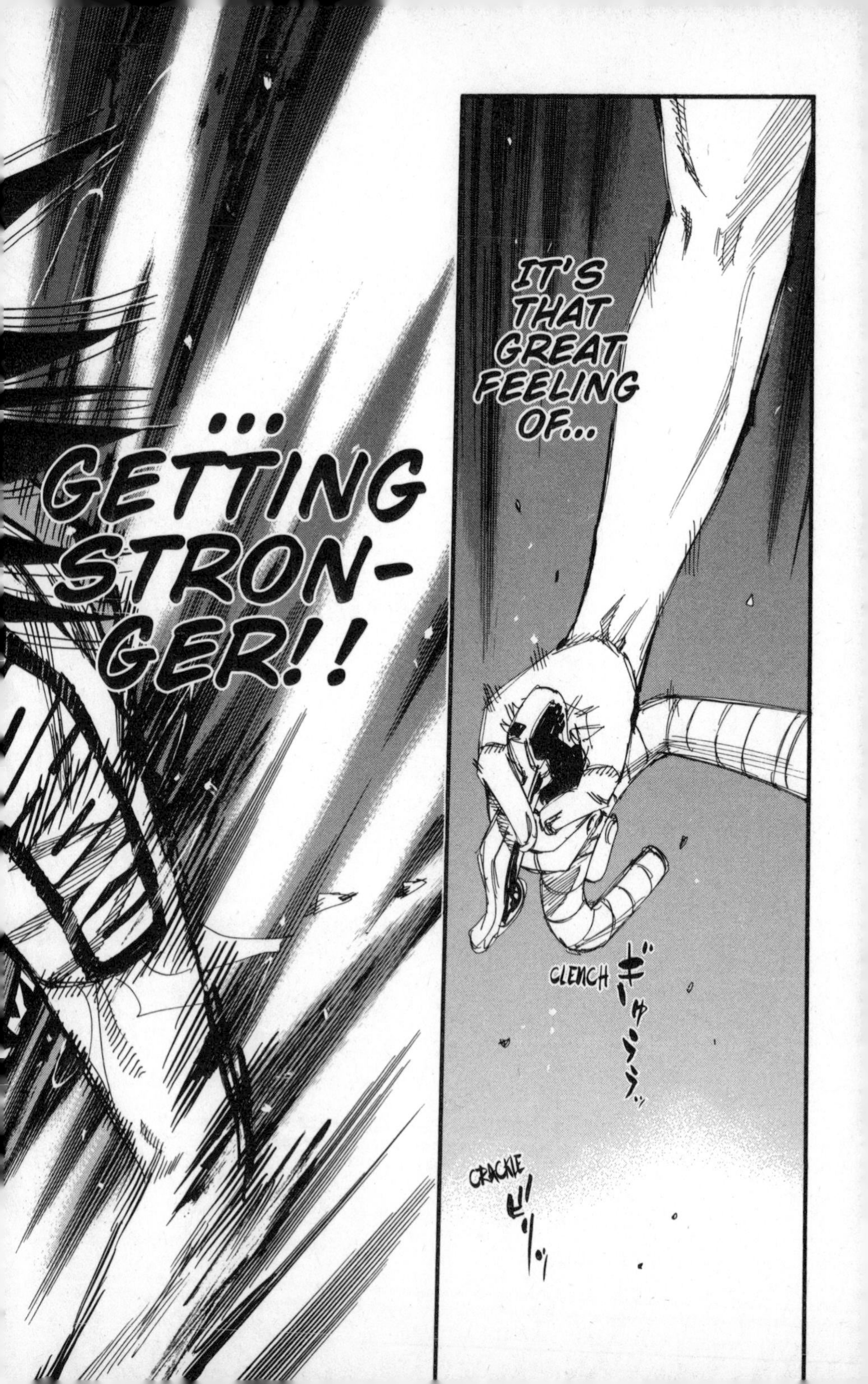
IT'S THAT GREAT FEELING OF...
CLENCH
CRACKLE
...GETTING STRON-GER!!

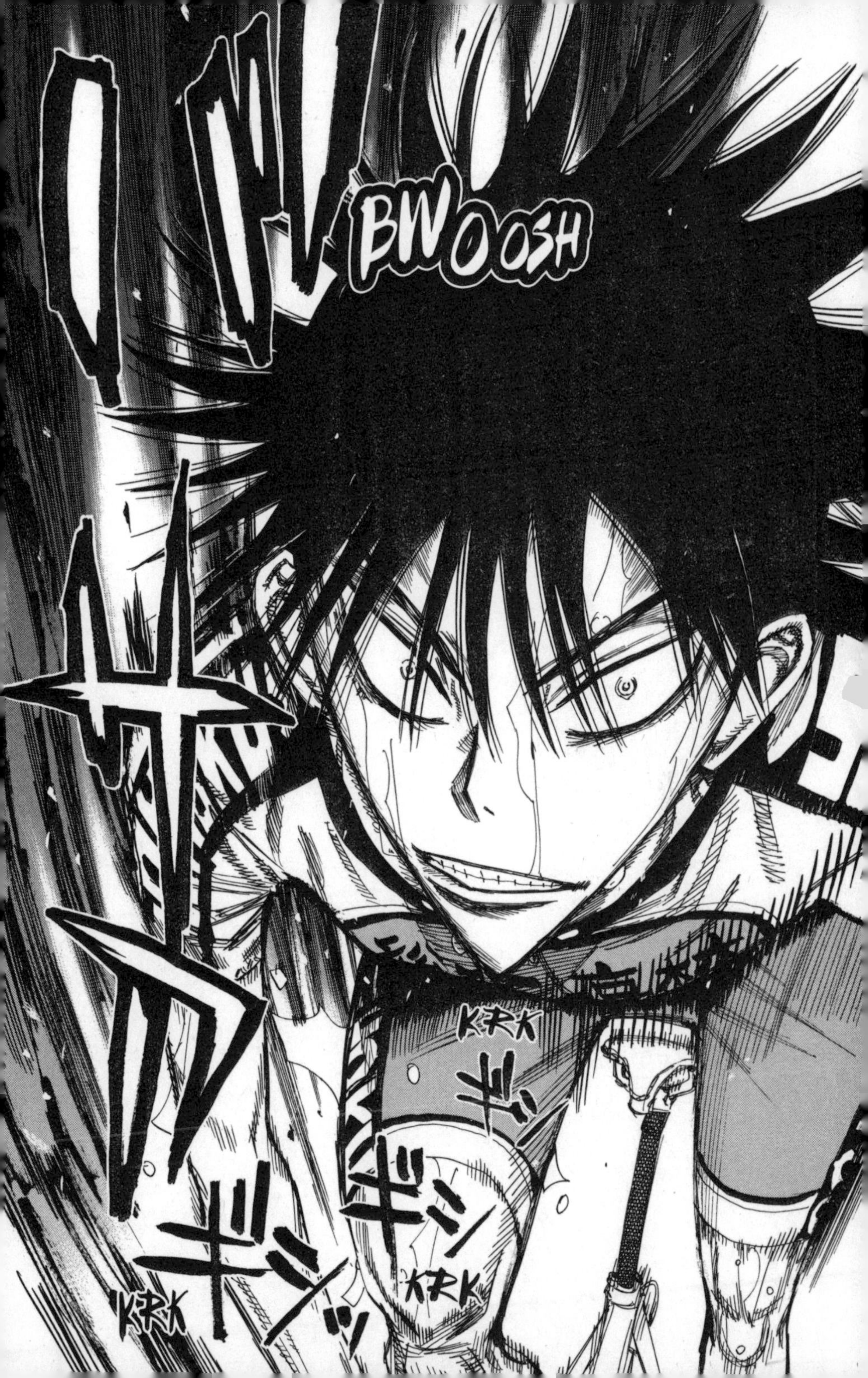
BWOOSH
KRK
KRK
KRK

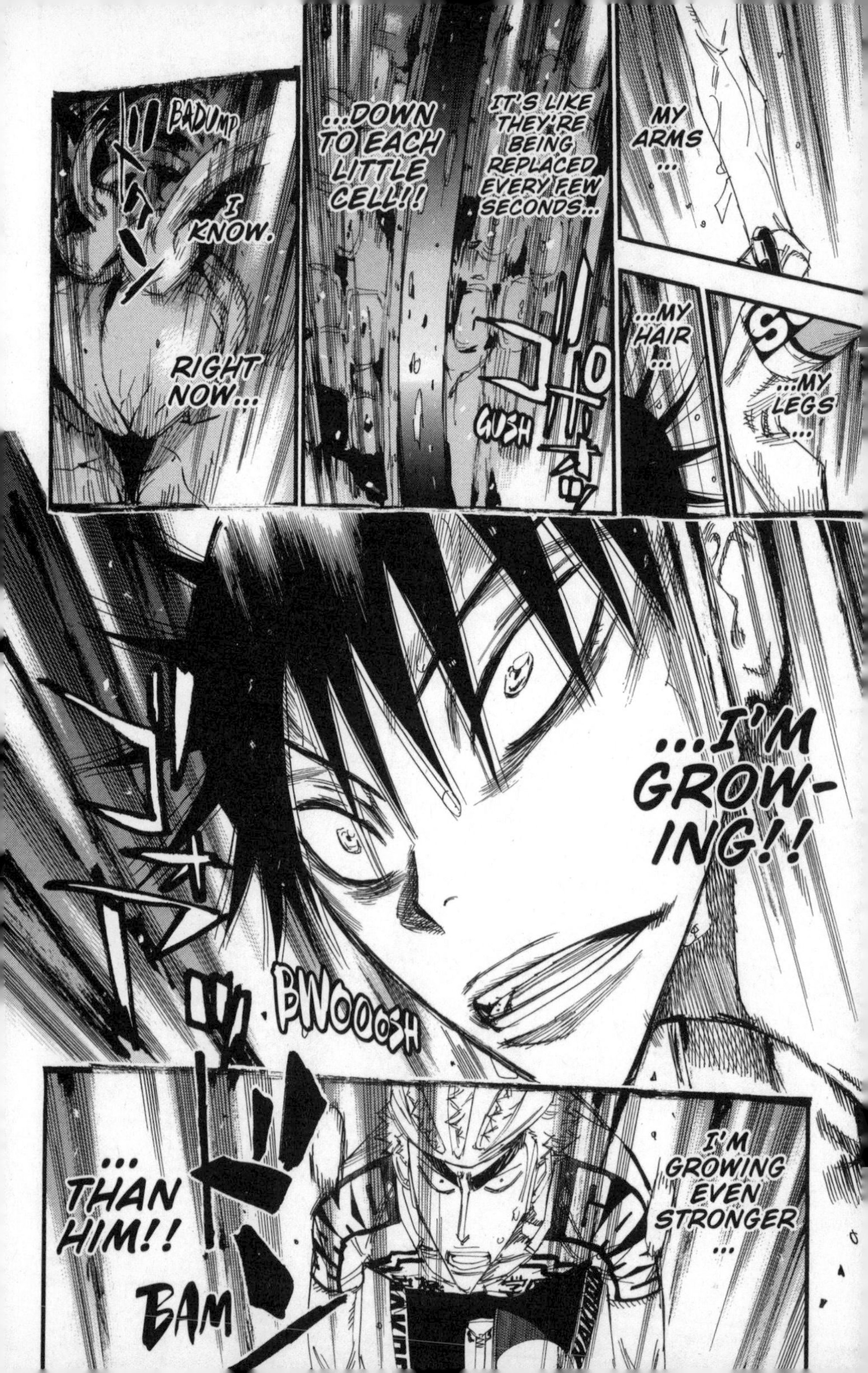
MY ARMS ...
...MY LEGS ...
...MY HAIR ...
IT'S LIKE THEY'RE BEING REPLACED EVERY FEW SECONDS...
...DOWN TO EACH LITTLE CELL!!
GUSH
BADUMP
I KNOW.
RIGHT NOW...
...I'M GROW-ING!!
BWOOOSH
I'M GROWING EVEN STRONGER ...
... THAN HIM!!
BAM

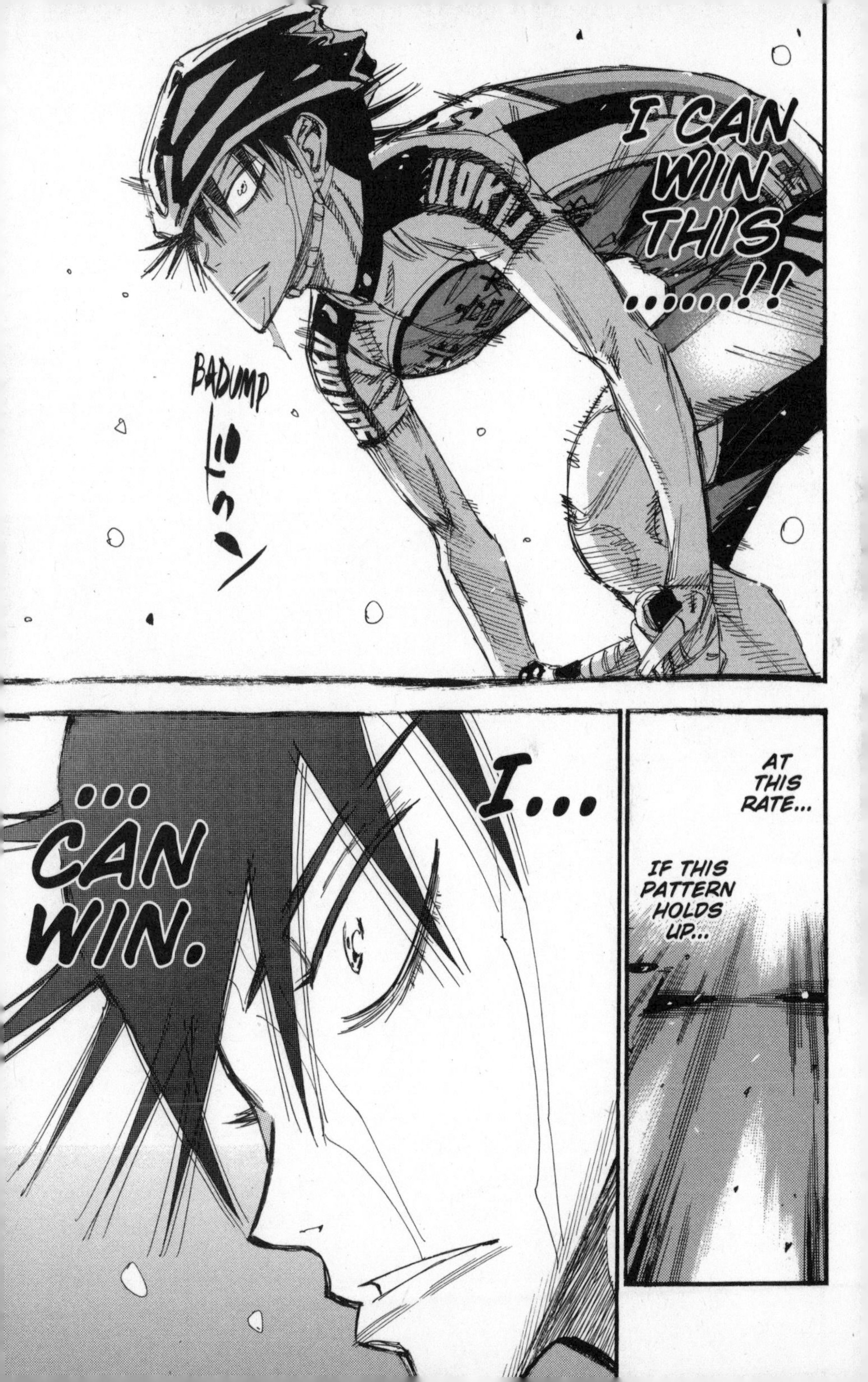
I CAN WIN THIS ......!!
BADUMP
AT THIS RATE...
IF THIS PATTERN HOLDS UP...
I...
...CAN WIN.

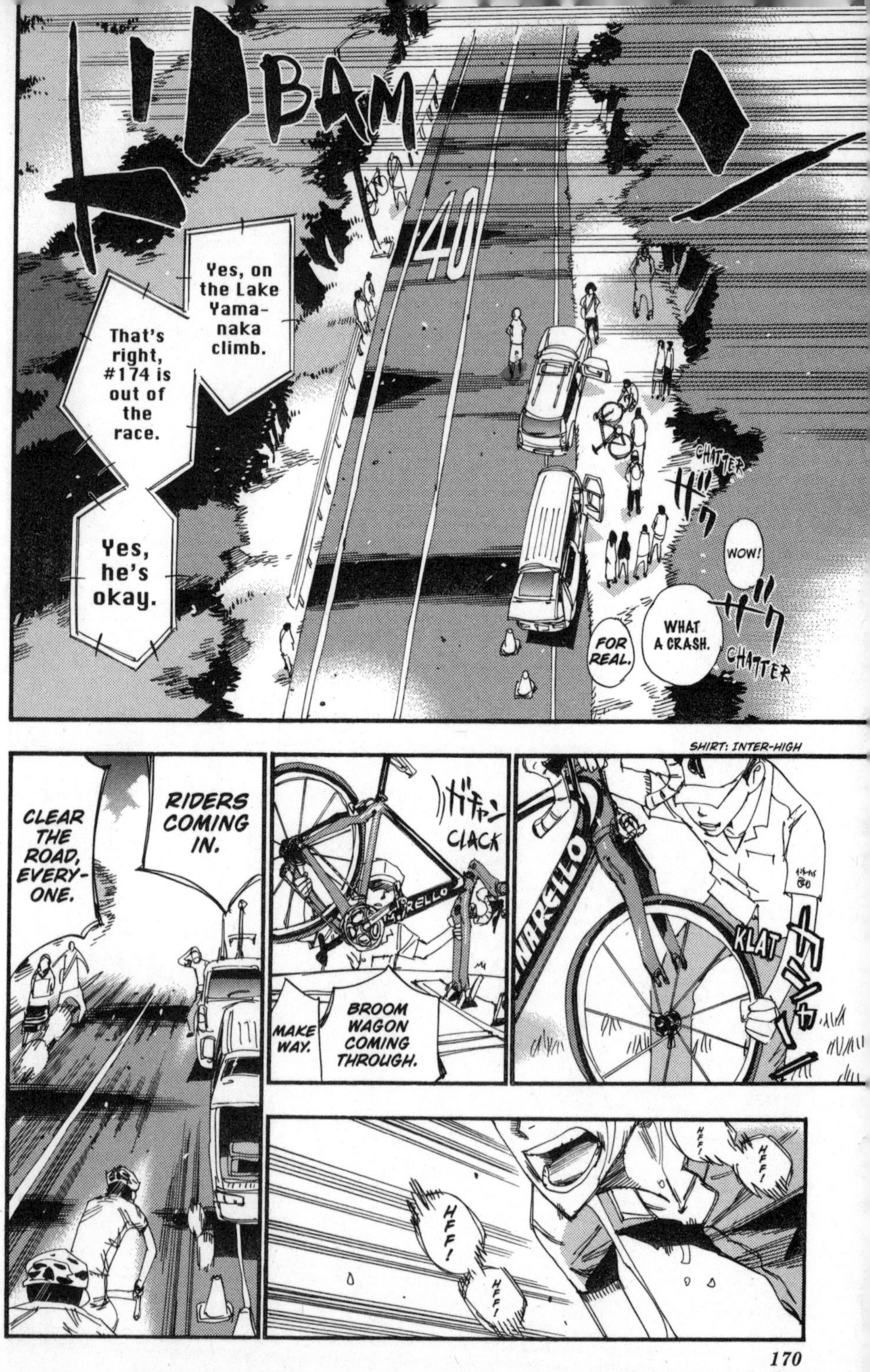
BAM
Yes, on the Lake Yamanaka climb.
That's right, #174 is out of the race.
Yes, he's okay.
CHATTER
WOW!
WHAT A CRASH.
FOR REAL.
CHATTER
SHIRT: INTER-HIGH
KLAT
CLACK
BROOM WAGON COMING THROUGH.
MAKE WAY.
HFF!
HFF!
HFF!
HFF!
RIDERS COMING IN.
CLEAR THE ROAD, EVERY-ONE.

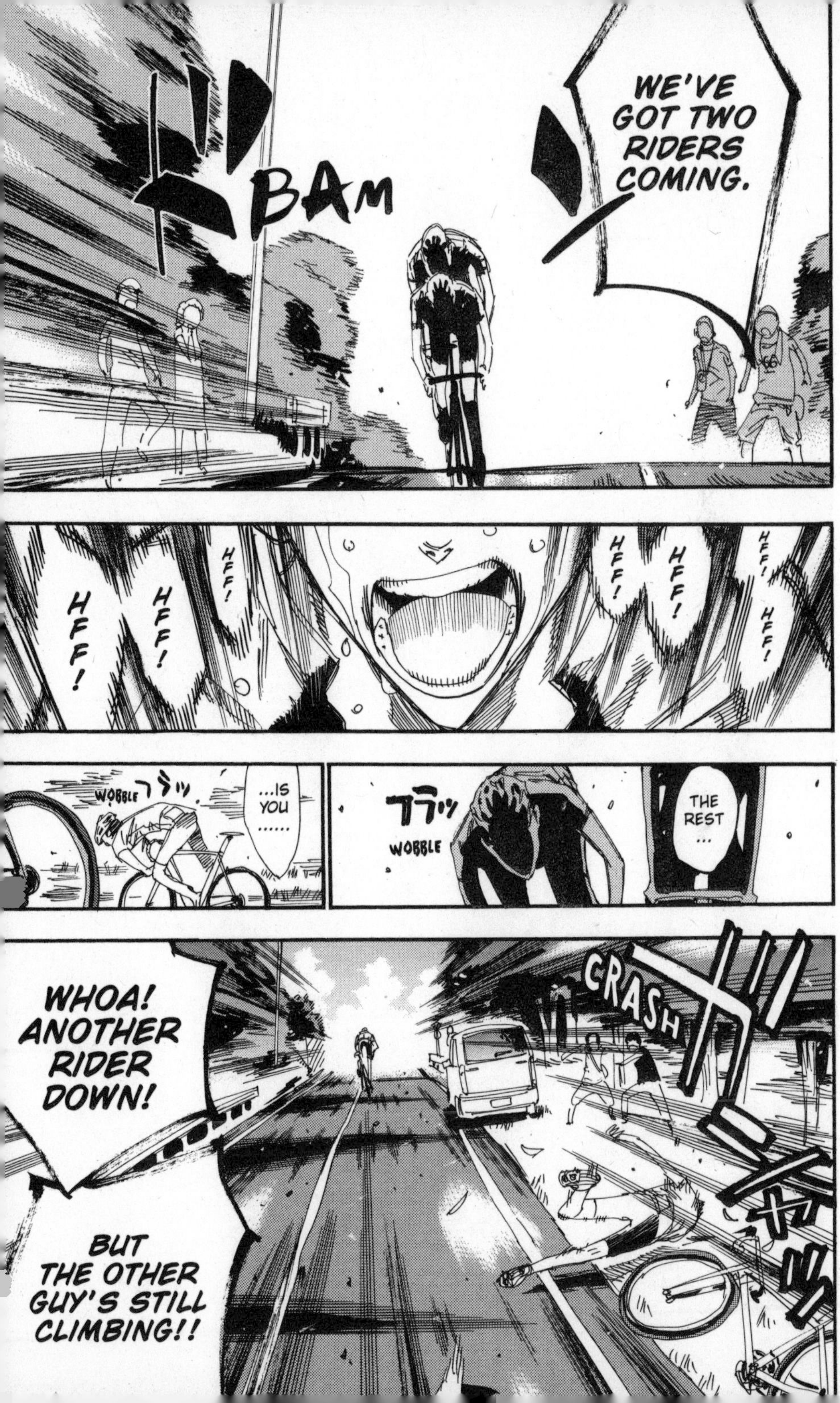
WE'VE GOT TWO RIDERS COMING.
BAM
HFF! HFF!
HFF! HFF!
HFF! HFF! HFF!
THE REST ...
フラッ
WOBBLE
...IS YOU ......
WOBBLE フラッ
CRASH
WHOA! ANOTHER RIDER DOWN!
BUT THE OTHER GUY'S STILL CLIMBING!!

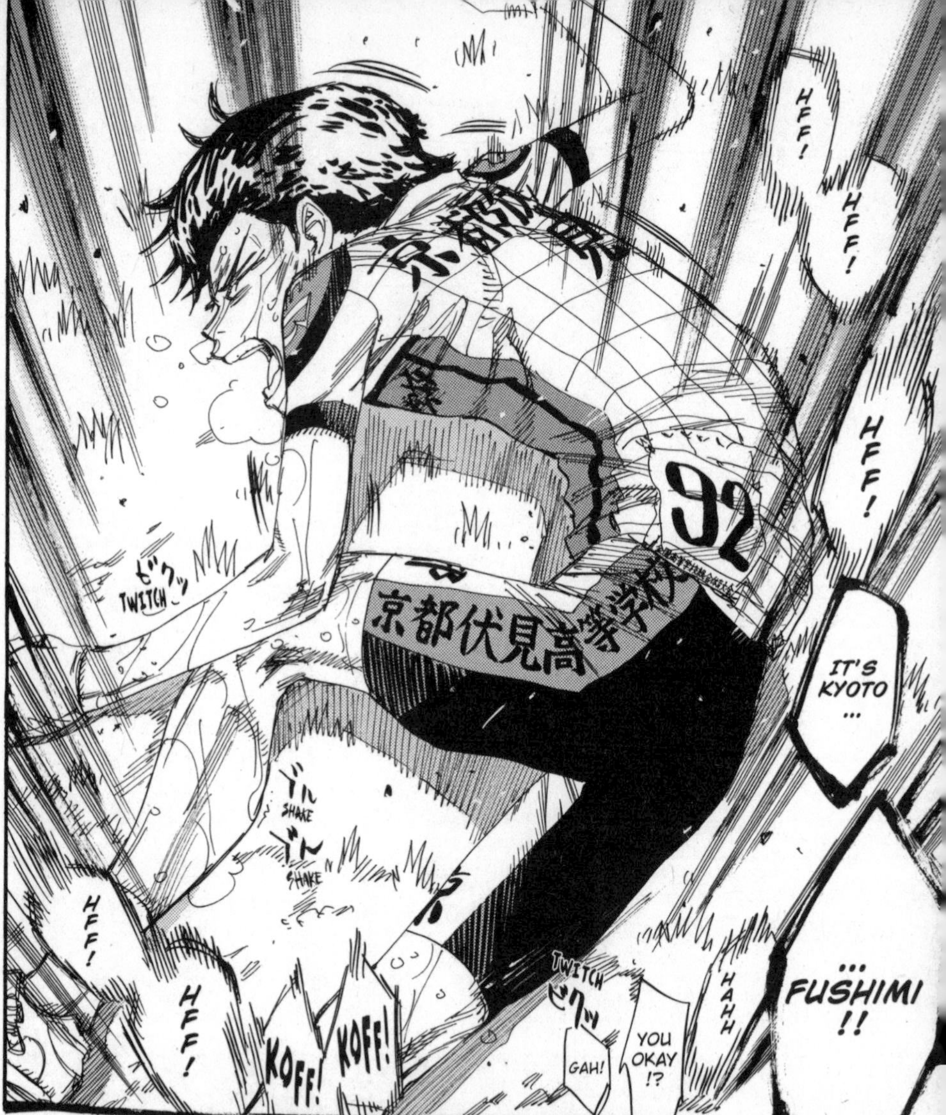
HFF!
HFF!
HFF!
IT'S KYOTO...
...FUSHIMI!!
HAHH
YOU OKAY!?
GAH!
TWITCH
KOFF!
KOFF!
HFF!
HFF!
SHAKE
SHAKE
TWITCH
京都伏見高等学校

JERSEY: KYOTO-FUSHIMI HIGH SCHOOL

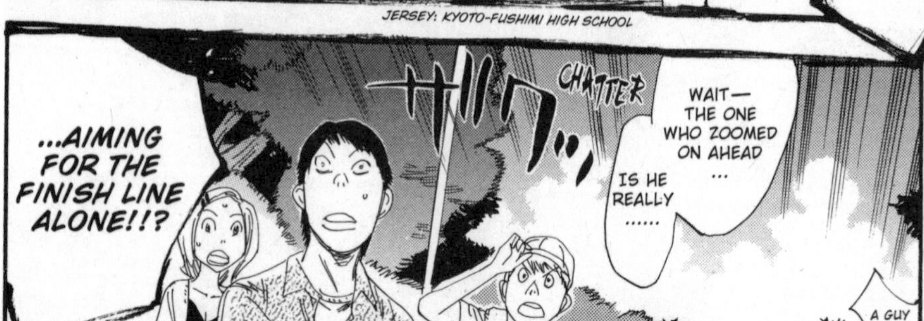
A GUY FELL!
CHATTER
WAIT— THE ONE WHO ZOOMED ON AHEAD...
IS HE REALLY......
CHATTER
...AIMING FOR THE FINISH LINE ALONE!!?

RIDE.199 TENACIOUS GUY

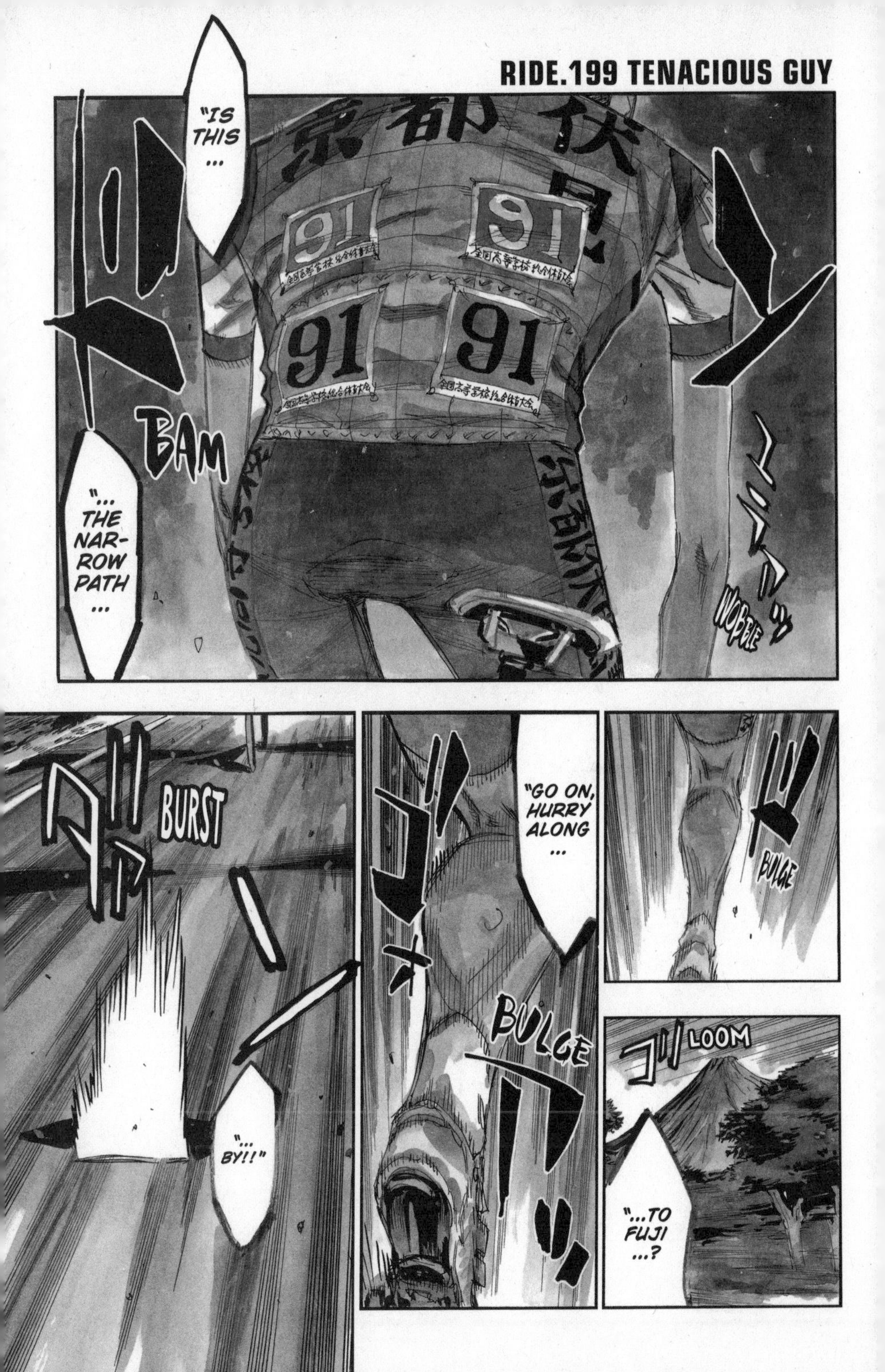
"IS THIS ...
BAM
"... THE NAR-ROW PATH ...
WOBBLE
BULGE
LOOM
"...TO FUJI ...?
"GO ON, HURRY ALONG ...
BULGE
BURST
"... BY!!"

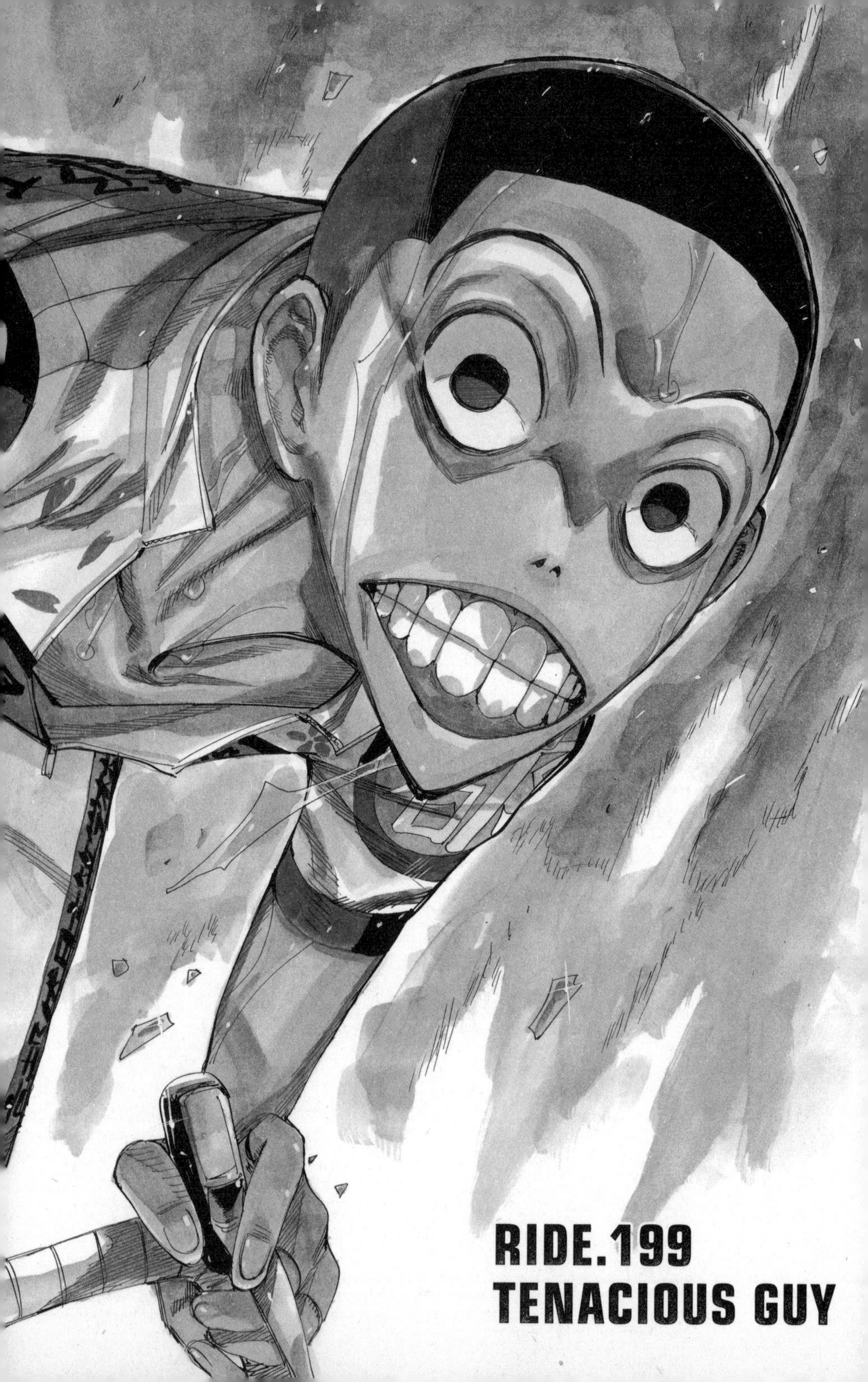

RIDE.199
TENACIOUS GUY

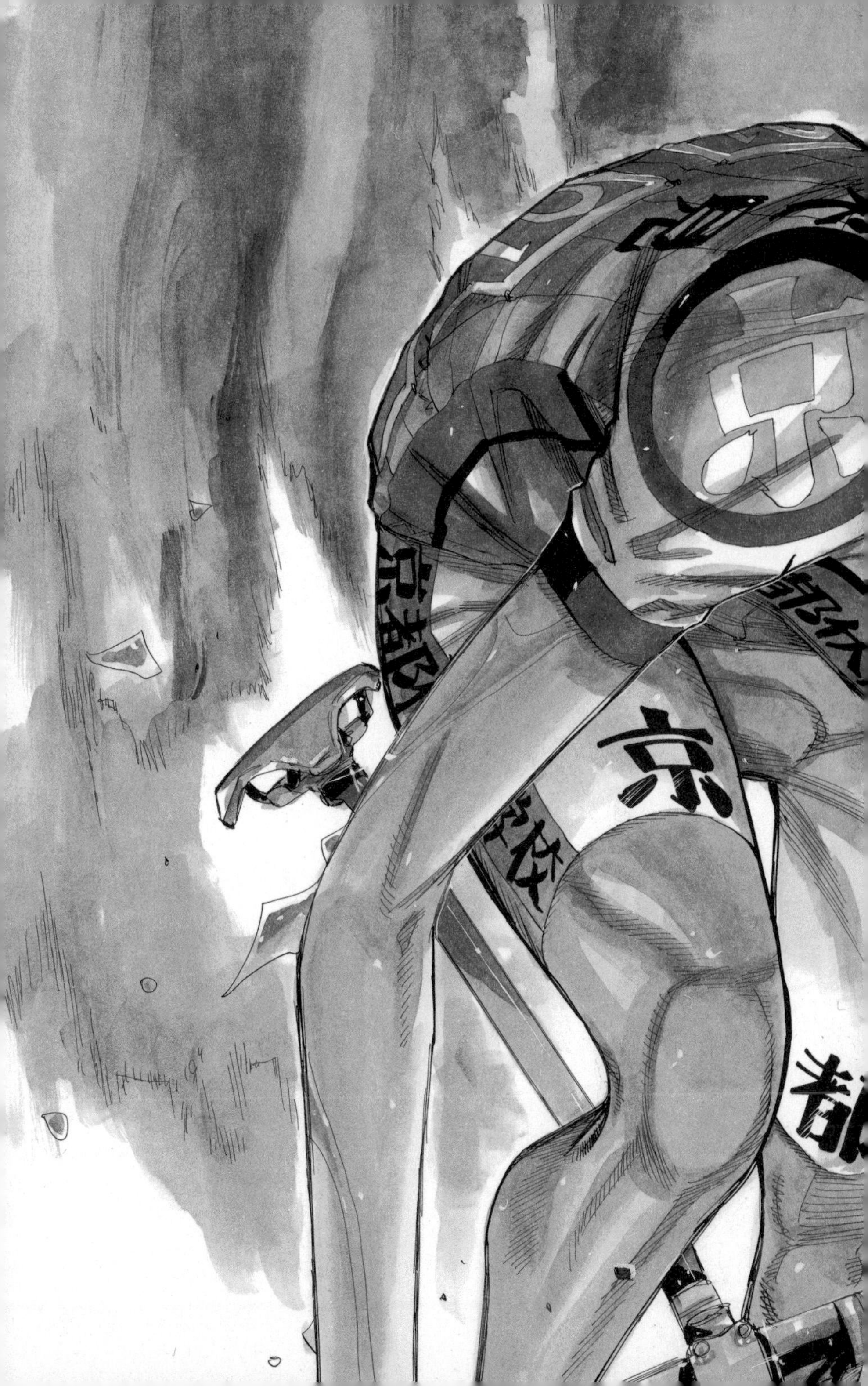

SHUNSUKE IMAIZUMI

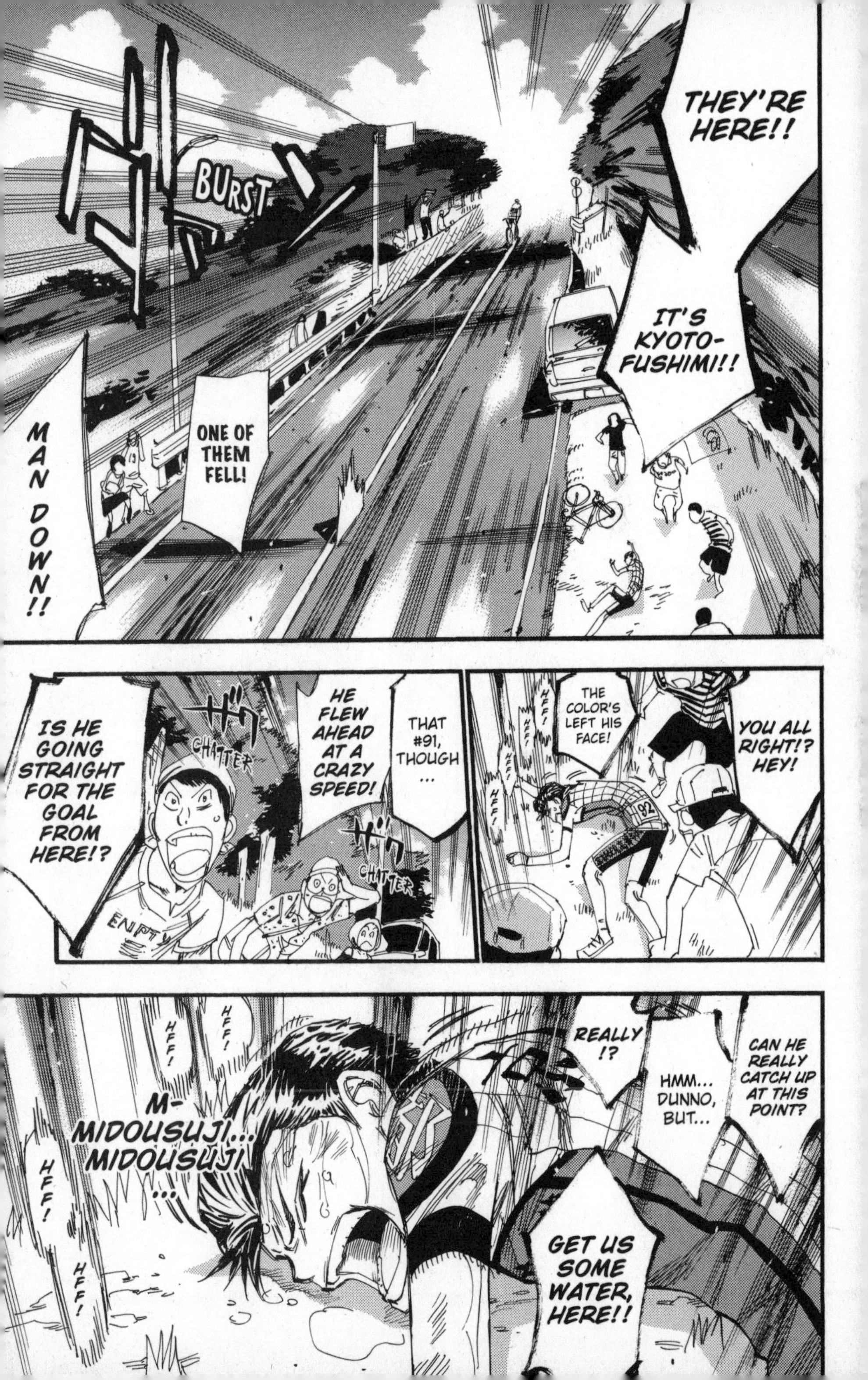
THEY'RE HERE!!
IT'S KYOTO-FUSHIMI!!
BURST
ONE OF THEM FELL!
MAN DOWN!!
YOU ALL RIGHT!? HEY!
THE COLOR'S LEFT HIS FACE!
HFF! HFF!
HFF! HFF!
THAT #91, THOUGH...
HE FLEW AHEAD AT A CRAZY SPEED!
CHATTER
IS HE GOING STRAIGHT FOR THE GOAL FROM HERE!?
CHATTER
CAN HE REALLY CATCH UP AT THIS POINT?
HMM... DUNNO, BUT...
REALLY!?
GET US SOME WATER, HERE!!
HFF! HFF!
M-MIDOUSUJI... MIDOUSUJI...
HFF! HFF!

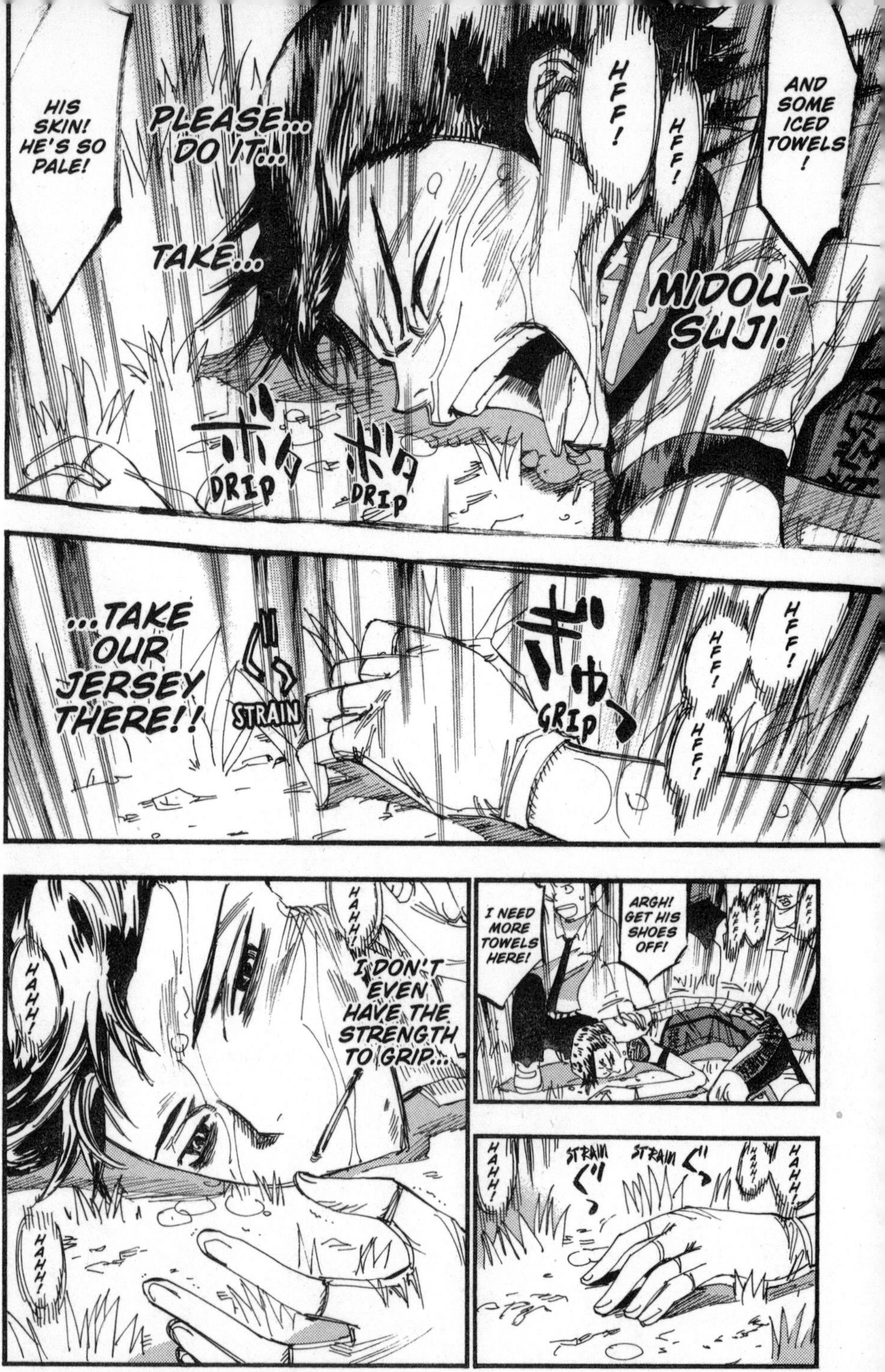
AND SOME ICED TOWELS!
HFF!
HFF!
MIDOU-SUJI.
PLEASE... DO IT...
HIS SKIN! HE'S SO PALE!
TAKE...
DRIP
DRIP
HFF!
HFF!
HFF!
GRIP
STRAIN
...TAKE OUR JERSEY THERE!!
HFF!
ARGH! GET HIS SHOES OFF!
I NEED MORE TOWELS HERE!
HAHH!
HAHH!
STRAIN
STRAIN
HAHH!
I DON'T EVEN HAVE THE STRENGTH TO GRIP...
HAHH!
HAHH!

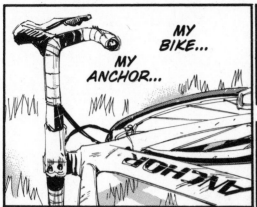

MY BIKE...

MY ANCHOR...

CALL THE BASE.

HURRY!

HAHH!

HAHH!

HAHH!

HAHH!

CLENCH

HAHH!

HAHH!

HAHH!

HAHH!

HAHH!

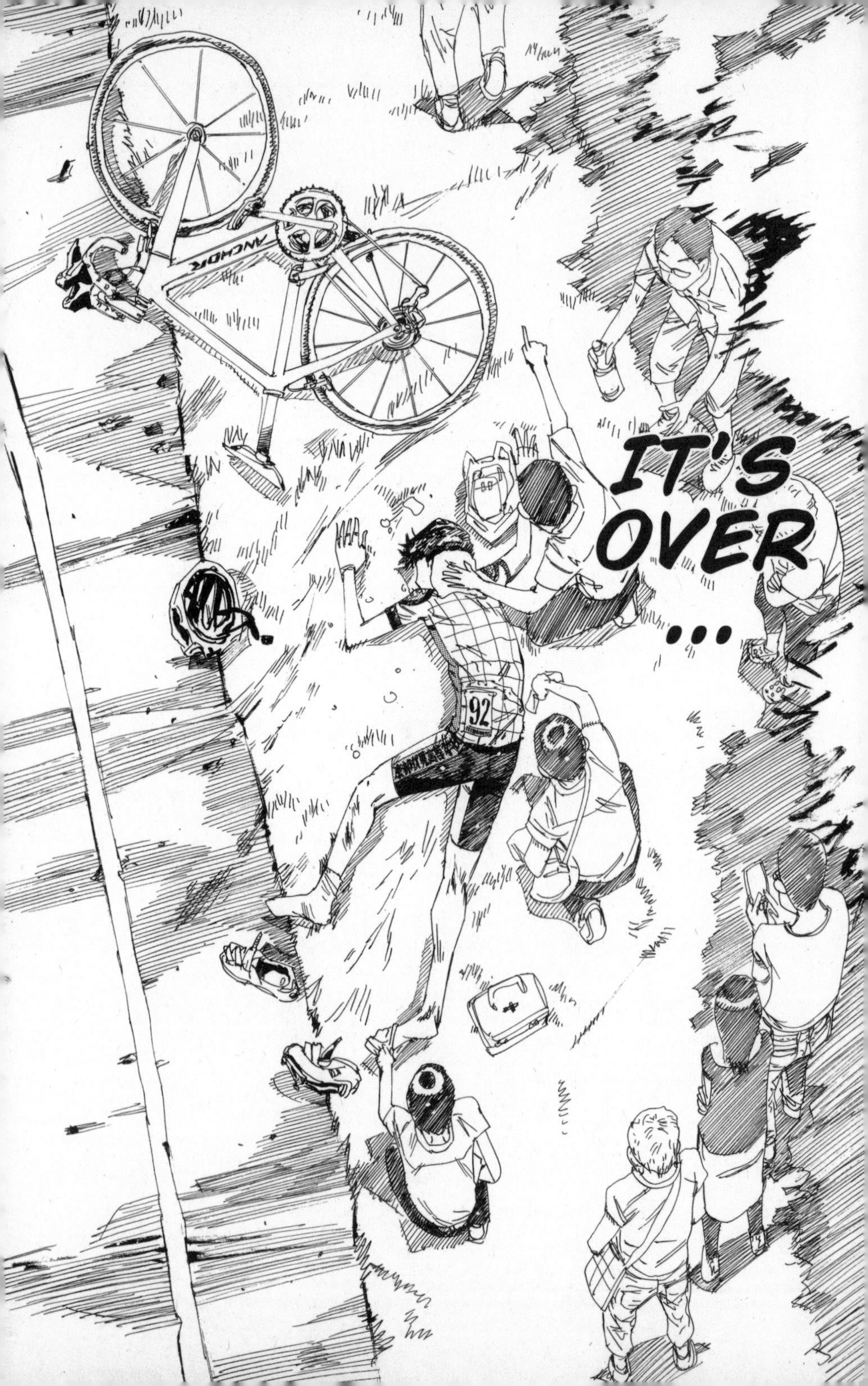
IT'S OVER
...

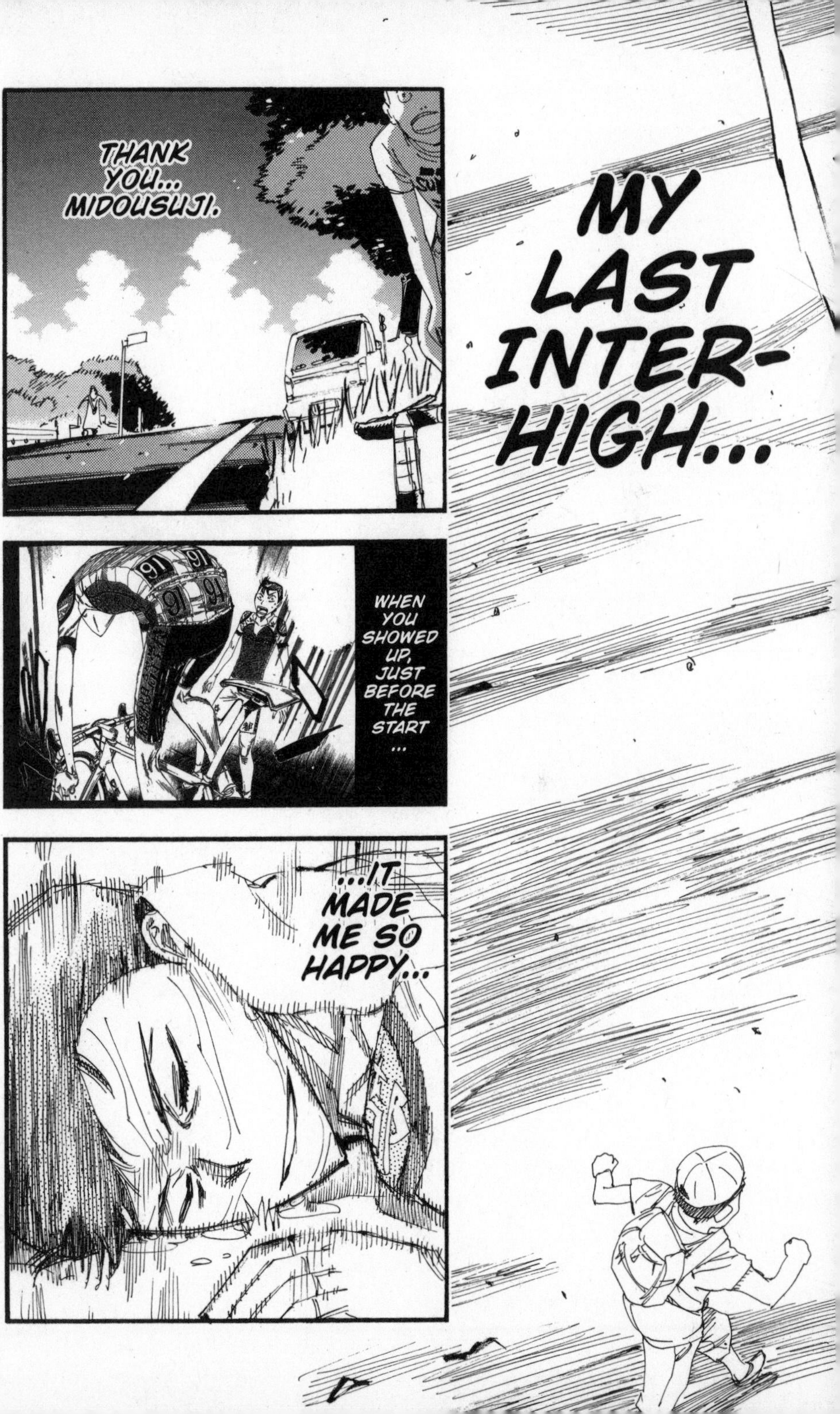
MY LAST INTER-HIGH...
THANK YOU... MIDOUSUJI.
WHEN YOU SHOWED UP, JUST BEFORE THE START...
...IT MADE ME SO HAPPY...

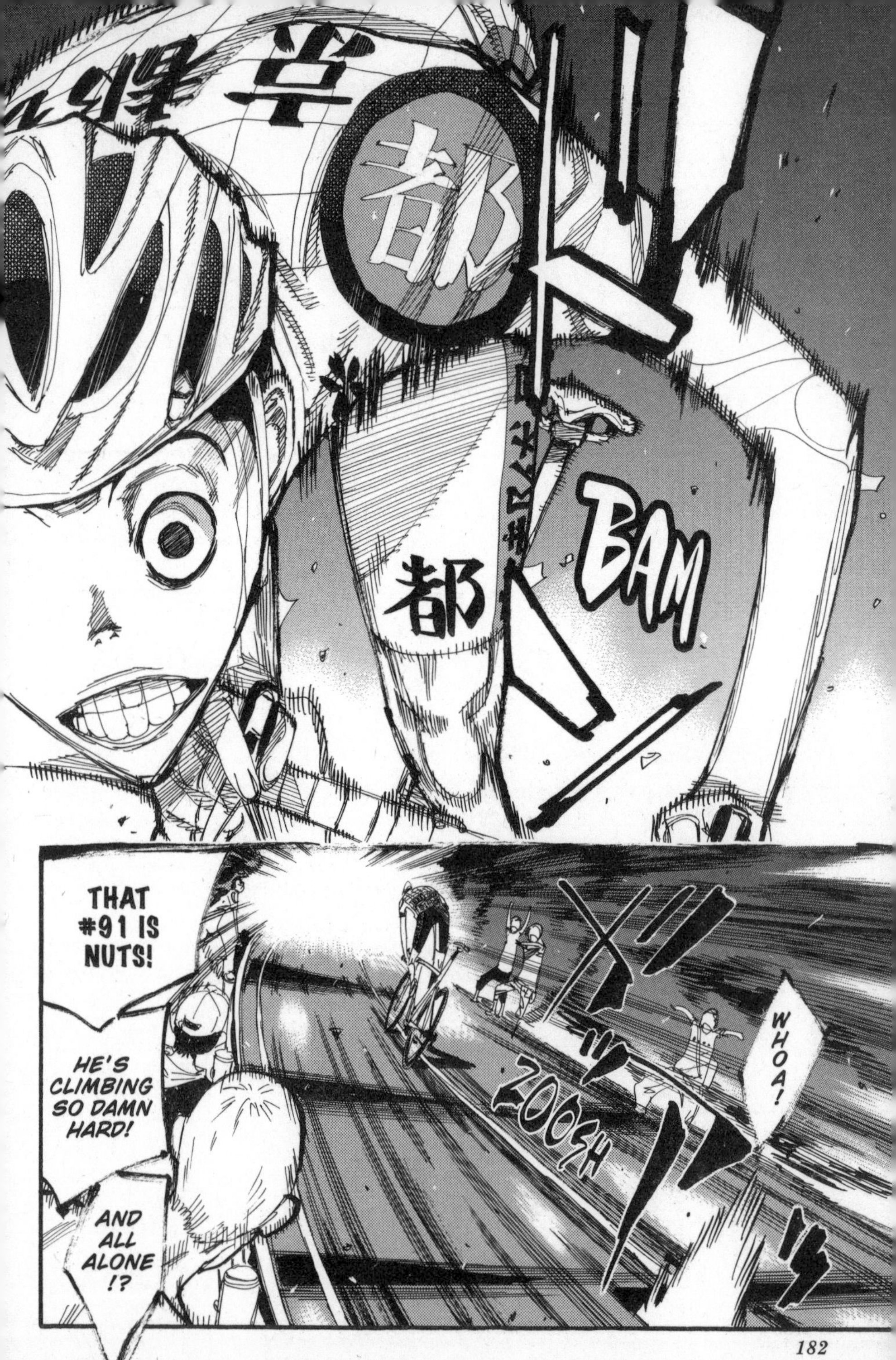

都
BAM
WHOA!
ZOOSH
THAT #91 IS NUTS!
HE'S CLIMBING SO DAMN HARD!
AND ALL ALONE !?

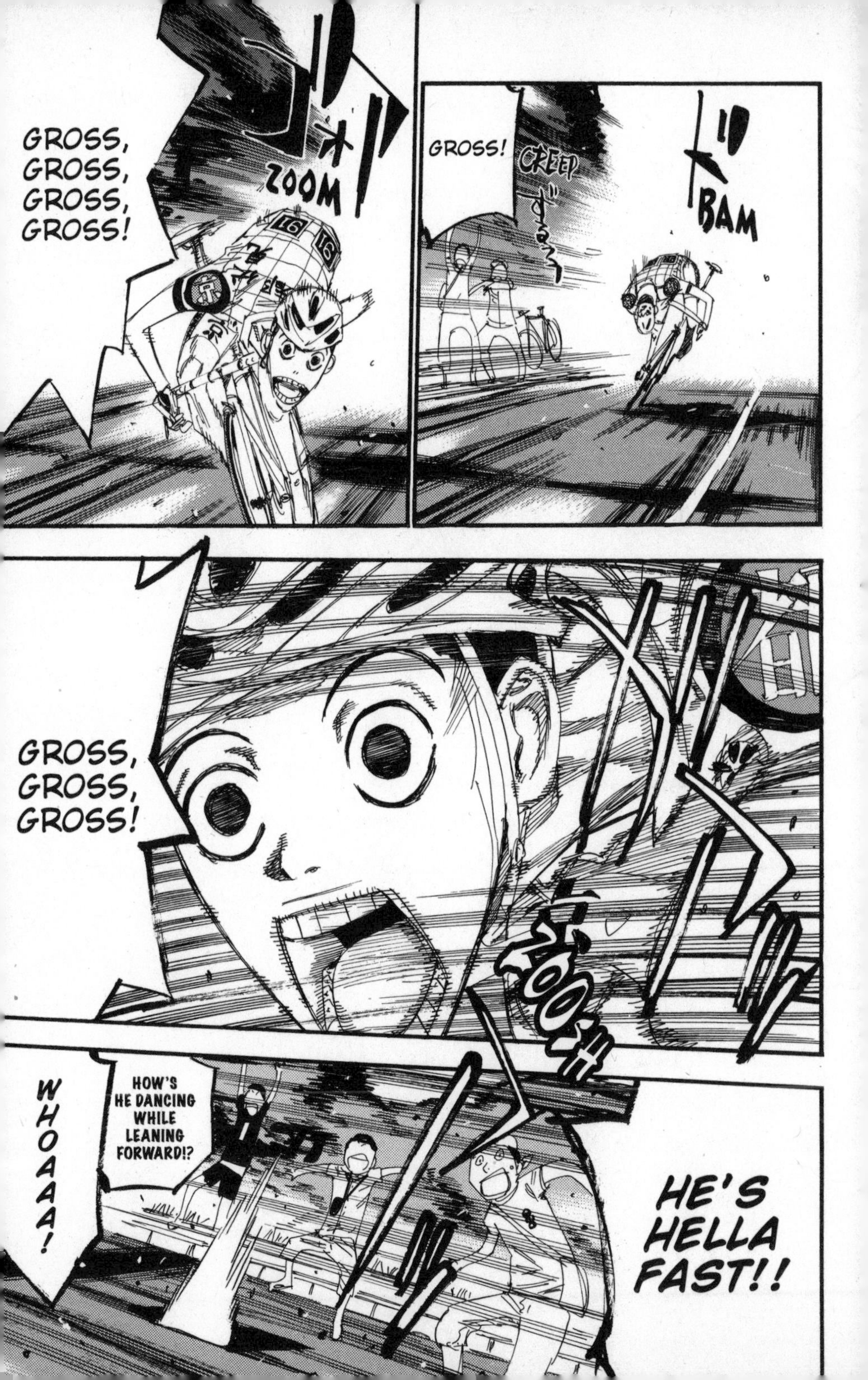
GROSS!
CREEP
BAM
GROSS, GROSS, GROSS, GROSS!
ZOOM
GROSS, GROSS, GROSS!
ZOOOSH
HE'S HELLA FAST!!
HOW'S HE DANCING WHILE LEANING FORWARD!?
WHOAAAA!

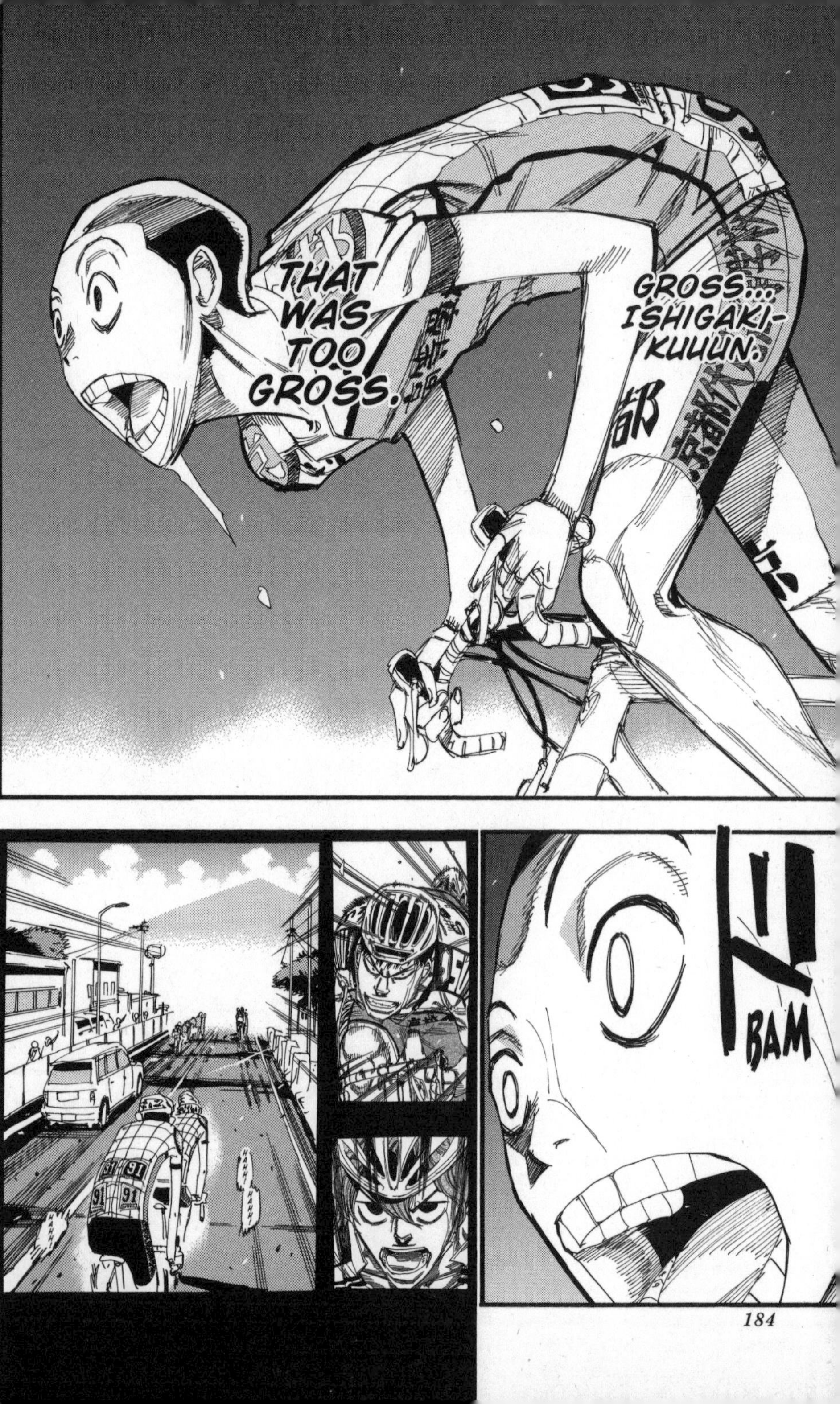
GROSS... ISHIGAKI-KUUUN.
THAT WAS TOO GROSS.
BAM

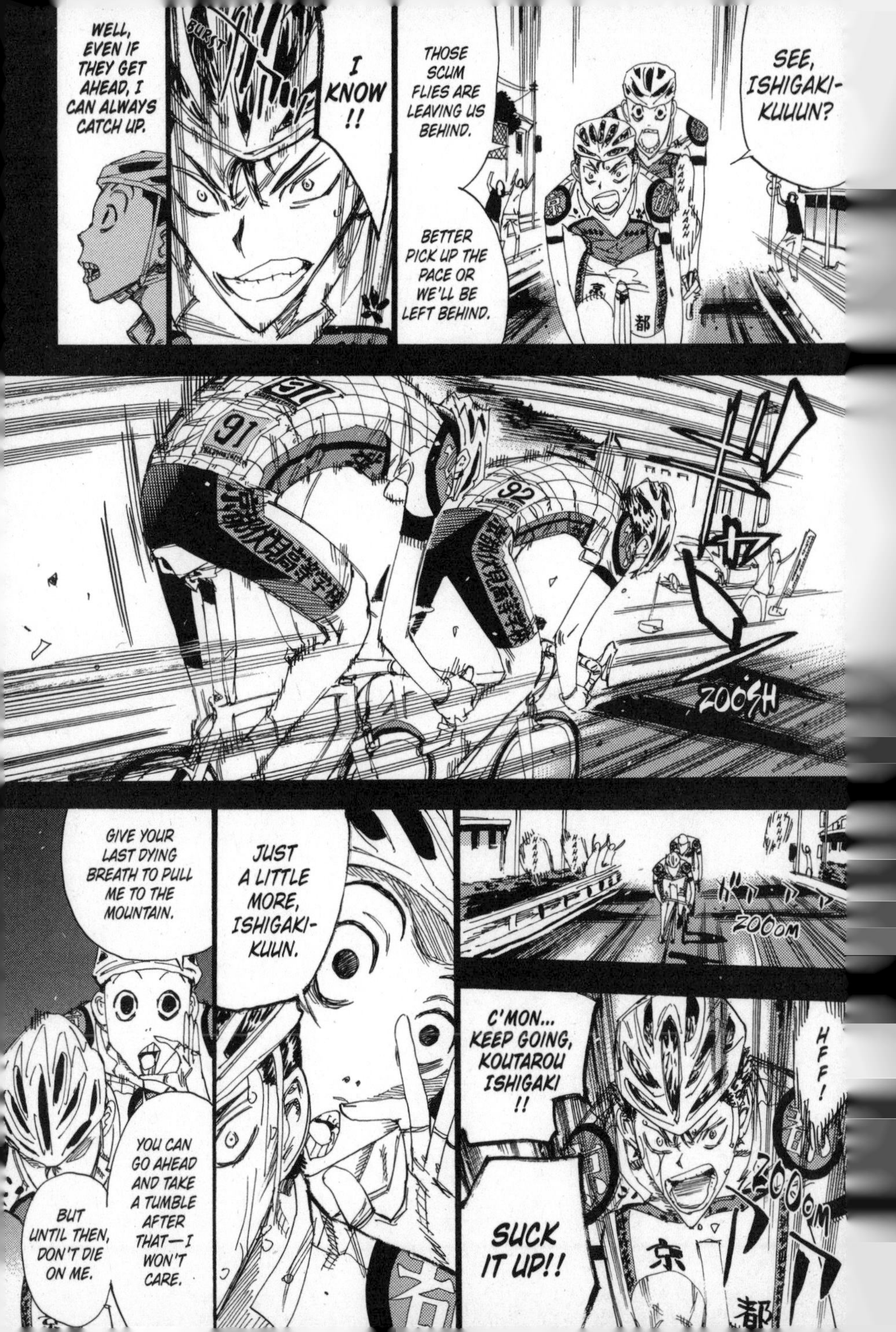
SEE, ISHIGAKI-KUUUN?
THOSE SCUM FLIES ARE LEAVING US BEHIND.
BETTER PICK UP THE PACE OR WE'LL BE LEFT BEHIND.
BURST
I KNOW !!
WELL, EVEN IF THEY GET AHEAD, I CAN ALWAYS CATCH UP.
ZOOSH
ZOOOM
HFF!
C'MON... KEEP GOING, KOUTAROU ISHIGAKI !!
ZOOOM
SUCK IT UP!!
JUST A LITTLE MORE, ISHIGAKI-KUUN.
GIVE YOUR LAST DYING BREATH TO PULL ME TO THE MOUNTAIN.
YOU CAN GO AHEAD AND TAKE A TUMBLE AFTER THAT—I WON'T CARE.
BUT UNTIL THEN, DON'T DIE ON ME.

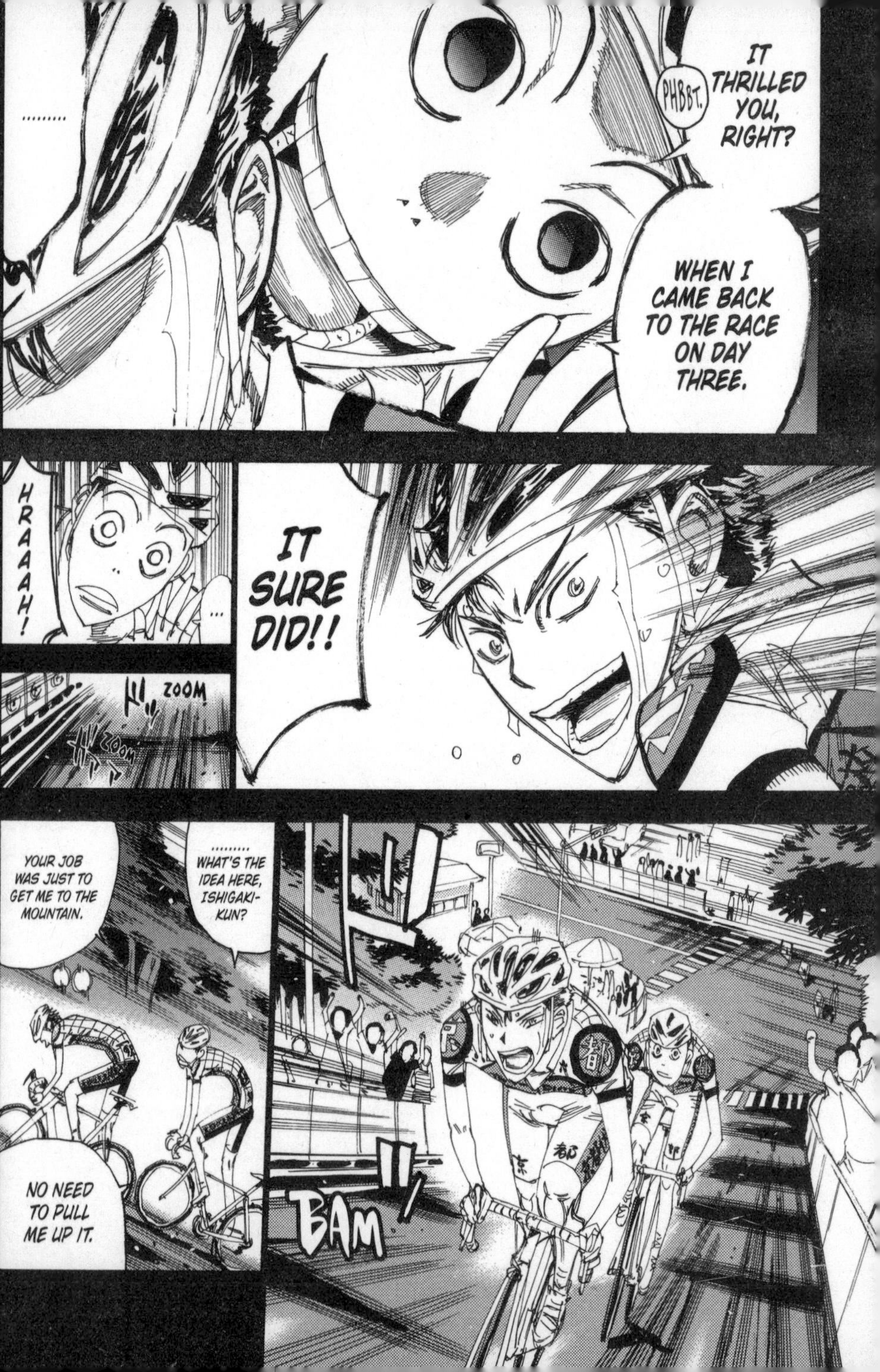
PHBBT.
IT THRILLED YOU, RIGHT?
WHEN I CAME BACK TO THE RACE ON DAY THREE.
....
IT SURE DID!!
HRAAAAH!
...
ZOOM
ZOOM
BAM
.... WHAT'S THE IDEA HERE, ISHIGAKI-KUN?
YOUR JOB WAS JUST TO GET ME TO THE MOUNTAIN.
NO NEED TO PULL ME UP IT.

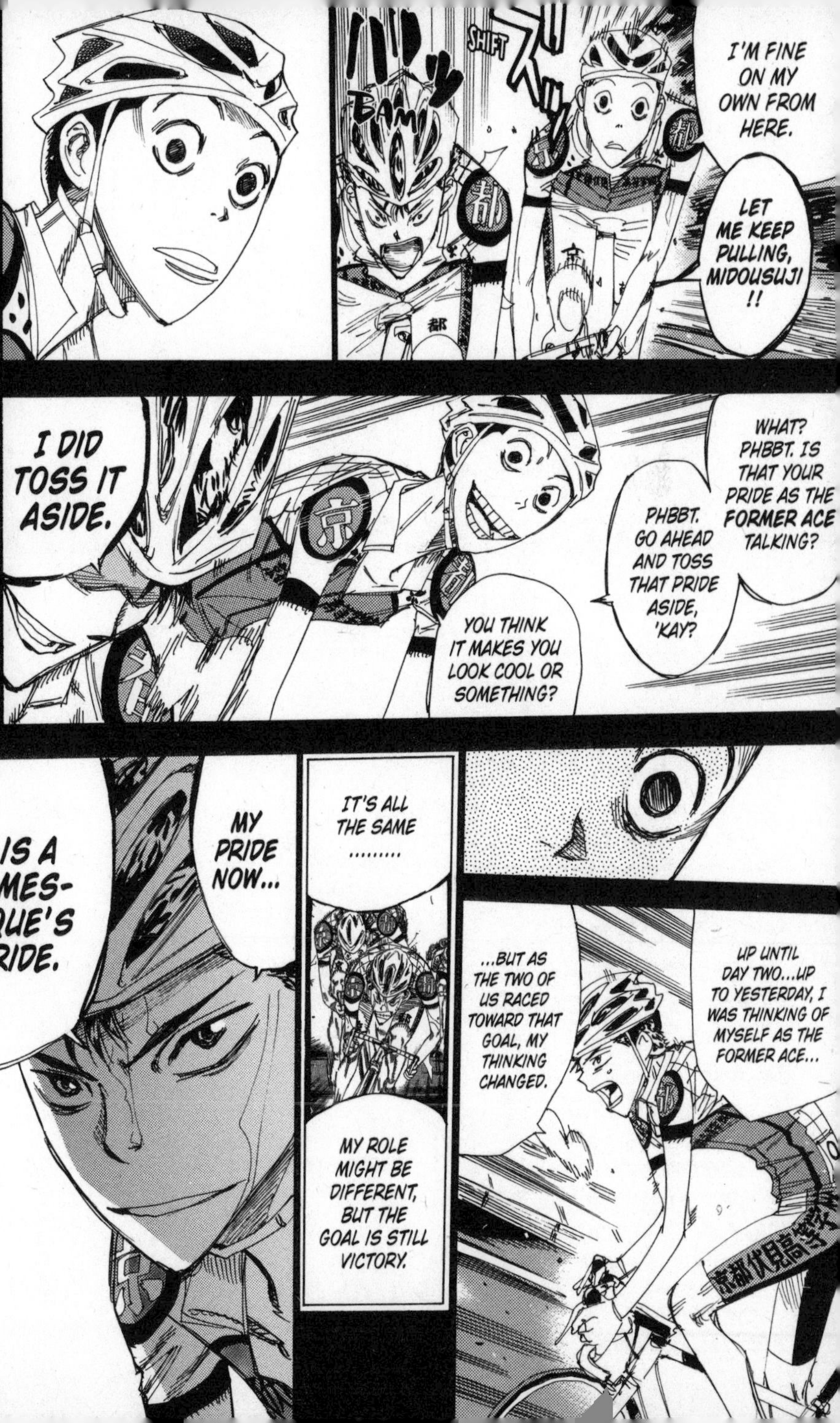
I'M FINE ON MY OWN FROM HERE.
LET ME KEEP PULLING, MIDOUSUJI!!
SHIFT
BAM
WHAT? PHBBT. IS THAT YOUR PRIDE AS THE FORMER ACE TALKING?
PHBBT. GO AHEAD AND TOSS THAT PRIDE ASIDE, 'KAY?
YOU THINK IT MAKES YOU LOOK COOL OR SOMETHING?
I DID TOSS IT ASIDE.
UP UNTIL DAY TWO...UP TO YESTERDAY, I WAS THINKING OF MYSELF AS THE FORMER ACE...
...BUT AS THE TWO OF US RACED TOWARD THAT GOAL, MY THINKING CHANGED.
IT'S ALL THE SAME ....
MY ROLE MIGHT BE DIFFERENT, BUT THE GOAL IS STILL VICTORY.
MY PRIDE NOW...
...IS A DOMES-TIQUE'S PRIDE.

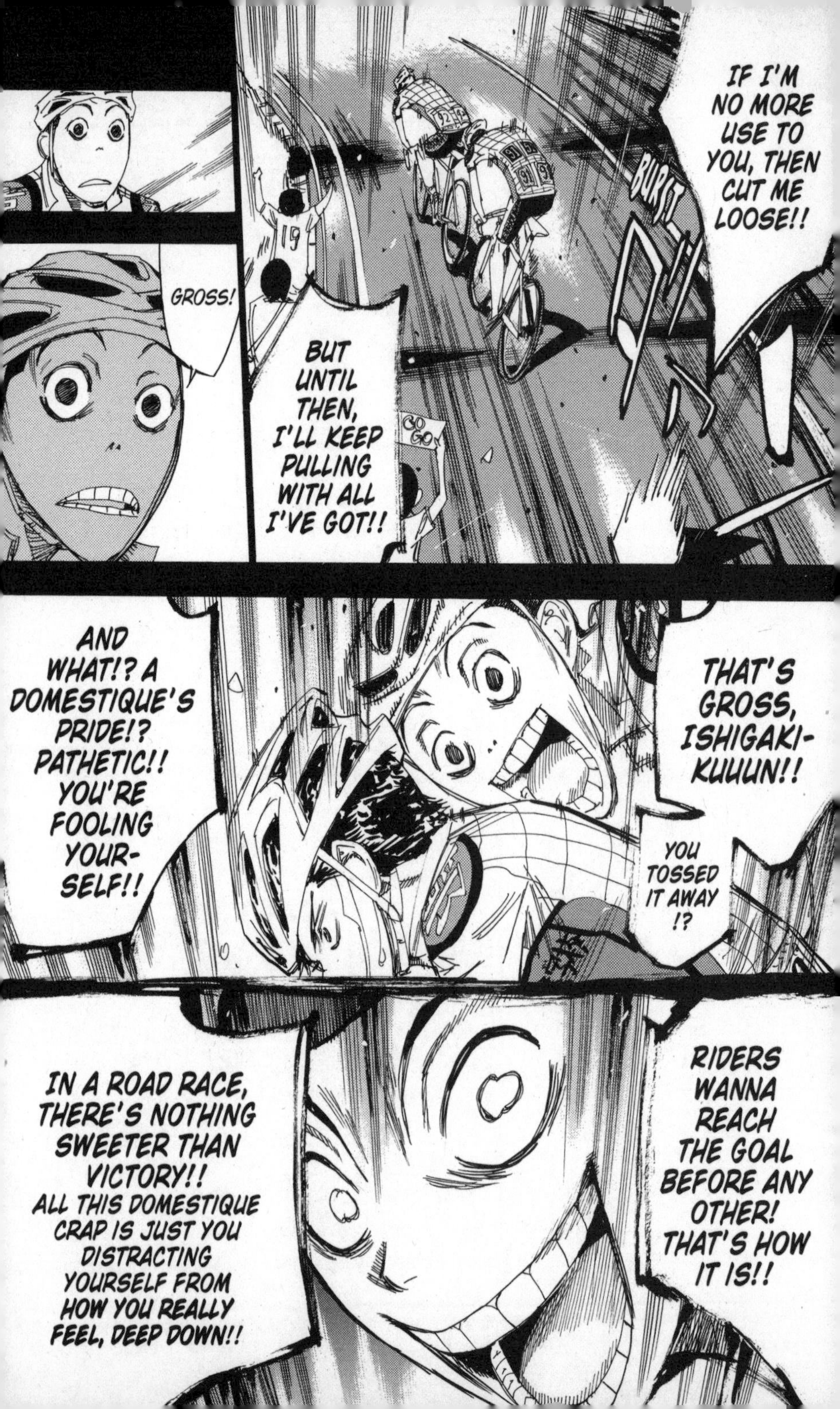
IF I'M NO MORE USE TO YOU, THEN CUT ME LOOSE!!
BURST
GO GO
BUT UNTIL THEN, I'LL KEEP PULLING WITH ALL I'VE GOT!!
GROSS!
THAT'S GROSS, ISHIGAKI-KUUUN!!
YOU TOSSED IT AWAY!?
AND WHAT!? A DOMESTIQUE'S PRIDE!? PATHETIC!! YOU'RE FOOLING YOURSELF!!
RIDERS WANNA REACH THE GOAL BEFORE ANY OTHER! THAT'S HOW IT IS!!
IN A ROAD RACE, THERE'S NOTHING SWEETER THAN VICTORY!!
ALL THIS DOMESTIQUE CRAP IS JUST YOU DISTRACTING YOURSELF FROM HOW YOU REALLY FEEL, DEEP DOWN!!

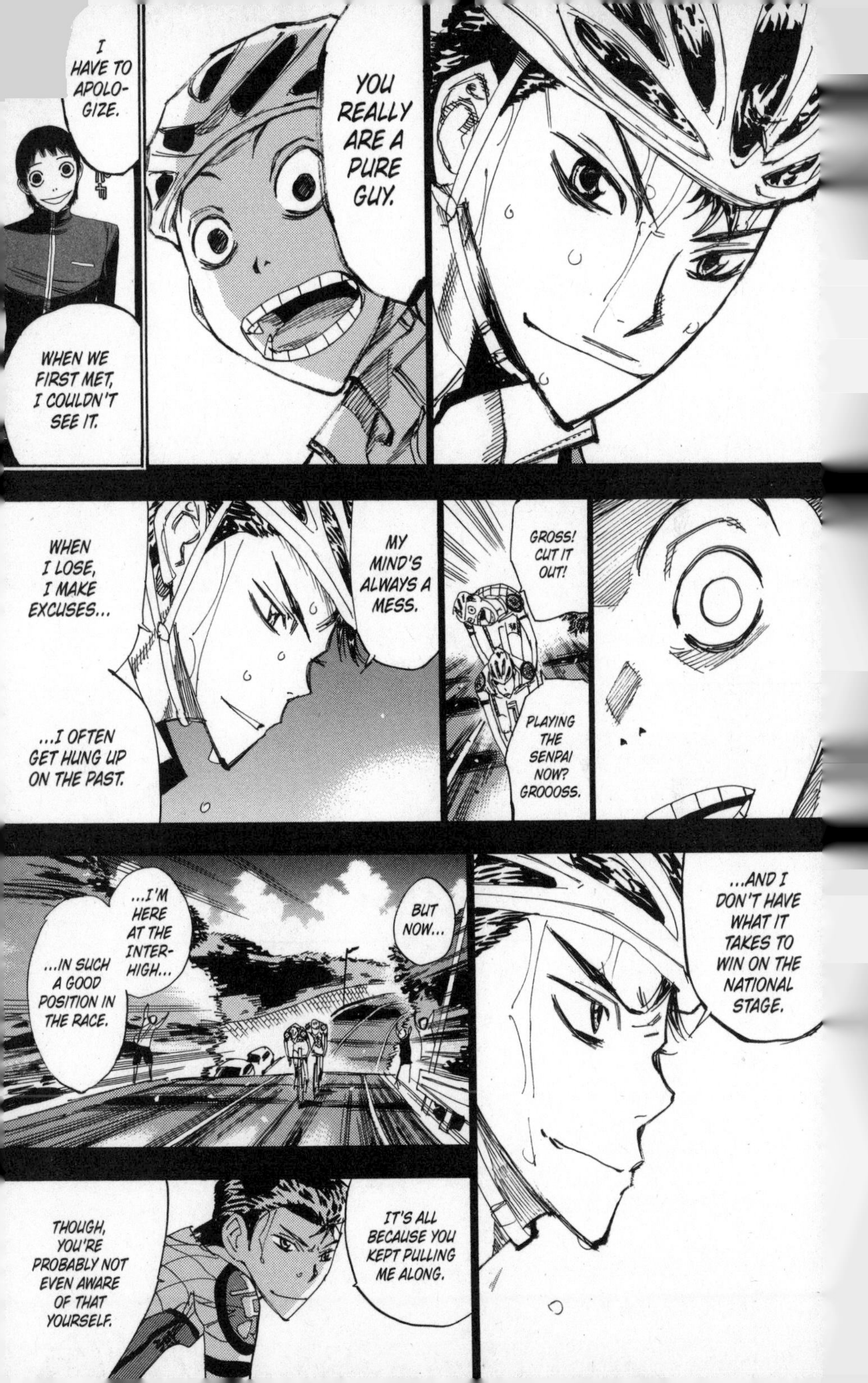
YOU REALLY ARE A PURE GUY.
I HAVE TO APOLOGIZE.
WHEN WE FIRST MET, I COULDN'T SEE IT.
GROSS! CUT IT OUT!
PLAYING THE SENPAI NOW? GROOOSS.
MY MIND'S ALWAYS A MESS.
WHEN I LOSE, I MAKE EXCUSES...
...I OFTEN GET HUNG UP ON THE PAST.
...AND I DON'T HAVE WHAT IT TAKES TO WIN ON THE NATIONAL STAGE.
BUT NOW...
...I'M HERE AT THE INTER-HIGH...
...IN SUCH A GOOD POSITION IN THE RACE.
IT'S ALL BECAUSE YOU KEPT PULLING ME ALONG.
THOUGH, YOU'RE PROBABLY NOT EVEN AWARE OF THAT YOURSELF.

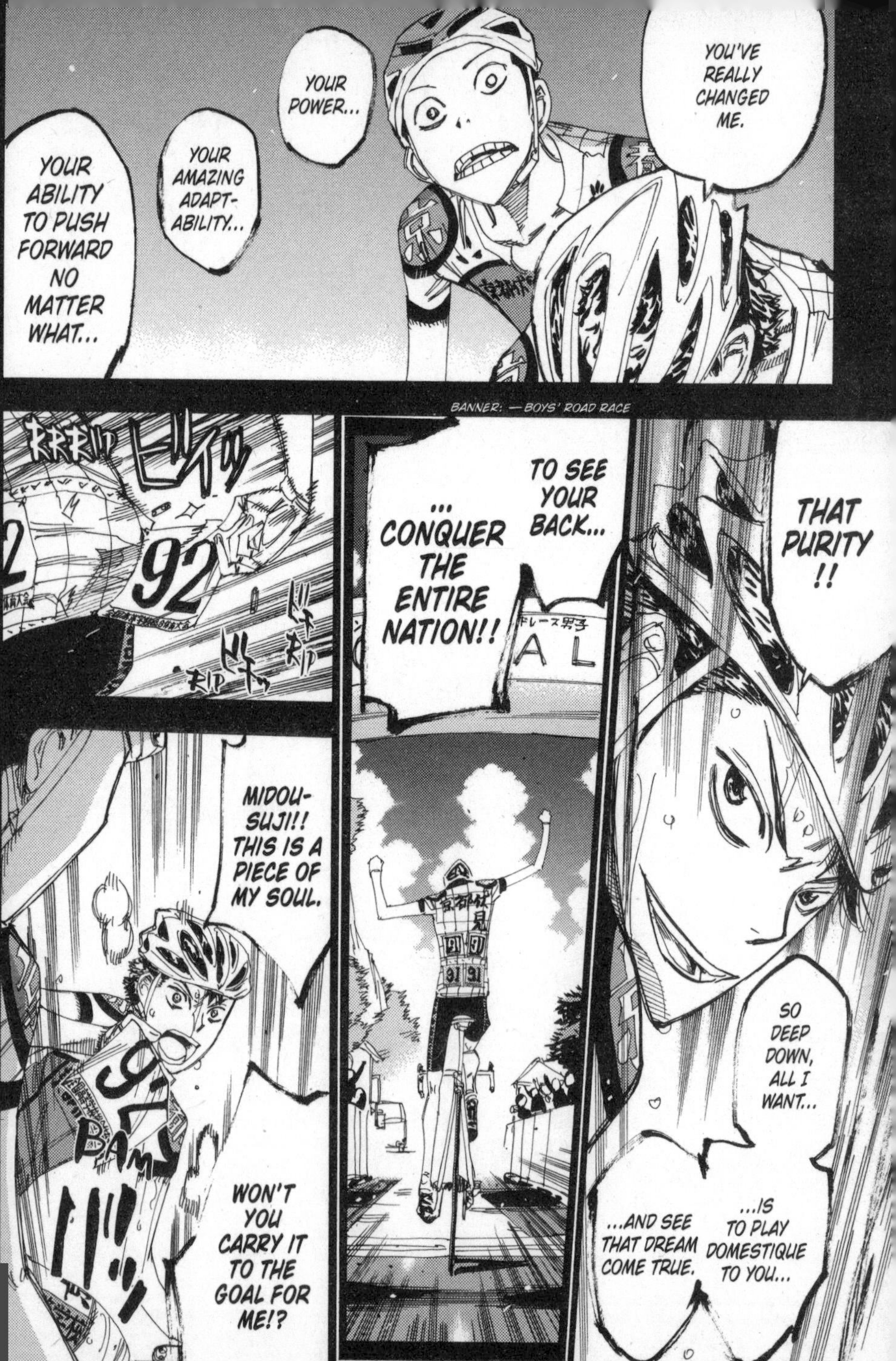
YOU'VE REALLY CHANGED ME.
YOUR POWER...
YOUR AMAZING ADAPT-ABILITY...
YOUR ABILITY TO PUSH FORWARD NO MATTER WHAT...
BANNER: —BOYS' ROAD RACE
THAT PURITY!!
SO DEEP DOWN, ALL I WANT...
...IS TO PLAY DOMESTIQUE TO YOU...
...AND SEE THAT DREAM COME TRUE.
TO SEE YOUR BACK...
...CONQUER THE ENTIRE NATION!!
RRRRIP
RIP
RIP
MIDOU-SUJI!! THIS IS A PIECE OF MY SOUL.
BAM
WON'T YOU CARRY IT TO THE GOAL FOR ME!?

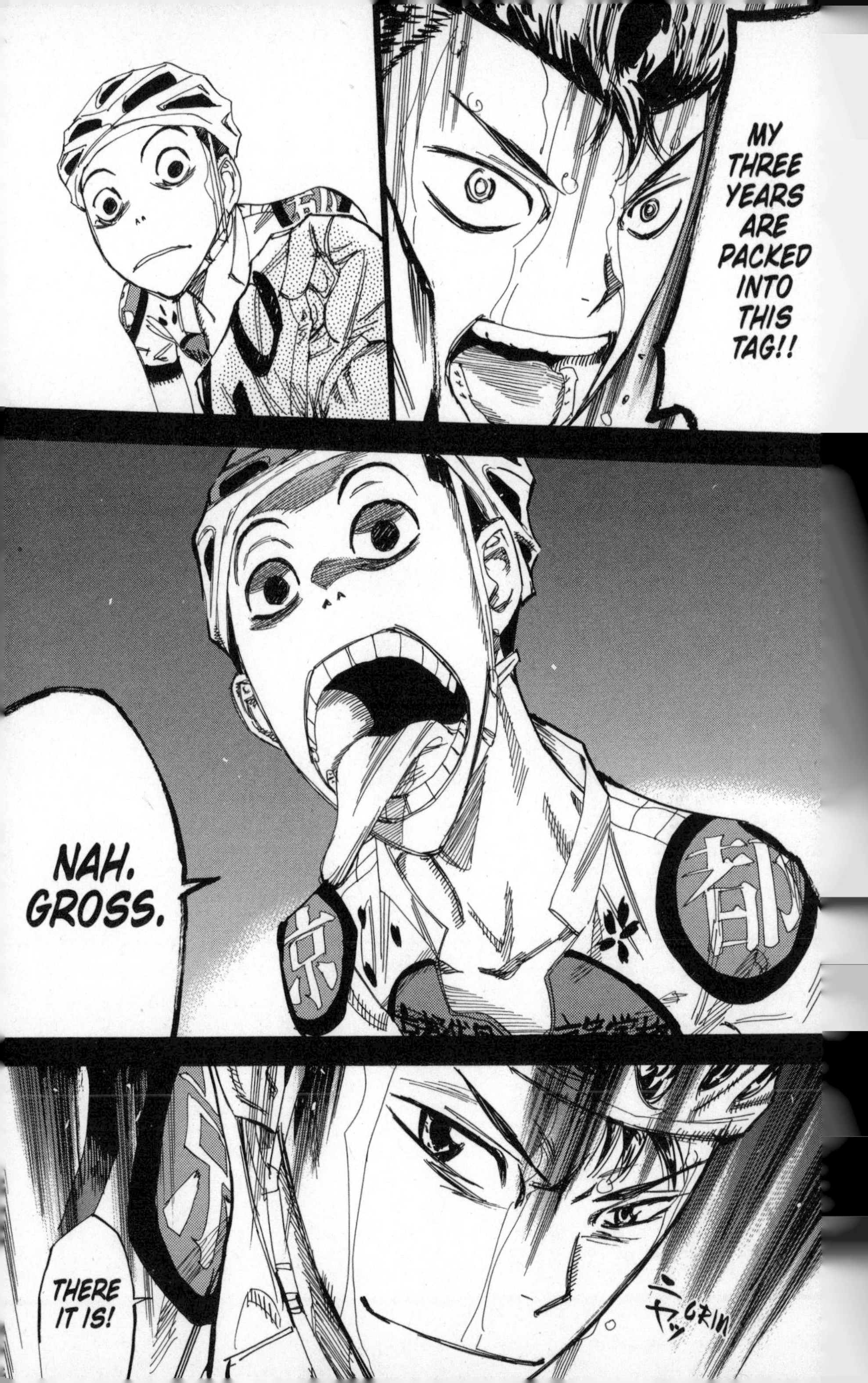
MY THREE YEARS ARE PACKED INTO THIS TAG!!
NAH. GROSS.
ニヤッ GRIN
THERE IT IS!

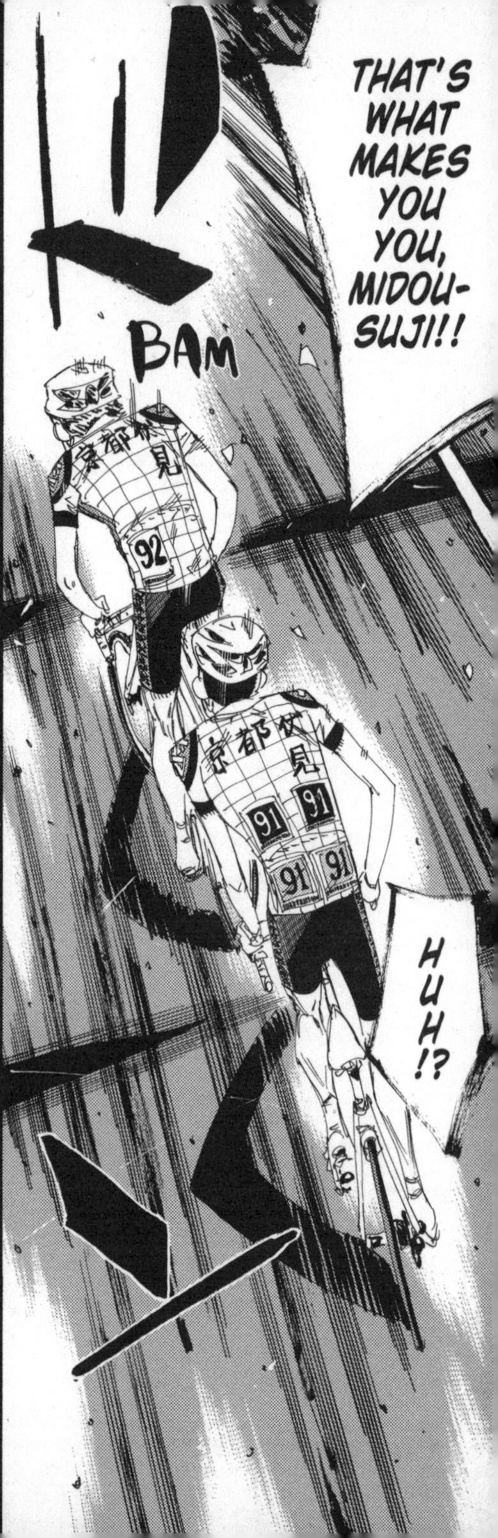
THAT'S WHAT MAKES YOU YOU, MIDOU-SUJI!!
BAM
HUH!?
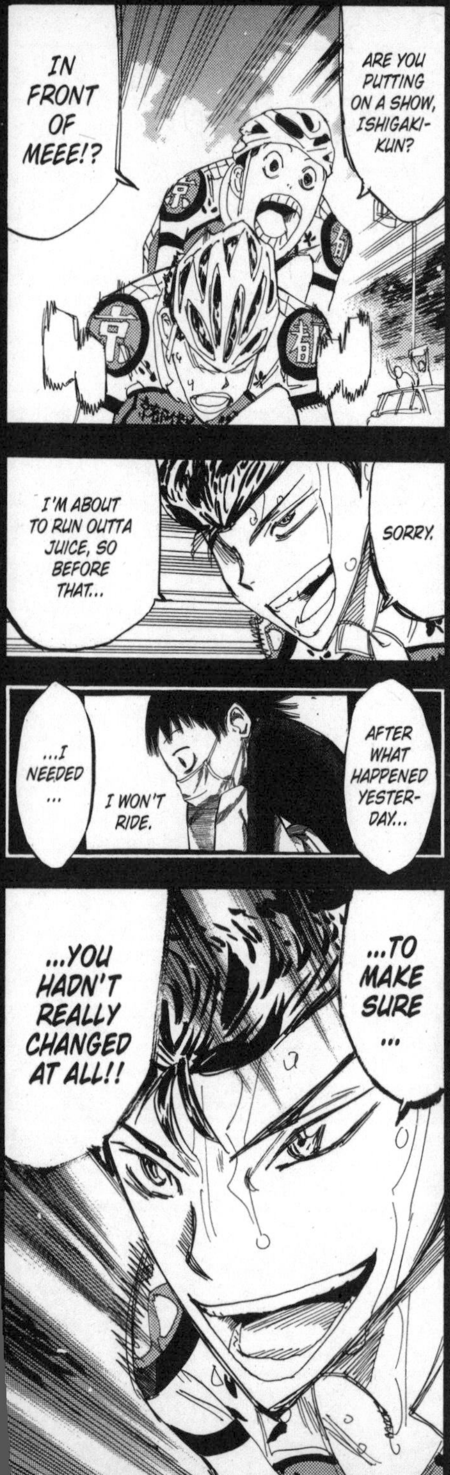
ARE YOU PUTTING ON A SHOW, ISHIGAKI-KUN?
IN FRONT OF MEEE!?
SORRY.
I'M ABOUT TO RUN OUTTA JUICE, SO BEFORE THAT...
AFTER WHAT HAPPENED YESTER-DAY...
I WON'T RIDE.
...I NEEDED ...
...TO MAKE SURE ...
...YOU HADN'T REALLY CHANGED AT ALL!!

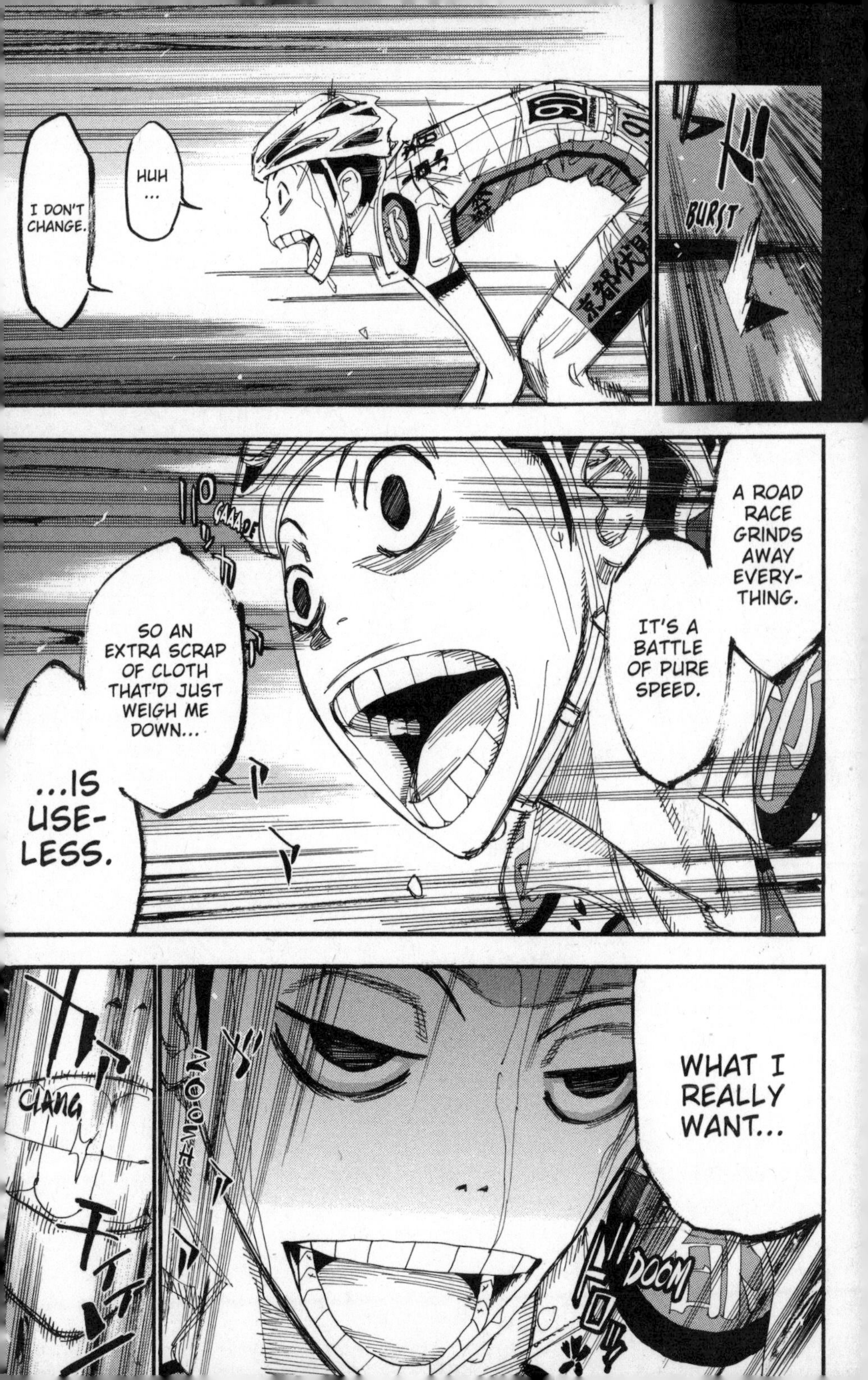
BURST
HUH ...
I DON'T CHANGE.
A ROAD RACE GRINDS AWAY EVERYTHING.
IT'S A BATTLE OF PURE SPEED.
SO AN EXTRA SCRAP OF CLOTH THAT'D JUST WEIGH ME DOWN...
...IS USELESS.
WHAT I REALLY WANT...
DOOM
CLANG

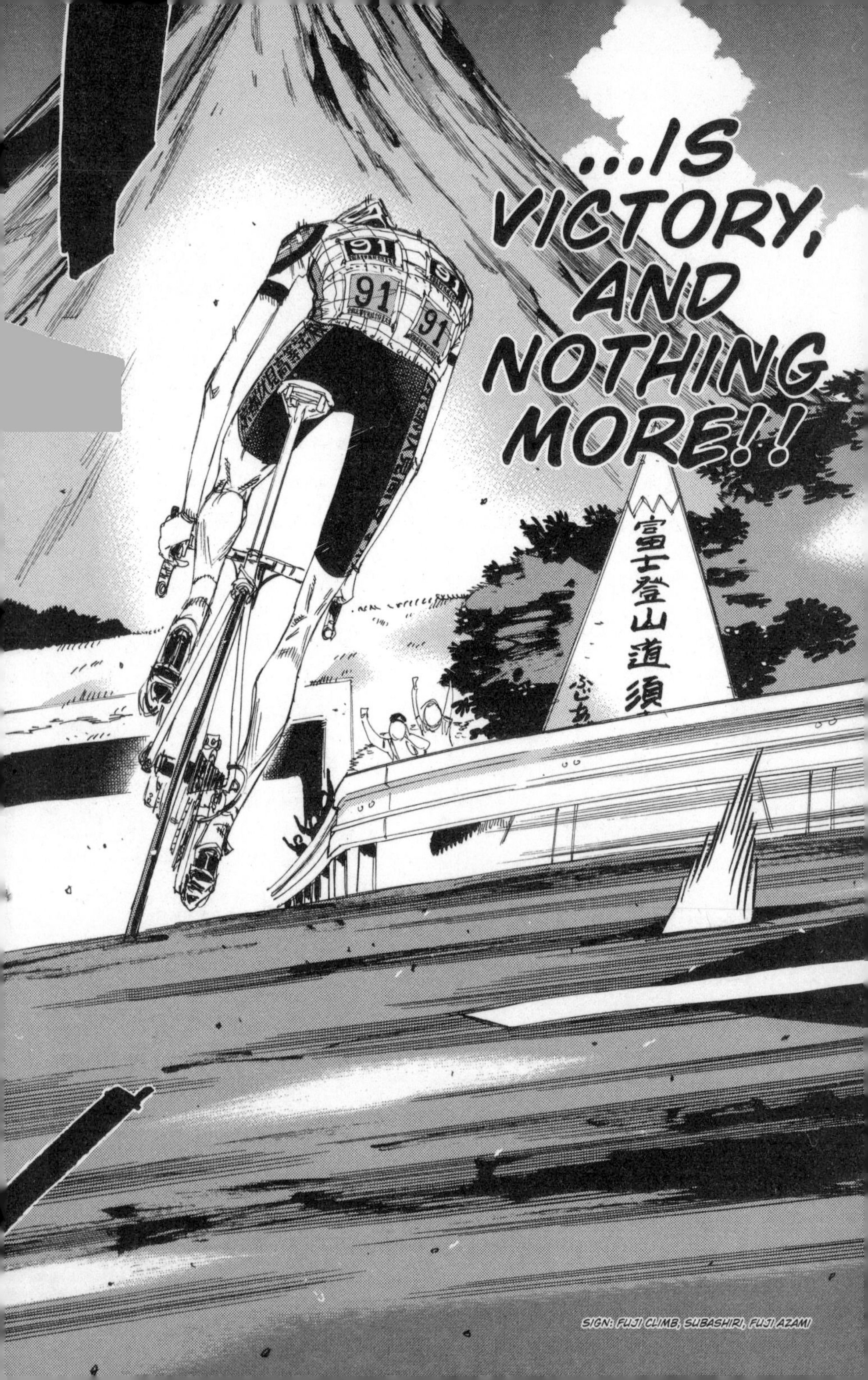
...IS VICTORY, AND NOTHING MORE!!
SIGN: FUJI CLIMB, SUBASHIRI, FUJI AZAMI

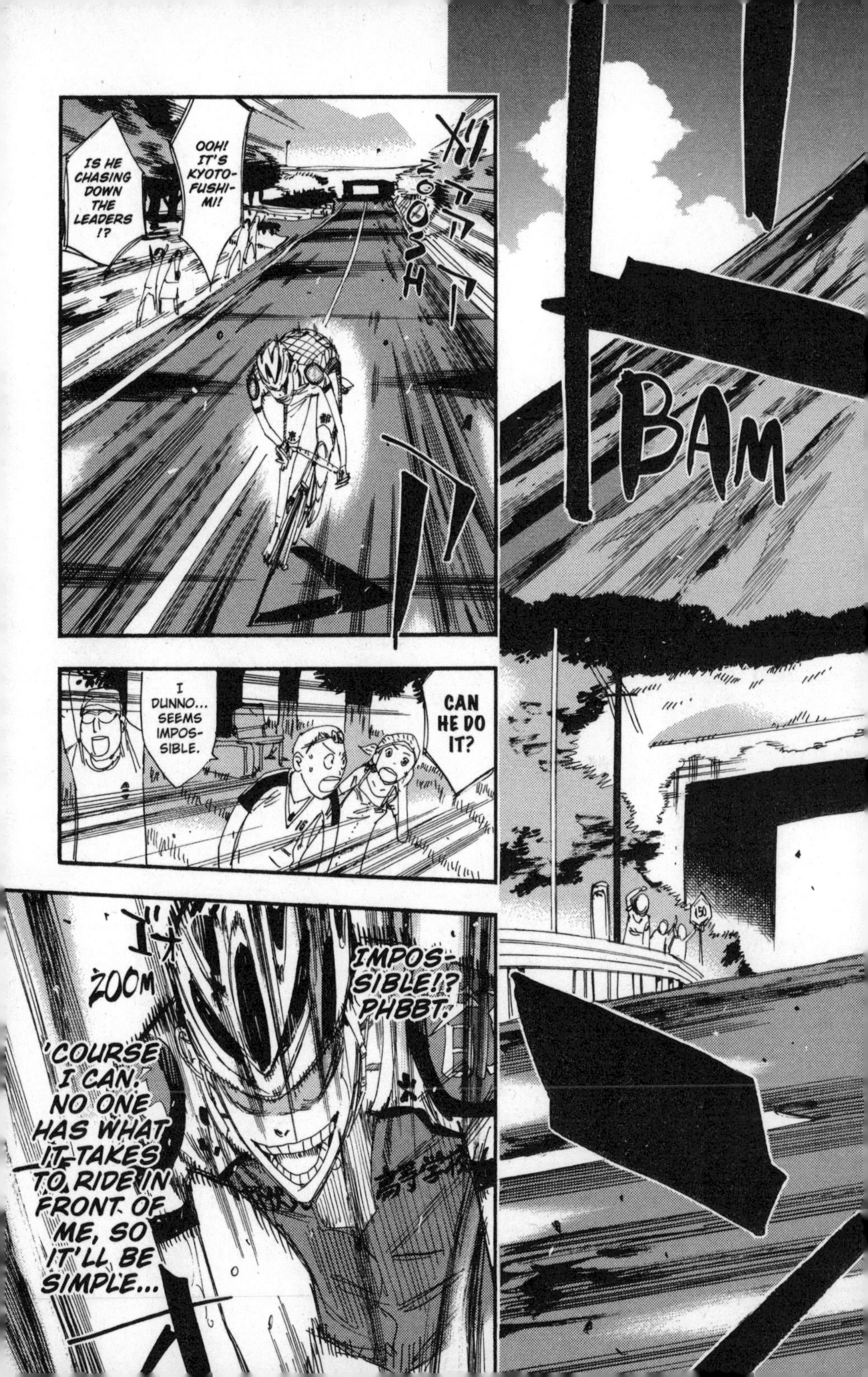
BAM
ZOOOSH
OOH! IT'S KYOTO-FUSHIMI!
IS HE CHASING DOWN THE LEADERS!?
CAN HE DO IT?
I DUNNO... SEEMS IMPOSSIBLE.
ZOOM
IMPOSSIBLE!? PHBBT.
'COURSE I CAN. NO ONE HAS WHAT IT TAKES TO RIDE IN FRONT OF ME, SO IT'LL BE SIMPLE...

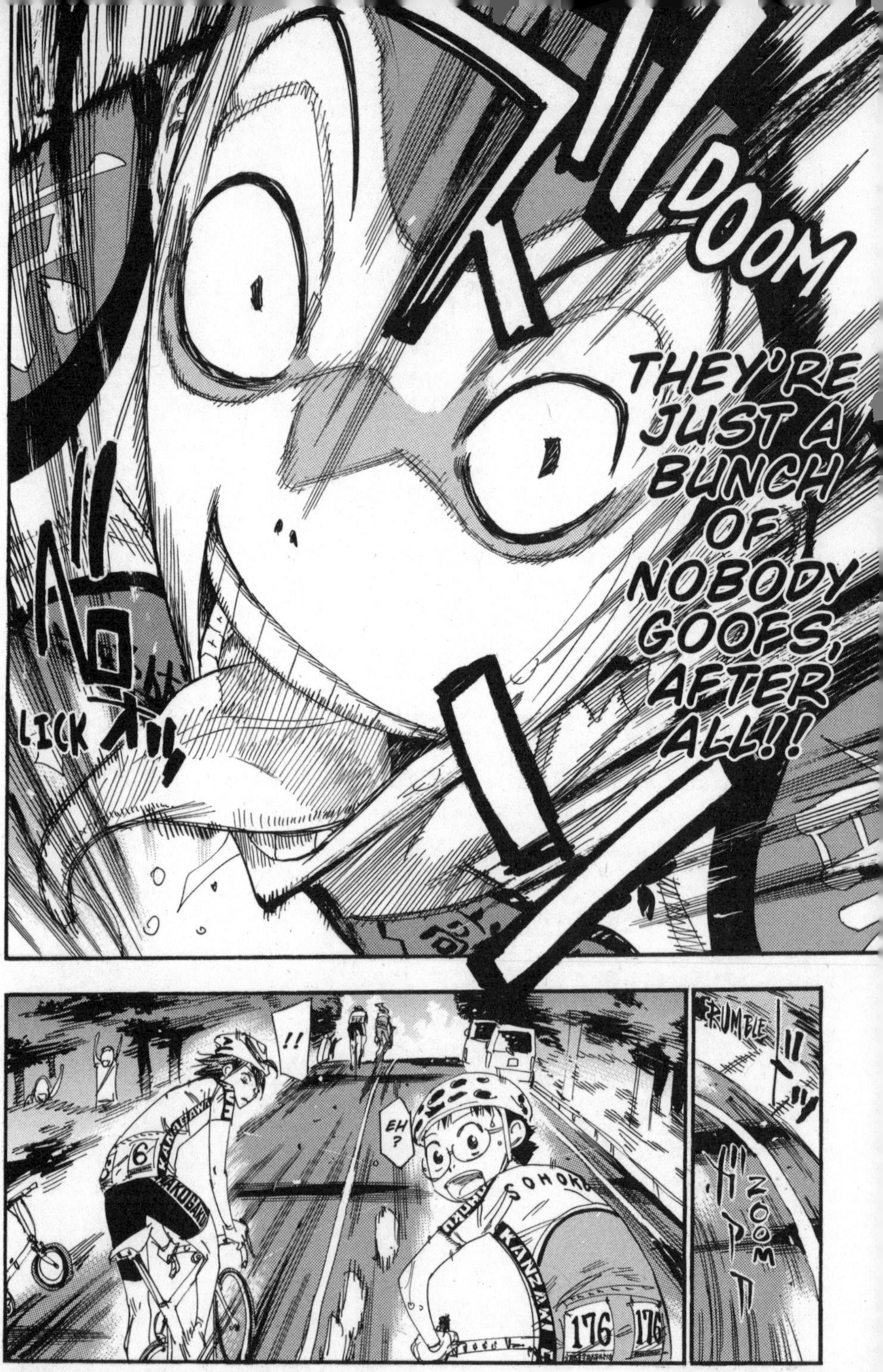
DOOM
THEY'RE JUST A BUNCH OF NOBODY GOOFS, AFTER ALL!!
LICK
RUMBLE
ZOOM
!!
EH?

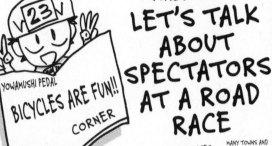

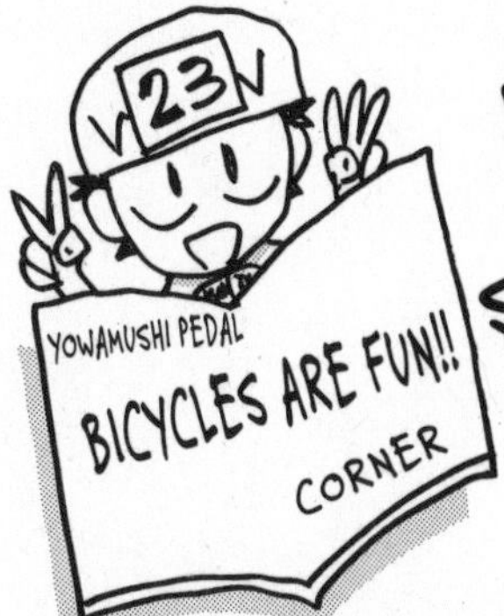
23
YOWAMUSHI PEDAL
BICYCLES ARE FUN!!
CORNER

THE THING THAT GETS NARUKO FIRED UP:

LET'S TALK ABOUT SPECTATORS AT A ROAD RACE

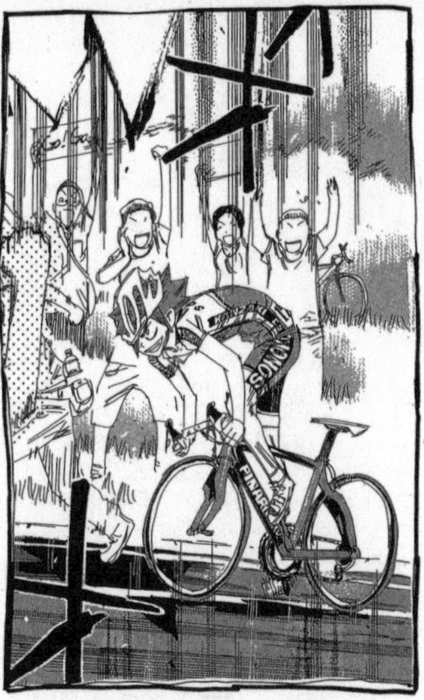

AMATEUR RACES ARE POPULAR TOO. ← MANY TOWNS AND CITIES HAVE THEIR OWN AMATEUR TEAMS.

ROAD RACES ARE ALWAYS HAPPENING IN EUROPE, THE HOME OF CYCLING! THE SEASON RUNS FROM MARCH (FEBRUARY AT THE EARLIEST) UNTIL OCTOBER, AND BOTH MEN AND WOMEN, YOUNG AND OLD, COME OUT TO WATCH. RACES ARE USUALLY ABOUT 200KM LONG. THERE'S A UNIQUE, FUN QUALITY YOU DON'T GET WITH OTHER SPORTS, SO LET'S GO OVER SOME OF THE JUICIER POINTS!

1 SPECTATING IS **FREE!!**

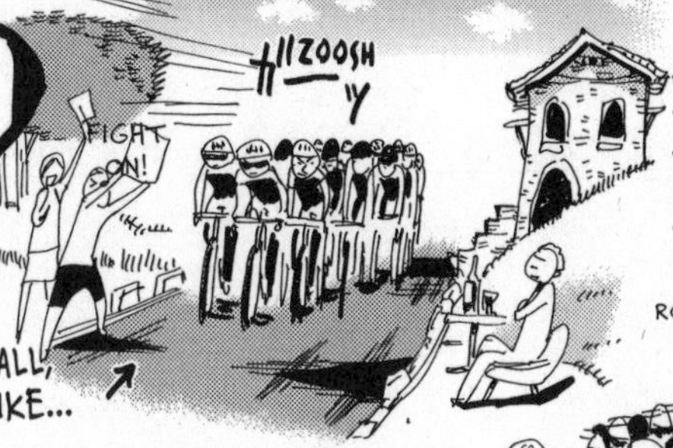
ZOOSH
FIGHT ON!

BICYCLE ROAD RACES MAKE USE OF PUBLIC ROADS, SO UNLIKE WITH BASEBALL, SOCCER, AND THE LIKE...

...SPECTATING IS TOTALLY **FREE!!** YOU CAN HEAD OUT TO WATCH THE RACE WHENEVER THE HECK YOU FEEL LIKE IT!!

ROAD RACES IN JAPAN ARE ALSO FREE TO VIEW!

2 IT'S IN YOUR FACE!!

THERE AREN'T A LOT OF FENCES AROUND APART FROM THE START AND FINISH LINES, SO YOU CAN GET UP CLOSE AND PERSONAL WITH THE RIDERS.

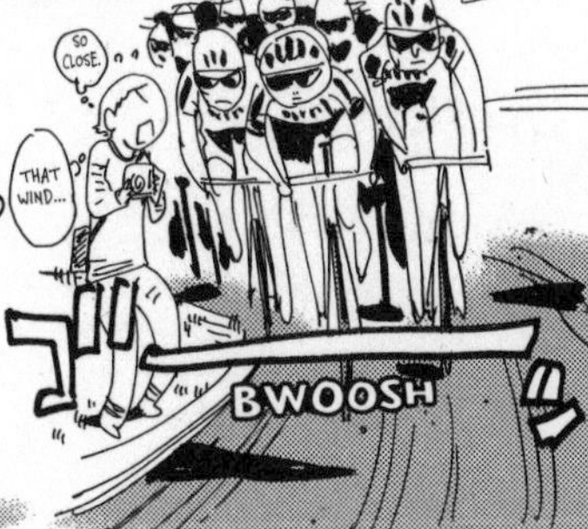
SO CLOSE.
THAT WIND...
BWOOSH

ROAD RACES ARE KNOWN AS THE PRO SPORT THAT LETS FANS GET CLOSER TO COMPETITORS THAN ANY OTHER. NOTE: OF COURSE, DON'T TRY TOUCHING THE RIDERS OR BLOCKING THE ROAD IN ANY WAY.

3 YOU CAN GET AUTOGRAPHS!

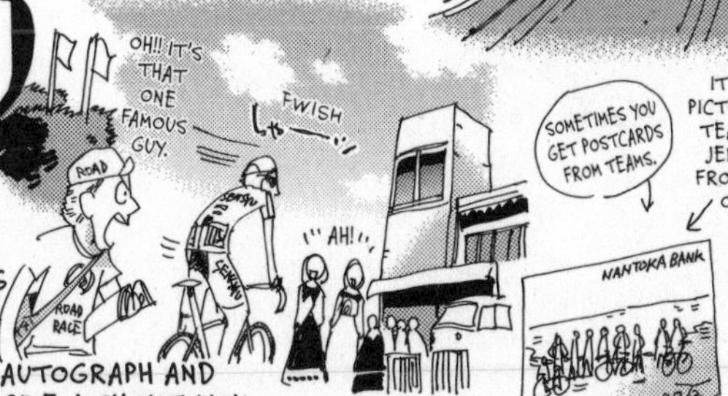
OH!! IT'S THAT ONE FAMOUS GUY.
FWISH
AH!!
SOMETIMES YOU GET POSTCARDS FROM TEAMS.
NANTOKA BANK
2012

ANOTHER WAY TO GET "CLOSE" TO THE ACTION. IT'S NOT UNCOMMON FOR RIDERS TO BE WANDERING AROUND AT THE START AND FINISH LINES. MOST WILL HAPPILY GIVE YOU AN AUTOGRAPH AND SHAKE YOUR HAND IF YOU GIVE A SHOUT. YOU MIGHT EVEN GET A POSTCARD FROM THE TEAM!

IT'LL USUALLY BE A PICTURE OF THE WHOLE TEAM, CLAD IN THEIR JERSEYS, POSING IN FRONT OF THE OCEAN OR SOME OTHER GORGEOUS BACKGROUND.

IF YOU'RE REALLY LUCKY, THEY'LL SIGN THIS FOR YOU. ♪

4 MOUNTAINS ARE SPECIAL

EVEN PROS WILL BE GOING A LITTLE SLOWER DURING A MOUNTAIN **CLIMB**, WHICH MEANS YOU GET LONGER TO CHEER THEM ON THAN ON FLATTER SECTIONS. IT'S ALSO YOUR CHANCE TO SNAP A PHOTO OF YOUR FAVORITE RIDER, OR GIVE THEM A SHOUT-OUT WHERE THEY'LL ACTUALLY HEAR YOU! THAT'S WHY MANY SPECTATORS PREFER MOUNTAIN SECTIONS.

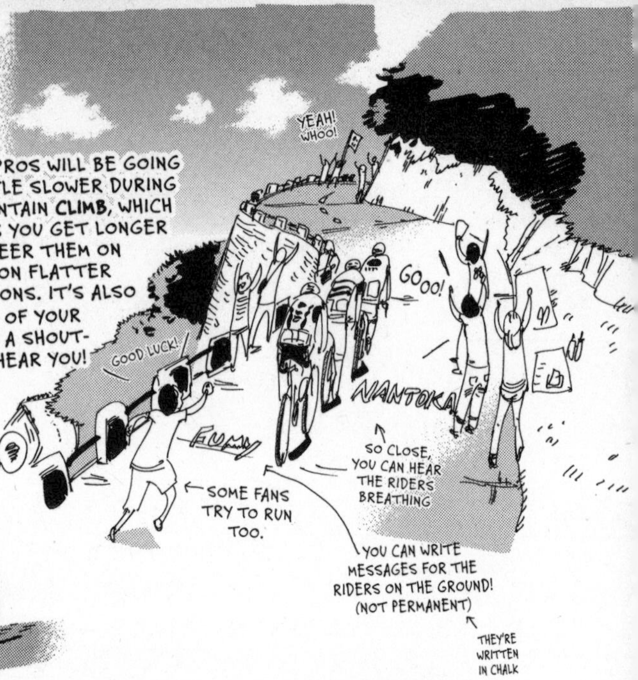
YEAH! WHOO!
GOooo!
GOOD LUCK!
NANTOKA
FUMI
SO CLOSE, YOU CAN HEAR THE RIDERS BREATHING
SOME FANS TRY TO RUN TOO.
YOU CAN WRITE MESSAGES FOR THE RIDERS ON THE GROUND! (NOT PERMANENT)
THEY'RE WRITTEN IN CHALK

SOME PEOPLE TRY TO GIVE RIDERS A BOOST BY SMACKING THEIR BUTTS, BUT TRY TO REFRAIN FROM DOING SO.

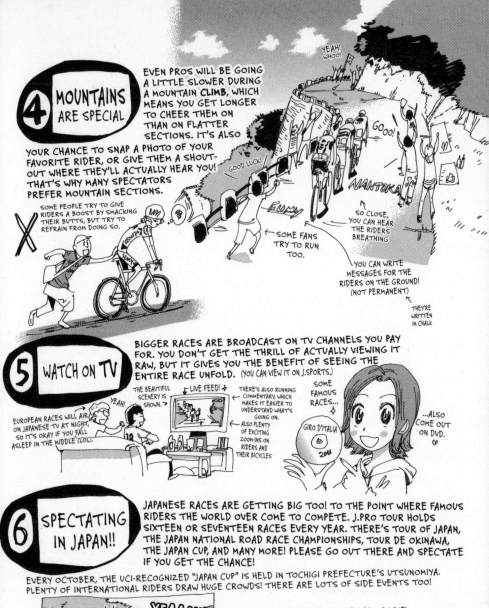

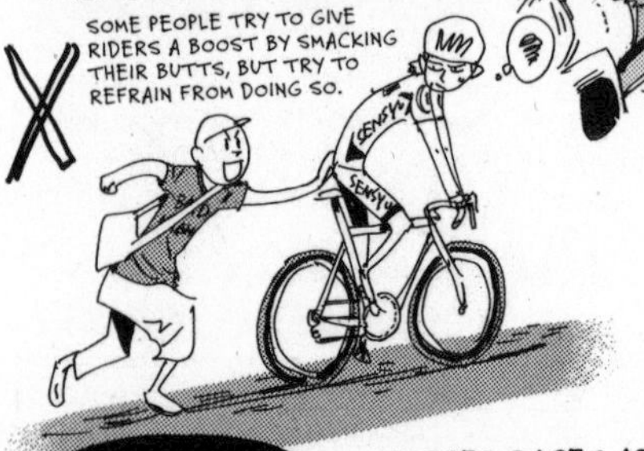
SENSYU
SENSYU

5 WATCH ON TV

BIGGER RACES ARE BROADCAST ON TV CHANNELS YOU PAY FOR. YOU DON'T GET THE THRILL OF ACTUALLY VIEWING IT RAW, BUT IT GIVES YOU THE BENEFIT OF SEEING THE ENTIRE RACE UNFOLD. (YOU CAN VIEW IT ON J.SPORTS.)

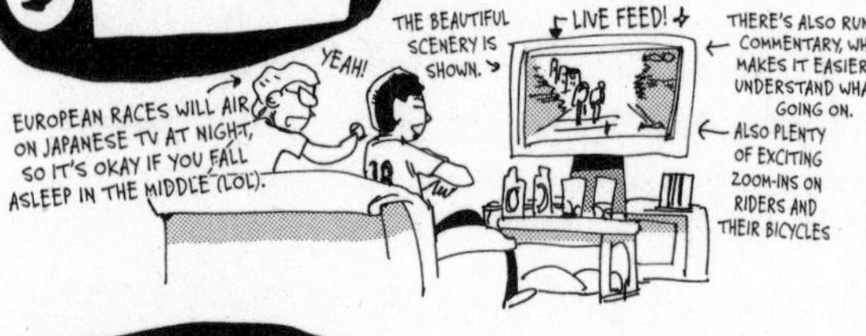
THE BEAUTIFUL SCENERY IS SHOWN.
LIVE FEED!
THERE'S ALSO RUNNING COMMENTARY, WHICH MAKES IT EASIER TO UNDERSTAND WHAT'S GOING ON.
ALSO PLENTY OF EXCITING ZOOM-INS ON RIDERS AND THEIR BICYCLES
YEAH!
EUROPEAN RACES WILL AIR ON JAPANESE TV AT NIGHT, SO IT'S OKAY IF YOU FALL ASLEEP IN THE MIDDLE (LOL).

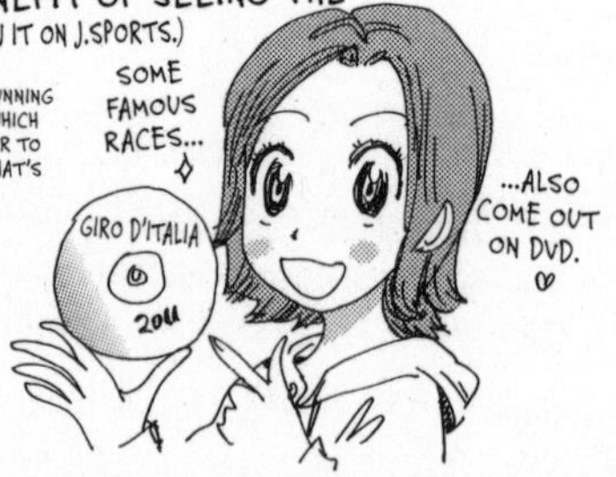
SOME FAMOUS RACES...
GIRO D'ITALIA
2011
...ALSO COME OUT ON DVD.

6 SPECTATING IN JAPAN!!

JAPANESE RACES ARE GETTING BIG TOO! TO THE POINT WHERE FAMOUS RIDERS THE WORLD OVER COME TO COMPETE. J.PRO TOUR HOLDS SIXTEEN OR SEVENTEEN RACES EVERY YEAR. THERE'S TOUR OF JAPAN, THE JAPAN NATIONAL ROAD RACE CHAMPIONSHIPS, TOUR DE OKINAWA, THE JAPAN CUP, AND MANY MORE! PLEASE GO OUT THERE AND SPECTATE IF YOU GET THE CHANCE!

EVERY OCTOBER, THE UCI-RECOGNIZED "JAPAN CUP" IS HELD IN TOCHIGI PREFECTURE'S UTSUNOMIYA. PLENTY OF INTERNATIONAL RIDERS DRAW HUGE CROWDS! THERE ARE LOTS OF SIDE EVENTS TOO!

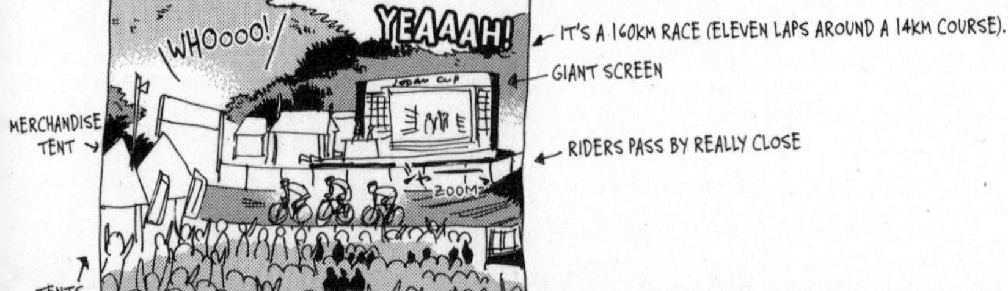
WHOOOO!
YEAAAH!
JAPAN CUP
ZOOM
IT'S A 160KM RACE (ELEVEN LAPS AROUND A 14KM COURSE).
GIANT SCREEN
MERCHANDISE TENT
RIDERS PASS BY REALLY CLOSE
TENTS OFFERING FOOD

IT'S FREE TO SPECTATE!

SOME COMMENTARY ON THE FINAL STAGE OF THE INTER-HIGH:

THE ROADS UP MT. FUJI

MT. FUJI SERVES AS THE SETTING FOR THE FINAL STAGE OF THE INTER-HIGH, AND THERE ARE ACTUALLY THREE ROADS GOING UP IT. (ALL THREE END AT THEIR OWN FIFTH STATIONS).

◄ PUBLIC LOTS FOR MOUNTAIN-CLIMBING TOURISTS

MT. FUJI: 3,776M ①

CLIMBING FROM THE YAMANASHI PREFECTURE SIDE: FUJI SUBARU LINE (TOLL ROAD)

LAKE KAWAGUCHI

LAKE YAMANAKA

LAKE MOTOSU

③ FUJI AZAMI LINE

② CLIMBING FROM THE SHIZUOKA PREFECTURE SIDE: FUJI SKYLINE

FUJINOMIYA CITY

139

GOTEMBA

246 → TOKYO

←SHIZUOKA

FUJI CITY

LAKE ASHI

NUMAZU CITY

HAKONE CITY

ODAWARA CITY

1

SURUGA BAY

▲ ENTRANCE TO MT. FUJI'S AZAMI LINE

● THE FUJI AZAMI LINE IS THE ONE THAT SHOWS UP IN THE STORY, AND OUT OF ALL THREE, THAT'S THE NARROWEST ROAD WITH THE STEEPEST GRADE.

ALL THREE OF THE ROADS SHOWCASED HERE ARE USED FOR HILL CLIMB RACES THROUGHOUT THE YEAR. I'VE ACTUALLY COMPETED ON ① (FUJI SUBARU LINE RACE) AND ③ (FUJI AZAMI LINE RACE) AND ③ WAS SERIOUSLY HARD. THE GRADE GETS UP TO 20% IN SOME SPOTS, AND IT TOOK ALL I HAD TO KEEP DANCING UP THE SLOPES.☆ CHALLENGE THESE ROADS, IF YOU DARE?

► YOU'LL SEE A LOT OF BARE ROCKS SINCE THE FIFTH STATION IS RIGHT ABOUT WHERE VEGETATION STOPS GROWING. AT AN ELEVATION OF 2,000M, IT'S CHILLY EVEN IN THE SUMMER.

BONUS

◄ ABOUT THE ILLUSTRATION ON THE NEXT PAGE... IT RAN WITH A SPECIAL ARTICLE ABOUT *YOWAMUSHI PEDAL* IN AKITA SHOTEN'S SHOUJO MAGAZINE *PRINCESS* AT THE SAME TIME AS THE STAGE PLAY IN 2012. I DREW IT JUST FOR THAT OCCASION. ONE OF THE EDITORS AT *PRINCESS* (←A BIG *YOWAPEDA* FAN) FERVENTLY ASKED FOR THE BOYS IN THEIR STREET CLOTHES, WHICH IS WHY THEY'RE NOT WEARING THEIR USUAL JERSEYS. IT'S TEAM SOHOKU IN THEIR REGULAR CLOTHES! THEY'RE WEARING WINTERY OUTFITS BECAUSE THIS WAS THE JANUARY ISSUE OF THE MAGAZINE!

"YOWAMUSHI PEDAL: THE PLAY"

YOU DON'T SEE THEM IN STREET CLOTHES TOO MUCH DURING THE STORY, SO I HOPE YOU ENJOY IT (LOL). IT MAY BE WINTER, BUT TADOKORO IS STILL IN SHORT SLEEVES!

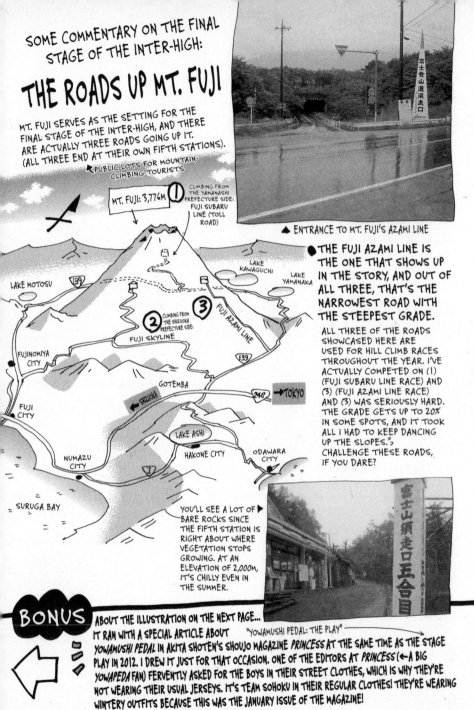

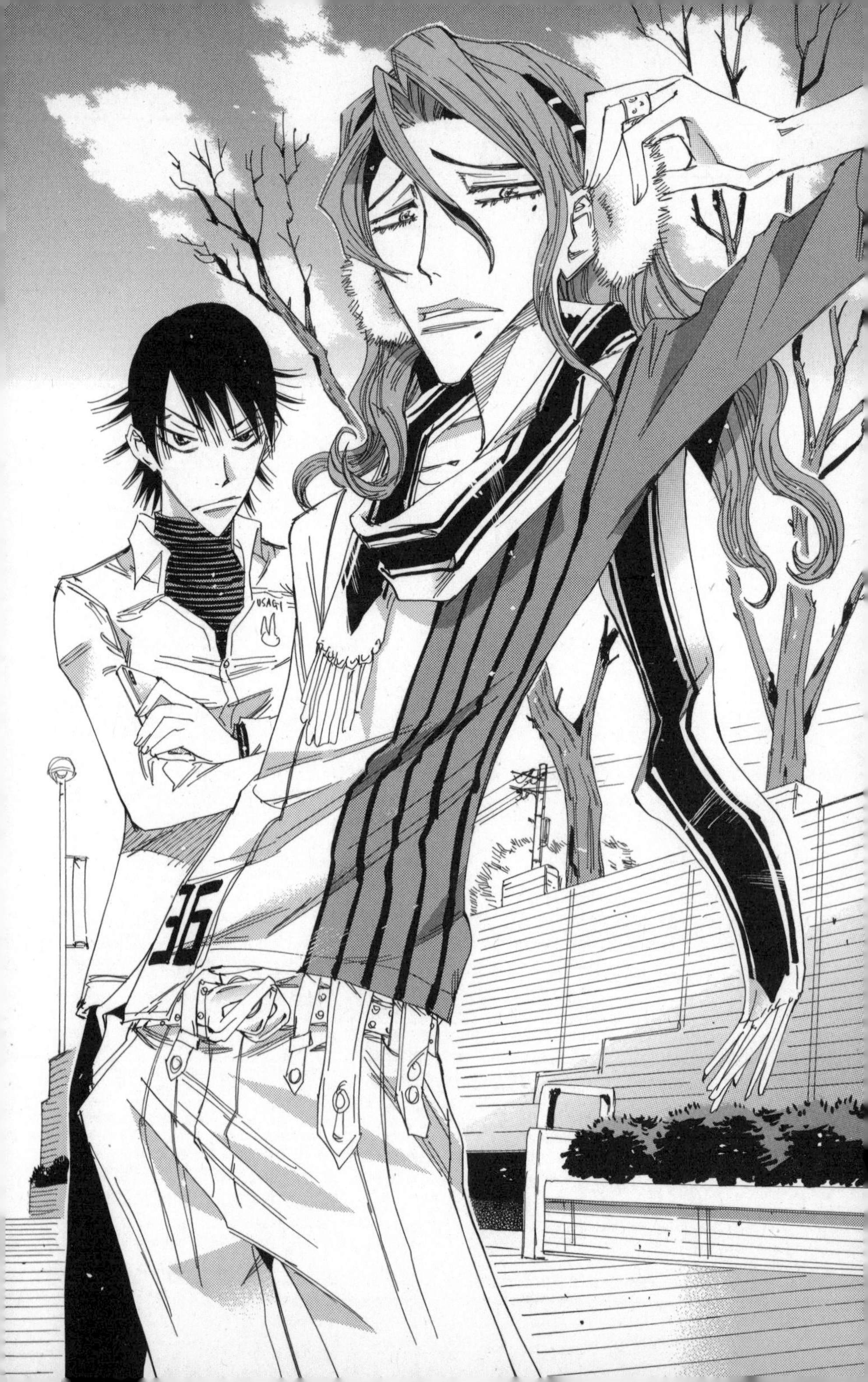
USAGI
36

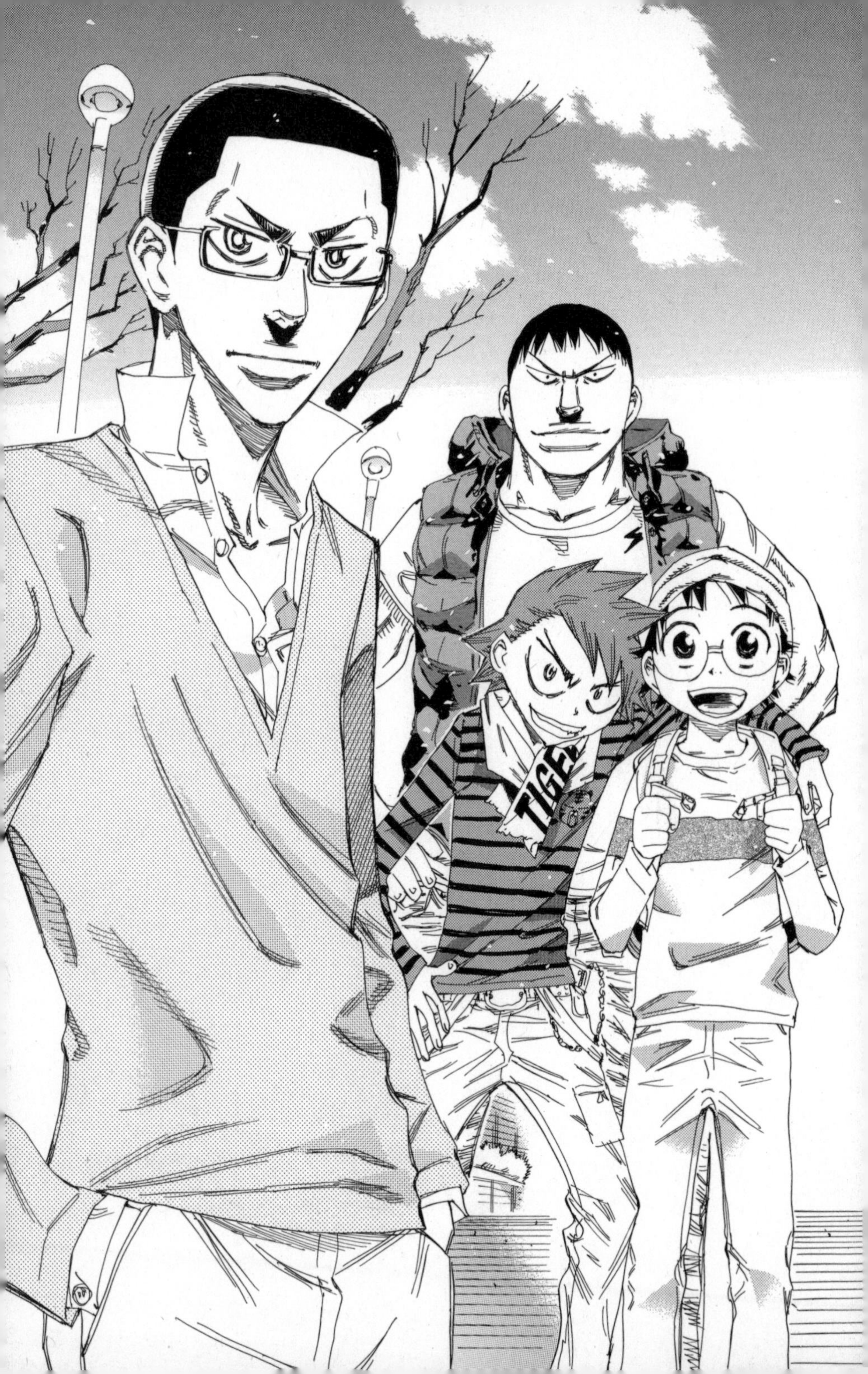
TIGE

YOWAMUSHI PEDAL

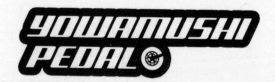

RIDE.200 UNFORESEEN

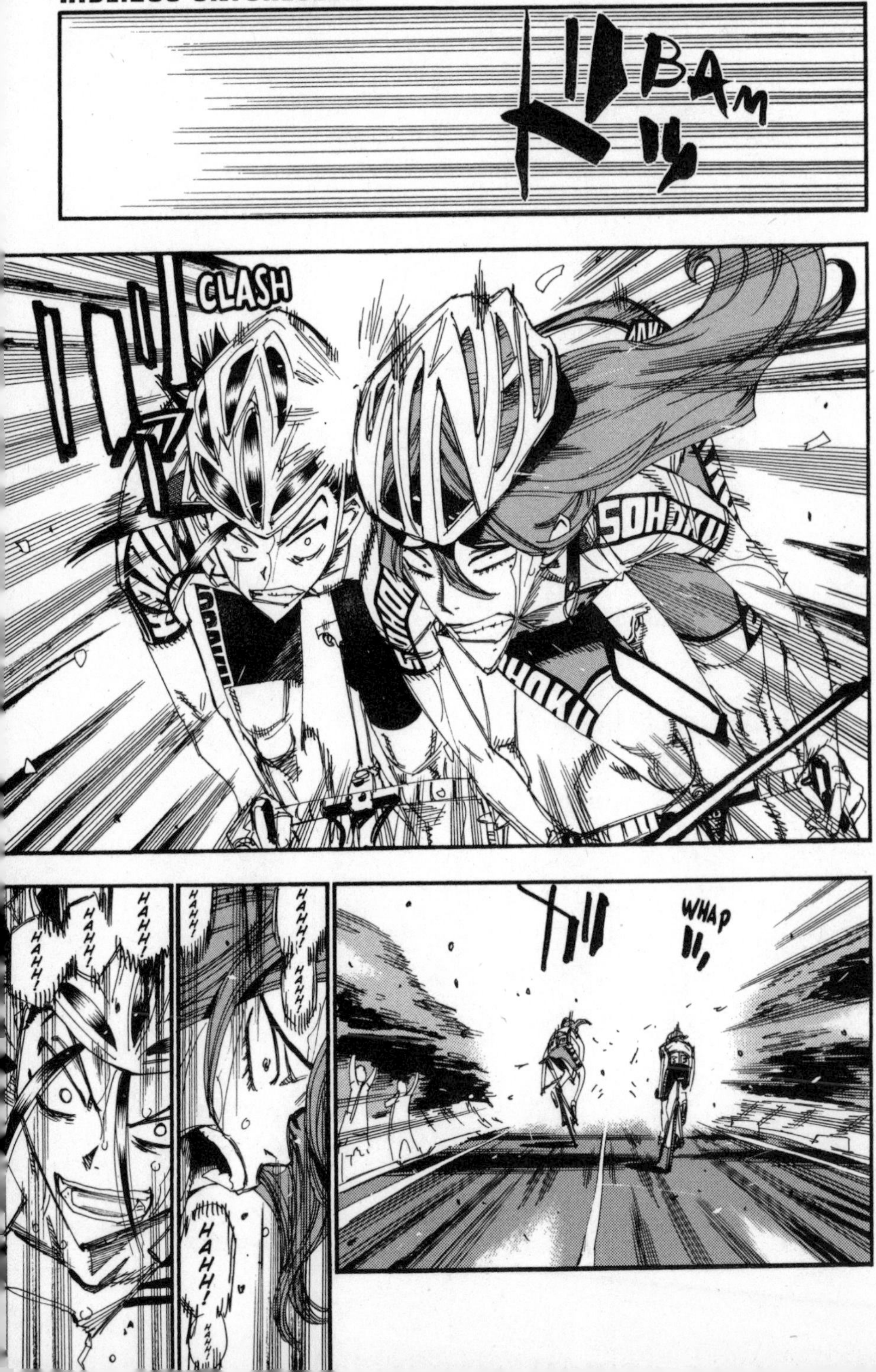
BAM
CLASH
WHAP
HAHH!
HAHH!
HAHH!
HAHH!
HAHH!
HAHH!
HAHH!
HAHH!

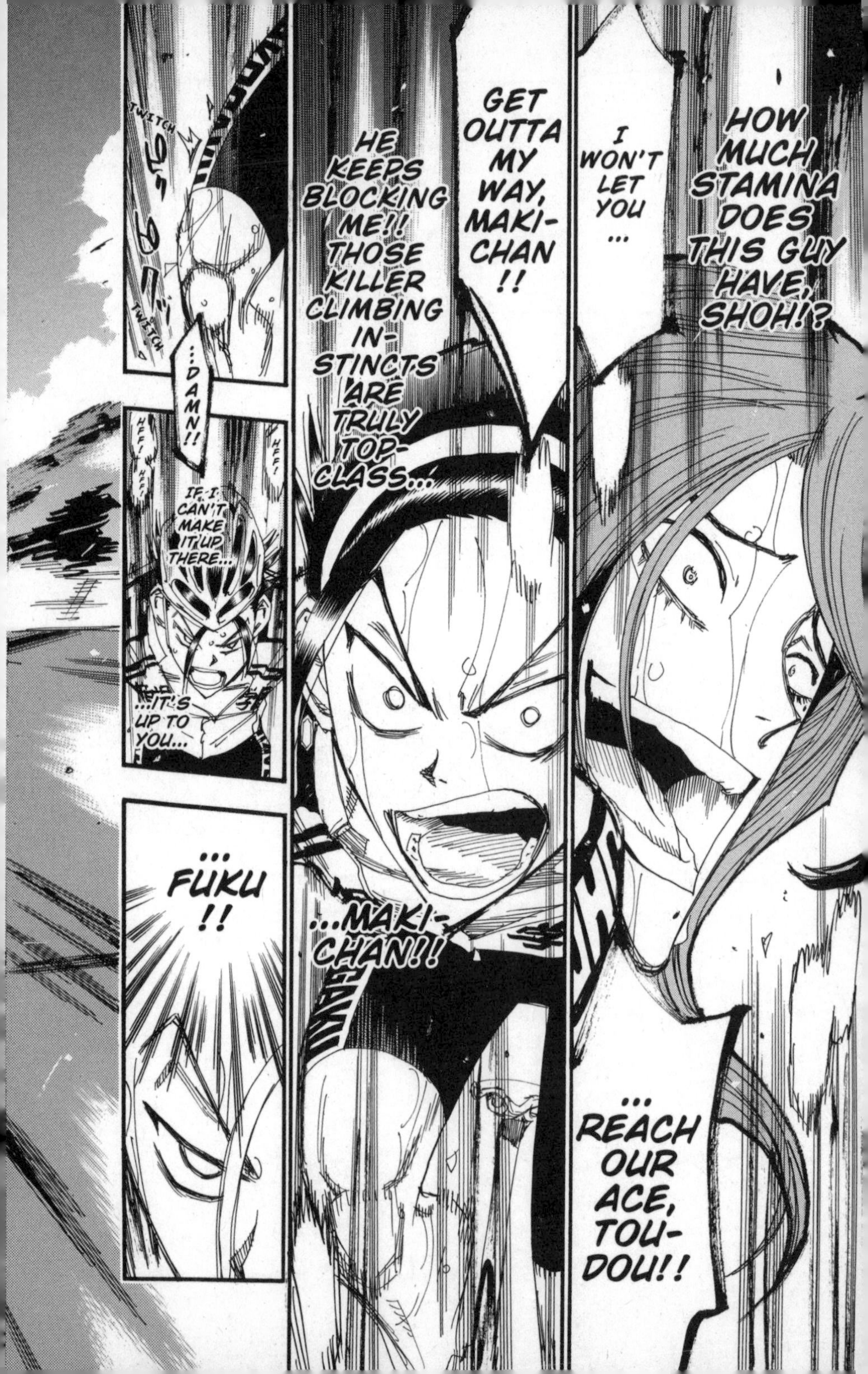
HOW MUCH STAMINA DOES THIS GUY HAVE, SHOH!?
I WON'T LET YOU ...
... REACH OUR ACE, TOU-DOU!!
GET OUTTA MY WAY, MAKI-CHAN!!
HE KEEPS BLOCKING ME!! THOSE KILLER CLIMBING IN-STINCTS ARE TRULY TOP-CLASS...
...MAKI-CHAN!!
TWITCH
TWITCH
...DAMN!!
HFF! HFF! HFF!
IF I CAN'T MAKE IT UP THERE...
...IT'S UP TO YOU...
... FŪKU !!

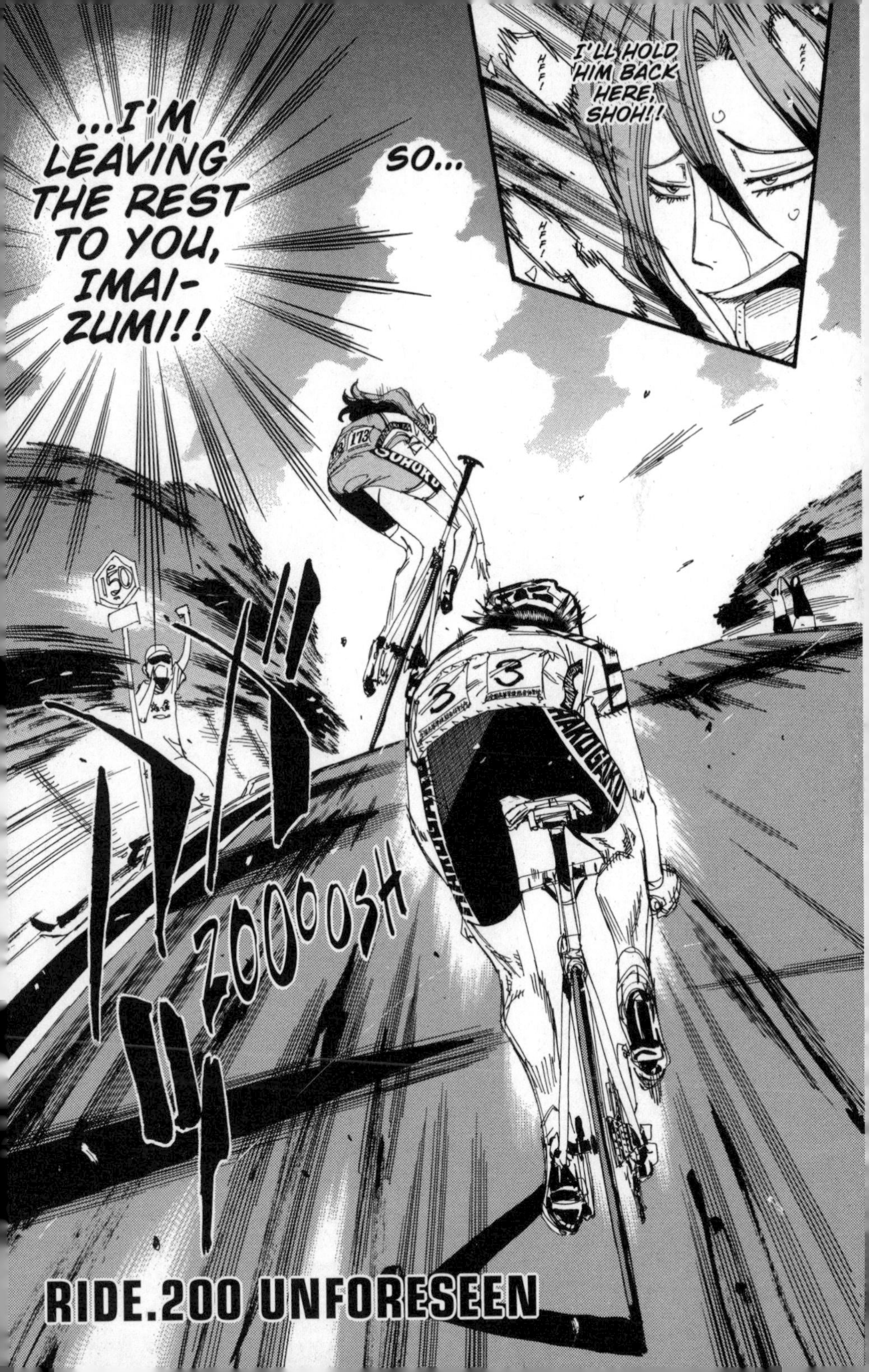
HFF!
I'LL HOLD HIM BACK HERE, SHOH!!
HFF!
HFF!
SO...
...I'M LEAVING THE REST TO YOU, IMAI-ZUMI!!
ZOOOOSH

RIDE.200 UNFORESEEN

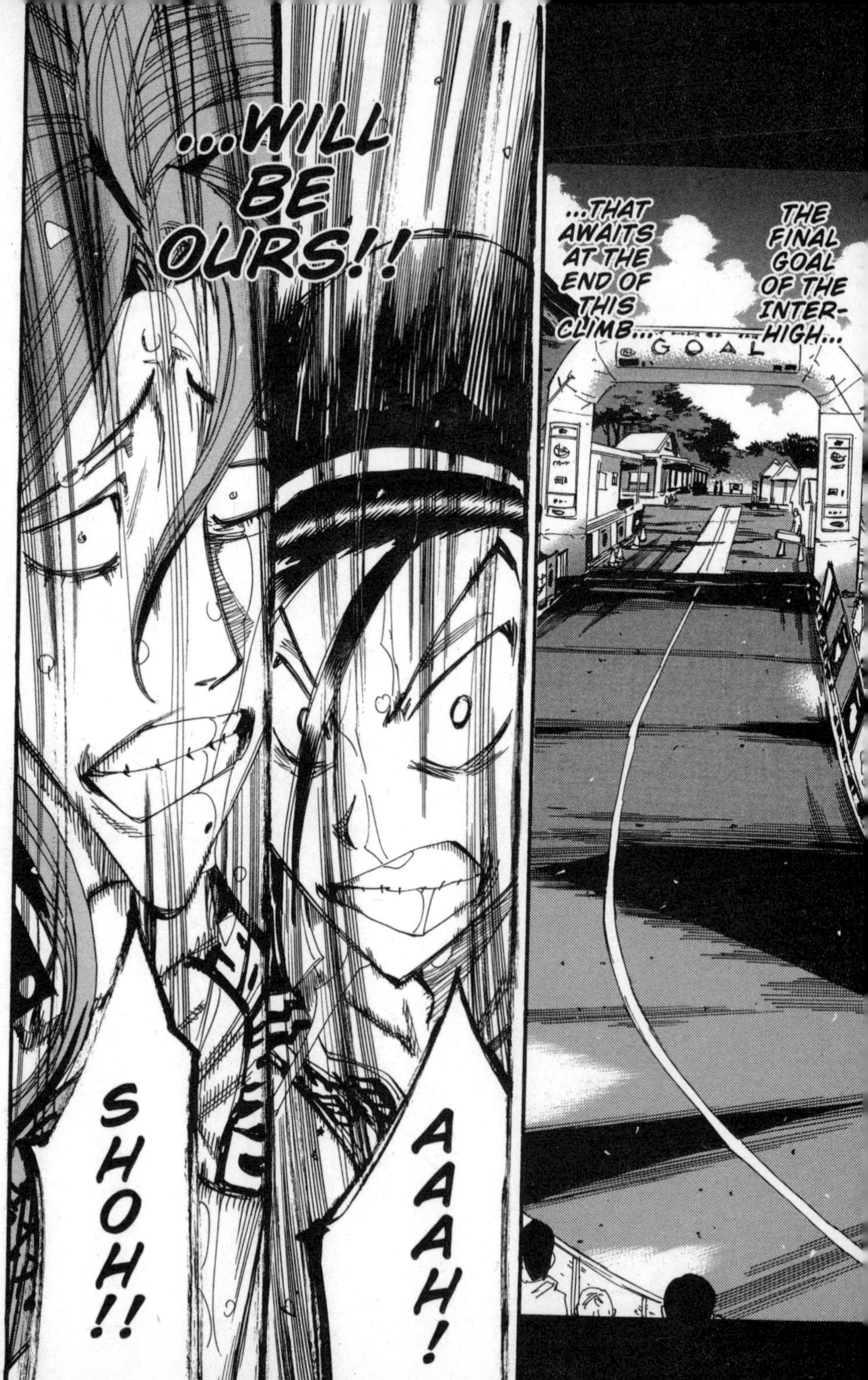
THE FINAL GOAL OF THE INTER-HIGH...
...THAT AWAITS AT THE END OF THIS CLIMB...
GOAL
...WILL BE OURS!!
AAAH!
SHOH!!

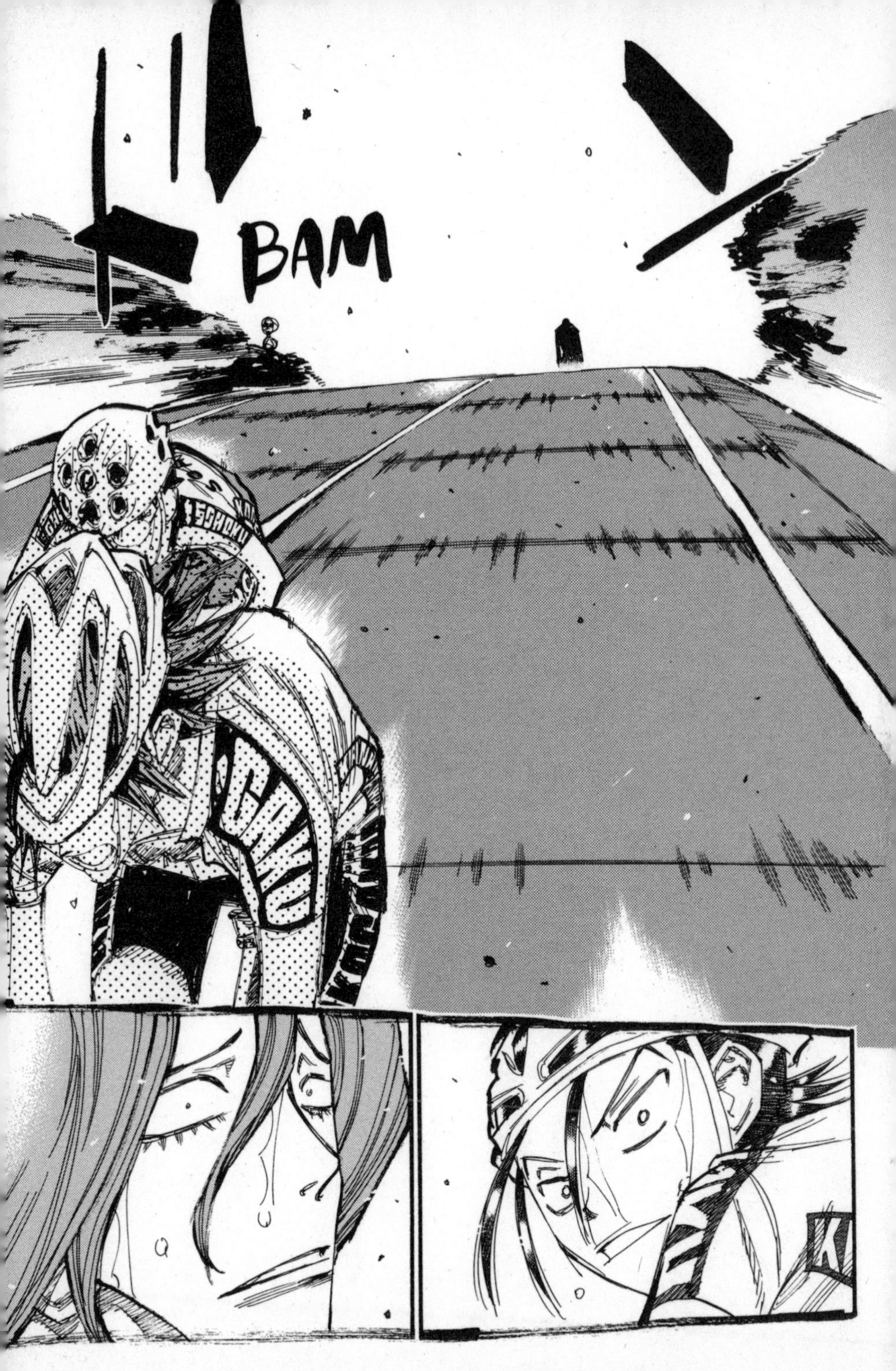
BAM

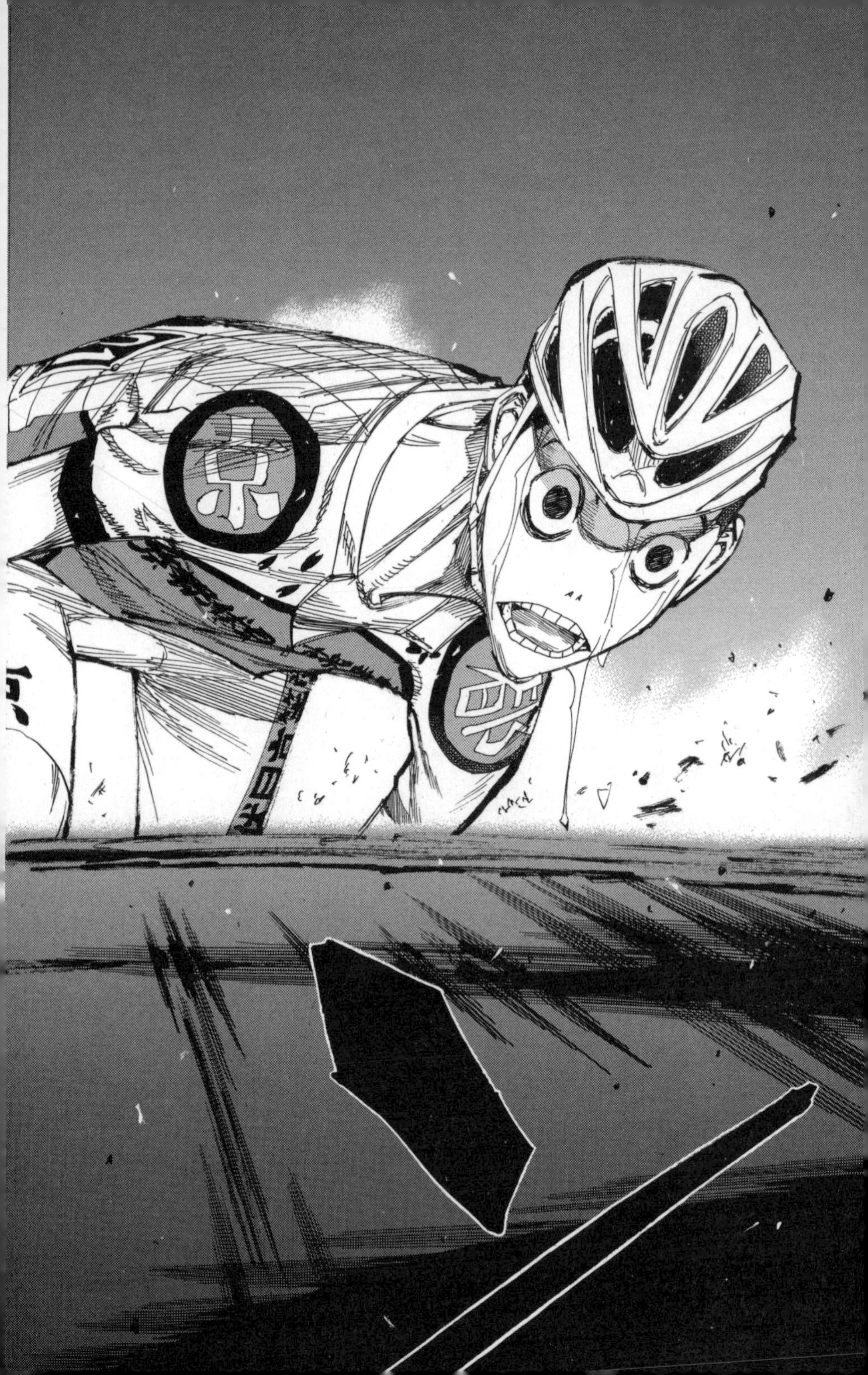
京

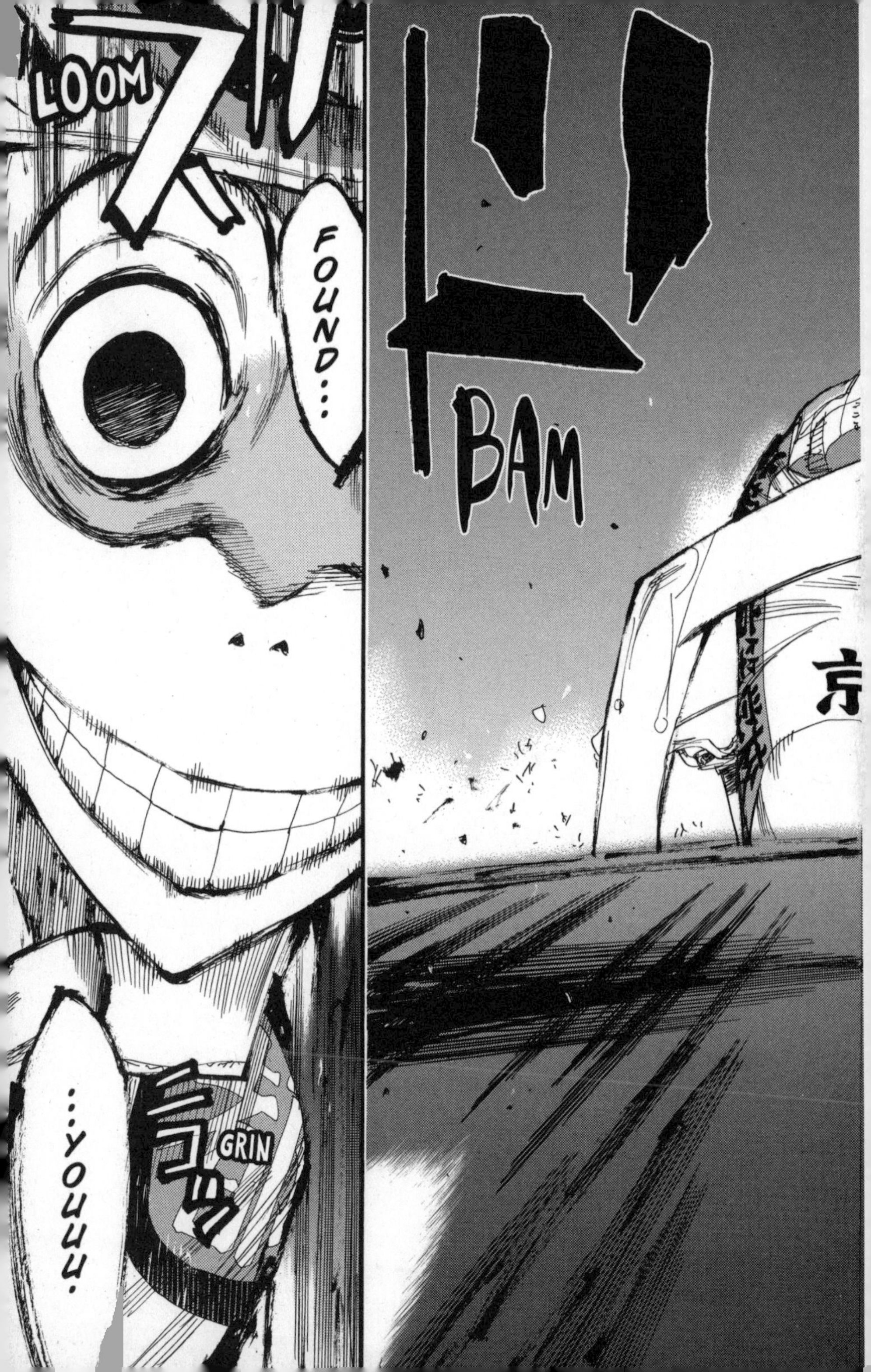
BAM
LOOM
FOUND...
GRIN
...YOUUUU.

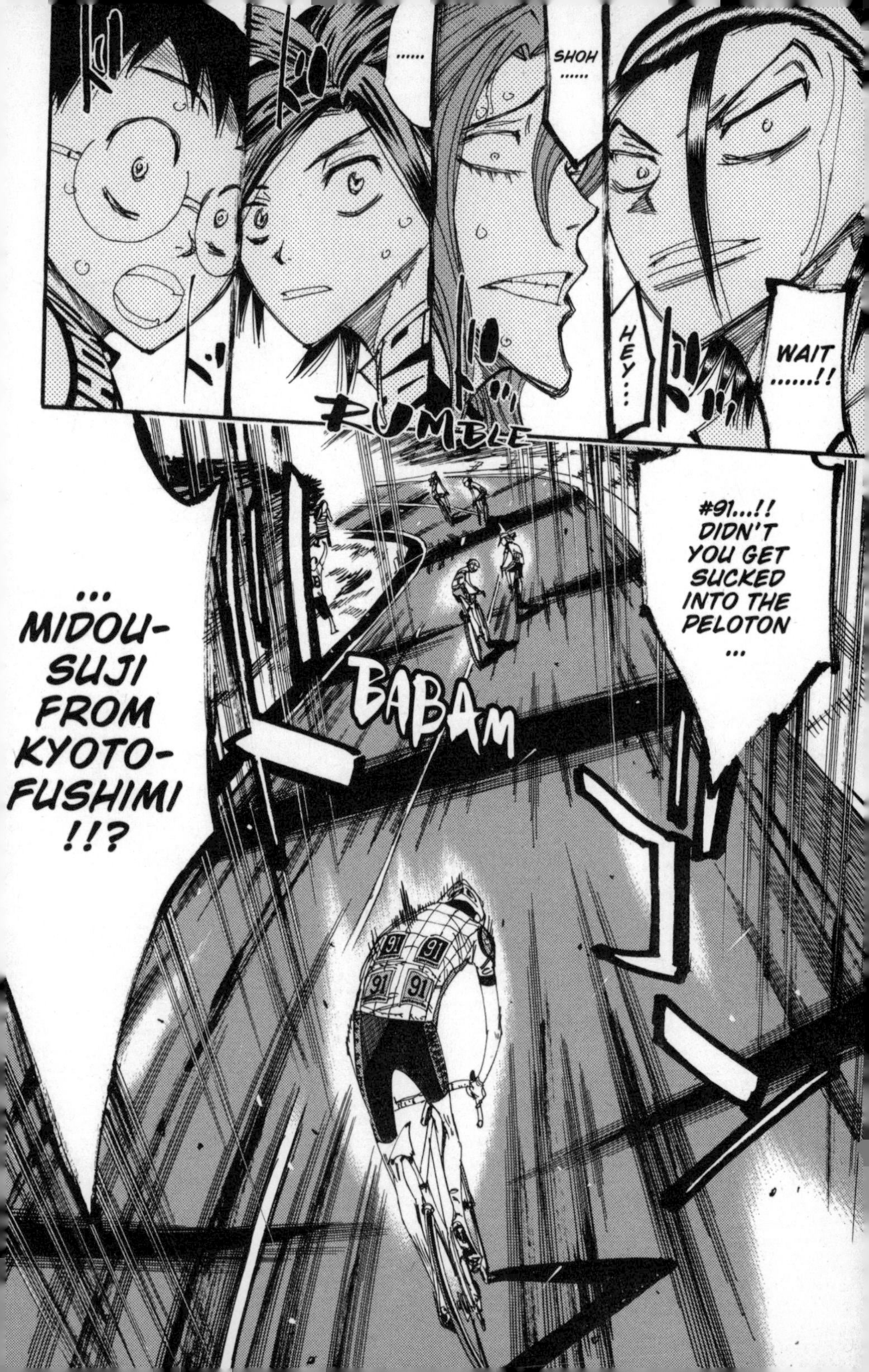
WAIT ......!!
HEY...
SHOH ......
......
RUMBLE
#91...!! DIDN'T YOU GET SUCKED INTO THE PELOTON ...
BABAM
... MIDOU-SUJI FROM KYOTO-FUSHIMI !!?

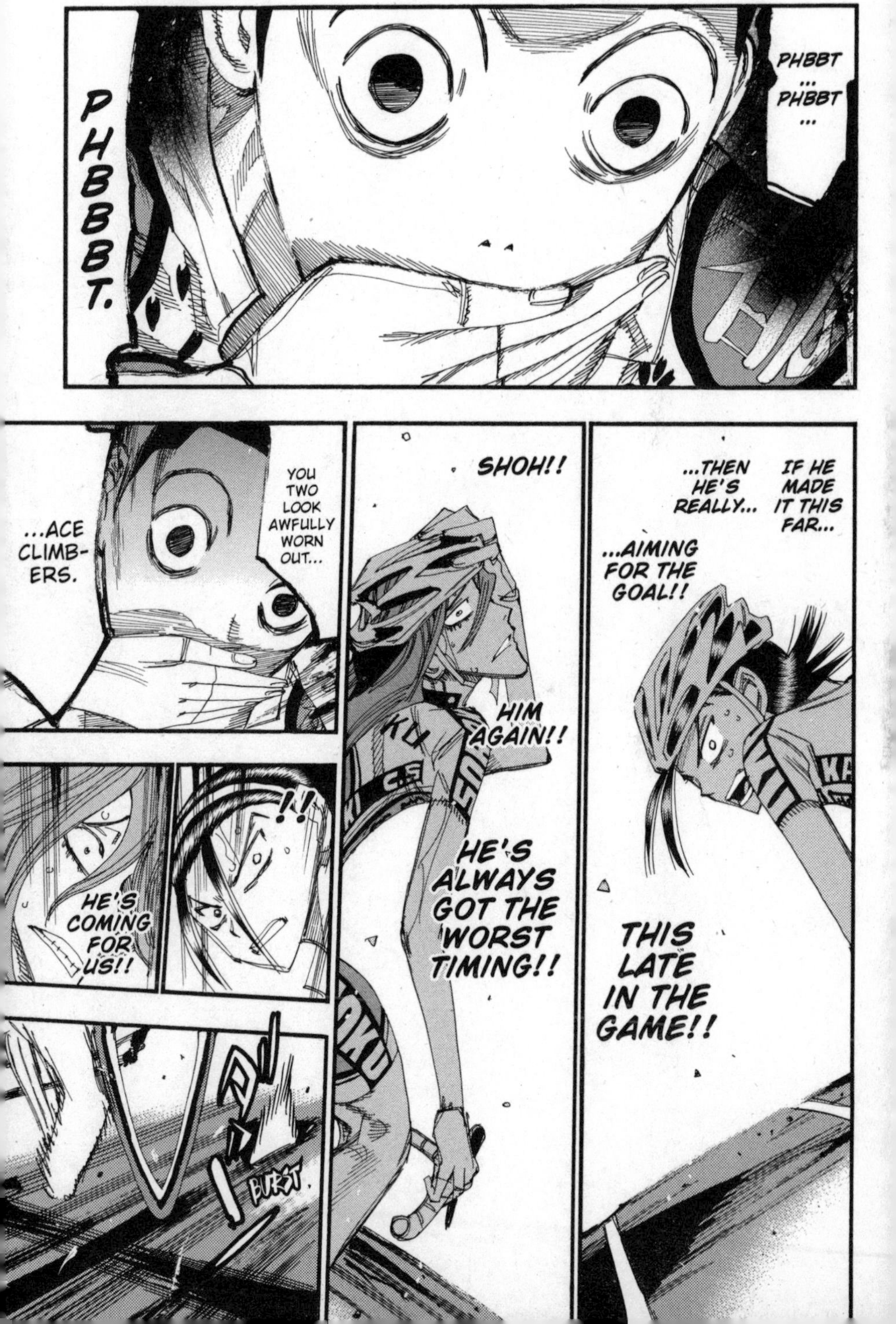
PHBBT ... PHBBT ...
PHBBBT.
IF HE MADE IT THIS FAR...
...THEN HE'S REALLY...
...AIMING FOR THE GOAL!!
THIS LATE IN THE GAME!!
SHOH!!
HIM AGAIN!!
HE'S ALWAYS GOT THE WORST TIMING!!
YOU TWO LOOK AWFULLY WORN OUT...
...ACE CLIMBERS.
!!
HE'S COMING FOR US!!
BURST

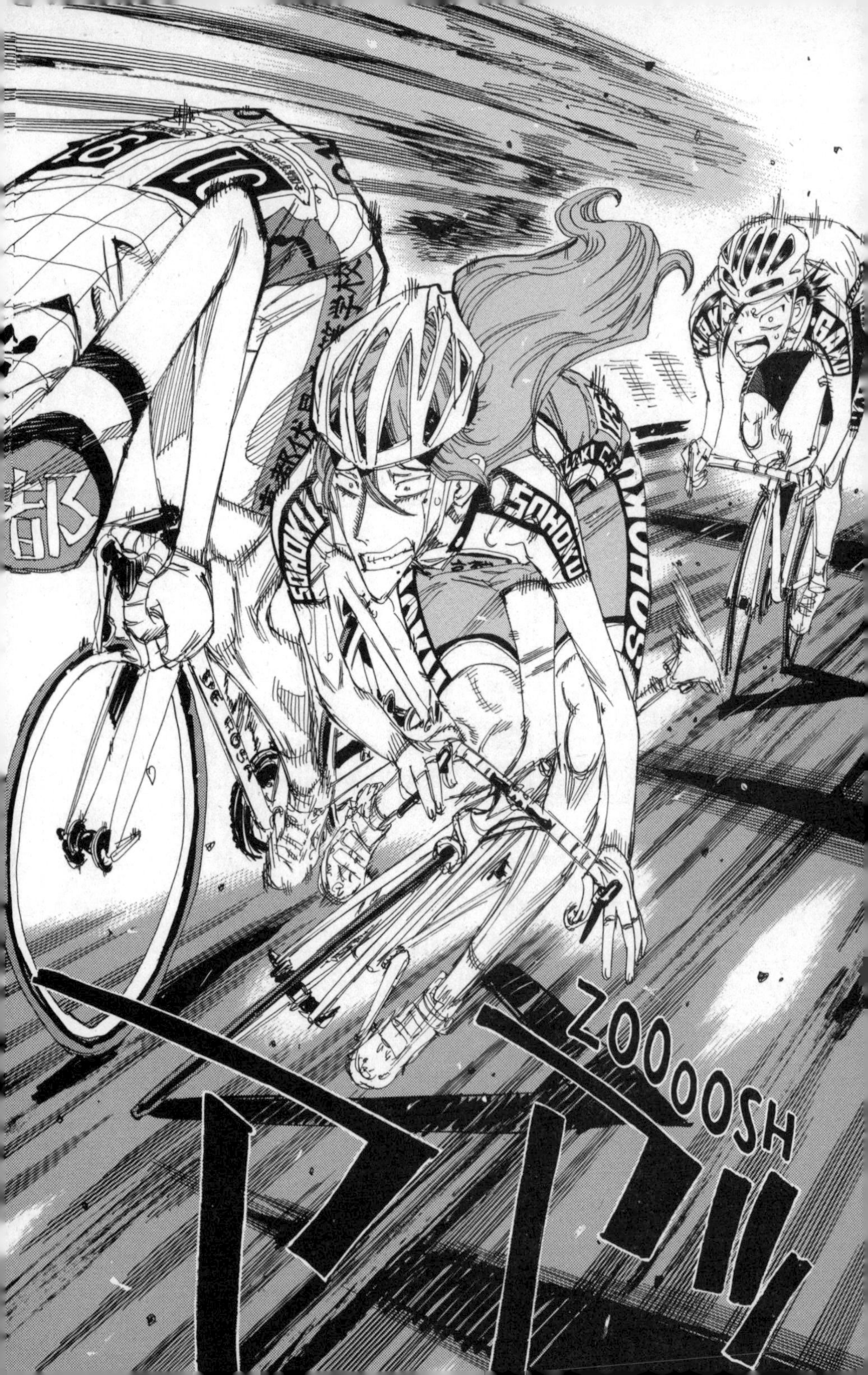
ZOOOOSH
SOHOKU

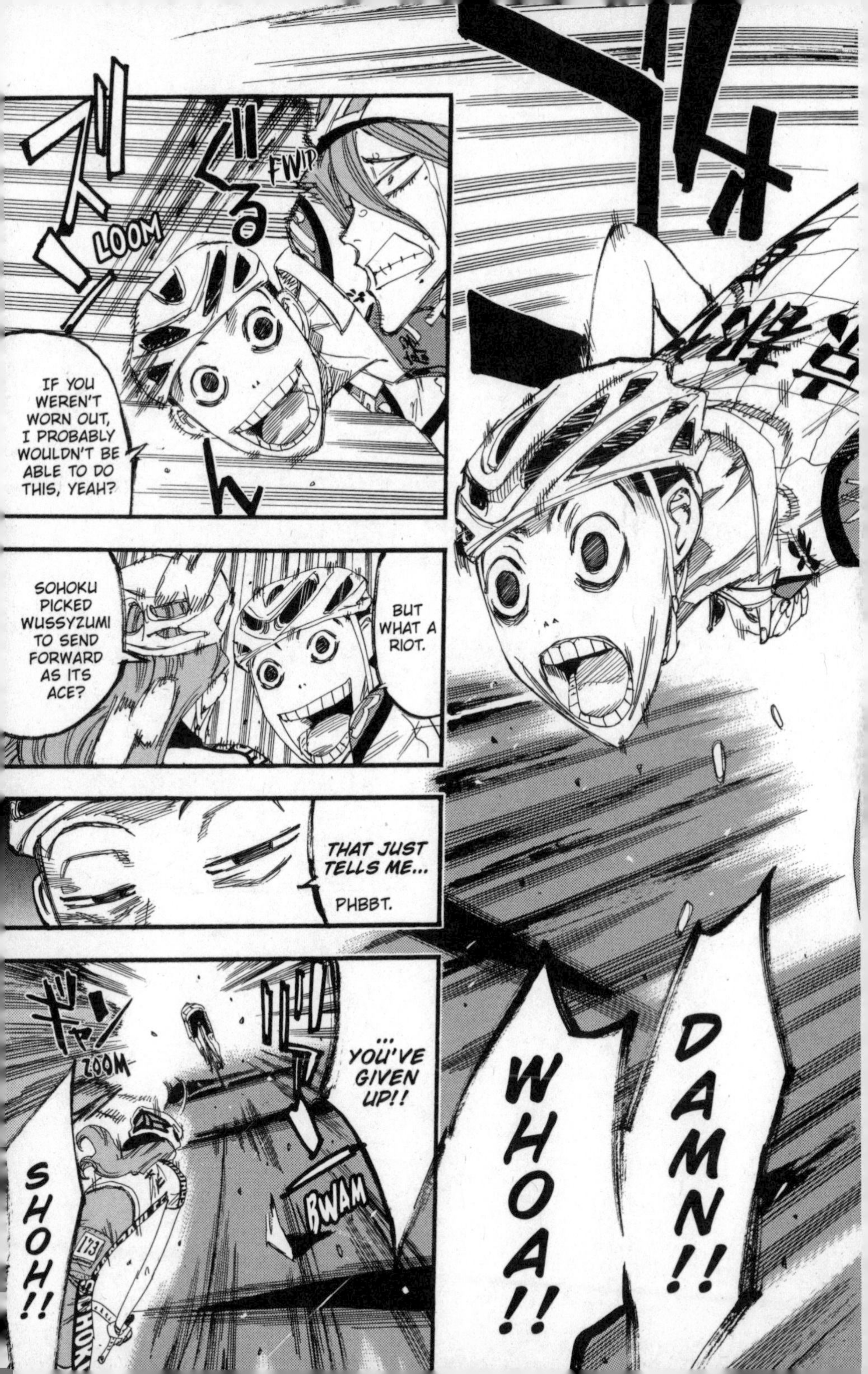
DAMN!!
WHOA!!
FWIP
LOOM
IF YOU WEREN'T WORN OUT, I PROBABLY WOULDN'T BE ABLE TO DO THIS, YEAH?
BUT WHAT A RIOT.
SOHOKU PICKED WUSSYZUMI TO SEND FORWARD AS ITS ACE?
THAT JUST TELLS ME...
PHBBT.
...YOU'VE GIVEN UP!!
ZOOM
BWAM
SHOH!!
173

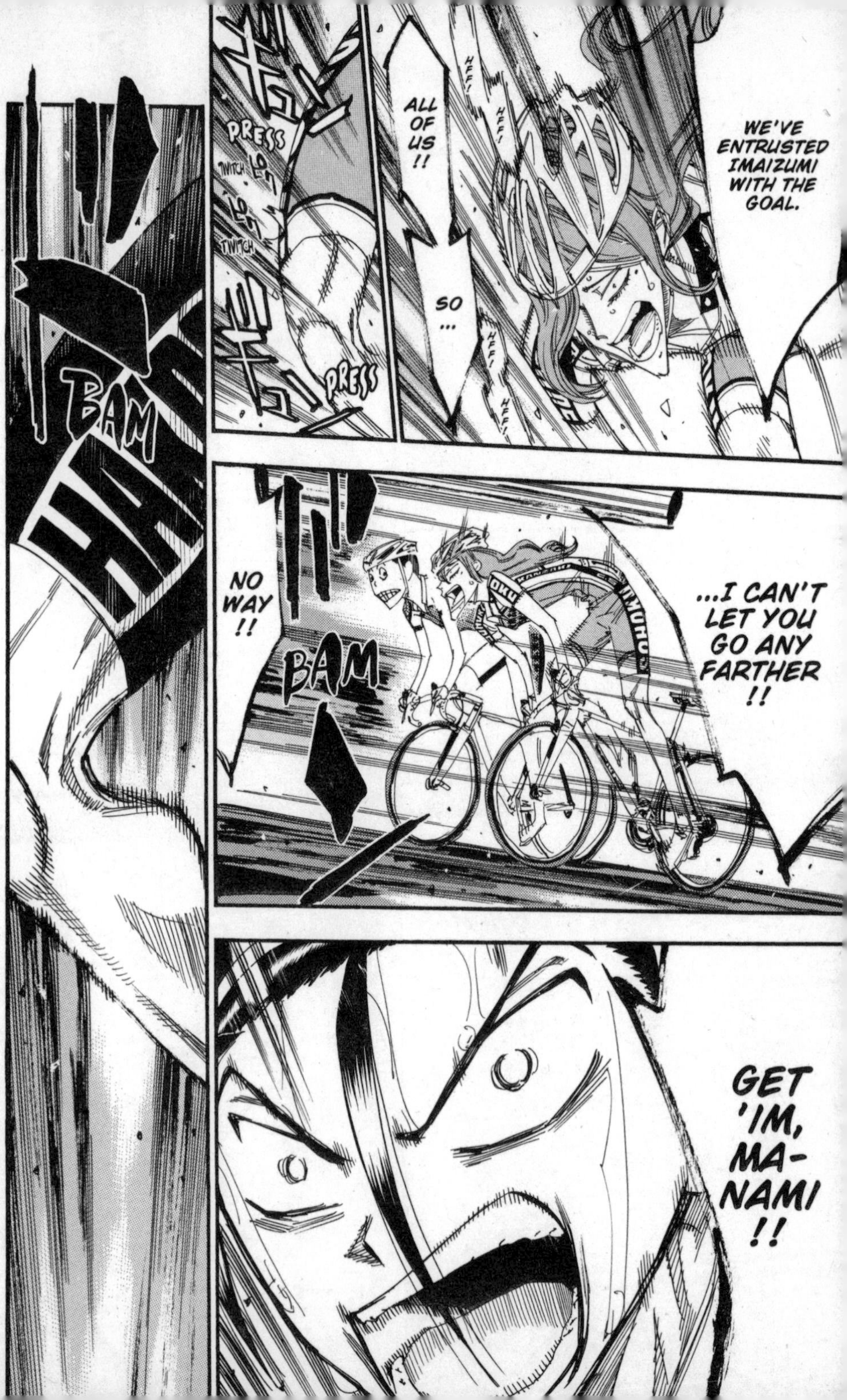

WE'VE ENTRUSTED IMAIZUMI WITH THE GOAL.
HFF! HFF!
HFF! HFF!
ALL OF US!!
SO...
PRESS
TWITCH
TWITCH
PRESS
...I CAN'T LET YOU GO ANY FARTHER!!
NO WAY!!
BAM
GET 'IM, MA-NAMI!!
BAM

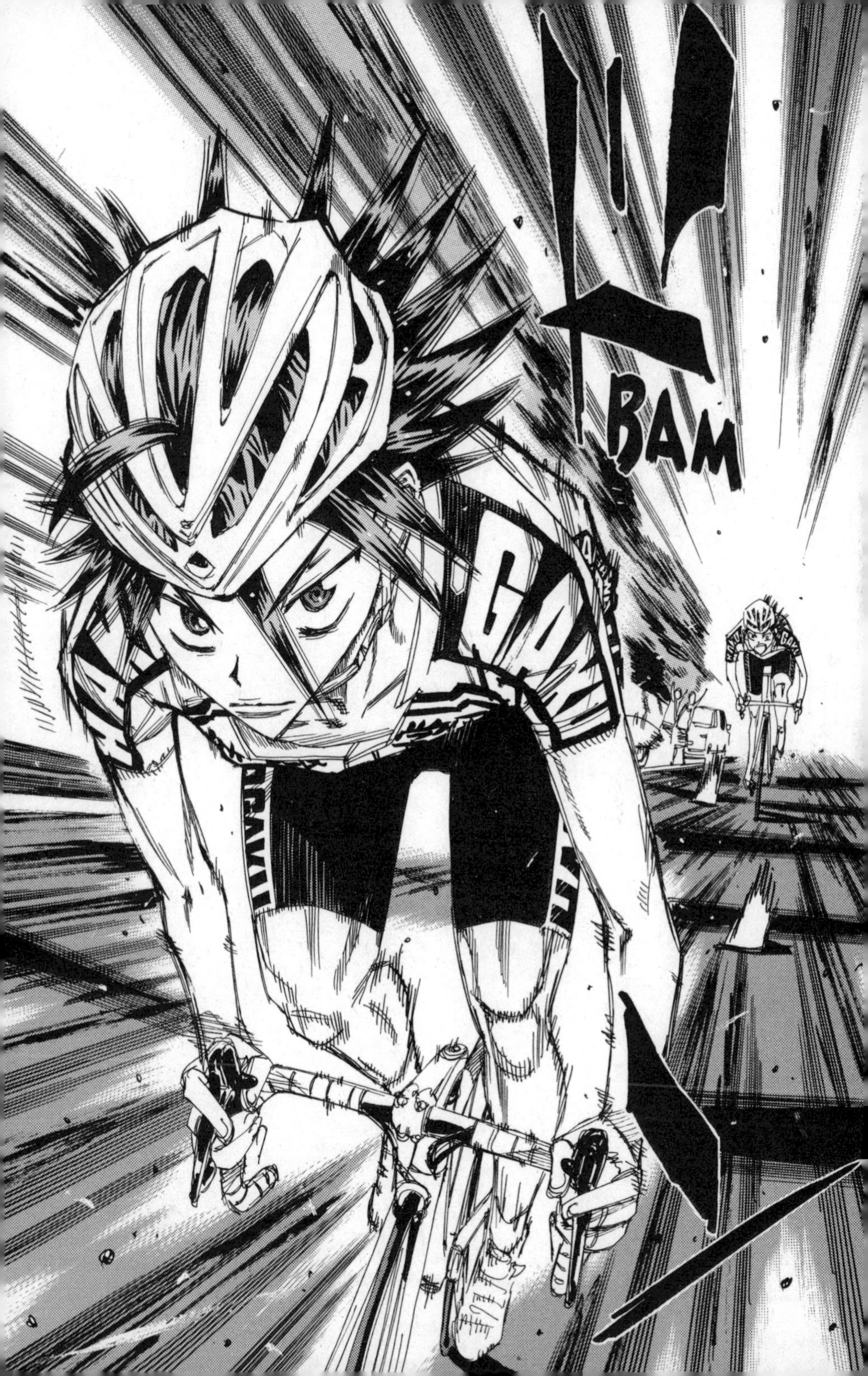
BAM

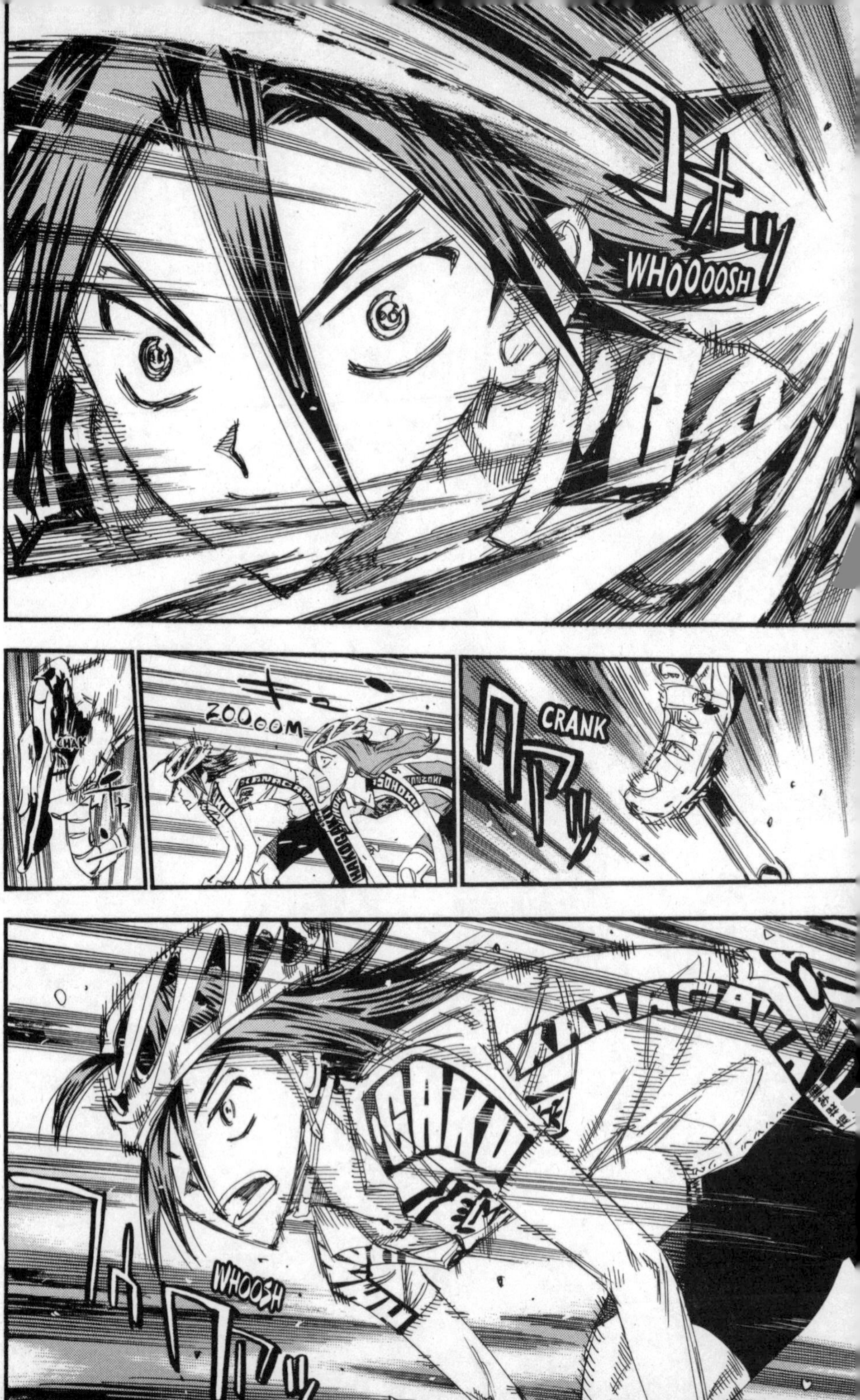
WHOOOOSH
CRANK
ZOOOOM
CHAK
WHOOSH

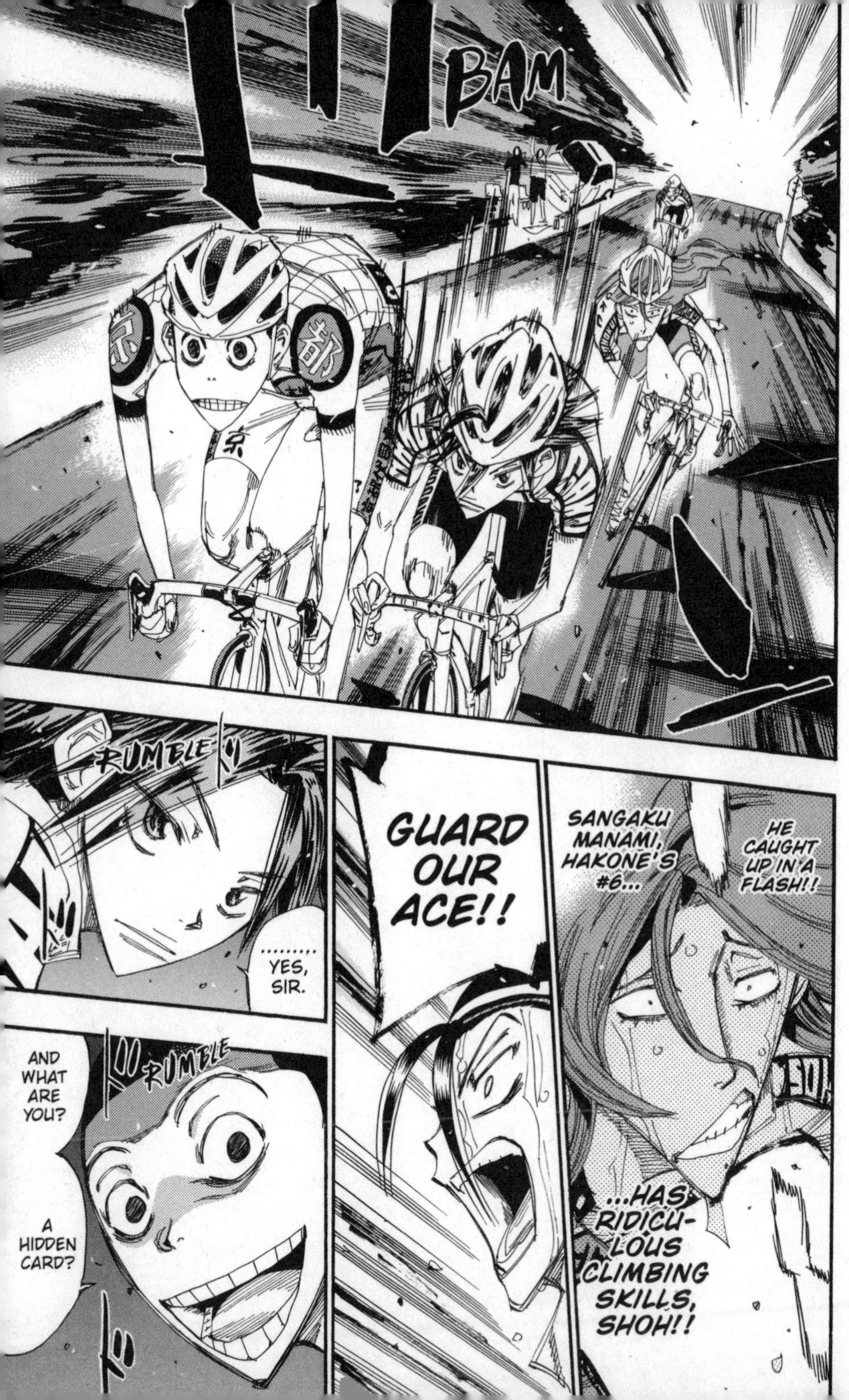
BAM
HE CAUGHT UP IN A FLASH!!
SANGAKU MANAMI, HAKONE'S #6...
...HAS RIDICULOUS CLIMBING SKILLS, SHOH!!
GUARD OUR ACE!!
RUMBLE
........, YES, SIR.
RUMBLE
AND WHAT ARE YOU?
A HIDDEN CARD?

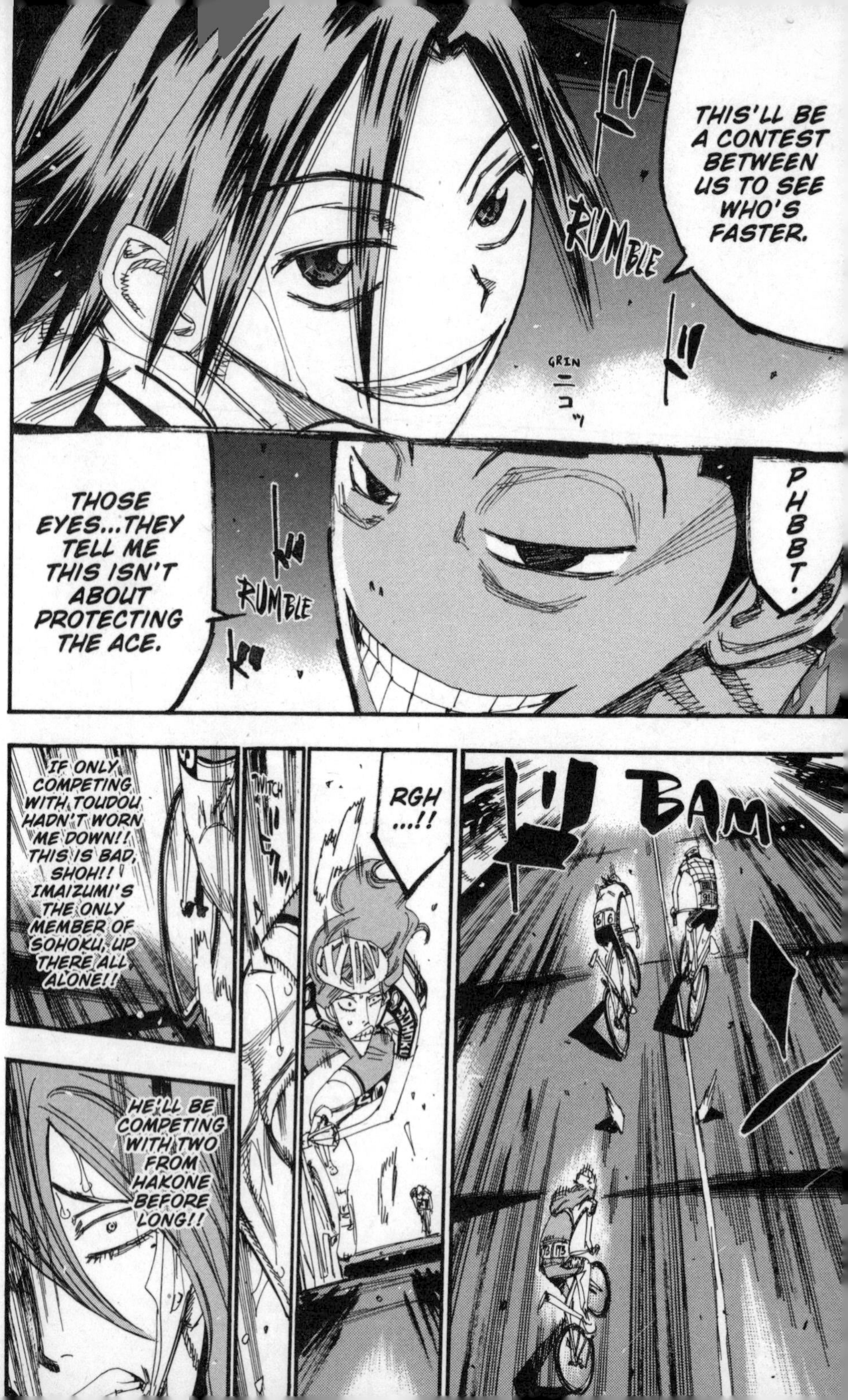
THIS'LL BE A CONTEST BETWEEN US TO SEE WHO'S FASTER.
RUMBLE
GRIN
PHBBT.
THOSE EYES...THEY TELL ME THIS ISN'T ABOUT PROTECTING THE ACE.
RUMBLE
BAM
RGH ...!!
TWITCH
IF ONLY COMPETING WITH TOUDOU HADN'T WORN ME DOWN!! THIS IS BAD, SHOH!! IMAIZUMI'S THE ONLY MEMBER OF SOHOKU UP THERE ALL ALONE!!
HE'LL BE COMPETING WITH TWO FROM HAKONE BEFORE LONG!!

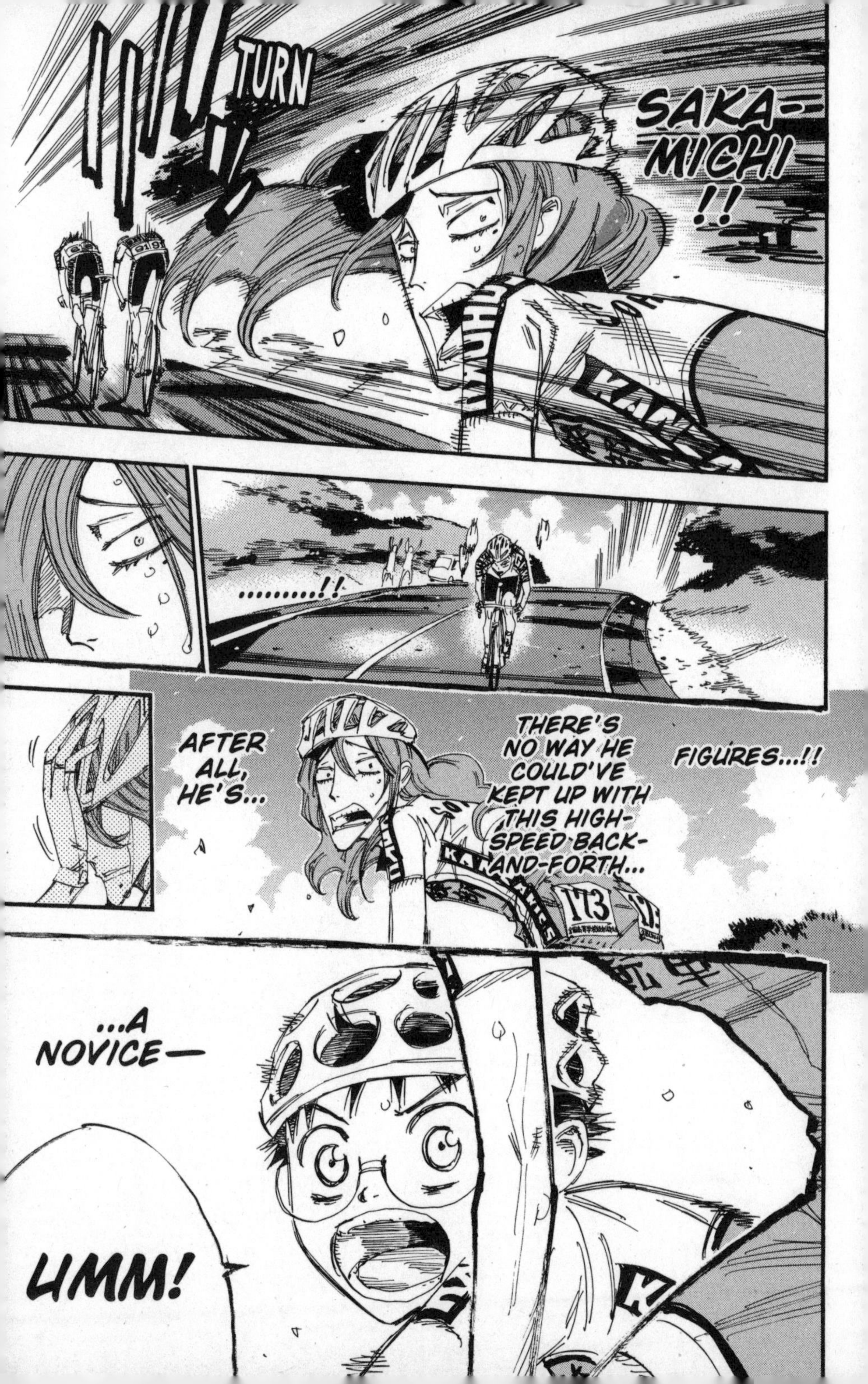
TURN
SAKA-MICHI!!
..........!!
FIGURES...!!
THERE'S NO WAY HE COULD'VE KEPT UP WITH THIS HIGH-SPEED BACK-AND-FORTH...
AFTER ALL, HE'S...
...A NOVICE—
UMM!

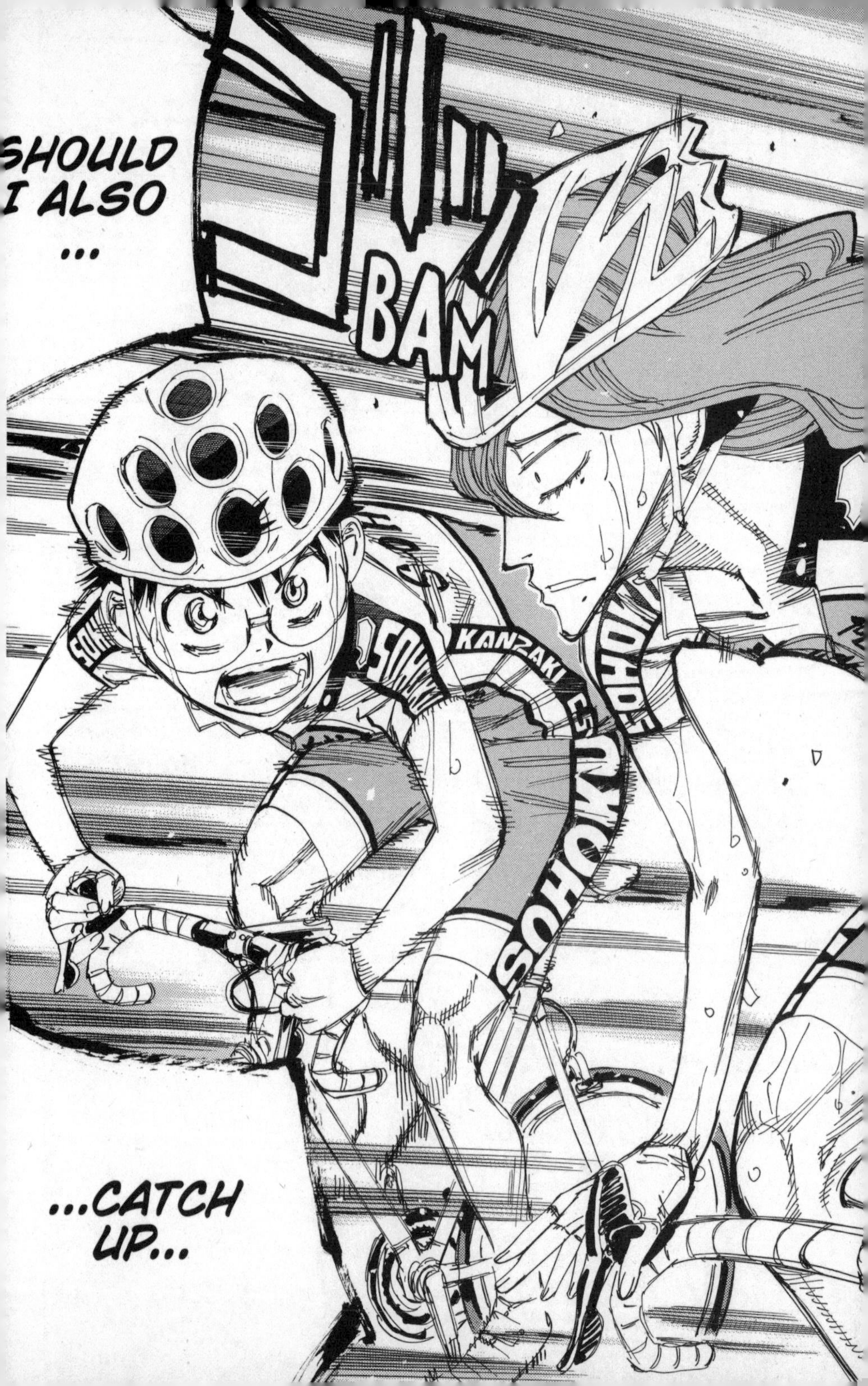
SHOULD I ALSO ...
BAM
KANZAKI
SOHOKU
...CATCH UP...

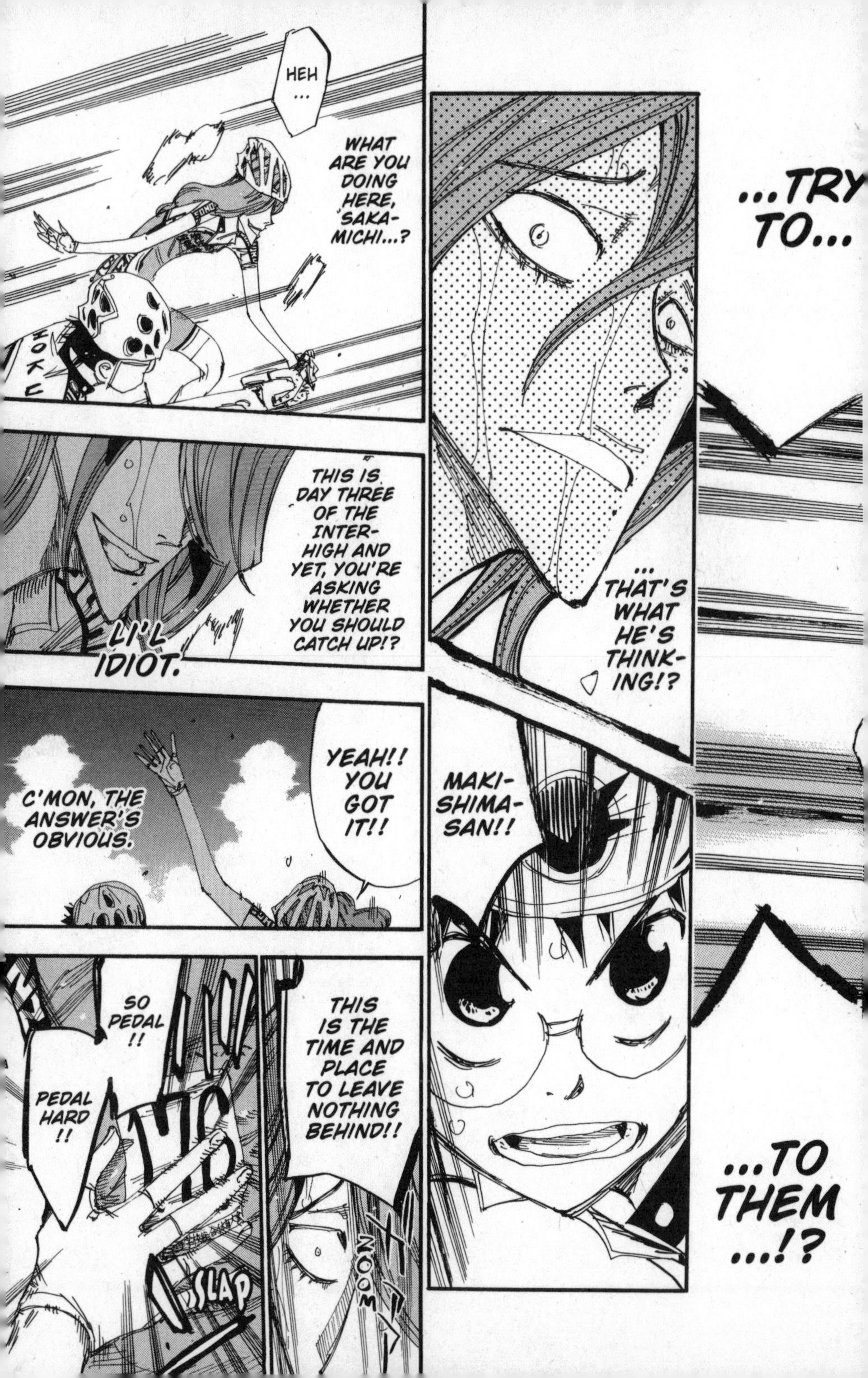
...TRY TO...
...TO THEM ...!?
...THAT'S WHAT HE'S THINK-ING!?
MAKI-SHIMA-SAN!!
HEH ...
WHAT ARE YOU DOING HERE, SAKA-MICHI...?
THIS IS DAY THREE OF THE INTER-HIGH AND YET, YOU'RE ASKING WHETHER YOU SHOULD CATCH UP!?
LI'L IDIOT.
YEAH!! YOU GOT IT!!
C'MON, THE ANSWER'S OBVIOUS.
THIS IS THE TIME AND PLACE TO LEAVE NOTHING BEHIND!!
ZOOM
SO PEDAL !!
PEDAL HARD !!
SLAP

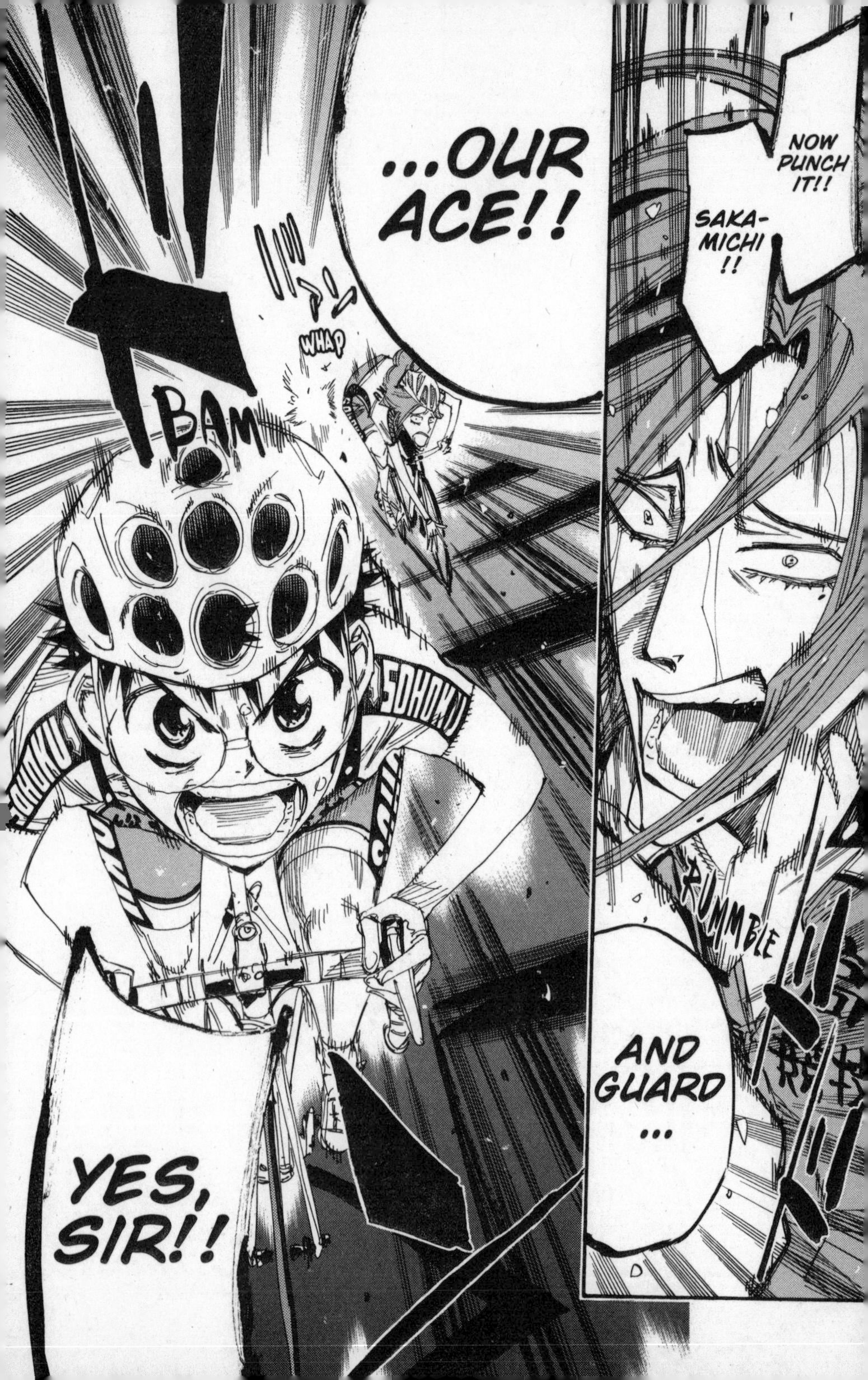
NOW PUNCH IT!!
SAKA-MICHI!!
RUMMBLE
AND GUARD...
...OUR ACE!!
WHAP
BAM
YES, SIR!!

RIDE.201 HAKONE'S #6 TAG

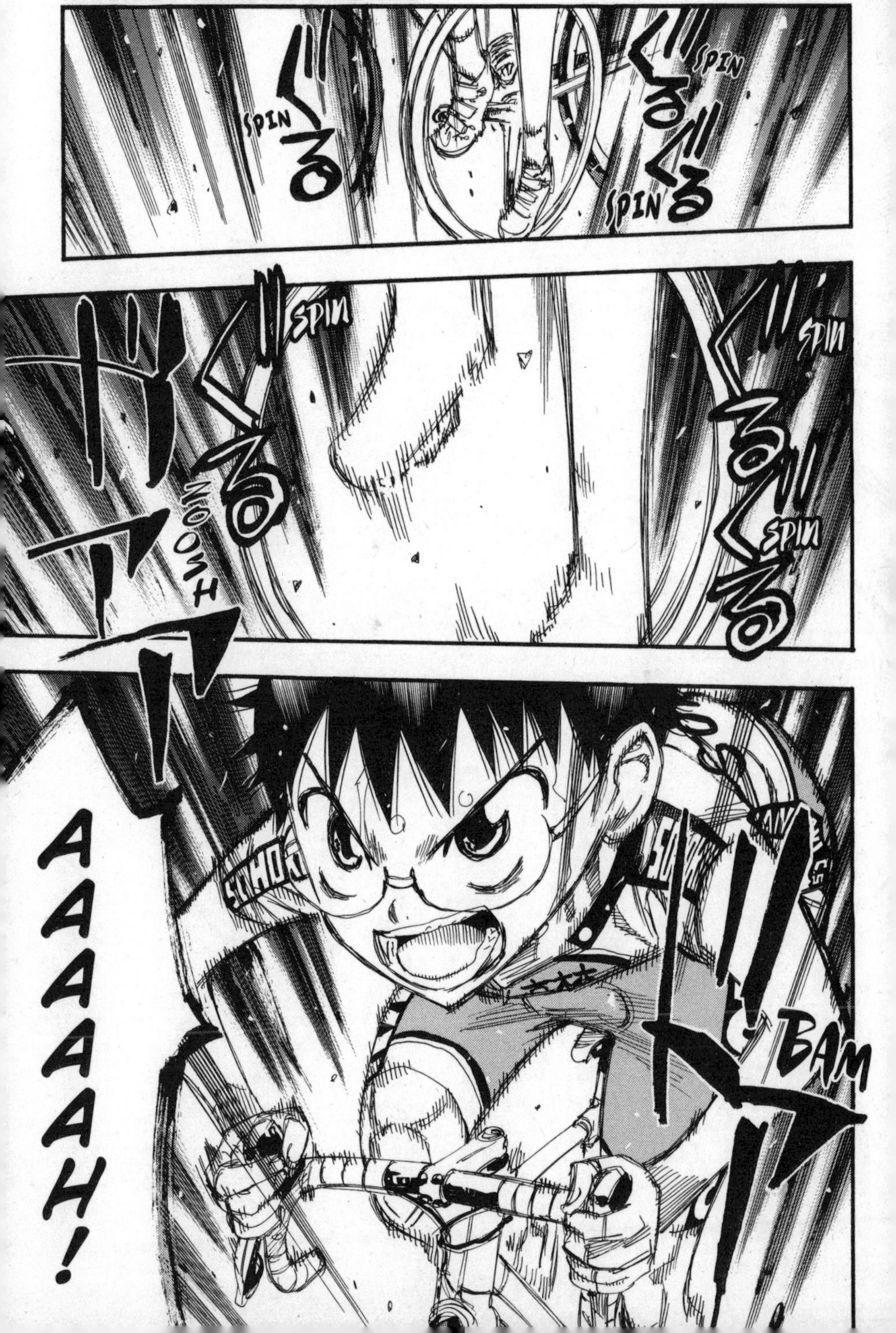
SPIN
SPIN
SPIN
SPIN
SPIN
SPIN
WOOSH
BAM
AAAAAAH!

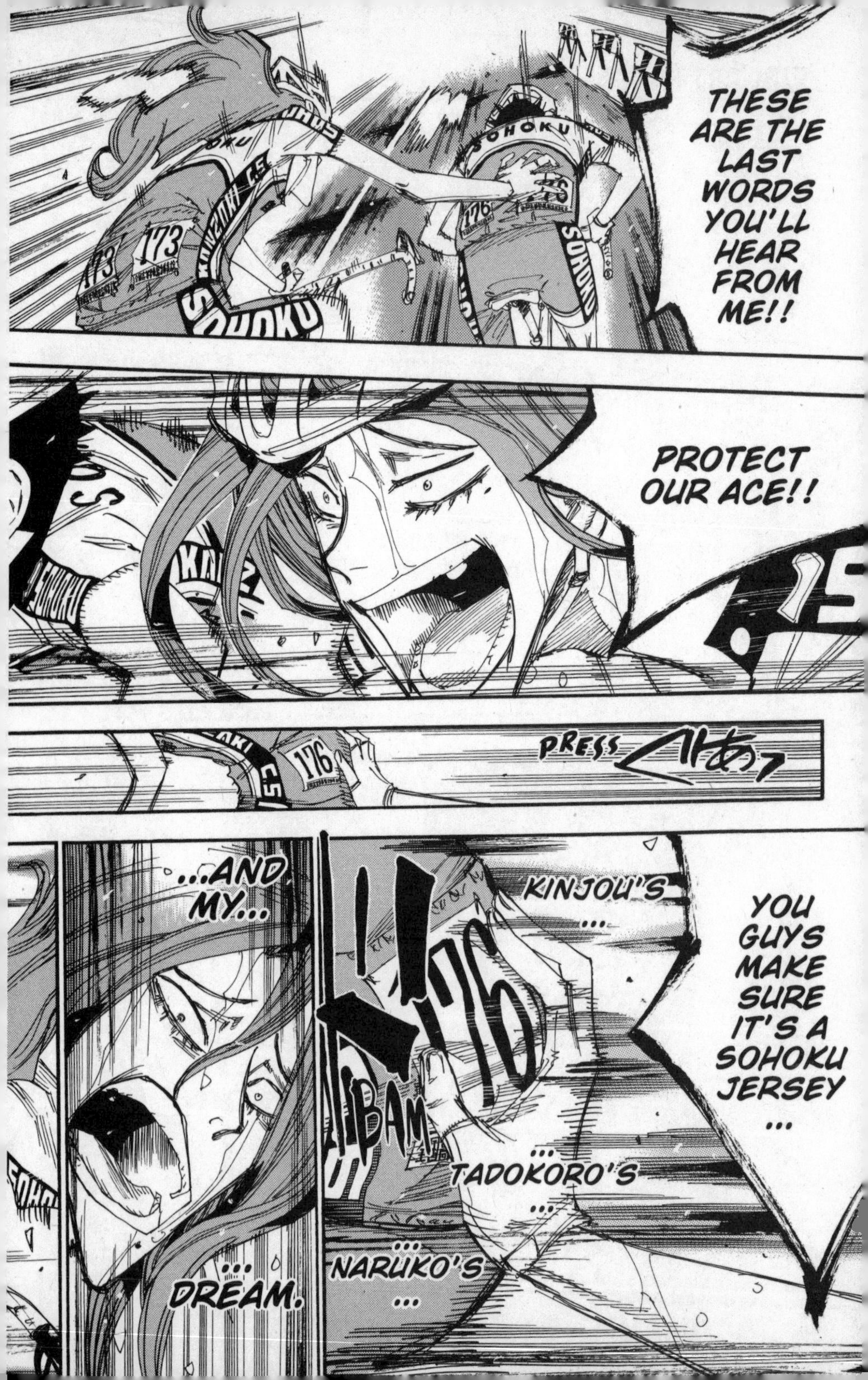
THESE ARE THE LAST WORDS YOU'LL HEAR FROM ME!!
PROTECT OUR ACE!!
PRESS
YOU GUYS MAKE SURE IT'S A SOHOKU JERSEY ...
KINJOU'S ...
... TADOKORO'S ...
... NARUKO'S ...
...AND MY...
... DREAM.
BAM

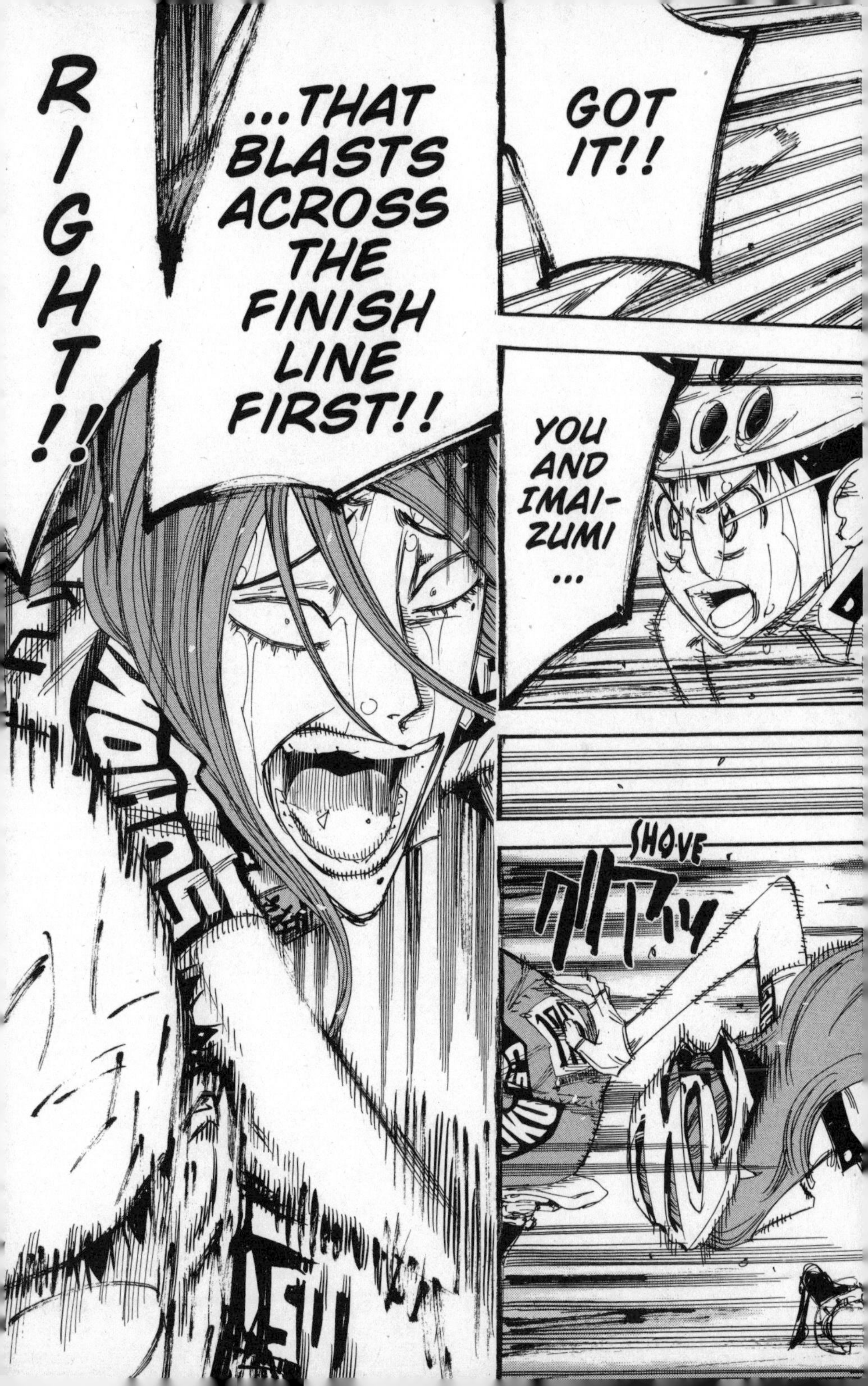
GOT IT!!
YOU AND IMAI-ZUMI...
SHOVE
...THAT BLASTS ACROSS THE FINISH LINE FIRST!!
RIGHT!!

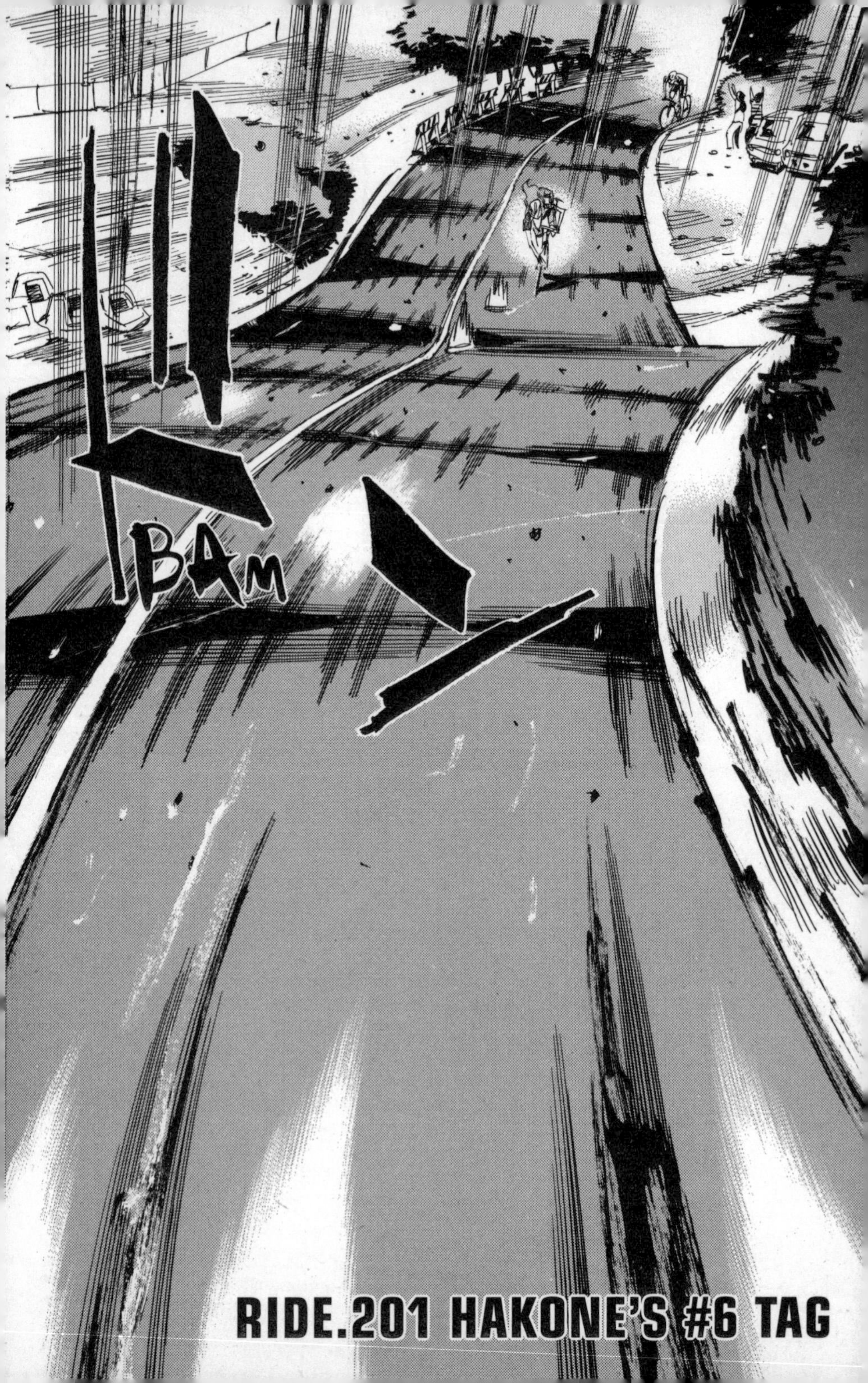
BAM

RIDE.201 HAKONE'S #6 TAG

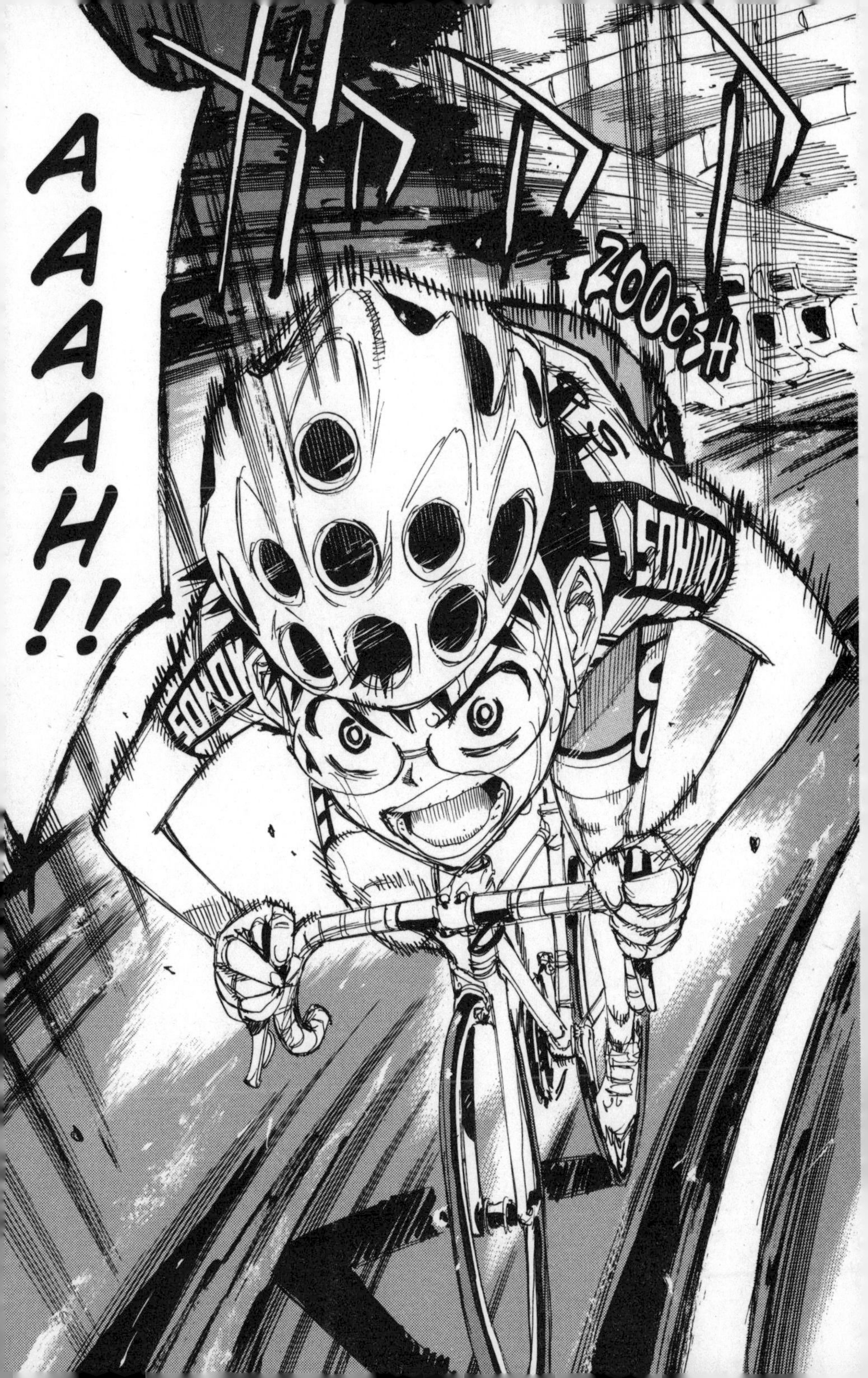

ZOOOSH
AAAAH!!

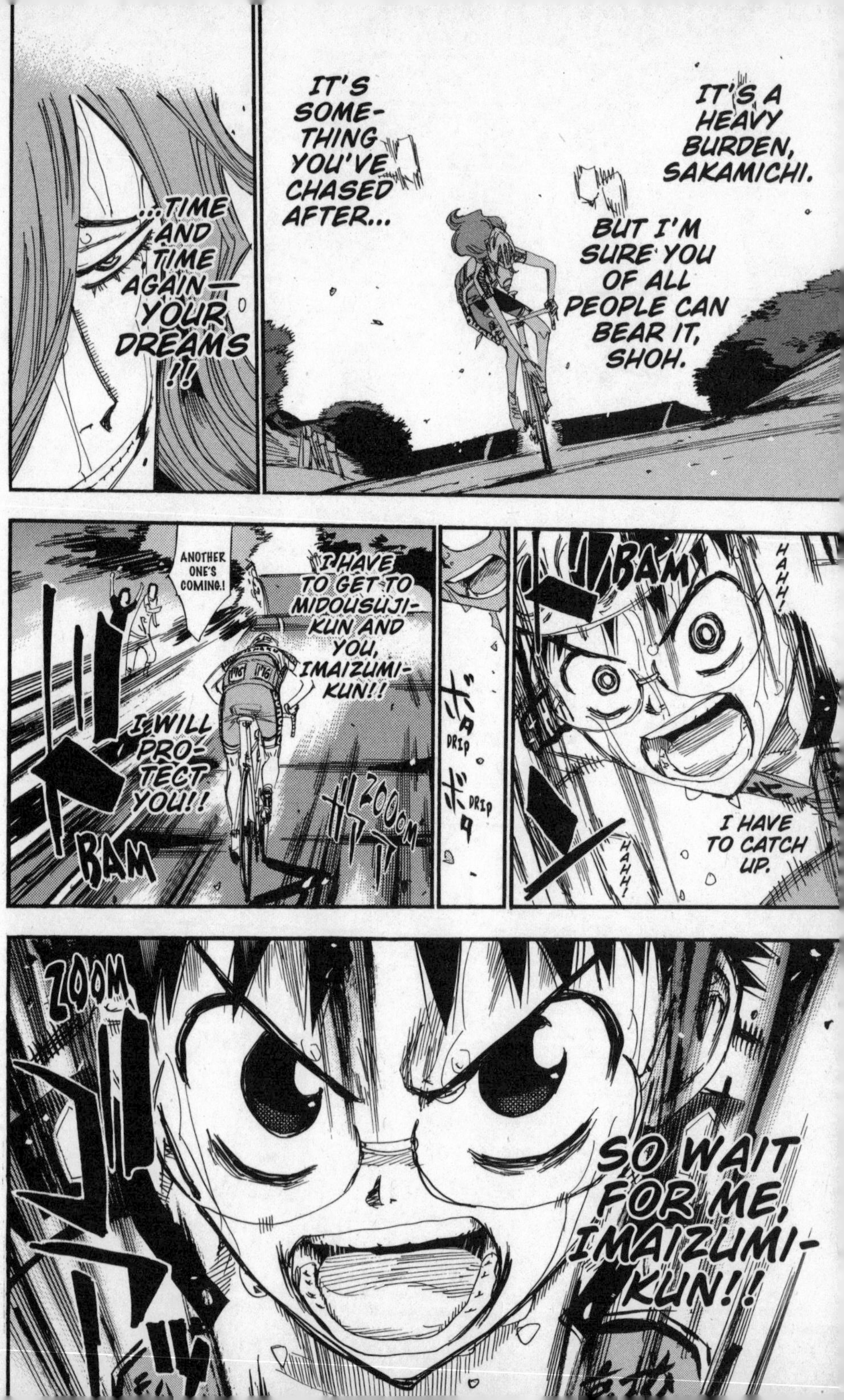
IT'S A HEAVY BURDEN, SAKAMICHI.
BUT I'M SURE YOU OF ALL PEOPLE CAN BEAR IT, SHOH.
IT'S SOMETHING YOU'VE CHASED AFTER...
...TIME AND TIME AGAIN—YOUR DREAMS!!
BAM
HAHH!
I HAVE TO CATCH UP.
HAHH!
DRIP
DRIP
I HAVE TO GET TO MIDOUSUJI-KUN AND YOU, IMAIZUMI-KUN!!
ANOTHER ONE'S COMING!
I WILL PROTECT YOU!!
ZOOOM
BAM
ZOOM
SO WAIT FOR ME, IMAIZUMI-KUN!!

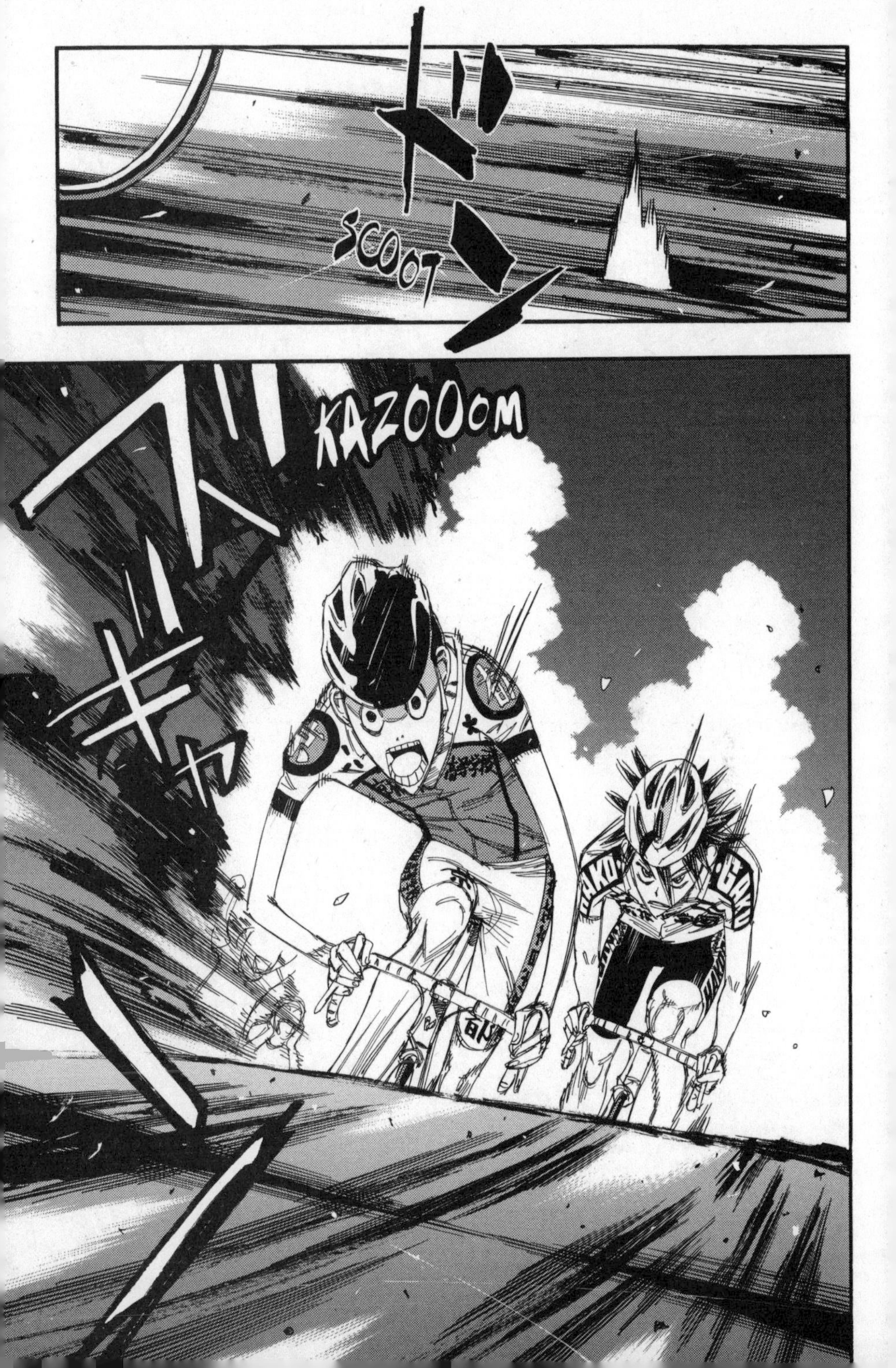
SCOOT
KAZOOOM

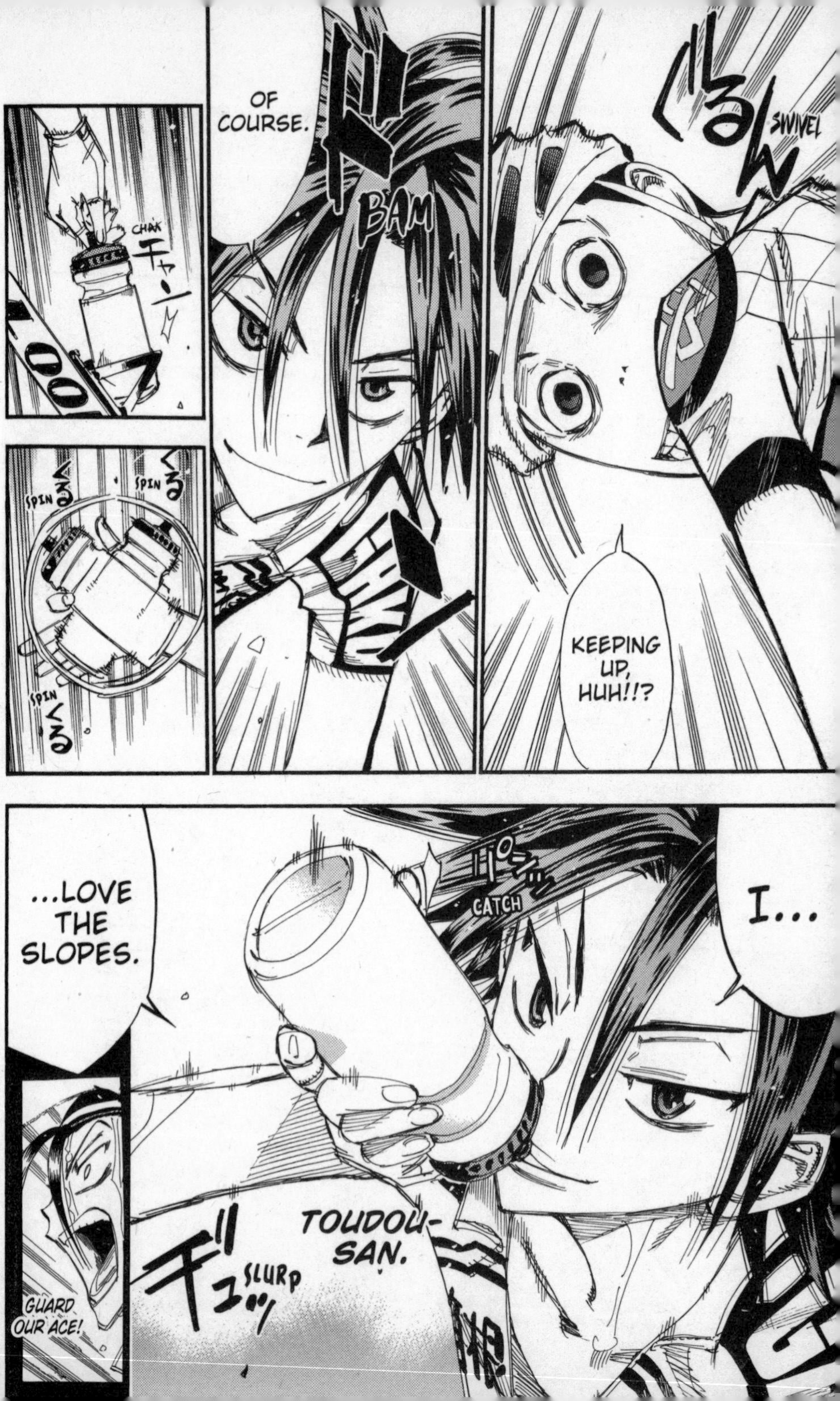
SWIVEL
KEEPING UP, HUH!!?
OF COURSE.
BAM
CHAK
SPIN
SPIN
SPIN
I...
CATCH
...LOVE THE SLOPES.
TOUDOU-SAN.
SLURP
GUARD OUR ACE!

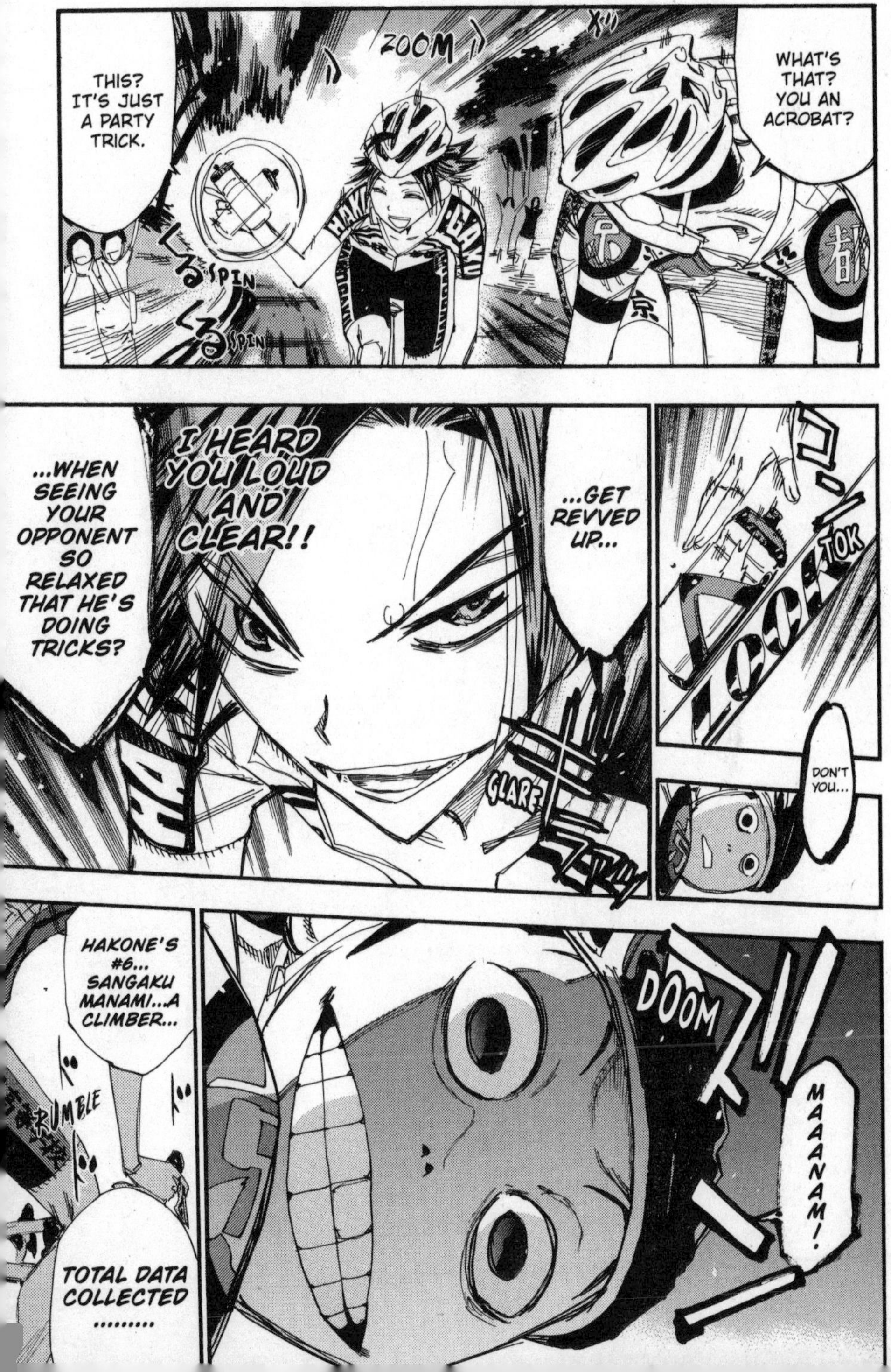
WHAT'S THAT? YOU AN ACROBAT?
ZOOM
THIS? IT'S JUST A PARTY TRICK.
SPIN
SPIN
TOK
DON'T YOU...
...GET REVVED UP...
I HEARD YOU LOUD AND CLEAR!!
...WHEN SEEING YOUR OPPONENT SO RELAXED THAT HE'S DOING TRICKS?
GLARE
DOOM
MAAAANAM!
HAKONE'S #6... SANGAKU MANAMI...A CLIMBER...
RUMBLE
TOTAL DATA COLLECTED ....

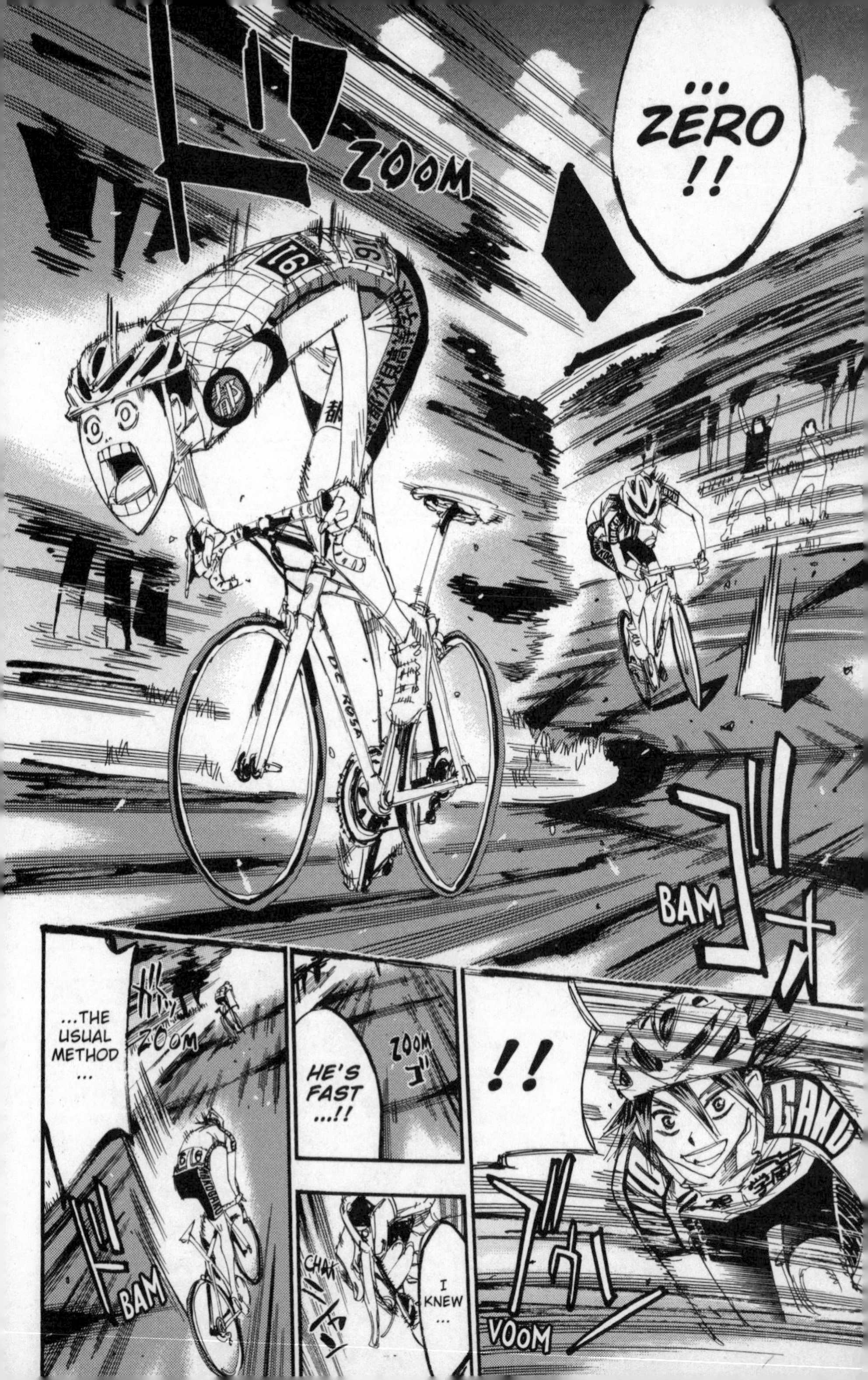
...ZERO!!
ZOOM
BAM
!!
VOOM
HE'S FAST...!!
ZOOM
I KNEW...
CHAK
...THE USUAL METHOD...
ZOOM
BAM

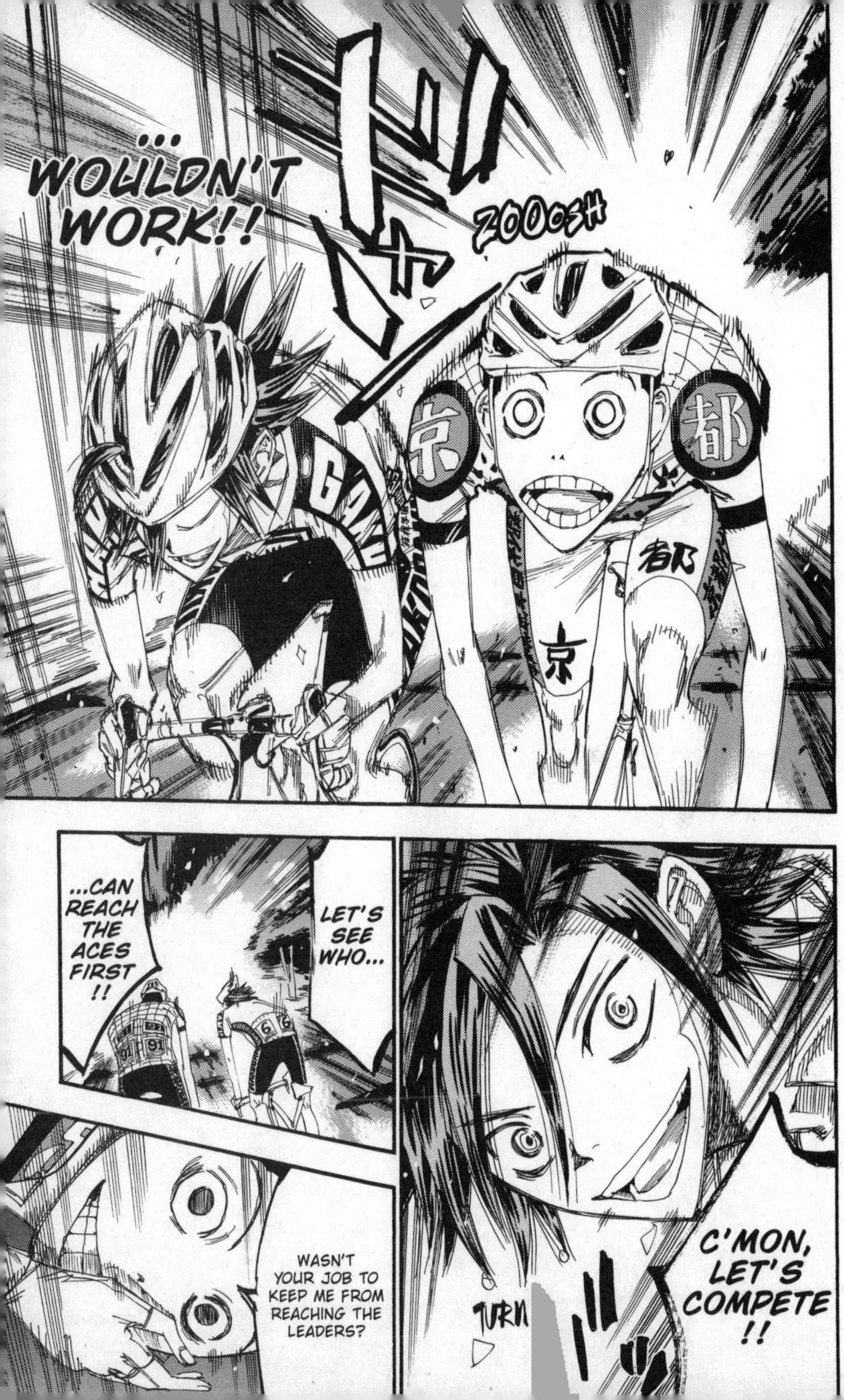
...WOULDN'T WORK!!
ZOOOSH
C'MON, LET'S COMPETE!!
TURN
LET'S SEE WHO...
...CAN REACH THE ACES FIRST!!
WASN'T YOUR JOB TO KEEP ME FROM REACHING THE LEADERS?

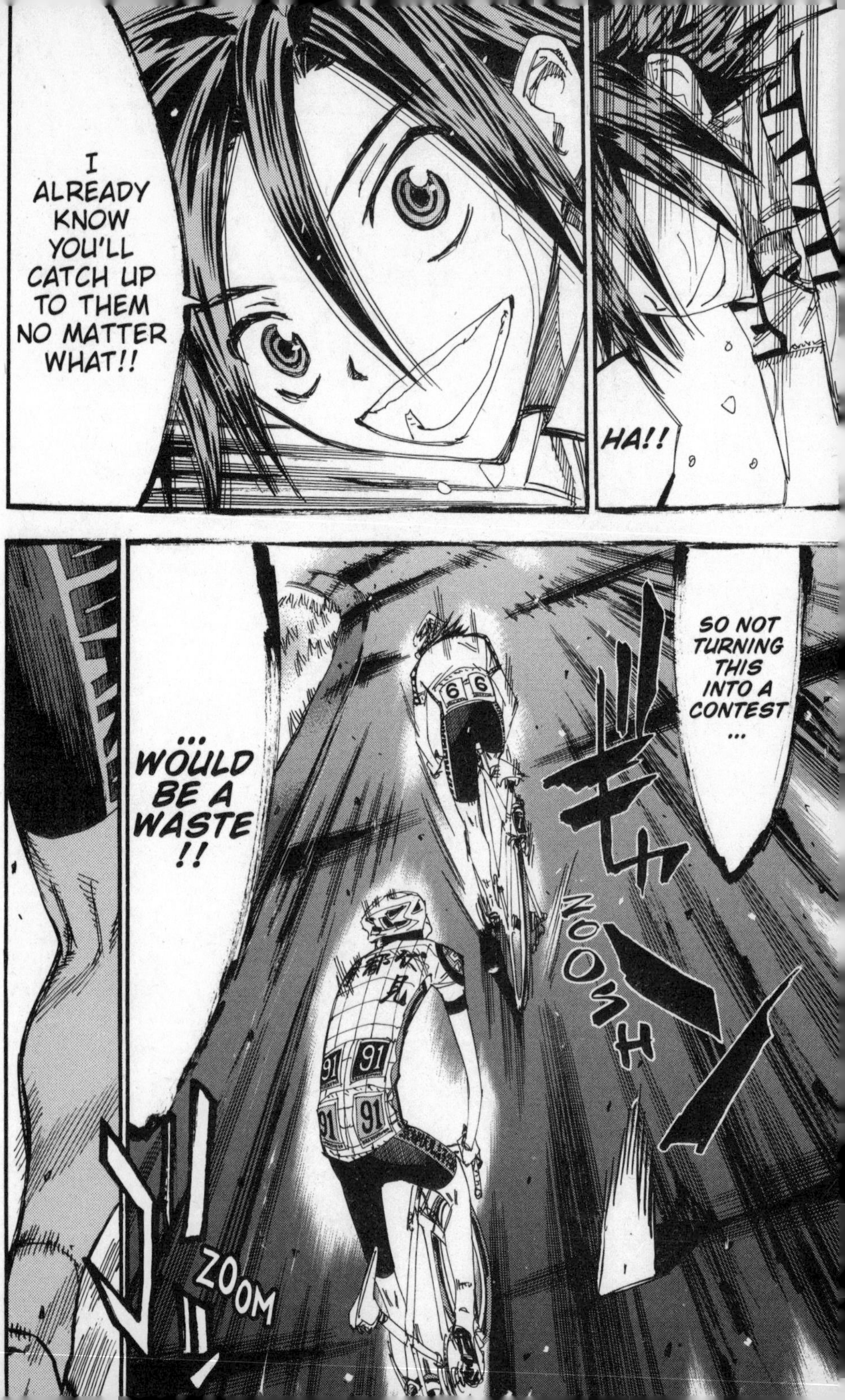
HA!!
I ALREADY KNOW YOU'LL CATCH UP TO THEM NO MATTER WHAT!!
SO NOT TURNING THIS INTO A CONTEST...
...WOULD BE A WASTE!!
WHOOSH
ZOOM

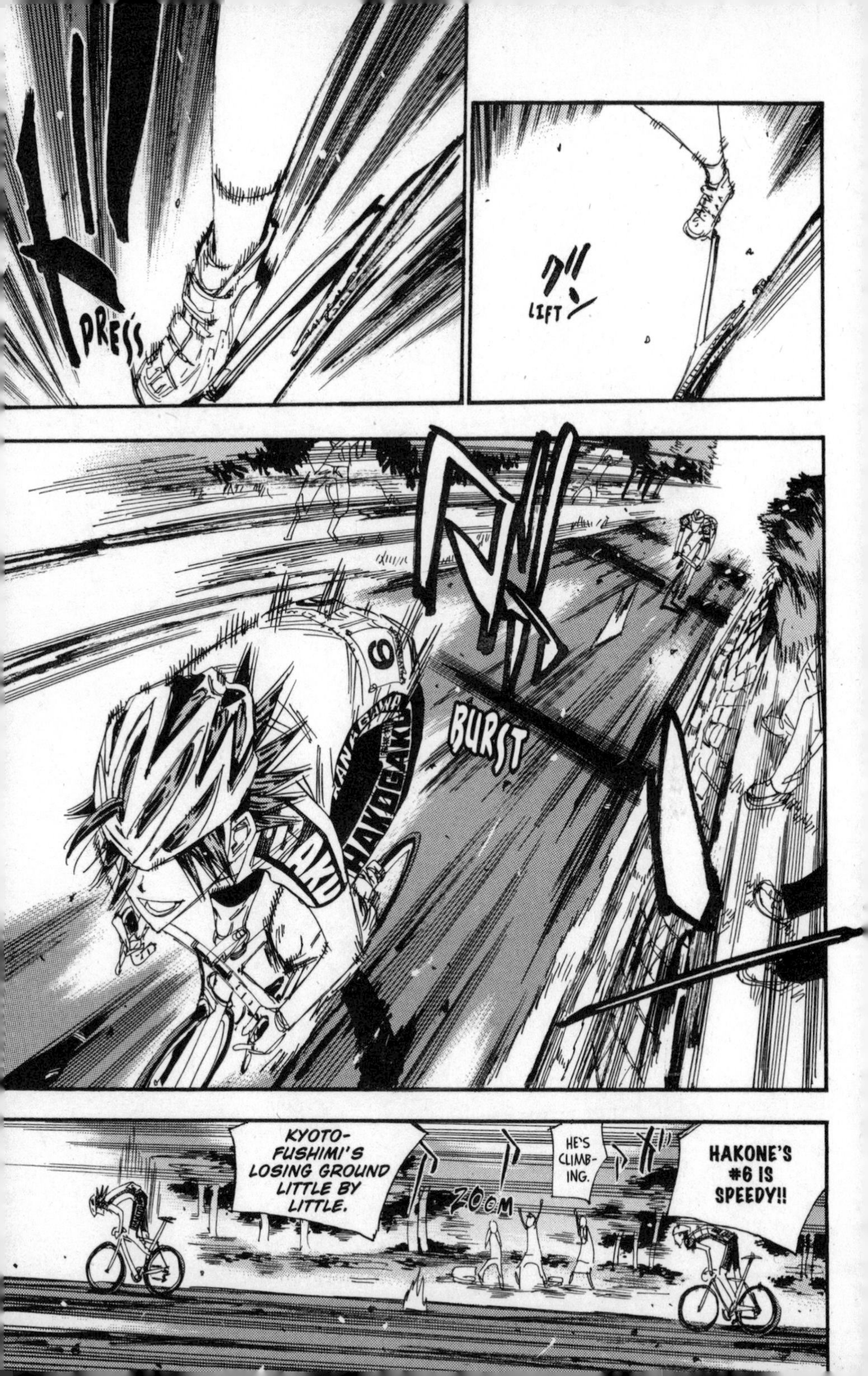
LIFT
PRESS
BURST
HAKONE'S #6 IS SPEEDY!!
HE'S CLIMB-ING.
ZOOM
KYOTO-FUSHIMI'S LOSING GROUND LITTLE BY LITTLE.

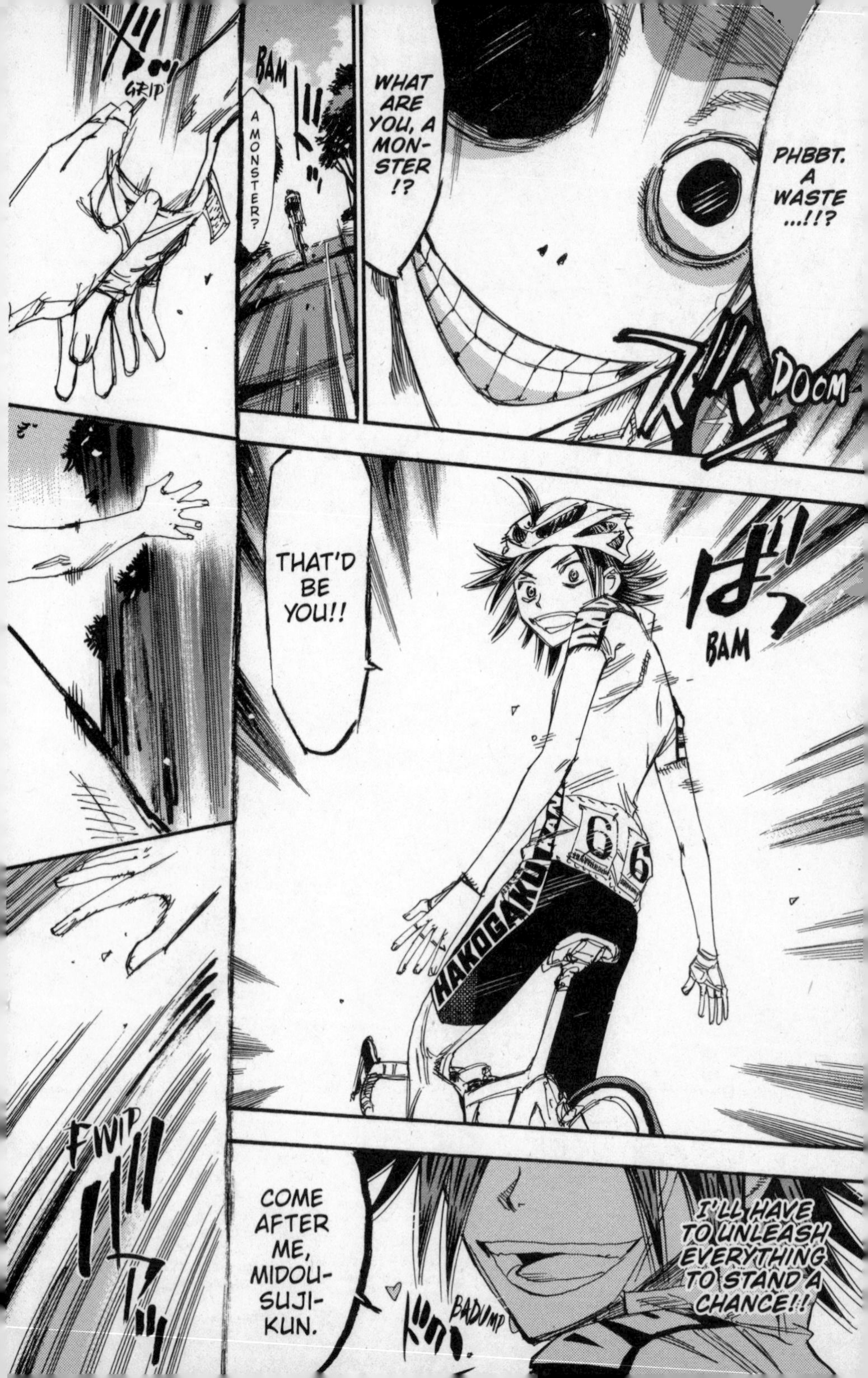
PHBBT. A WASTE ...!!?
DOOM
WHAT ARE YOU, A MONSTER!?
BAM
A MONSTER?
GRIP
BAM
THAT'D BE YOU!!
I'LL HAVE TO UNLEASH EVERYTHING TO STAND A CHANCE!!
BADUMP
COME AFTER ME, MIDOUSUJI-KUN.
FWIP

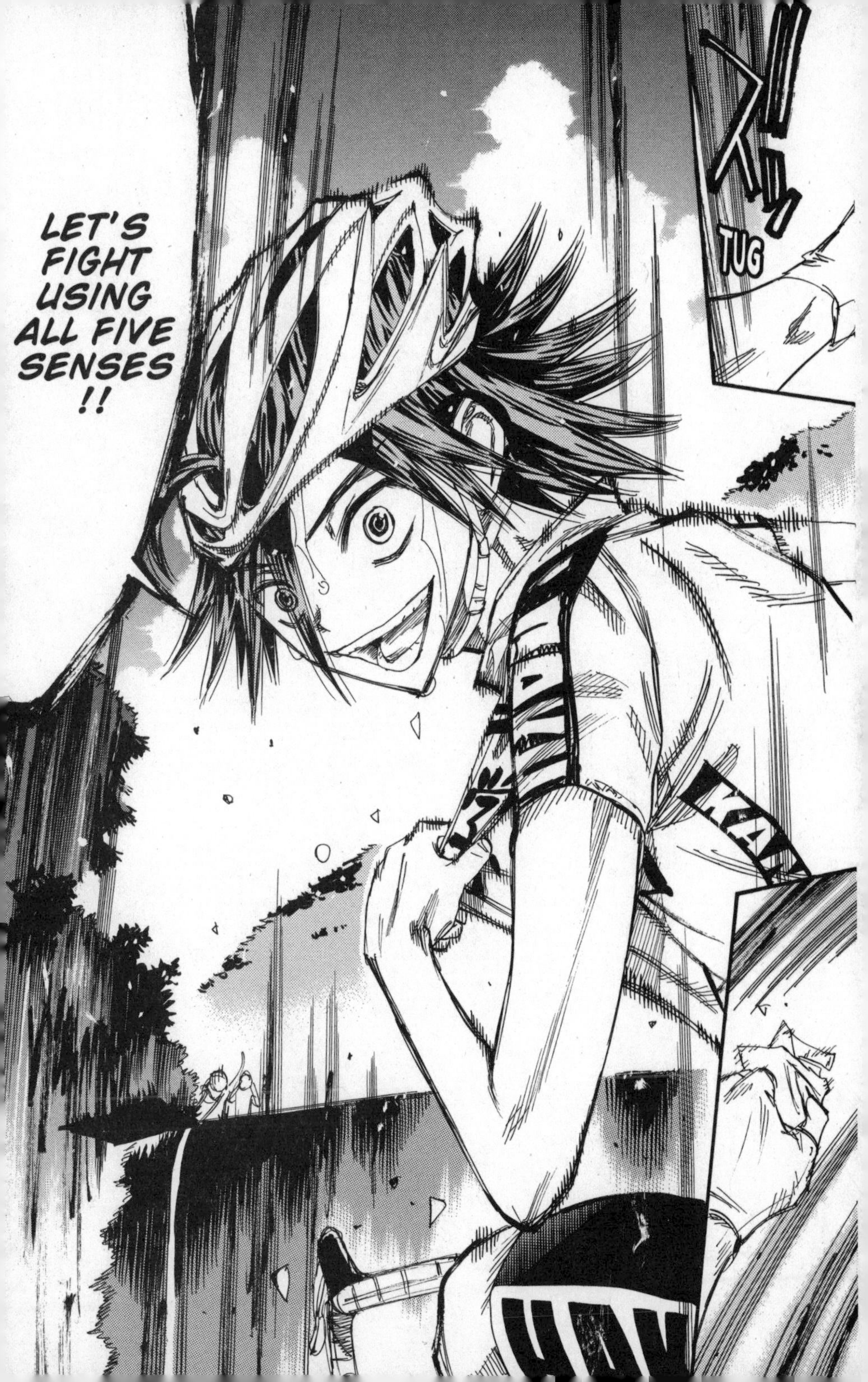
TUG
LET'S FIGHT USING ALL FIVE SENSES !!

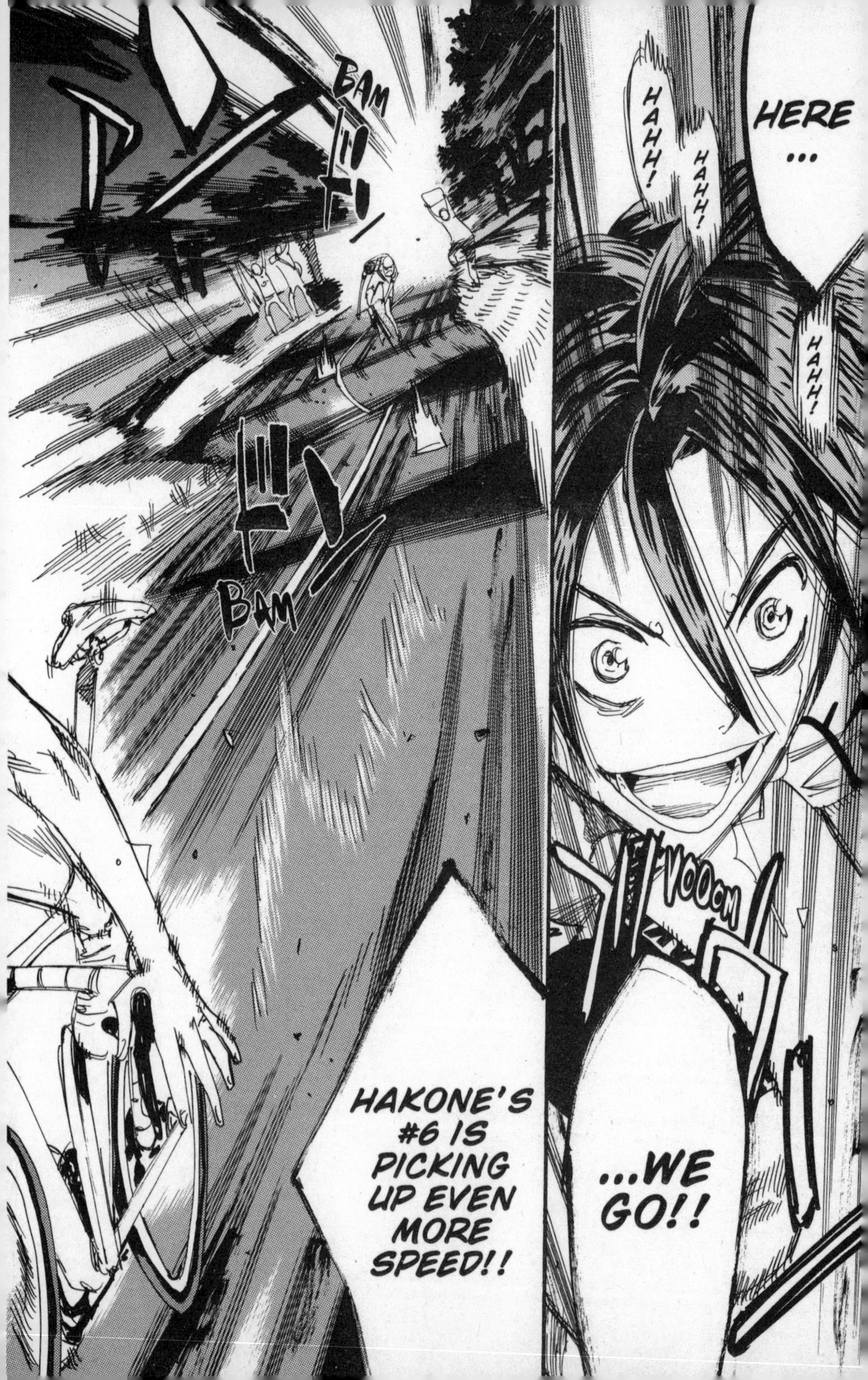
HERE ...
HAHH!
HAHH!
HAHH!
VOOOM
...WE GO!!
BAM
BAM
HAKONE'S #6 IS PICKING UP EVEN MORE SPEED!!

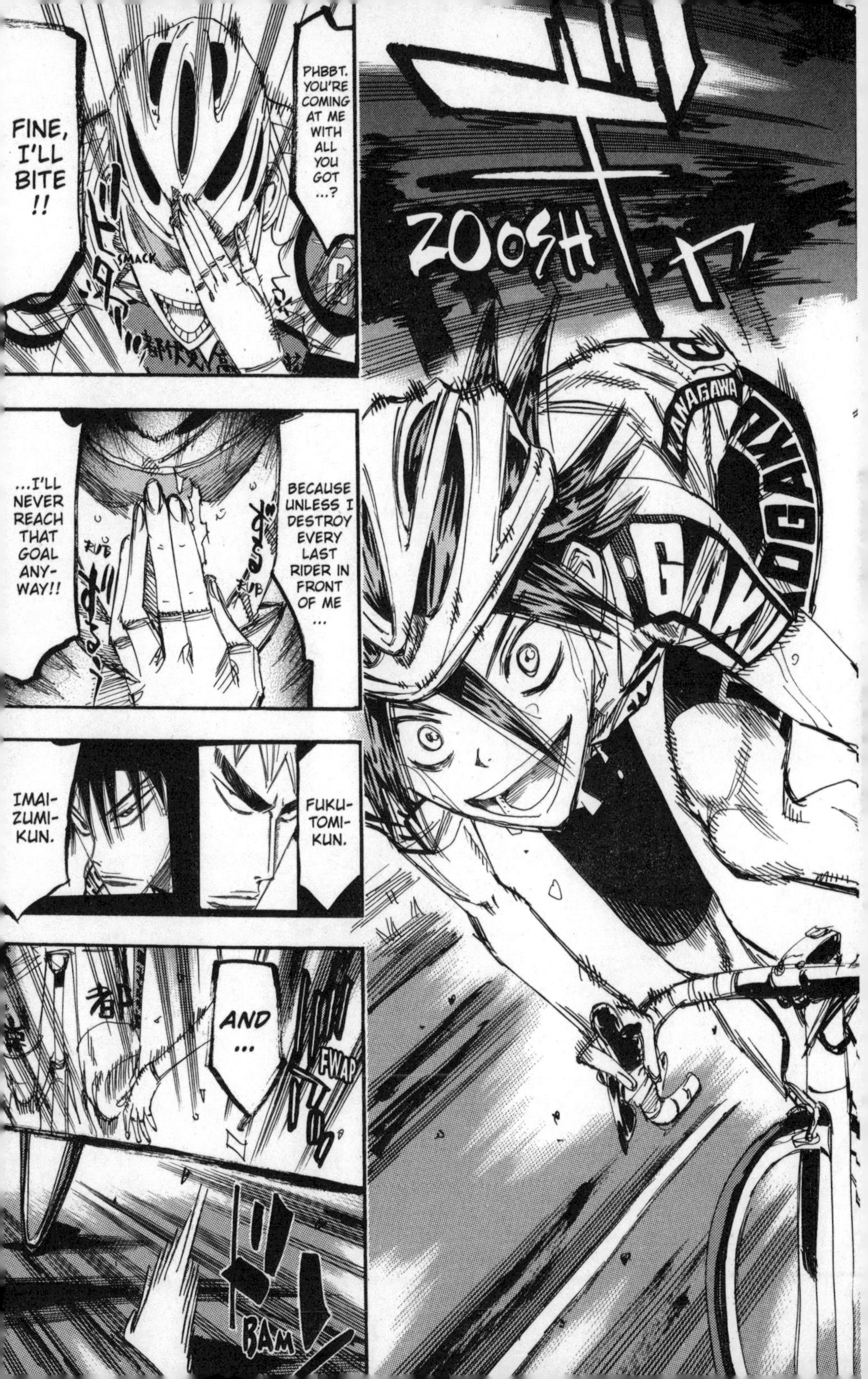
ZOOSH
PHBBT. YOU'RE COMING AT ME WITH ALL YOU GOT ...?
FINE, I'LL BITE !!
SMACK
BECAUSE UNLESS I DESTROY EVERY LAST RIDER IN FRONT OF ME ...
...I'LL NEVER REACH THAT GOAL ANY-WAY!!
RUB
RUB
FUKU-TOMI-KUN.
IMAI-ZUMI-KUN.
AND ...
FWAP
BAM

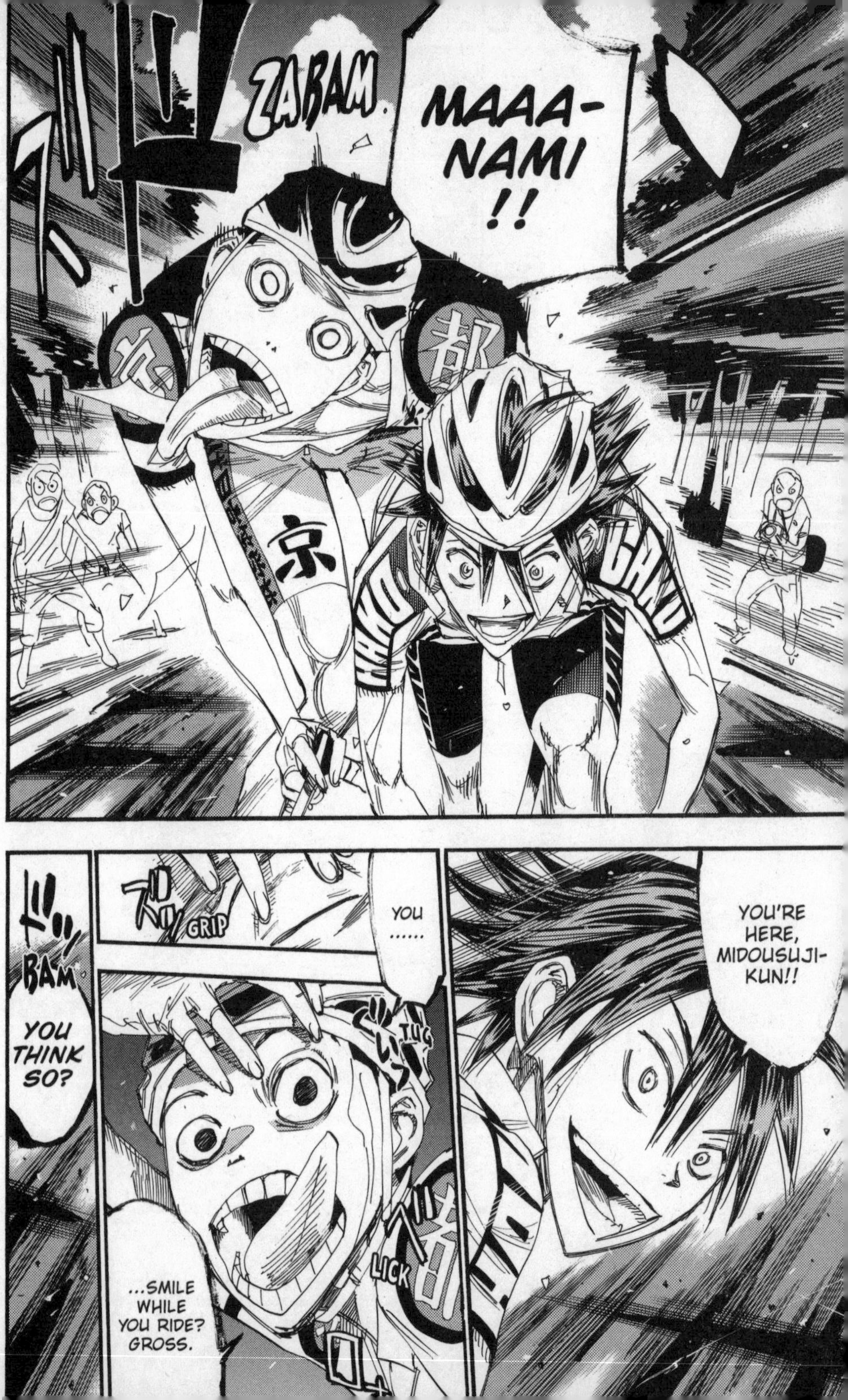
MAAA-NAMI!!
ZABAM
YOU'RE HERE, MIDOUSUJI-KUN!!
YOU ......
GRIP
BAM
YOU THINK SO?
TUG
LICK
...SMILE WHILE YOU RIDE? GROSS.

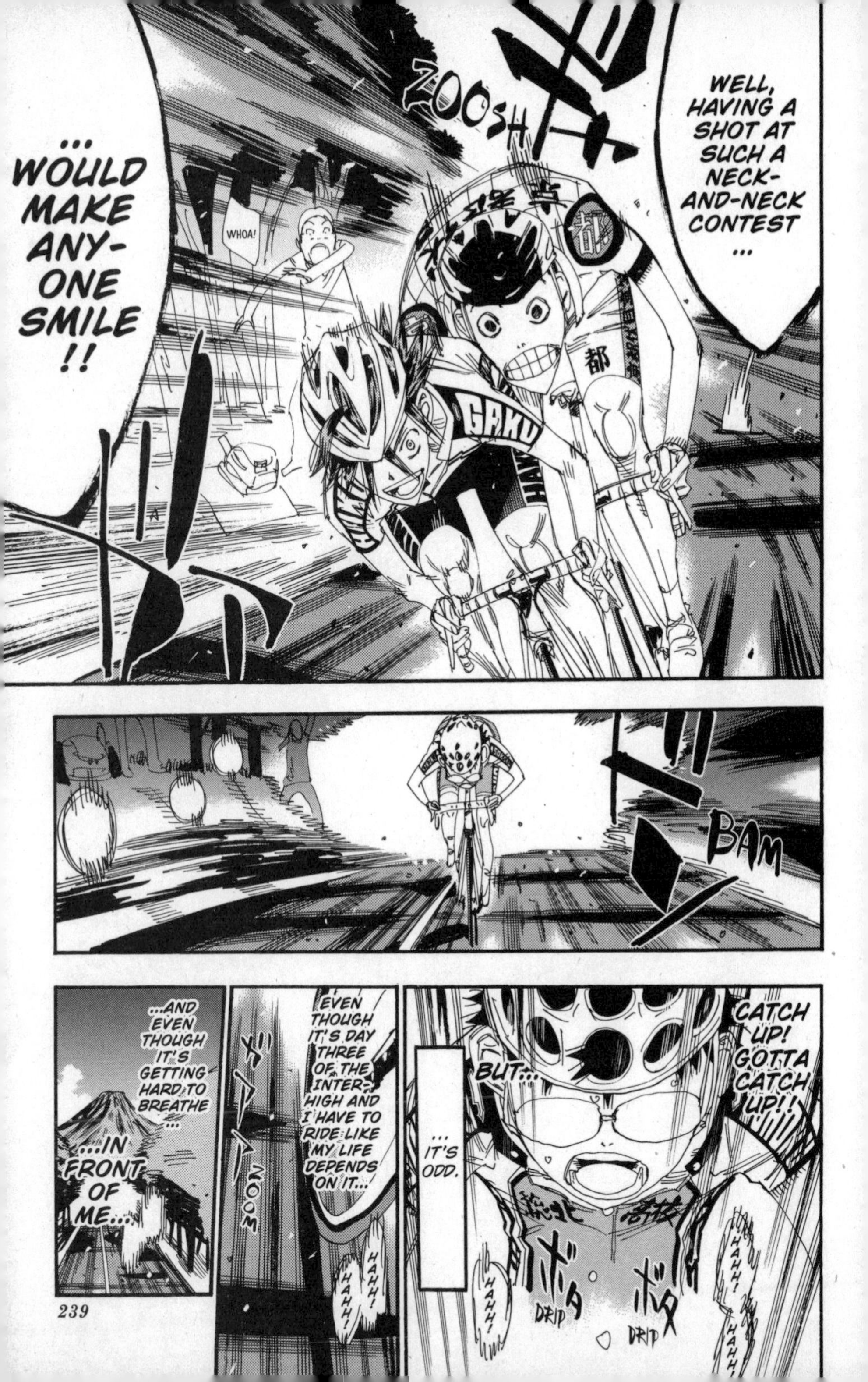
WELL, HAVING A SHOT AT SUCH A NECK-AND-NECK CONTEST...
ZOOSH
WHOA!
...WOULD MAKE ANY-ONE SMILE!!
BAM
CATCH UP! GOTTA CATCH UP!!
BUT...
...IT'S ODD.
HAHH!
HAHH!
DRIP
DRIP
EVEN THOUGH IT'S DAY THREE OF THE INTER-HIGH AND I HAVE TO RIDE LIKE MY LIFE DEPENDS ON IT...
ZOOM
HAHH!
HAHH!
...AND EVEN THOUGH IT'S GETTING HARD TO BREATHE...
...IN FRONT OF ME...

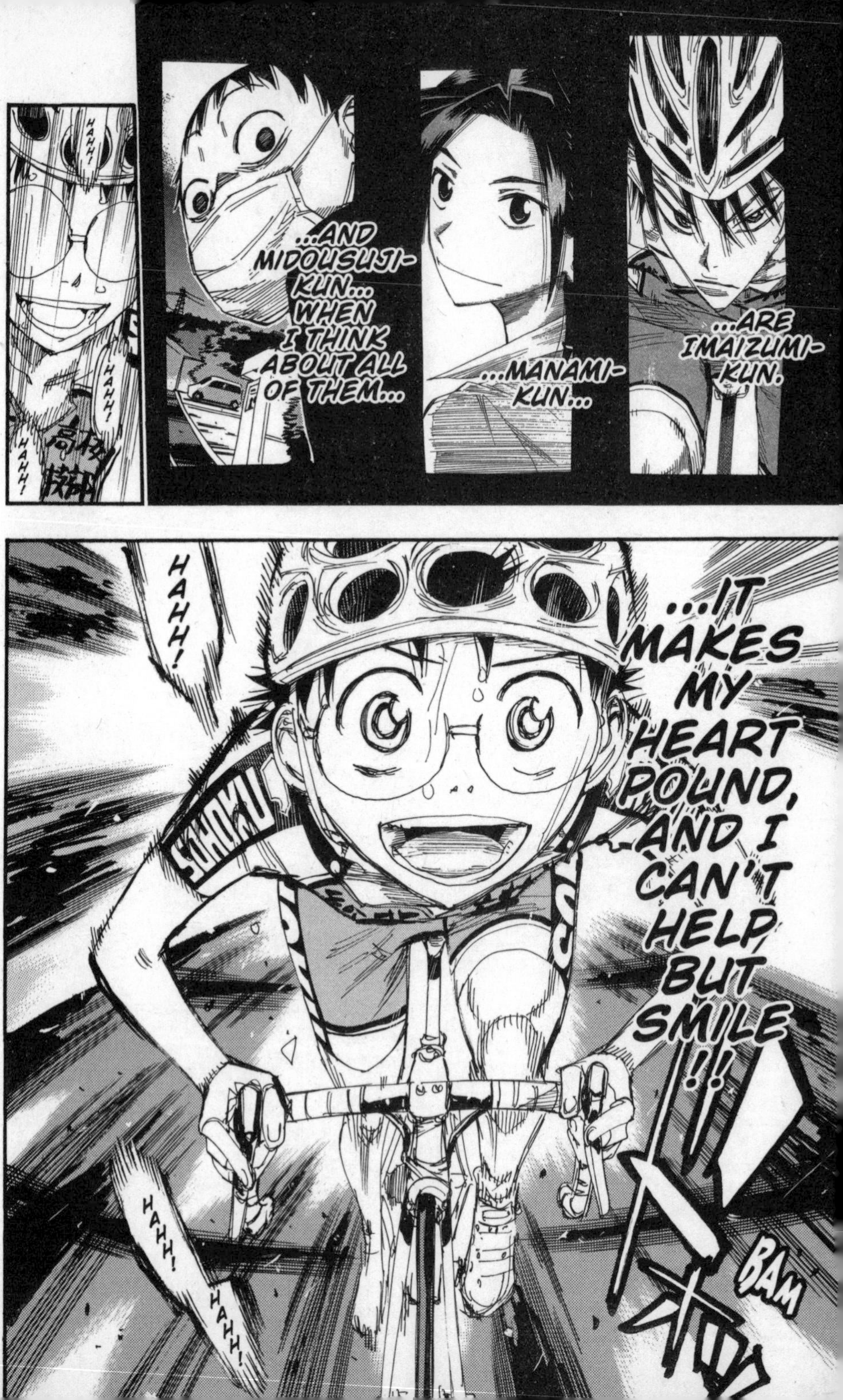
...ARE IMAIZUMI-KUN.
...MANAMI-KUN...
...AND MIDOUSUJI-KUN... WHEN I THINK ABOUT ALL OF THEM...
HAHH!
HAHH!
HAHH!
HAHH!
...IT MAKES MY HEART POUND, AND I CAN'T HELP BUT SMILE!!
HAHH!
HAHH!
HAHH!
BAM
SOHOKU

RIDE.202 MANAMI'S SMILE

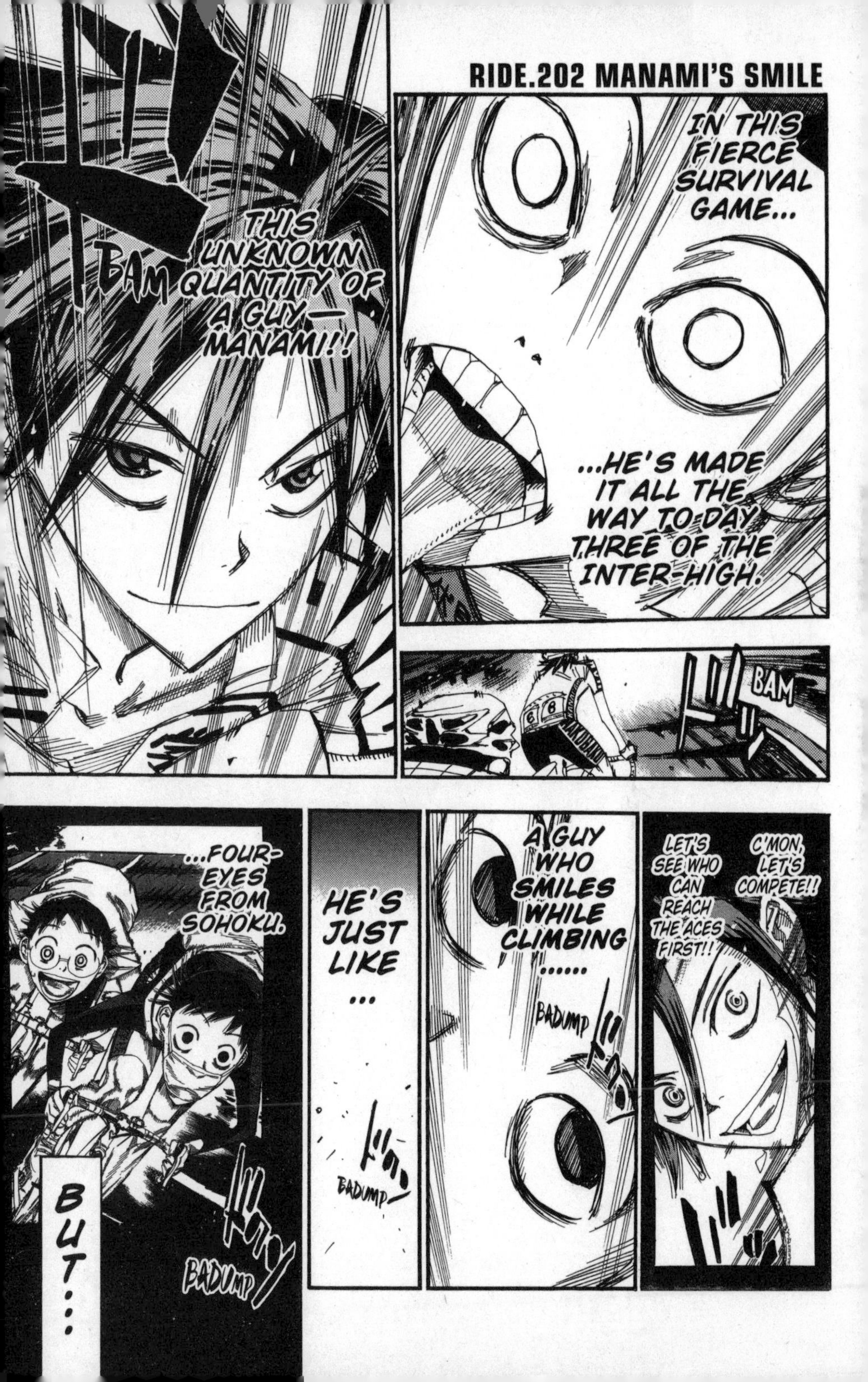
IN THIS FIERCE SURVIVAL GAME...
...HE'S MADE IT ALL THE WAY TO DAY THREE OF THE INTER-HIGH.
BAM
BAM
THIS UNKNOWN QUANTITY OF A GUY—MANAMI!!
C'MON, LET'S COMPETE!!
LET'S SEE WHO CAN REACH THE ACES FIRST!!
A GUY WHO SMILES WHILE CLIMBING ......
BADUMP
HE'S JUST LIKE ...
BADUMP
...FOUR-EYES FROM SOHOKU.
BADUMP
BUT...

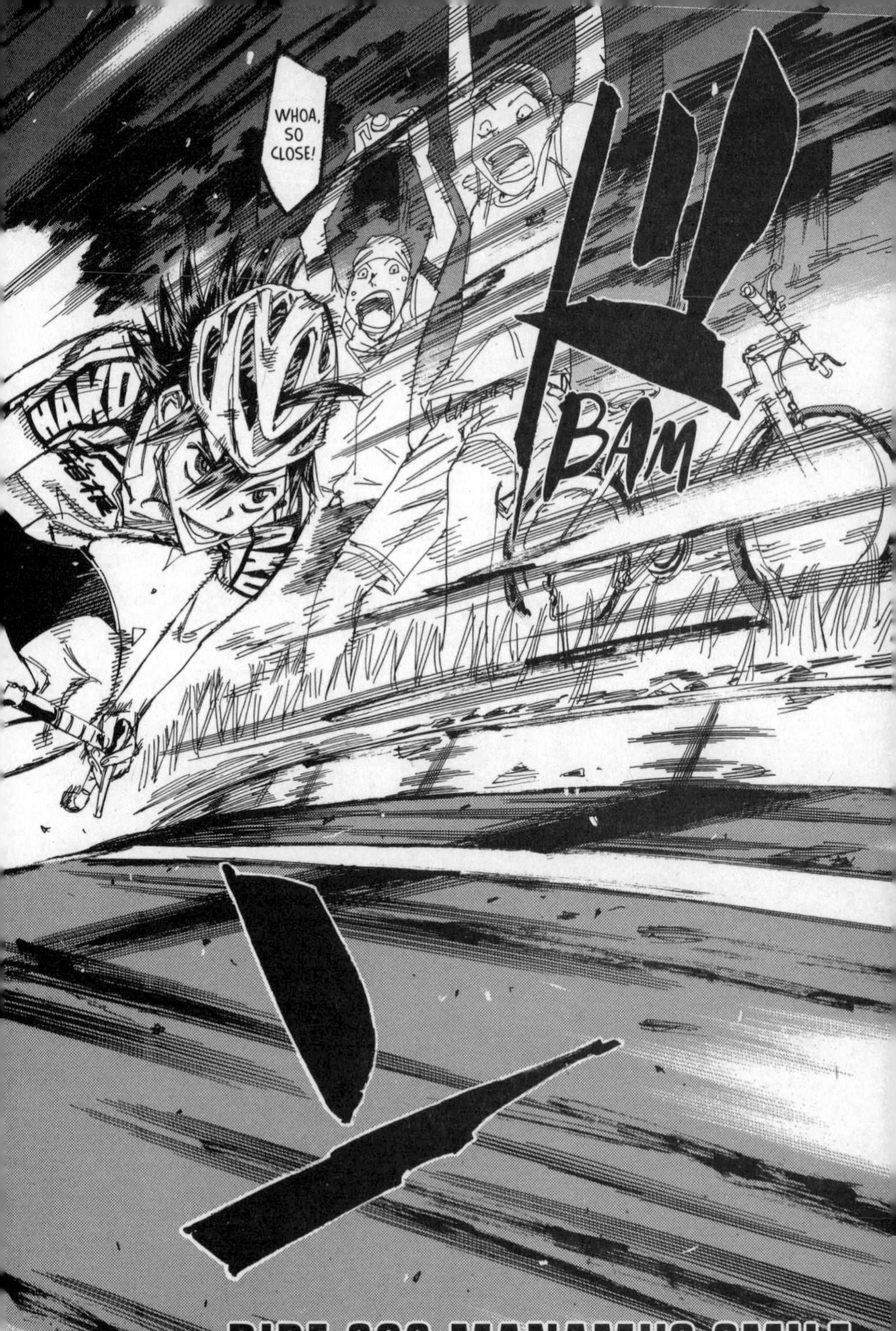
WHOA, SO CLOSE!
BAM

RIDE.202 MANAMI'S SMILE

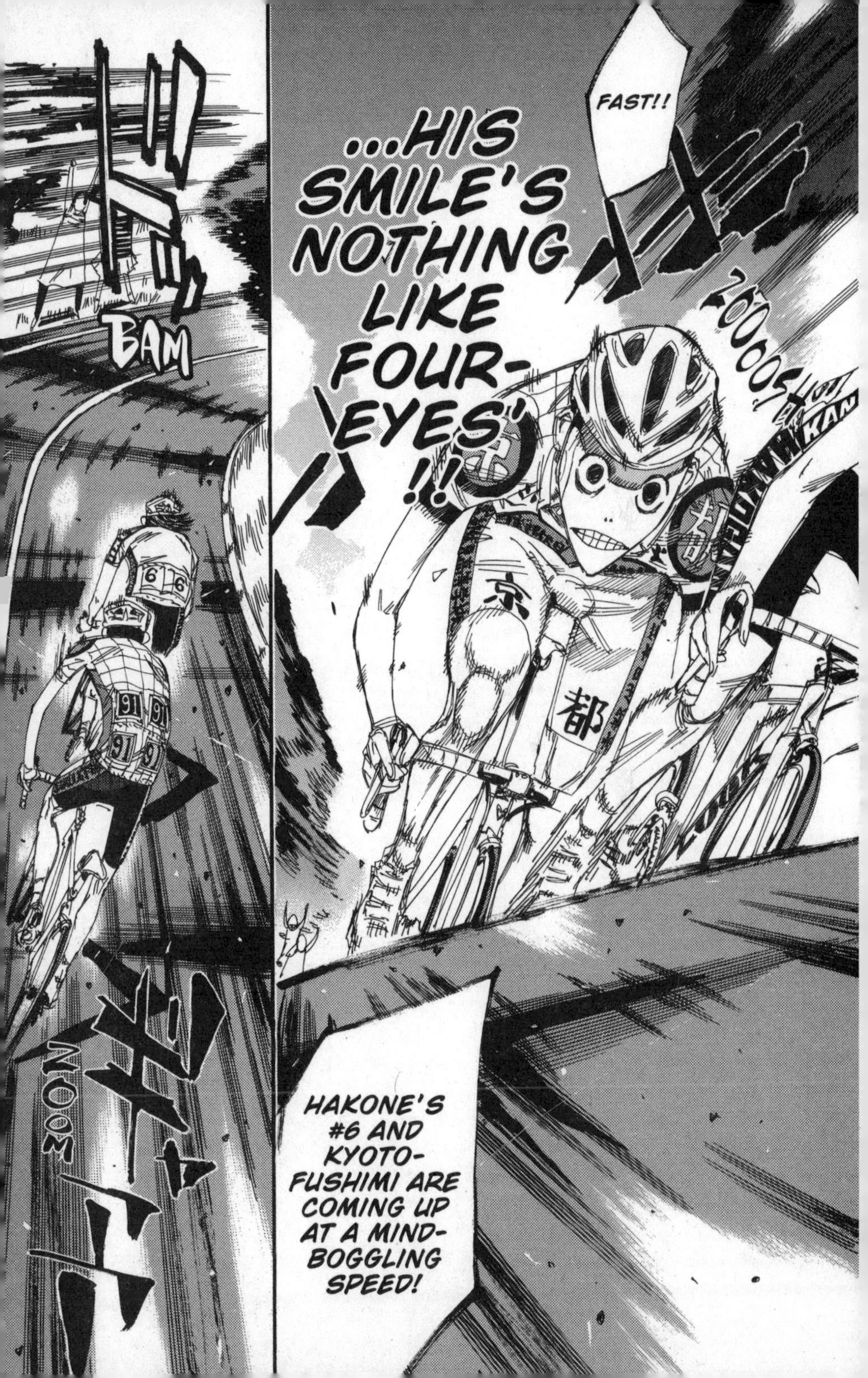
FAST!!
...HIS SMILE'S NOTHING LIKE FOUR-EYES'!!
ZOOOOSH
KAN
HAKONE'S #6 AND KYOTO-FUSHIMI ARE COMING UP AT A MIND-BOGGLING SPEED!
BAM
ZOOM

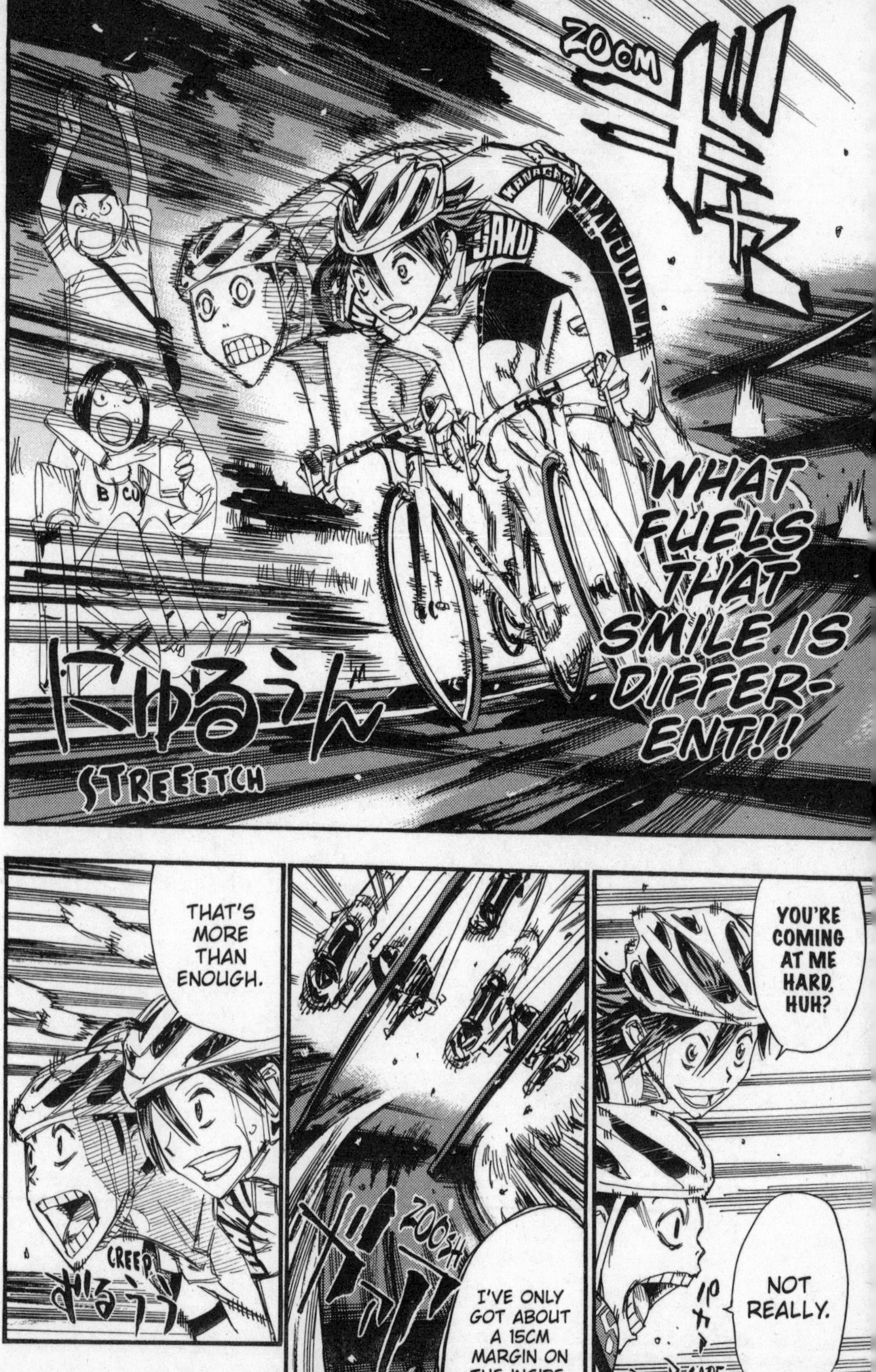
ZOOM
WHAT FUELS THAT SMILE IS DIFFER-ENT!!
にゅるうん
STREEETCH
YOU'RE COMING AT ME HARD, HUH?
NOT REALLY.
GAPE
ZOOM
I'VE ONLY GOT ABOUT A 15CM MARGIN ON THE INSIDE.
THAT'S MORE THAN ENOUGH.
CREEP

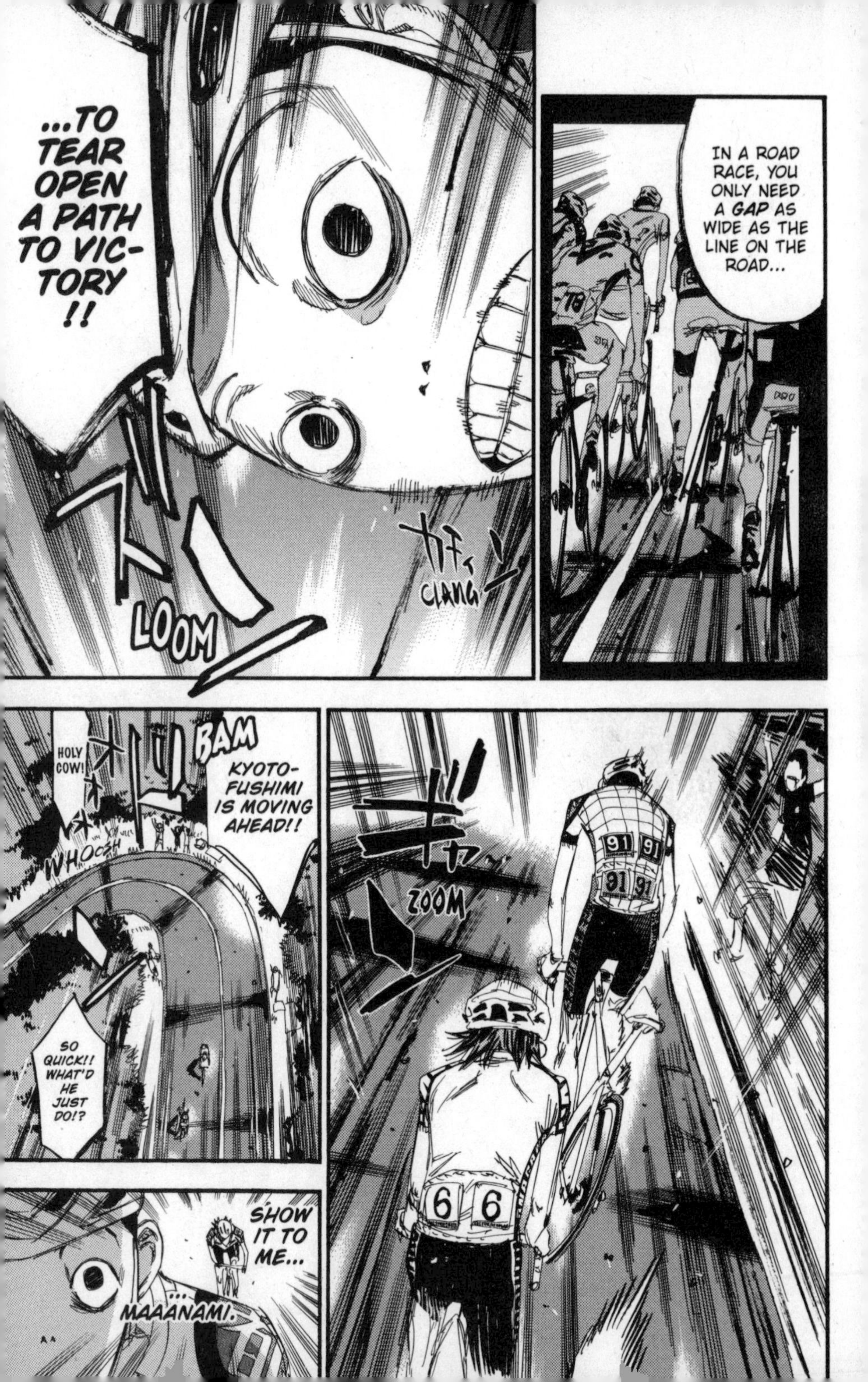
IN A ROAD RACE, YOU ONLY NEED A GAP AS WIDE AS THE LINE ON THE ROAD...
...TO TEAR OPEN A PATH TO VIC-TORY!!
CLANG
LOOM
ZOOM
BAM
KYOTO-FUSHIMI IS MOVING AHEAD!!
HOLY COW!
WHOOSH
SO QUICK!! WHAT'D HE JUST DO!?
SHOW IT TO ME...
...MAAANAMI.

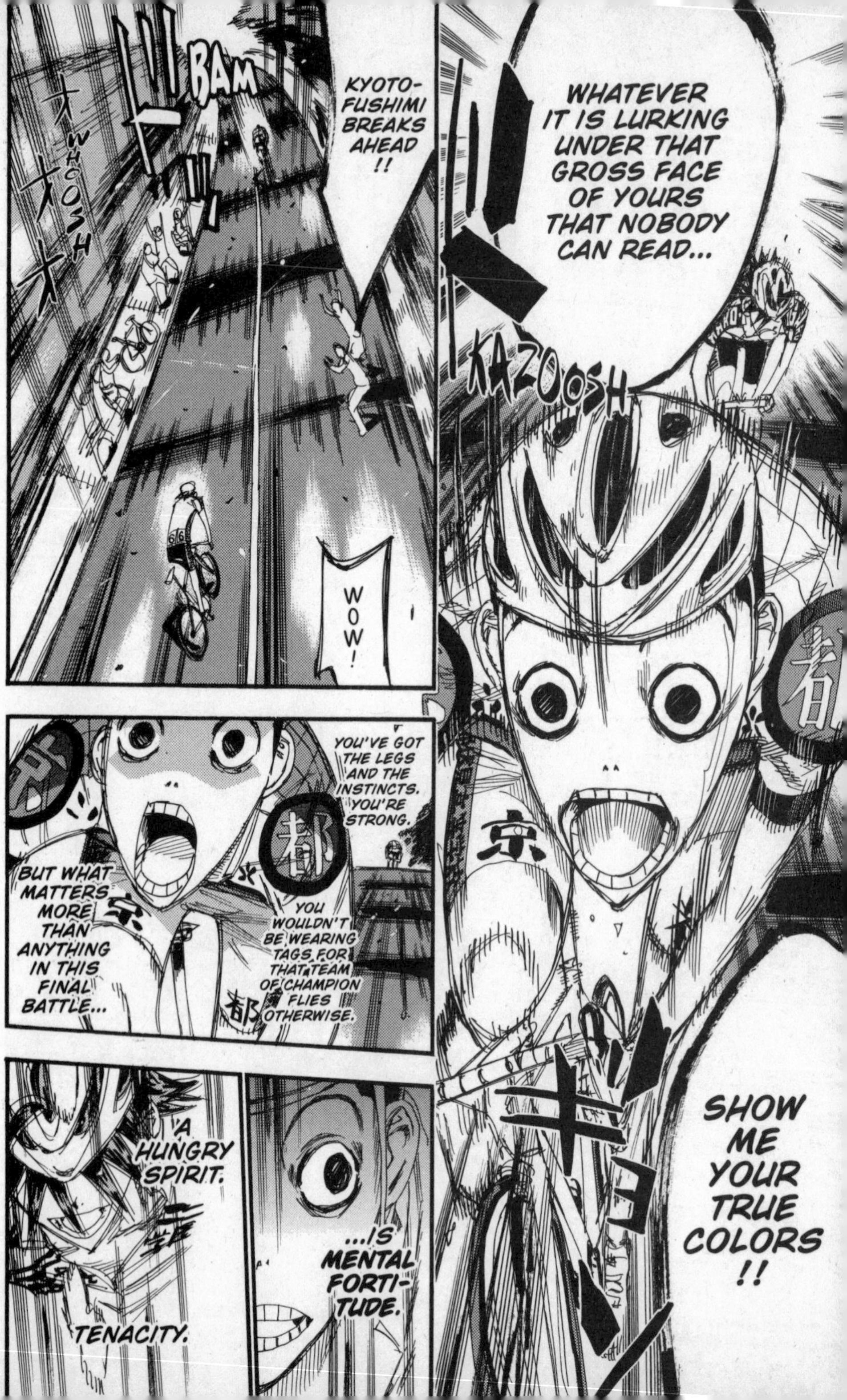
WHATEVER IT IS LURKING UNDER THAT GROSS FACE OF YOURS THAT NOBODY CAN READ...
KAZOOSH
SHOW ME YOUR TRUE COLORS !!
BAM
WHOOSH
KYOTO-FUSHIMI BREAKS AHEAD !!
WOW!
YOU'VE GOT THE LEGS AND THE INSTINCTS. YOU'RE STRONG.
YOU WOULDN'T BE WEARING TAGS FOR THAT TEAM OF CHAMPION FLIES OTHERWISE.
BUT WHAT MATTERS MORE THAN ANYTHING IN THIS FINAL BATTLE...
...IS MENTAL FORTITUDE.
A HUNGRY SPIRIT.
TENACITY.

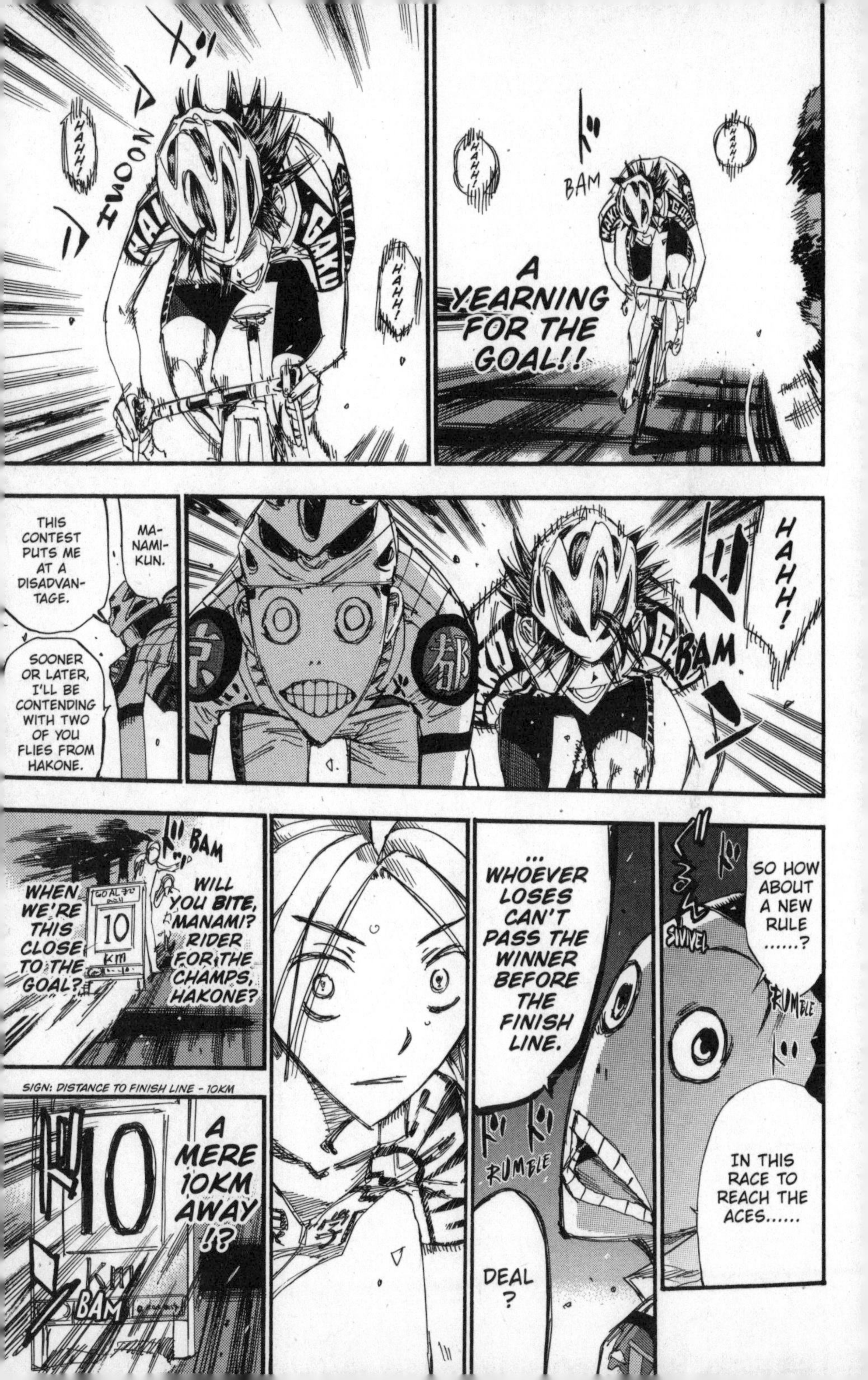
HAHH!
BAM
HAHH!
A YEARNING FOR THE GOAL!!
HAHH!
HAHH!
HAHH!
BAM
MANAMI-KUN.
THIS CONTEST PUTS ME AT A DISADVANTAGE.
SOONER OR LATER, I'LL BE CONTENDING WITH TWO OF YOU FLIES FROM HAKONE.
SO HOW ABOUT A NEW RULE ......?
SWIVEL
RUMBLE
IN THIS RACE TO REACH THE ACES......
... WHOEVER LOSES CAN'T PASS THE WINNER BEFORE THE FINISH LINE.
RUMBLE
DEAL ?
BAM
WILL YOU BITE, MANAMI? RIDER FOR THE CHAMPS, HAKONE?
WHEN WE'RE THIS CLOSE TO THE GOAL?
10
KM
SIGN: DISTANCE TO FINISH LINE - 10KM
A MERE 10KM AWAY!?
10
KM
BAM

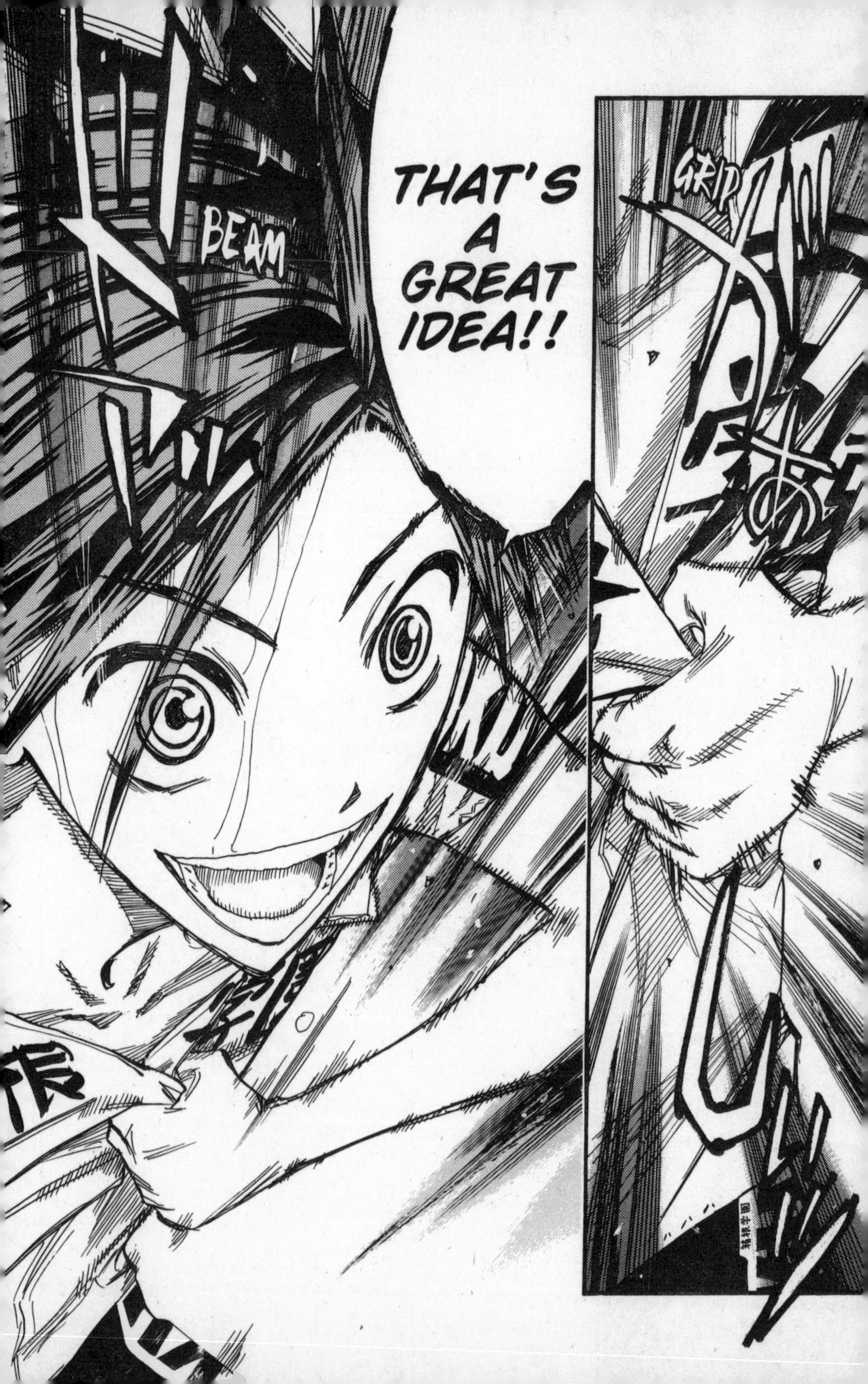
GRIP
THAT'S A GREAT IDEA!!
BEAM

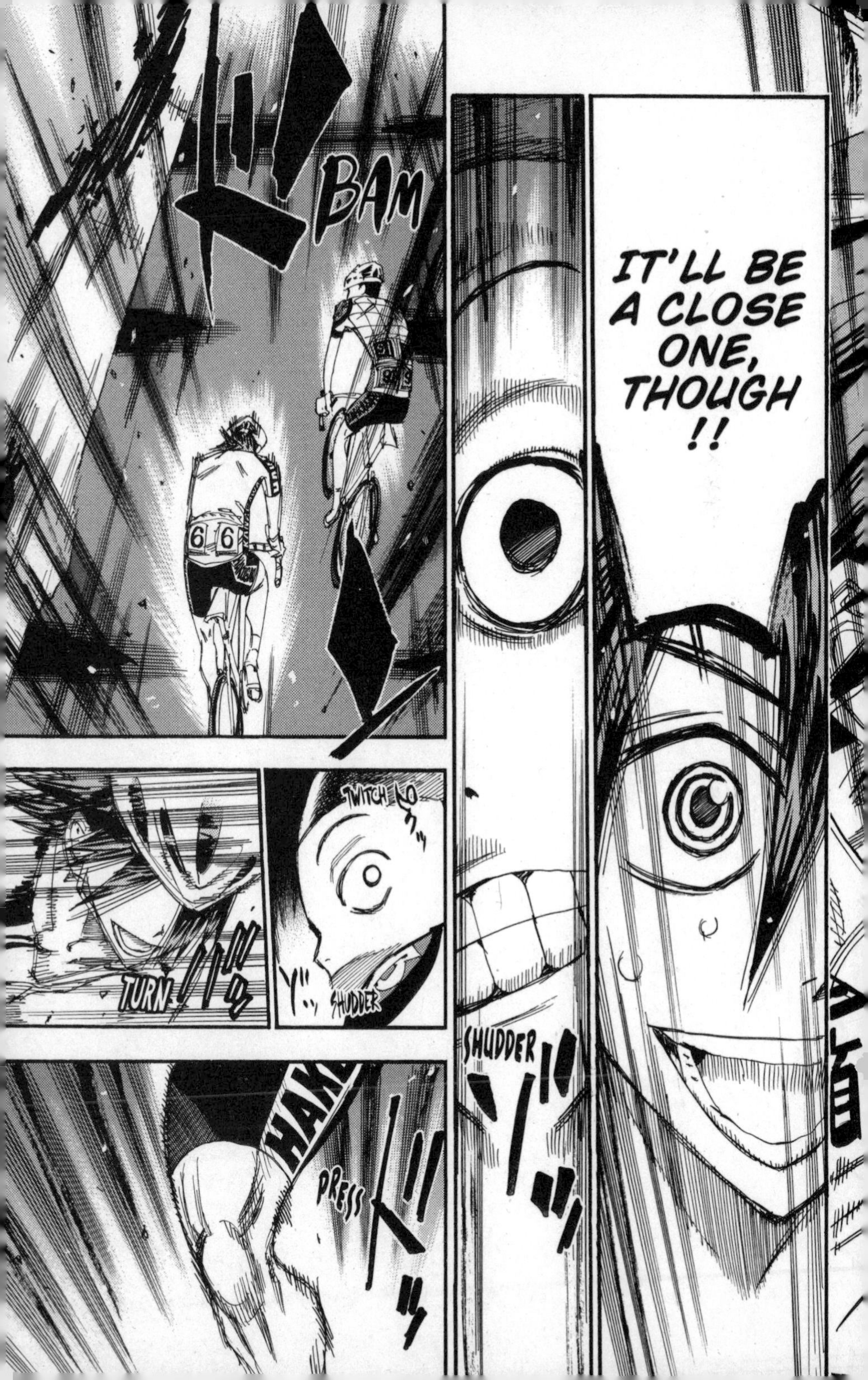
IT'LL BE A CLOSE ONE, THOUGH!!
SHUDDER
BAM
TWITCH
SHUDDER
TURN
PRESS

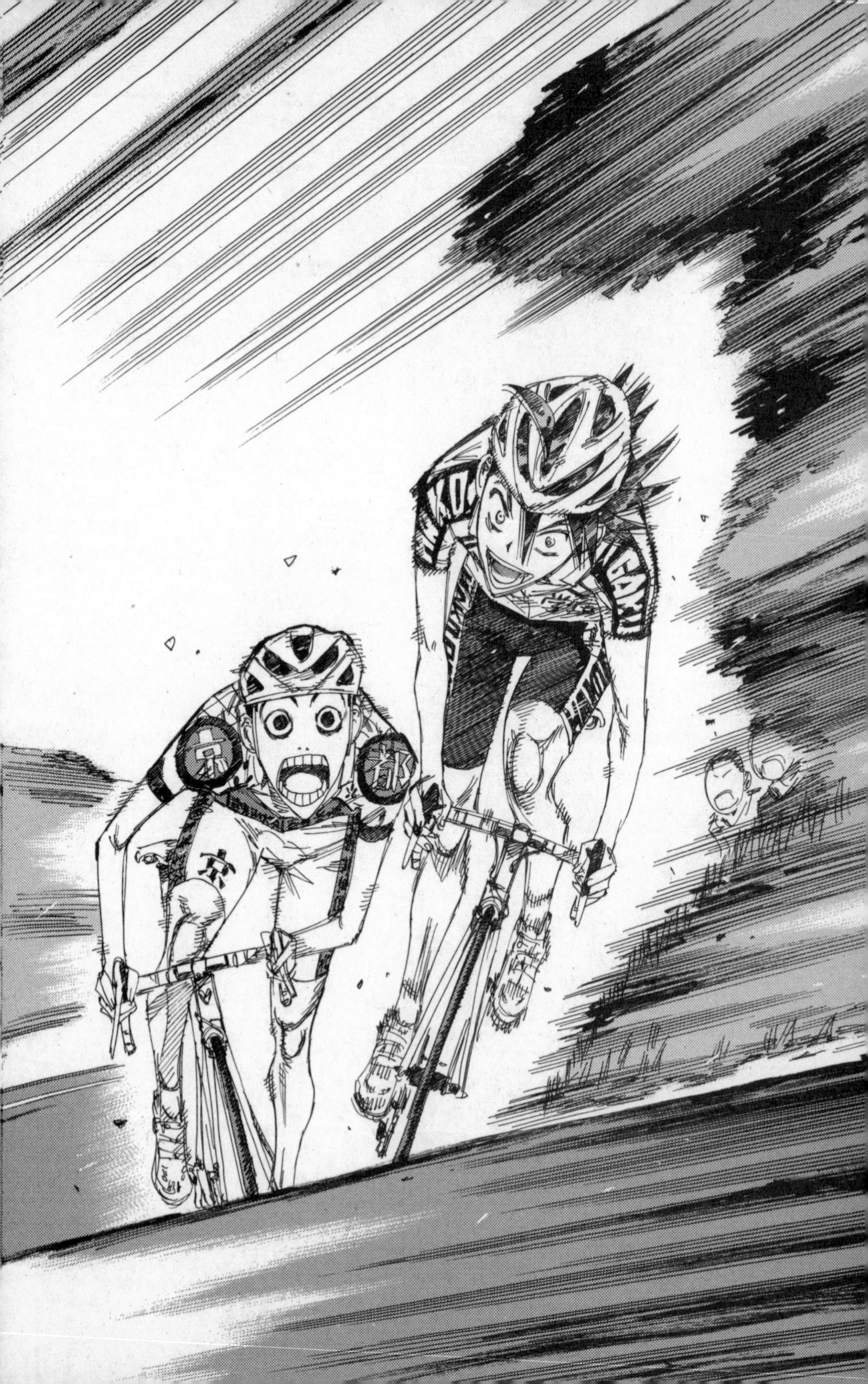

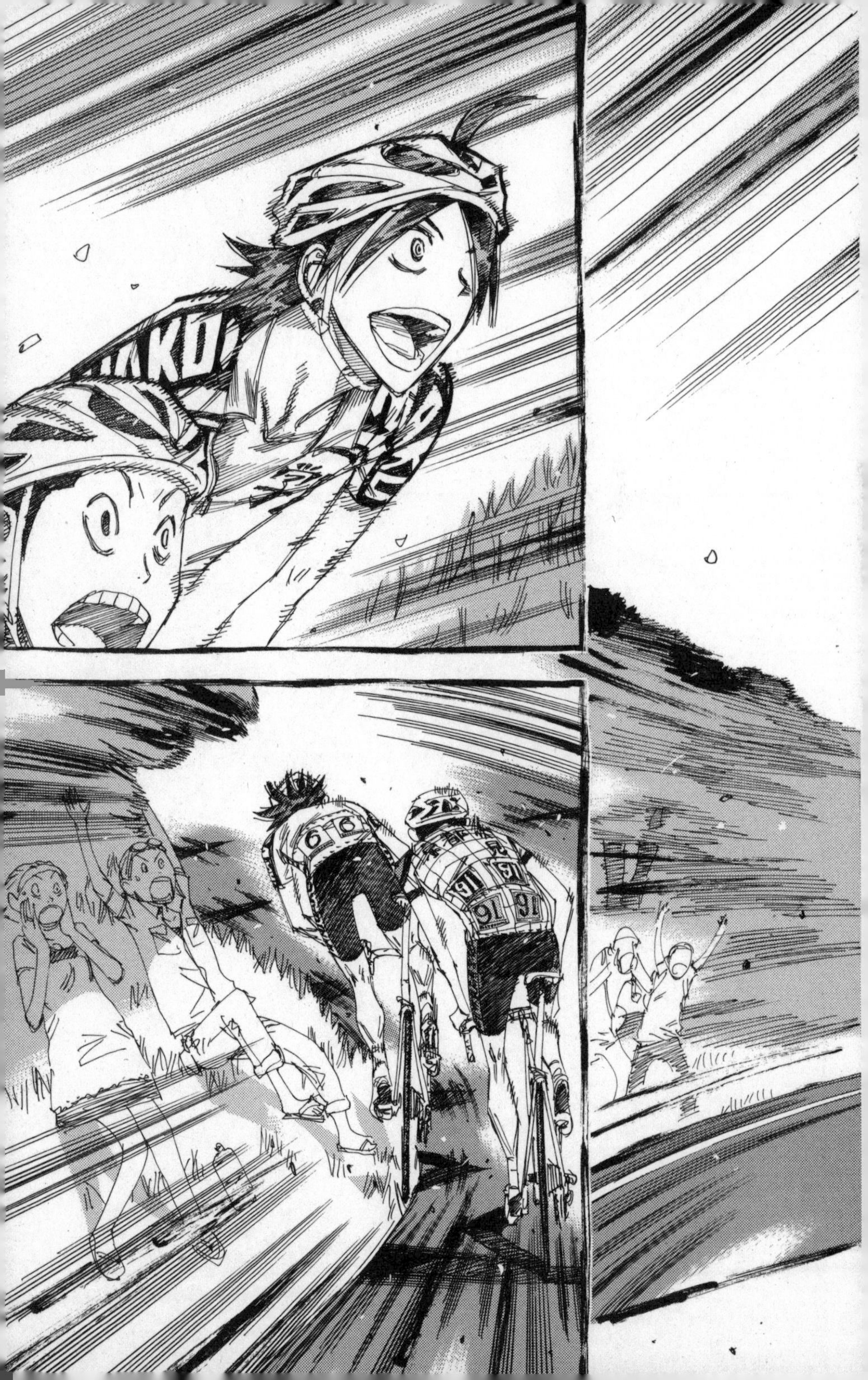

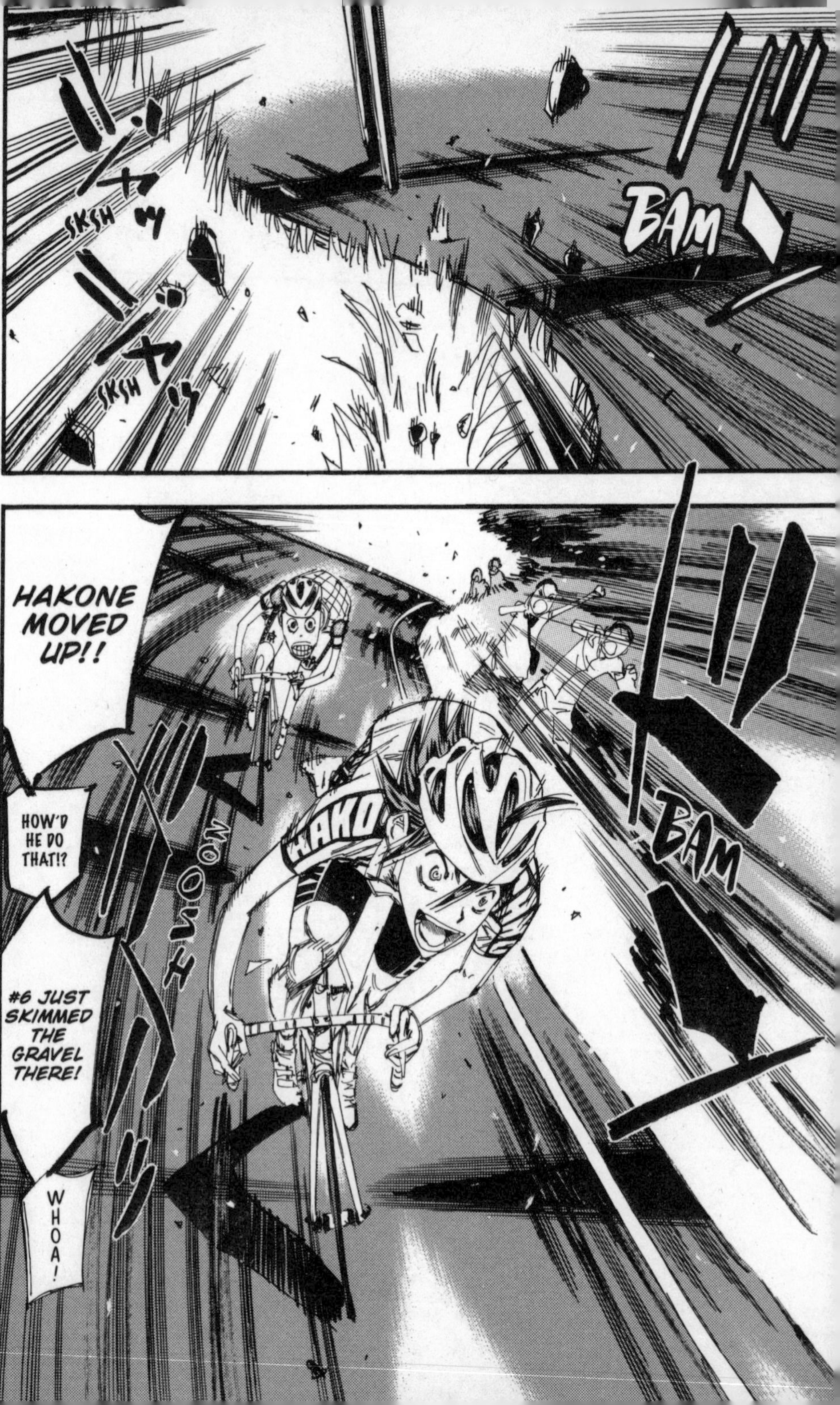
BAM
SKSH
SKSH
BAM
HAKONE MOVED UP!!
HOW'D HE DO THAT!?
#6 JUST SKIMMED THE GRAVEL THERE!
WHOA!
WHOOSH

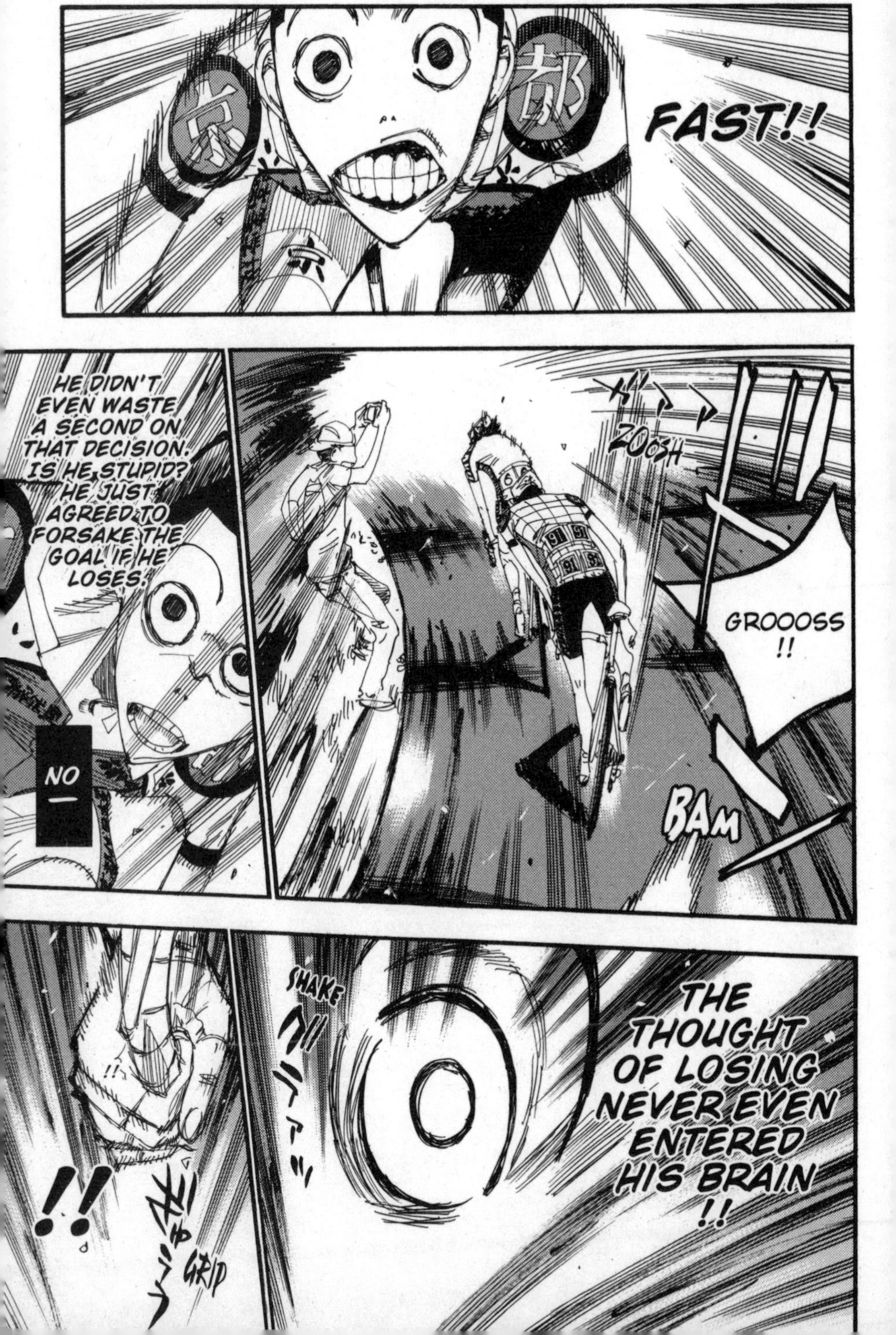
FAST!!
ZOOSH
GROOOSS!!
BAM
HE DIDN'T EVEN WASTE A SECOND ON THAT DECISION. IS HE STUPID? HE JUST AGREED TO FORSAKE THE GOAL IF HE LOSES.
NO—
THE THOUGHT OF LOSING NEVER EVEN ENTERED HIS BRAIN!!
SHAKE
!!
GRIP

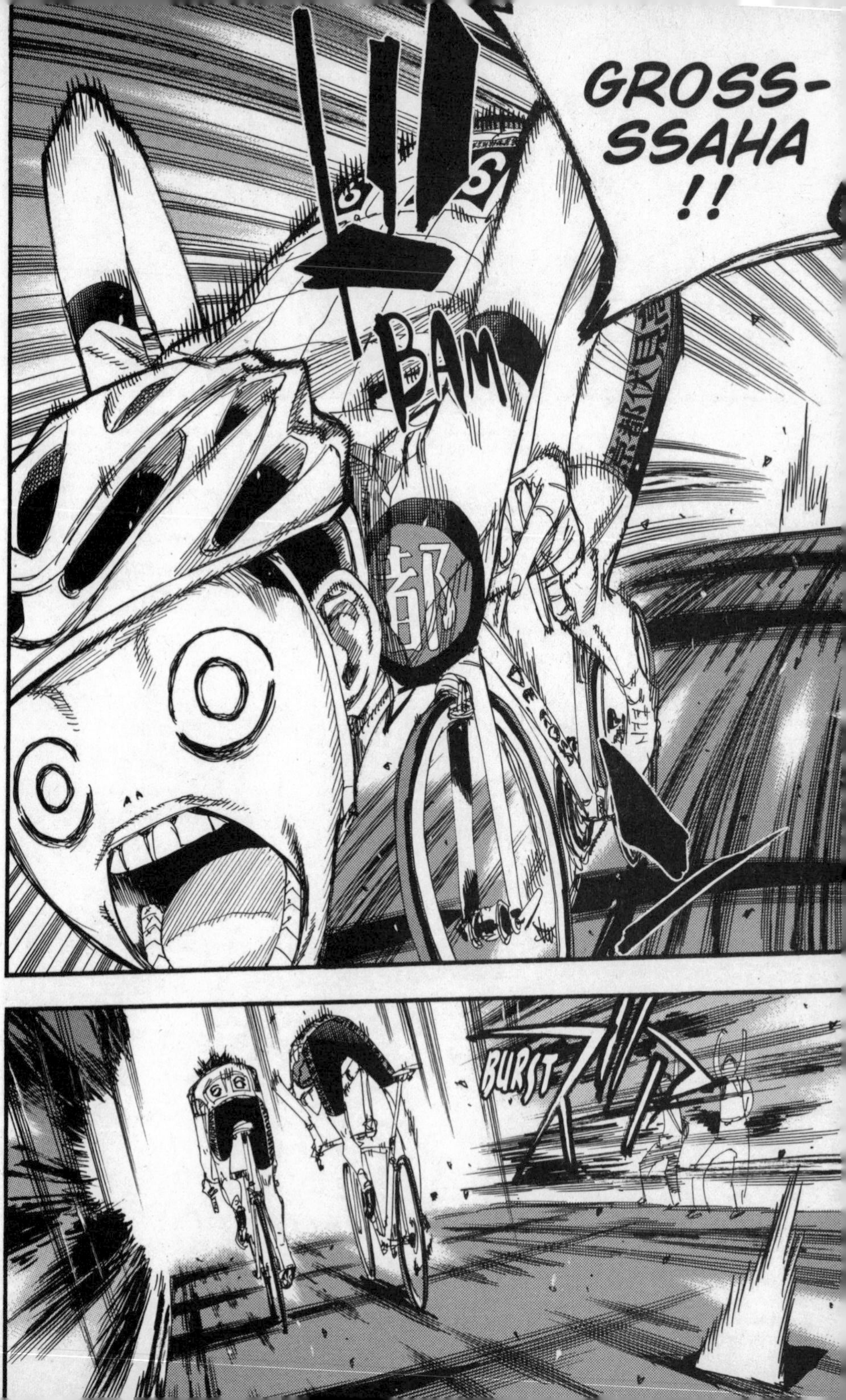
GROSS-SSAHA!!
BAM
BURST

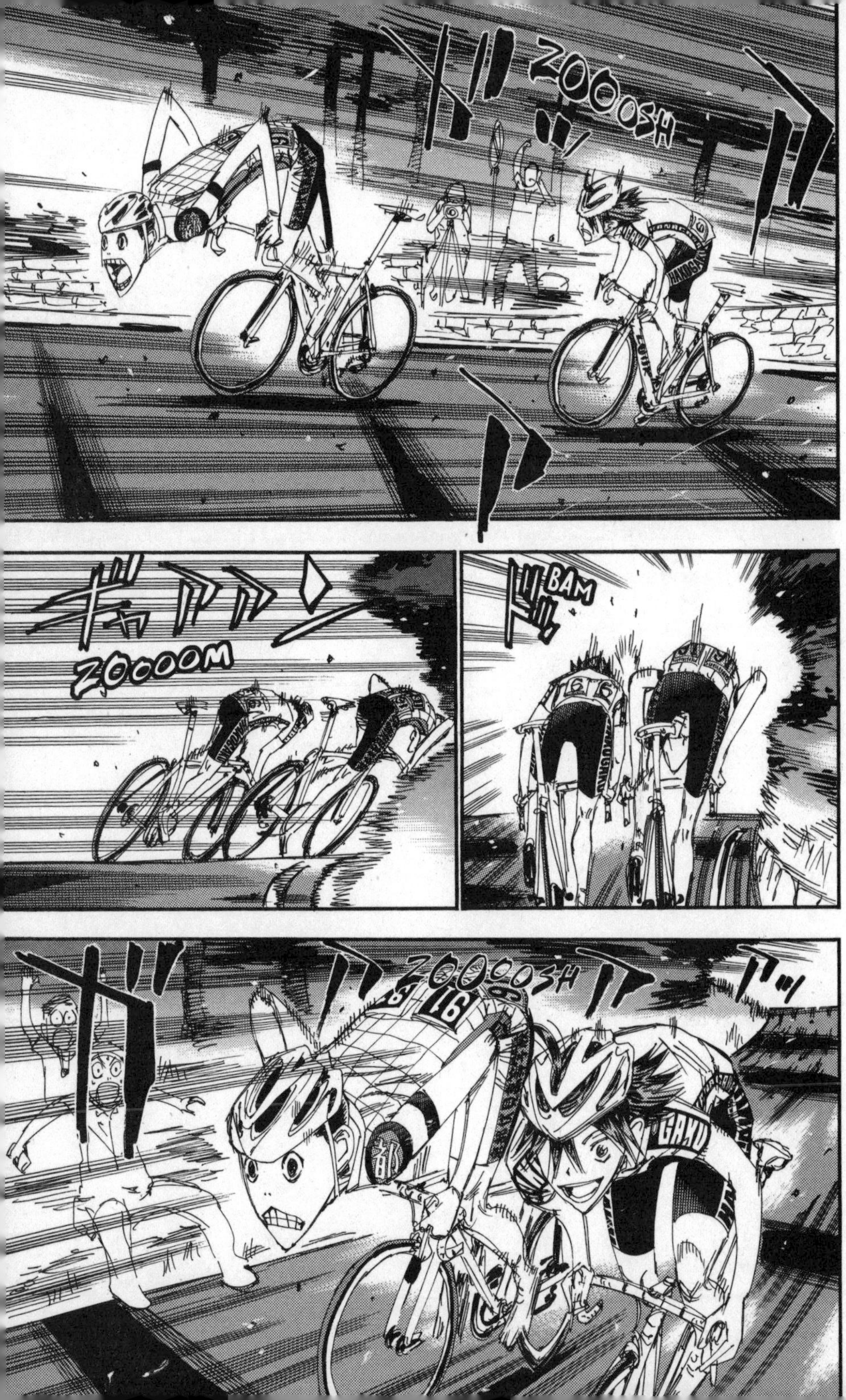
ZOOOOSH
BAM
ZOOOOM
ZOOOOOSH

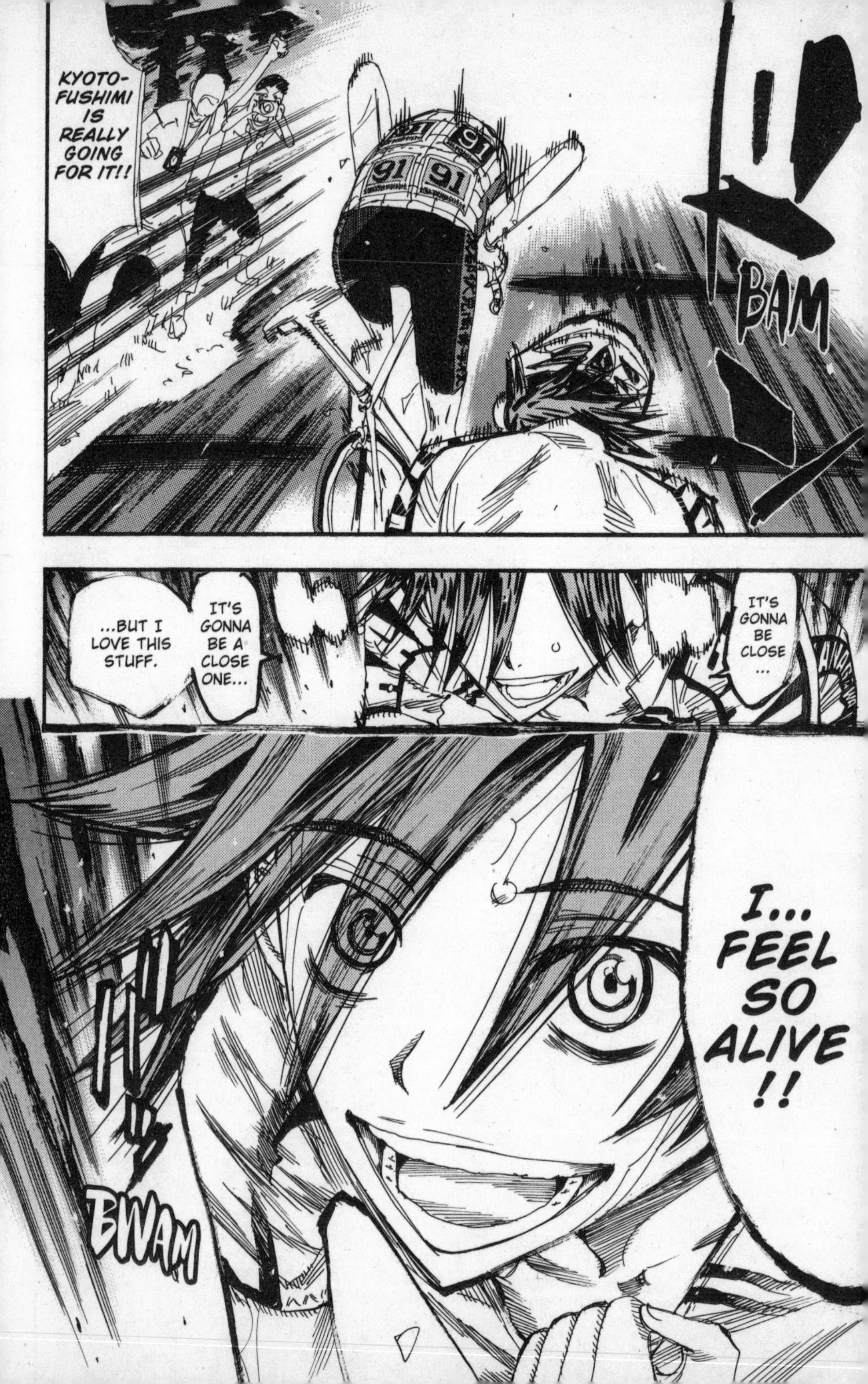
BAM
KYOTO-FUSHIMI IS REALLY GOING FOR IT!!
IT'S GONNA BE CLOSE ...
IT'S GONNA BE A CLOSE ONE...
...BUT I LOVE THIS STUFF.
I... FEEL SO ALIVE!!
BWAM

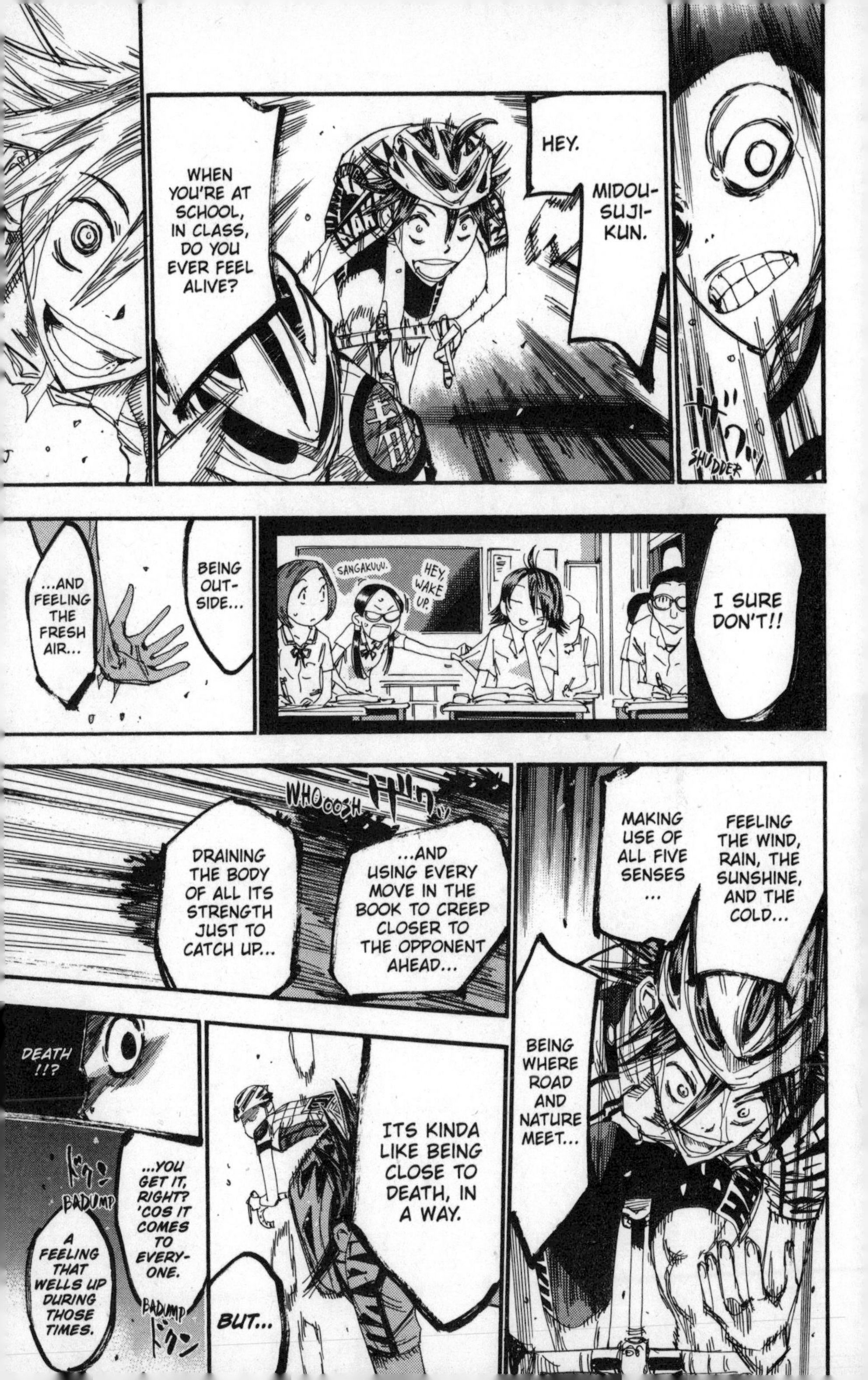
SHUDDER
HEY.
MIDOU-SUJI-KUN.
WHEN YOU'RE AT SCHOOL, IN CLASS, DO YOU EVER FEEL ALIVE?
I SURE DON'T!!
HEY, WAKE UP.
SANGAKUUU.
BEING OUT-SIDE...
...AND FEELING THE FRESH AIR...
FEELING THE WIND, RAIN, THE SUNSHINE, AND THE COLD...
MAKING USE OF ALL FIVE SENSES ...
BEING WHERE ROAD AND NATURE MEET...
WHOOOSH
...AND USING EVERY MOVE IN THE BOOK TO CREEP CLOSER TO THE OPPONENT AHEAD...
DRAINING THE BODY OF ALL ITS STRENGTH JUST TO CATCH UP...
ITS KINDA LIKE BEING CLOSE TO DEATH, IN A WAY.
BUT...
...YOU GET IT, RIGHT? 'COS IT COMES TO EVERY-ONE.
DEATH!!?
BADUMP
A FEELING THAT WELLS UP DURING THOSE TIMES.
BADUMP

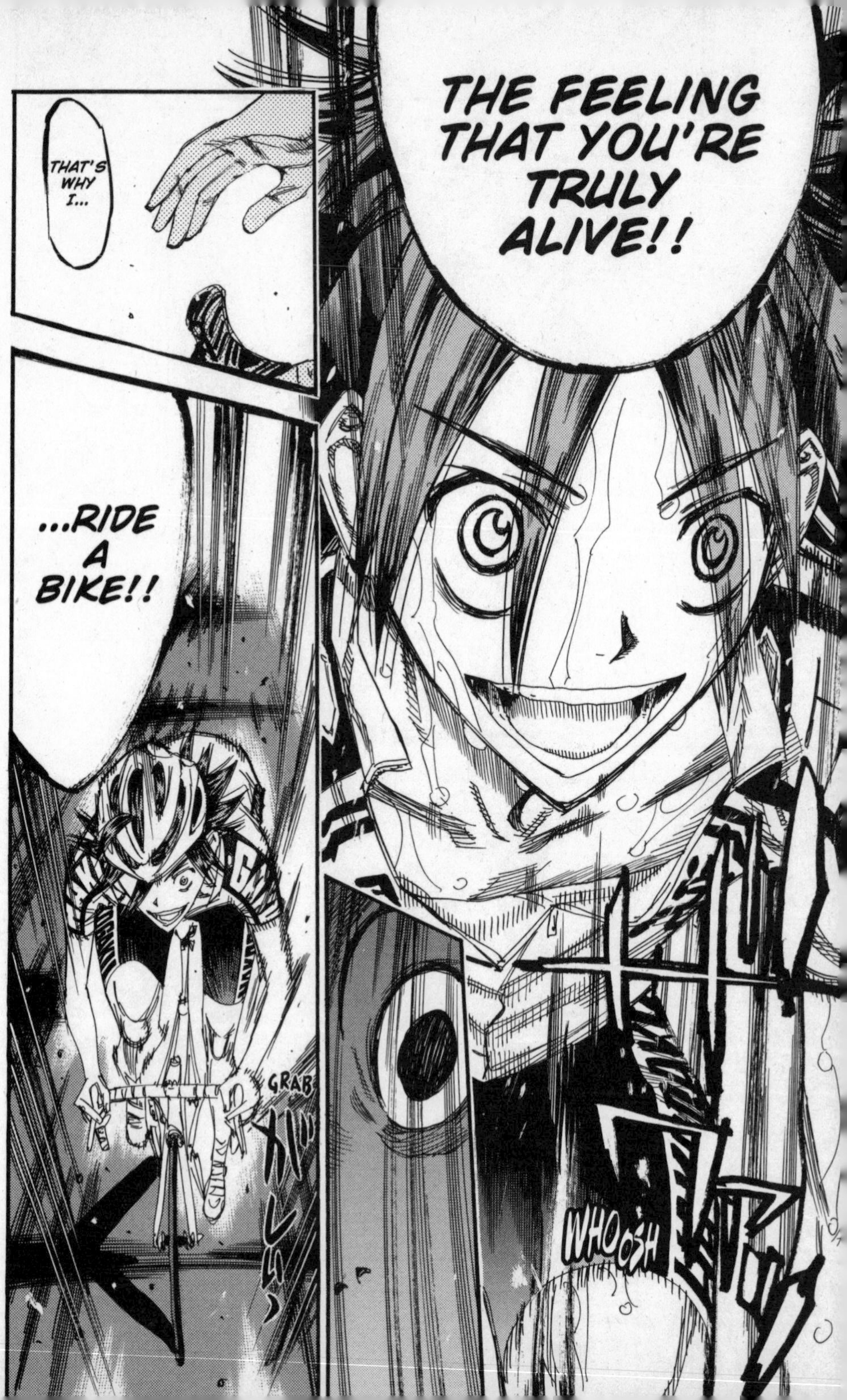
THE FEELING THAT YOU'RE TRULY ALIVE!!
WHOOSH
THAT'S WHY I...
...RIDE A BIKE!!
GRAB

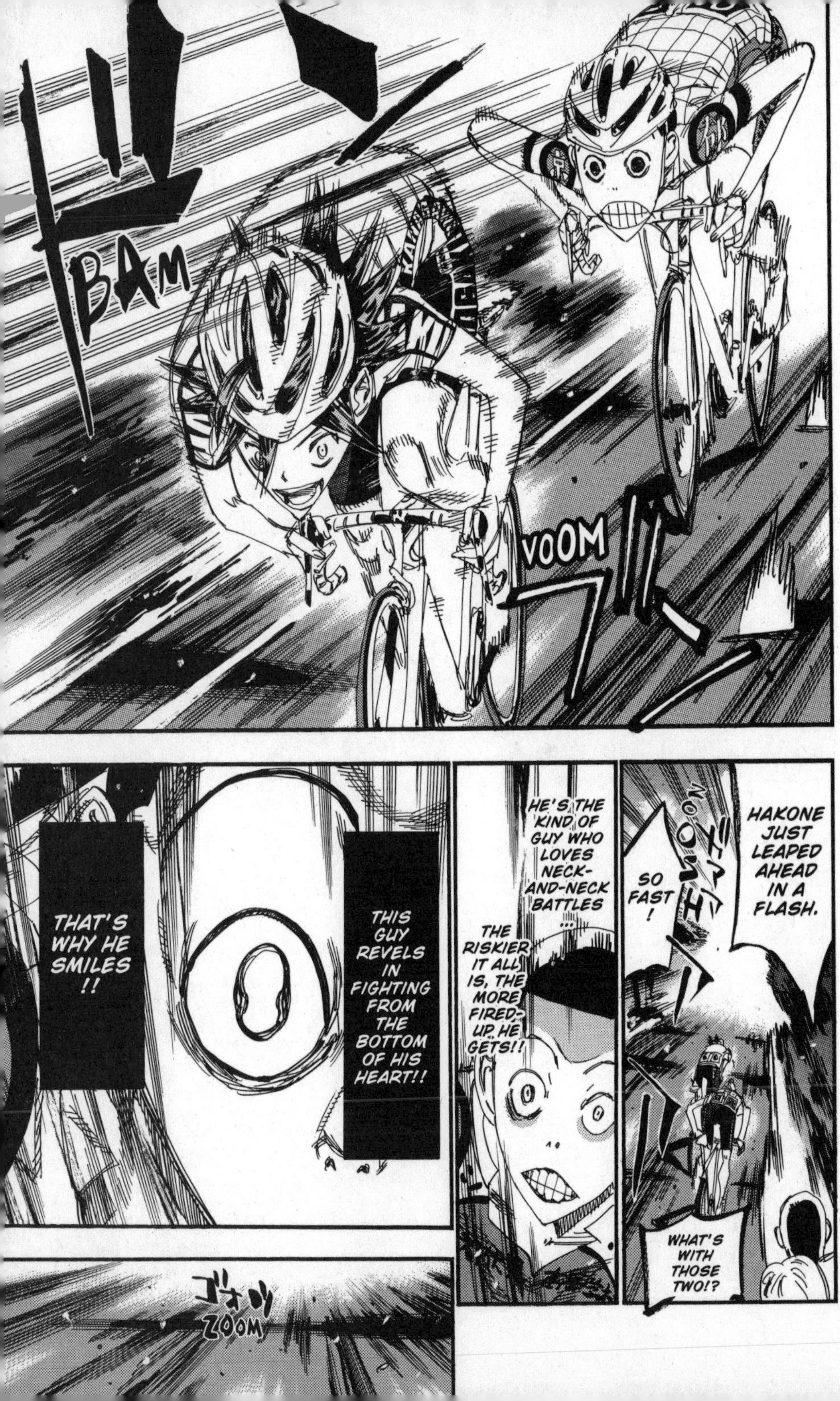
BAM
VOOM
HAKONE JUST LEAPED AHEAD IN A FLASH.
SO FAST!
WHAT'S WITH THOSE TWO!?
HE'S THE KIND OF GUY WHO LOVES NECK-AND-NECK BATTLES...
THE RISKIER IT ALL IS, THE MORE FIRED-UP HE GETS!!
THIS GUY REVELS IN FIGHTING FROM THE BOTTOM OF HIS HEART!!
THAT'S WHY HE SMILES!!
ゴオッ
ZOOM

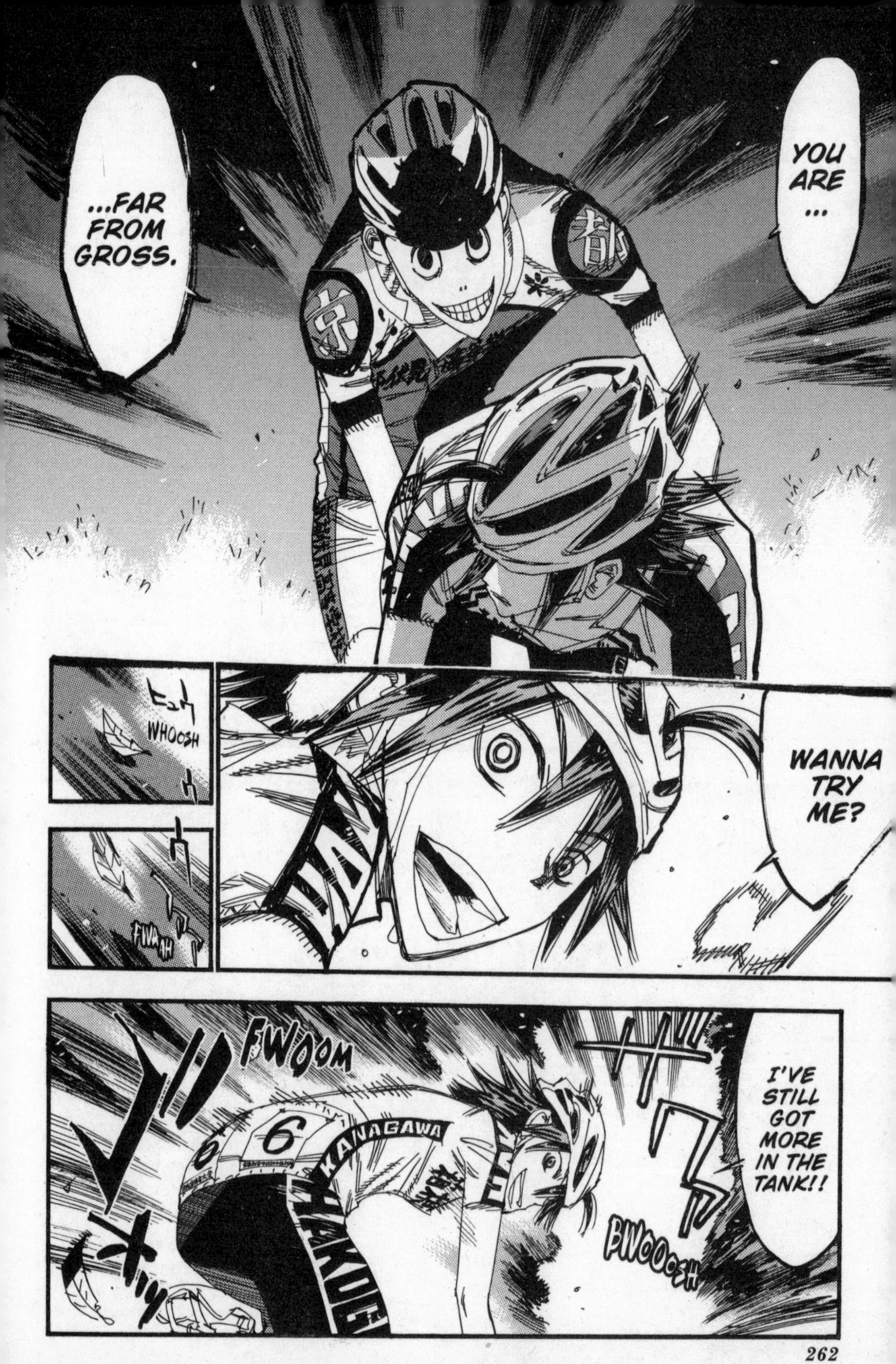
YOU ARE ...
...FAR FROM GROSS.
WANNA TRY ME?
WHOOSH
FWAAH
I'VE STILL GOT MORE IN THE TANK!!
BWOOOSH
FWOOM

RIDE.203 WIND

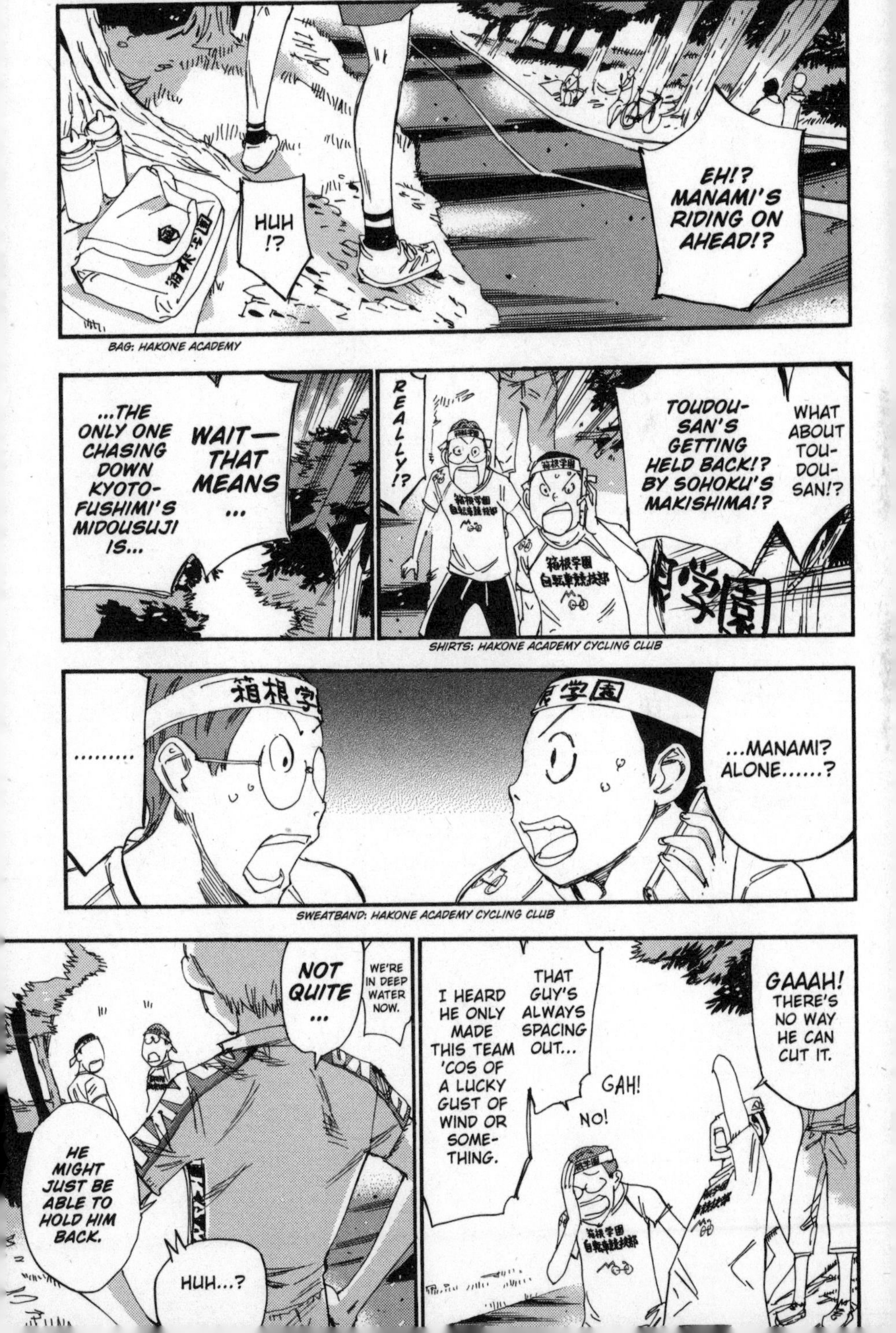
EH!? MANAMI'S RIDING ON AHEAD!?
HUH!?
BAG: HAKONE ACADEMY
WHAT ABOUT TOU-DOU-SAN!?
TOUDOU-SAN'S GETTING HELD BACK!? BY SOHOKU'S MAKISHIMA!?
REALLY!?
WAIT— THAT MEANS ...
...THE ONLY ONE CHASING DOWN KYOTO-FUSHIMI'S MIDOUSUJI IS...
SHIRTS: HAKONE ACADEMY CYCLING CLUB
...MANAMI? ALONE......?
....
SWEATBAND: HAKONE ACADEMY CYCLING CLUB
GAAAH! THERE'S NO WAY HE CAN CUT IT.
THAT GUY'S ALWAYS SPACING OUT...
I HEARD HE ONLY MADE THIS TEAM 'COS OF A LUCKY GUST OF WIND OR SOME-THING.
GAH!
NO!
WE'RE IN DEEP WATER NOW.
NOT QUITE ...
HE MIGHT JUST BE ABLE TO HOLD HIM BACK.
HUH...?

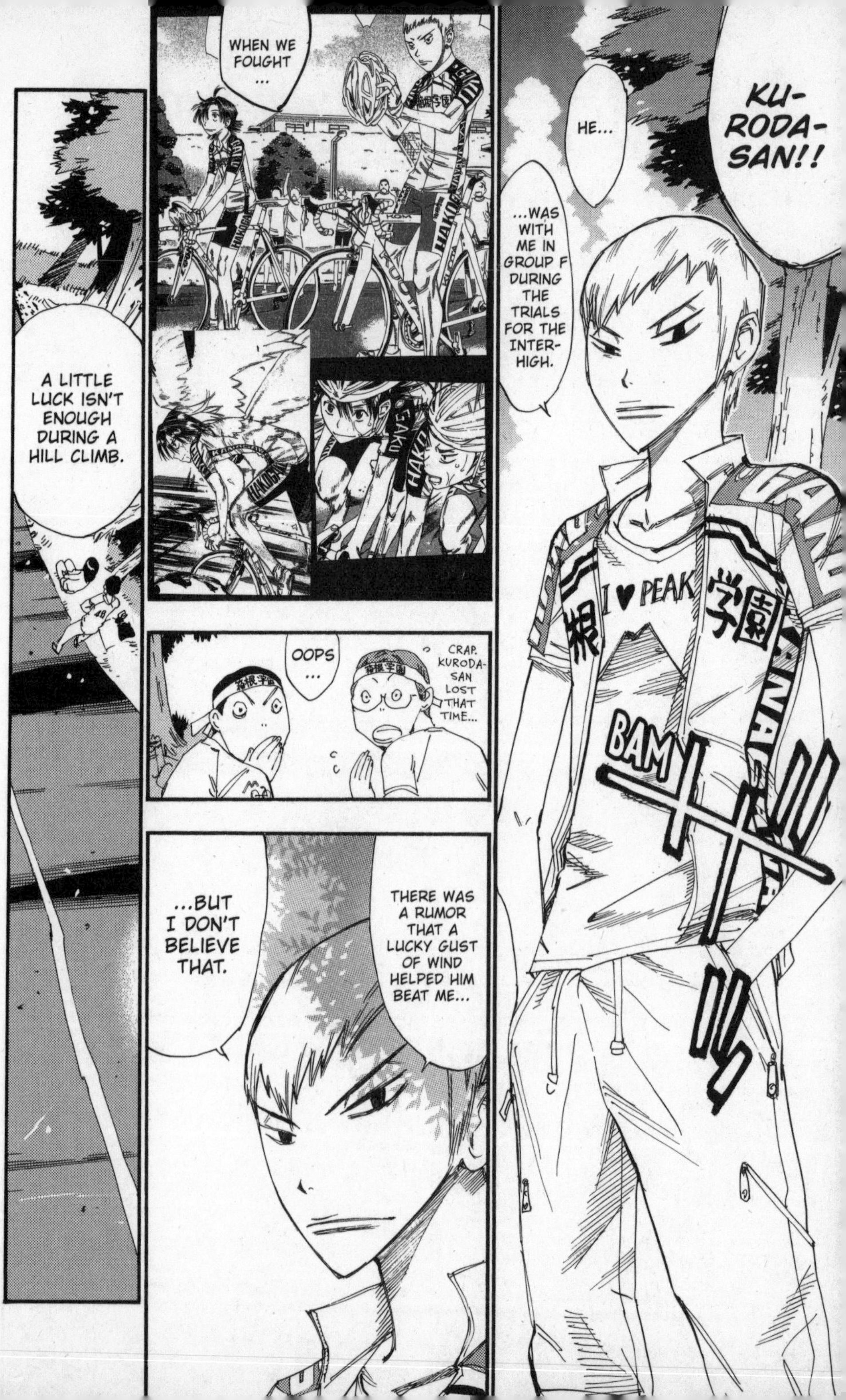
KURODA-SAN!!
HE...
...WAS WITH ME IN GROUP F DURING THE TRIALS FOR THE INTER-HIGH.
BAM
WHEN WE FOUGHT ...
OOPS ...
CRAP. KURODA-SAN LOST THAT TIME...
THERE WAS A RUMOR THAT A LUCKY GUST OF WIND HELPED HIM BEAT ME...
...BUT I DON'T BELIEVE THAT.
A LITTLE LUCK ISN'T ENOUGH DURING A HILL CLIMB.

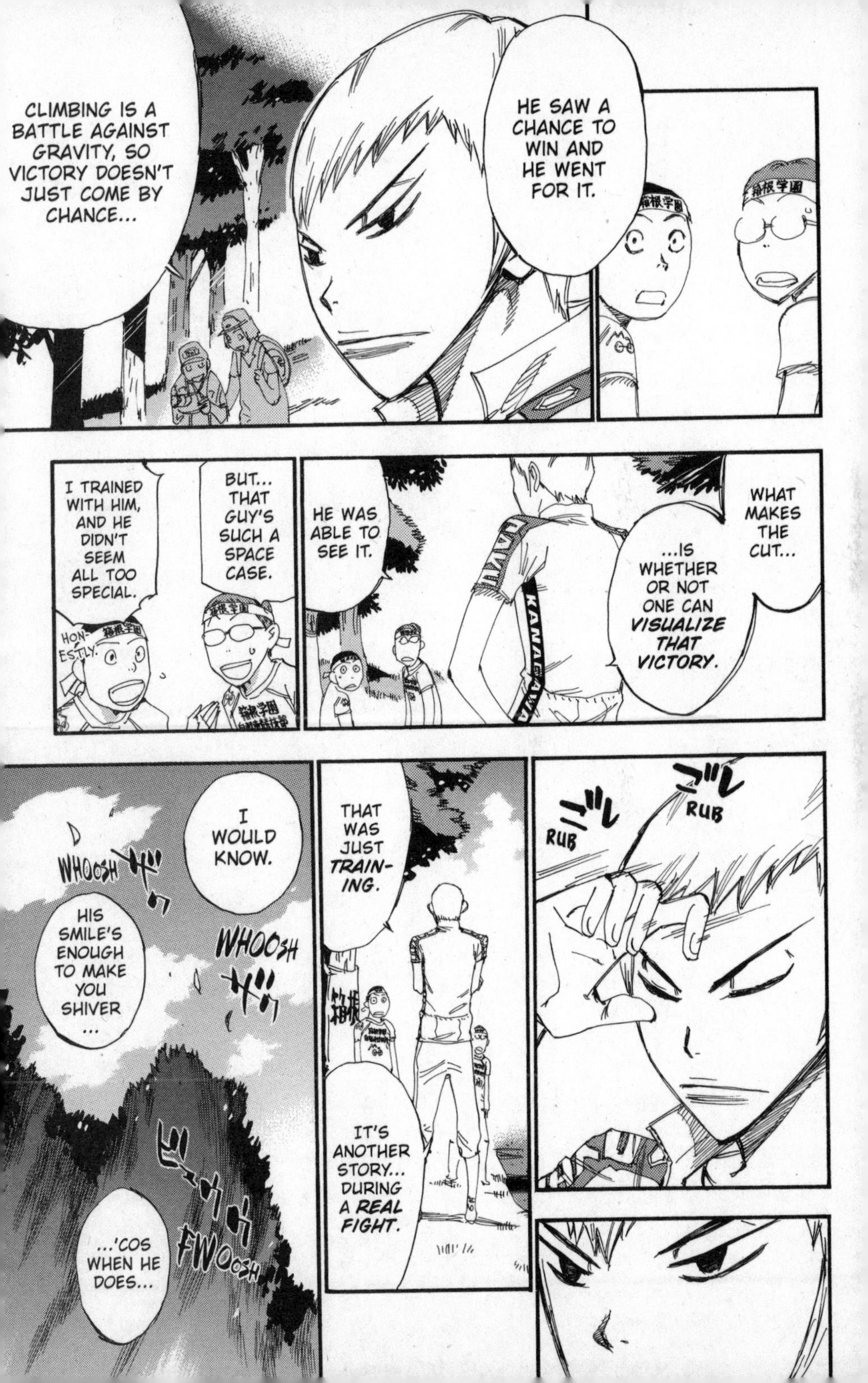
HE SAW A CHANCE TO WIN AND HE WENT FOR IT.
CLIMBING IS A BATTLE AGAINST GRAVITY, SO VICTORY DOESN'T JUST COME BY CHANCE...
WHAT MAKES THE CUT...
...IS WHETHER OR NOT ONE CAN VISUALIZE THAT VICTORY.
HE WAS ABLE TO SEE IT.
BUT... THAT GUY'S SUCH A SPACE CASE.
I TRAINED WITH HIM, AND HE DIDN'T SEEM ALL TOO SPECIAL.
HON-ESTLY.
RUB
RUB
THAT WAS JUST TRAINING.
IT'S ANOTHER STORY... DURING A REAL FIGHT.
I WOULD KNOW.
WHOOSH
HIS SMILE'S ENOUGH TO MAKE YOU SHIVER...
WHOOSH
FWOOSH
...'COS WHEN HE DOES...

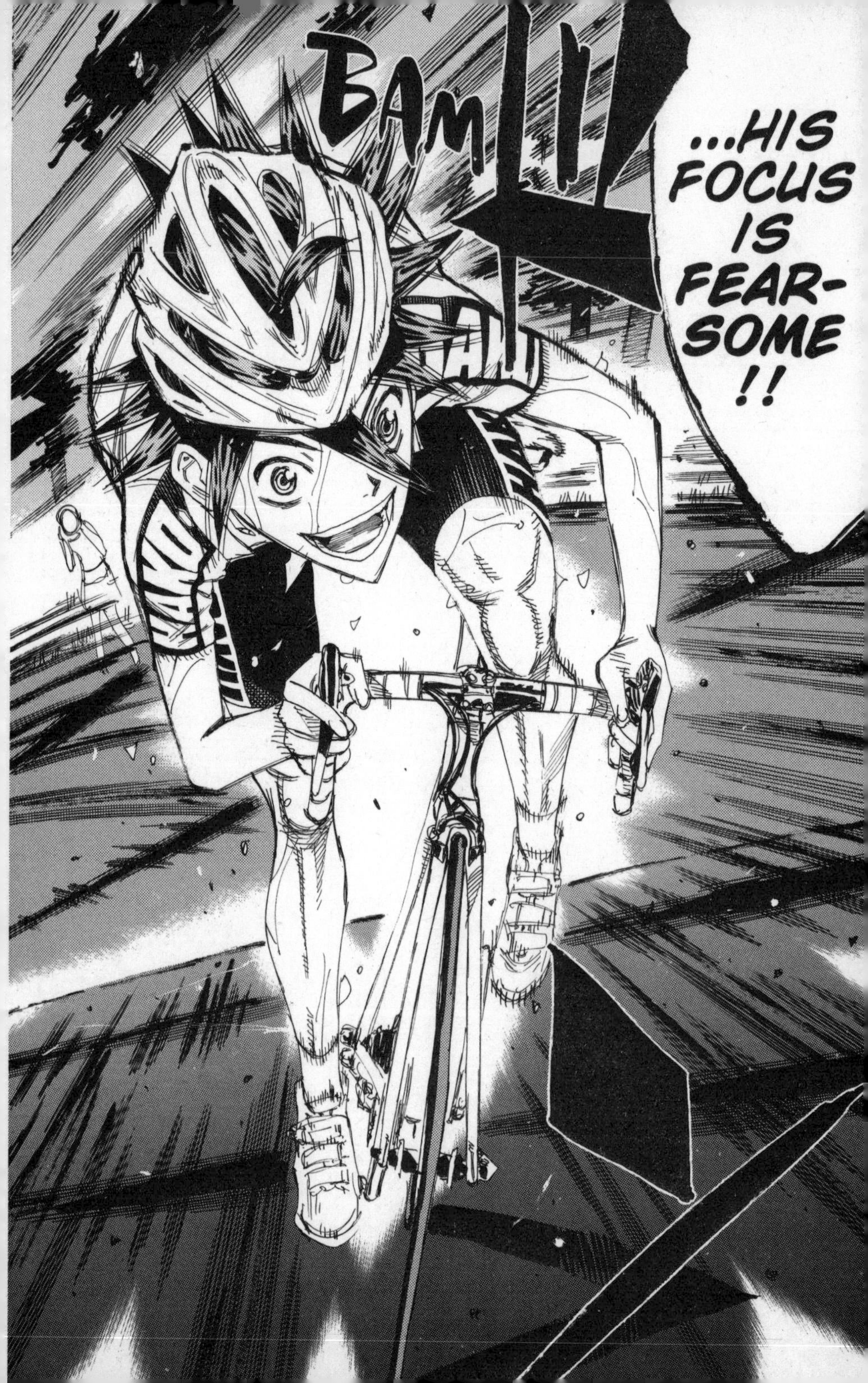
BAM!!
...HIS FOCUS IS FEAR-SOME!!

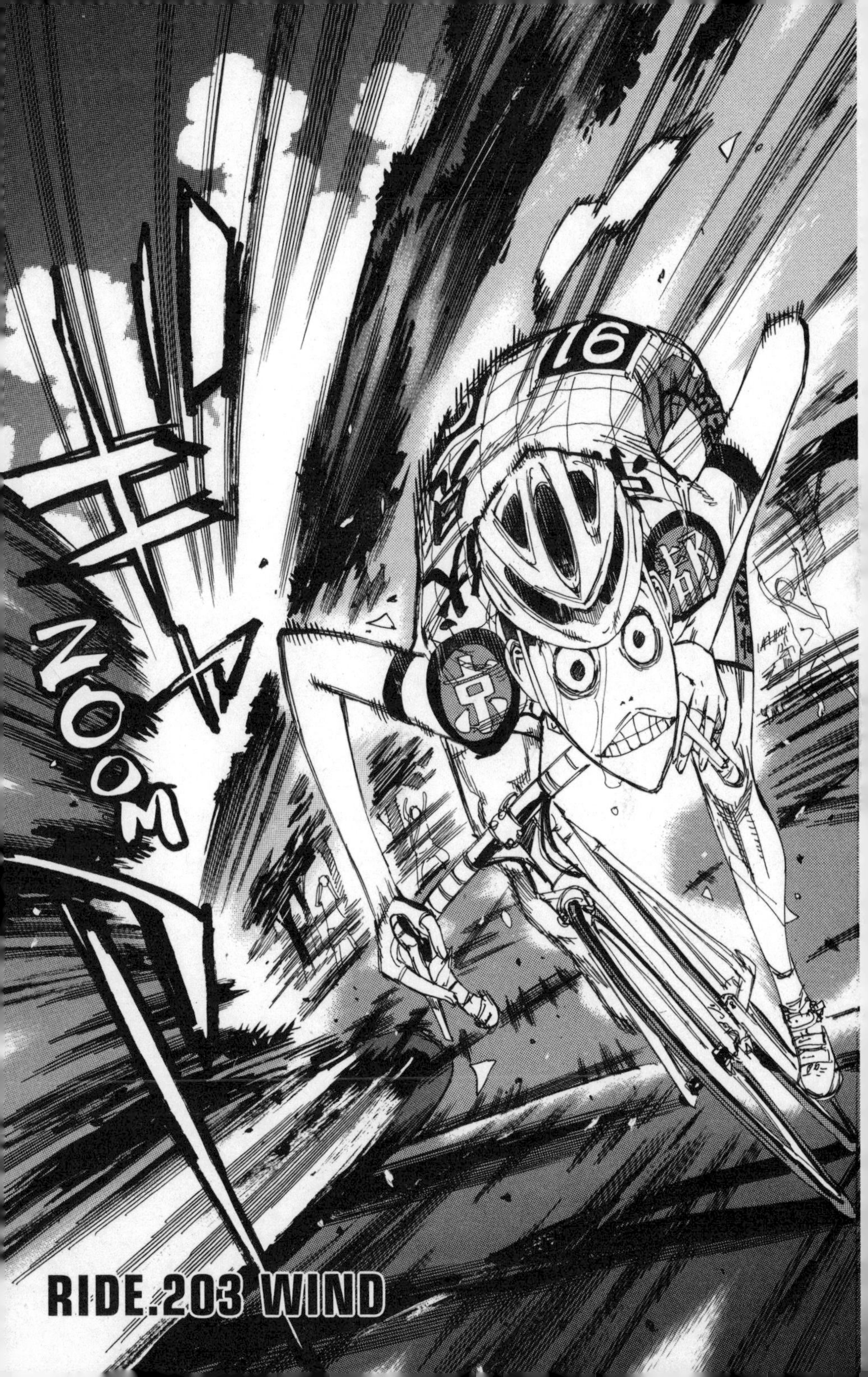
ZOOM

RIDE.203 WIND

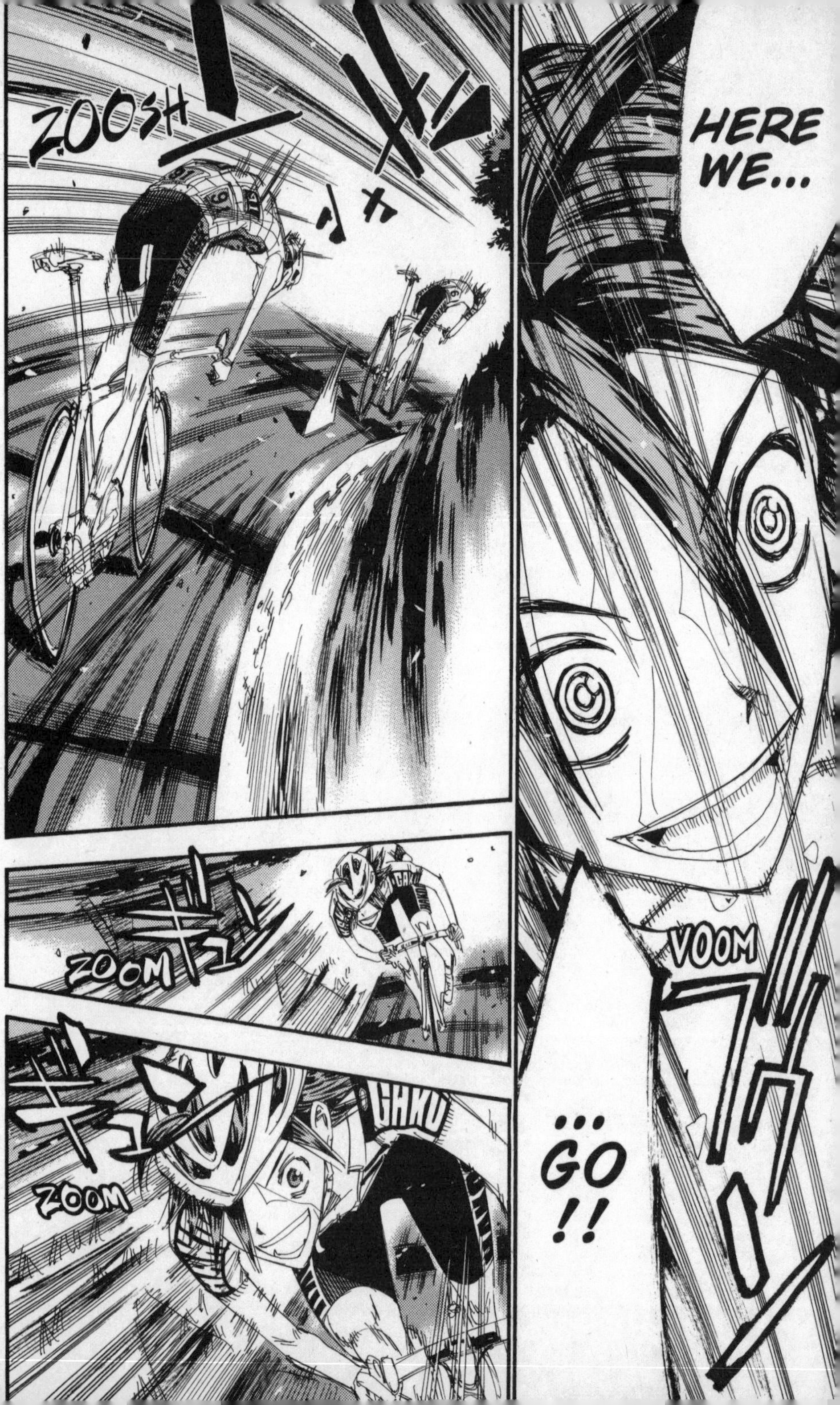
HERE WE...
VOOM
...GO!!
ZOOSH
ZOOM
ZOOM

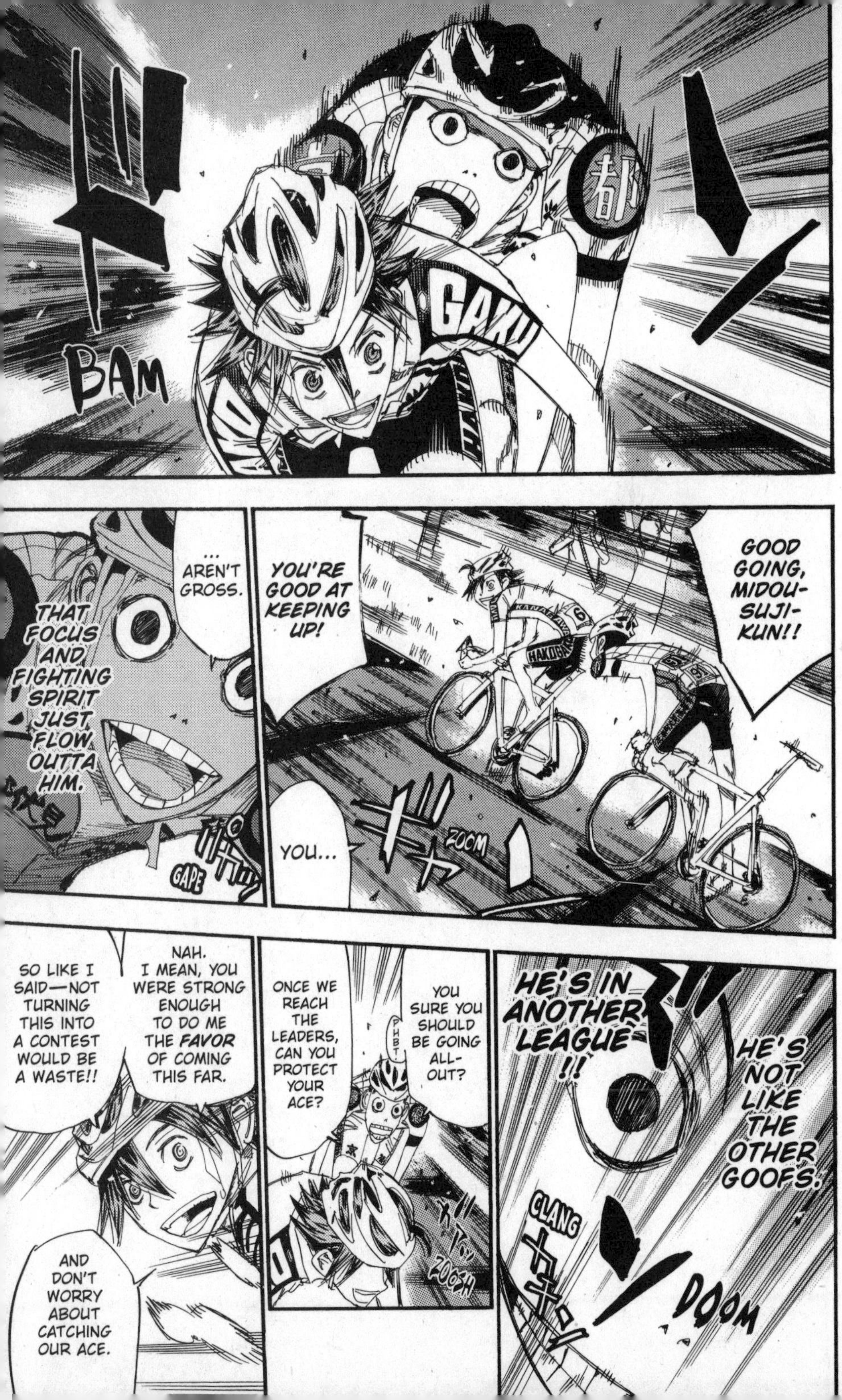
BAM
GOOD GOING, MIDOUSUJI-KUN!!
YOU'RE GOOD AT KEEPING UP!
YOU...
ZOOM
... AREN'T GROSS.
THAT FOCUS AND FIGHTING SPIRIT JUST FLOW OUTTA HIM.
GAPE
HE'S IN ANOTHER LEAGUE!!
HE'S NOT LIKE THE OTHER GOOFS.
CLANG
DOOM
YOU SURE YOU SHOULD BE GOING ALL-OUT?
PHBT
ONCE WE REACH THE LEADERS, CAN YOU PROTECT YOUR ACE?
ZOOSH
NAH. I MEAN, YOU WERE STRONG ENOUGH TO DO ME THE *FAVOR* OF COMING THIS FAR.
SO LIKE I SAID—NOT TURNING THIS INTO A CONTEST WOULD BE A WASTE!!
AND DON'T WORRY ABOUT CATCHING OUR ACE.

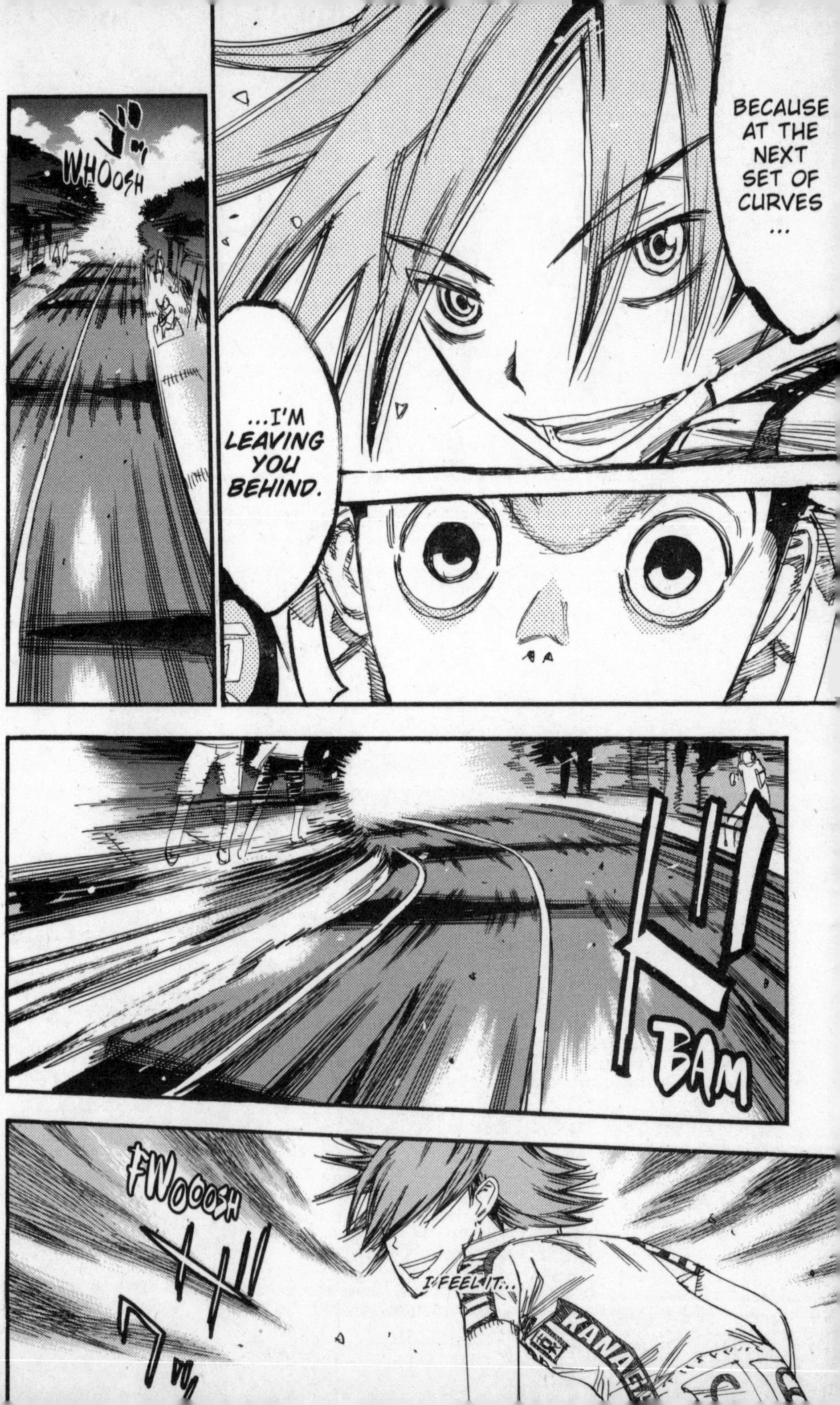
BECAUSE AT THE NEXT SET OF CURVES ...
...I'M LEAVING YOU BEHIND.
WHOOSH
BAM
FWOOOSH
I FEEL IT...

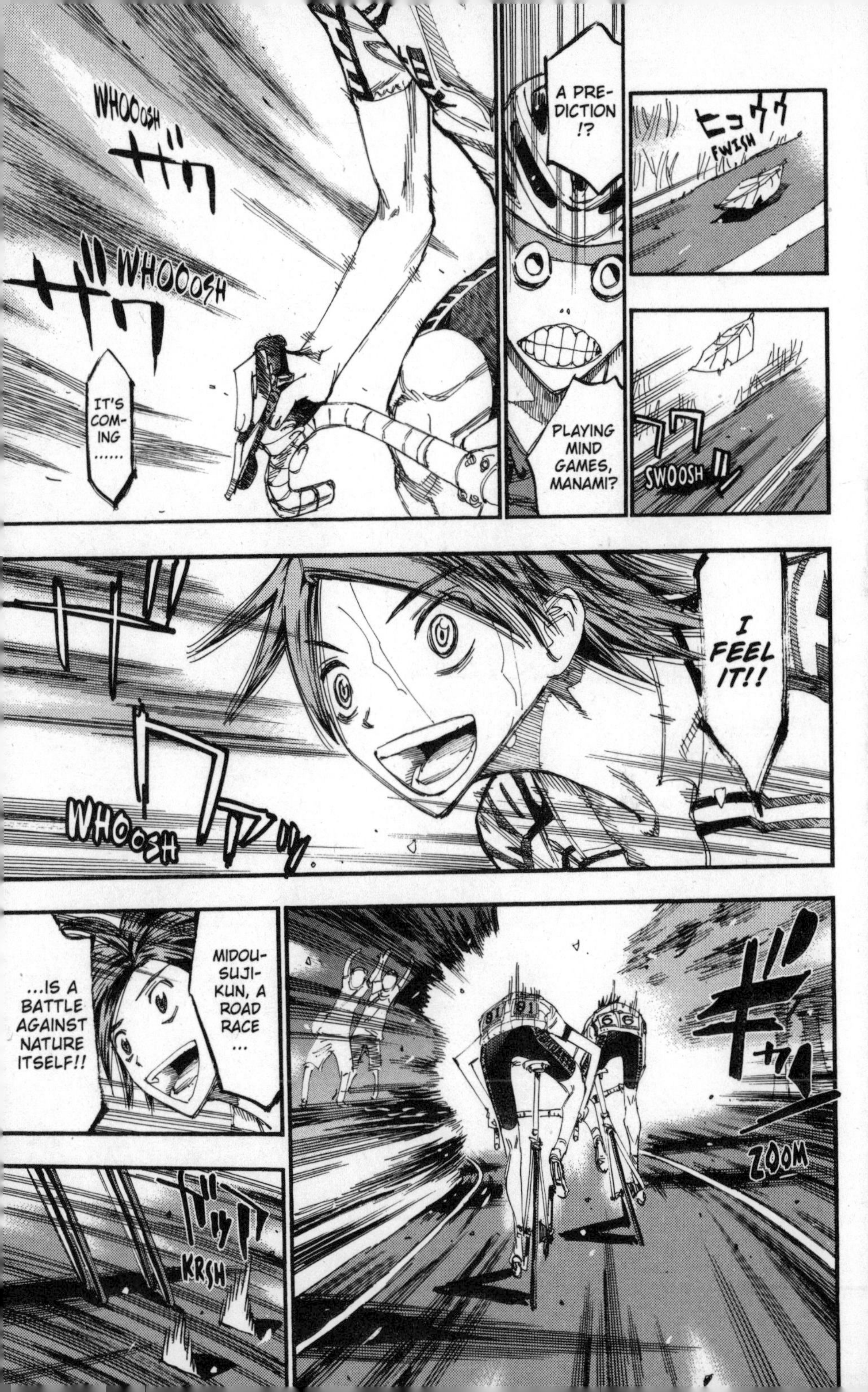
ヒュウウ
FWISH
SWOOSH
A PRE-DICTION!?
PLAYING MIND GAMES, MANAMI?
WHOOOSH
WHOOOSH
IT'S COMING......
I FEEL IT!!
WHOOOSH
ZOOM
MIDOU-SUJI-KUN, A ROAD RACE...
...IS A BATTLE AGAINST NATURE ITSELF!!
KRSH

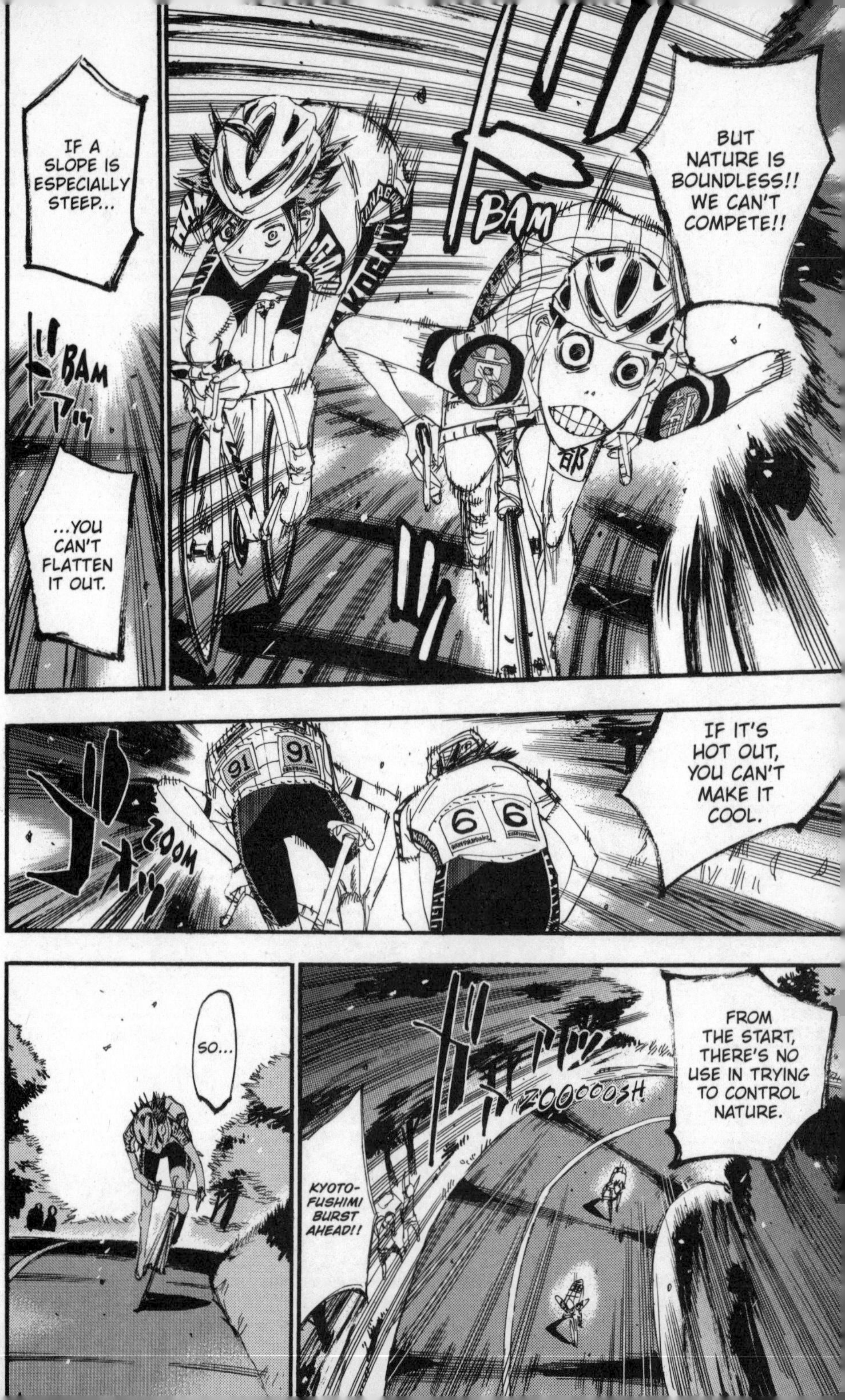
BUT NATURE IS BOUNDLESS!! WE CAN'T COMPETE!!
BAM
IF A SLOPE IS ESPECIALLY STEEP...
BAM
...YOU CAN'T FLATTEN IT OUT.
IF IT'S HOT OUT, YOU CAN'T MAKE IT COOL.
ZOOM
FROM THE START, THERE'S NO USE IN TRYING TO CONTROL NATURE.
ZOOOOOOSH
KYOTO-FUSHIMI BURST AHEAD!!
SO...

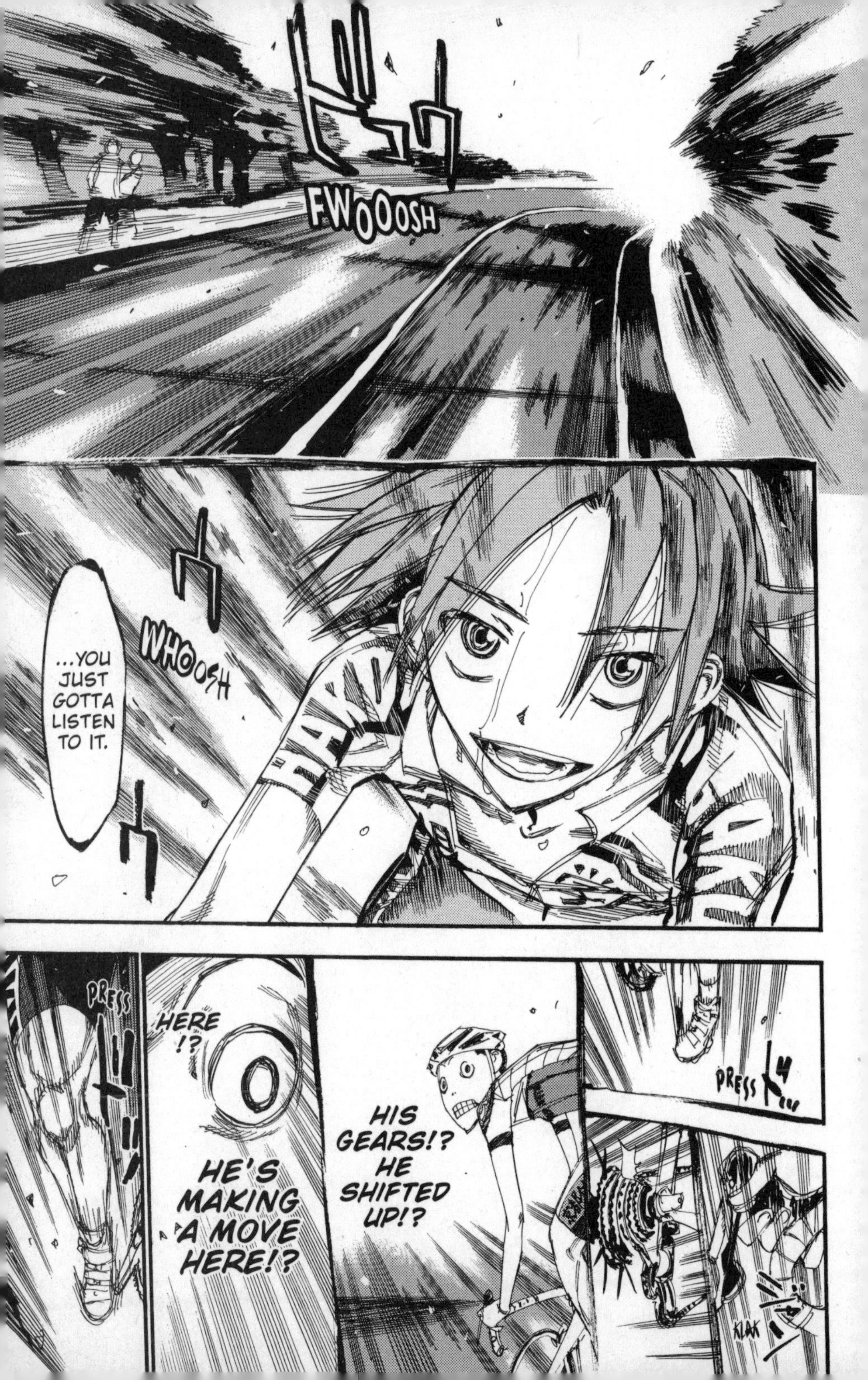
FWOOOSH
WHOOOSH
...YOU JUST GOTTA LISTEN TO IT.
PRESS
KLAK
HIS GEARS!? HE SHIFTED UP!?
HE'S MAKING A MOVE HERE!?
HERE!?
PRESS

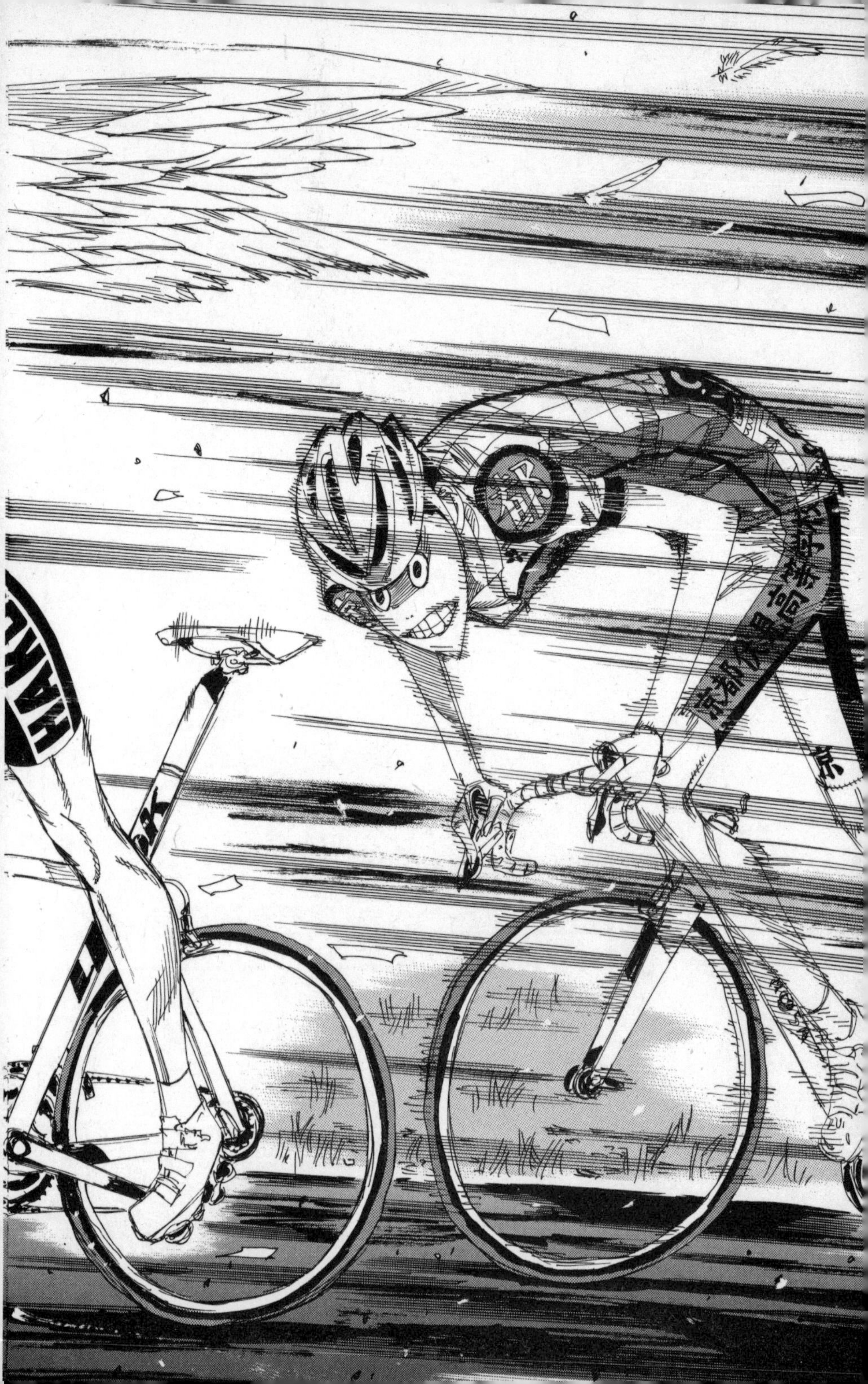
京都伏見高等
京

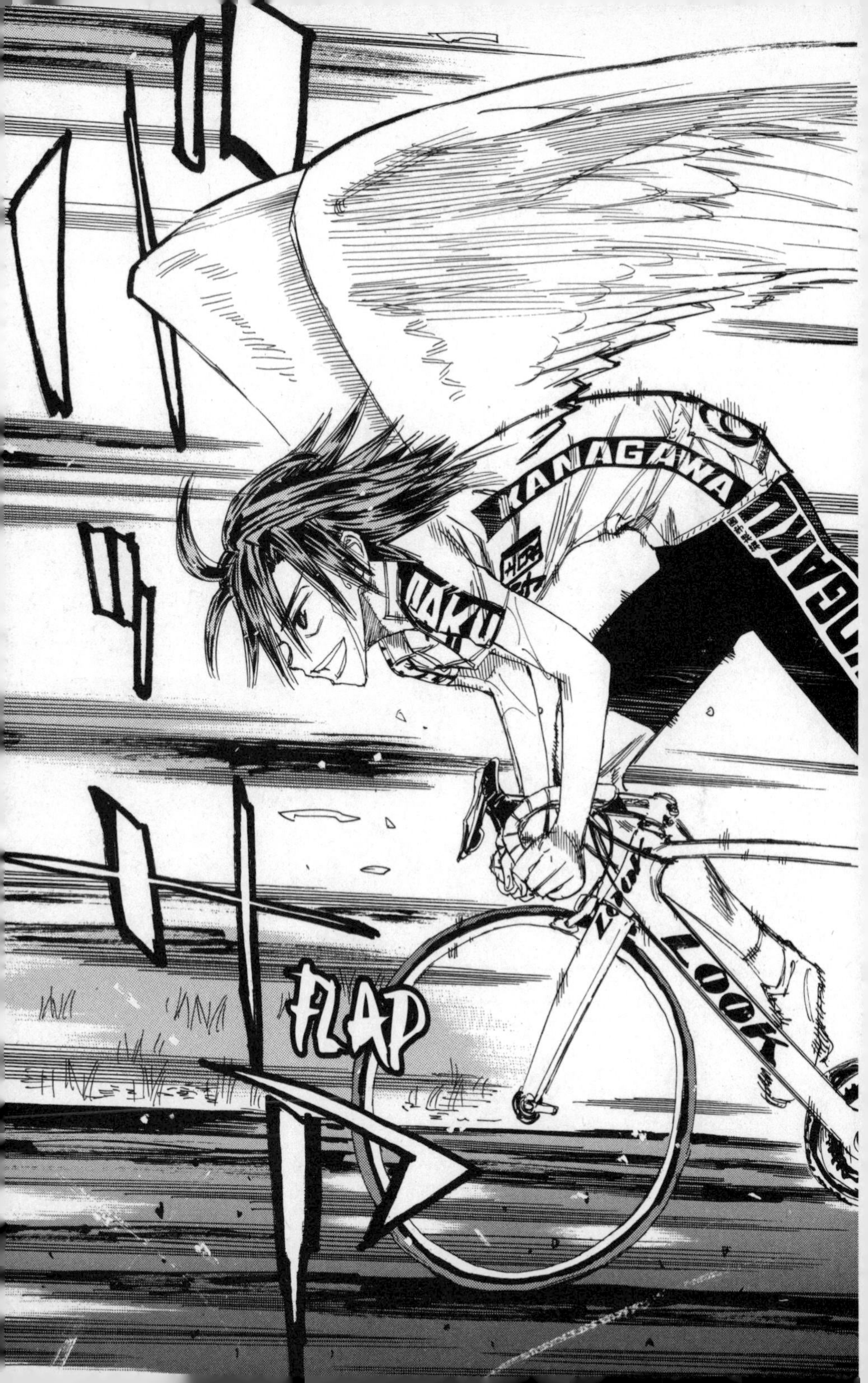
FLAP
KANAGAWA
LOOK

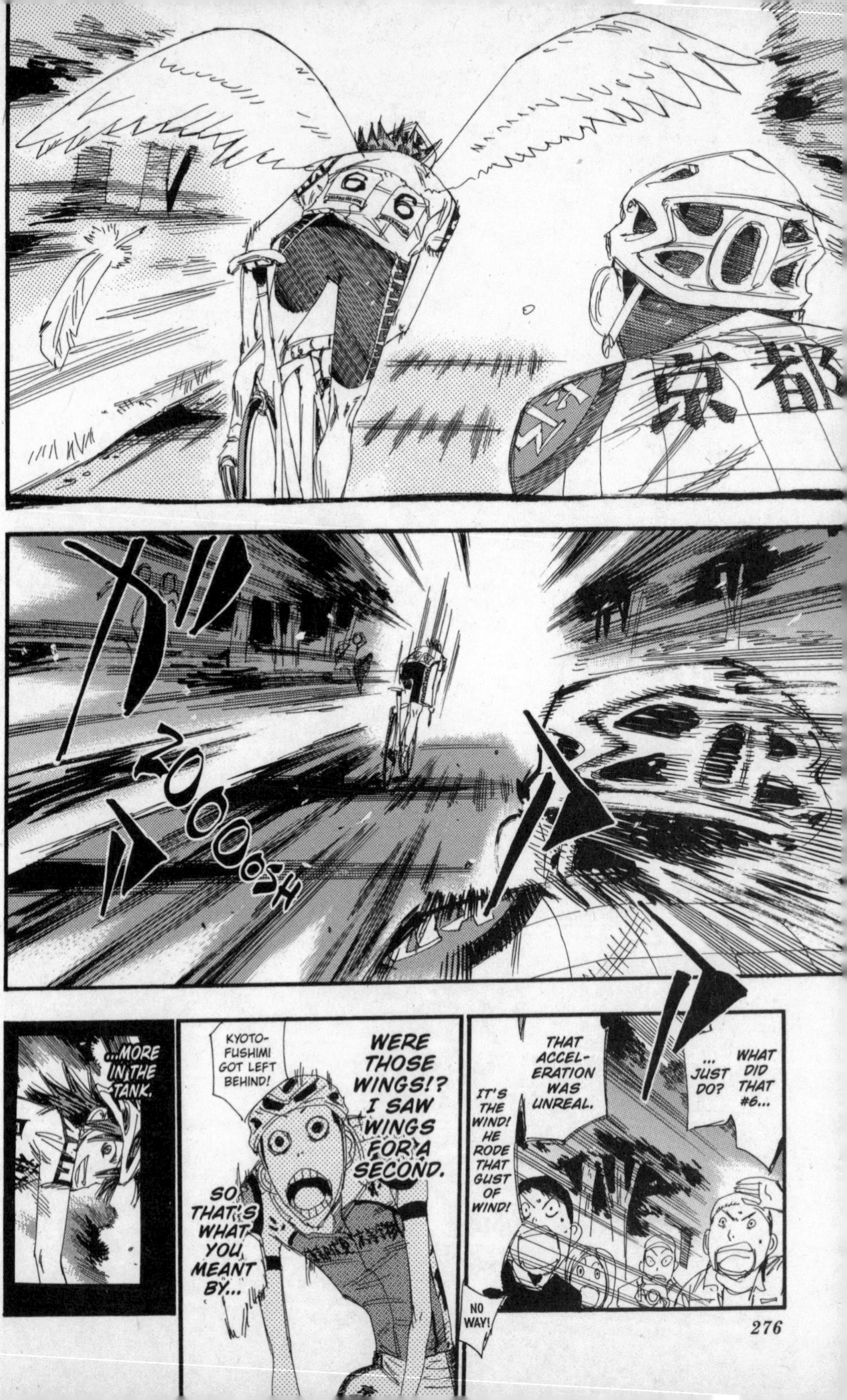
京都
ZOOOOOSH
WHAT DID THAT #6...
...JUST DO?
THAT ACCELERATION WAS UNREAL.
IT'S THE WIND! HE RODE THAT GUST OF WIND!
NO WAY!
WERE THOSE WINGS!? I SAW WINGS FOR A SECOND.
KYOTO-FUSHIMI GOT LEFT BEHIND!
SO THAT'S WHAT YOU MEANT BY...
...MORE IN THE TANK.

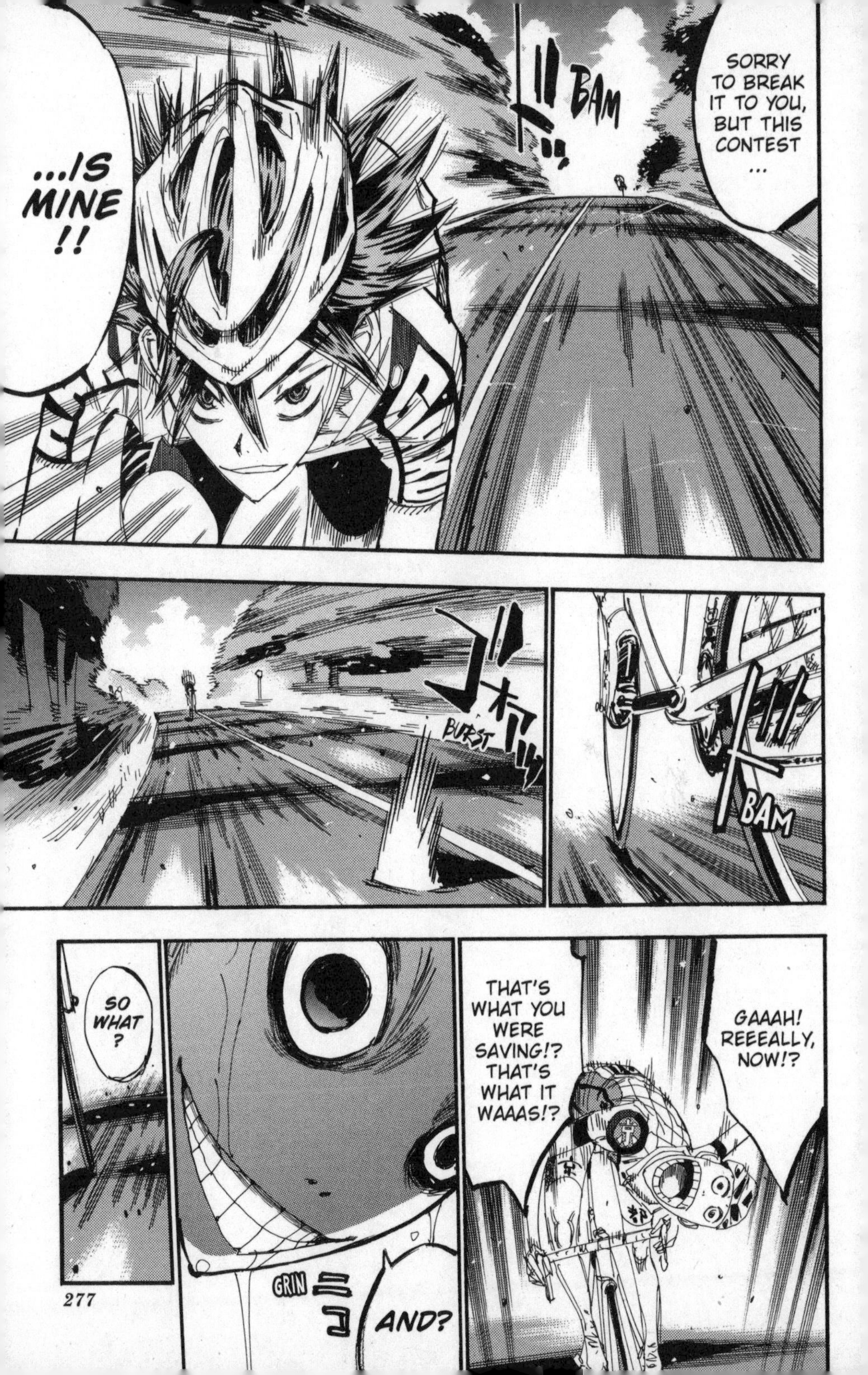
SORRY TO BREAK IT TO YOU, BUT THIS CONTEST ...
BAM
...IS MINE!!
BAM
BURST
GAAAH! REEEALLY, NOW!?
THAT'S WHAT YOU WERE SAVING!? THAT'S WHAT IT WAAAS!?
GRIN
AND?
SO WHAT?

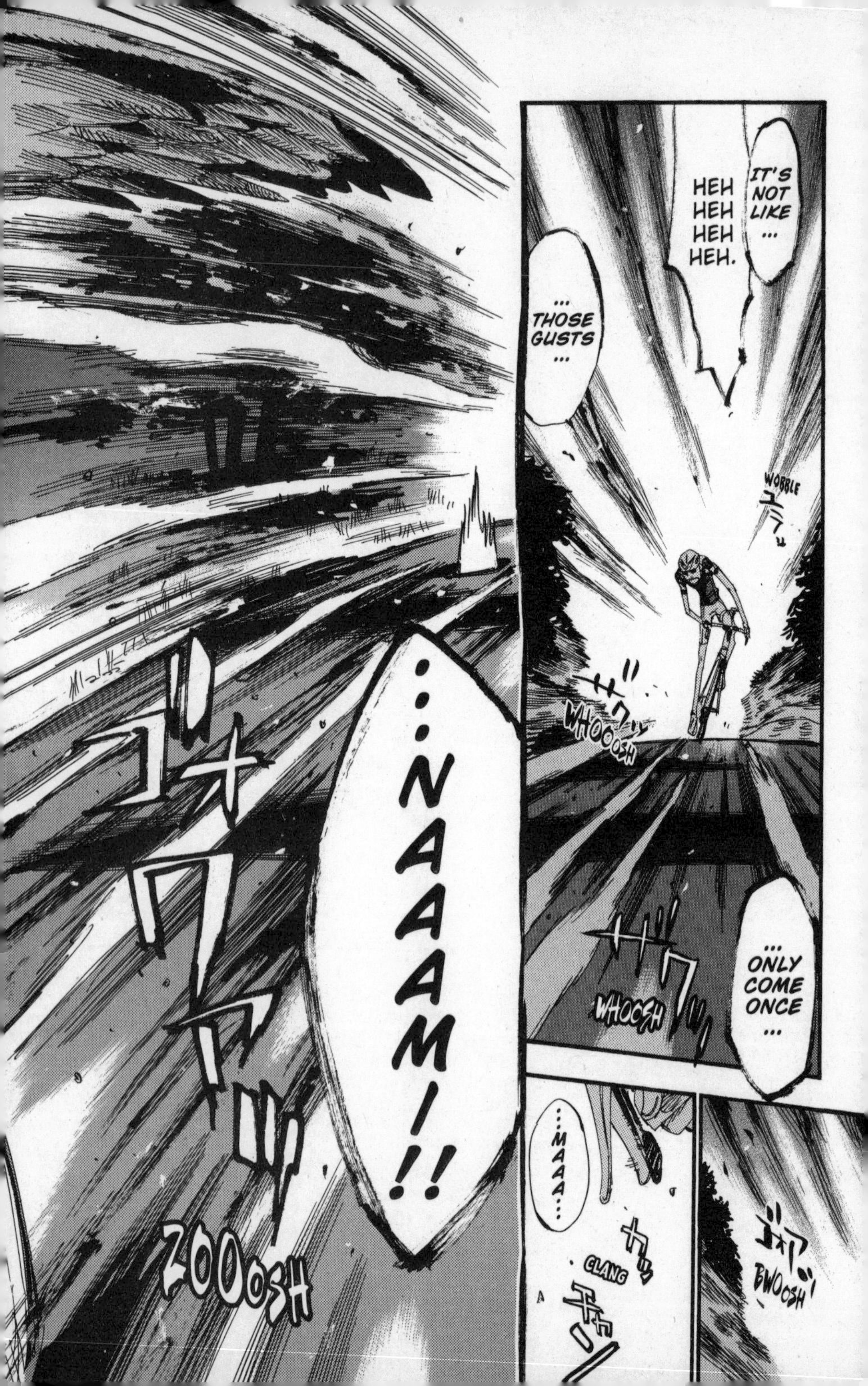
IT'S NOT LIKE ...
HEH HEH HEH HEH.
... THOSE GUSTS ...
WOBBLE
WHOOOSH
... ONLY COME ONCE ...
WHOOSH
BWOOSH
... MAAAA ...
CLANG
... NAAAAMI!!
ZOOOSH

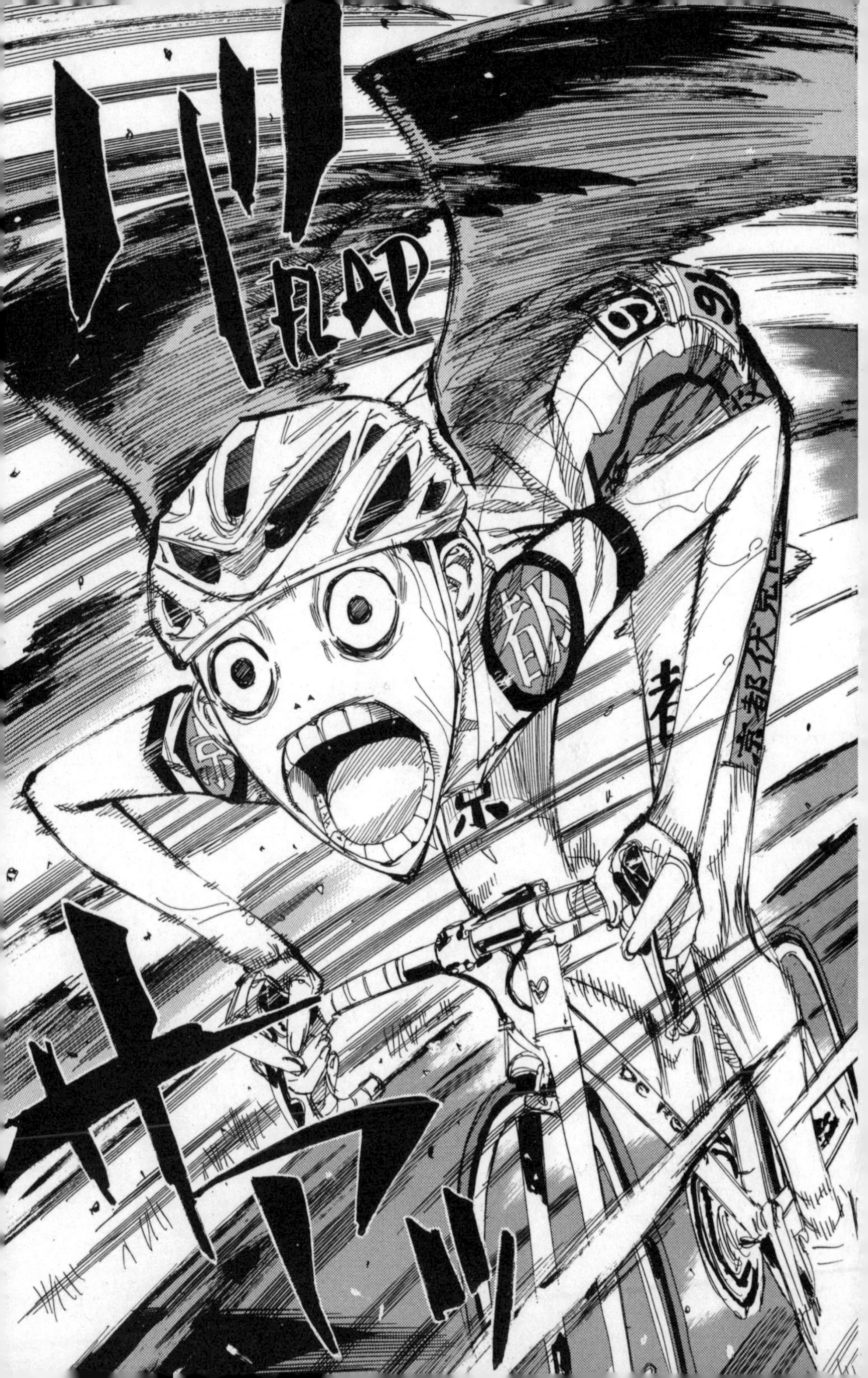
FLAP

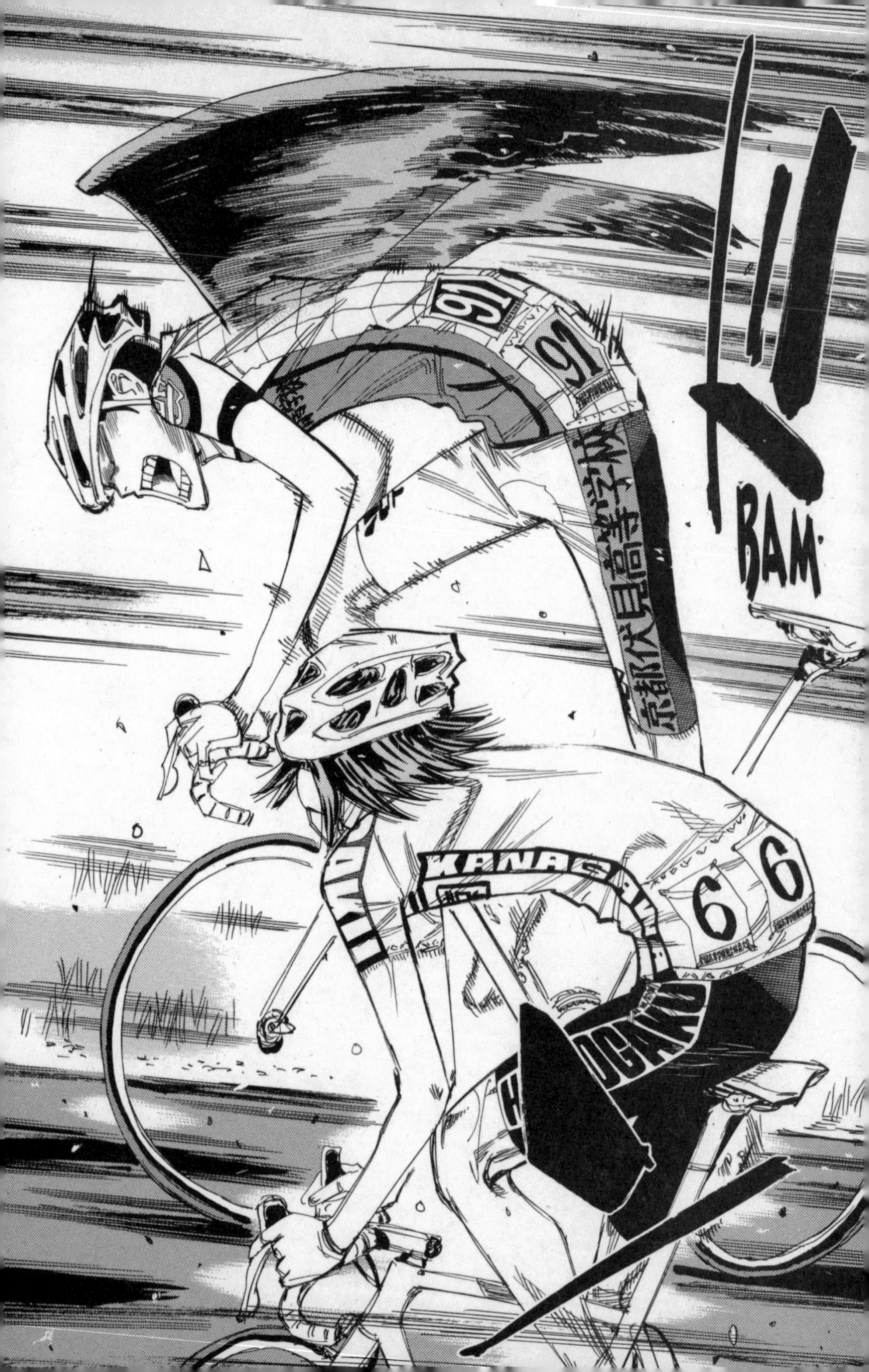
BAM

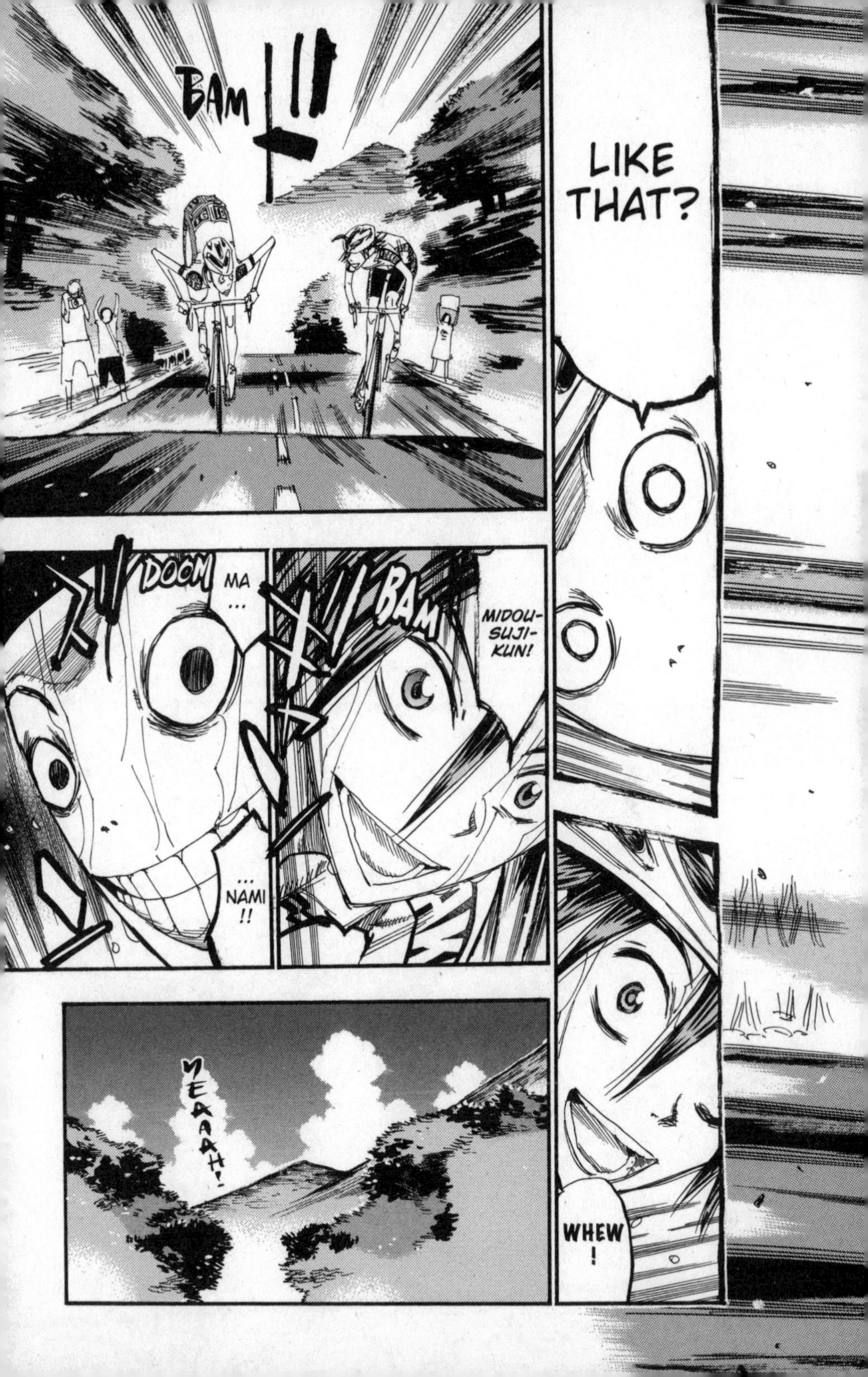
LIKE THAT?
WHEW!
BAM
BAM
MIDOUSUJI-KUN!
DOOM
MA...
...NAMI!!
YEAAAH!

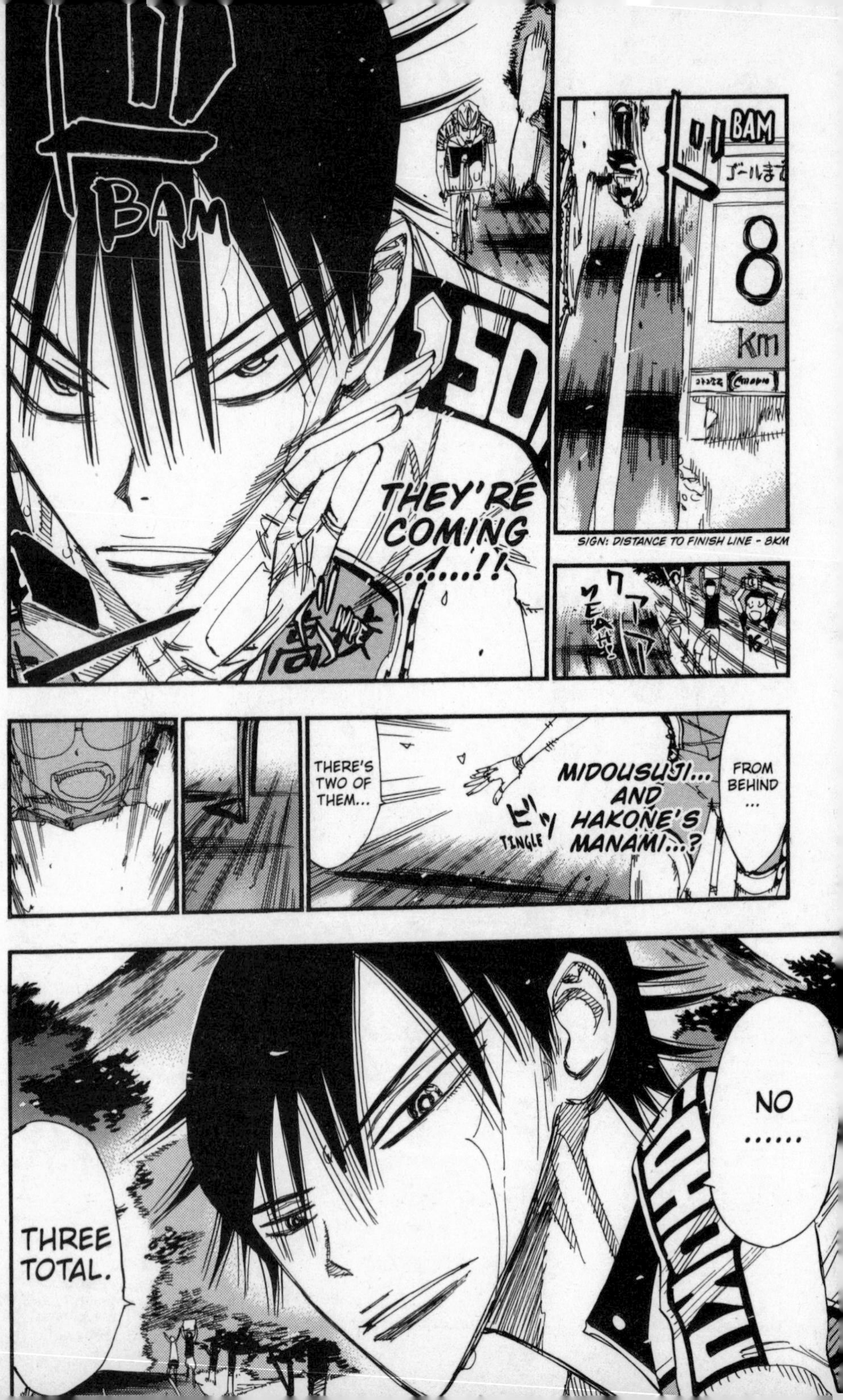

BAM
8
Km
SIGN: DISTANCE TO FINISH LINE - 8KM
WAAH!
BAM
THEY'RE COMING ......!!
FROM BEHIND ...
MIDOUSUJI... AND HAKONE'S MANAMI...?
TINGLE
THERE'S TWO OF THEM...
NO ......
THREE TOTAL.

RIDE.204 ONE STEP AT A TIME

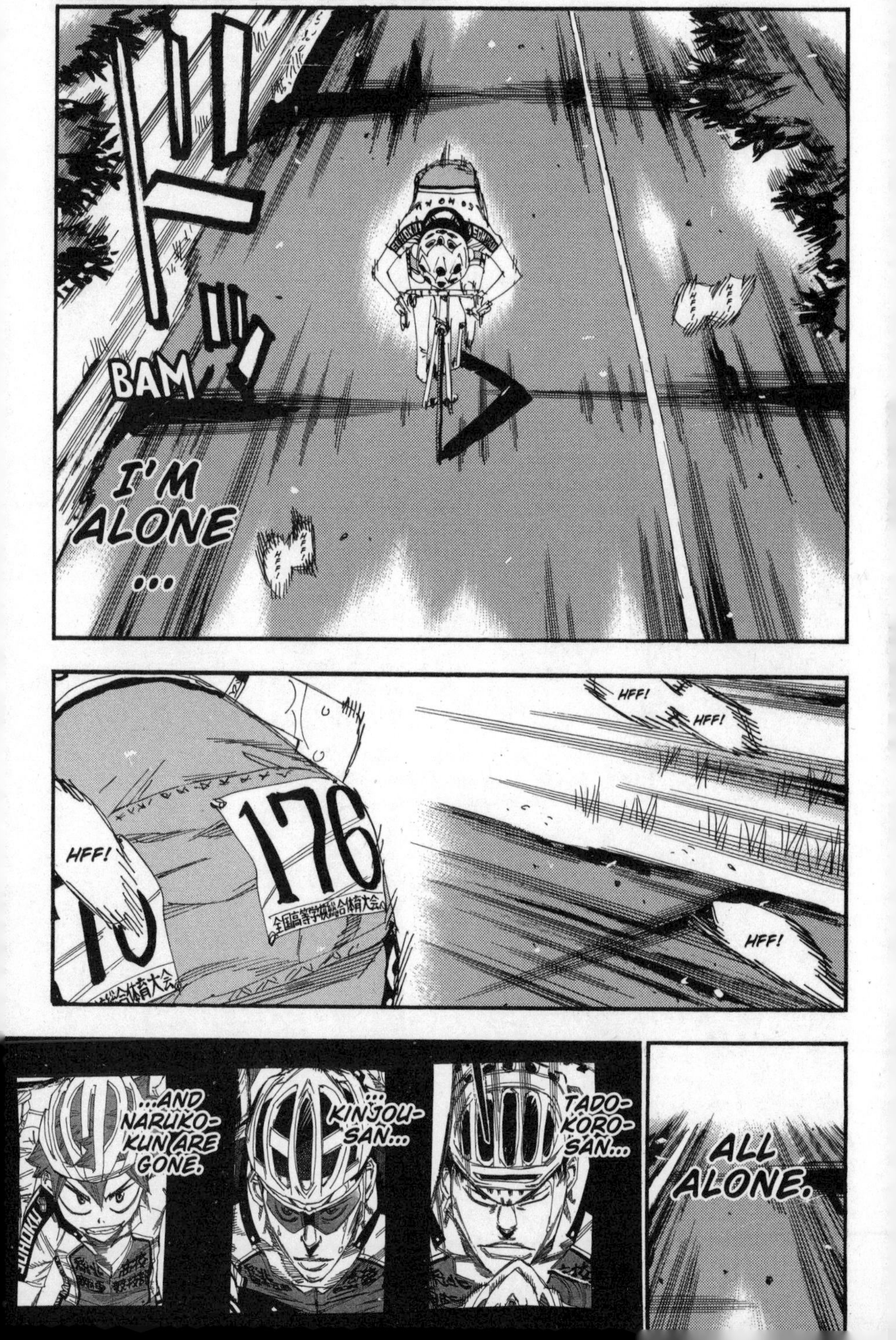
BAM
HFF! HFF!
I'M ALONE...
HFF! HFF!
HFF!
HFF!
176
HFF!
HFF!
ALL ALONE.
TADOKORO-SAN...
...KINJOU-SAN...
...AND NARUKO-KUN ARE GONE.

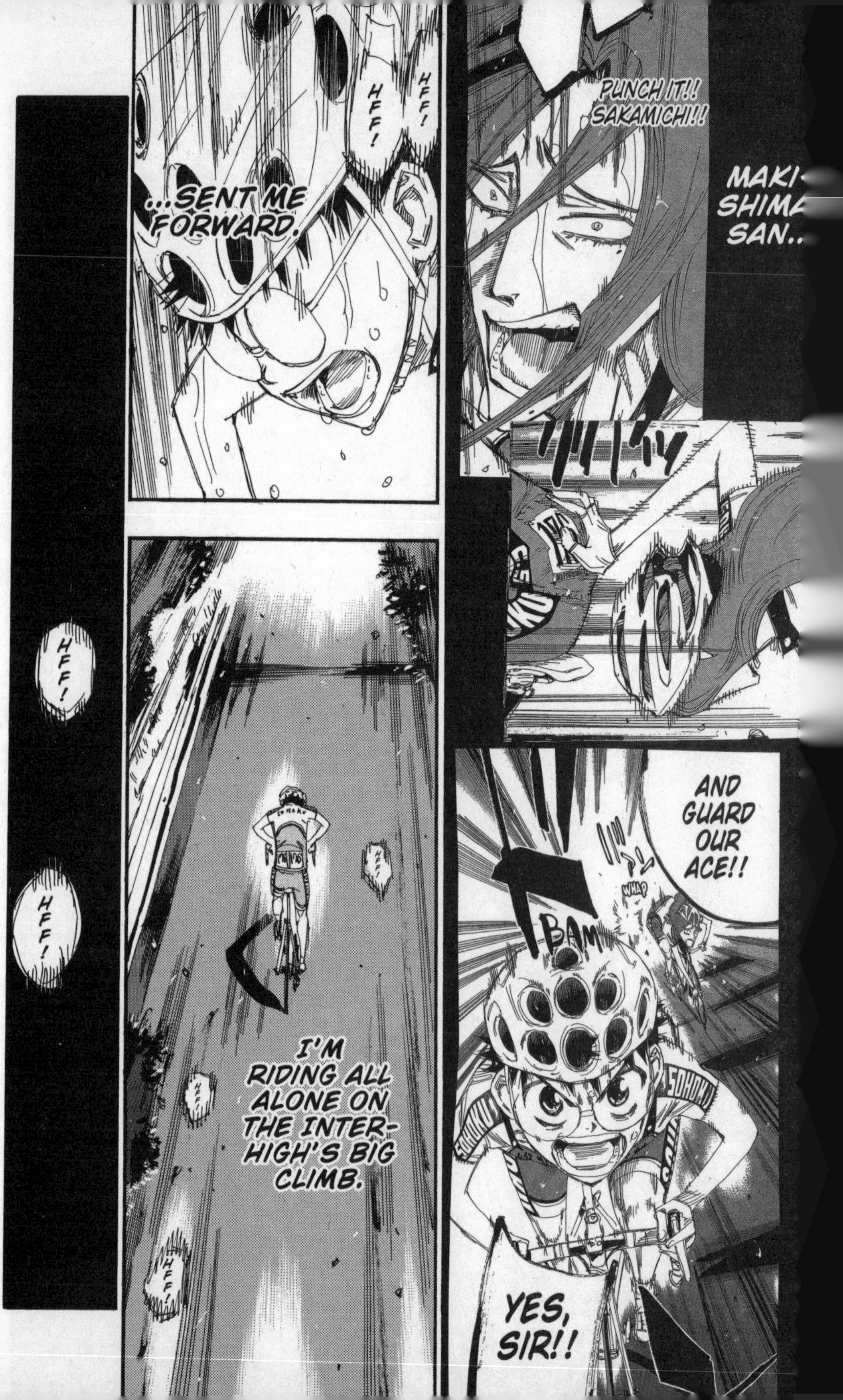
PUNCH IT!! SAKAMICHI!!
MAKI-SHIMA SAN..
AND GUARD OUR ACE!!
WHAP
BAM
YES, SIR!!
HFF! HFF!
...SENT ME FORWARD.
HFF!
HFF!
HFF!
I'M RIDING ALL ALONE ON THE INTER-HIGH'S BIG CLIMB.
HFF!
HFF!
HFF!

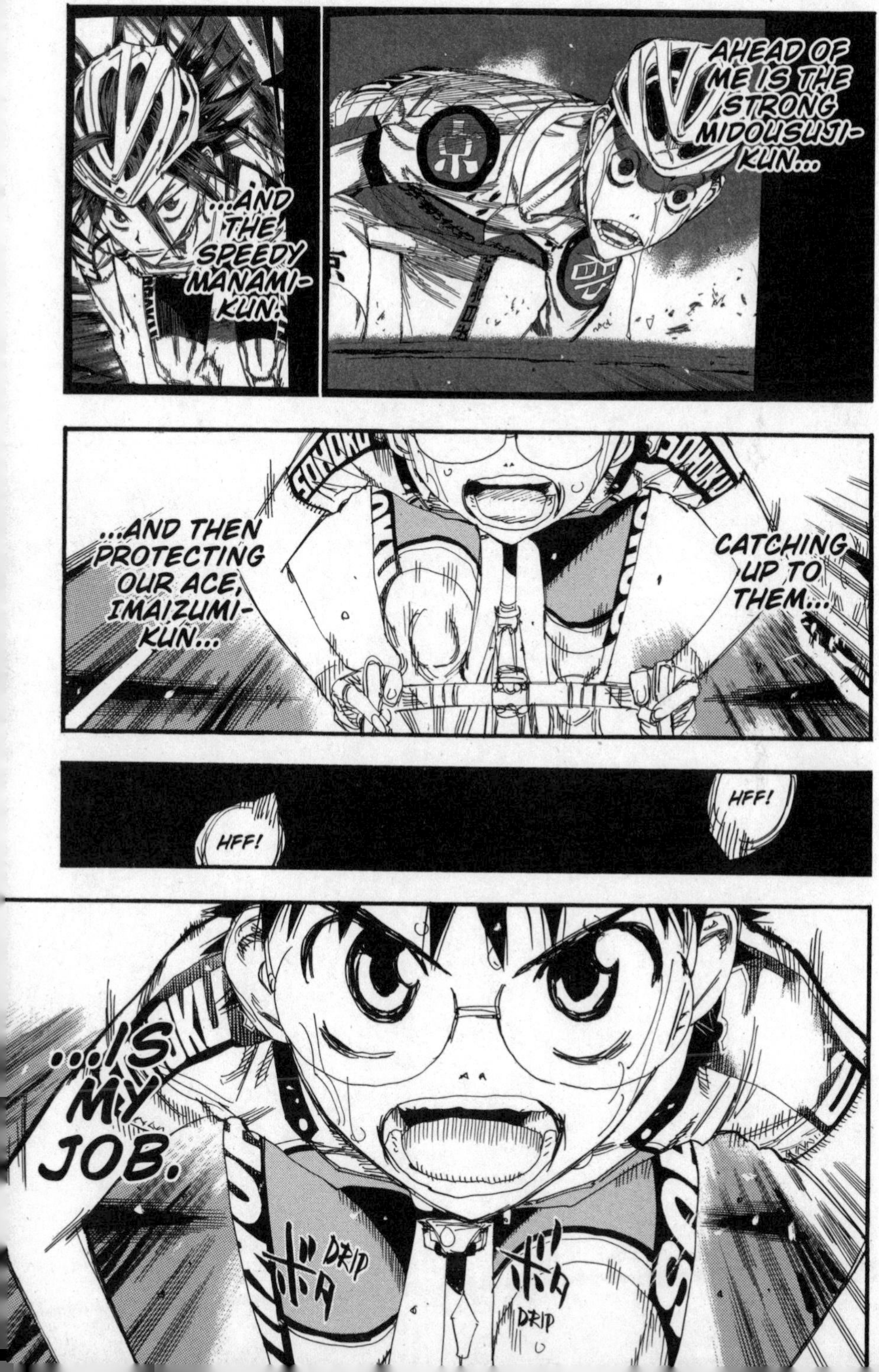
AHEAD OF ME IS THE STRONG MIDOUSUJI-KUN...
...AND THE SPEEDY MANAMI-KUN.
CATCHING UP TO THEM...
...AND THEN PROTECTING OUR ACE, IMAIZUMI-KUN...
HFF!
HFF!
...IS MY JOB.
DRIP
DRIP

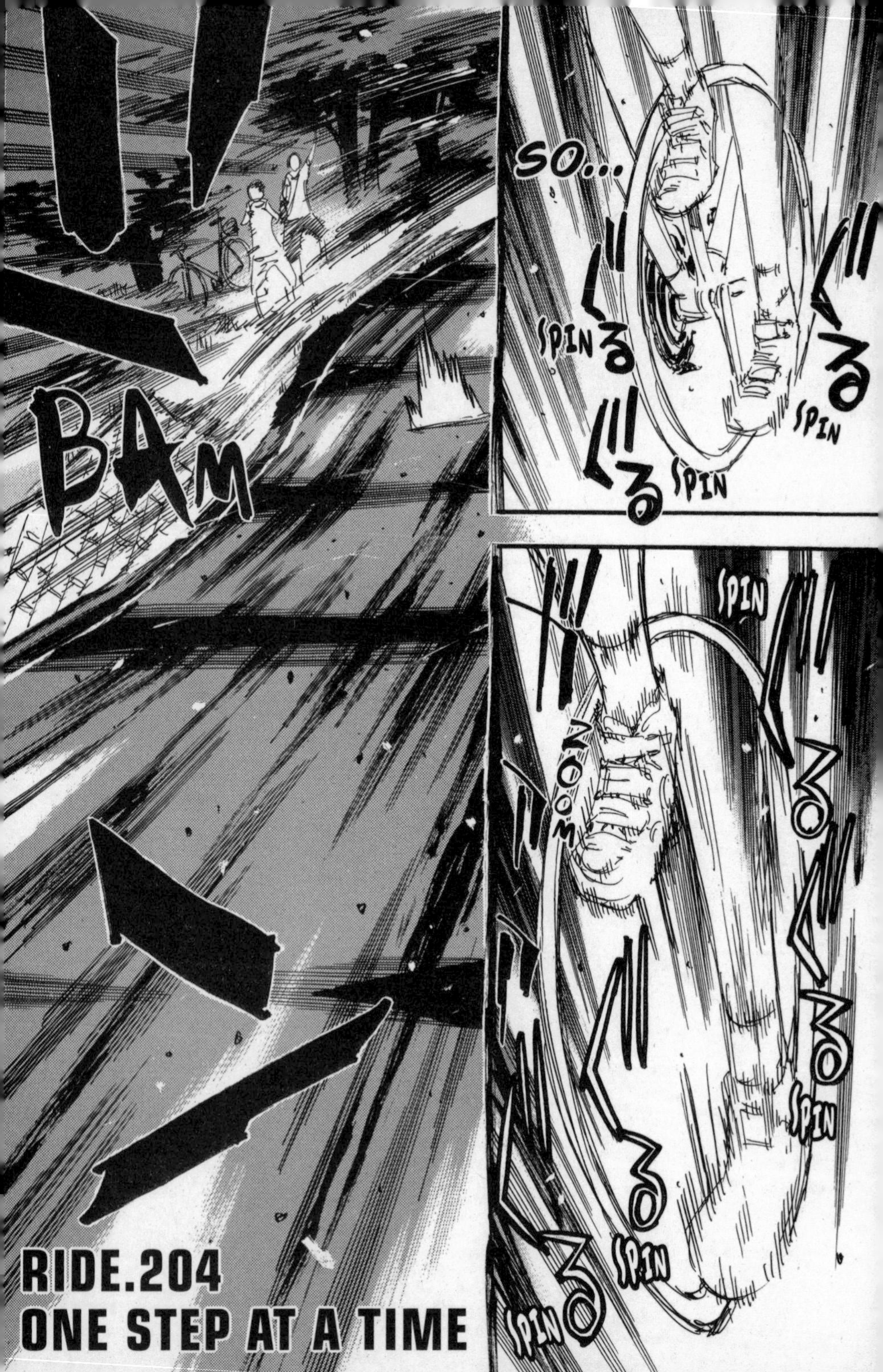
SO...
ぐる
SPIN
ぐる
SPIN
ぐる
SPIN
SPIN
ZOOM
ぐる
SPIN
ぐる
SPIN
ぐる
SPIN
BAM

RIDE.204
ONE STEP AT A TIME

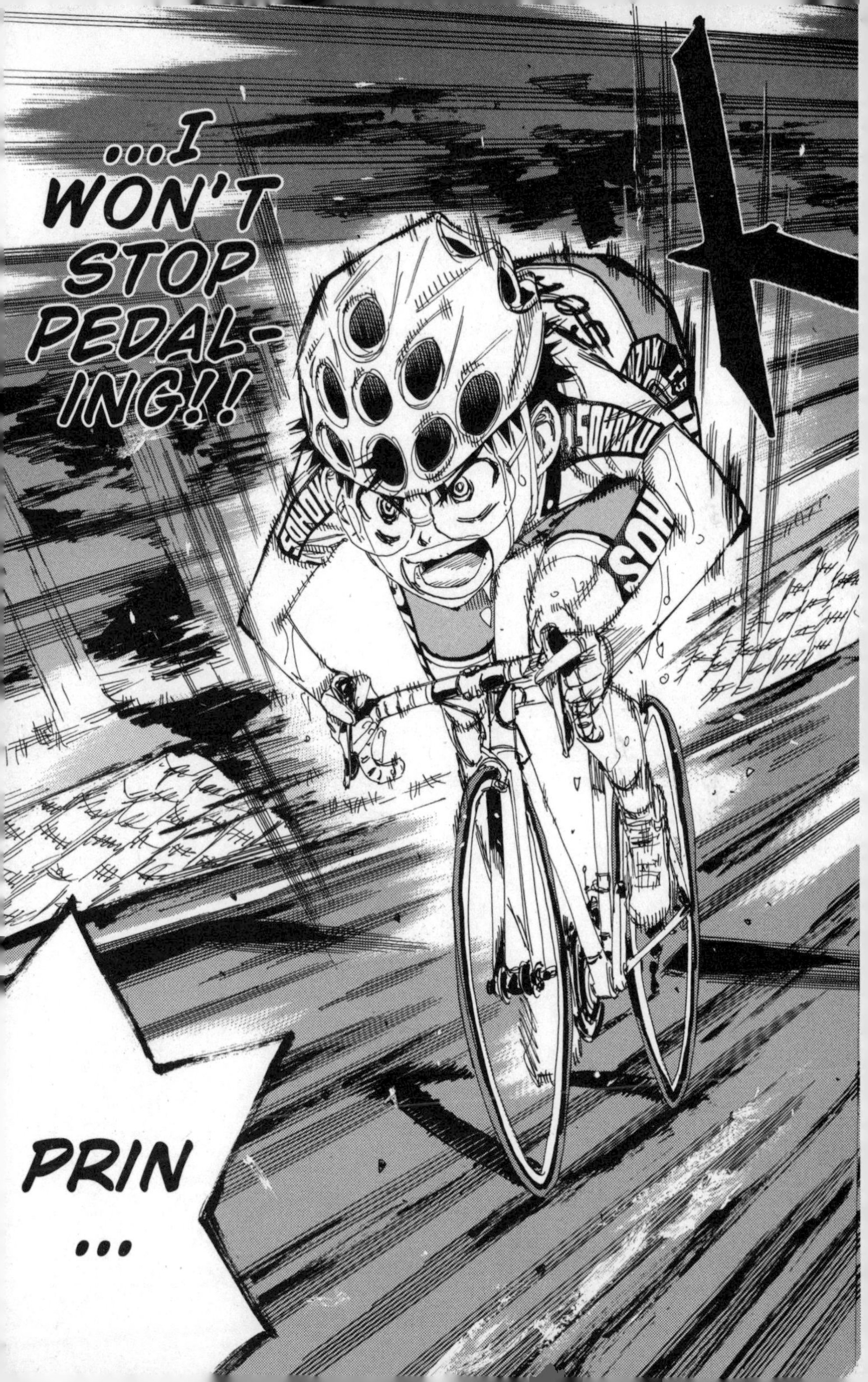
...I WON'T STOP PEDAL-ING!!
PRIN ...

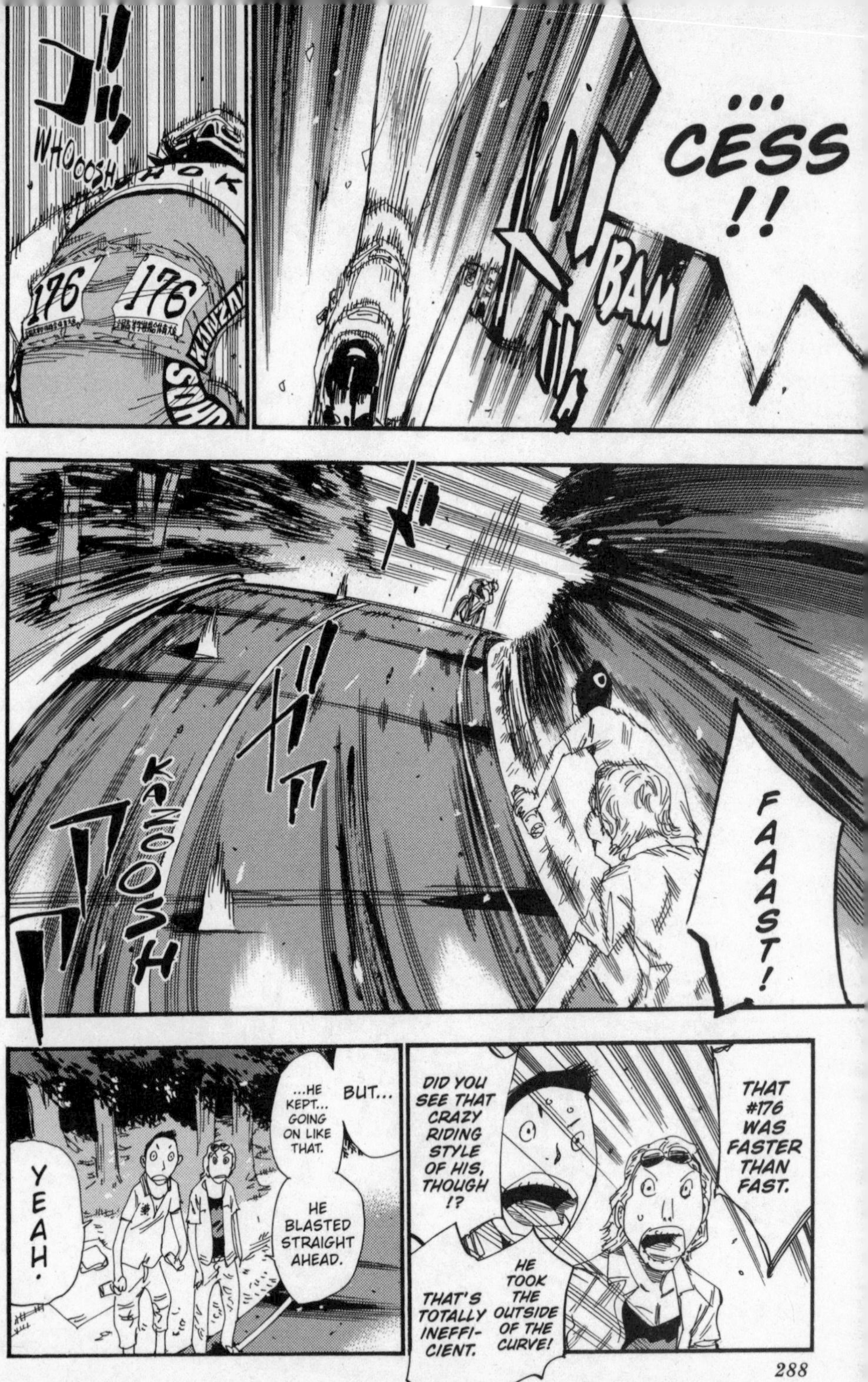
...CESS!!
BAM
WHOOOSH
176
176
FAAAAST!
KAZOOOSH
THAT #176 WAS FASTER THAN FAST.
DID YOU SEE THAT CRAZY RIDING STYLE OF HIS, THOUGH!?
HE TOOK THE OUTSIDE OF THE CURVE!
THAT'S TOTALLY INEFFICIENT.
BUT...
...HE KEPT... GOING ON LIKE THAT.
HE BLASTED STRAIGHT AHEAD.
YEAH.

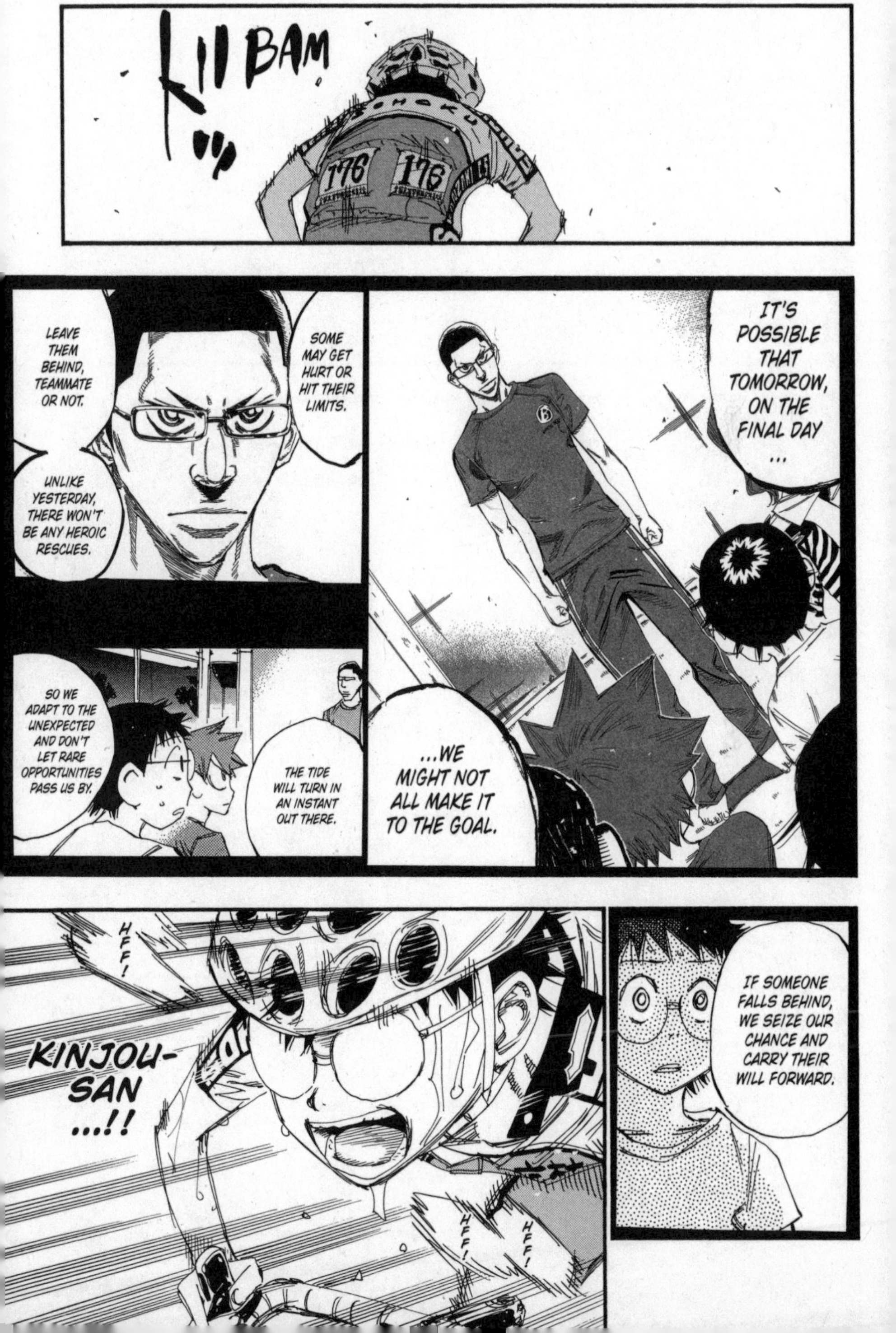
BAM
IT'S POSSIBLE THAT TOMORROW, ON THE FINAL DAY ...
...WE MIGHT NOT ALL MAKE IT TO THE GOAL.
SOME MAY GET HURT OR HIT THEIR LIMITS.
LEAVE THEM BEHIND, TEAMMATE OR NOT.
UNLIKE YESTERDAY, THERE WON'T BE ANY HEROIC RESCUES.
THE TIDE WILL TURN IN AN INSTANT OUT THERE.
SO WE ADAPT TO THE UNEXPECTED AND DON'T LET RARE OPPORTUNITIES PASS US BY.
IF SOMEONE FALLS BEHIND, WE SEIZE OUR CHANCE AND CARRY THEIR WILL FORWARD.
HFF!
KINJOU-SAN ...!!
HFF!
HFF!

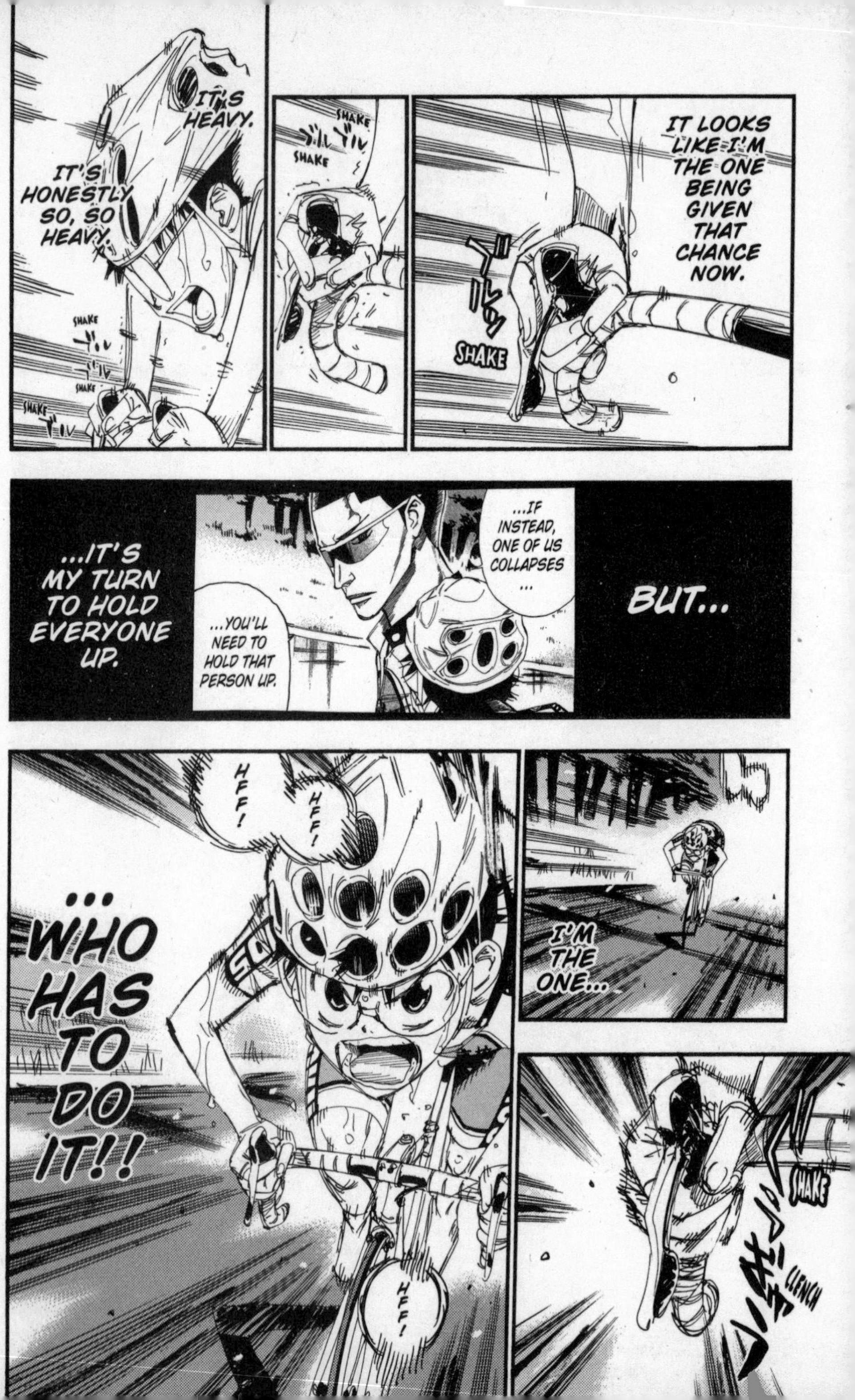
IT LOOKS LIKE I'M THE ONE BEING GIVEN THAT CHANCE NOW.
SHAKE
SHAKE
SHAKE
IT'S HEAVY.
IT'S HONESTLY SO, SO HEAVY.
SHAKE
SHAKE
SHAKE
BUT...
...IF INSTEAD, ONE OF US COLLAPSES...
...YOU'LL NEED TO HOLD THAT PERSON UP.
...IT'S MY TURN TO HOLD EVERYONE UP.
I'M THE ONE...
SHAKE
CLENCH
HFF!
HFF!
...WHO HAS TO DO IT!!
HFF!

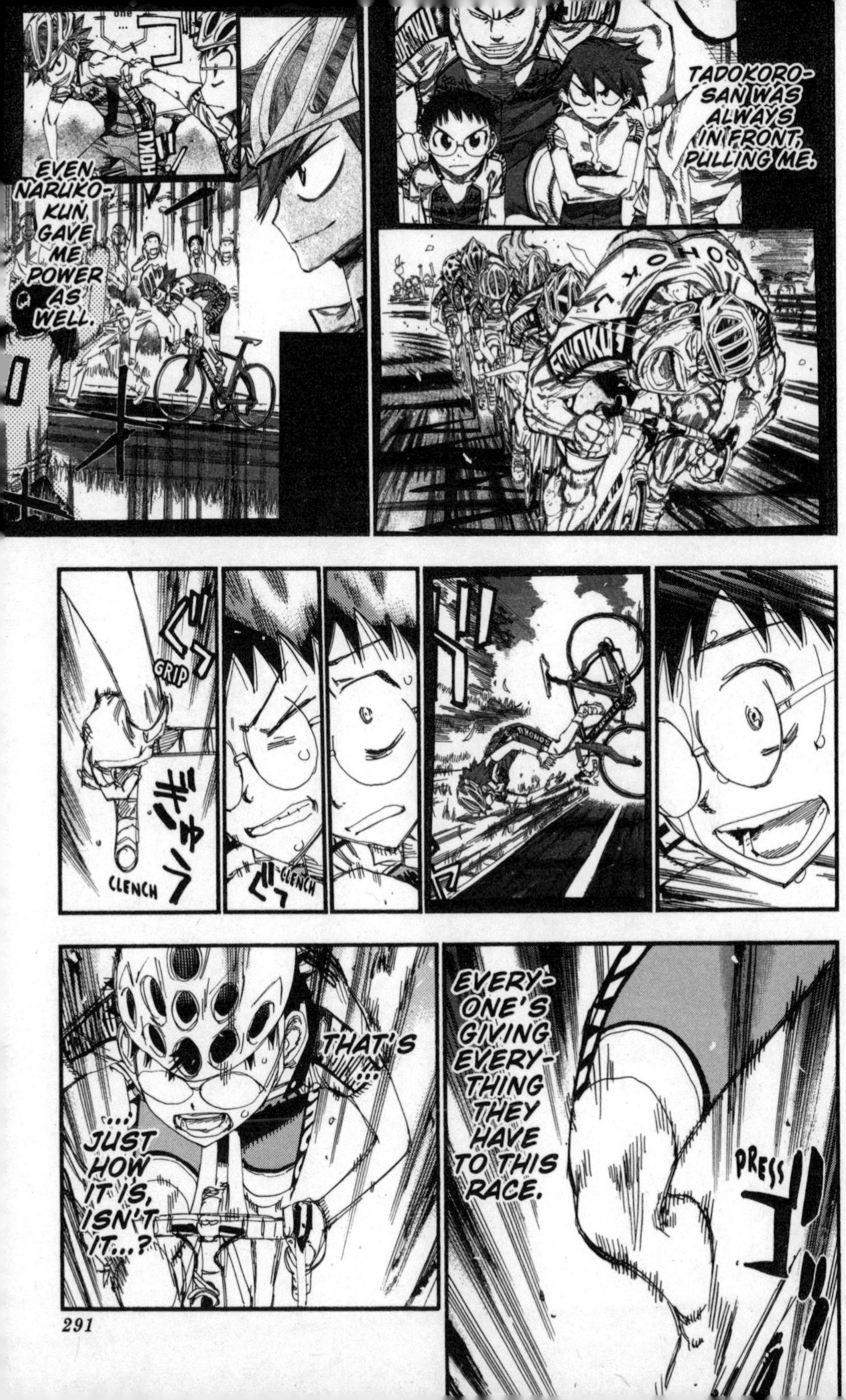
TADOKORO-SAN WAS ALWAYS IN FRONT, PULLING ME.
EVEN NARUKO-KUN GAVE ME POWER AS WELL.
CLENCH
GRIP
CLENCH
EVERY-ONE'S GIVING EVERY-THING THEY HAVE TO THIS RACE.
PRESS
THAT'S ...
... JUST HOW IT IS, ISN'T IT...?

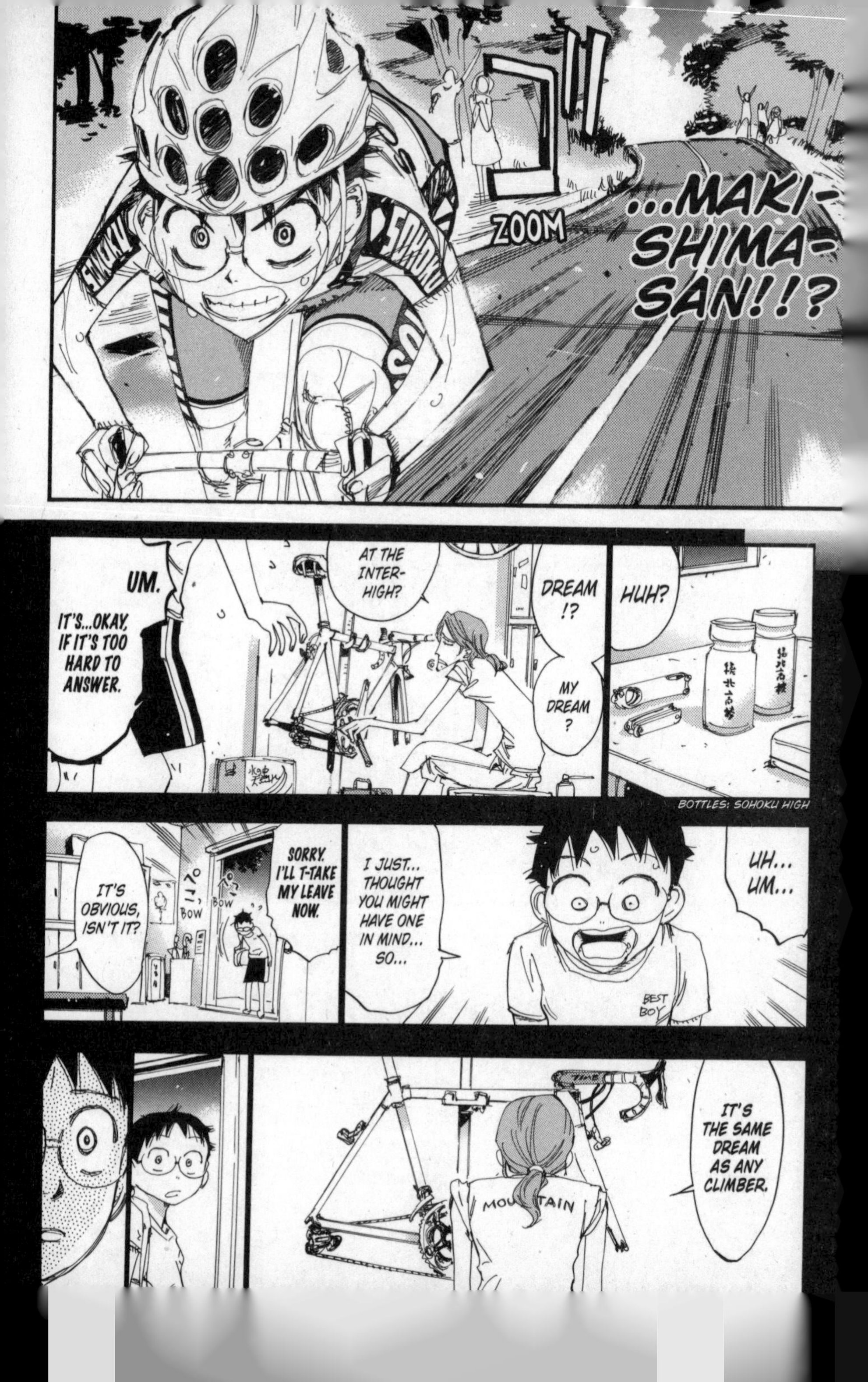
...MAKI-SHIMA-SAN!!?
ZOOM
HUH?
BOTTLES: SOHOKU HIGH
DREAM!?
AT THE INTER-HIGH?
MY DREAM?
UM.
IT'S...OKAY, IF IT'S TOO HARD TO ANSWER.
UH... UM...
I JUST... THOUGHT YOU MIGHT HAVE ONE IN MIND... SO...
BEST BOY
SORRY. I'LL T-TAKE MY LEAVE NOW.
BOW
BOW
IT'S OBVIOUS, ISN'T IT?
IT'S THE SAME DREAM AS ANY CLIMBER.
MOUNTAIN

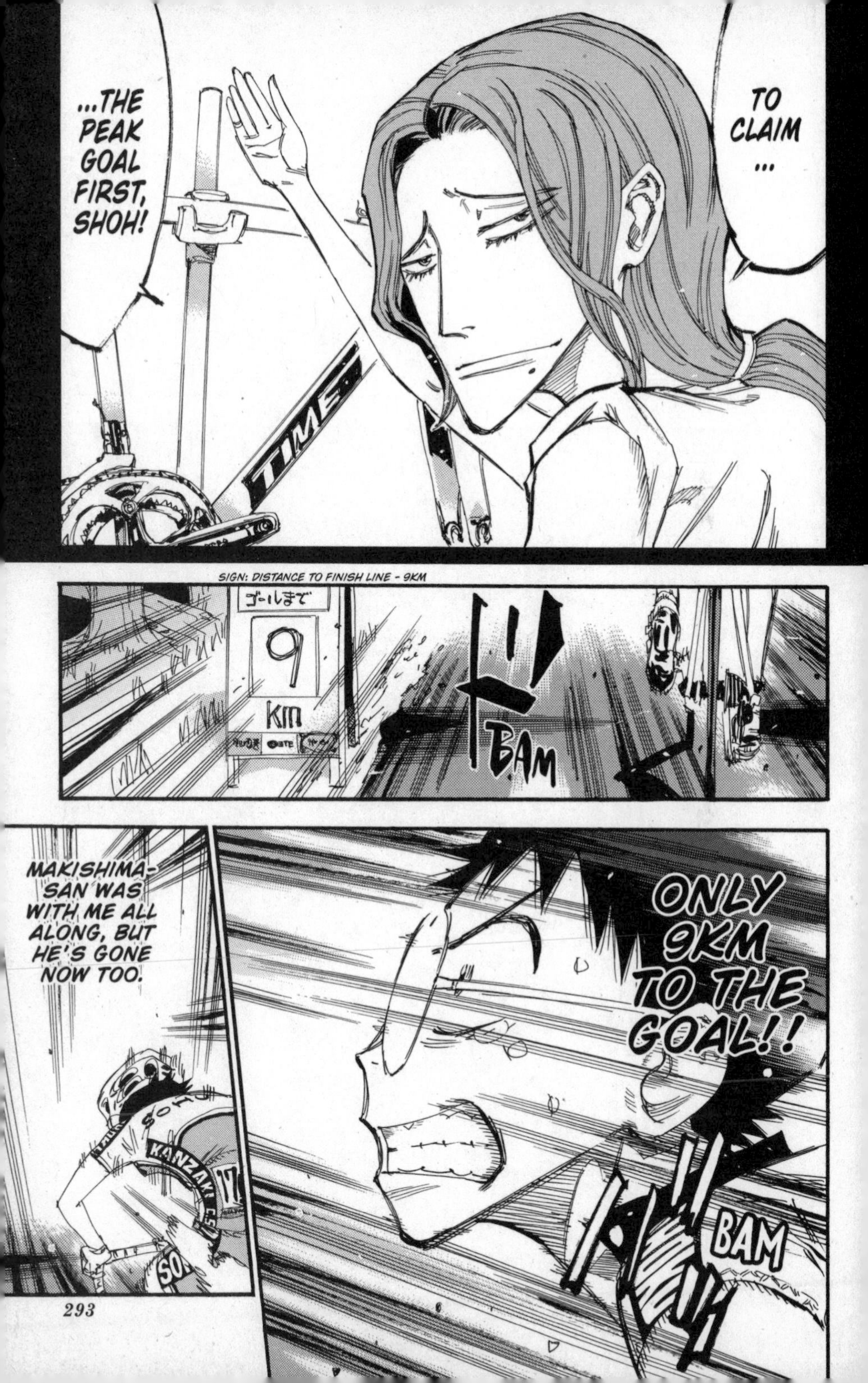

TO CLAIM ...
...THE PEAK GOAL FIRST, SHOH!
SIGN: DISTANCE TO FINISH LINE - 9KM
ゴールまで
9
km
BAM
ONLY 9KM TO THE GOAL!!
BAM
MAKISHIMA-SAN WAS WITH ME ALL ALONG, BUT HE'S GONE NOW TOO.

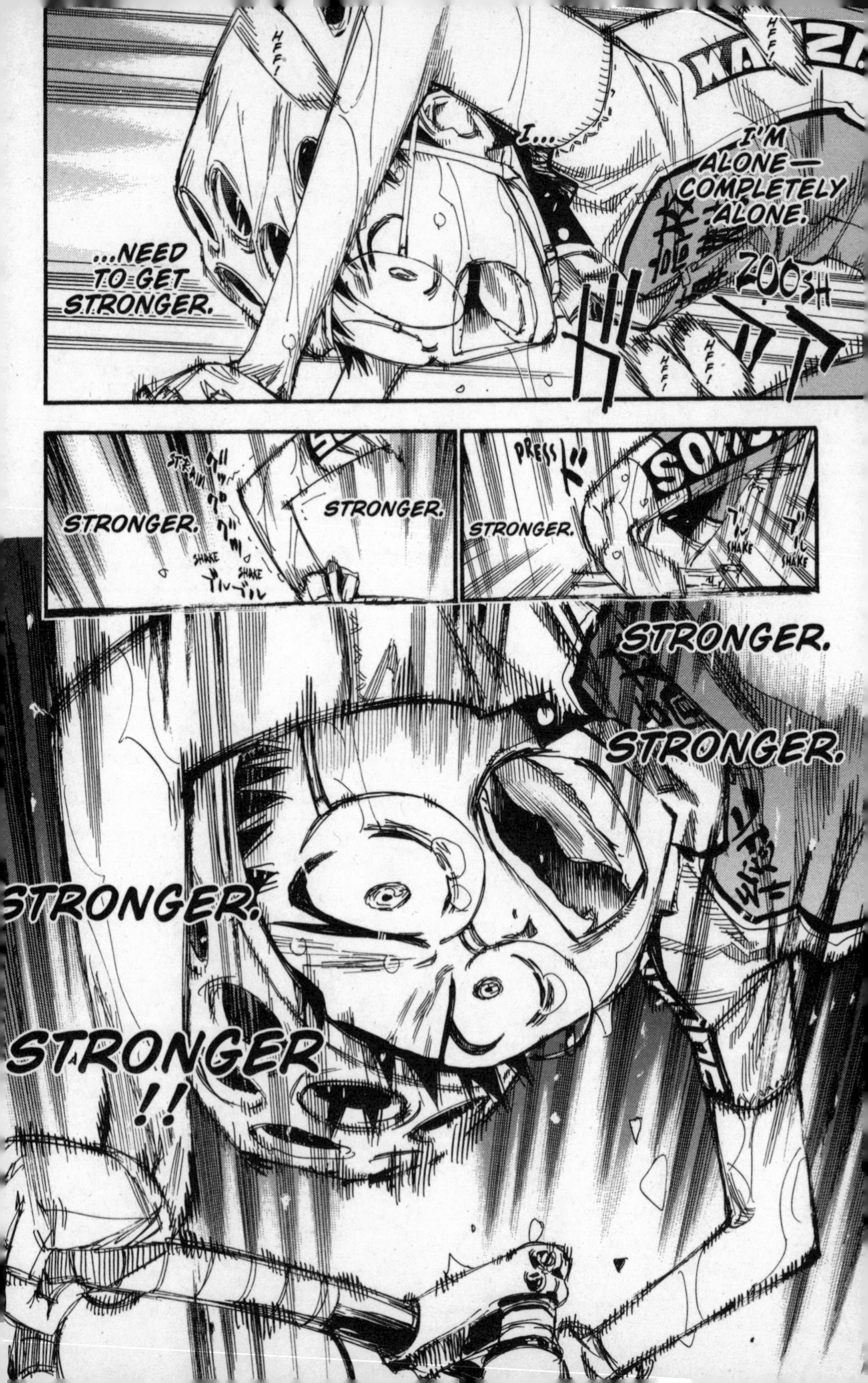
HFF!
HFF!
I...
I'M ALONE—COMPLETELY ALONE.
ZOOSH
HFF!
...NEED TO GET STRONGER.
PRESS
STRONGER.
SHAKE
SHAKE
STRONGER.
STRAIN
STRONGER.
SHAKE
SHAKE
STRONGER.
STRONGER.
STRONGER.
STRONGER!!

STRON-
GER!!

BAM

FWAP

WIPE

BAM

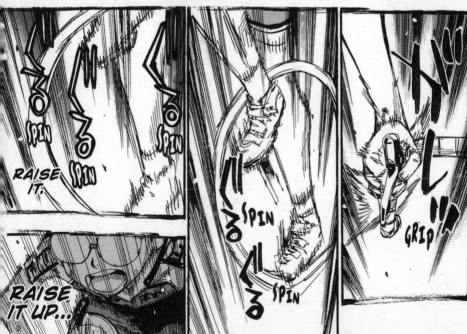

RAISE
IT.

RAISE
IT UP...

SPIN

SPIN

SPIN

SPIN

SPIN

GRIP

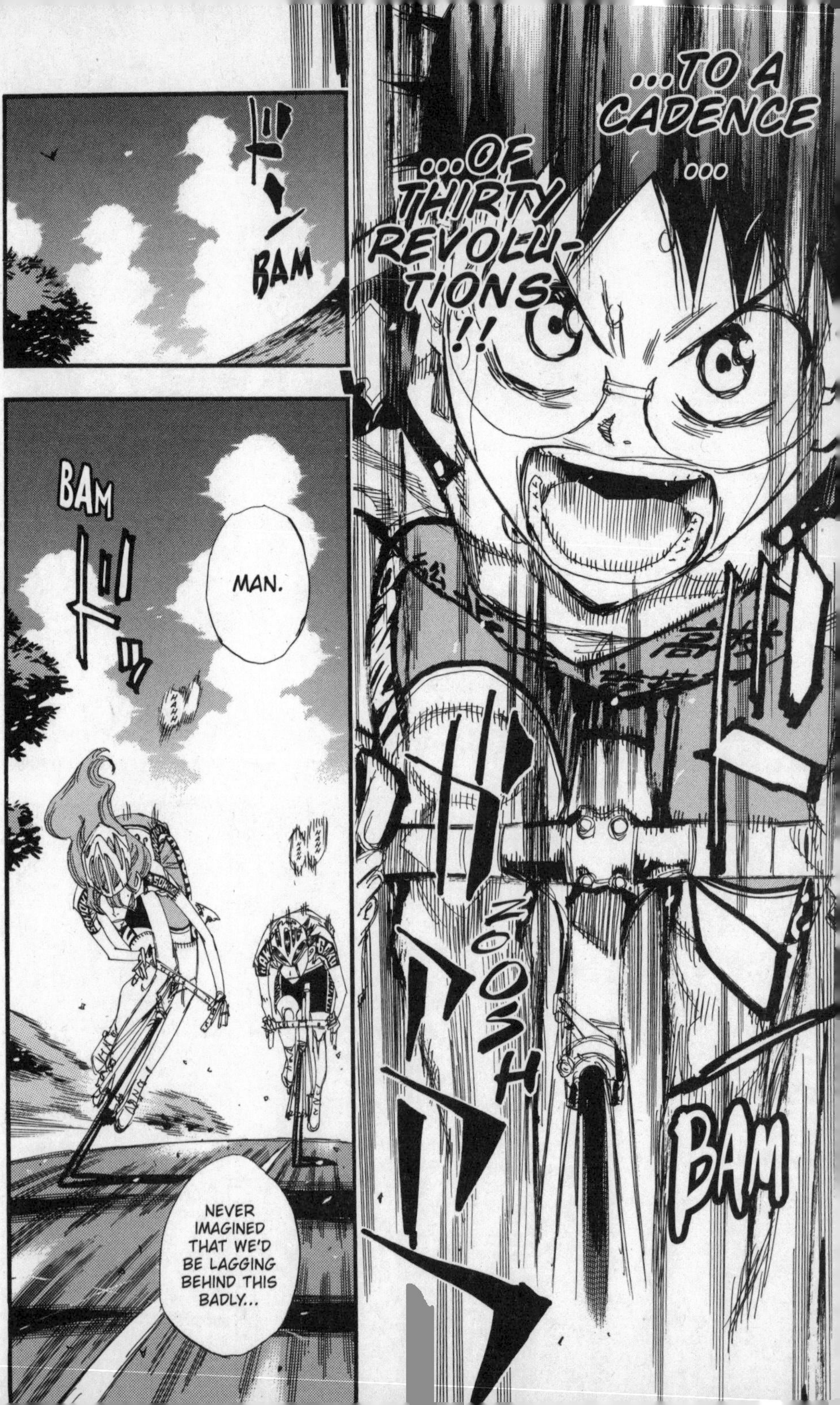
...TO A CADENCE ...
...OF THIRTY REVOLU-TIONS!!
ZOOSH
BAM
BAM
BAM
MAN.
NEVER IMAGINED THAT WE'D BE LAGGING BEHIND THIS BADLY...

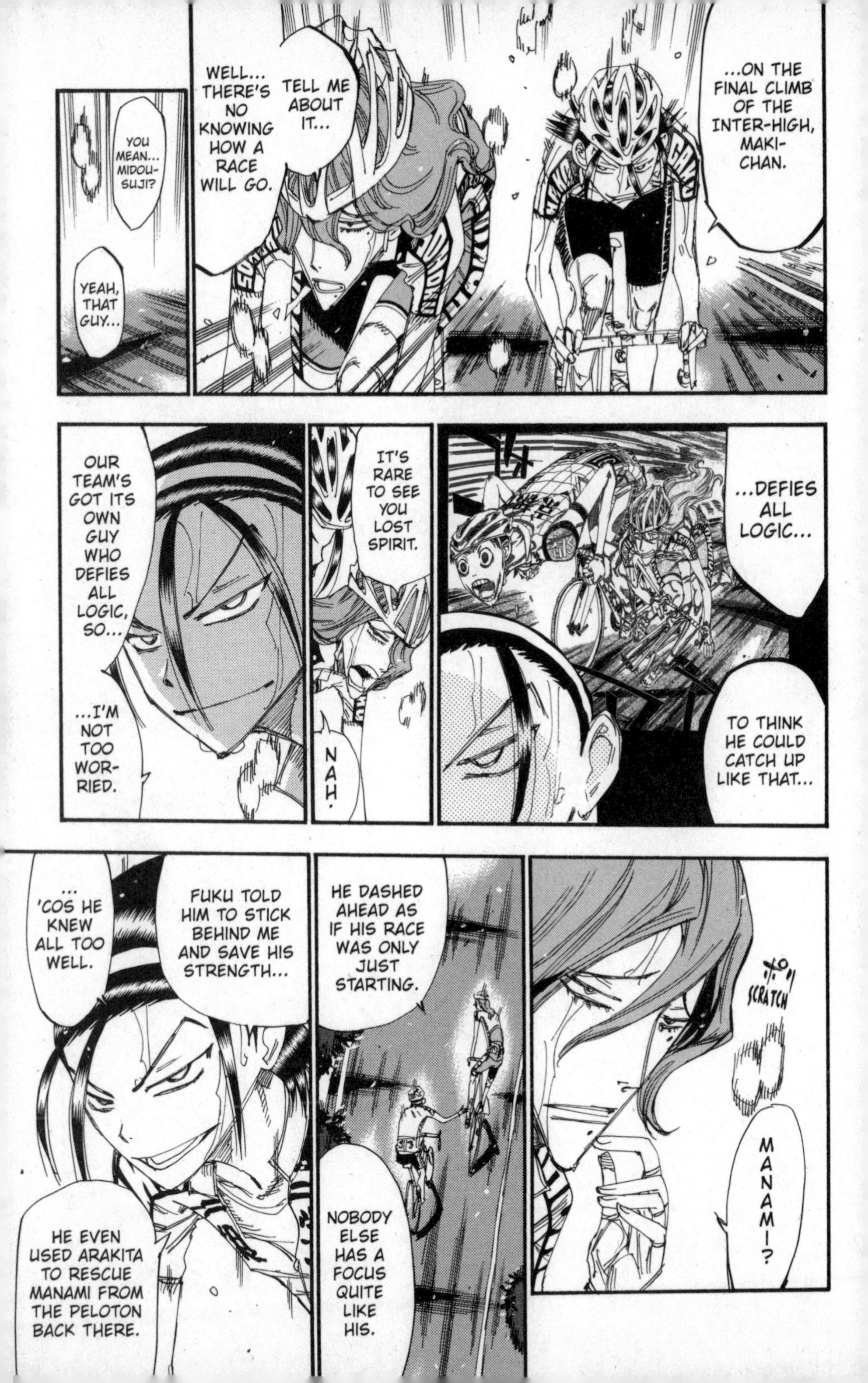
...ON THE FINAL CLIMB OF THE INTER-HIGH, MAKI-CHAN.
TELL ME ABOUT IT...
WELL... THERE'S NO KNOWING HOW A RACE WILL GO.
YOU MEAN... MIDOUSUJI?
YEAH, THAT GUY...
...DEFIES ALL LOGIC...
TO THINK HE COULD CATCH UP LIKE THAT...
IT'S RARE TO SEE YOU LOST SPIRIT.
NAH.
OUR TEAM'S GOT ITS OWN GUY WHO DEFIES ALL LOGIC, SO...
...I'M NOT TOO WORRIED.
SCRATCH
MANAMI-?
HE DASHED AHEAD AS IF HIS RACE WAS ONLY JUST STARTING.
NOBODY ELSE HAS A FOCUS QUITE LIKE HIS.
FUKU TOLD HIM TO STICK BEHIND ME AND SAVE HIS STRENGTH...
...'COS HE KNEW ALL TOO WELL.
HE EVEN USED ARAKITA TO RESCUE MANAMI FROM THE PELOTON BACK THERE.

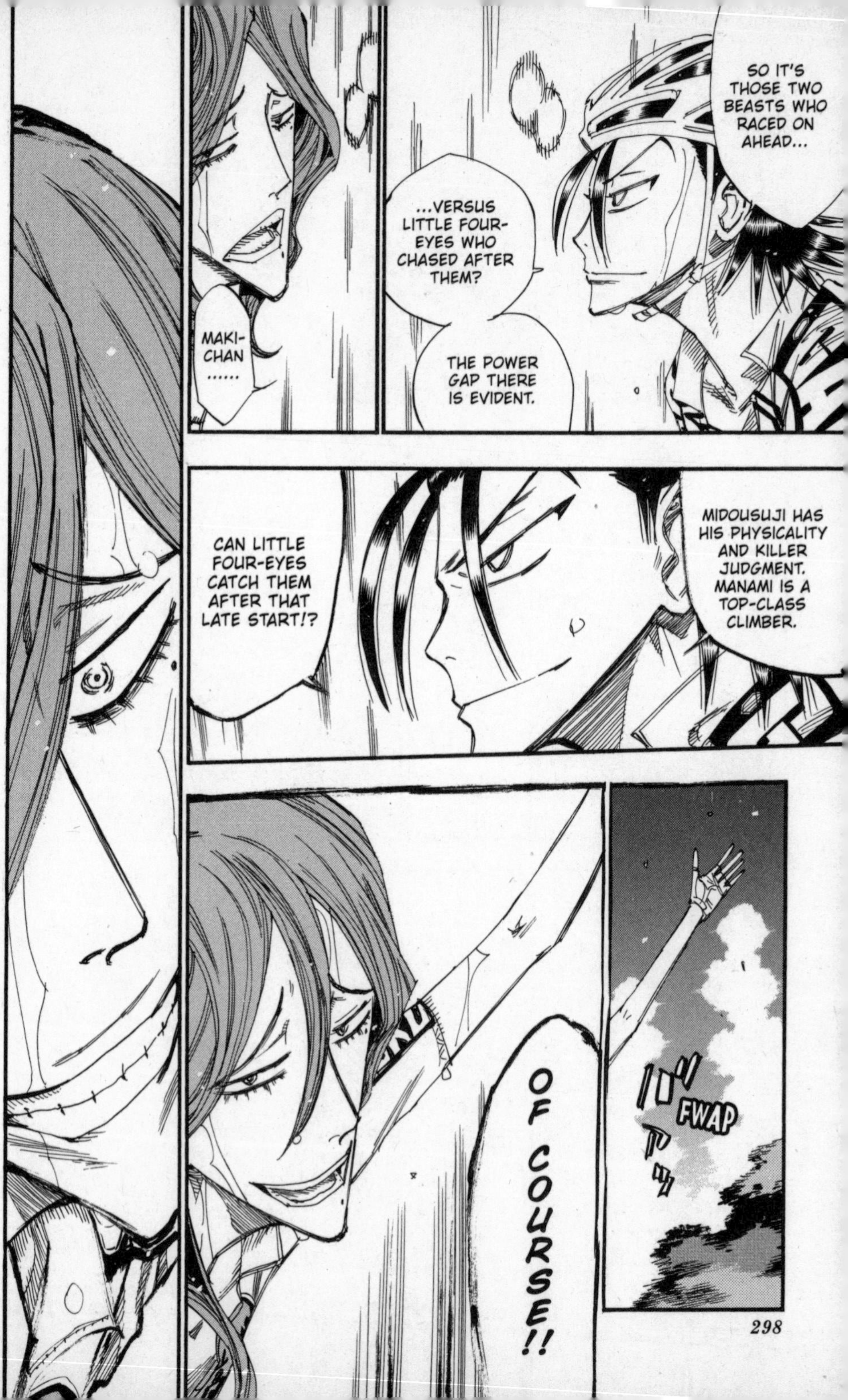
SO IT'S THOSE TWO BEASTS WHO RACED ON AHEAD...
...VERSUS LITTLE FOUR-EYES WHO CHASED AFTER THEM?
THE POWER GAP THERE IS EVIDENT.
MAKI-CHAN ......
MIDOUSUJI HAS HIS PHYSICALITY AND KILLER JUDGMENT. MANAMI IS A TOP-CLASS CLIMBER.
CAN LITTLE FOUR-EYES CATCH THEM AFTER THAT LATE START!?
FWAP
OF COURSE!!

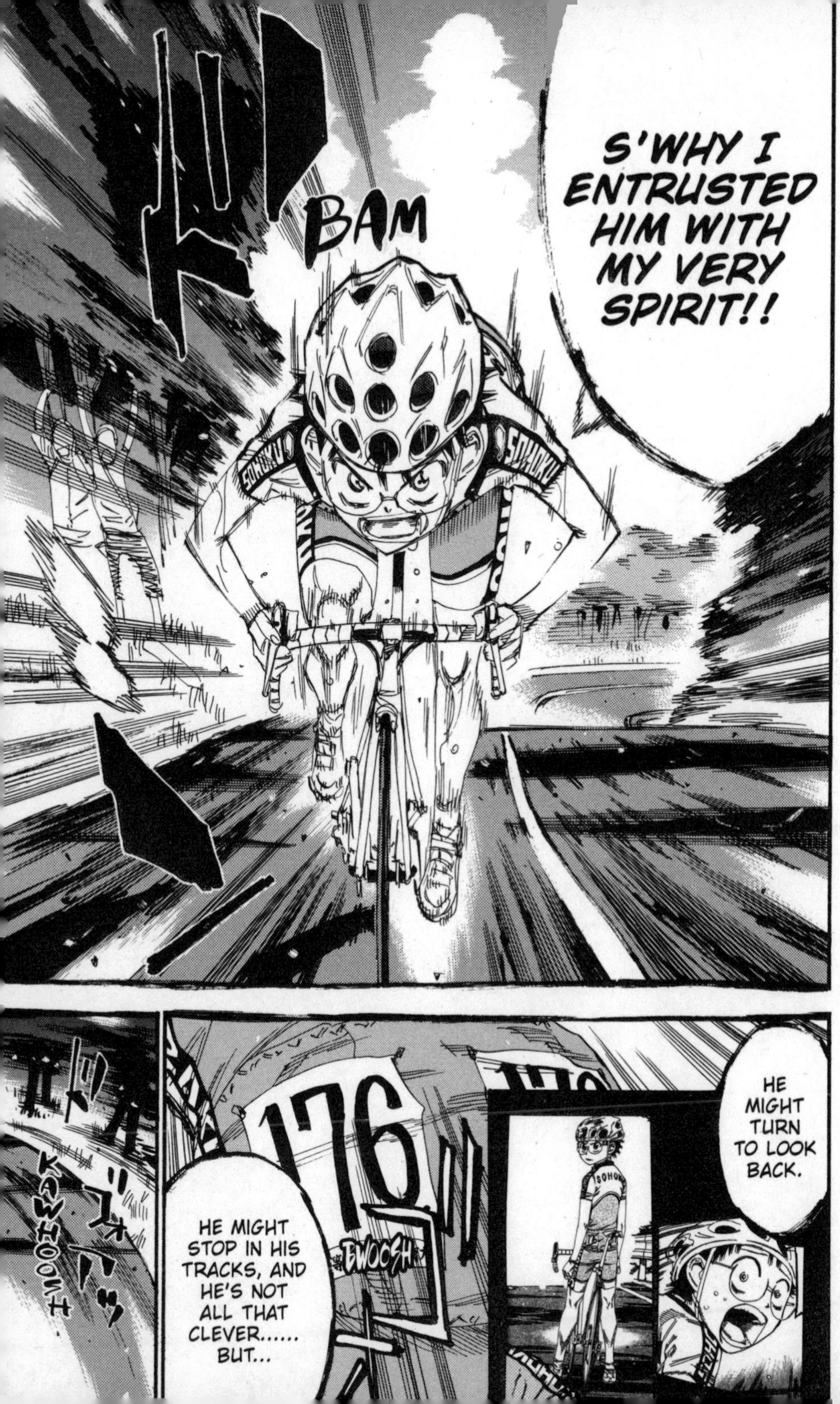
BAM
S'WHY I ENTRUSTED HIM WITH MY VERY SPIRIT!!
HE MIGHT TURN TO LOOK BACK.
176
HE MIGHT STOP IN HIS TRACKS, AND HE'S NOT ALL THAT CLEVER...... BUT...
BWOOSH
KAWHOOSH

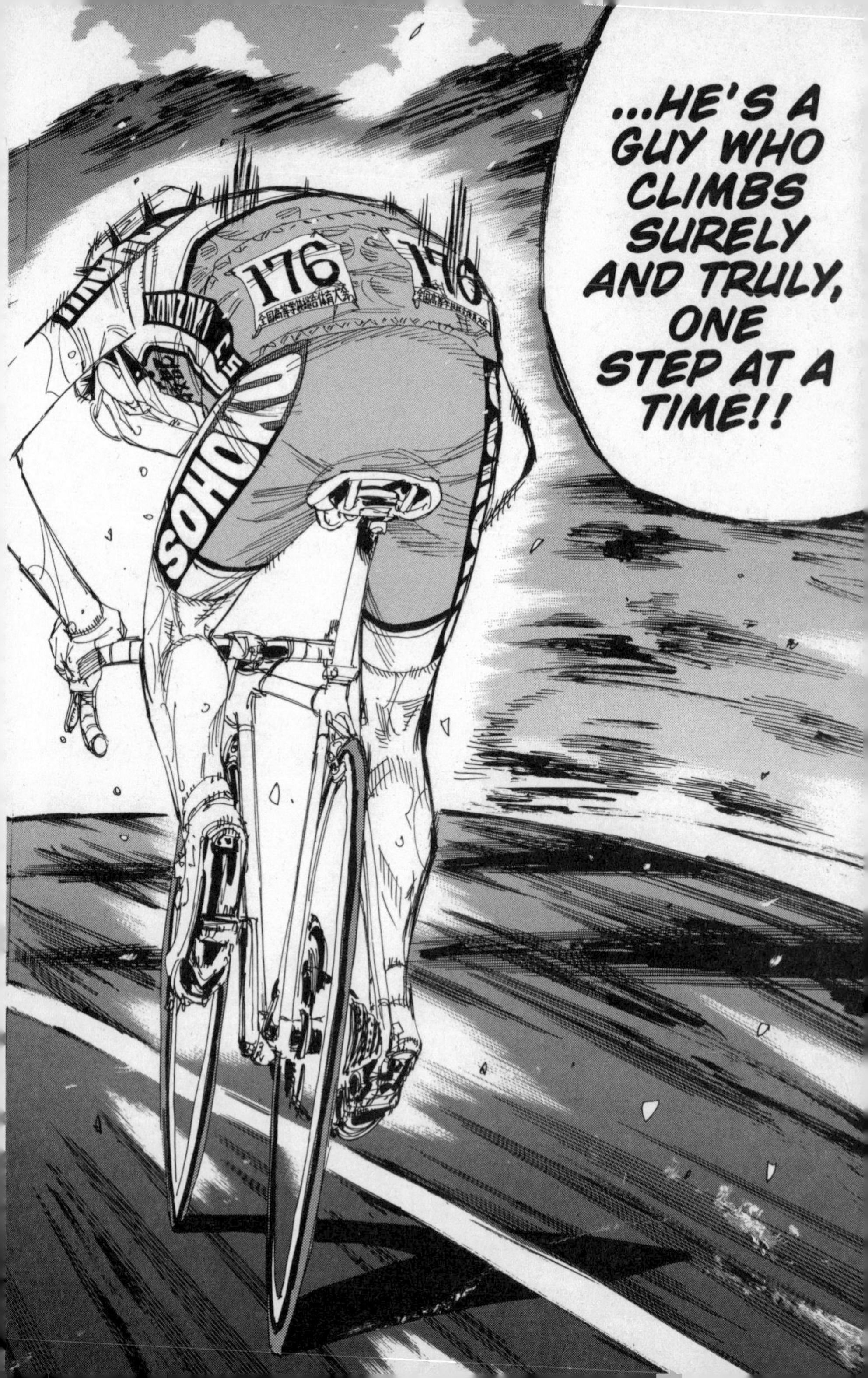
...HE'S A GUY WHO CLIMBS SURELY AND TRULY, ONE STEP AT A TIME!!
176
176

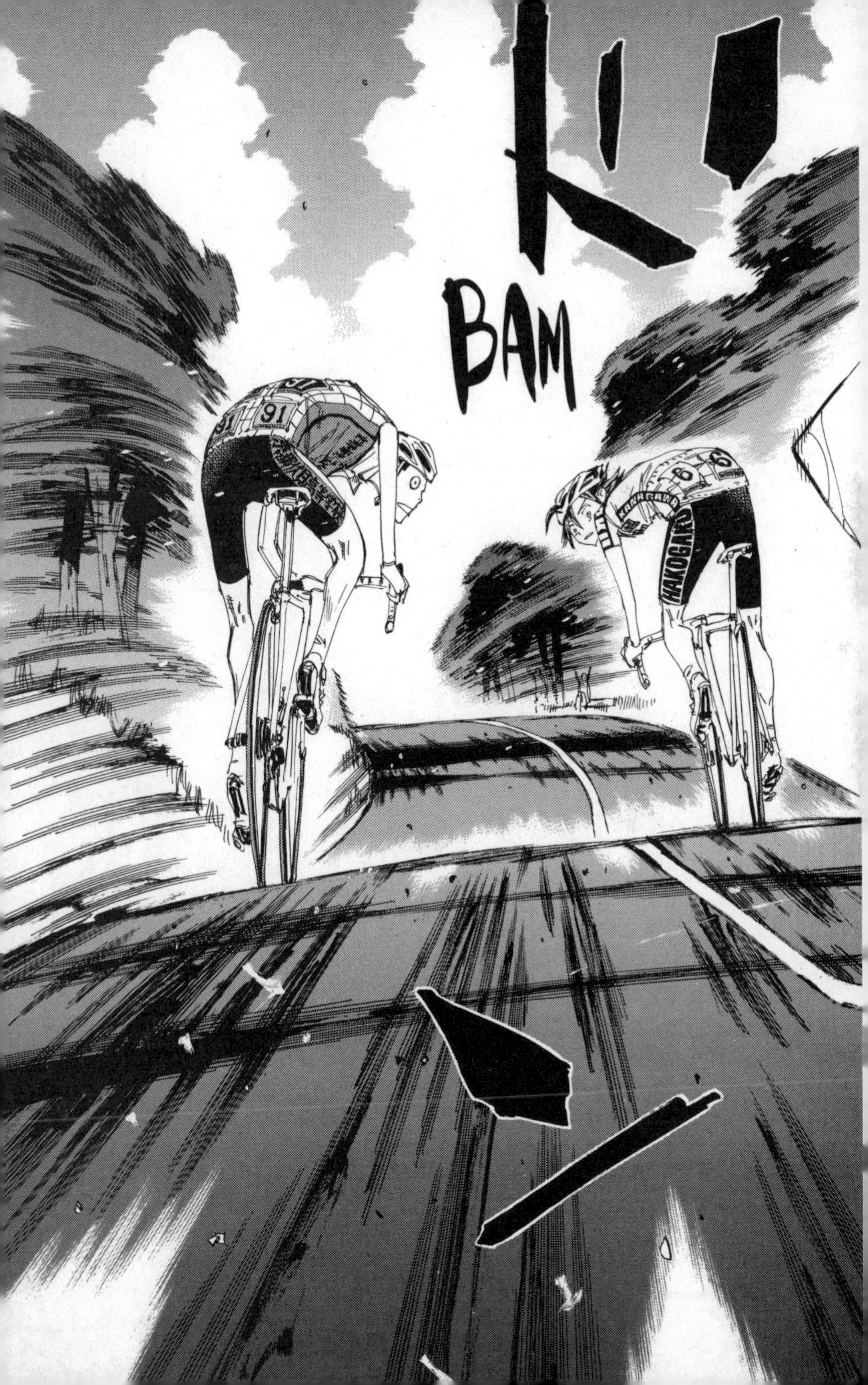
BAM

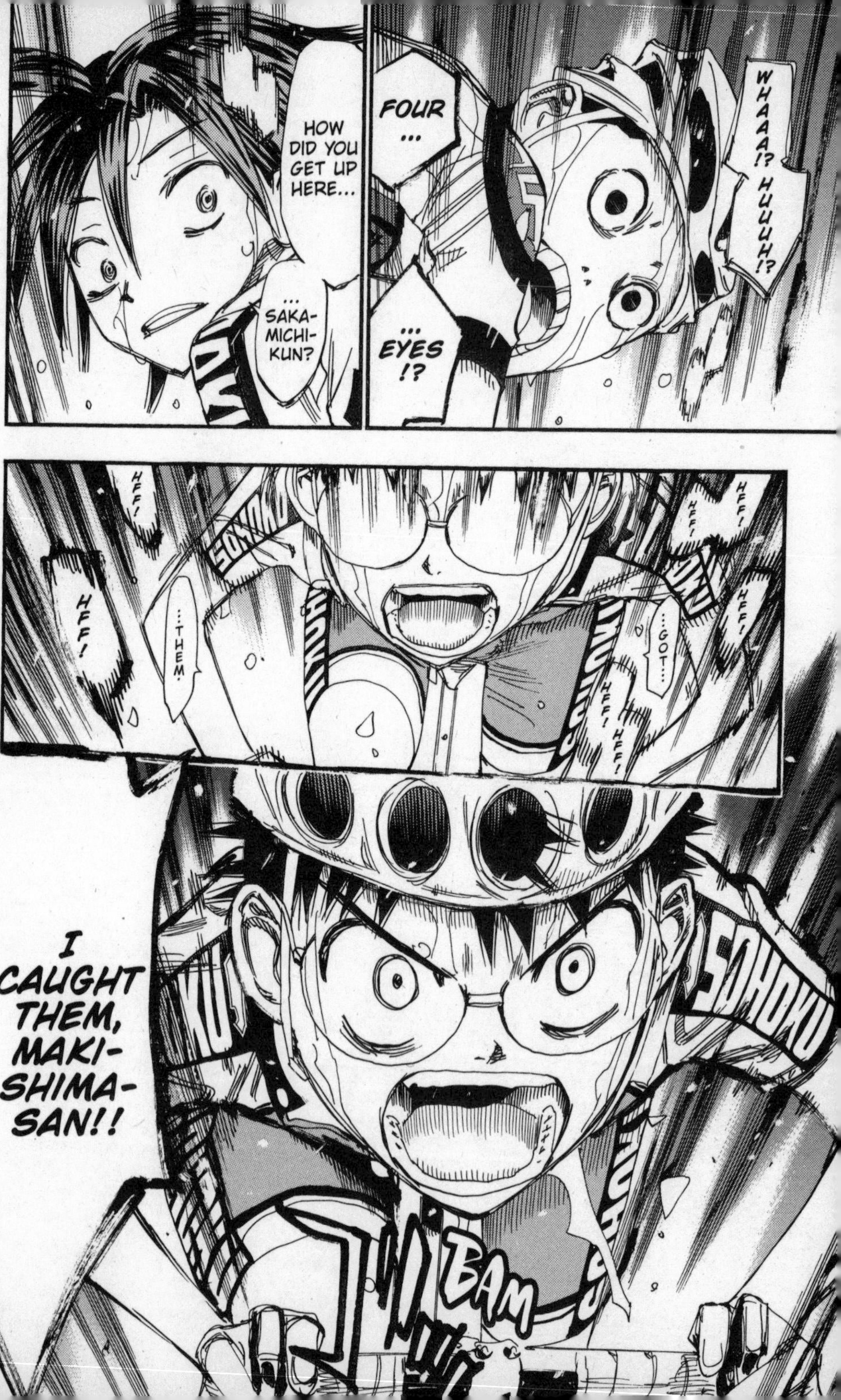
WHAAAA!? HUUUH!?
FOUR...
...EYES!?
HOW DID YOU GET UP HERE...
...SAKAMICHI-KUN?
HFF! HFF!
...GOT...
HFF! HFF!
HFF! HFF!
...THEM.
HFF!
HFF!
BAM
I CAUGHT THEM, MAKISHIMA-SAN!!

RIDE.205 SOHOKU'S FOUR-EYES

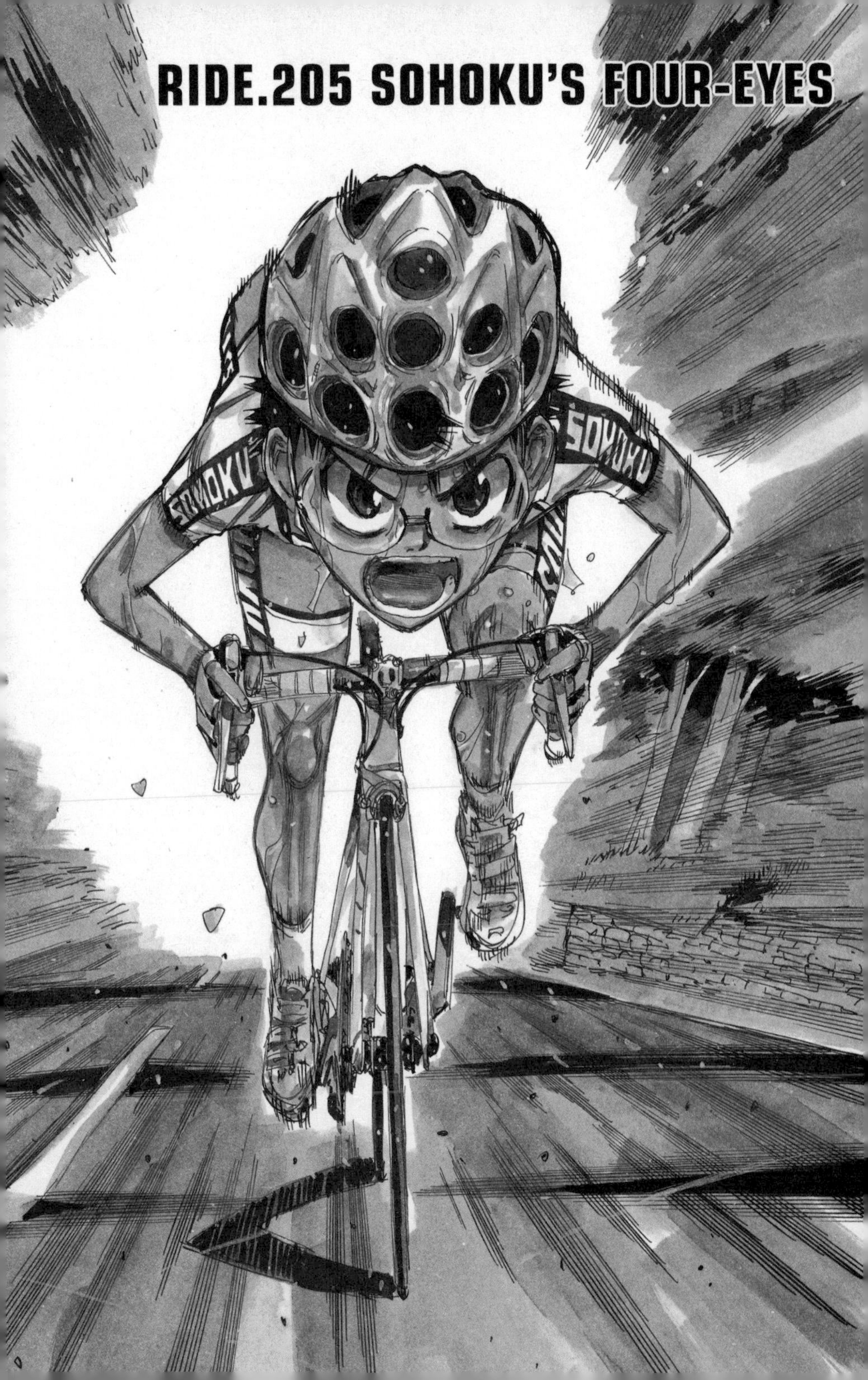
SOHOKU
SOHOKU

SAKAMICHI ONODA

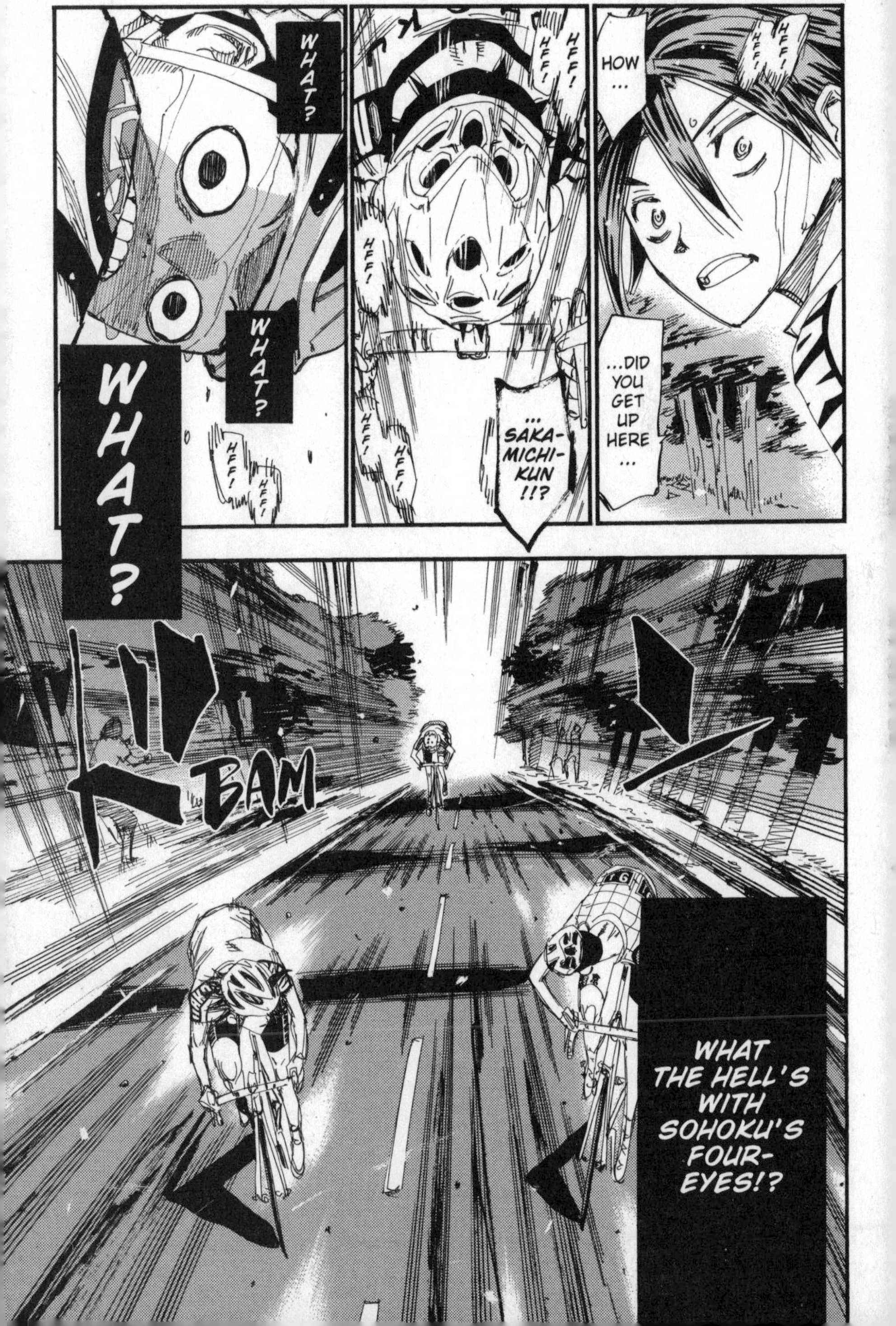
HFF! HFF!
HOW...
...DID YOU GET UP HERE...
HFF! HFF!
HFF!
...SAKAMICHI-KUN!!?
HFF! HFF!
WHAT?
WHAT?
WHAT?
HFF! HFF!
BAM
WHAT THE HELL'S WITH SOHOKU'S FOUR-EYES!?

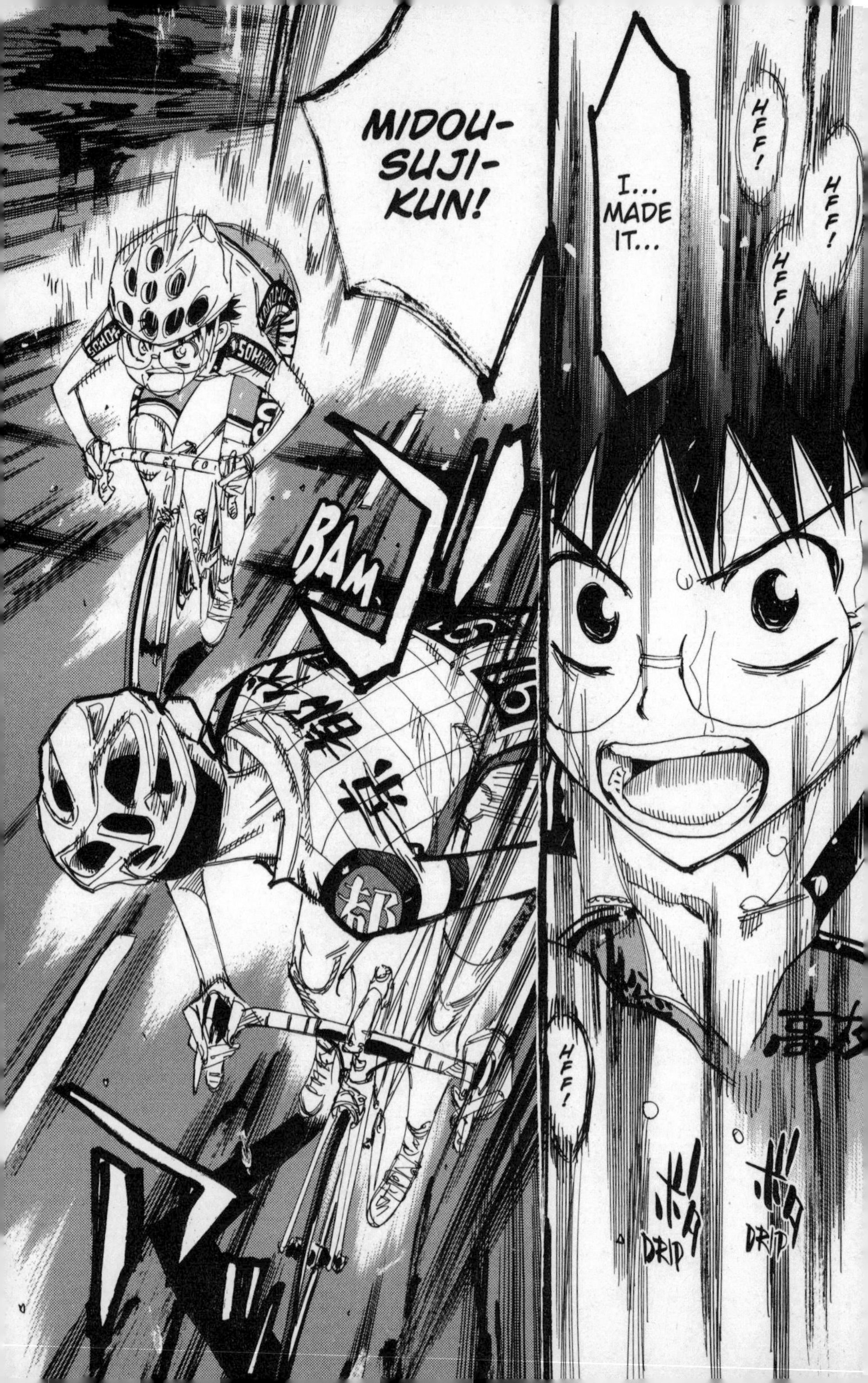
HFF!
HFF!
HFF!
I... MADE IT...
HFF!
DRIP
DRIP
MIDOU-SUJI-KUN!
BAM

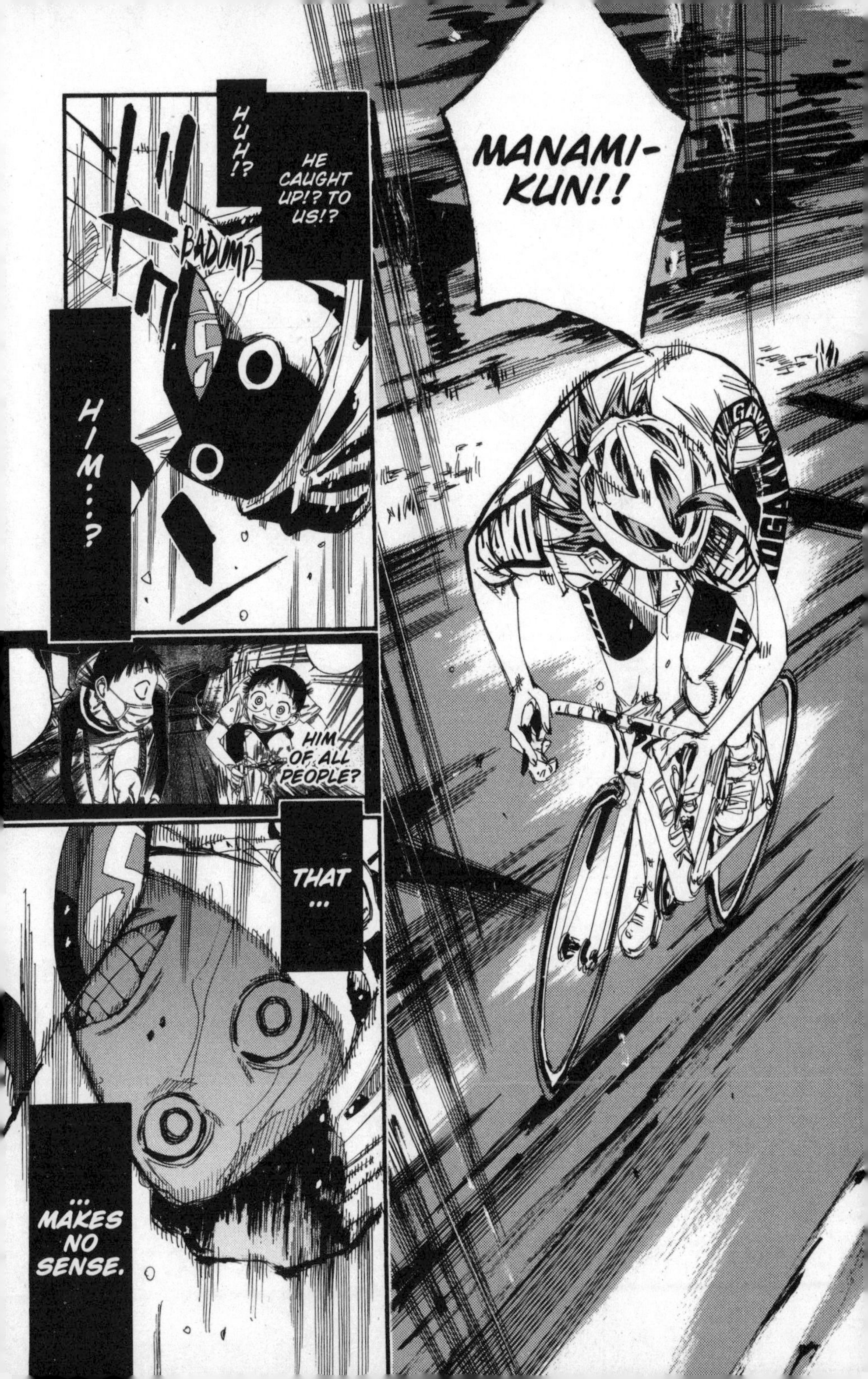
MANAMI-KUN!!
HUH!?
HE CAUGHT UP!? TO US!?
BADUMP
HIM...?
HIM OF ALL PEOPLE?
THAT...
...MAKES NO SENSE.

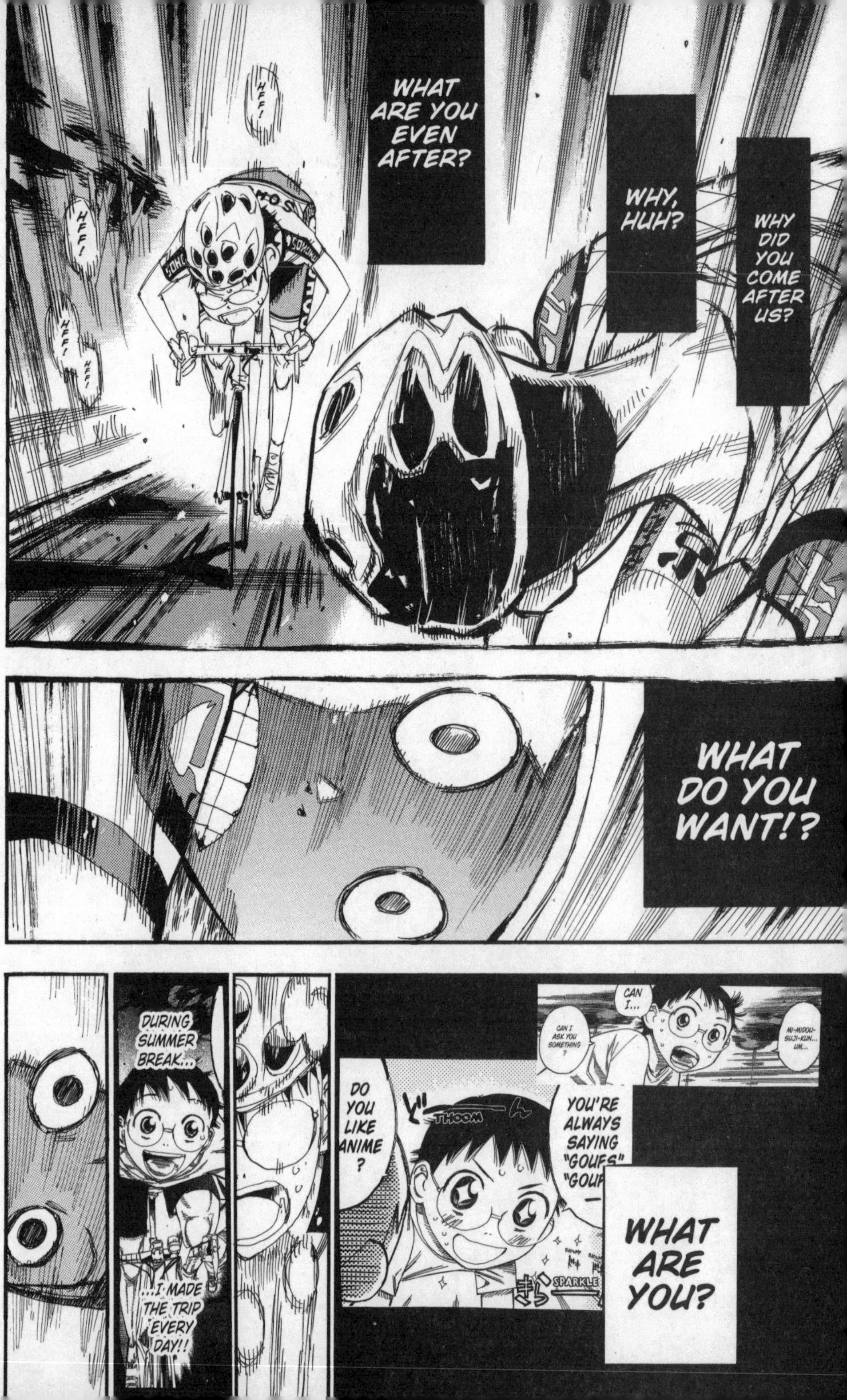
WHY DID YOU COME AFTER US?
WHY, HUH?
WHAT ARE YOU EVEN AFTER?
HFF!
HFF!
HFF!
HFF!
WHAT DO YOU WANT!?
MI-MIDOU-SUJI-KUN... UM...
CAN I...
CAN I ASK YOU SOMETHING?
WHAT ARE YOU?
YOU'RE ALWAYS SAYING "GOUFS" "GOUF
THOOM
DO YOU LIKE ANIME?
BADUMP BADUMP
SPARKLE
DURING SUMMER BREAK...
...I MADE THE TRIP EVERY DAY!!

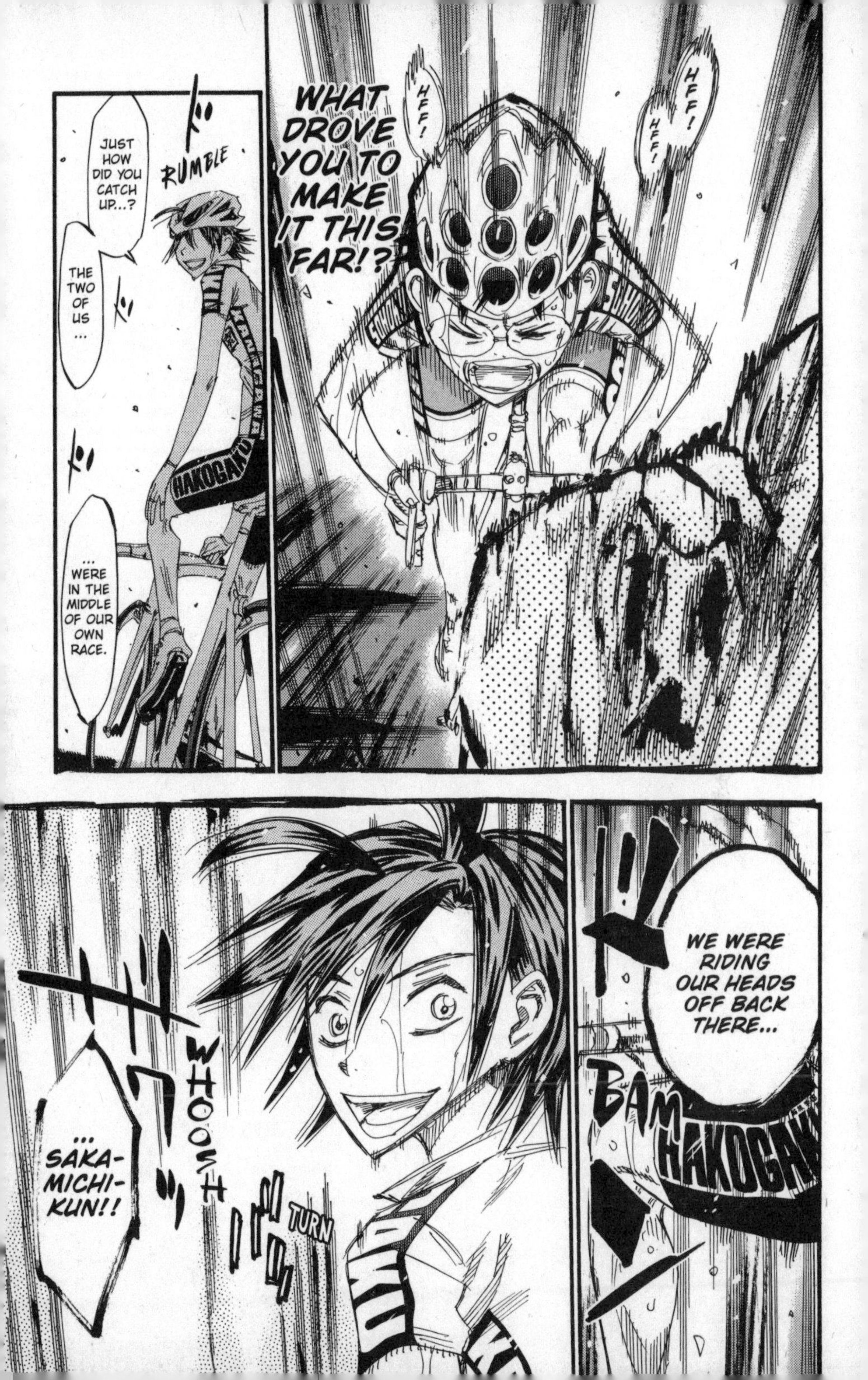
HFF!
HFF!
HFF!
WHAT DROVE YOU TO MAKE IT THIS FAR!?
RUMBLE
JUST HOW DID YOU CATCH UP...?
THE TWO OF US...
...WERE IN THE MIDDLE OF OUR OWN RACE.
HAKOGAKU
WE WERE RIDING OUR HEADS OFF BACK THERE...
BAM
WHOOSH
...SAKAMICHI-KUN!!
TURN

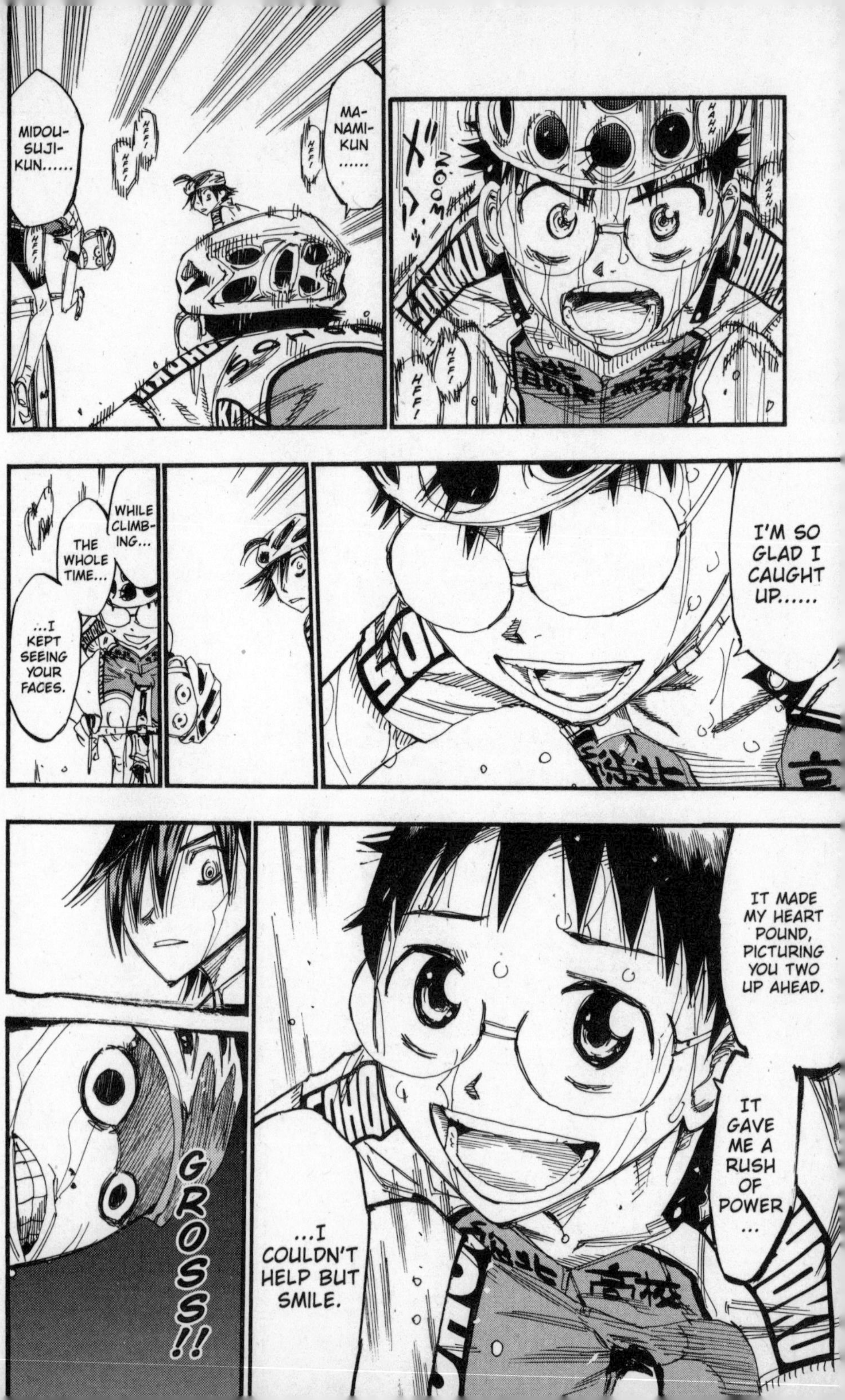
HAHH
ZOOM
HAHH
HFF!
HFF!
MA-NAMI-KUN......
HFF!
HFF!
HFF!
HFF!
MIDOU-SUJI-KUN......
HFF!
I'M SO GLAD I CAUGHT UP......
WHILE CLIMBING...
THE WHOLE TIME...
...I KEPT SEEING YOUR FACES.
IT MADE MY HEART POUND, PICTURING YOU TWO UP AHEAD.
IT GAVE ME A RUSH OF POWER...
...I COULDN'T HELP BUT SMILE.
GROSS!!

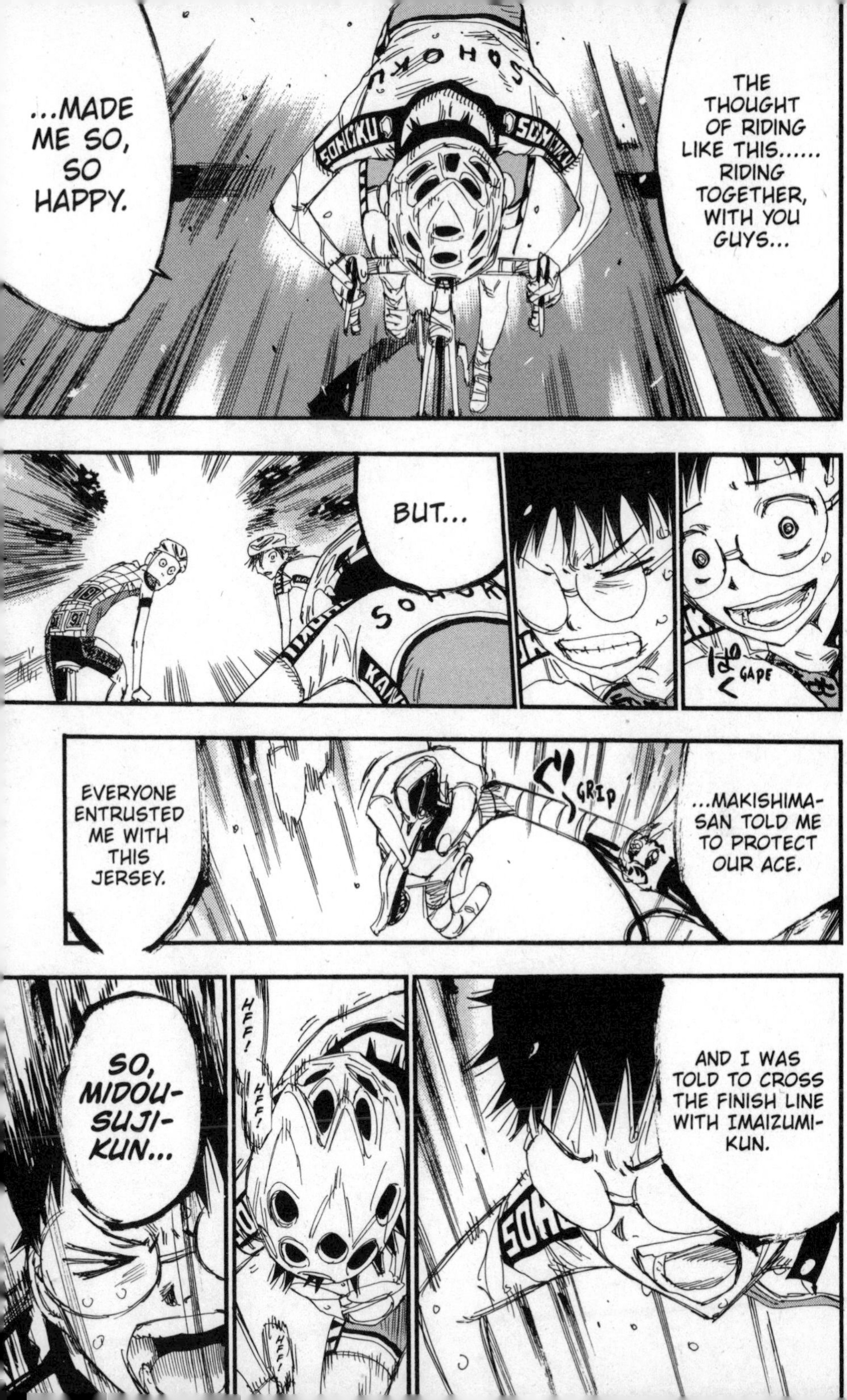
THE THOUGHT OF RIDING LIKE THIS...... RIDING TOGETHER, WITH YOU GUYS...
...MADE ME SO, SO HAPPY.
GAPE
BUT...
...MAKISHIMA-SAN TOLD ME TO PROTECT OUR ACE.
GRIP
EVERYONE ENTRUSTED ME WITH THIS JERSEY.
AND I WAS TOLD TO CROSS THE FINISH LINE WITH IMAIZUMI-KUN.
HFF! HFF!
HFF!
SO, MIDOU-SUJI-KUN...

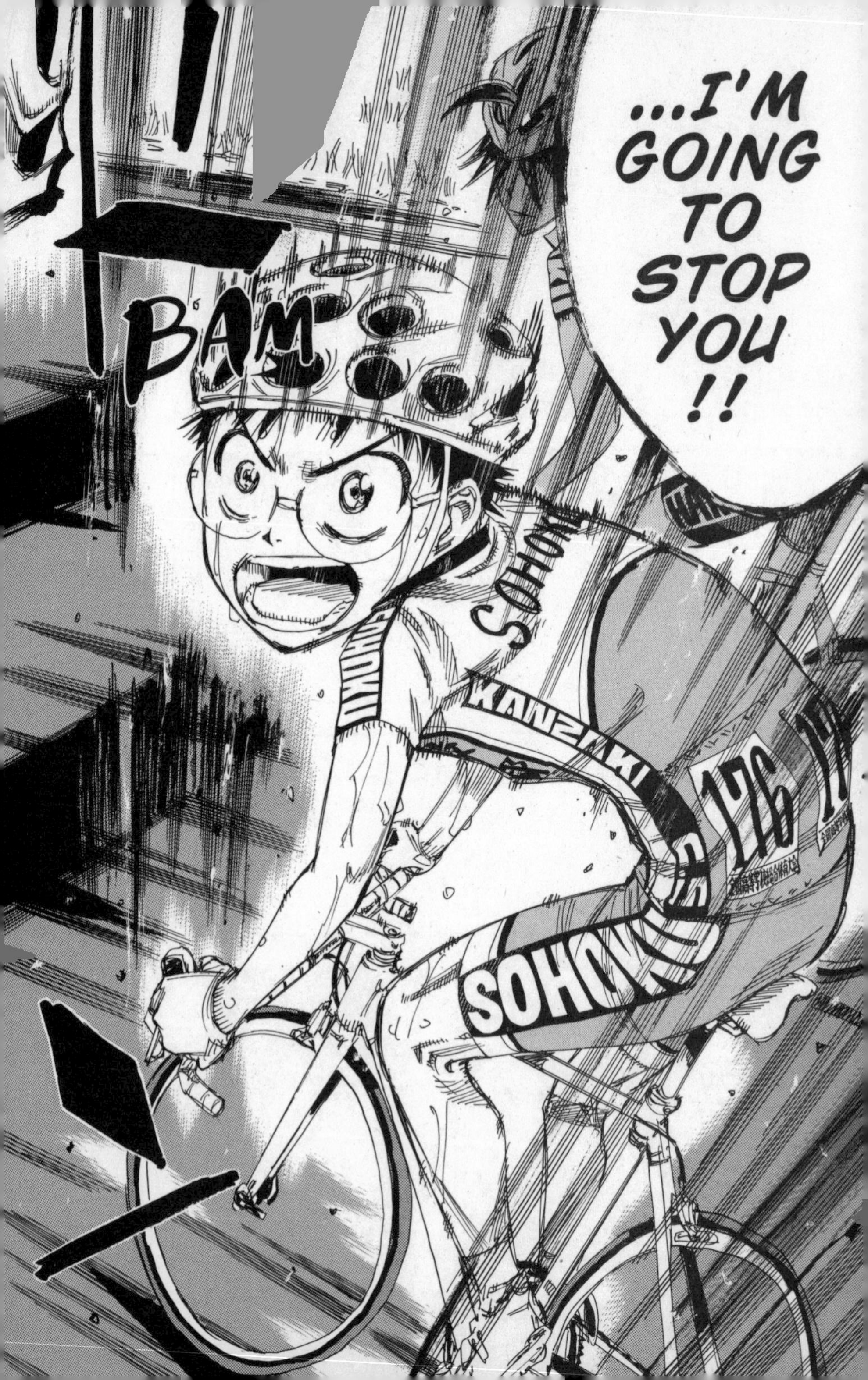
...I'M GOING TO STOP YOU!!
BAM

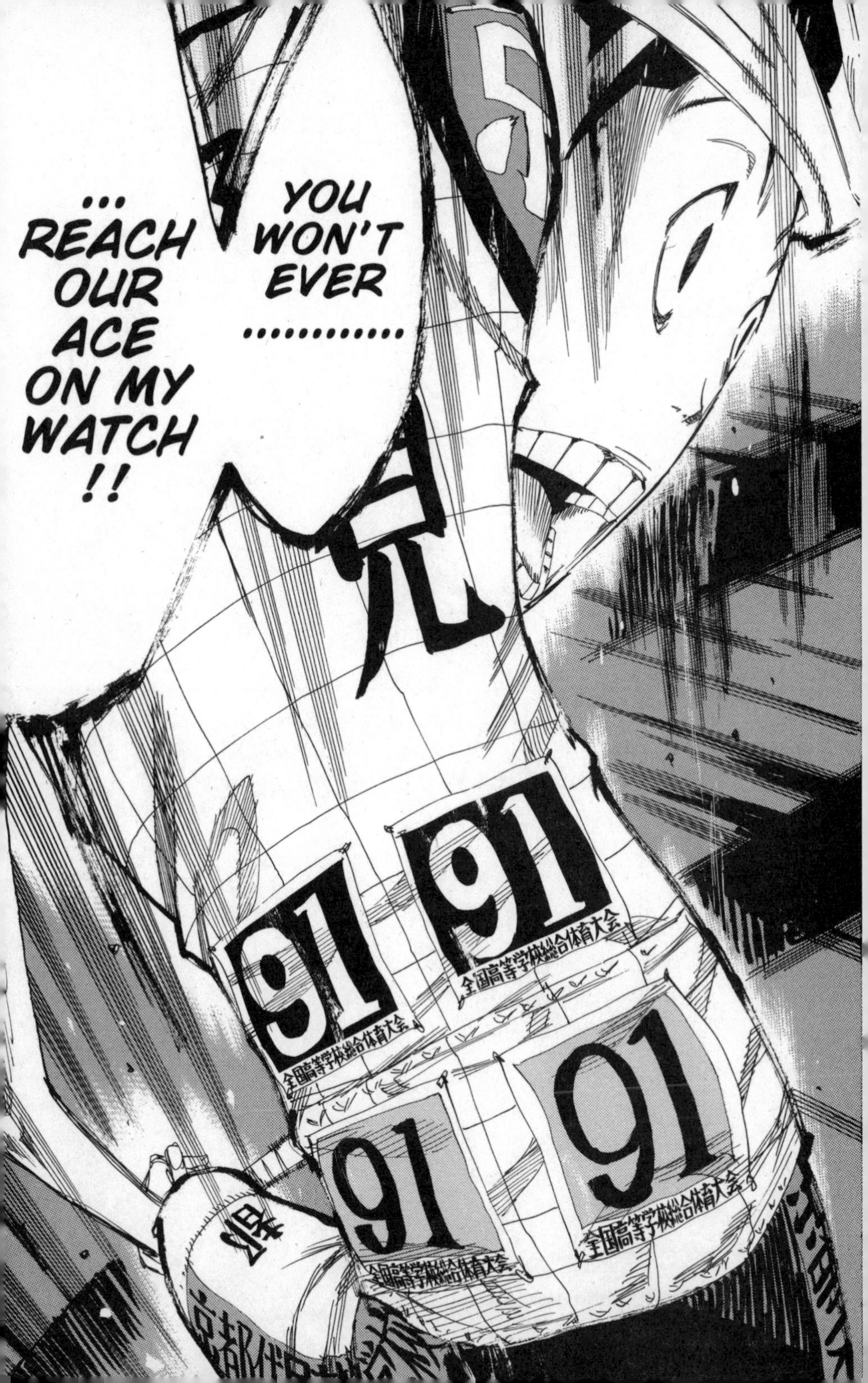
YOU WON'T EVER ....
... REACH OUR ACE ON MY WATCH!!

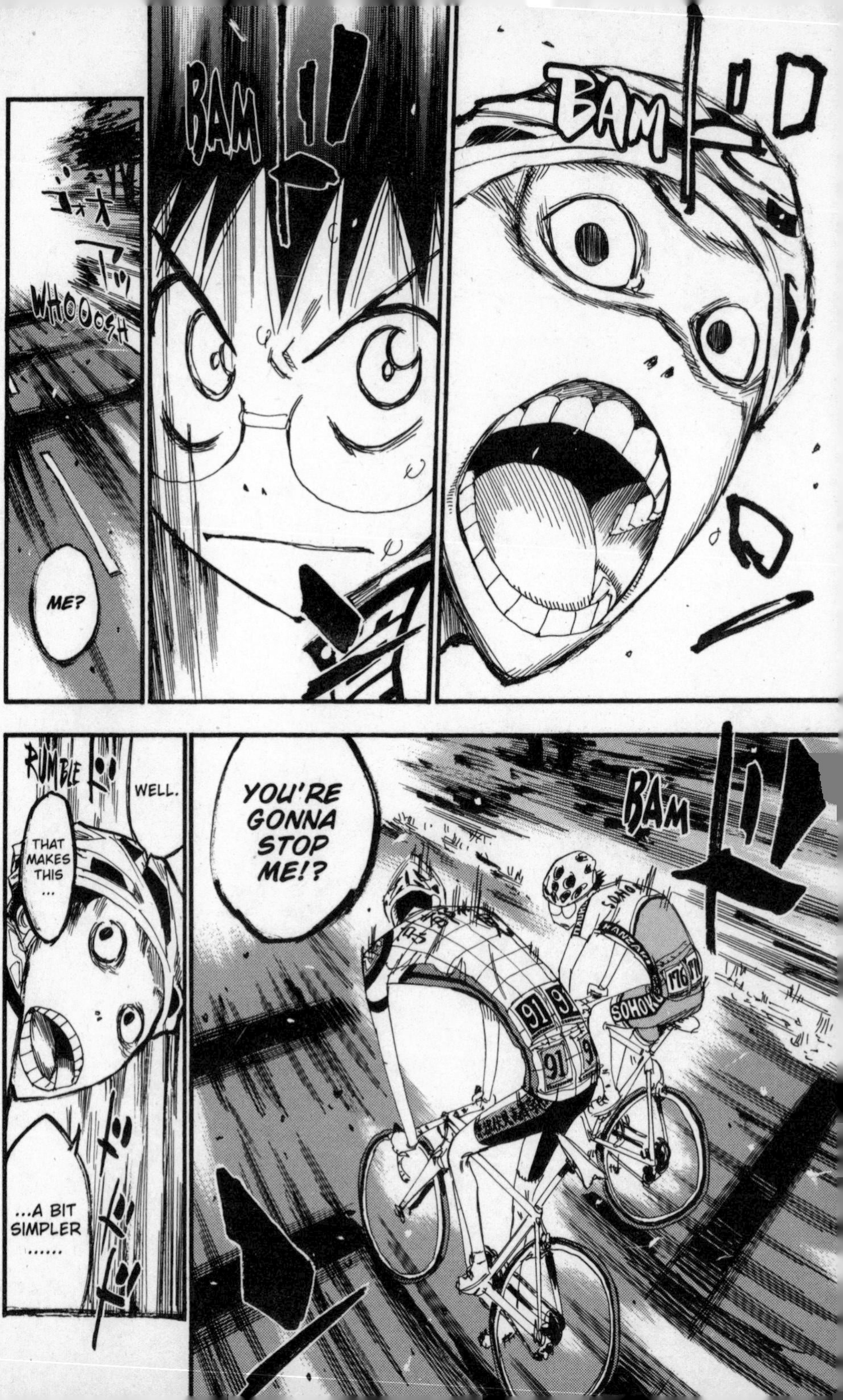
BAM
BAM
WHOOOSH
ME?
BAM
YOU'RE GONNA STOP ME!?
RUMBLE
WELL.
THAT MAKES THIS ...
...A BIT SIMPLER ....

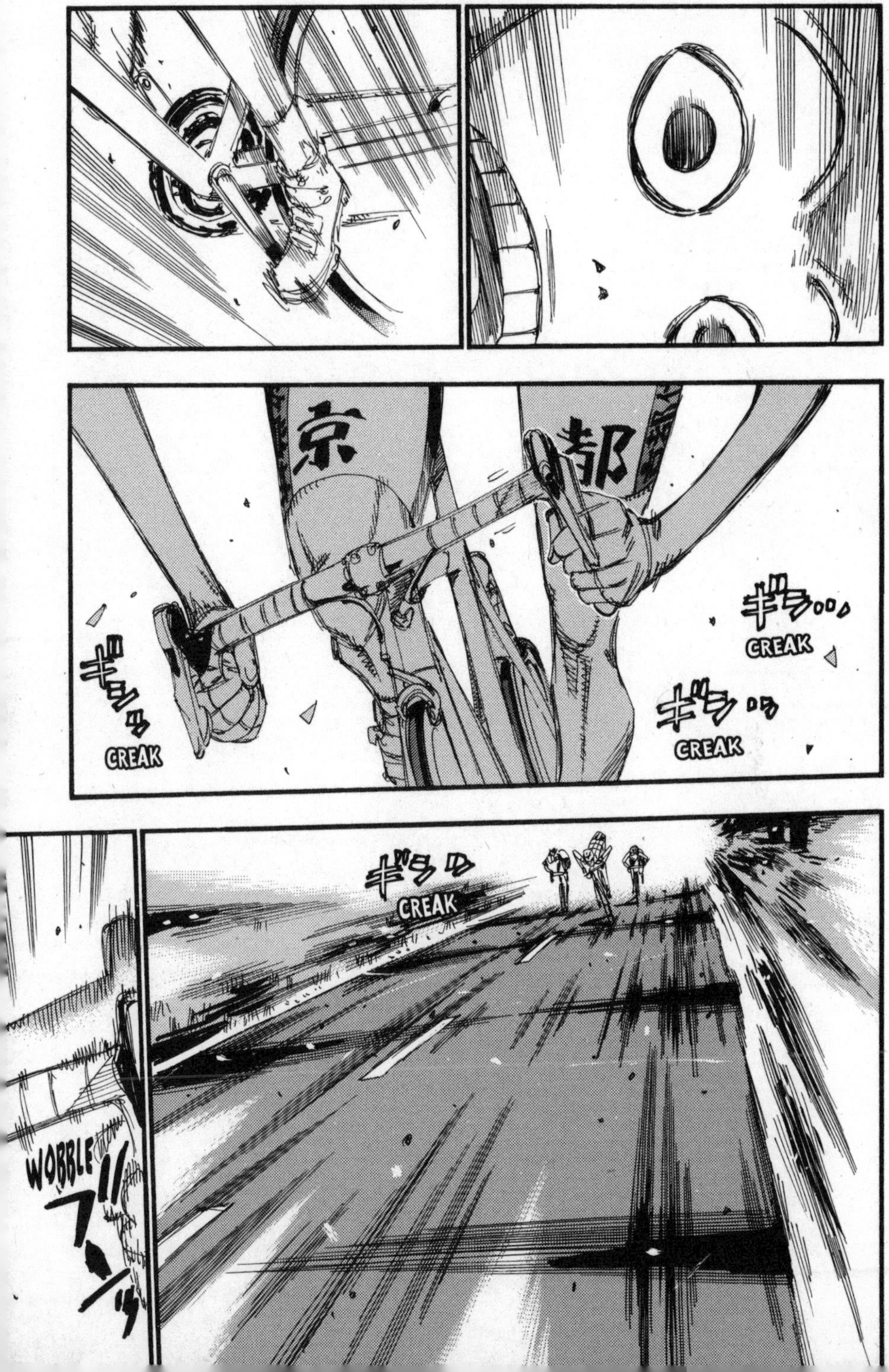
京 都
CREAK
CREAK
CREAK
CREAK
WOBBLE

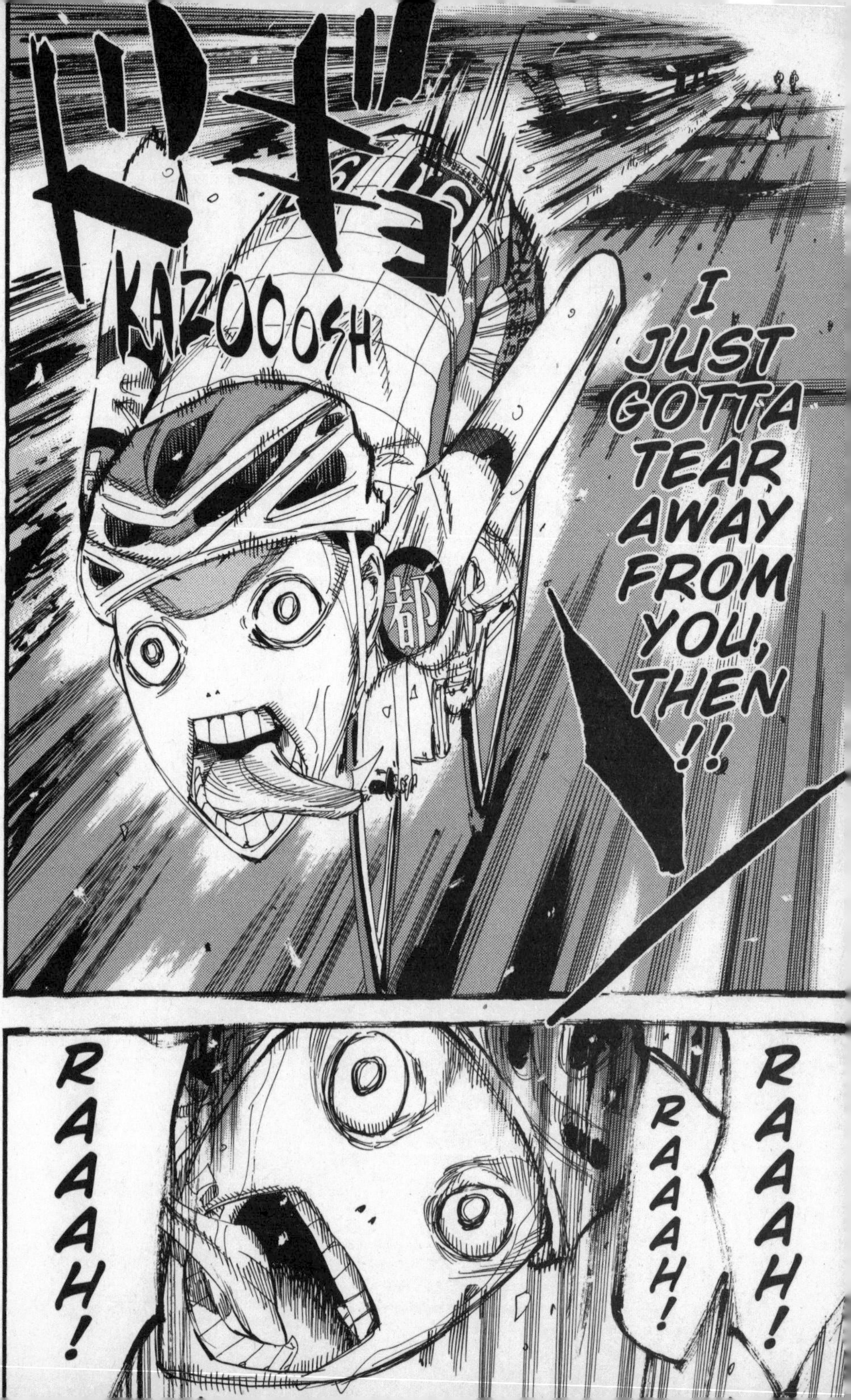
KAZOOOSH
I JUST GOTTA TEAR AWAY FROM YOU, THEN!!
RAAAAH!
RAAAAH!
RAAAAH!

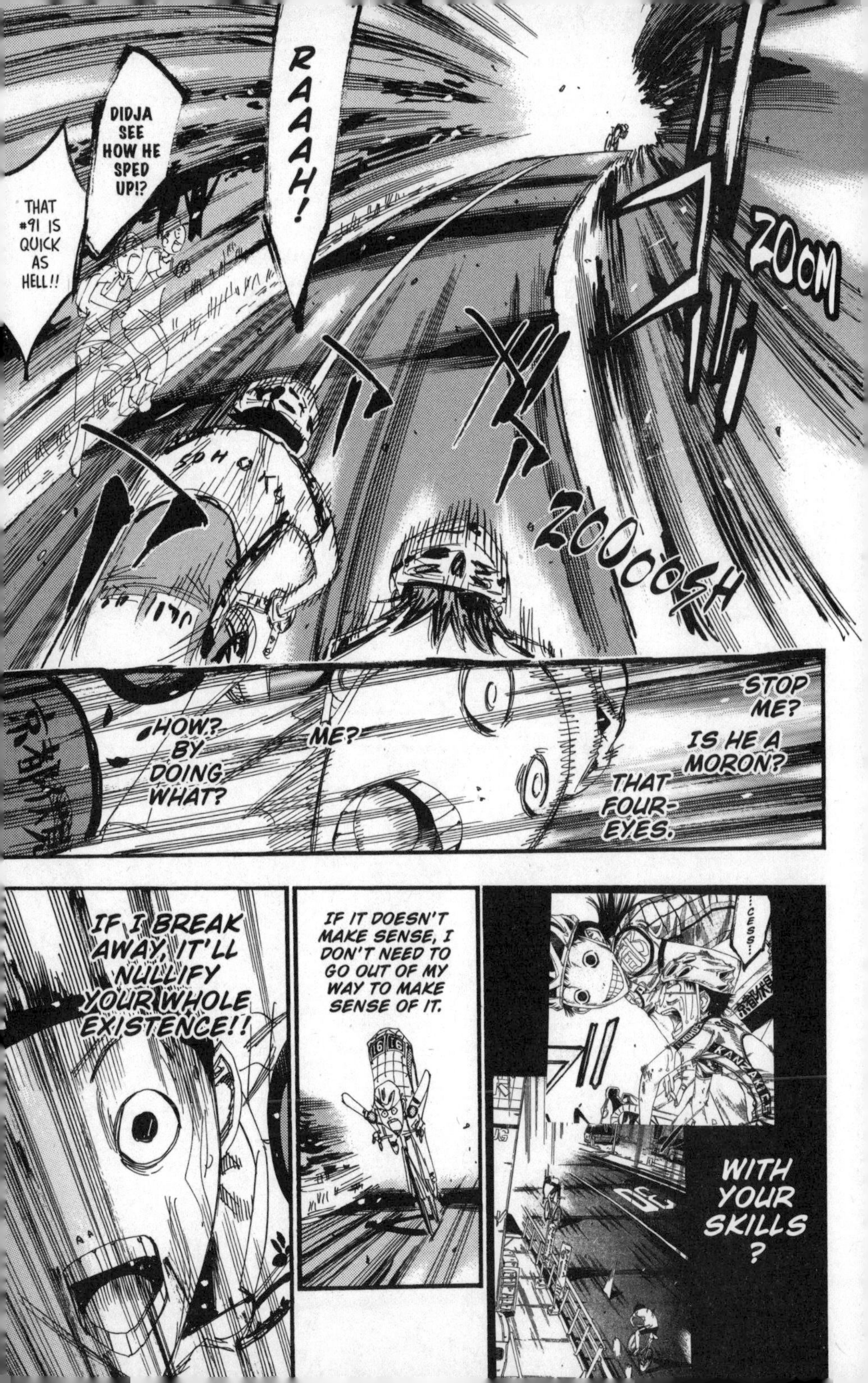
ZOOM
RAAAAH!
DIDJA SEE HOW HE SPED UP!?
THAT #91 IS QUICK AS HELL!!
ZOOOOSH
STOP ME?
IS HE A MORON?
THAT FOUR-EYES.
ME?
HOW? BY DOING WHAT?
...CESS...
WITH YOUR SKILLS?
IF IT DOESN'T MAKE SENSE, I DON'T NEED TO GO OUT OF MY WAY TO MAKE SENSE OF IT.
IF I BREAK AWAY, IT'LL NULLIFY YOUR WHOLE EXISTENCE!!

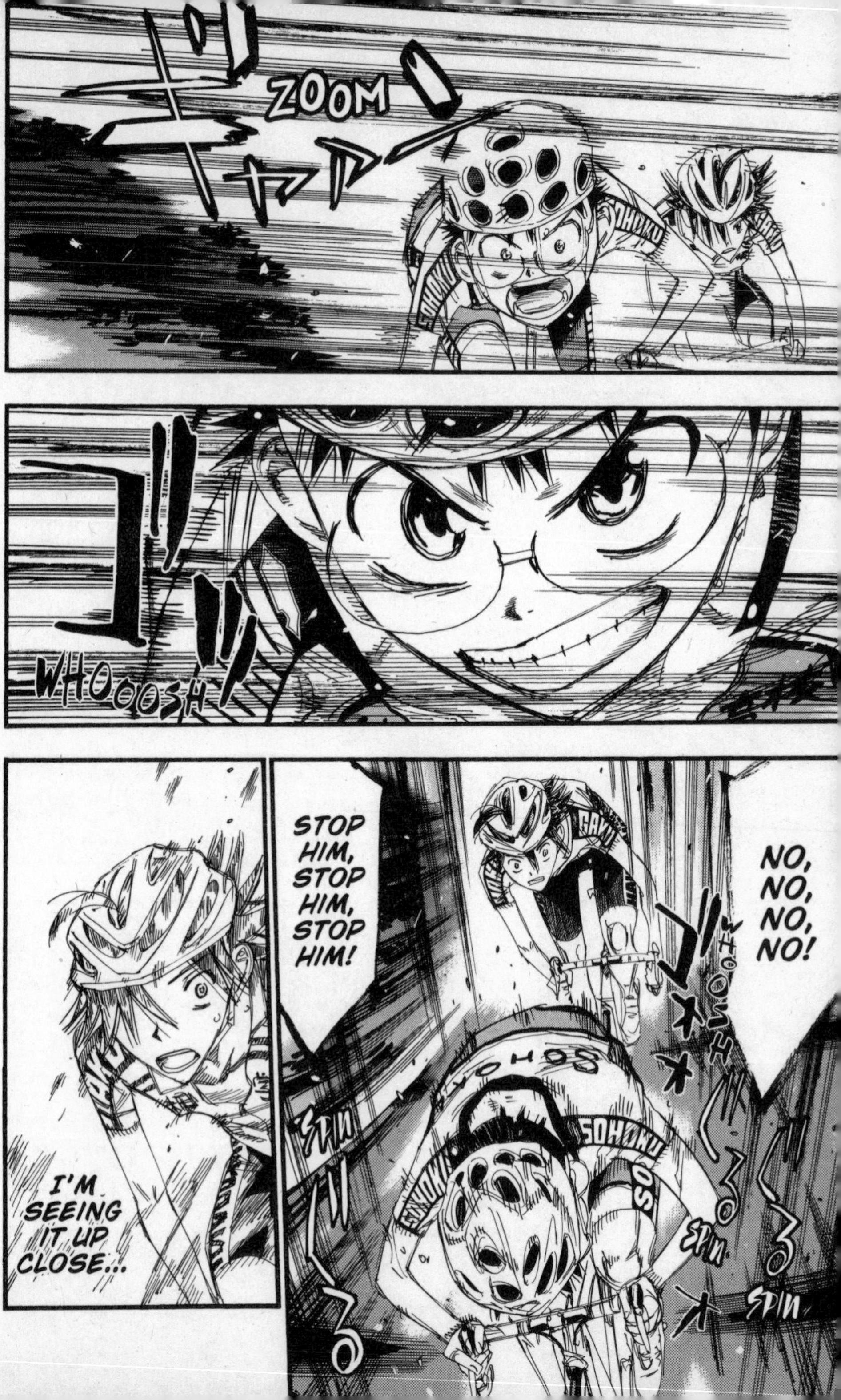
ZOOM
WHOOOSH!
NO, NO, NO, NO!
STOP HIM, STOP HIM, STOP HIM!
WHOOOSH
SPIN
SPIN
SPIN
I'M SEEING IT UP CLOSE...

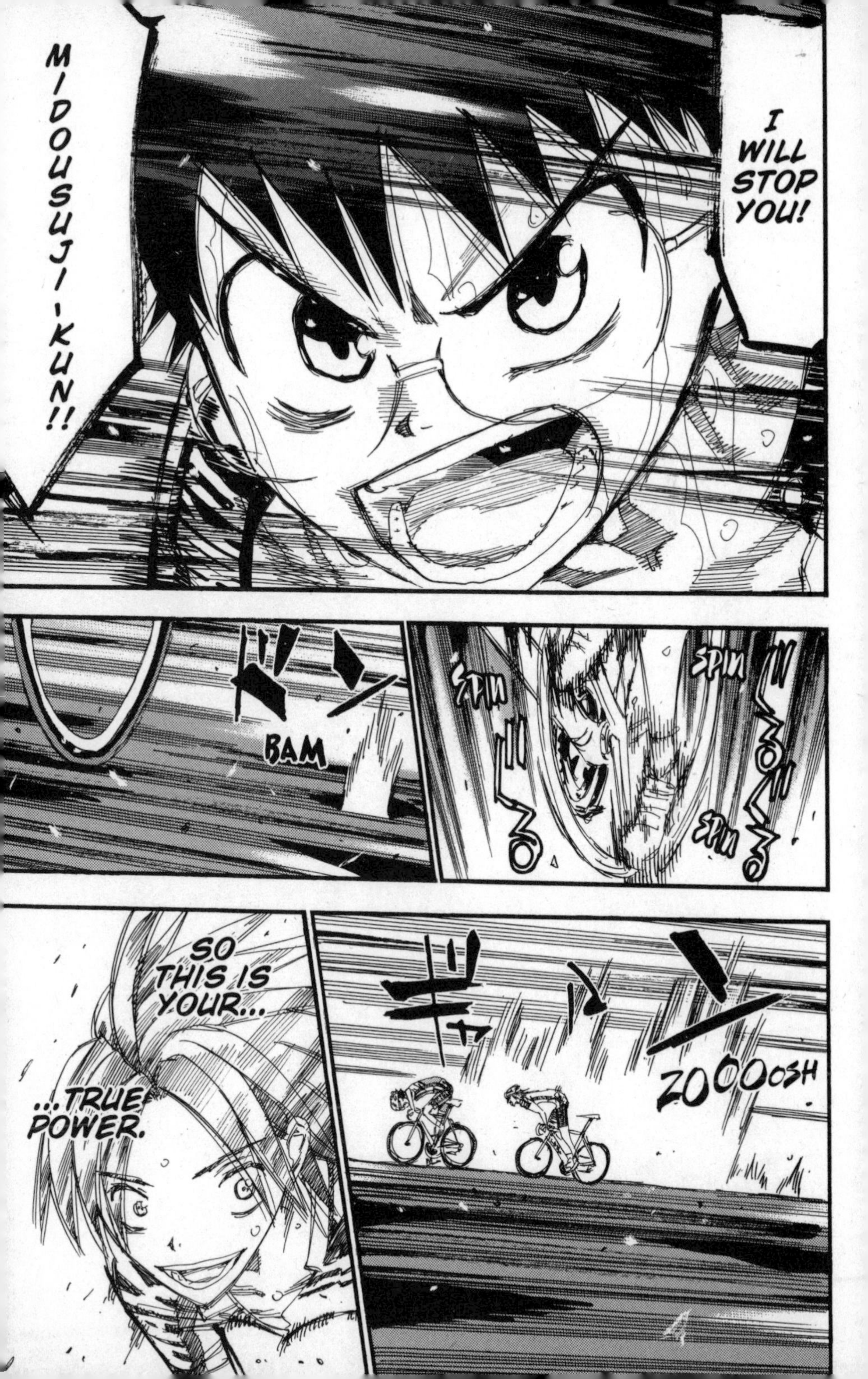
I WILL STOP YOU!
MIDOUSUJI-KUN!!
SPIN
SPIN
SPIN
ドン
BAM
ZOOOOSH
SO THIS IS YOUR...
...TRUE POWER.

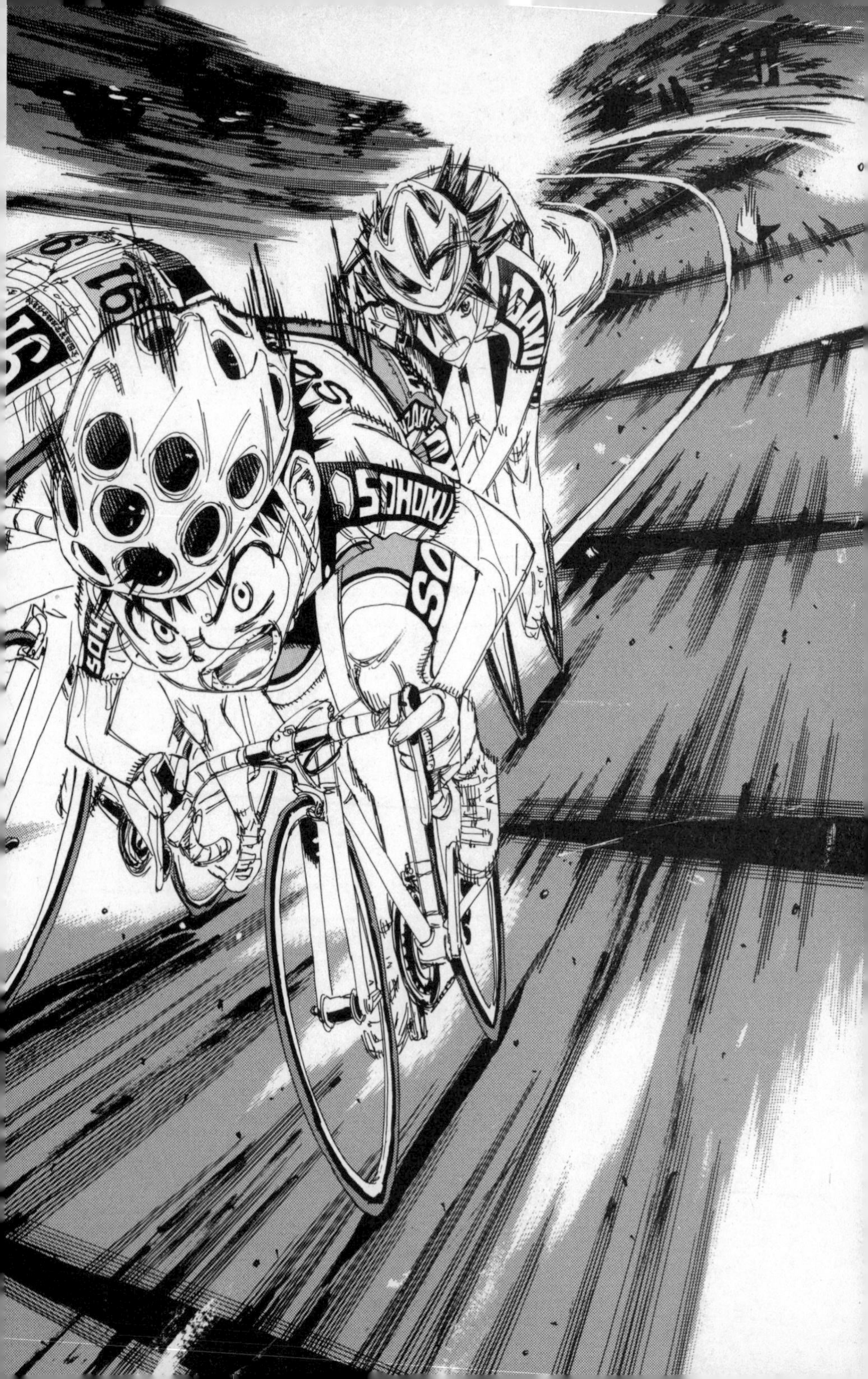
SOHOKU

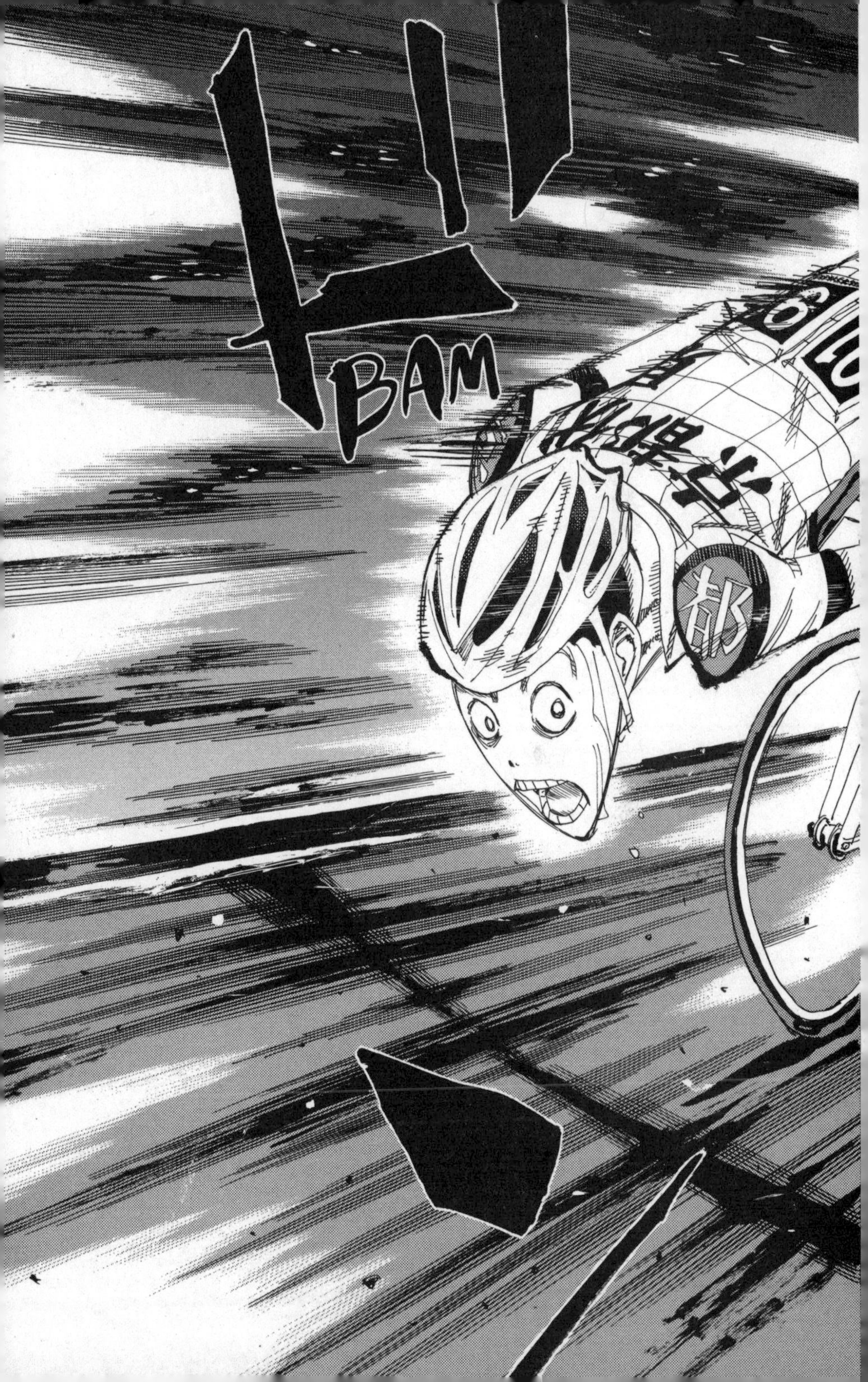
BAM

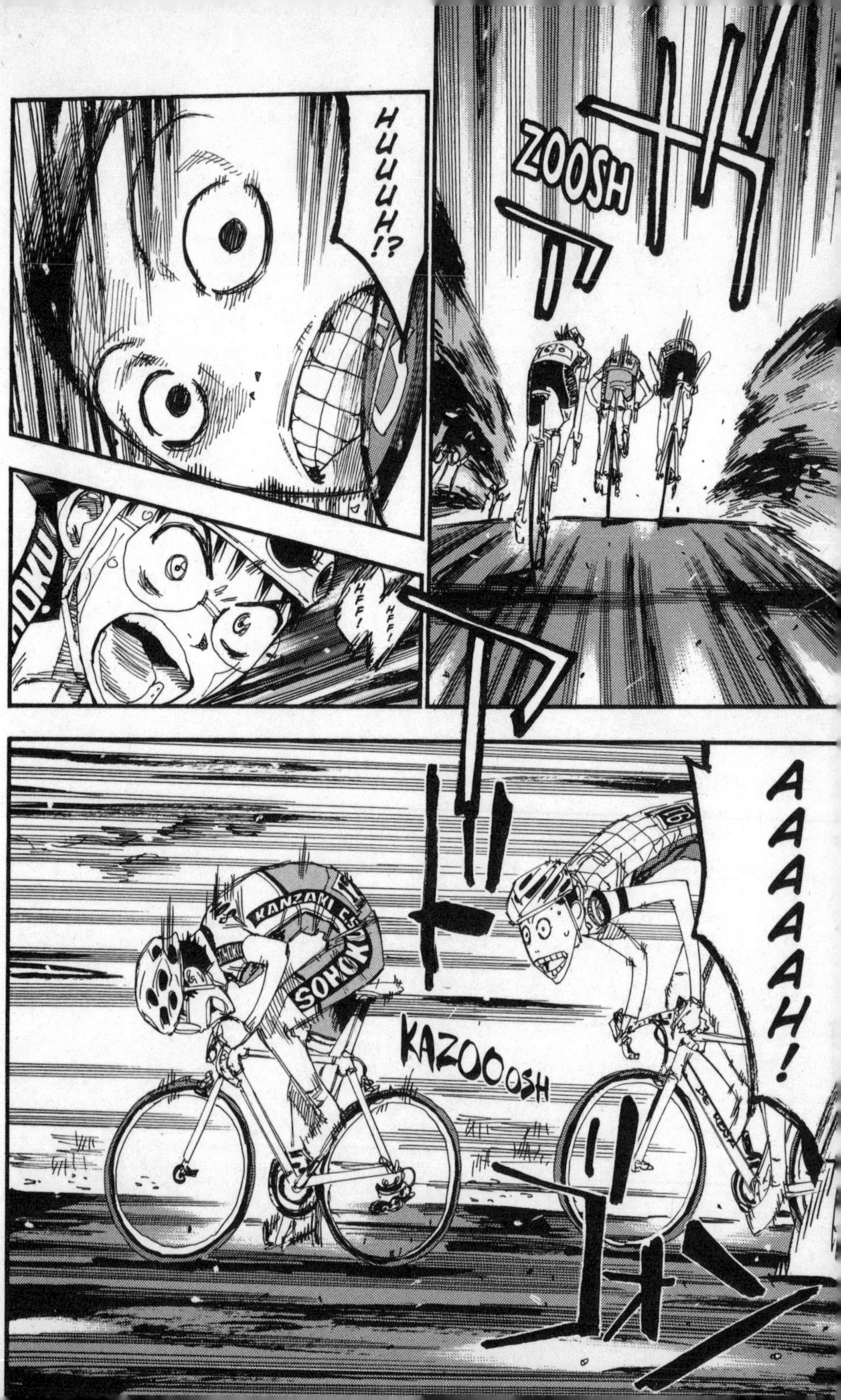
ZOOSH
HUUUUH!?
HFF! HFF!
AAAAAAH!
KAZOOOSH
SOHOKU

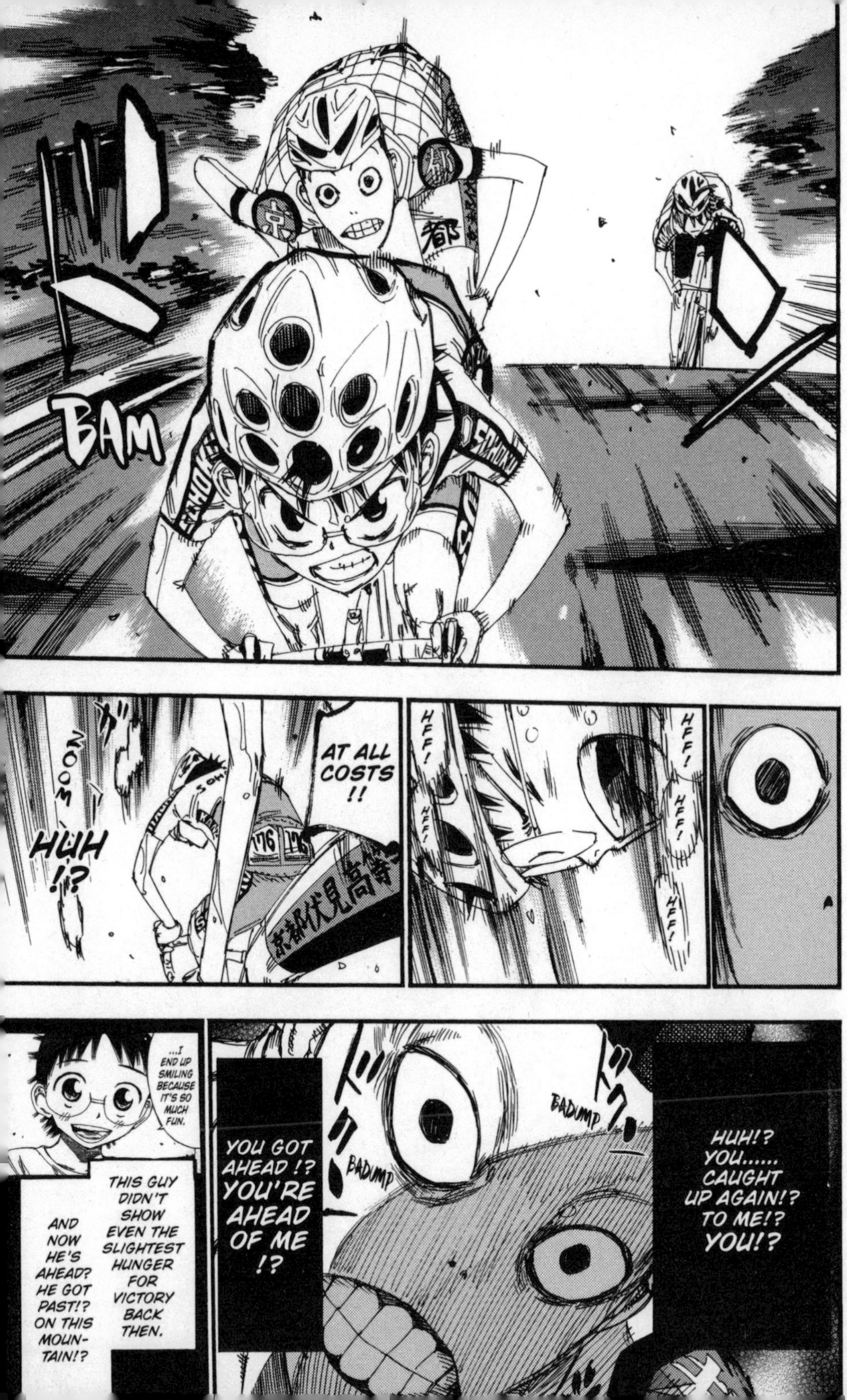
BAM
HFF! HFF!
HFF! HFF!
HFF!
AT ALL COSTS!!
ZOOM
HUH!?
HUH!? YOU...... CAUGHT UP AGAIN!? TO ME!? YOU!?
BADUMP
BADUMP
YOU GOT AHEAD!? YOU'RE AHEAD OF ME!?
...I END UP SMILING BECAUSE IT'S SO MUCH FUN.
THIS GUY DIDN'T SHOW EVEN THE SLIGHTEST HUNGER FOR VICTORY BACK THEN.
AND NOW HE'S AHEAD? HE GOT PAST!? ON THIS MOUN-TAIN!?

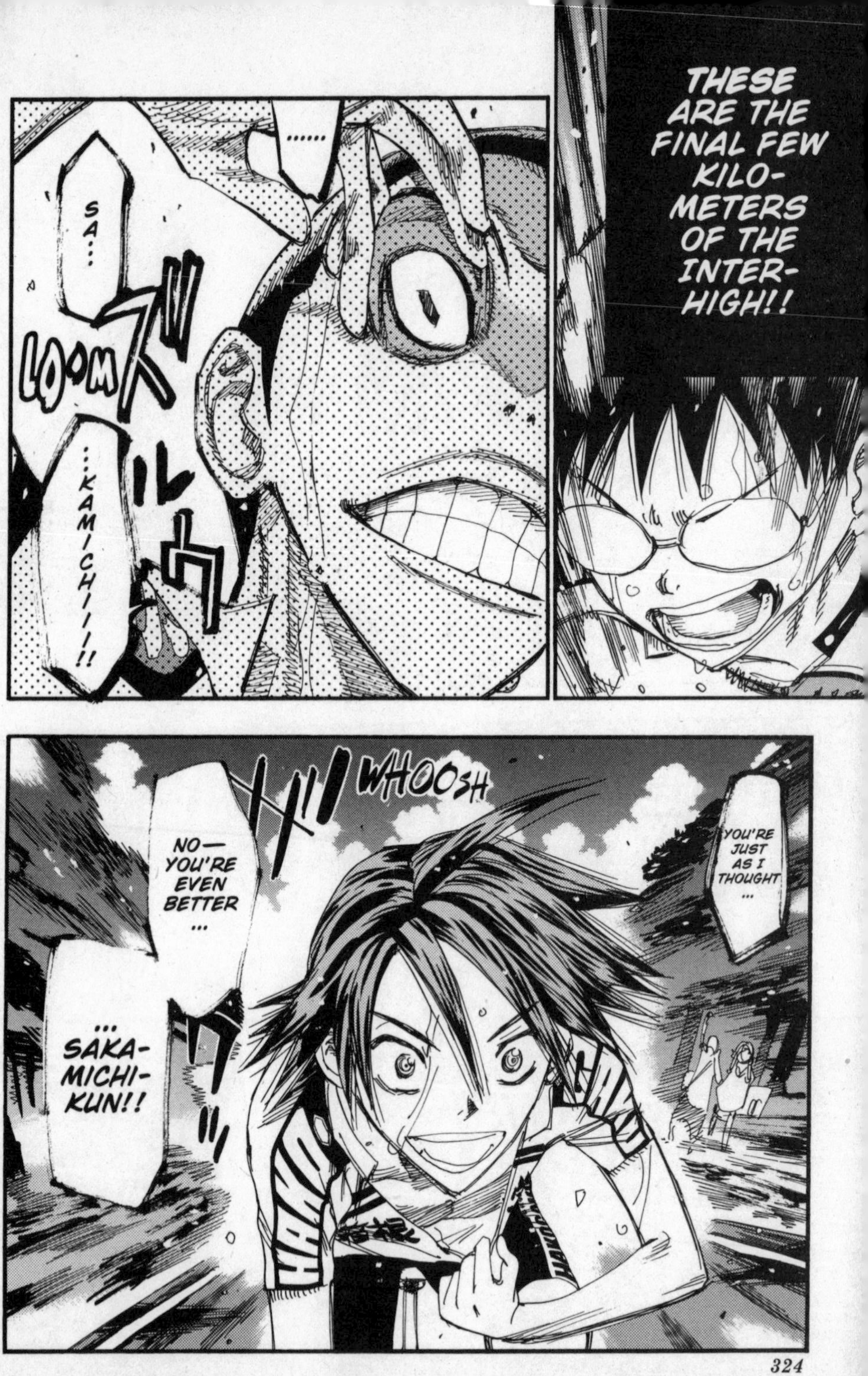
THESE ARE THE FINAL FEW KILO-METERS OF THE INTER-HIGH!!
......
SA...
LOOM
...KAMICHI!!!!!
YOU'RE JUST AS I THOUGHT...
WHOOSH
NO— YOU'RE EVEN BETTER...
...SAKA-MICHI-KUN!!

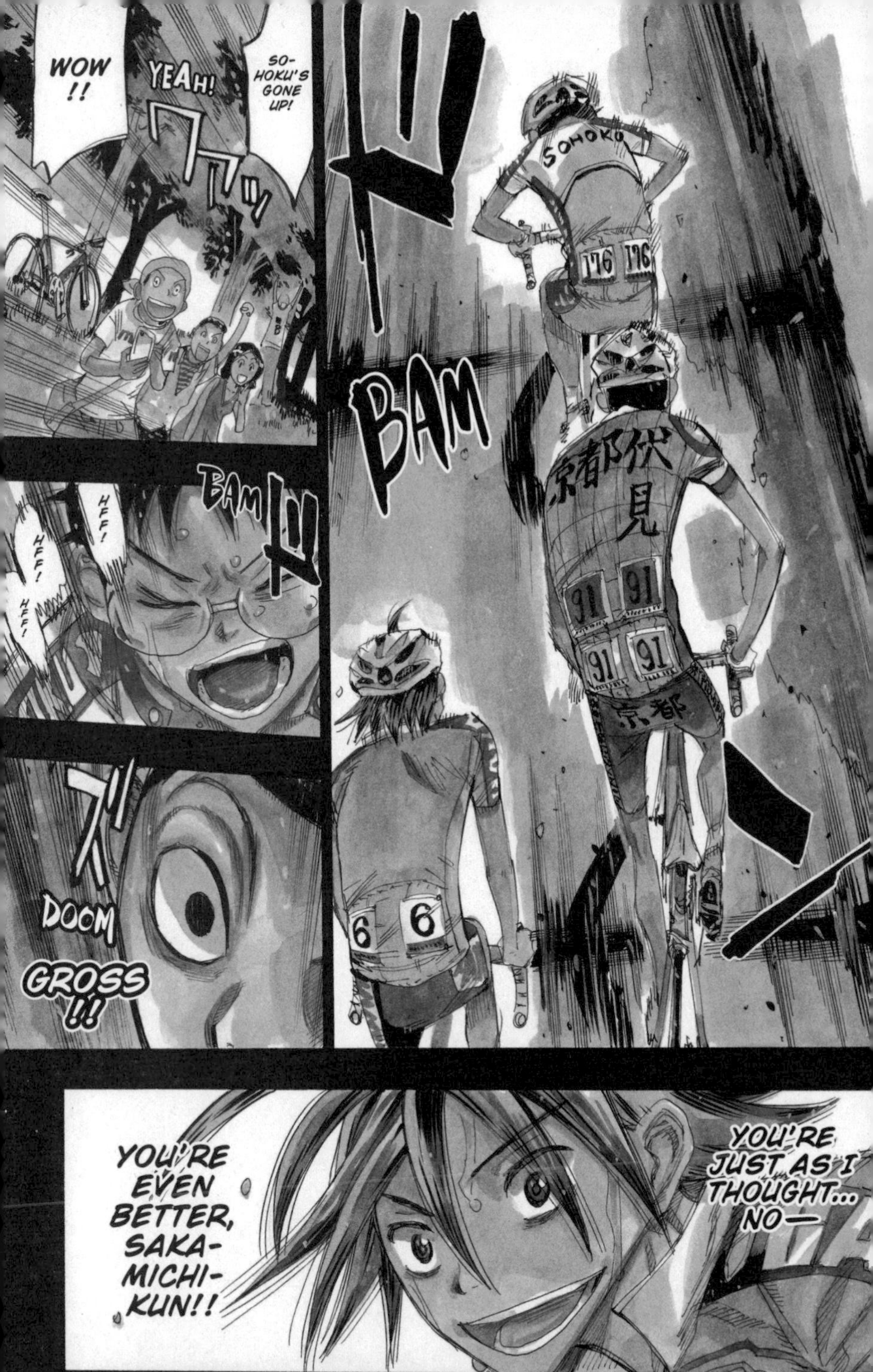
BAM
SOHOKU
京都伏見
SO-HOKU'S GONE UP!
YEAH!
WOW !!
BAM
HFF!
HFF!
HFF!
DOOM
GROSS !!
YOU'RE JUST AS I THOUGHT... NO—
YOU'RE EVEN BETTER, SAKA-MICHI-KUN!!

RIDE.206 SAKAMICHI OFF COURSE

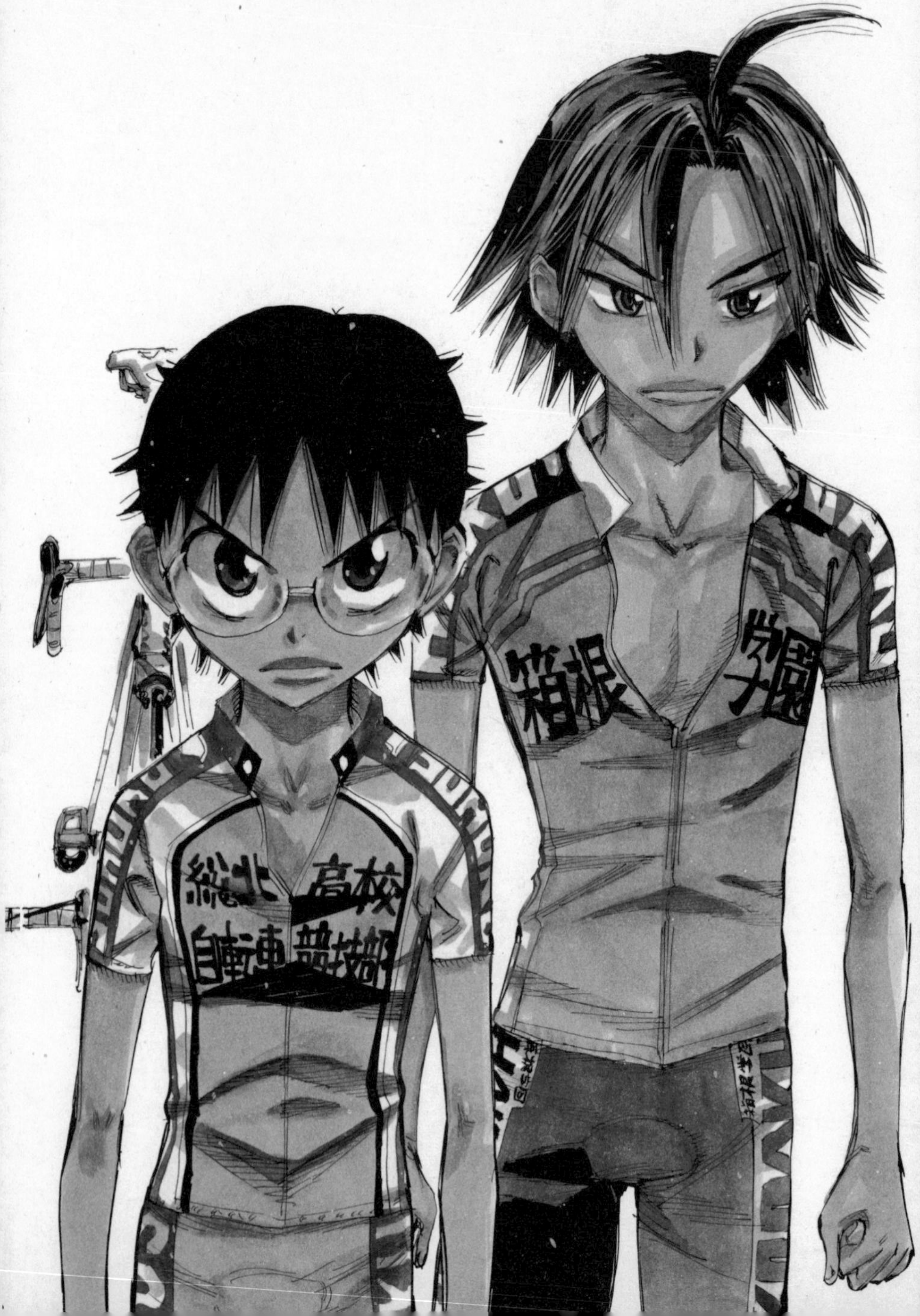
箱根学園
総北高校
自転車競技部

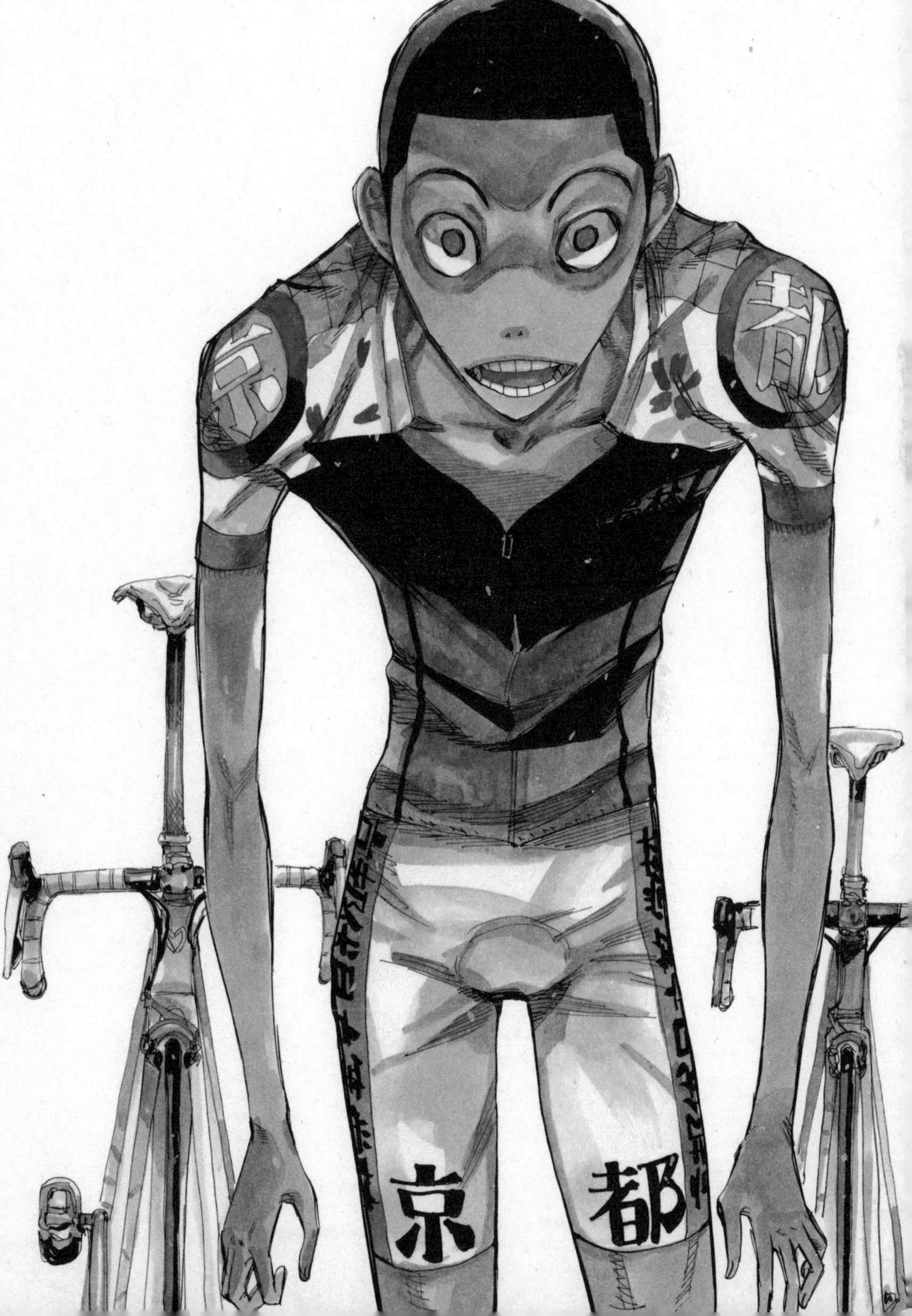
京都
京都

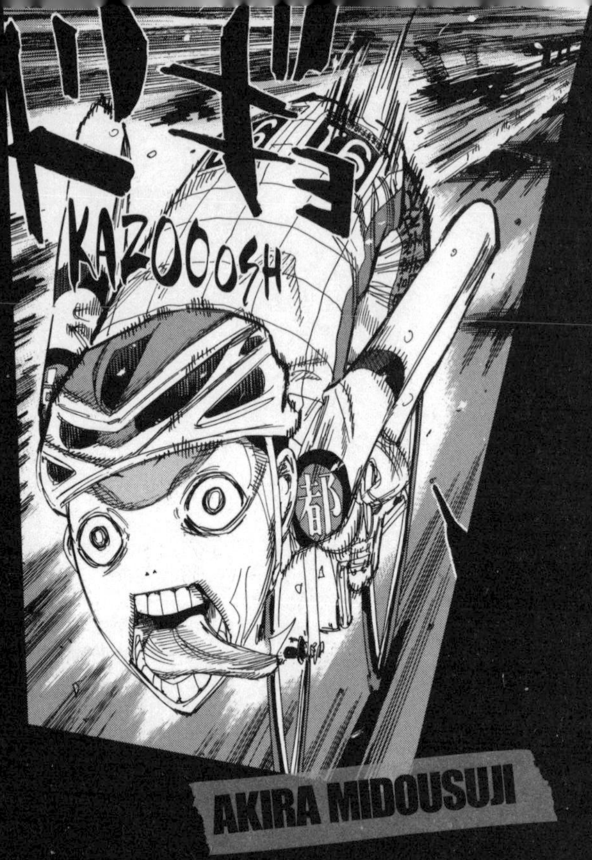
KAZOOOSH
AKIRA MIDOUSUJI

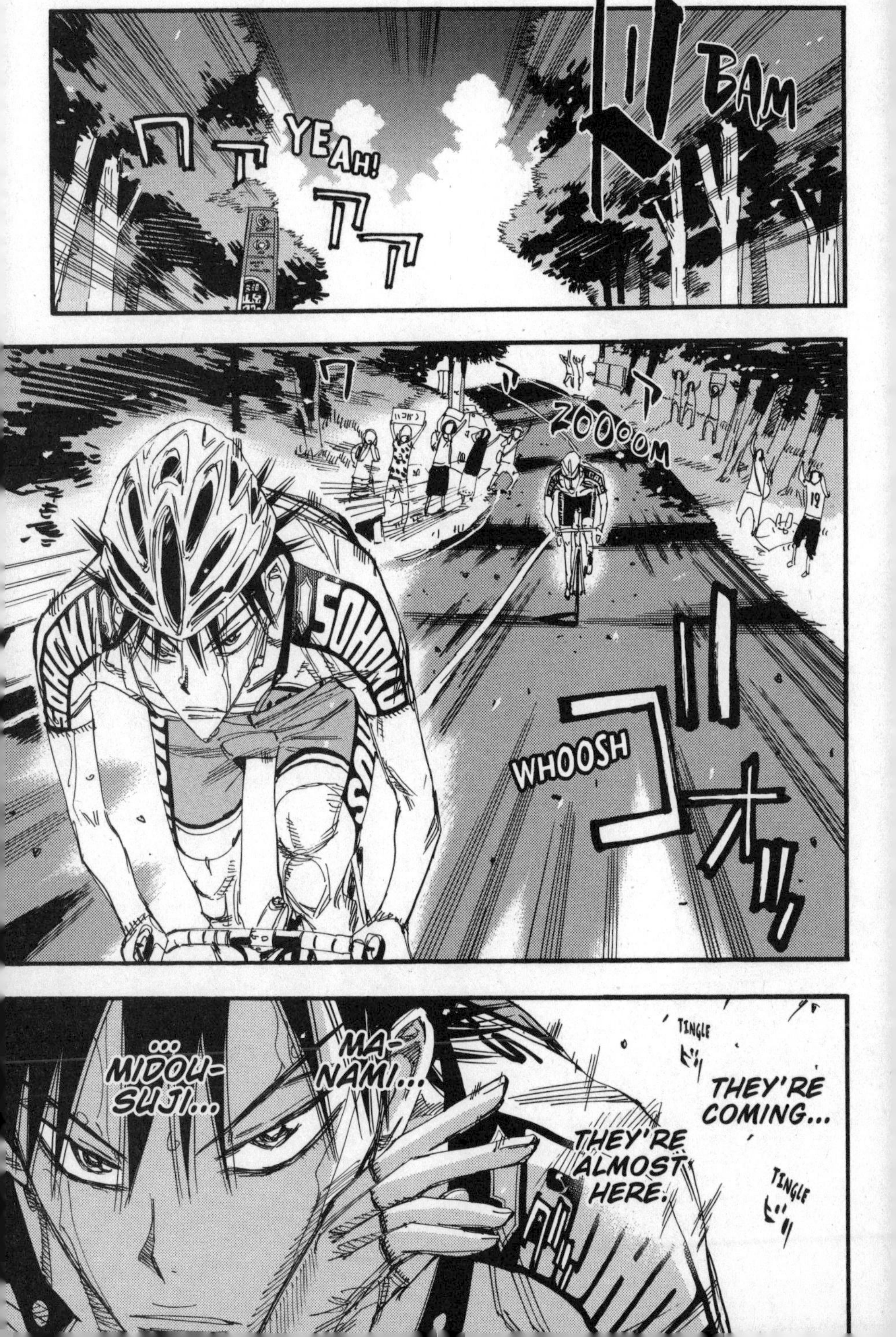
BAM
YEAH!
ZOOOOOM
WHOOSH
TINGLE
THEY'RE COMING...
THEY'RE ALMOST HERE.
TINGLE
MA-NAMI...
...MIDOU-SUJI...

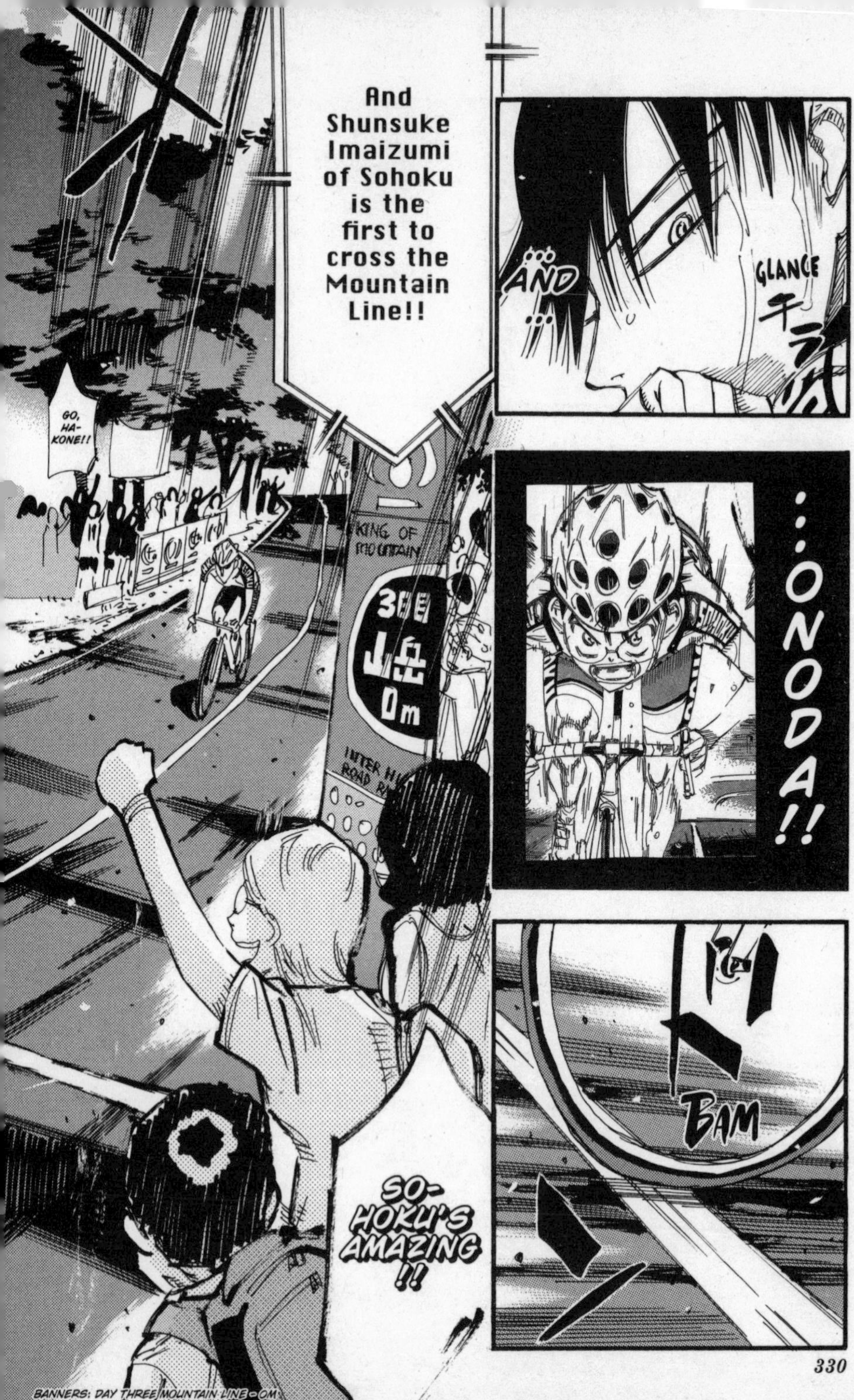
...AND...
GLANCE
...ONODA!!
BAM
And Shunsuke Imaizumi of Sohoku is the first to cross the Mountain Line!!
GO, HAKONE!!
KING OF MOUNTAIN
0m
SO-HOKU'S AMAZING!!

BANNERS: DAY THREE MOUNTAIN LINE - 0M

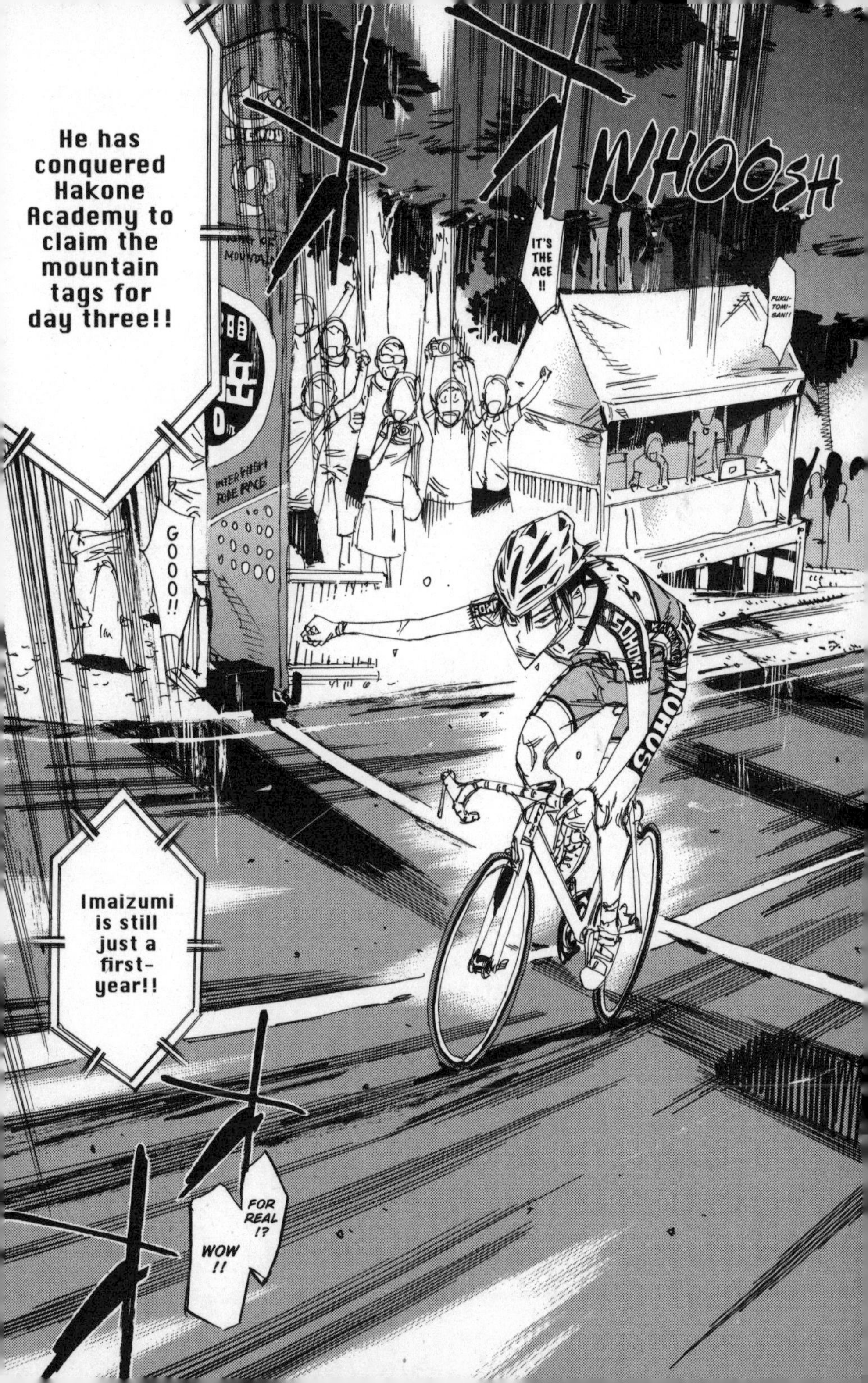
WHOOSH
FUKU-TOMI-SAN!!
IT'S THE ACE!!
He has conquered Hakone Academy to claim the mountain tags for day three!!
GOOOO!!
Imaizumi is still just a first-year!!
FOR REAL!?
WOW!!

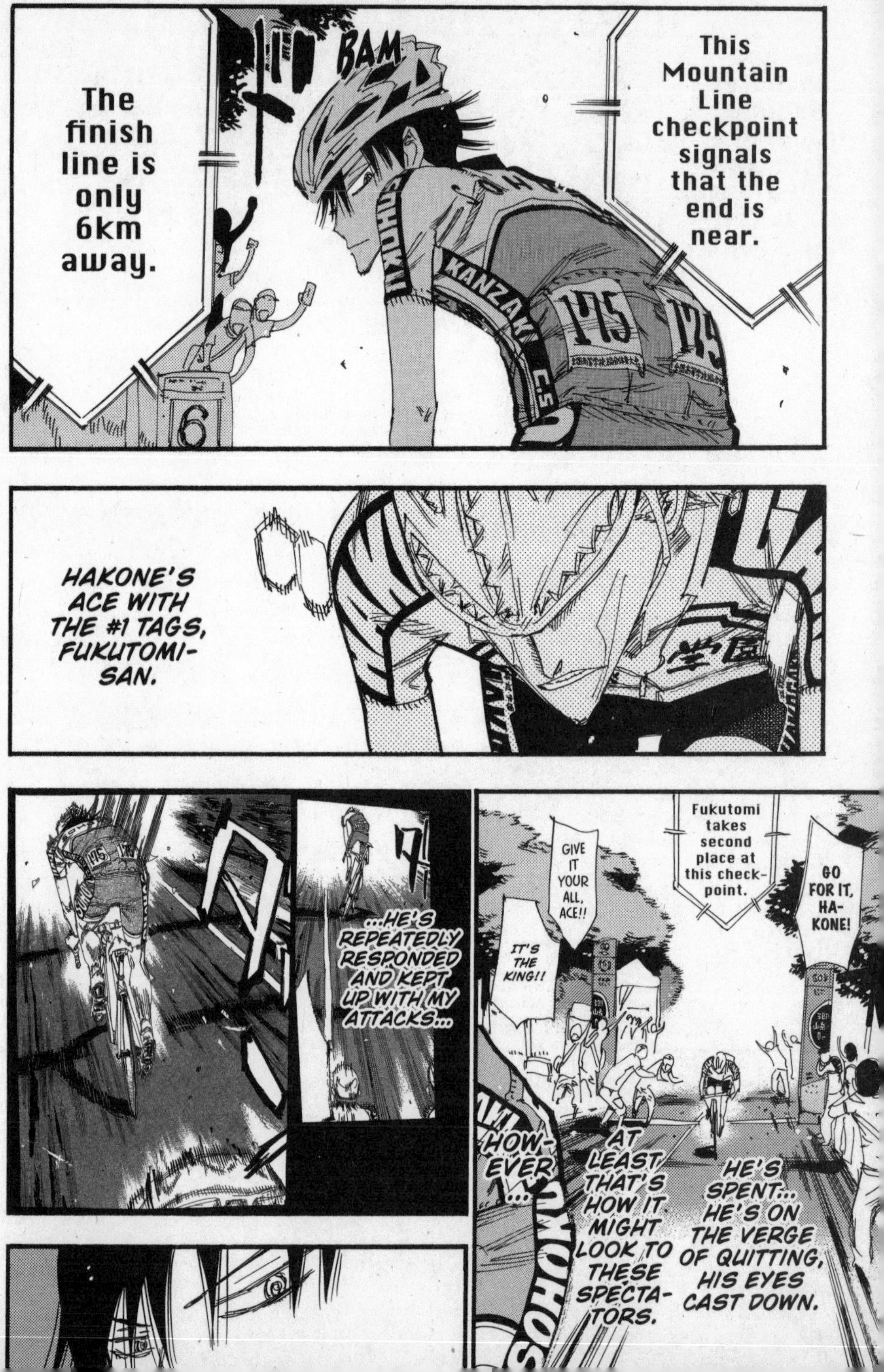
BAM
This Mountain Line checkpoint signals that the end is near.
The finish line is only 6km away.
HAKONE'S ACE WITH THE #1 TAGS, FUKUTOMI-SAN.
Fukutomi takes second place at this checkpoint.
GO FOR IT, HAKONE!
GIVE IT YOUR ALL, ACE!!
IT'S THE KING!!
HE'S SPENT... HE'S ON THE VERGE OF QUITTING, HIS EYES CAST DOWN.
AT LEAST THAT'S HOW IT MIGHT LOOK TO THESE SPECTATORS.
HOW-EVER...
...HE'S REPEATEDLY RESPONDED AND KEPT UP WITH MY ATTACKS...

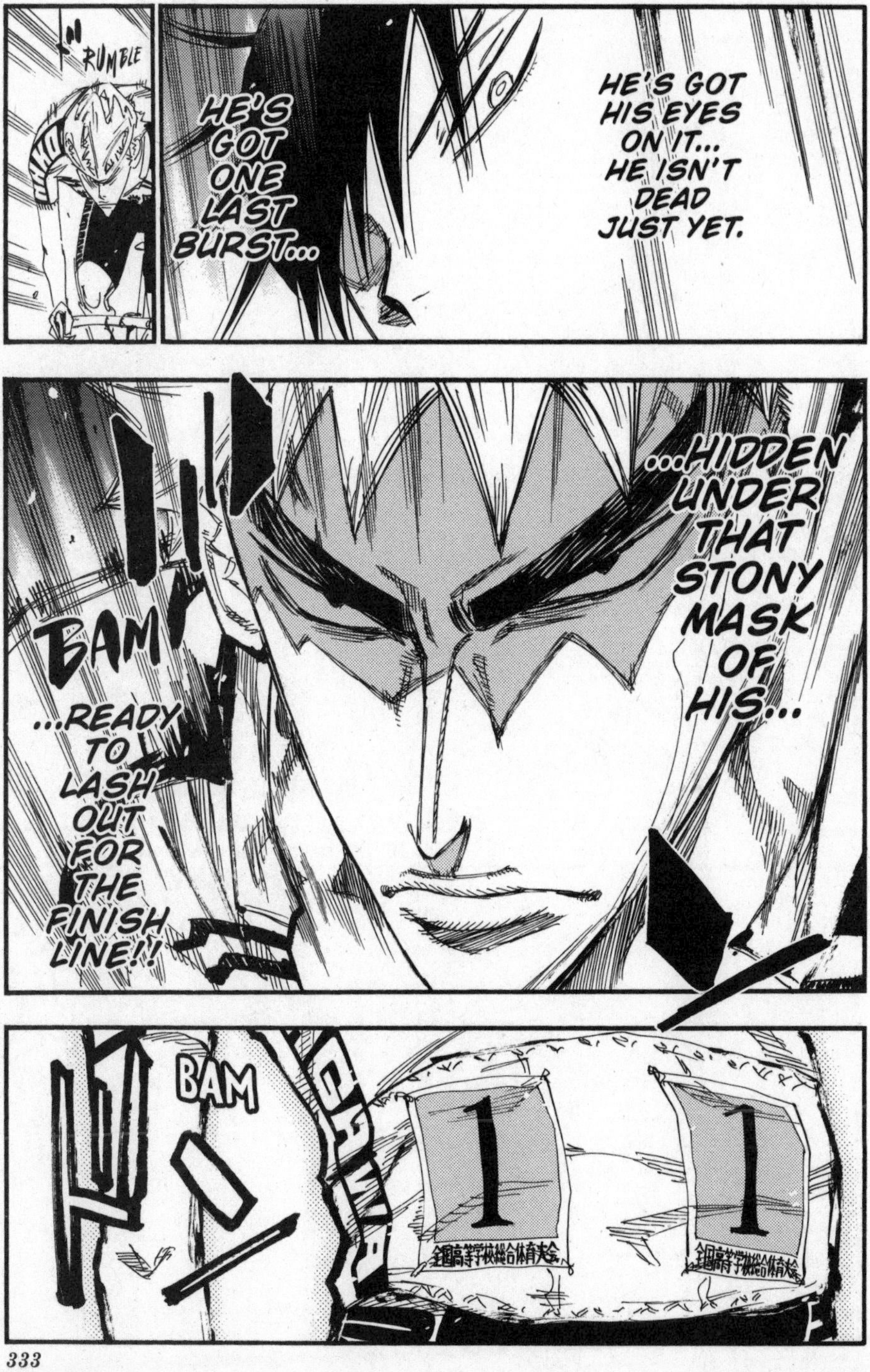
HE'S GOT HIS EYES ON IT... HE ISN'T DEAD JUST YET.
HE'S GOT ONE LAST BURST...
RUMBLE
...HIDDEN UNDER THAT STONY MASK OF HIS...
BAM
...READY TO LASH OUT FOR THE FINISH LINE!!
BAM
全国高等学校総合体育大会
全国高等学校総合体育大会

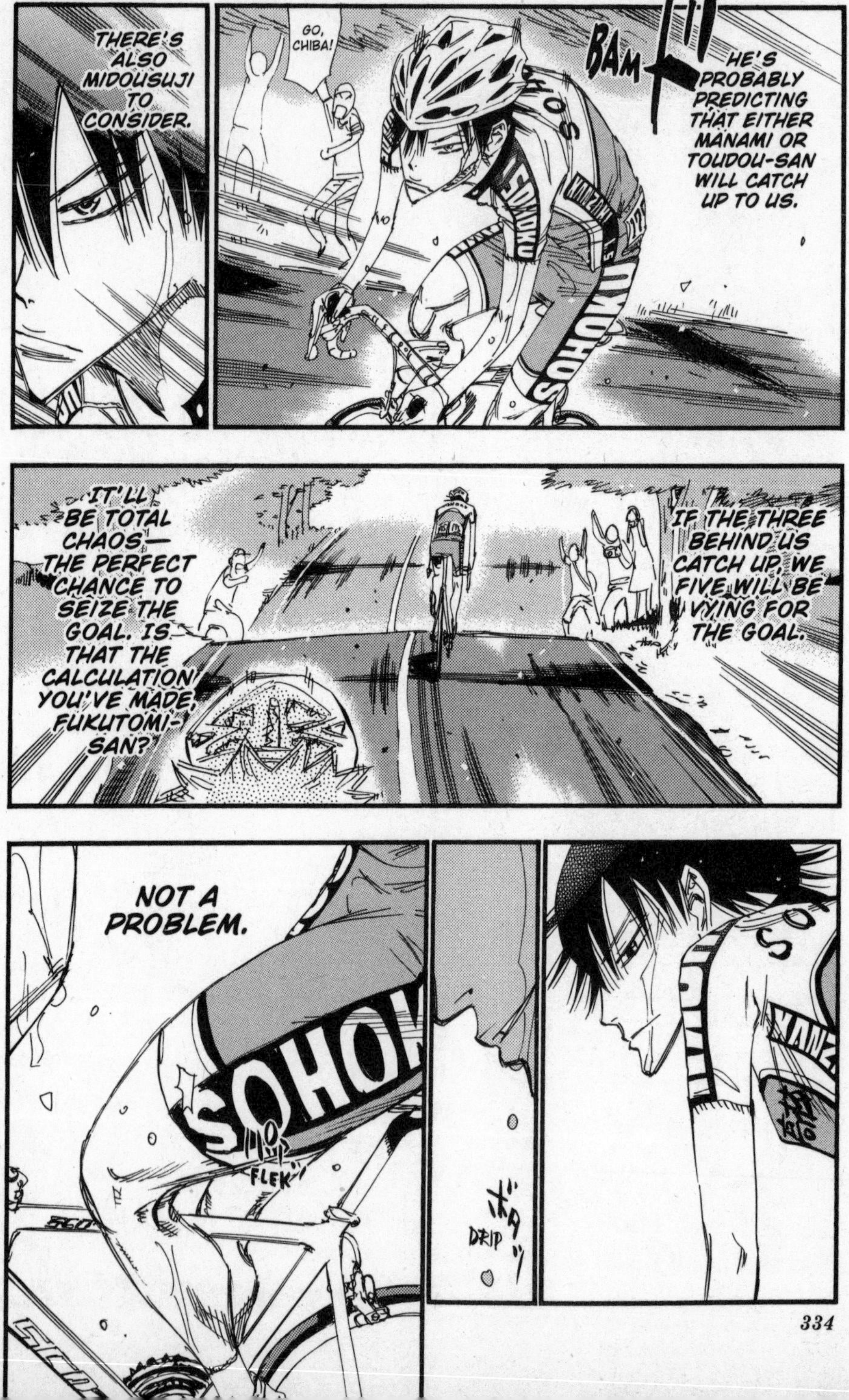
BAM
HE'S PROBABLY PREDICTING THAT EITHER MANAMI OR TOUDOU-SAN WILL CATCH UP TO US.
GO, CHIBA!
THERE'S ALSO MIDOUSUJI TO CONSIDER.
IF THE THREE BEHIND US CATCH UP, WE FIVE WILL BE VYING FOR THE GOAL.
IT'LL BE TOTAL CHAOS—THE PERFECT CHANCE TO SEIZE THE GOAL. IS THAT THE CALCULATION YOU'VE MADE, FUKUTOMI-SAN?
ぼたッ
DRIP
NOT A PROBLEM.
FLEK

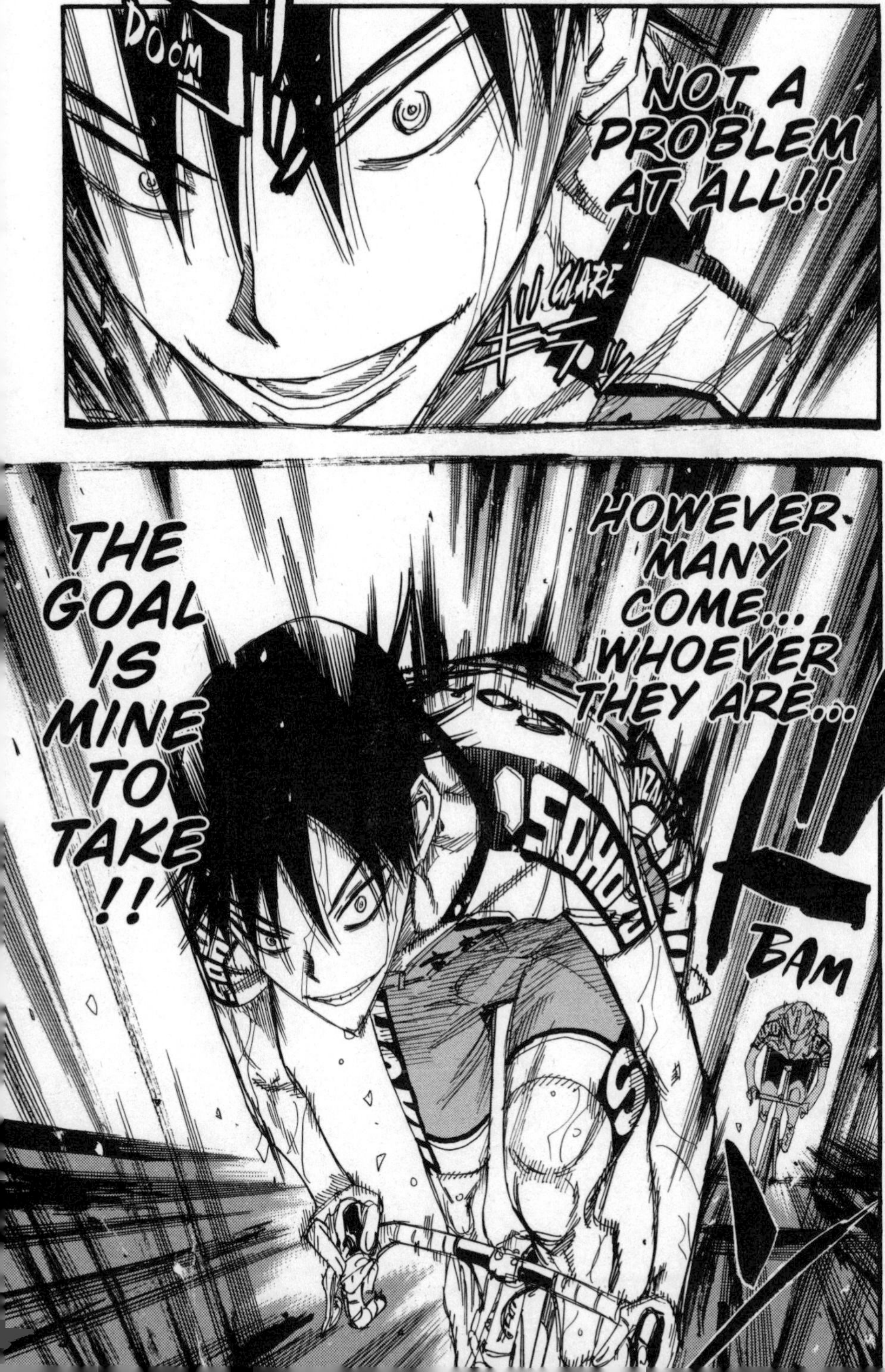
DOOM
NOT A PROBLEM AT ALL!!
GLARE
HOWEVER MANY COME... WHOEVER THEY ARE...
BAM
THE GOAL IS MINE TO TAKE!!

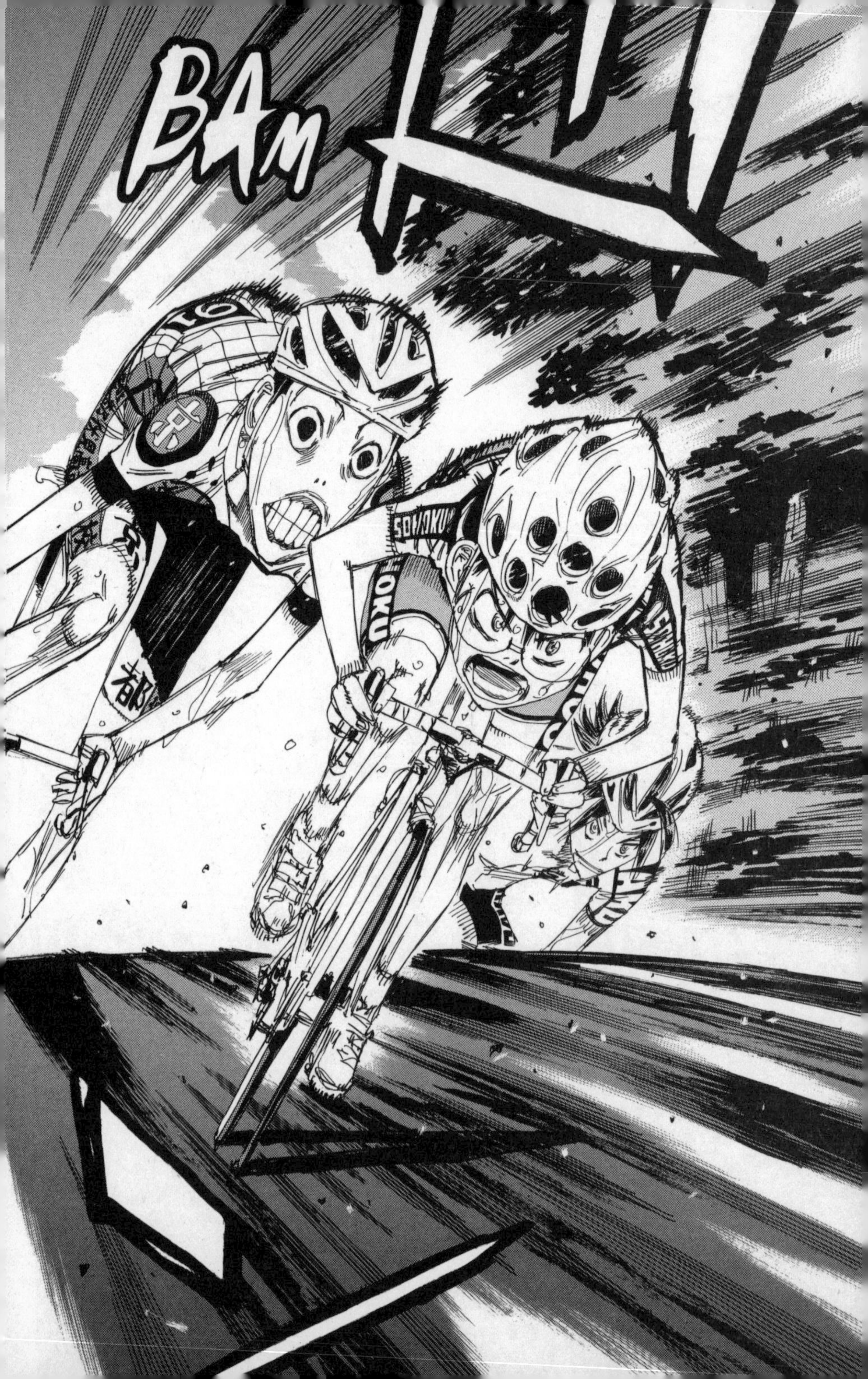
BAM

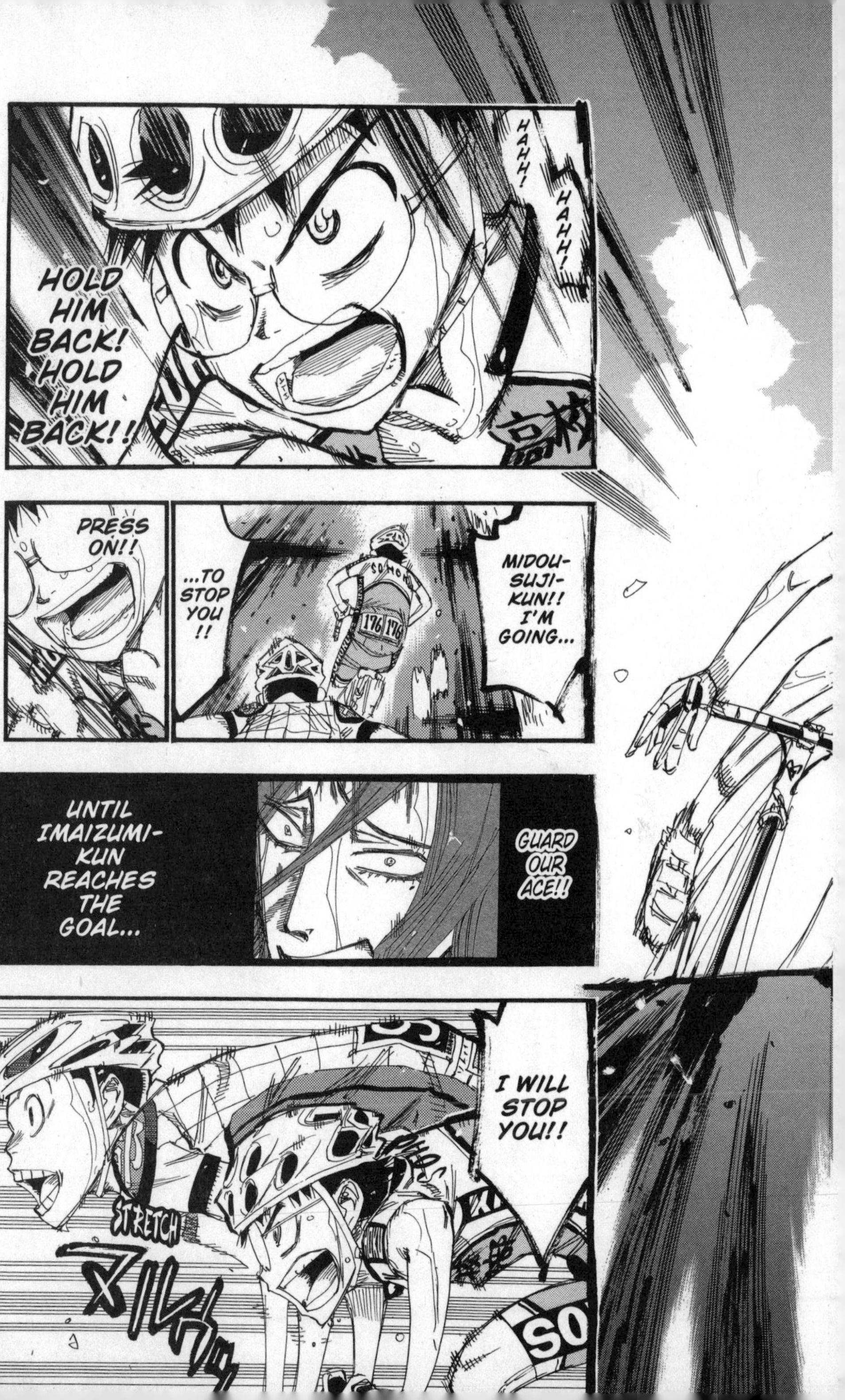
HAHH! HAHH!
HOLD HIM BACK! HOLD HIM BACK!!
MIDOU-SUJI-KUN!! I'M GOING...
...TO STOP YOU!!
PRESS ON!!
GUARD OUR ACE!!
UNTIL IMAIZUMI-KUN REACHES THE GOAL...
I WILL STOP YOU!!
STRETCH

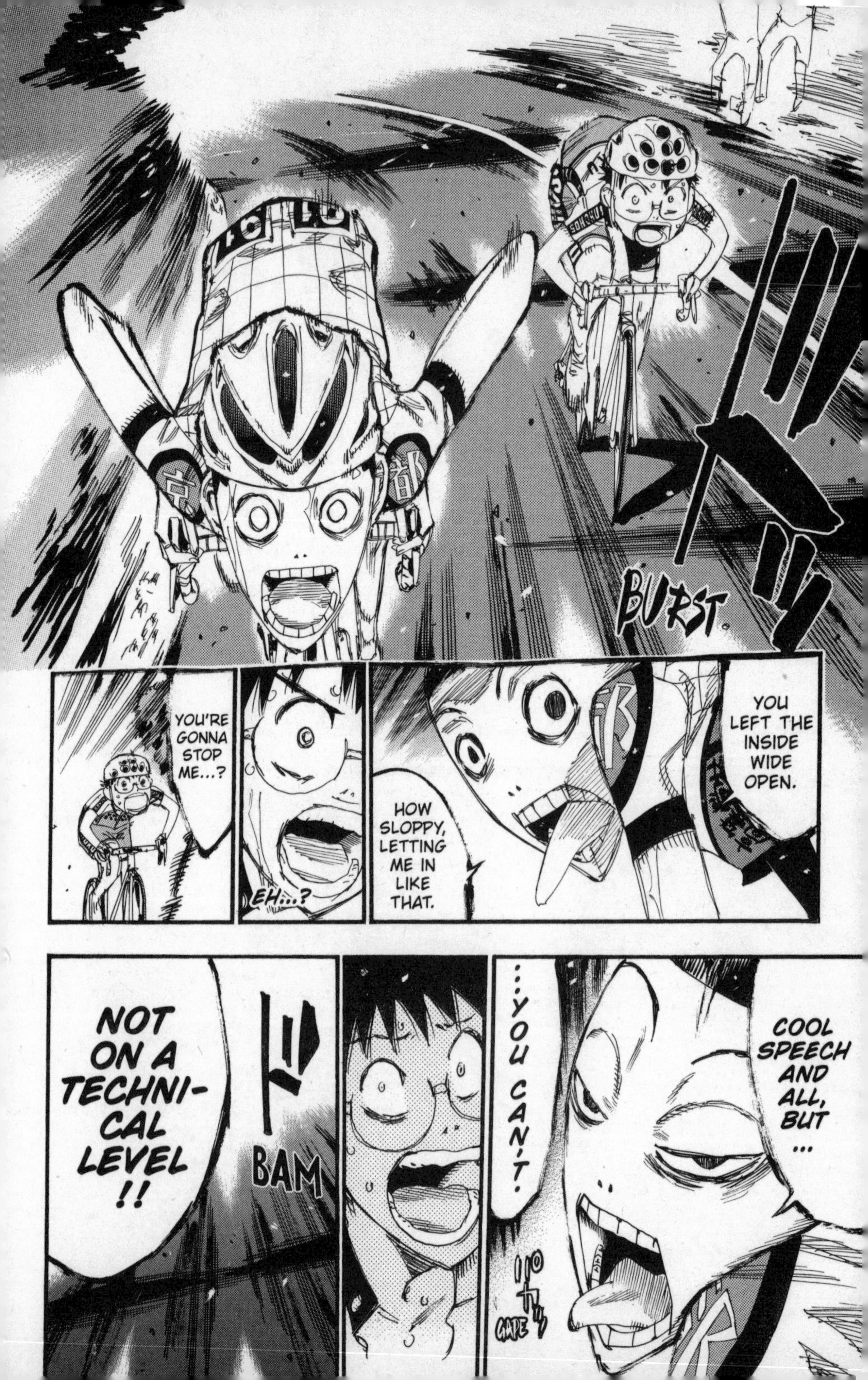
BURST
YOU LEFT THE INSIDE WIDE OPEN.
HOW SLOPPY, LETTING ME IN LIKE THAT.
EH...?
YOU'RE GONNA STOP ME...?
COOL SPEECH AND ALL, BUT ...
...YOU CAN'T.
GAPE
BAM
NOT ON A TECHNI-CAL LEVEL!!

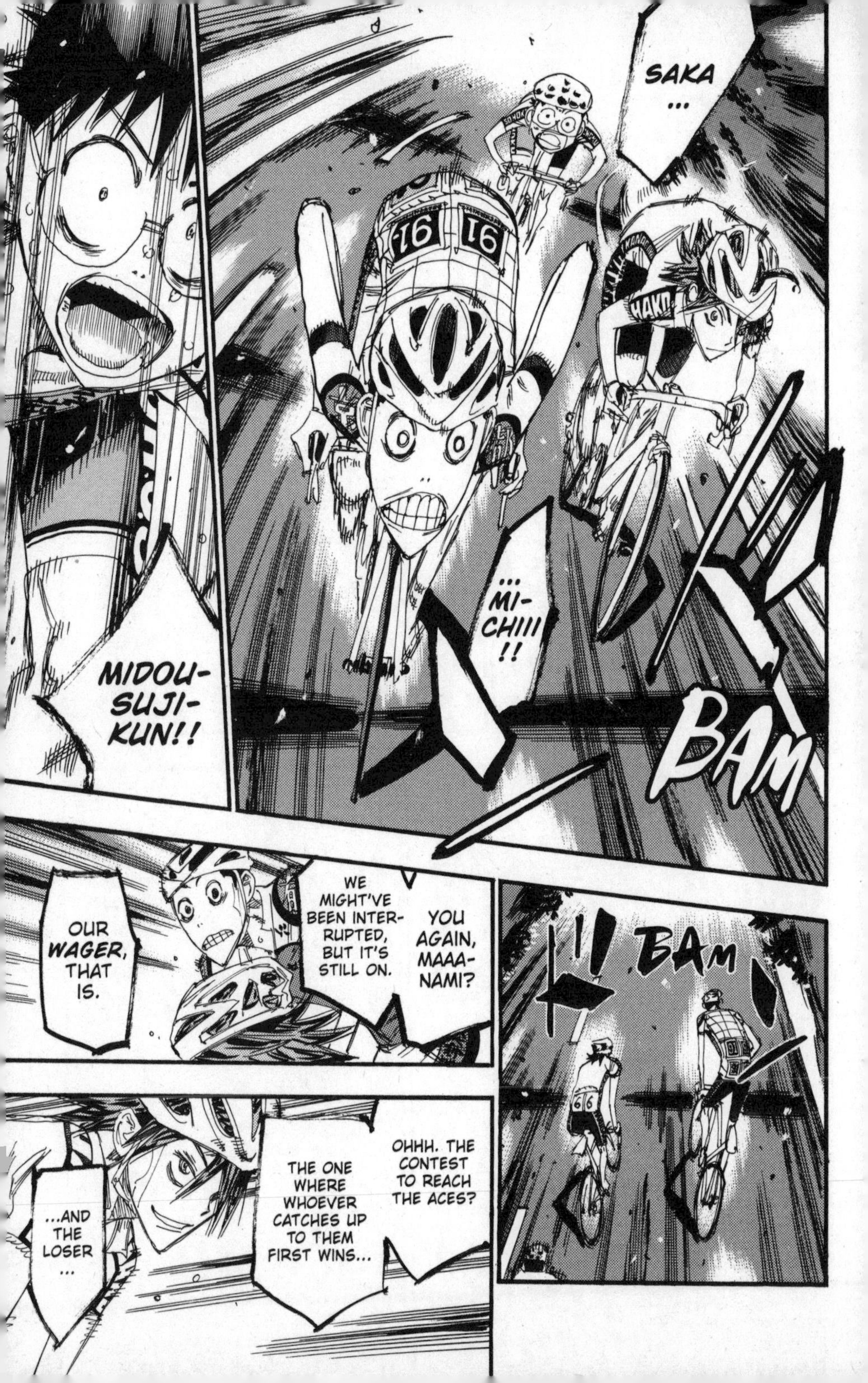
SAKA...
...MI-CHIIII!!
BAM
MIDOU-SUJI-KUN!!
!!
BAM
YOU AGAIN, MAAA-NAMI?
WE MIGHT'VE BEEN INTER-RUPTED, BUT IT'S STILL ON.
OUR WAGER, THAT IS.
OHHH. THE CONTEST TO REACH THE ACES?
THE ONE WHERE WHOEVER CATCHES UP TO THEM FIRST WINS...
...AND THE LOSER...

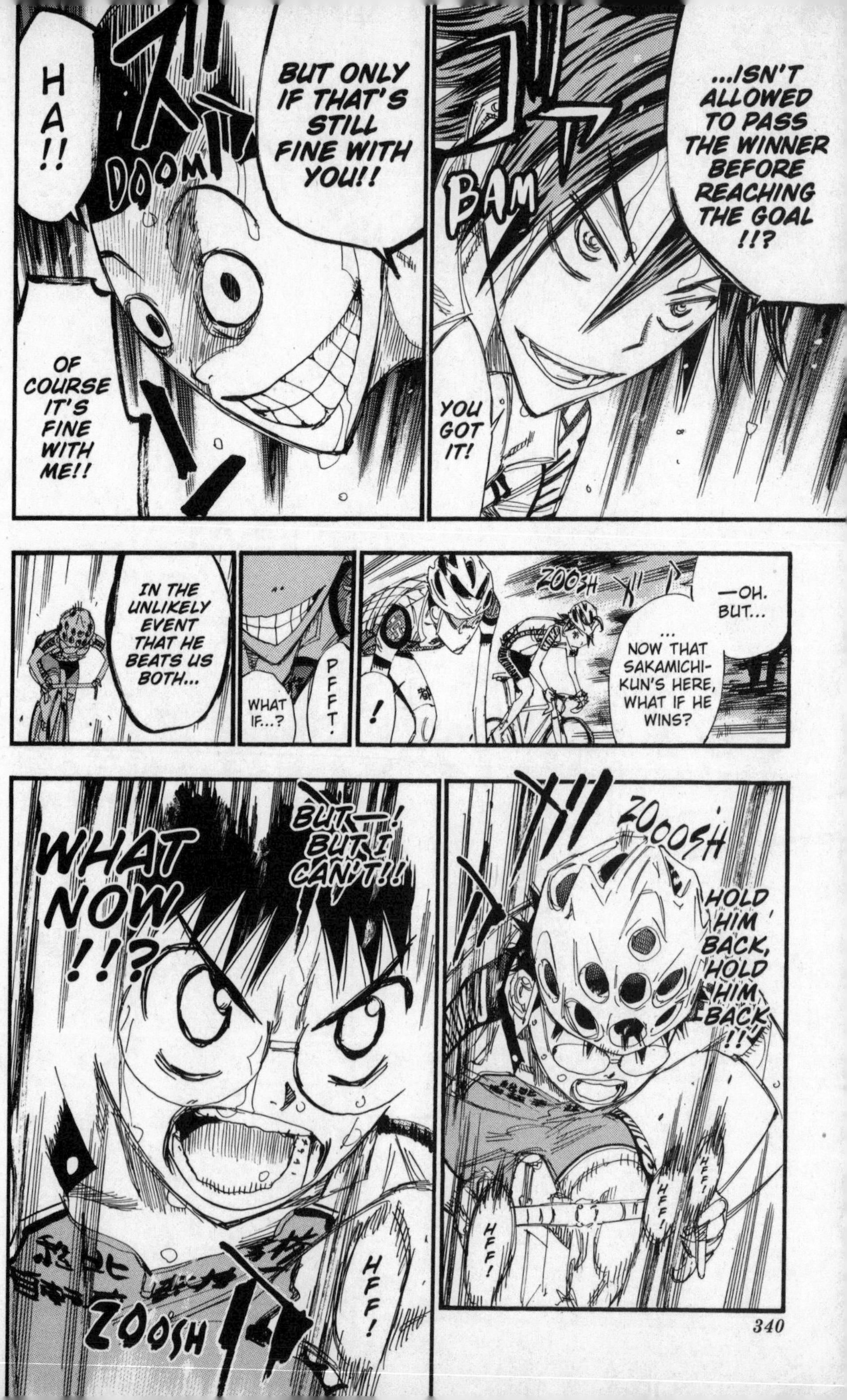
...ISN'T ALLOWED TO PASS THE WINNER BEFORE REACHING THE GOAL!!?
BAM
YOU GOT IT!
BUT ONLY IF THAT'S STILL FINE WITH YOU!!
HA!!
DOOM
OF COURSE IT'S FINE WITH ME!!
—OH. BUT...
...NOW THAT SAKAMICHI-KUN'S HERE, WHAT IF HE WINS?
ZOOSH
!
PFFT
WHAT IF...?
IN THE UNLIKELY EVENT THAT HE BEATS US BOTH...
ZOOOSH
HOLD HIM BACK, HOLD HIM BACK!!
HFF!
HFF!
HFF!
BUT—! BUT I CAN'T!!
WHAT NOW!!?
HFF!
ZOOSH

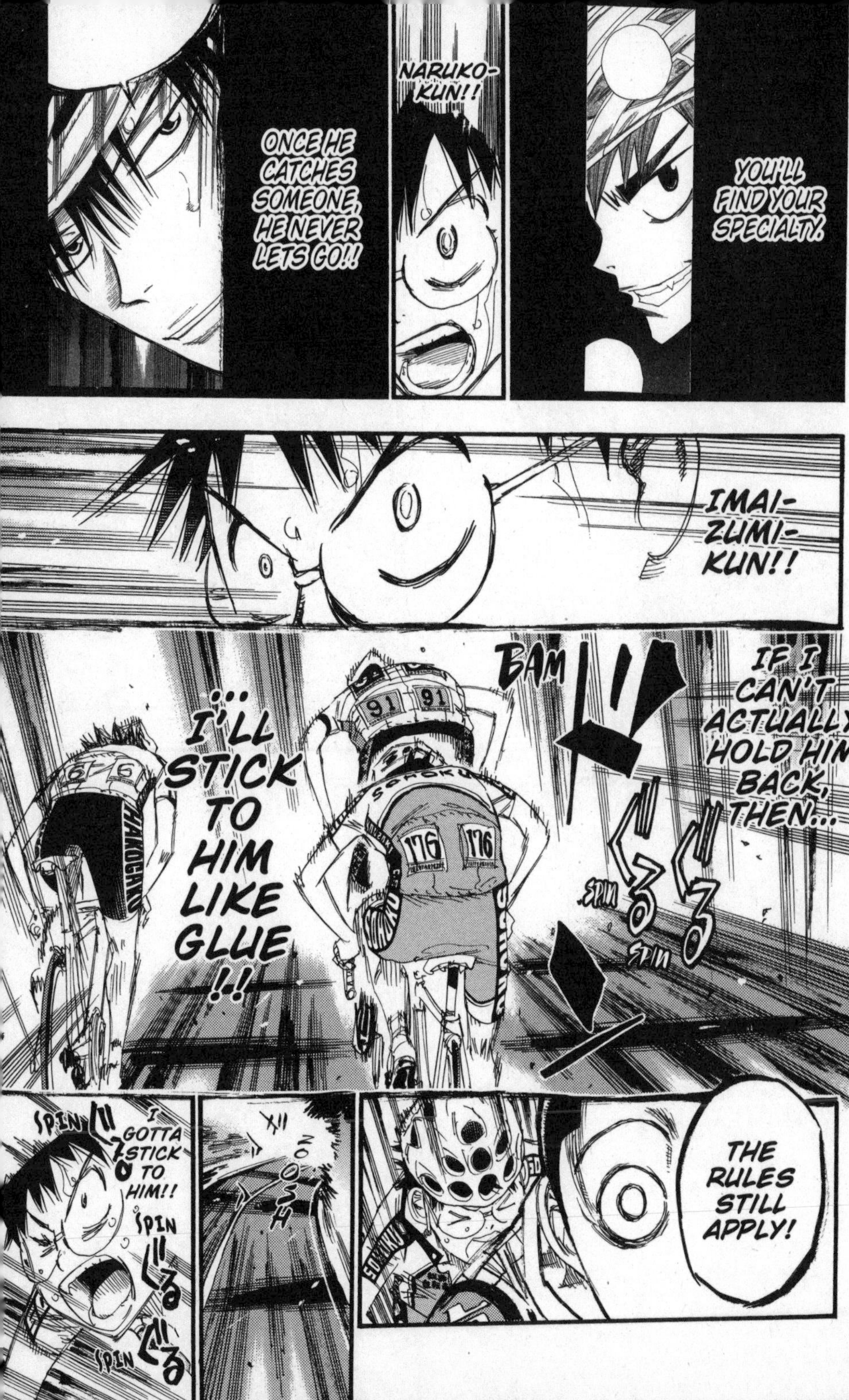
YOU'LL FIND YOUR SPECIALTY.
NARUKO-KUN!!
ONCE HE CATCHES SOMEONE, HE NEVER LETS GO!!
IMAI-ZUMI-KUN!!
IF I CAN'T ACTUALLY HOLD HIM BACK, THEN...
BAM
SPIN
SPIN
...I'LL STICK TO HIM LIKE GLUE!!
THE RULES STILL APPLY!
WHOOSH
SPIN
I GOTTA STICK TO HIM!!
SPIN
SPIN

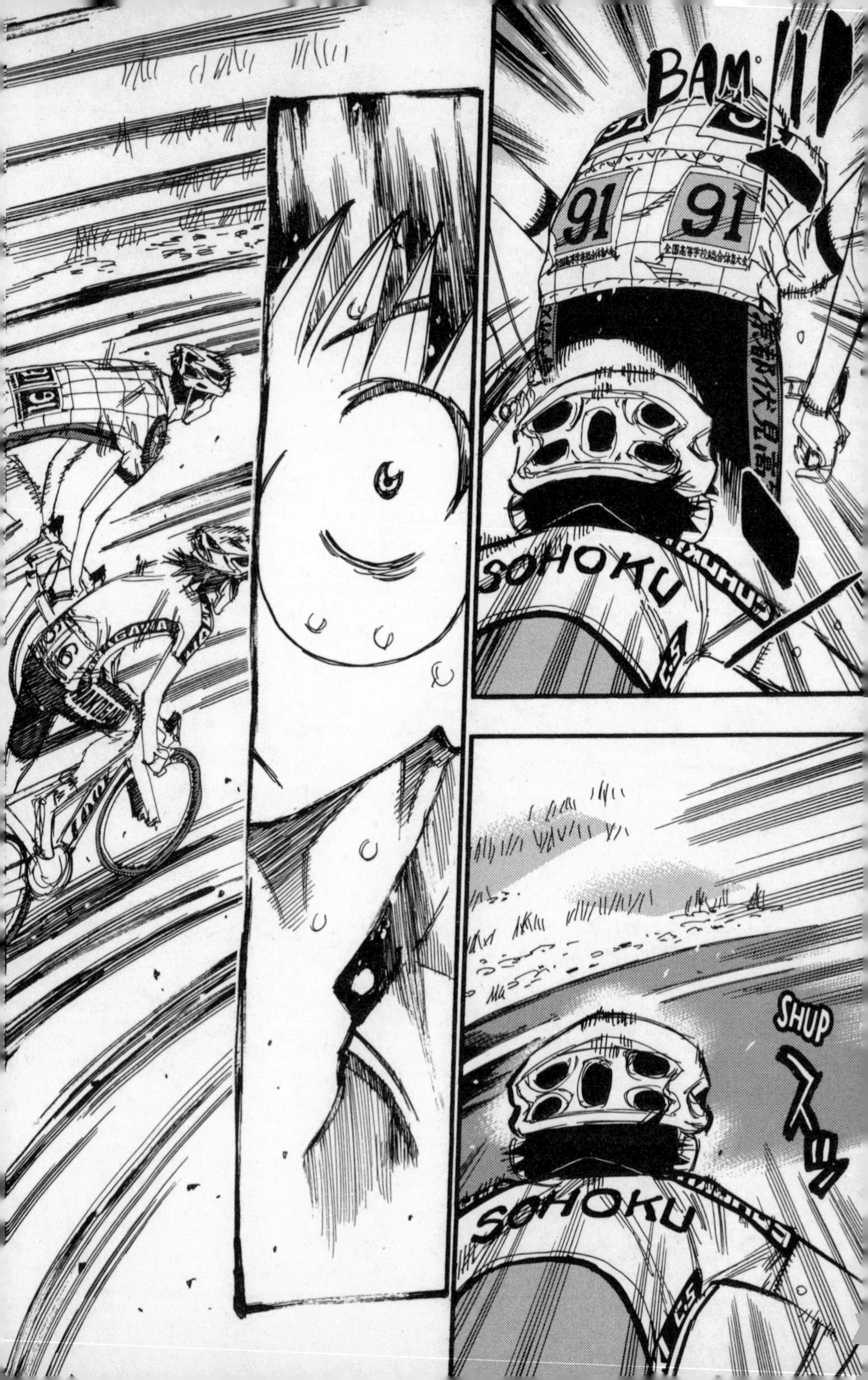
BAM!!
SHUP

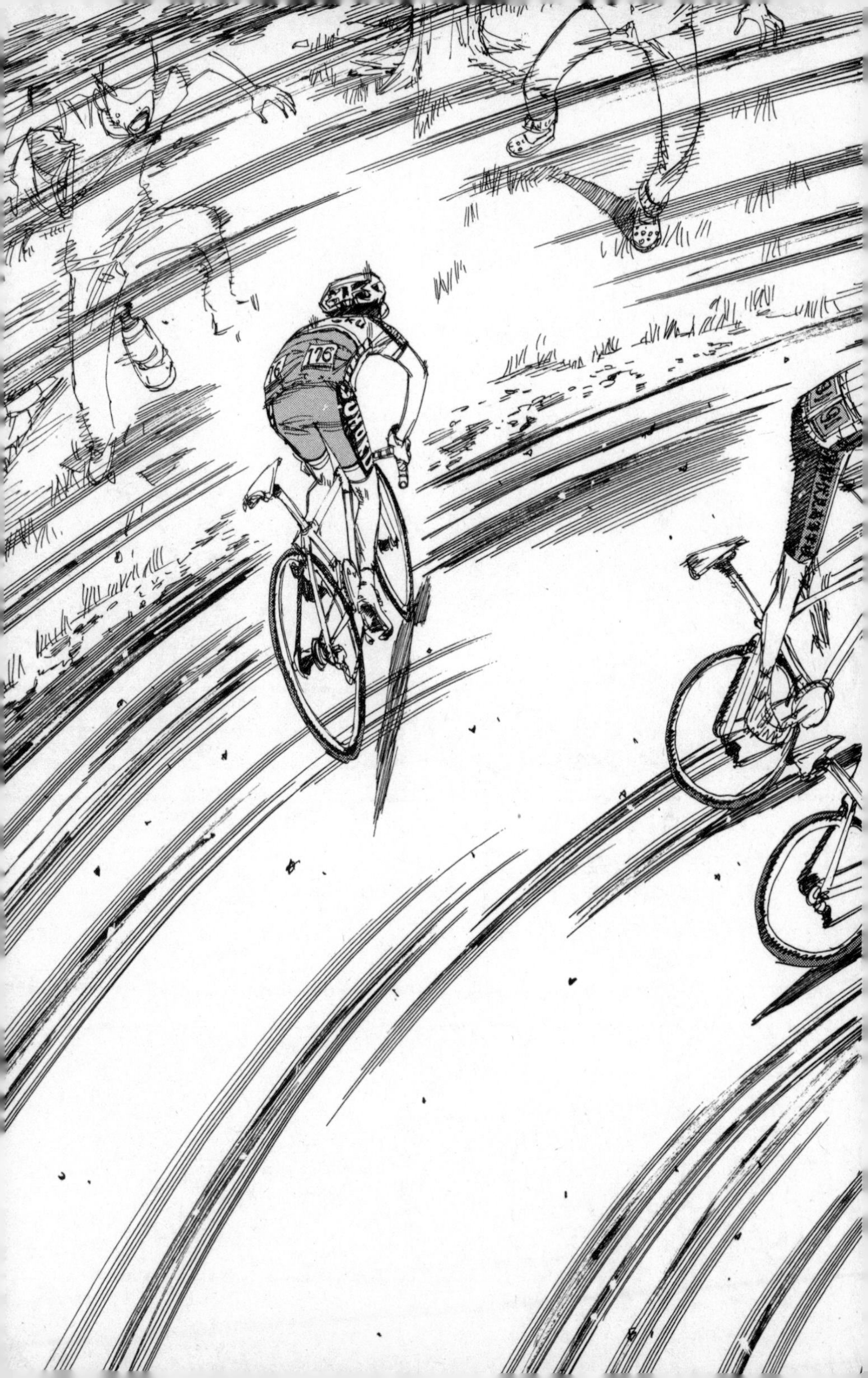
176

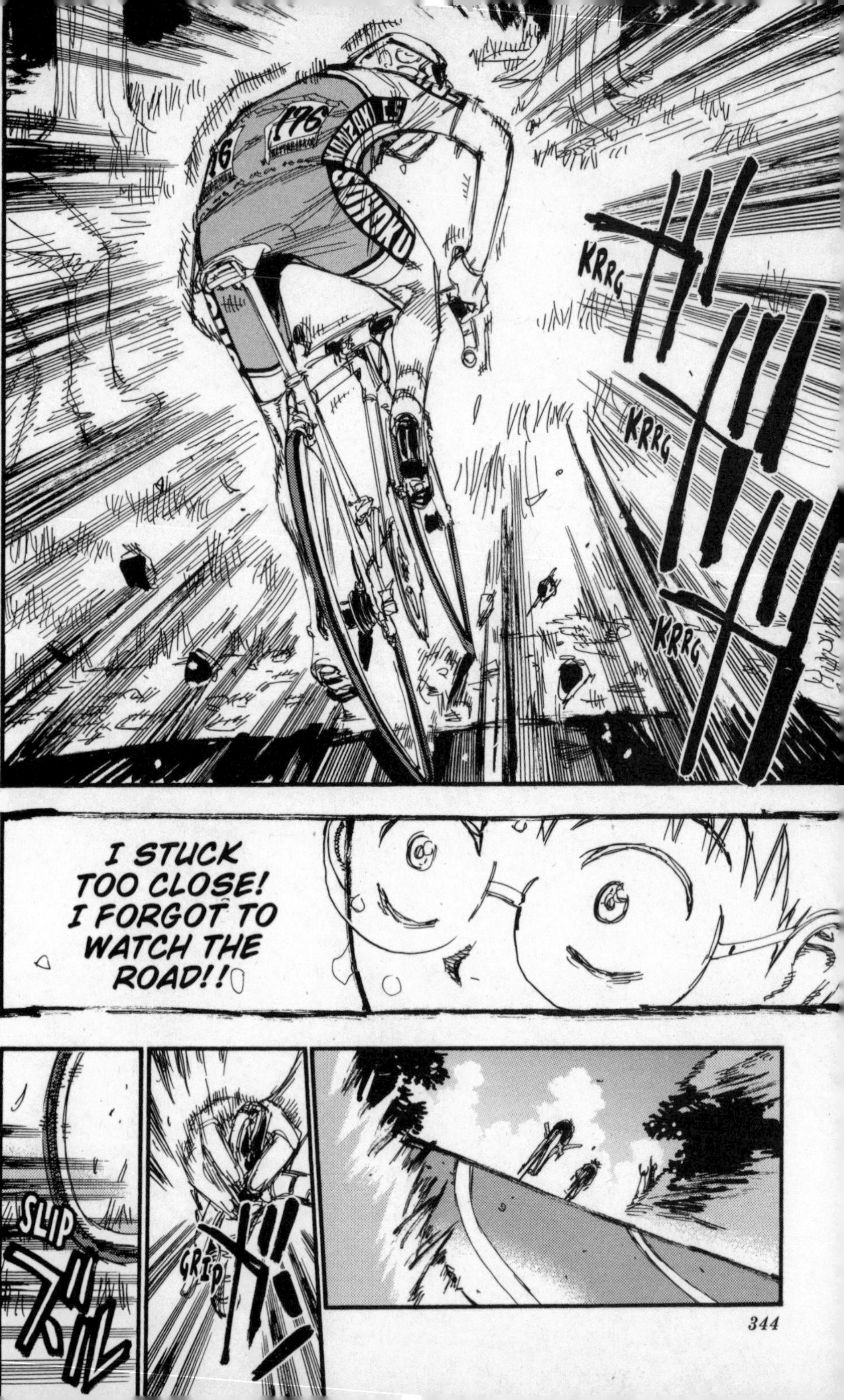
KRRG
KRRG
KRRG
I STUCK TOO CLOSE! I FORGOT TO WATCH THE ROAD!!
GRIP
SLIP

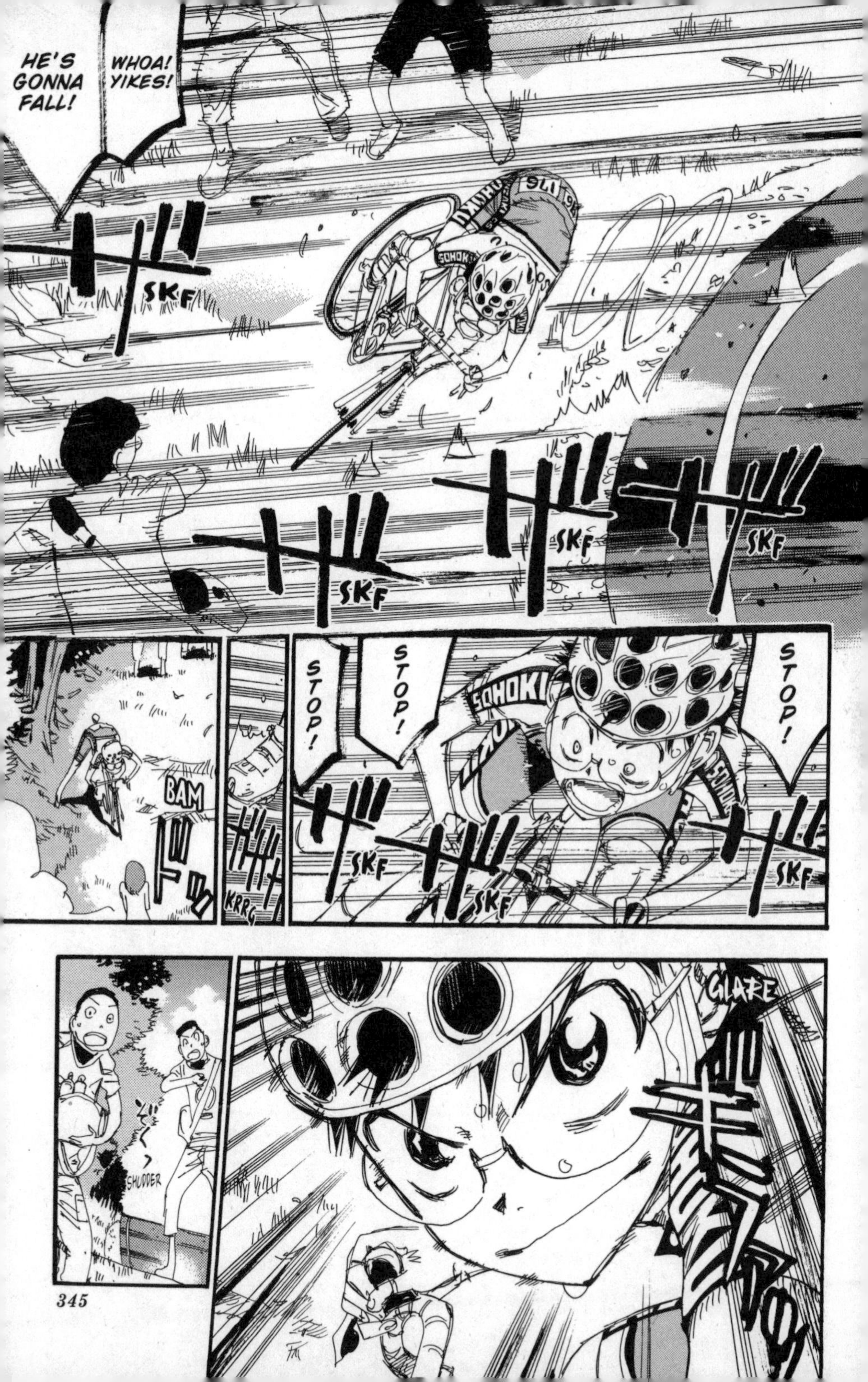
WHOA! YIKES!
HE'S GONNA FALL!
SKF
SKF
SKF
SKF
STOP!
STOP!
SKF
SKF
SKF
STOP!
KRRG
BAM
GLARE
SHUDDER

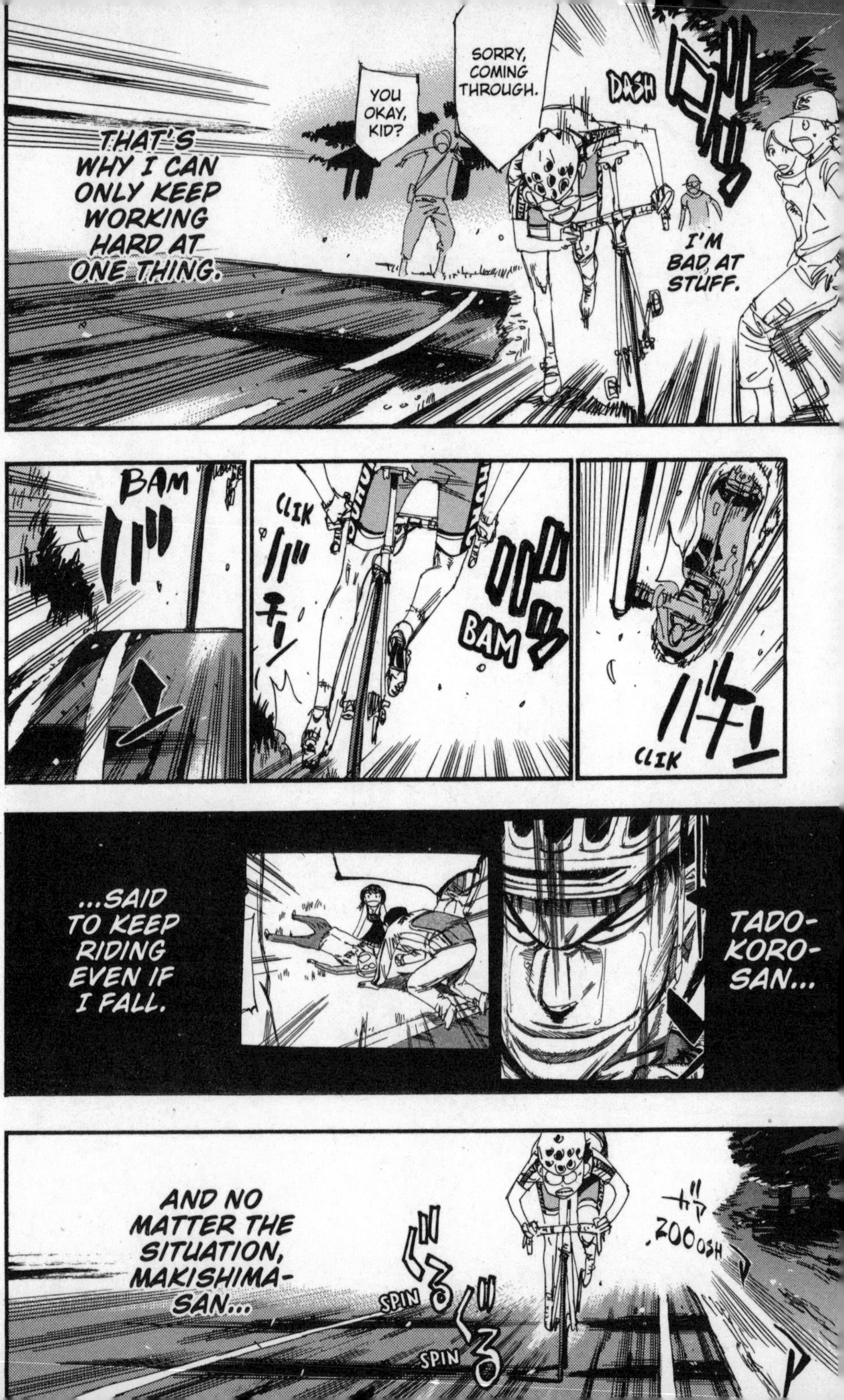
DASH
I'M BAD AT STUFF.
SORRY, COMING THROUGH.
YOU OKAY, KID?
THAT'S WHY I CAN ONLY KEEP WORKING HARD AT ONE THING.
CLIK
BAM
CLIK
BAM
TADO-KORO-SAN...
...SAID TO KEEP RIDING EVEN IF I FALL.
ZOOOSH
AND NO MATTER THE SITUATION, MAKISHIMA-SAN...
SPIN
SPIN

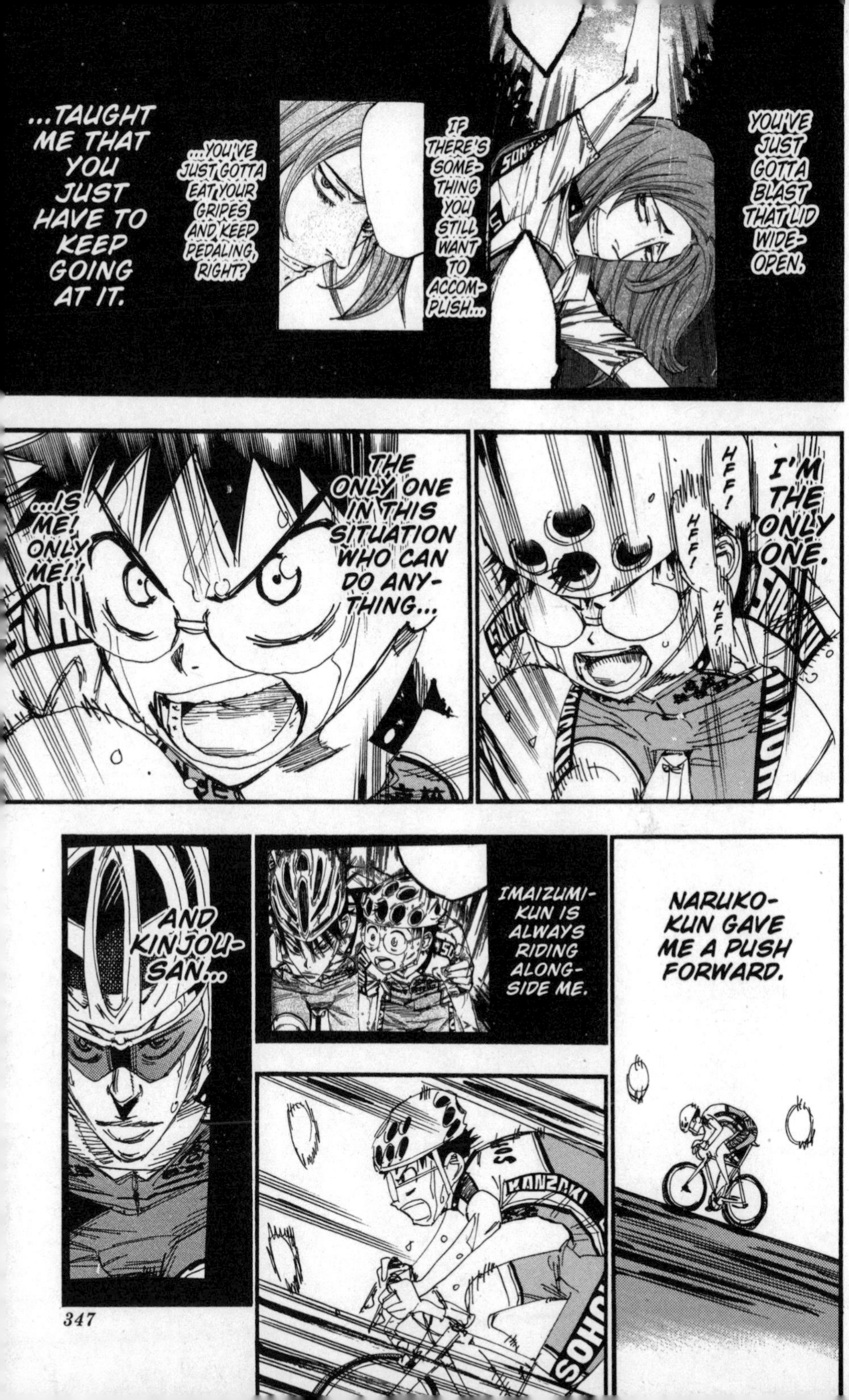
YOU'VE JUST GOTTA BLAST THAT LID WIDE-OPEN.
IF THERE'S SOME-THING YOU STILL WANT TO ACCOM-PLISH...
...YOU'VE JUST GOTTA EAT YOUR GRIPES AND KEEP PEDALING, RIGHT?
...TAUGHT ME THAT YOU JUST HAVE TO KEEP GOING AT IT.
I'M THE ONLY ONE.
HFF! HFF! HFF!
THE ONLY ONE IN THIS SITUATION WHO CAN DO ANY-THING...
...IS ME! ONLY ME!!
NARUKO-KUN GAVE ME A PUSH FORWARD.
IMAIZUMI-KUN IS ALWAYS RIDING ALONG-SIDE ME.
AND KINJOU-SAN...

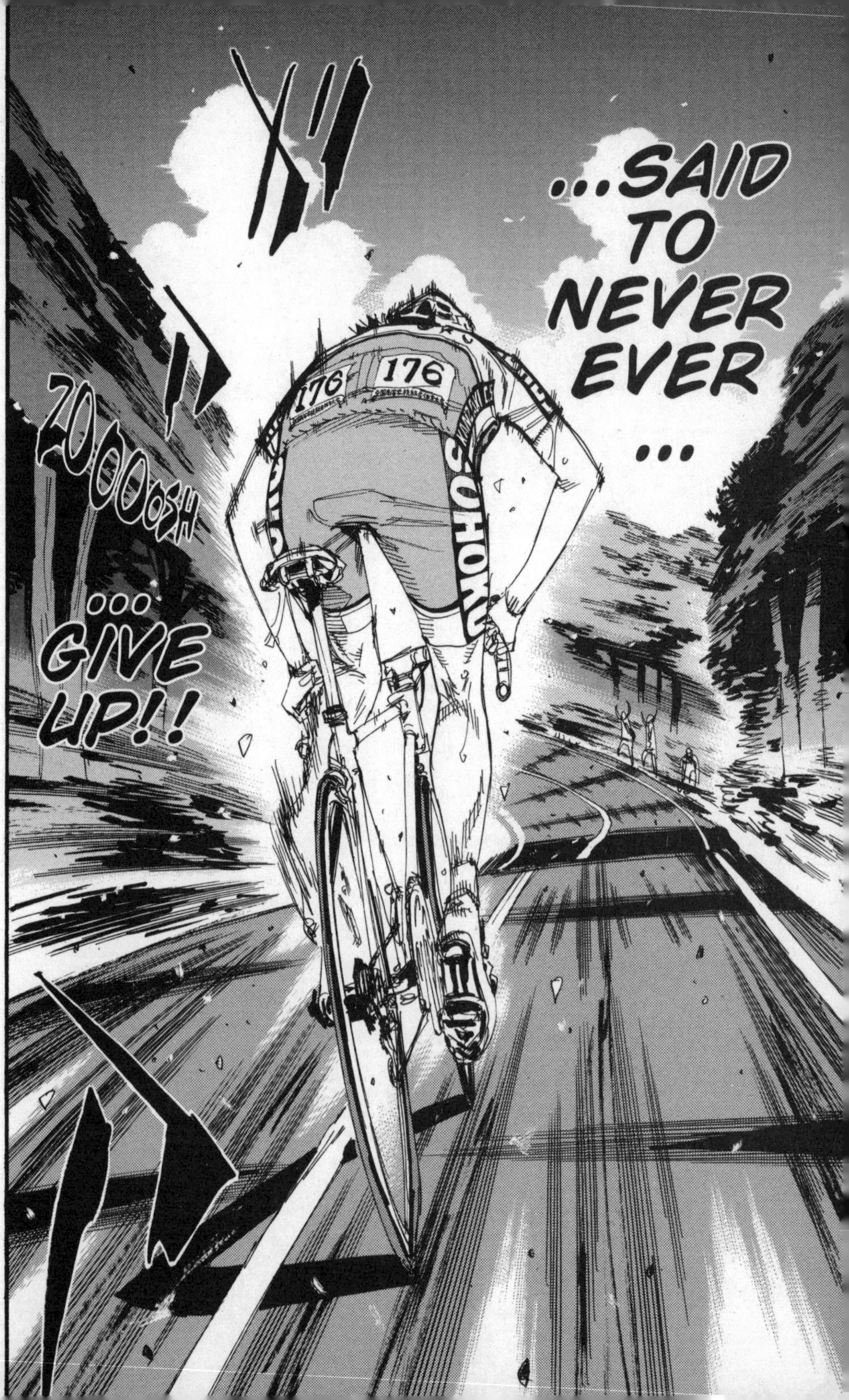
...SAID TO NEVER EVER ...
ZOOOOSH
...GIVE UP!!

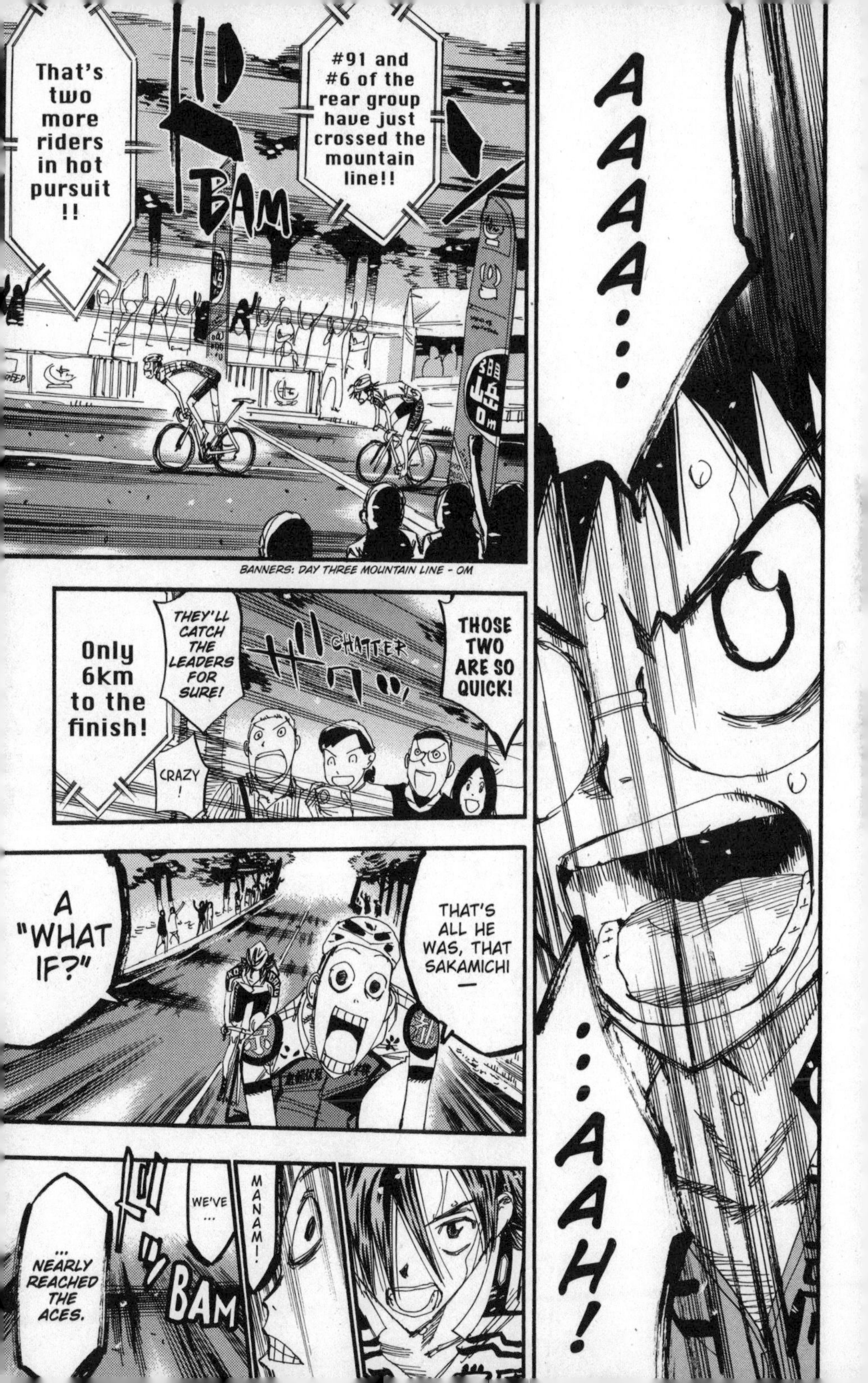
AAAA... ...AAAH!
#91 and #6 of the rear group have just crossed the mountain line!!
BAM
That's two more riders in hot pursuit!!
BANNERS: DAY THREE MOUNTAIN LINE - OM
THOSE TWO ARE SO QUICK!
CHATTER
THEY'LL CATCH THE LEADERS FOR SURE!
Only 6km to the finish!
CRAZY!
THAT'S ALL HE WAS, THAT SAKAMICHI —
A "WHAT IF?"
MANAMI!
WE'VE...
BAM
...NEARLY REACHED THE ACES.

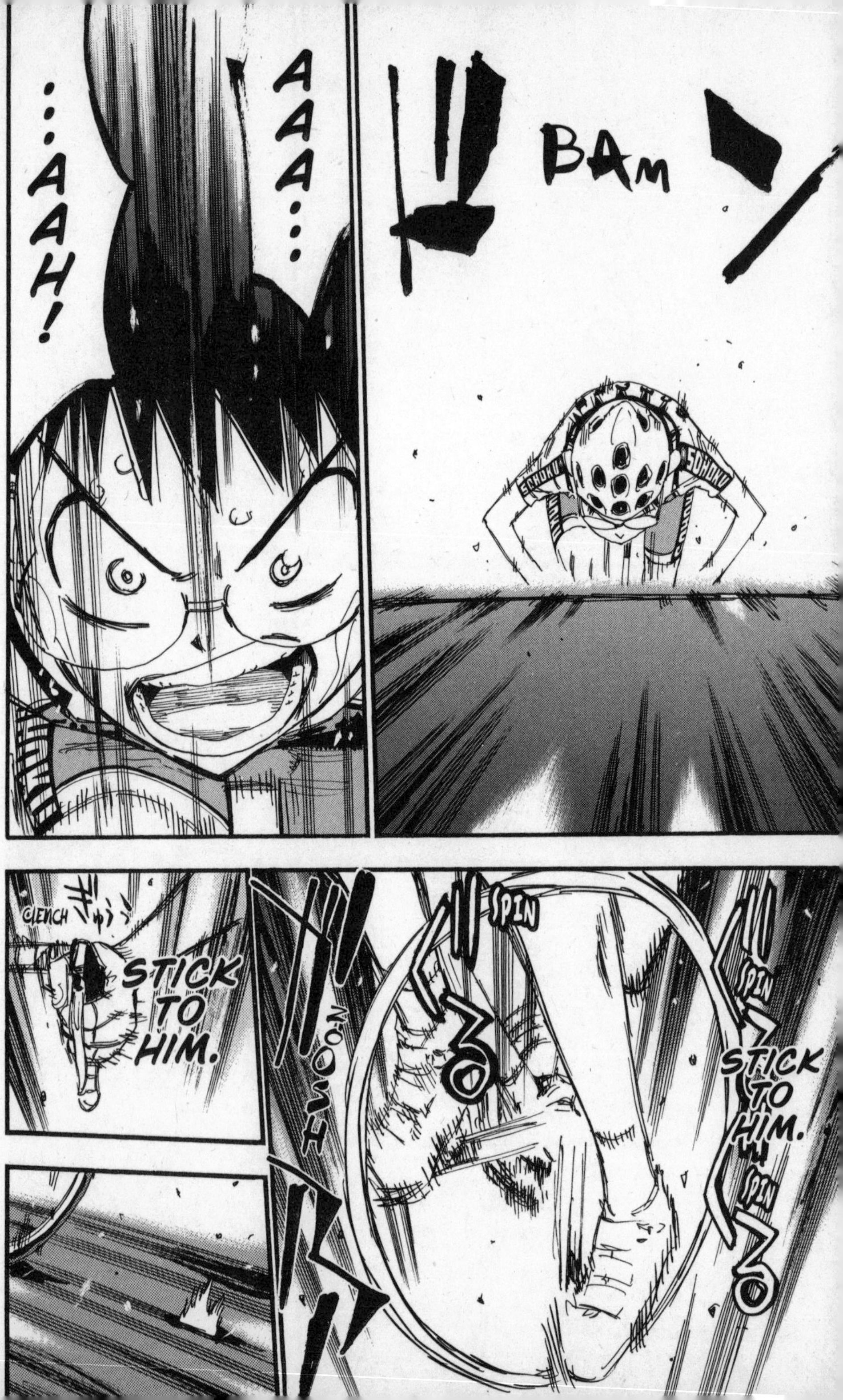
BAM
AAAA...
...AAAH!
SPIN
STICK TO HIM.
SPIN
SPIN
WHOOSH
CLENCH
STICK TO HIM.

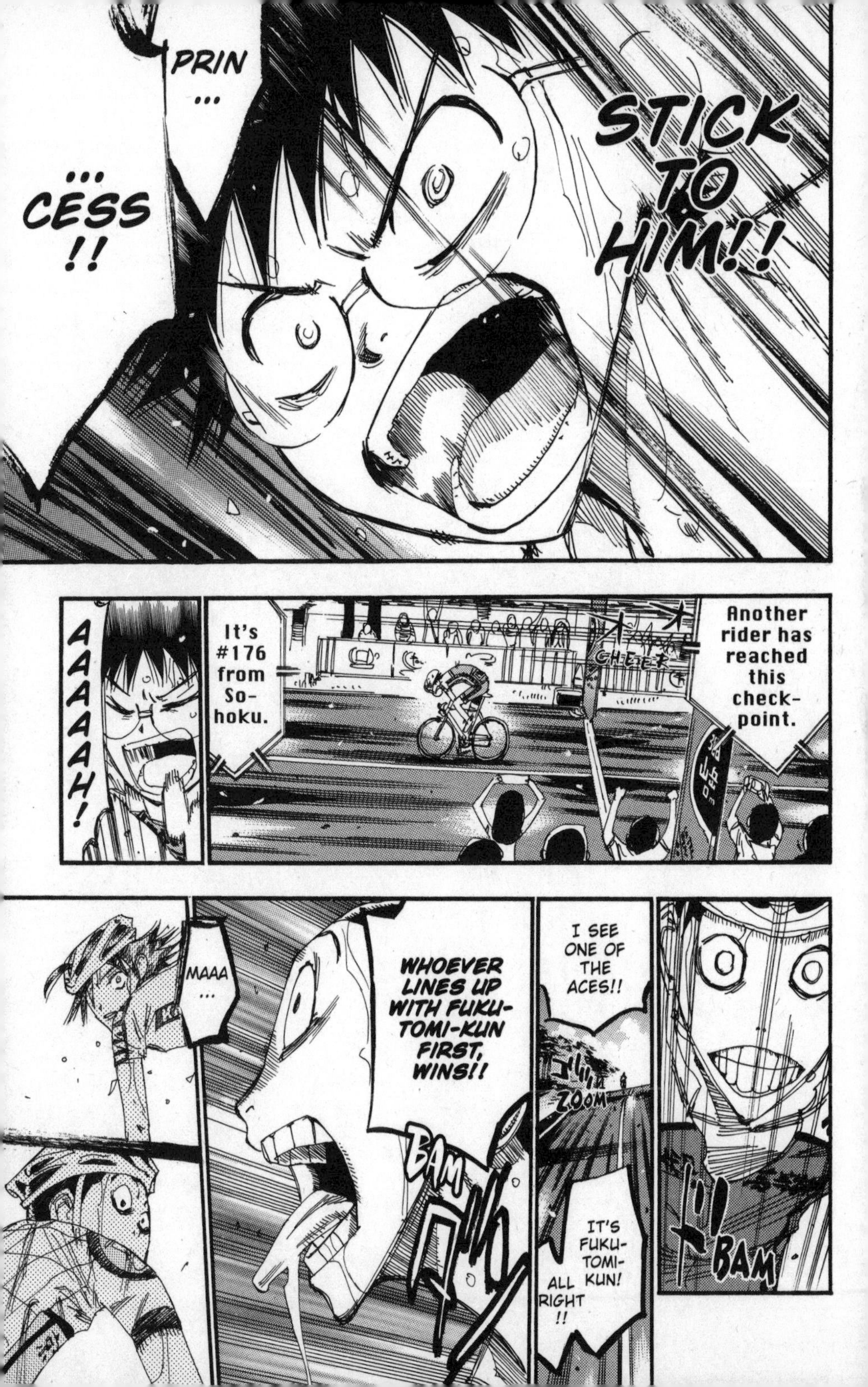
STICK TO HIM!!
PRIN ...
... CESS !!
Another rider has reached this check-point.
CHEER
It's #176 from So-hoku.
AAAAAAH!
BAM
I SEE ONE OF THE ACES!!
ZOOM
IT'S FUKU-TOMI-KUN!
ALL RIGHT !!
WHOEVER LINES UP WITH FUKU-TOMI-KUN FIRST, WINS!!
BAM
MAAA ...

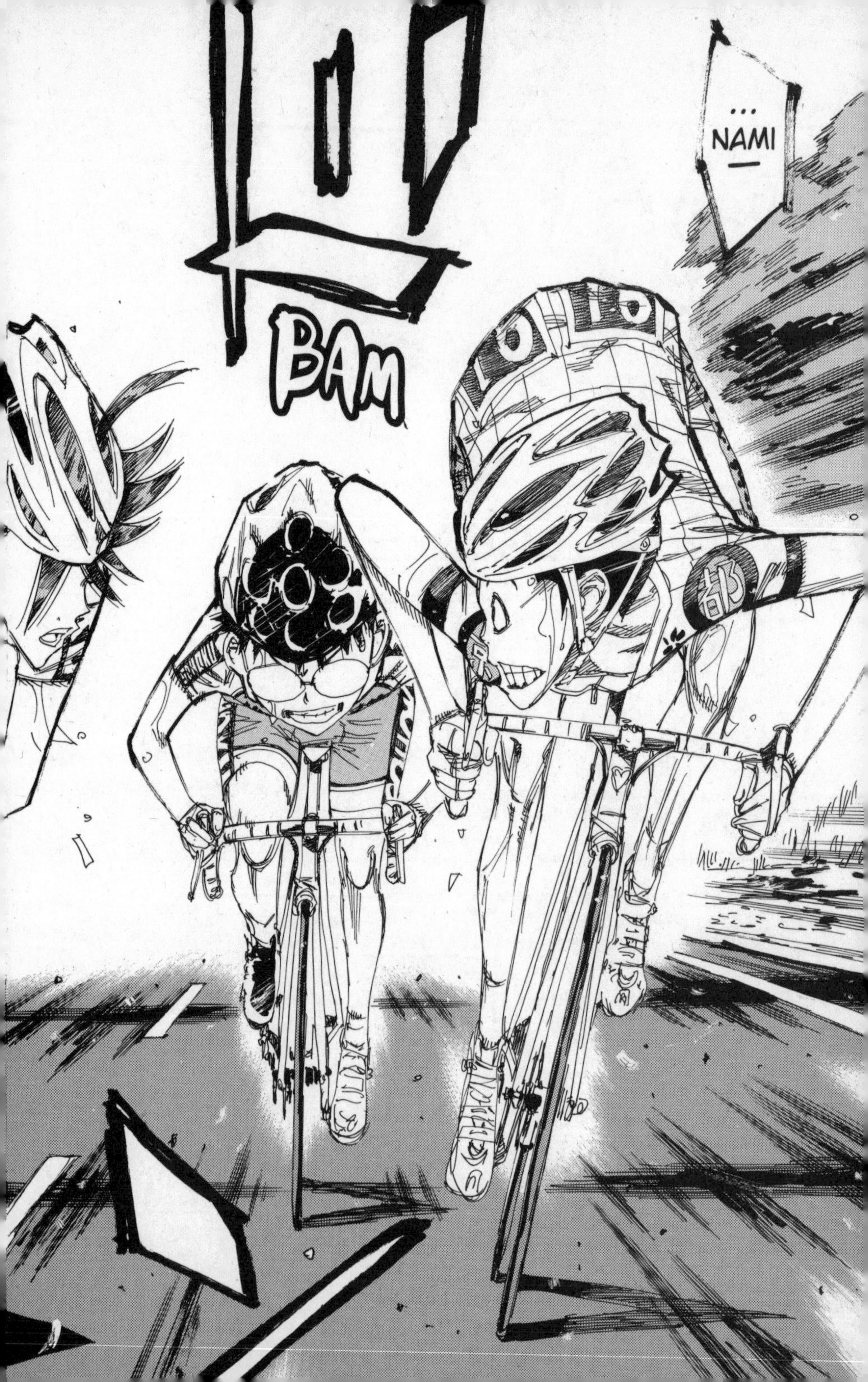
...NAMI—
BAM

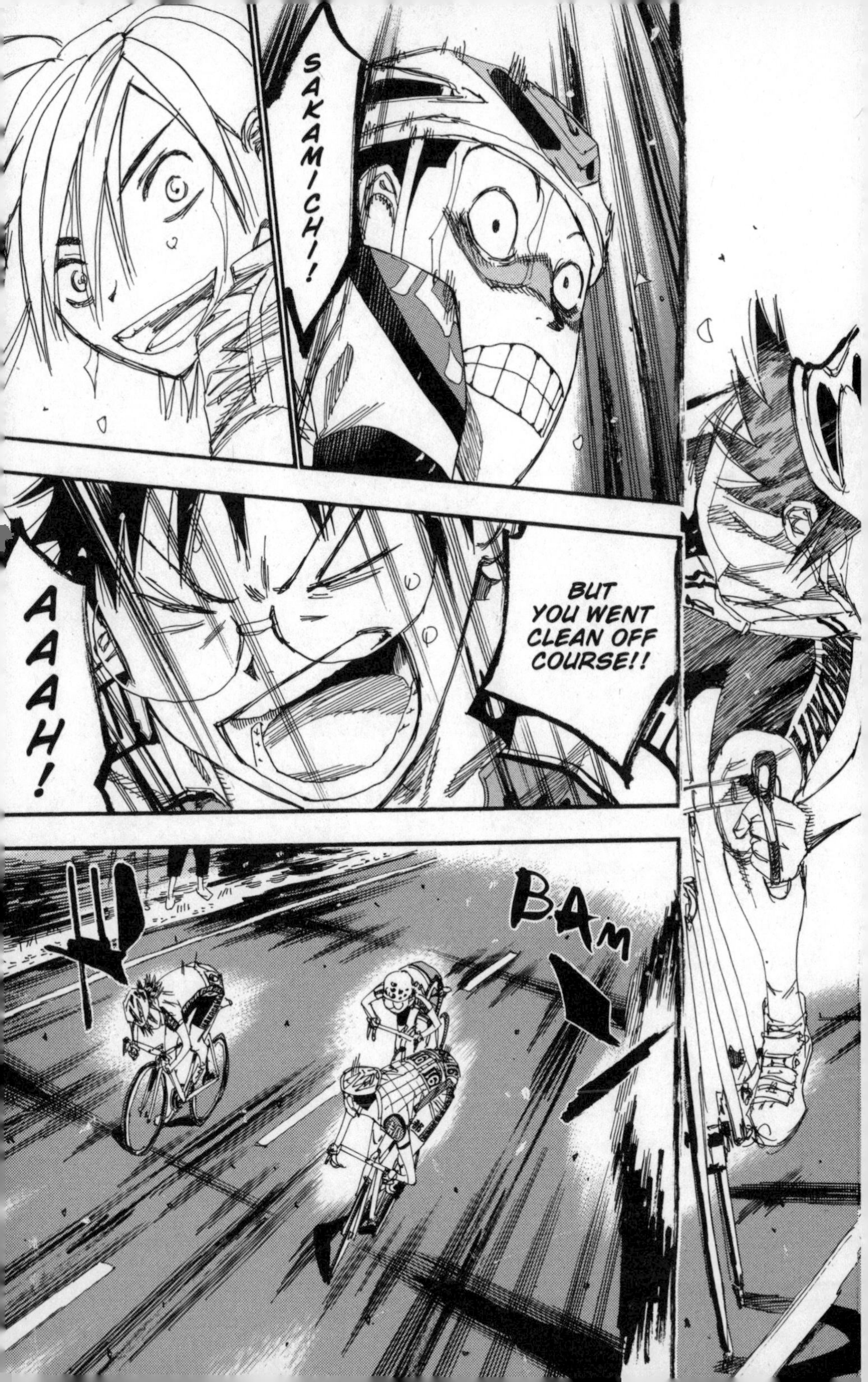
SAKAMICHI!!
BUT YOU WENT CLEAN OFF COURSE!!
AAAAH!
BAM

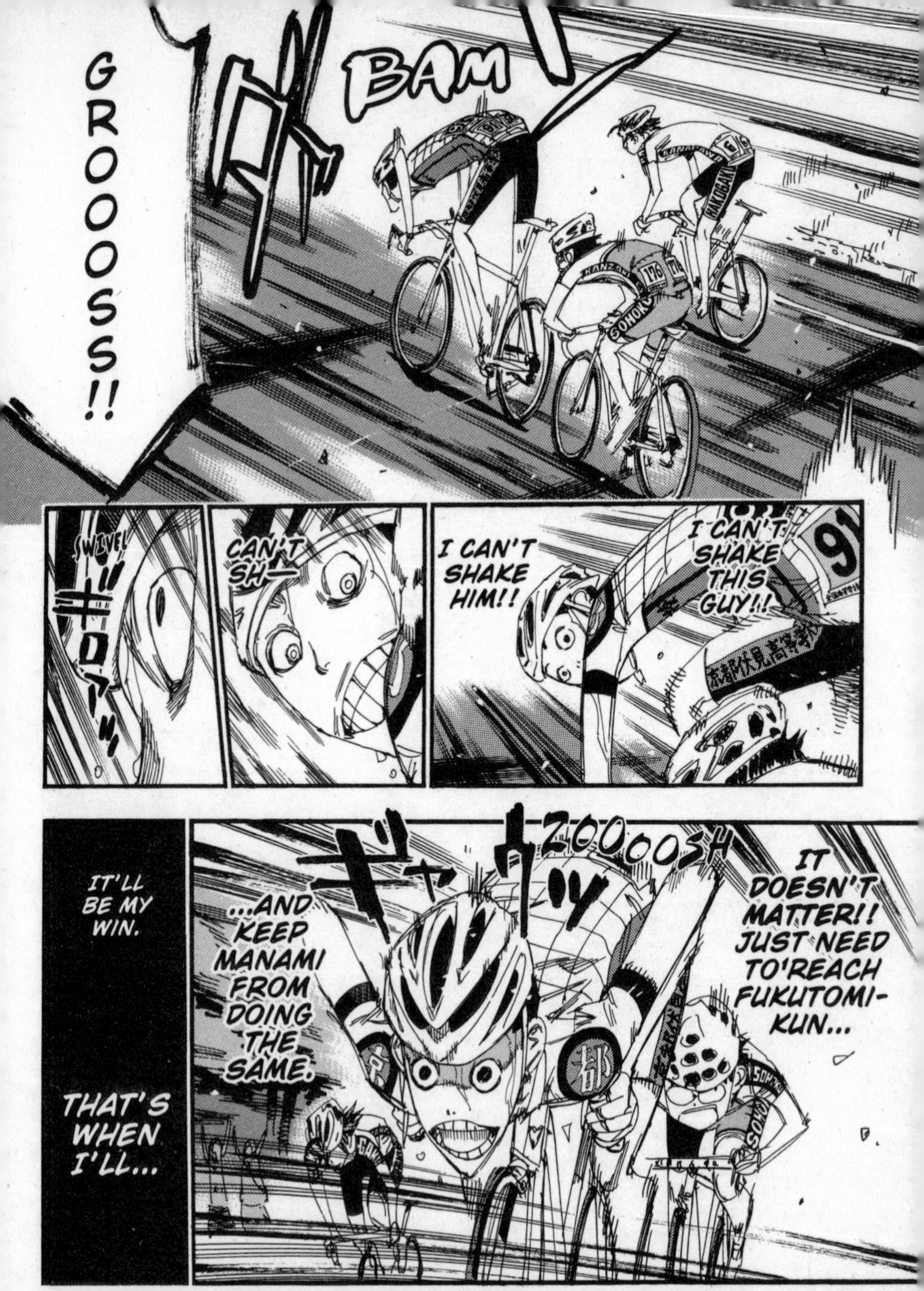
BAM
GROOOSS!!
I CAN'T SHAKE THIS GUY!!
I CAN'T SHAKE HIM!!
CAN'T SH—
SWIVEL
ZOOOOOSH
IT DOESN'T MATTER!! JUST NEED TO REACH FUKUTOMI-KUN...
...AND KEEP MANAMI FROM DOING THE SAME.
IT'LL BE MY WIN.
THAT'S WHEN I'LL...

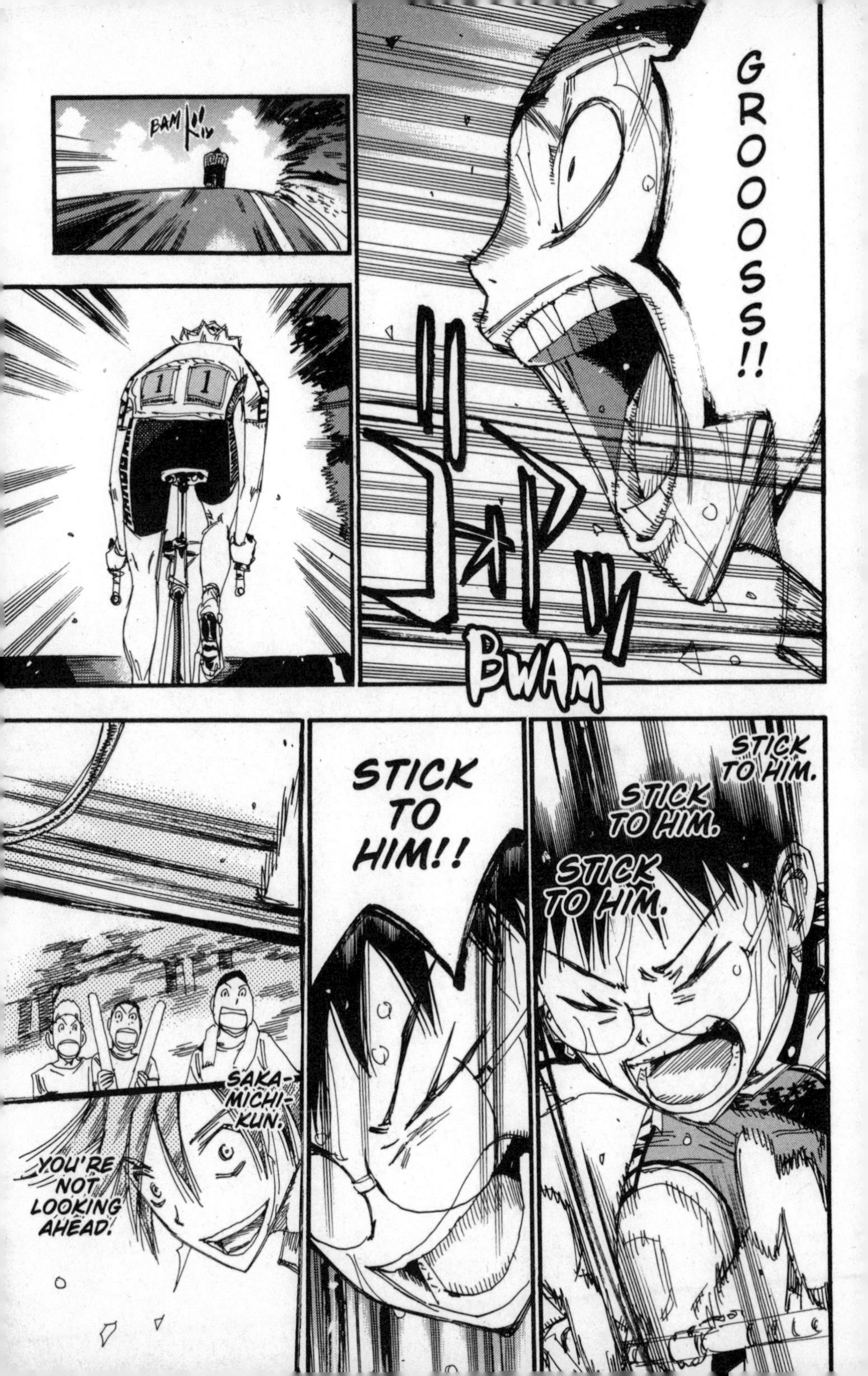
GROOOSS!!
BWAM
BAM
STICK TO HIM.
STICK TO HIM.
STICK TO HIM.
STICK TO HIM!!
SAKA-MICHI-KUN.
YOU'RE NOT LOOKING AHEAD.

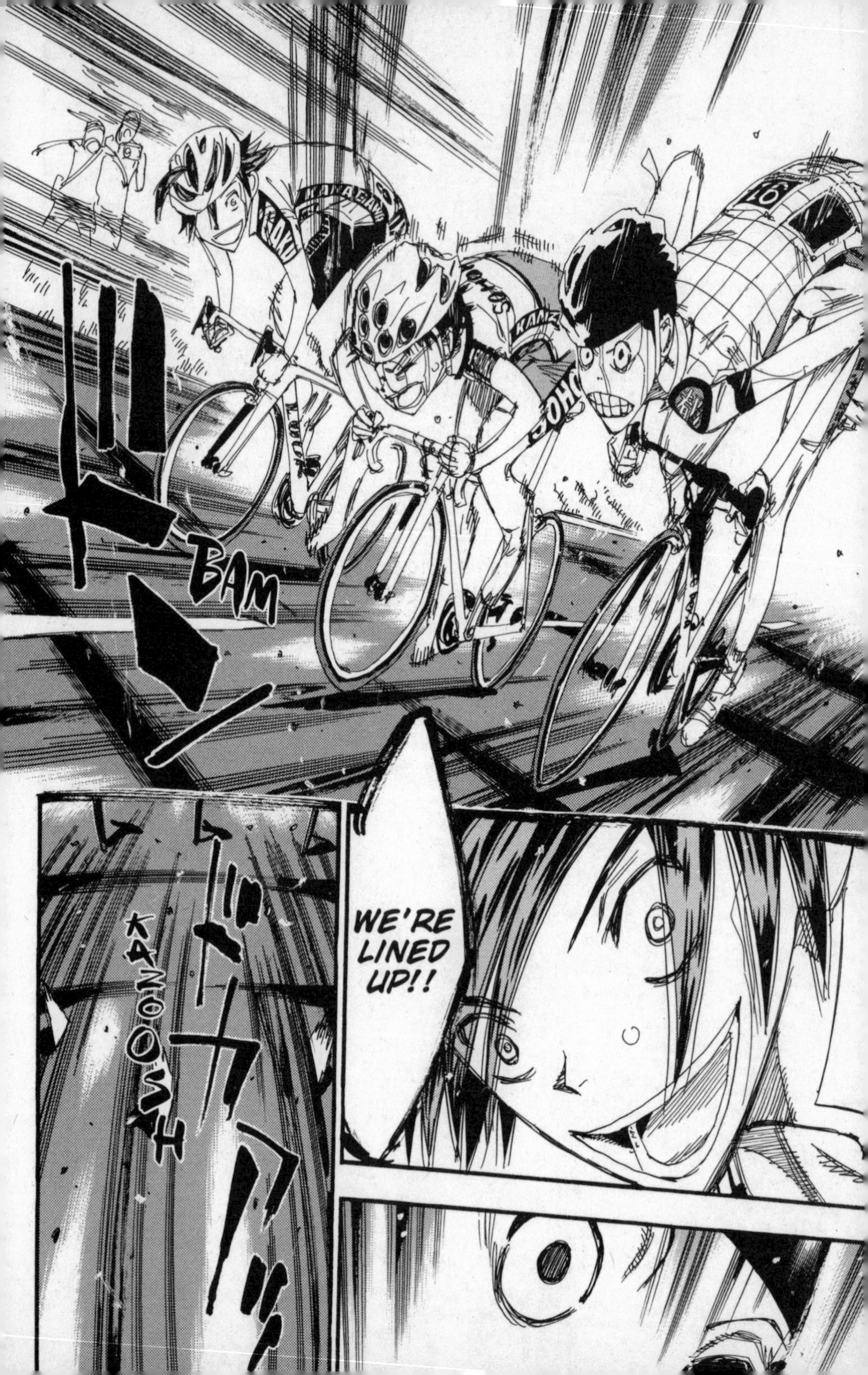
BAM
WE'RE LINED UP!!
KAZOOSH

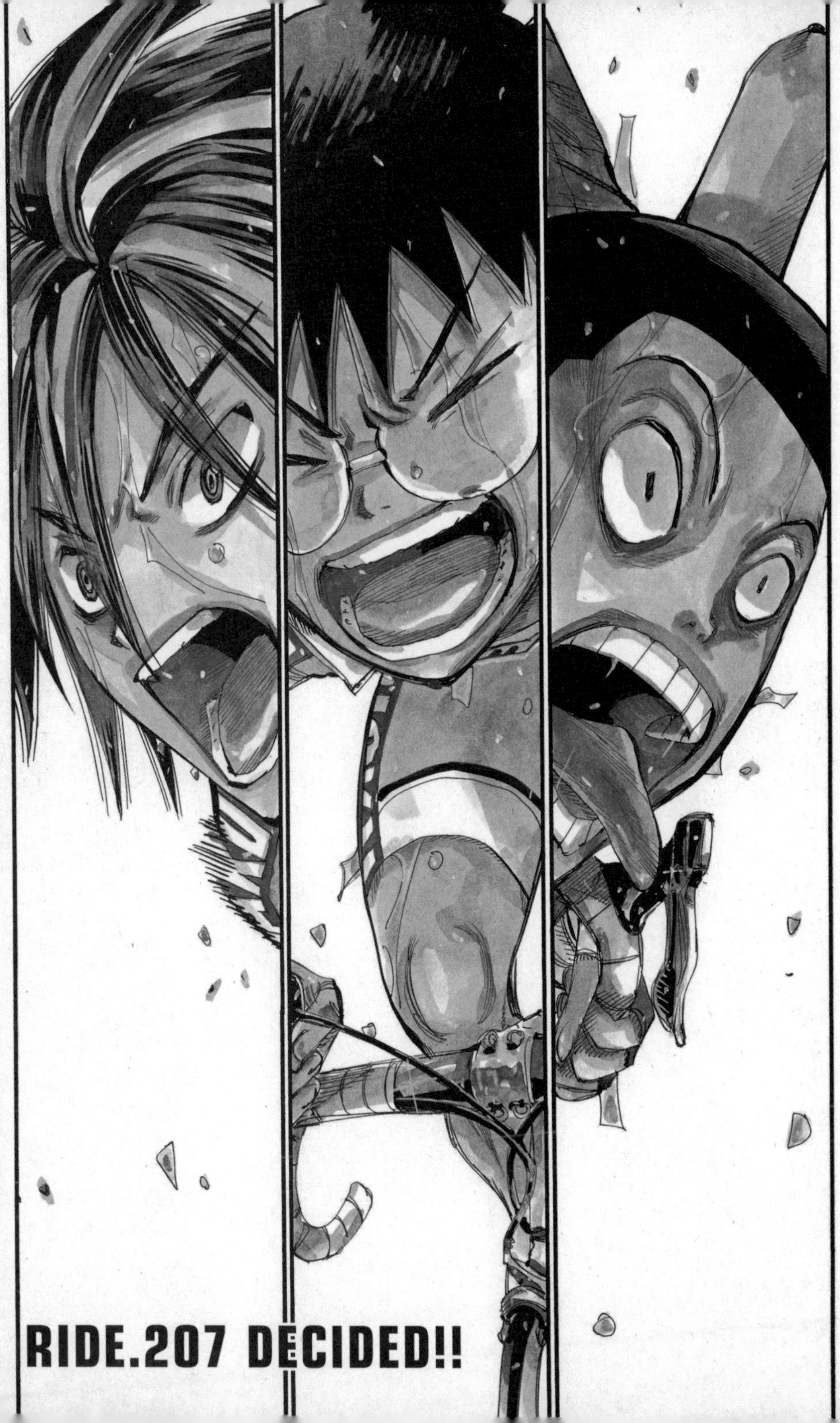

RIDE.207 DECIDED!!

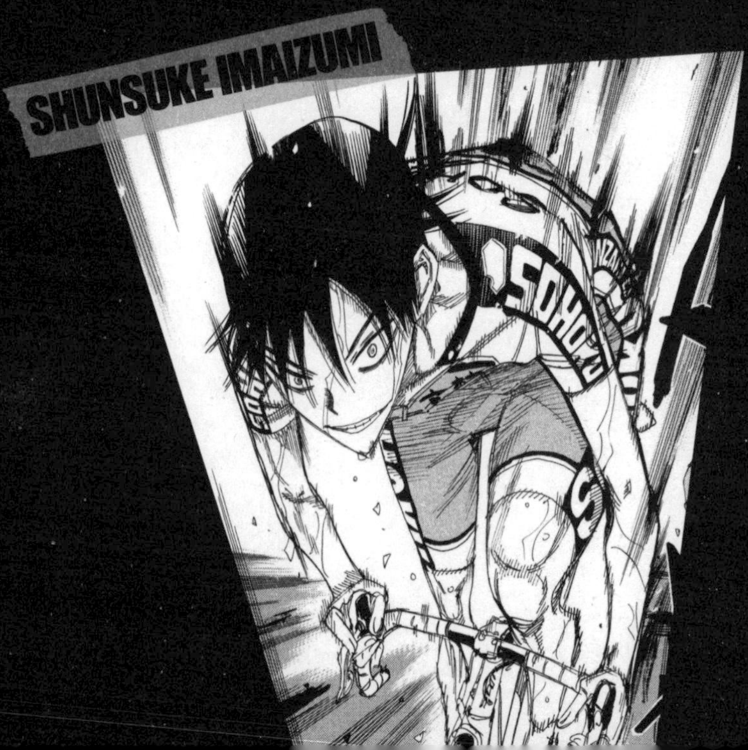
SHUNSUKE IMAIZUMI

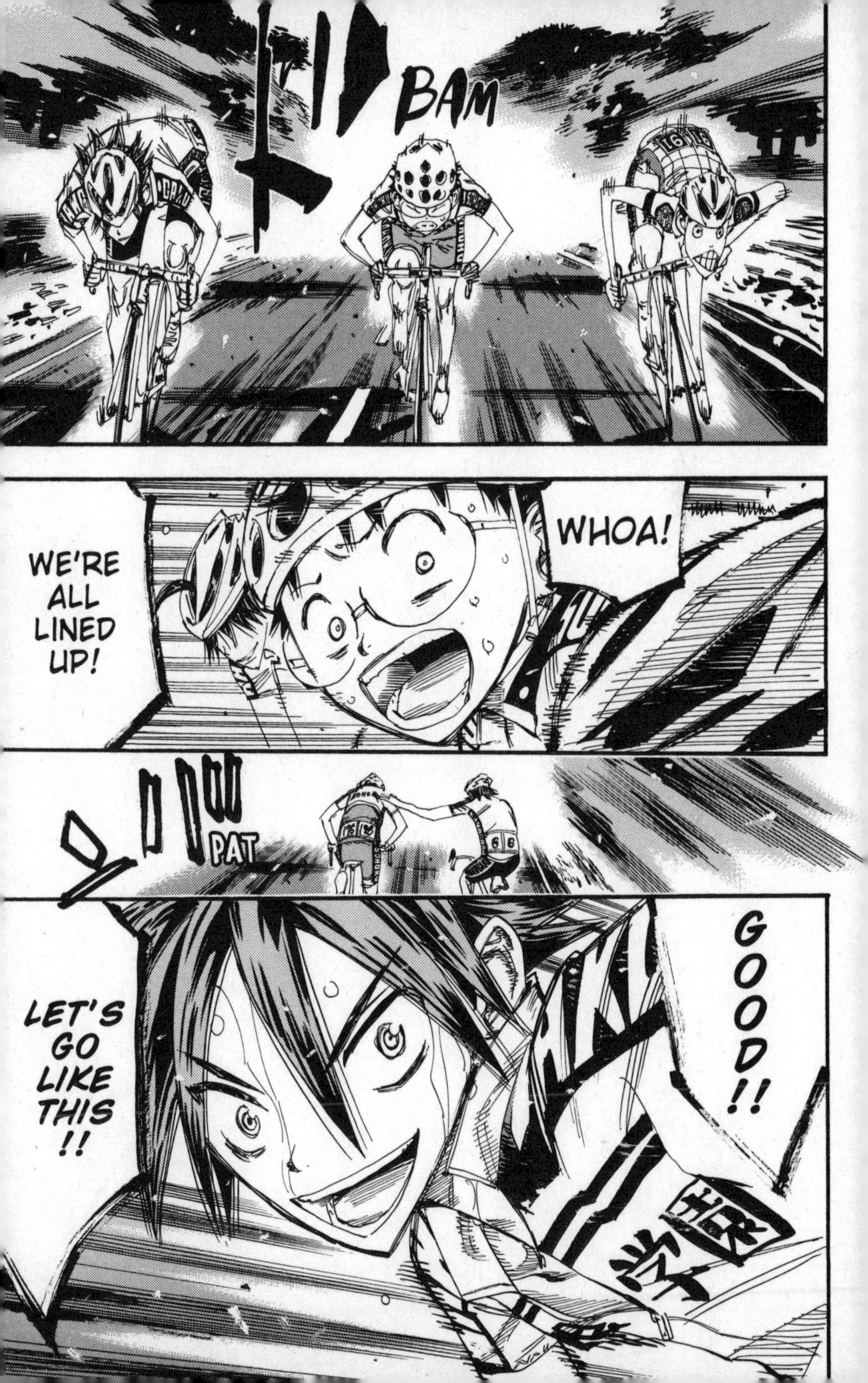
BAM
WHOA!
WE'RE ALL LINED UP!
PAT
GOOD!!
LET'S GO LIKE THIS!!

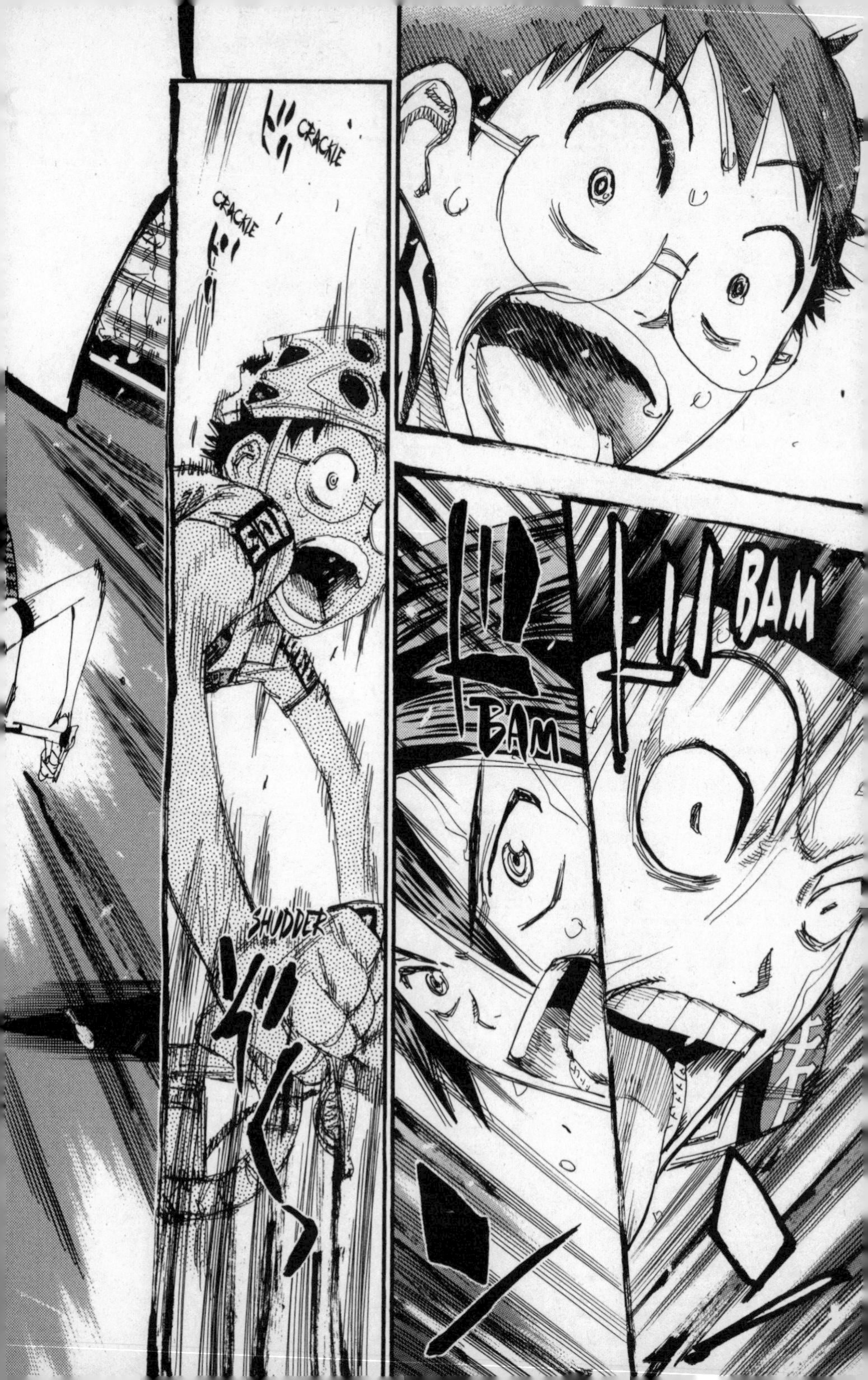
BAM
BAM
CRACKLE
CRACKLE
SHUDDER

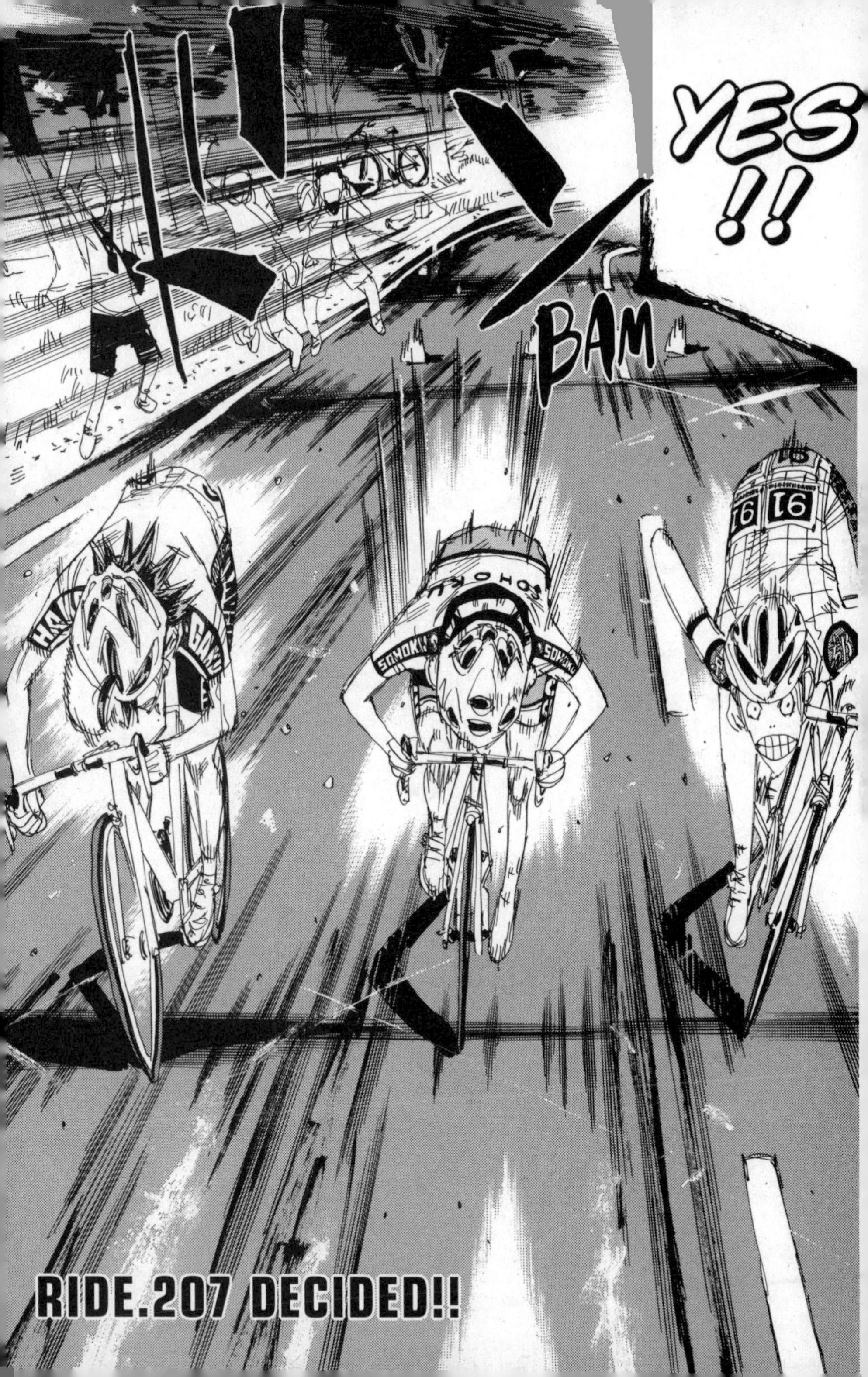
YES!!
BAM

RIDE.207 DECIDED!!

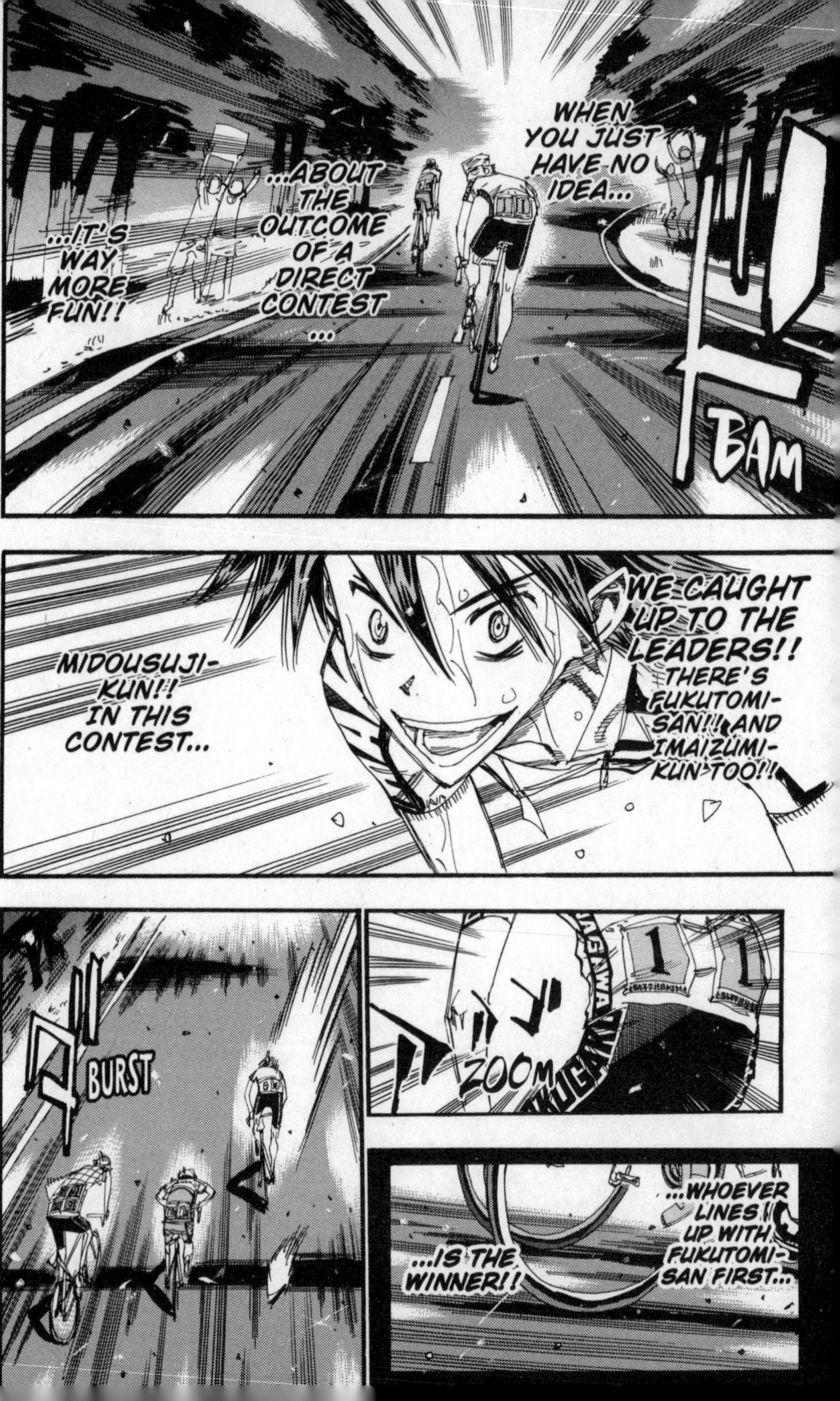
WHEN YOU JUST HAVE NO IDEA...
...ABOUT THE OUTCOME OF A DIRECT CONTEST...
...IT'S WAY MORE FUN!!
BAM
WE CAUGHT UP TO THE LEADERS!!
THERE'S FUKUTOMI-SAN!! AND IMAIZUMI-KUN TOO!!
MIDOUSUJI-KUN!! IN THIS CONTEST...
ZOOM
...WHOEVER LINES UP WITH FUKUTOMI-SAN FIRST...
...IS THE WINNER!!
BURST

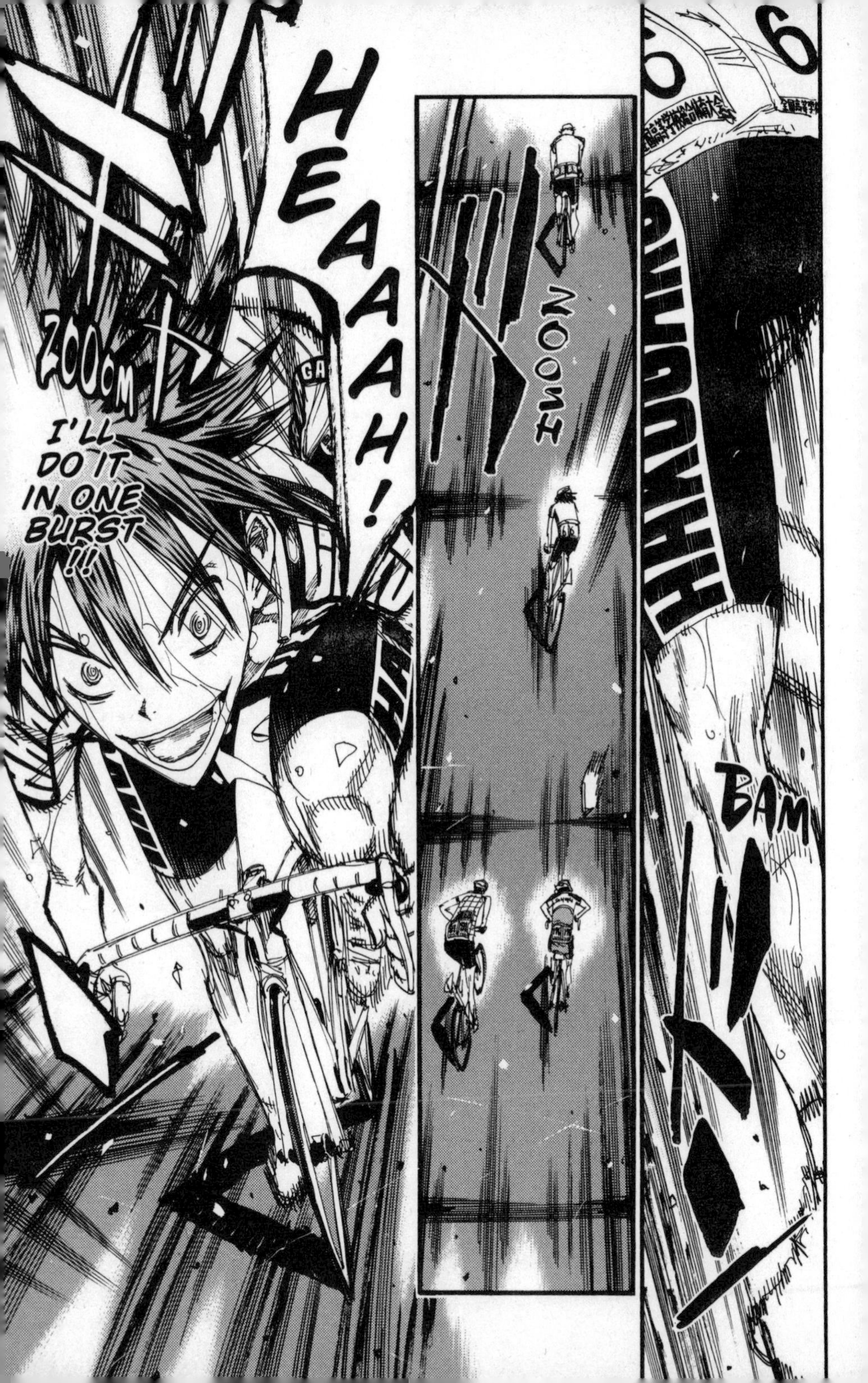
BAM
WHOOSH
HEAAAAH!
200M
I'LL DO IT IN ONE BURST!!!

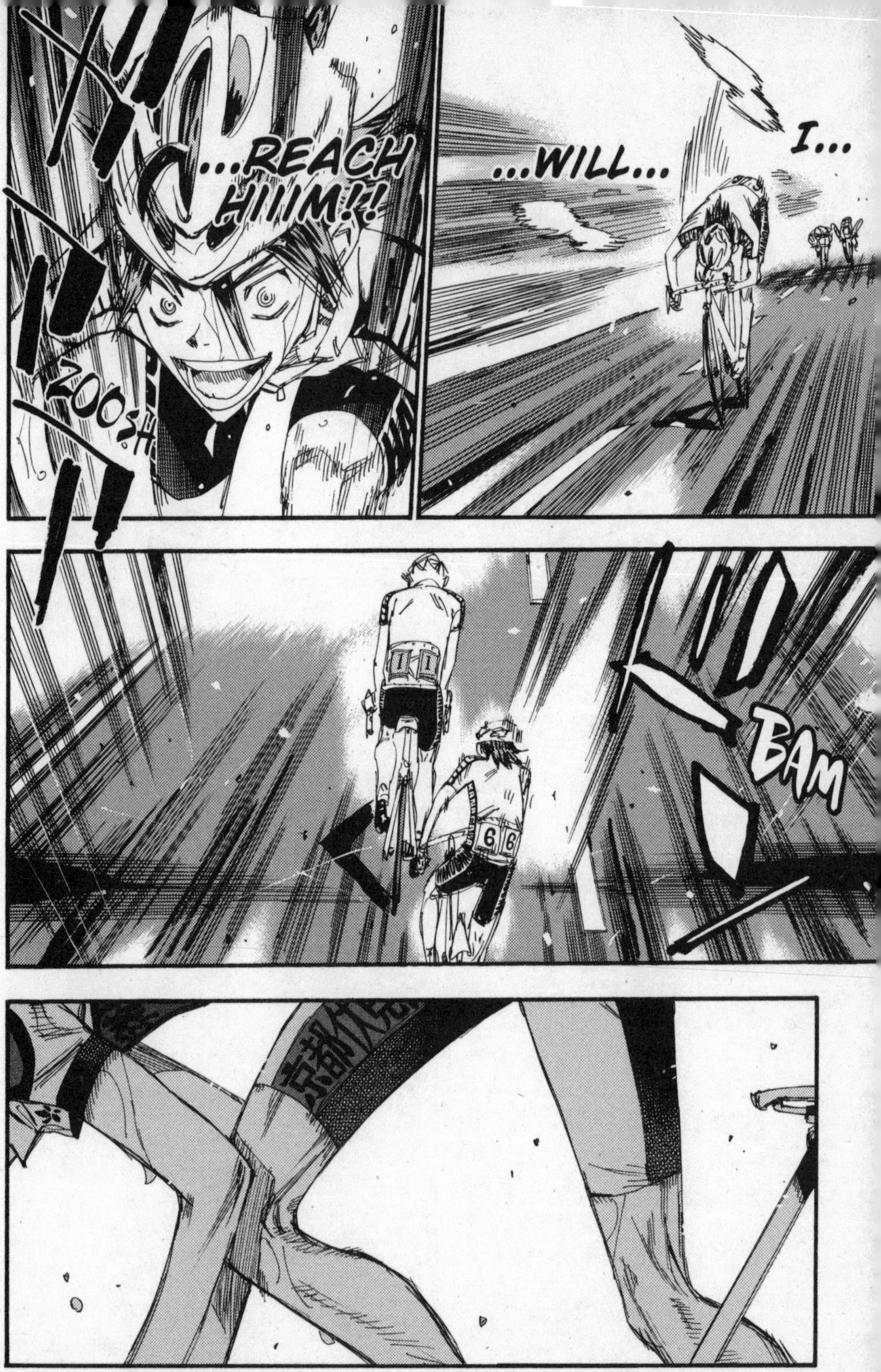
I...
...WILL...
...REACH HIIIM!!
ZOOSH
BAM

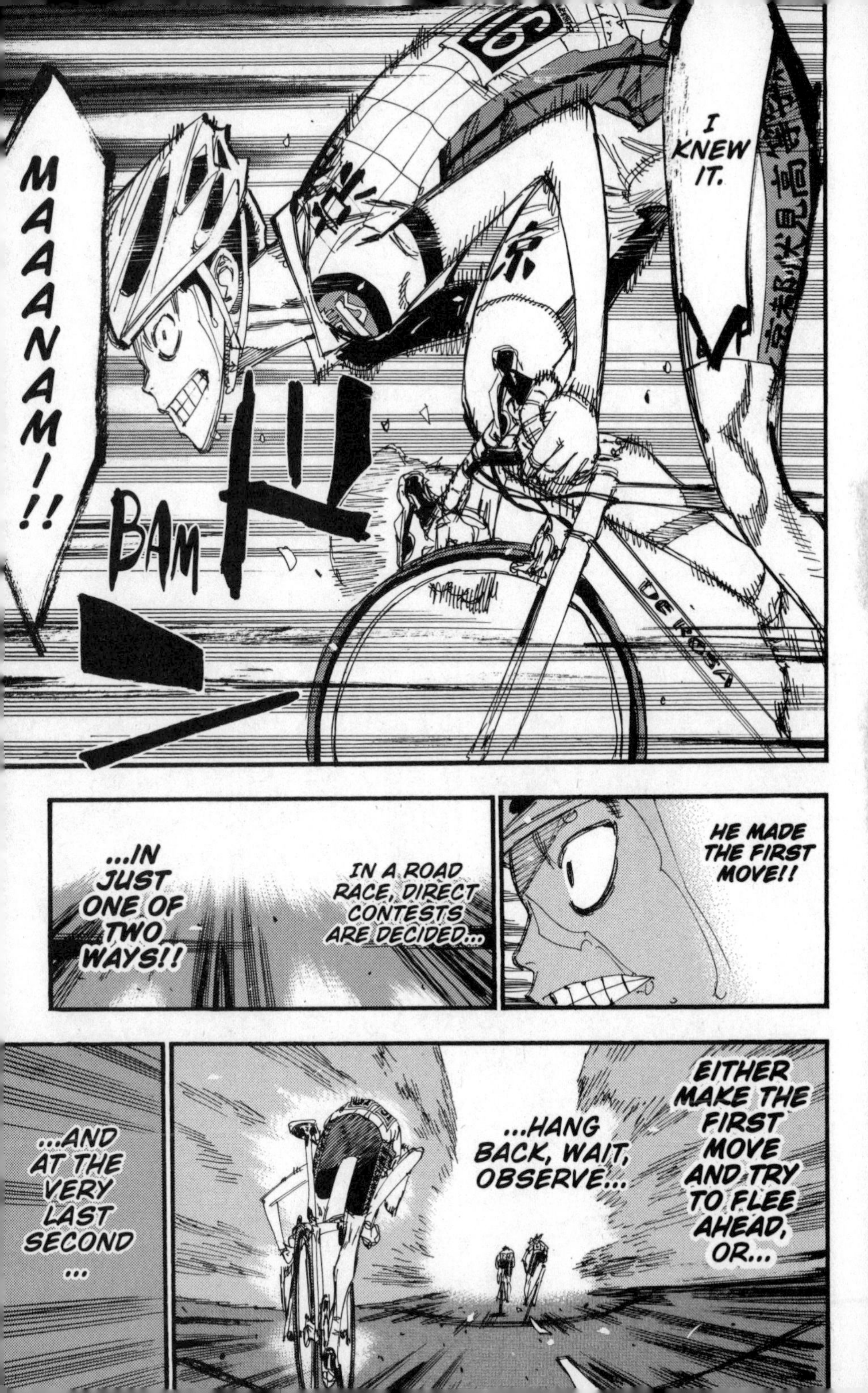
I KNEW IT.
MAAAANAMI!!
BAM
HE MADE THE FIRST MOVE!!
IN A ROAD RACE, DIRECT CONTESTS ARE DECIDED...
...IN JUST ONE OF TWO WAYS!!
EITHER MAKE THE FIRST MOVE AND TRY TO FLEE AHEAD, OR...
...HANG BACK, WAIT, OBSERVE...
...AND AT THE VERY LAST SECOND ...

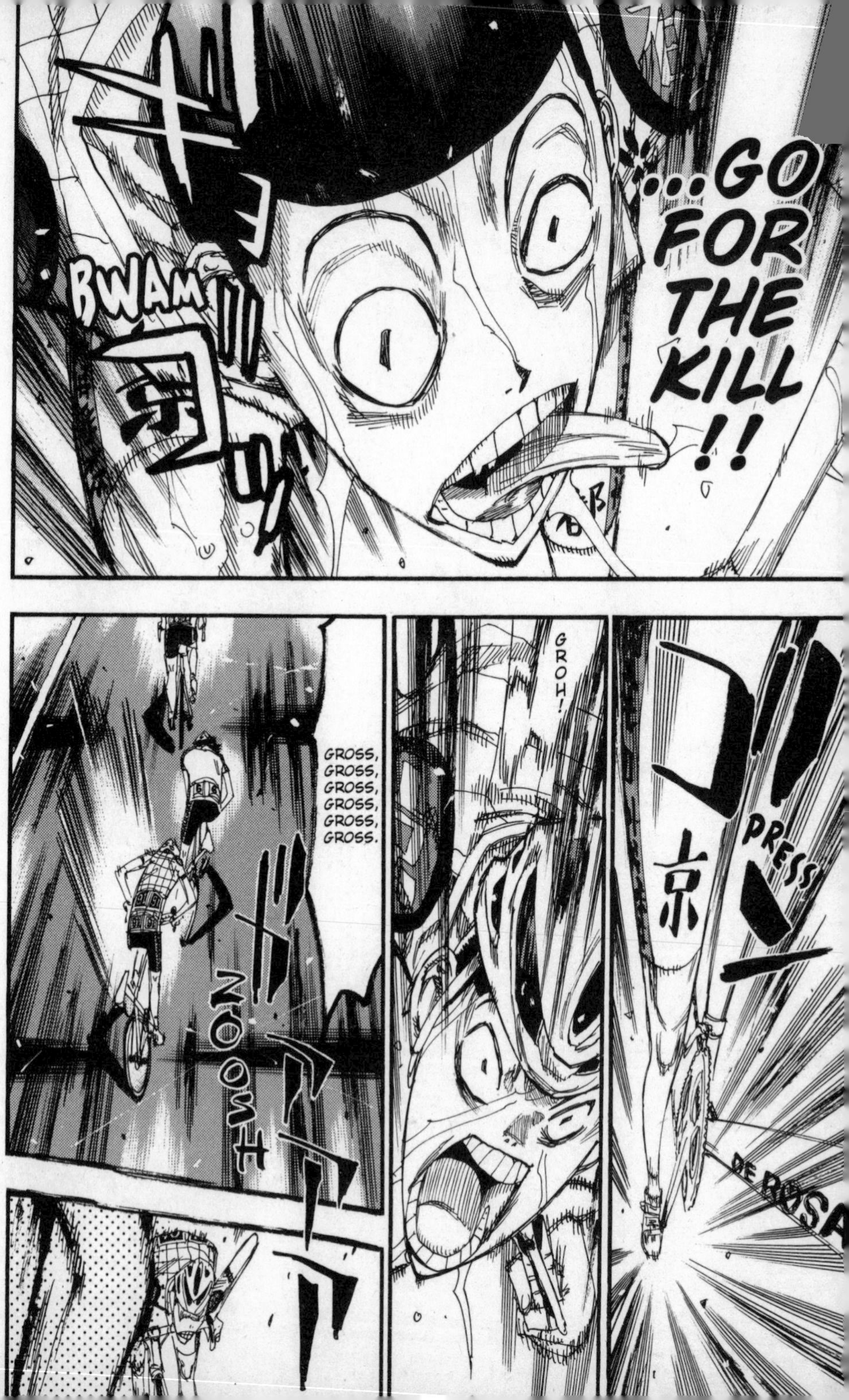
...GO FOR THE KILL!!
BWAM
PRESS
DE ROSA
GROH!
GROSS, GROSS, GROSS, GROSS, GROSS, GROSS.
ZOOSH

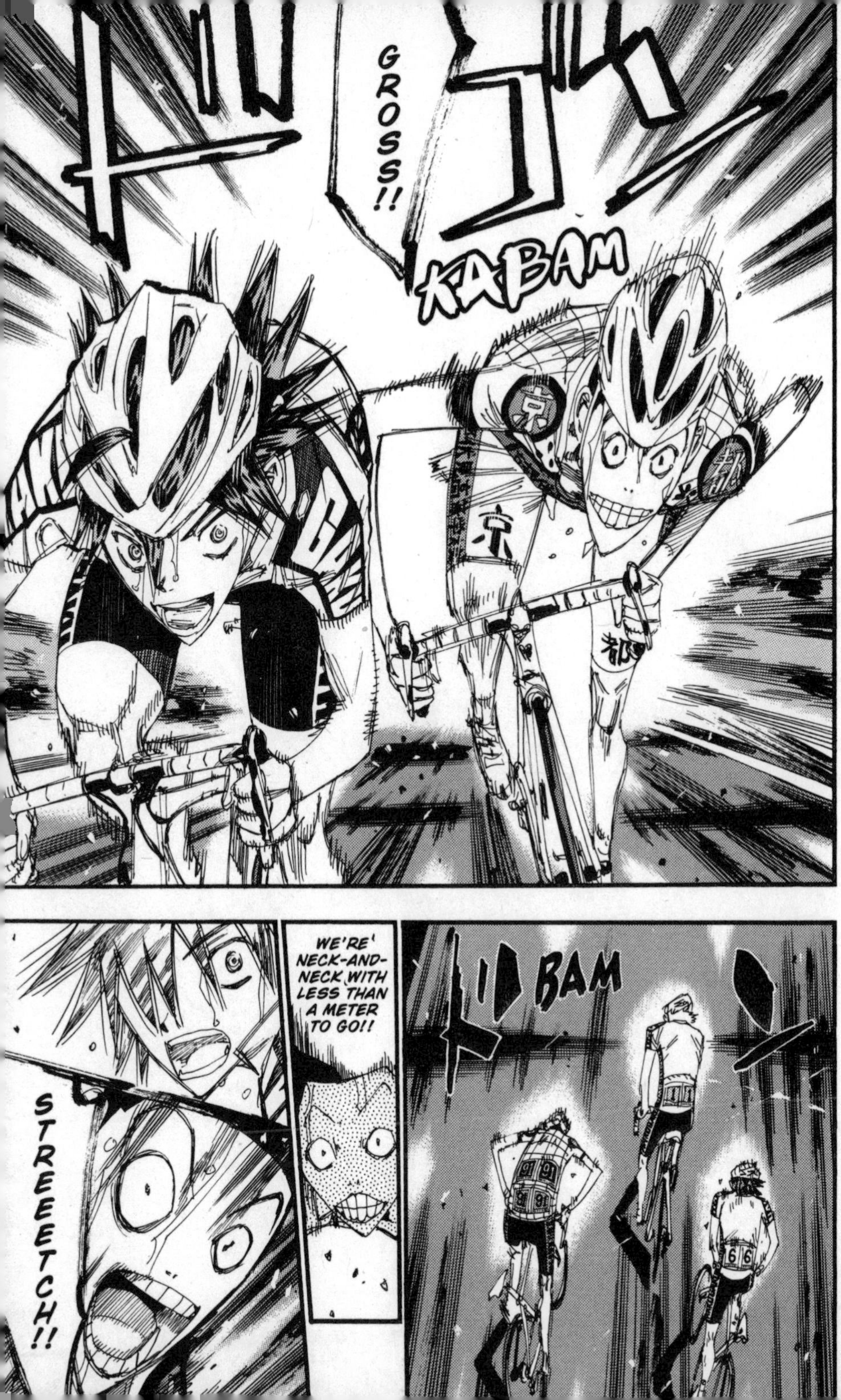
GROSS!!
KABAM
BAM
WE'RE NECK-AND-NECK WITH LESS THAN A METER TO GO!!
STREEETCH!!

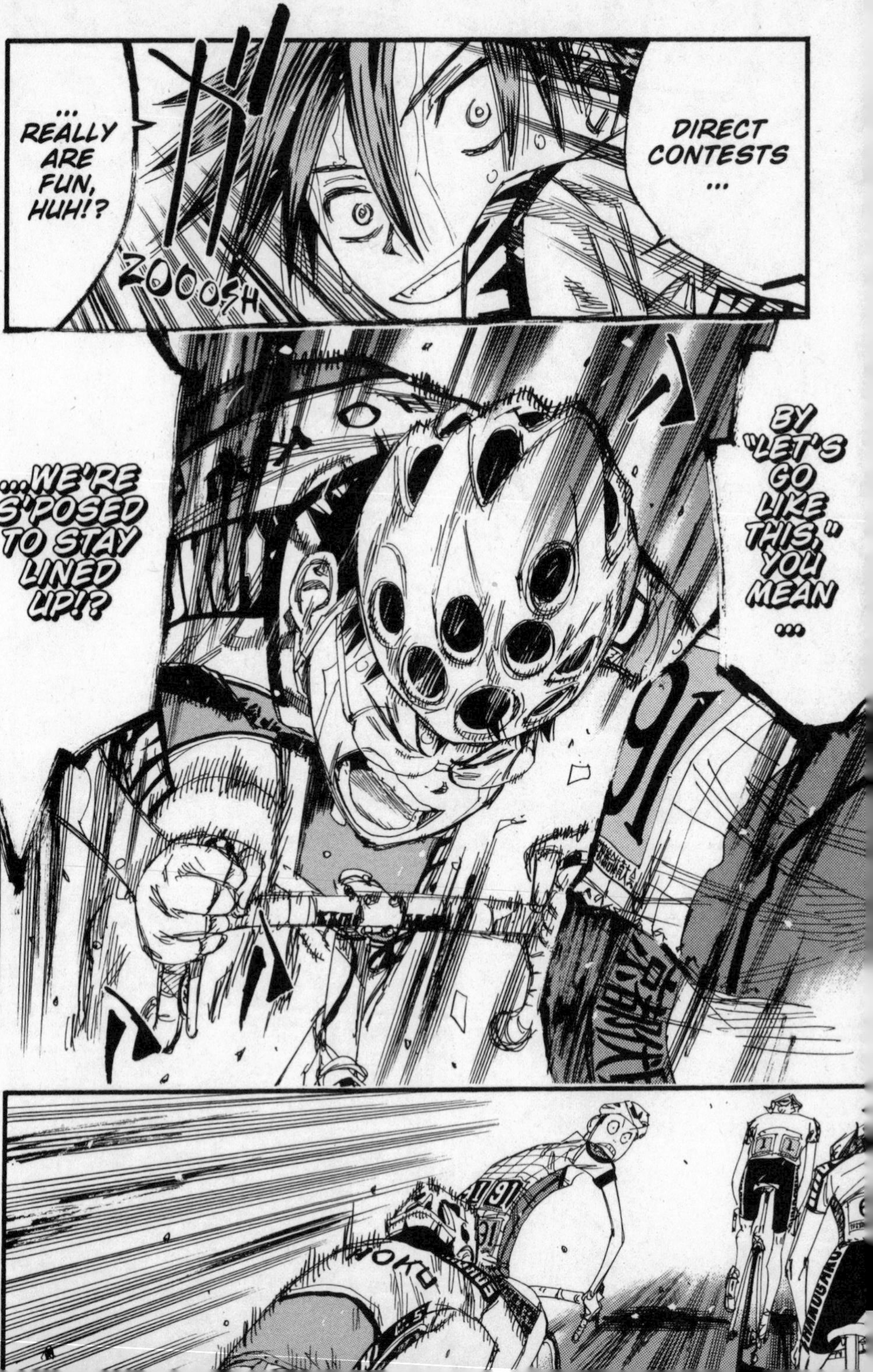
DIRECT CONTESTS ...
... REALLY ARE FUN, HUH!?
ZOOOSH
BY "LET'S GO LIKE THIS," YOU MEAN ...
...WE'RE S'POSED TO STAY LINED UP!?

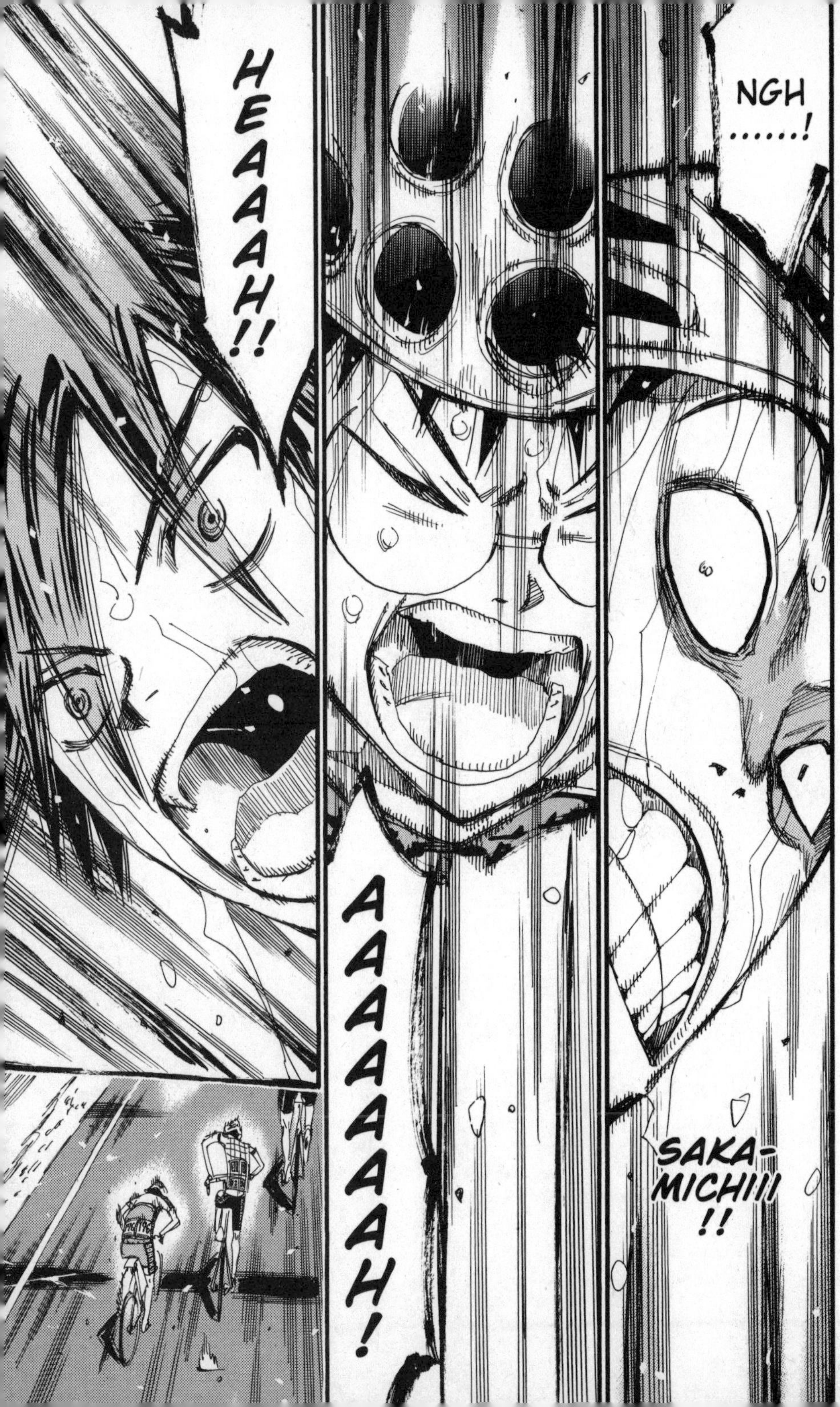
NGH
......!
SAKA-
MICHIII
!!
AAAAAAAH!
HEAAAAH!!

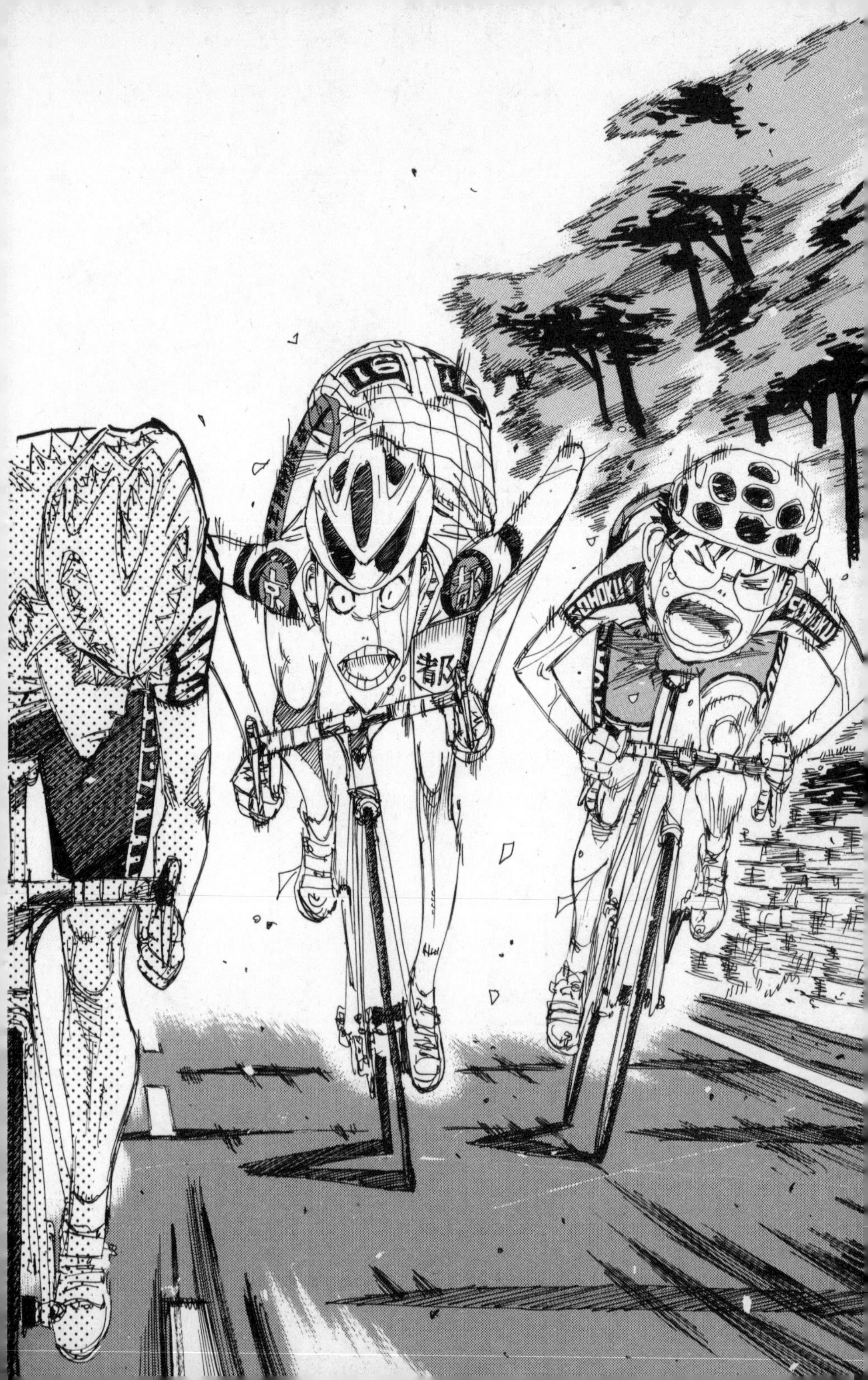

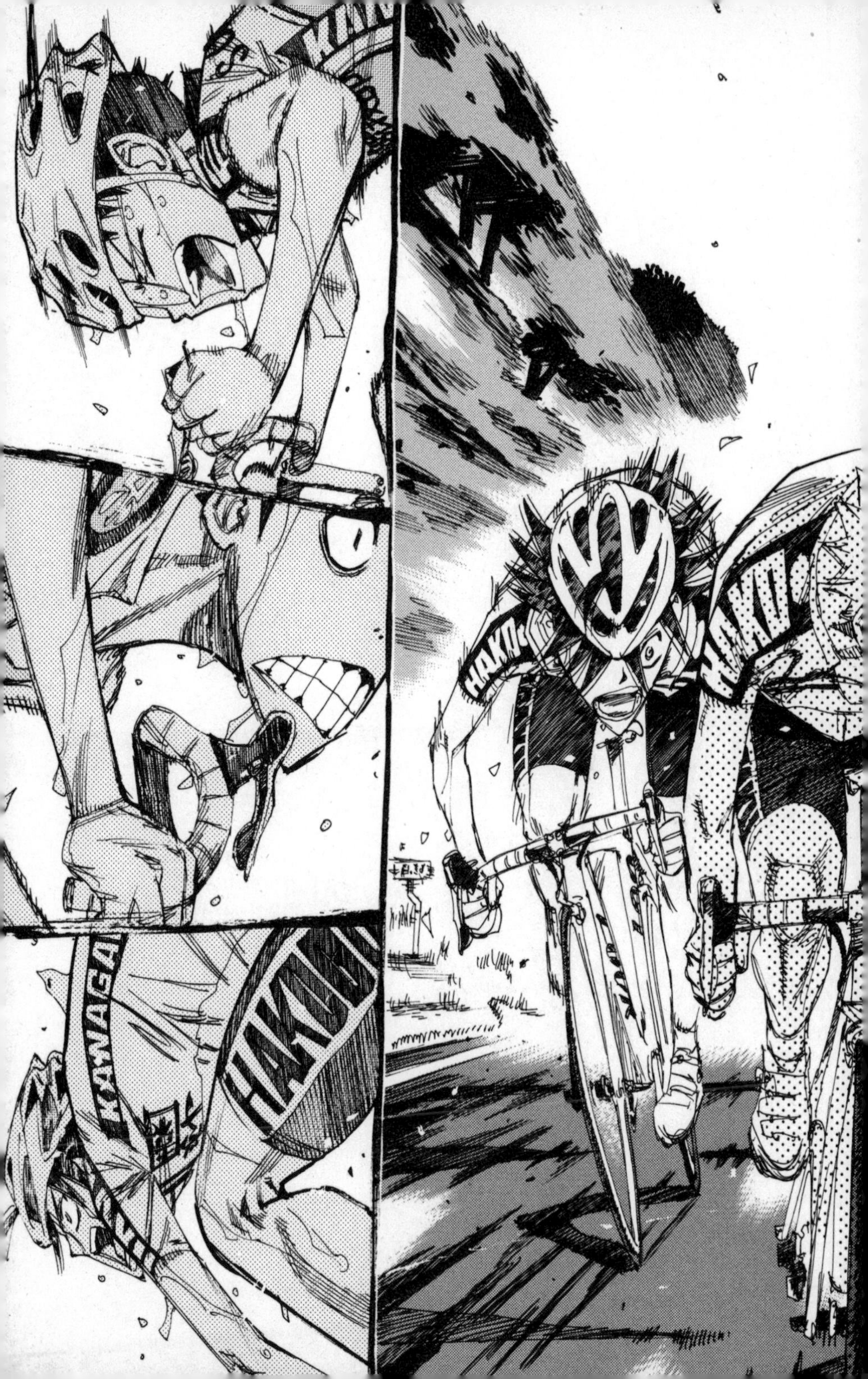

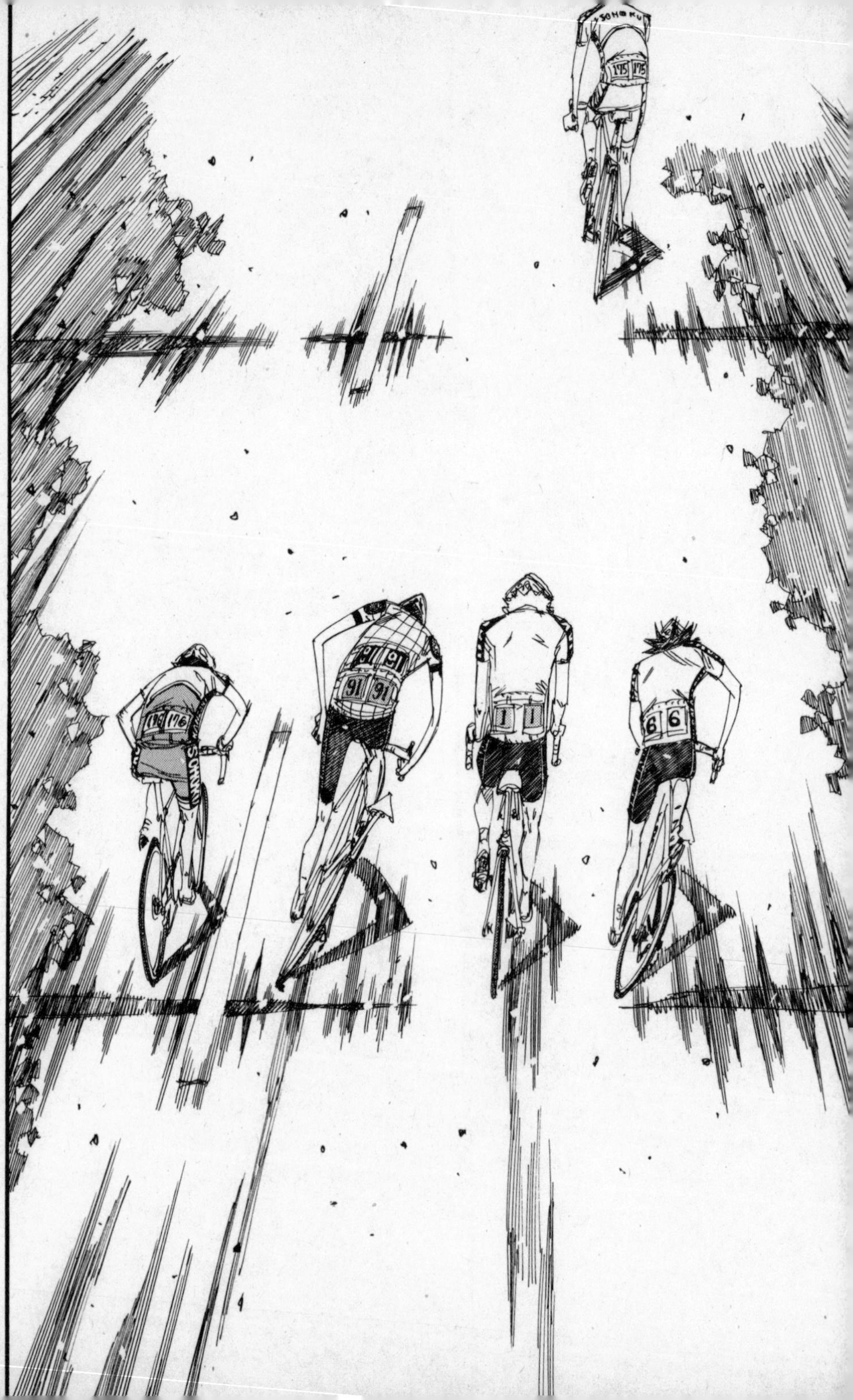

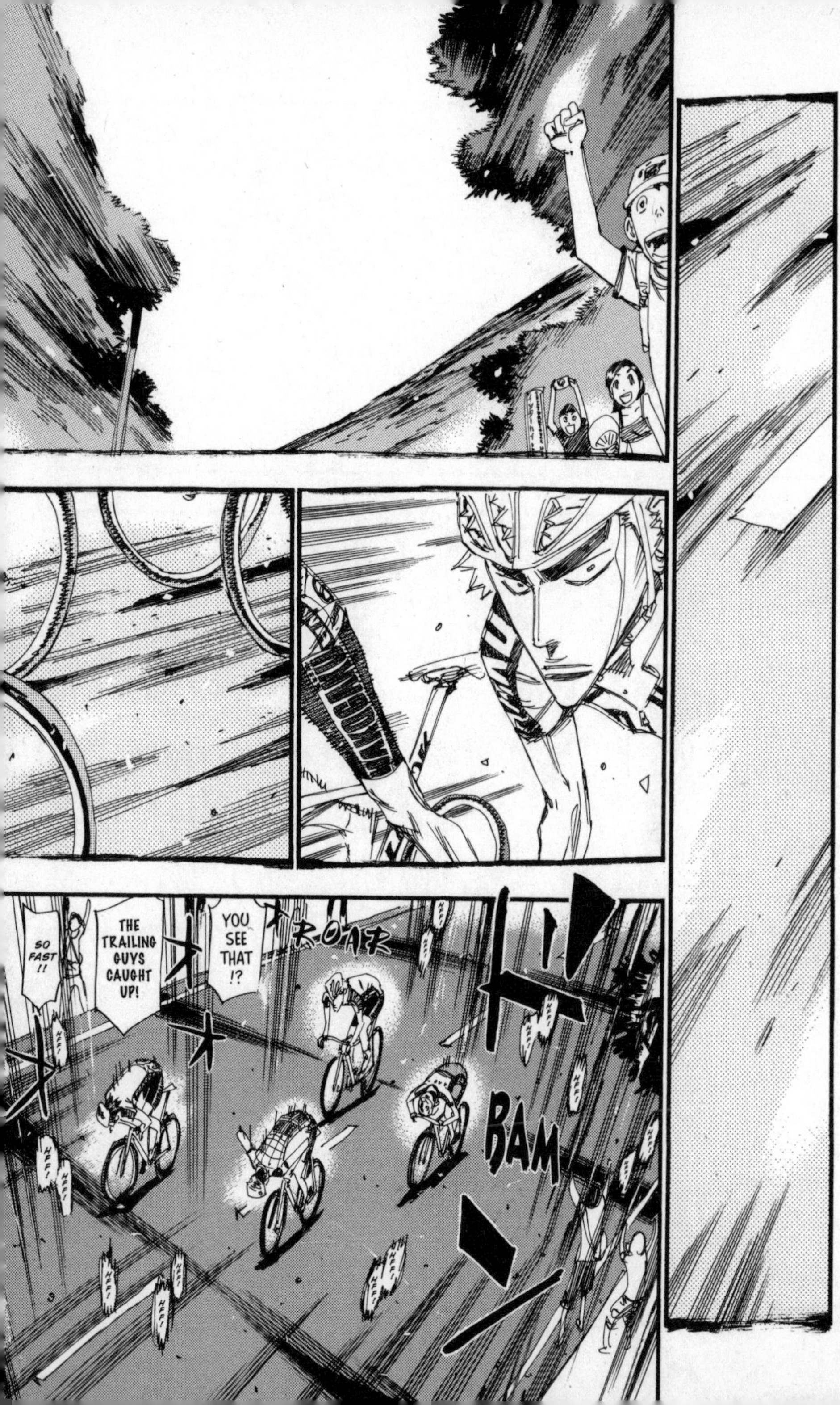
ROAR
BAM
YOU SEE THAT !?
THE TRAILING GUYS CAUGHT UP!
SO FAST !!

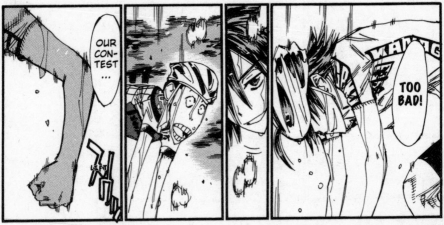

OUR CON-TEST ...

TOO BAD!

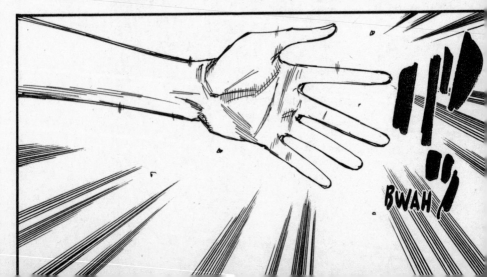

BWAH

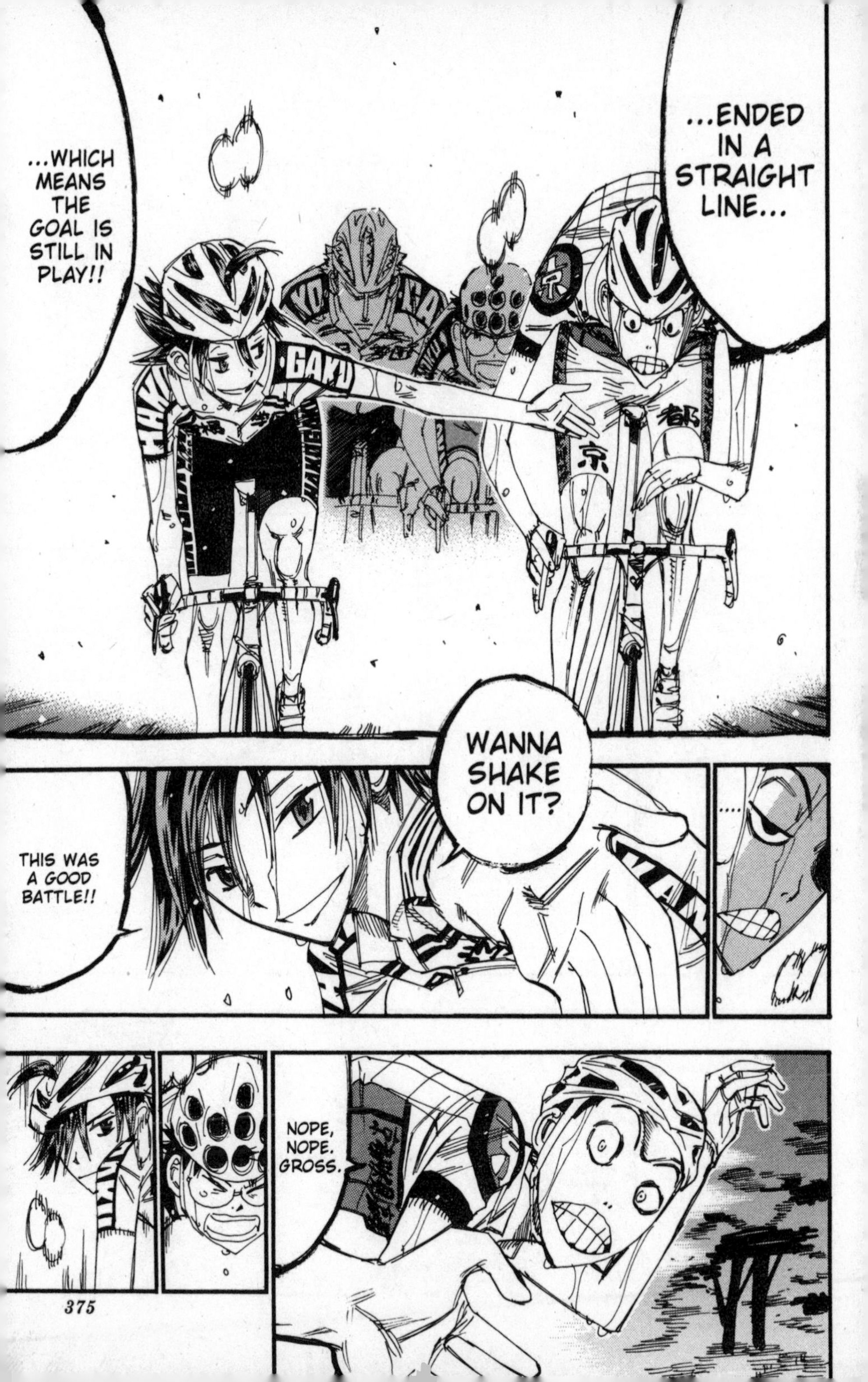
...ENDED IN A STRAIGHT LINE...
...WHICH MEANS THE GOAL IS STILL IN PLAY!!
....
WANNA SHAKE ON IT?
THIS WAS A GOOD BATTLE!!
NOPE, NOPE. GROSS.

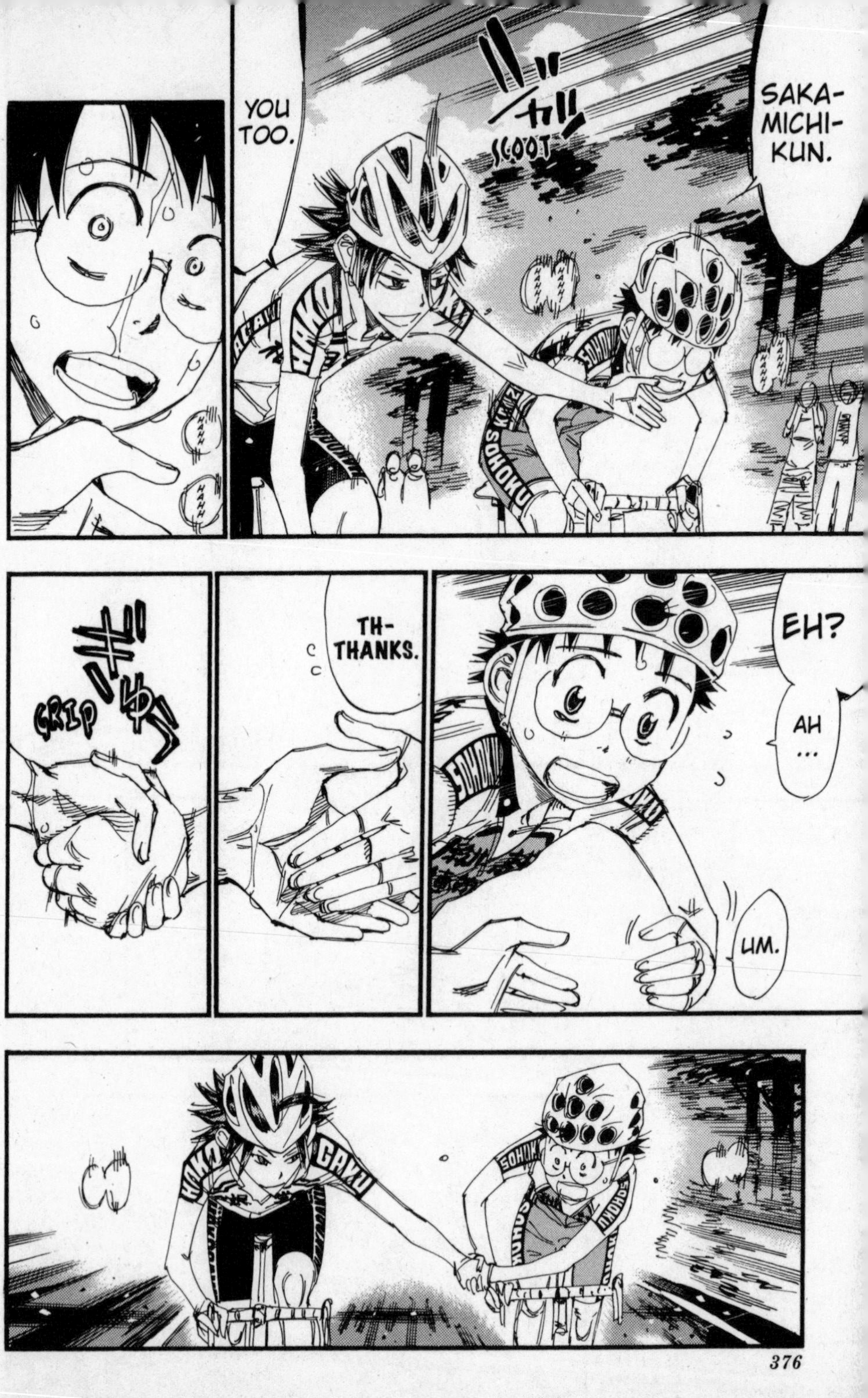
SAKA-MICHI-KUN.
SCOOT
YOU TOO.
EH?
AH ...
UM.
TH-THANKS.
GRIP

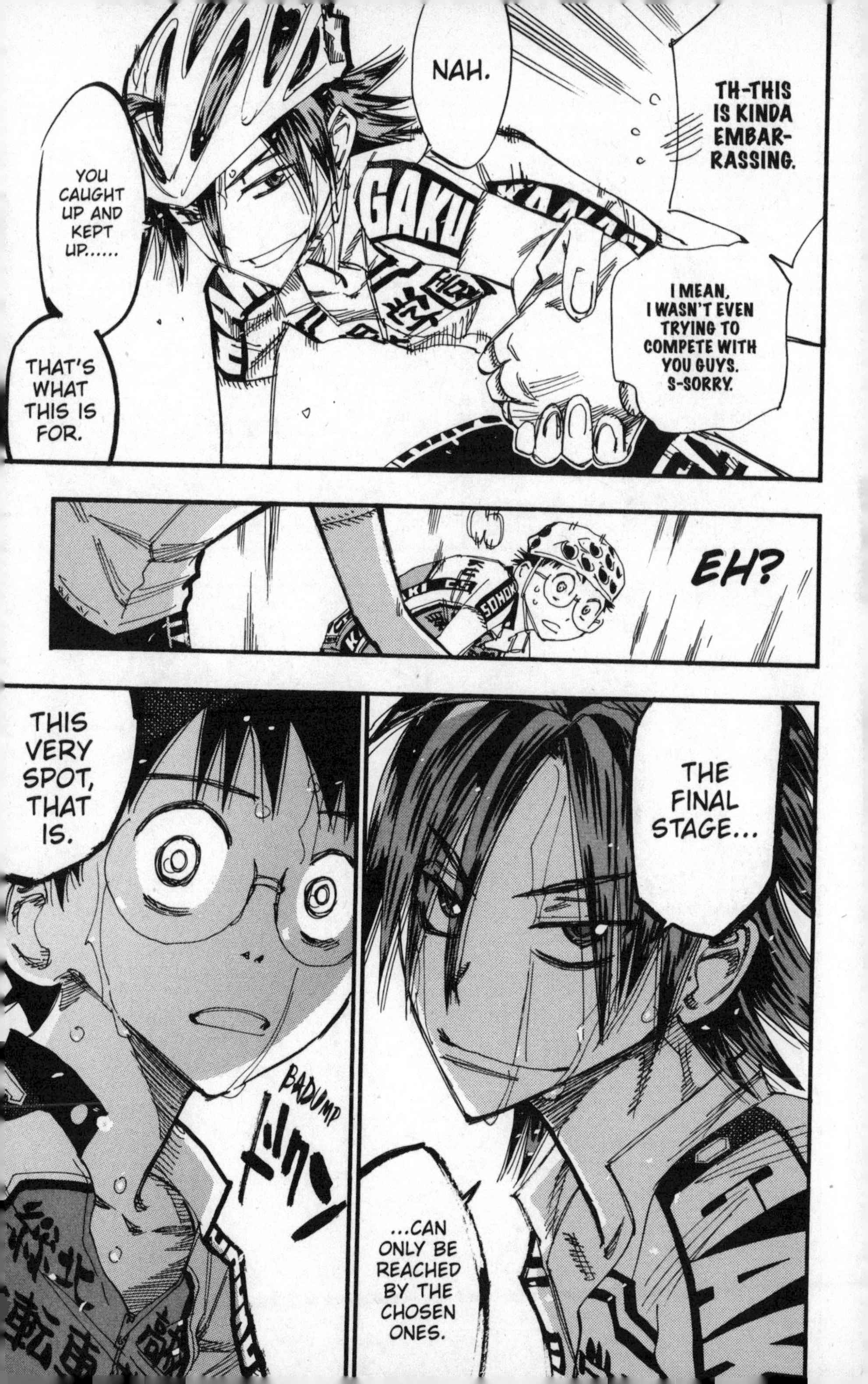

TH-THIS IS KINDA EMBARRASSING.
I MEAN, I WASN'T EVEN TRYING TO COMPETE WITH YOU GUYS. S-SORRY.
NAH.
YOU CAUGHT UP AND KEPT UP......
THAT'S WHAT THIS IS FOR.
EH?
THE FINAL STAGE...
...CAN ONLY BE REACHED BY THE CHOSEN ONES.
THIS VERY SPOT, THAT IS.
BADUMP

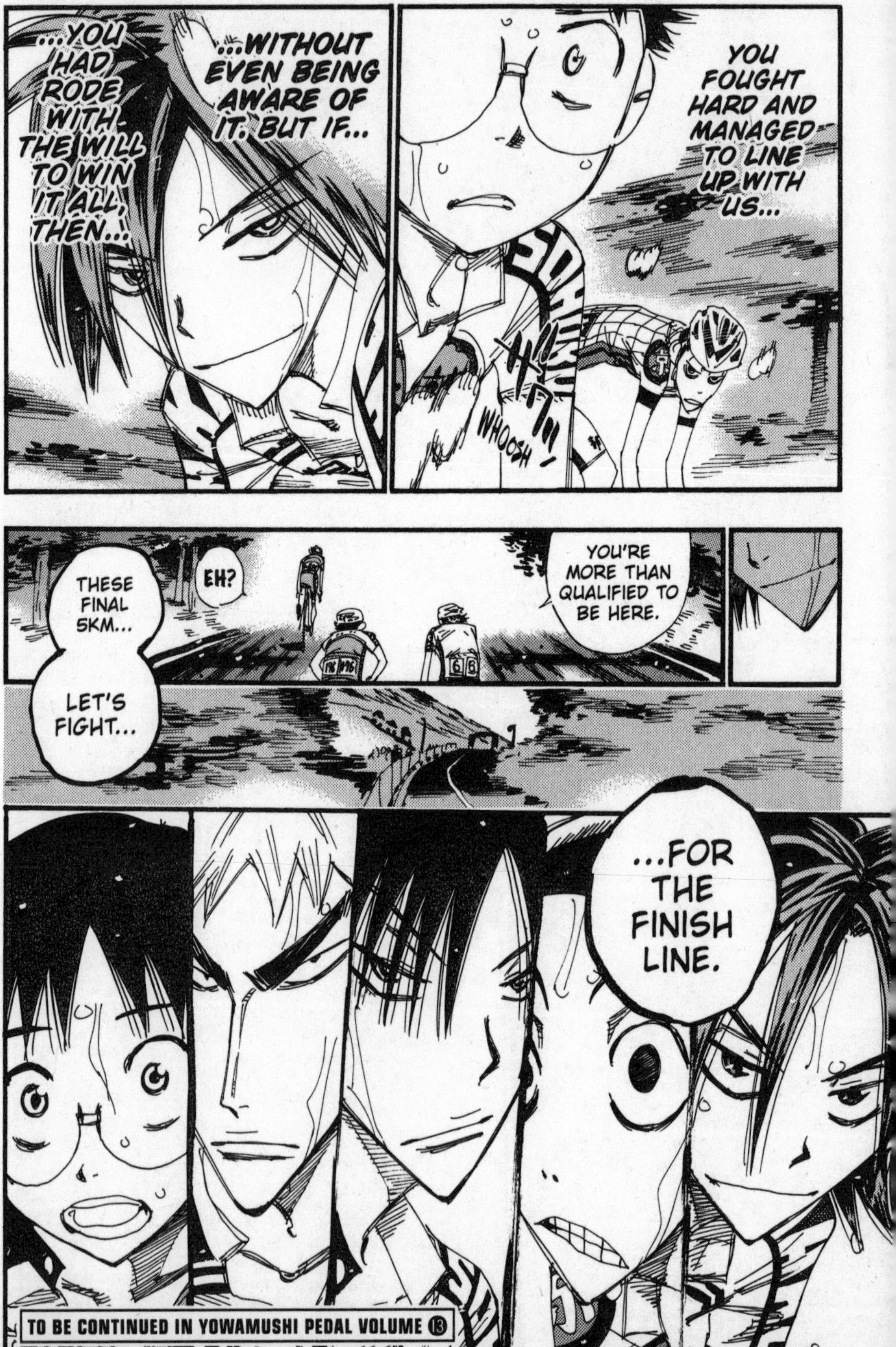
YOU FOUGHT HARD AND MANAGED TO LINE UP WITH US...
WHOOSH
...WITHOUT EVEN BEING AWARE OF IT. BUT IF...
...YOU HAD RODE WITH THE WILL TO WIN IT ALL, THEN...
YOU'RE MORE THAN QUALIFIED TO BE HERE.
EH?
THESE FINAL 5KM...
LET'S FIGHT...
...FOR THE FINISH LINE.
TO BE CONTINUED IN YOWAMUSHI PEDAL VOLUME 13

YOWAMUSHI PEDAL SPECIAL SIDE STORY: SOHOKU CYCLING CLUB: CLUBHOUSE BALLAD

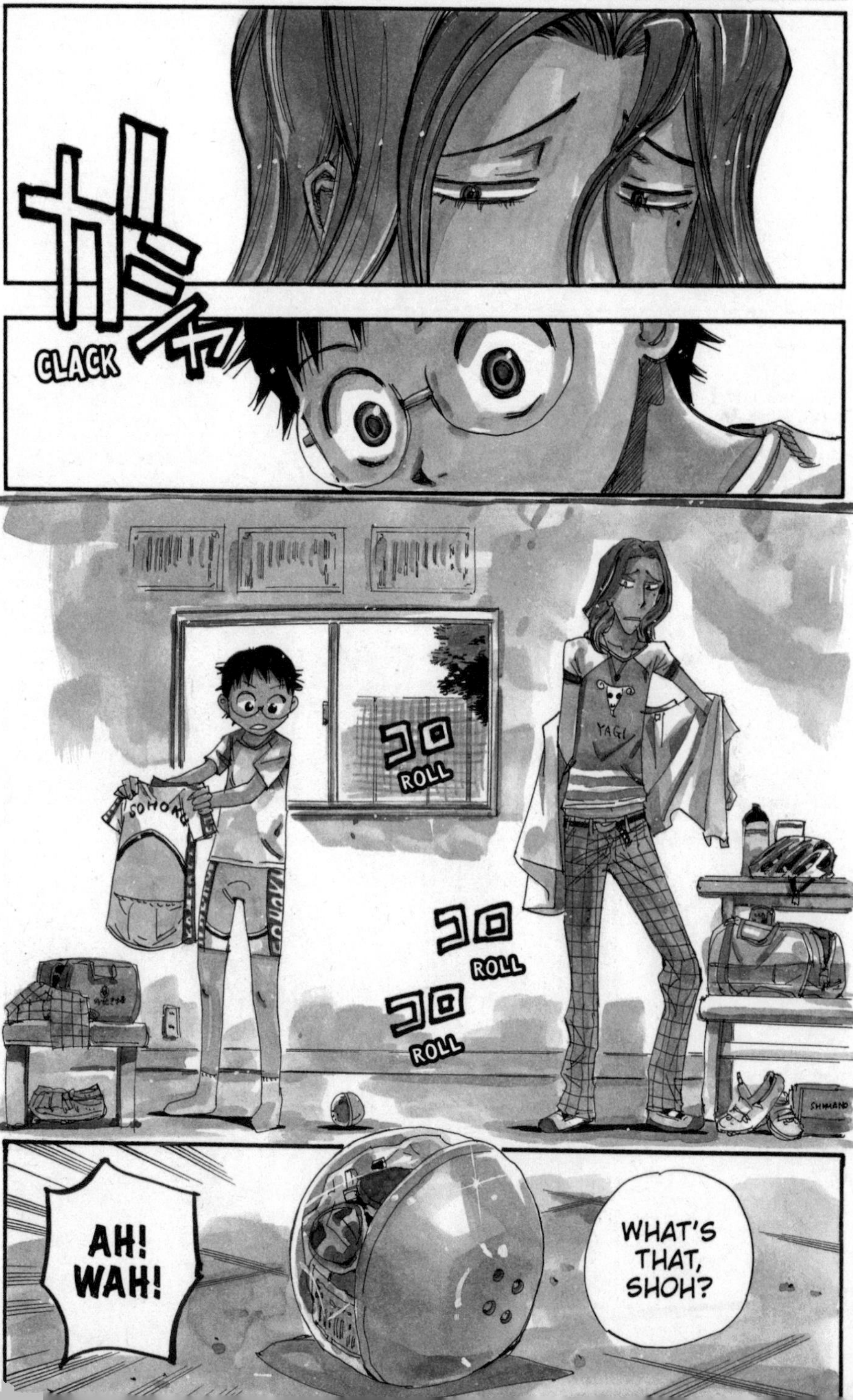
ガシャ
CLACK
コロ
ROLL
YAGI
コロ
ROLL
コロ
ROLL
SHIMANO
WHAT'S THAT, SHOH?
AH! WAH!

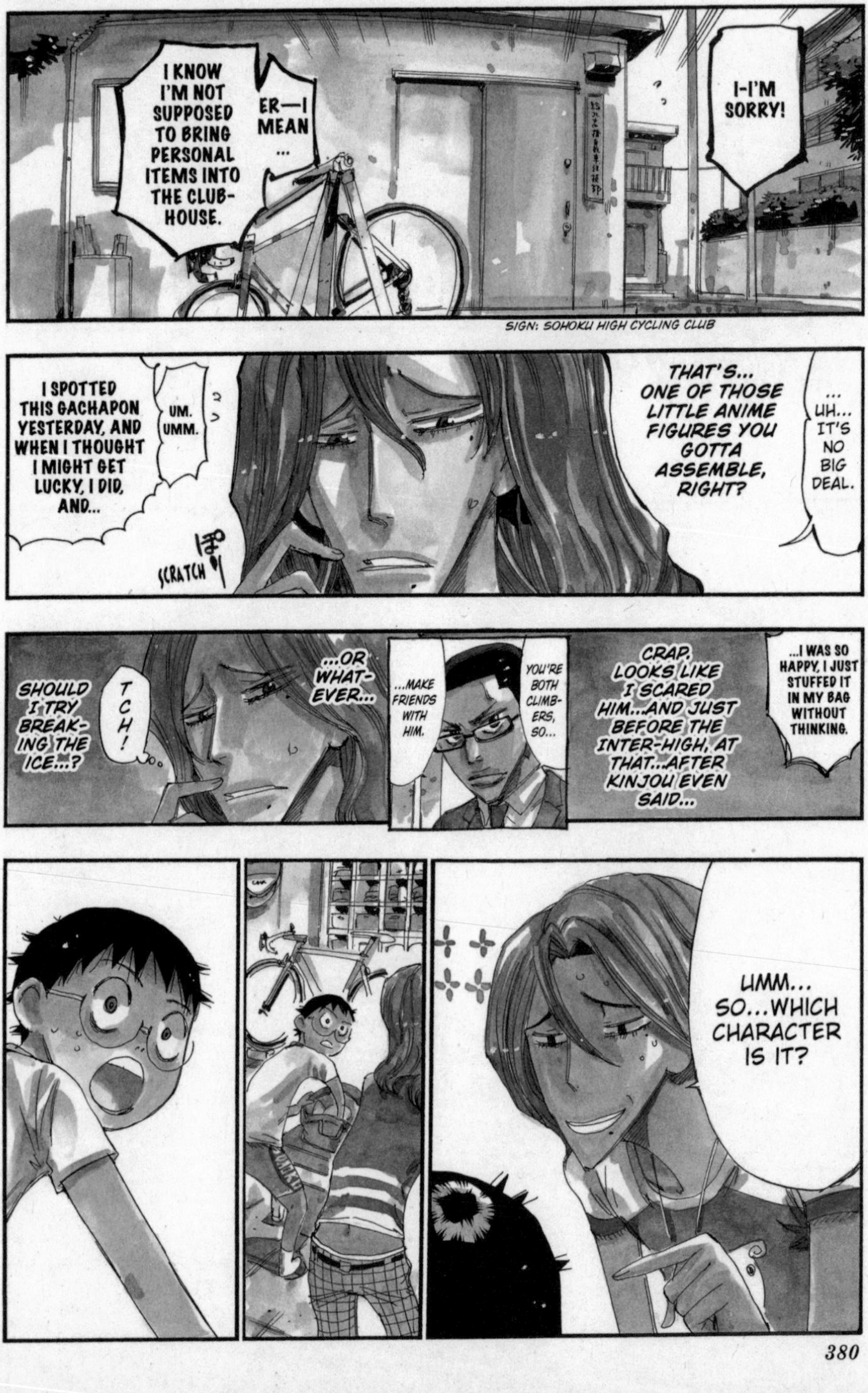
I-I'M SORRY!
ER—I MEAN ...
I KNOW I'M NOT SUPPOSED TO BRING PERSONAL ITEMS INTO THE CLUB-HOUSE.
SIGN: SOHOKU HIGH CYCLING CLUB
... UH... IT'S NO BIG DEAL.
THAT'S... ONE OF THOSE LITTLE ANIME FIGURES YOU GOTTA ASSEMBLE, RIGHT?
UM. UMM.
I SPOTTED THIS GACHAPON YESTERDAY, AND WHEN I THOUGHT I MIGHT GET LUCKY, I DID, AND...
SCRATCH
...I WAS SO HAPPY, I JUST STUFFED IT IN MY BAG WITHOUT THINKING.
CRAP, LOOKS LIKE I SCARED HIM...AND JUST BEFORE THE INTER-HIGH, AT THAT...AFTER KINJOU EVEN SAID...
YOU'RE BOTH CLIMB-ERS, SO...
...MAKE FRIENDS WITH HIM.
...OR WHAT-EVER...
TCH!
SHOULD I TRY BREAK-ING THE ICE...?
UMM... SO...WHICH CHARACTER IS IT?

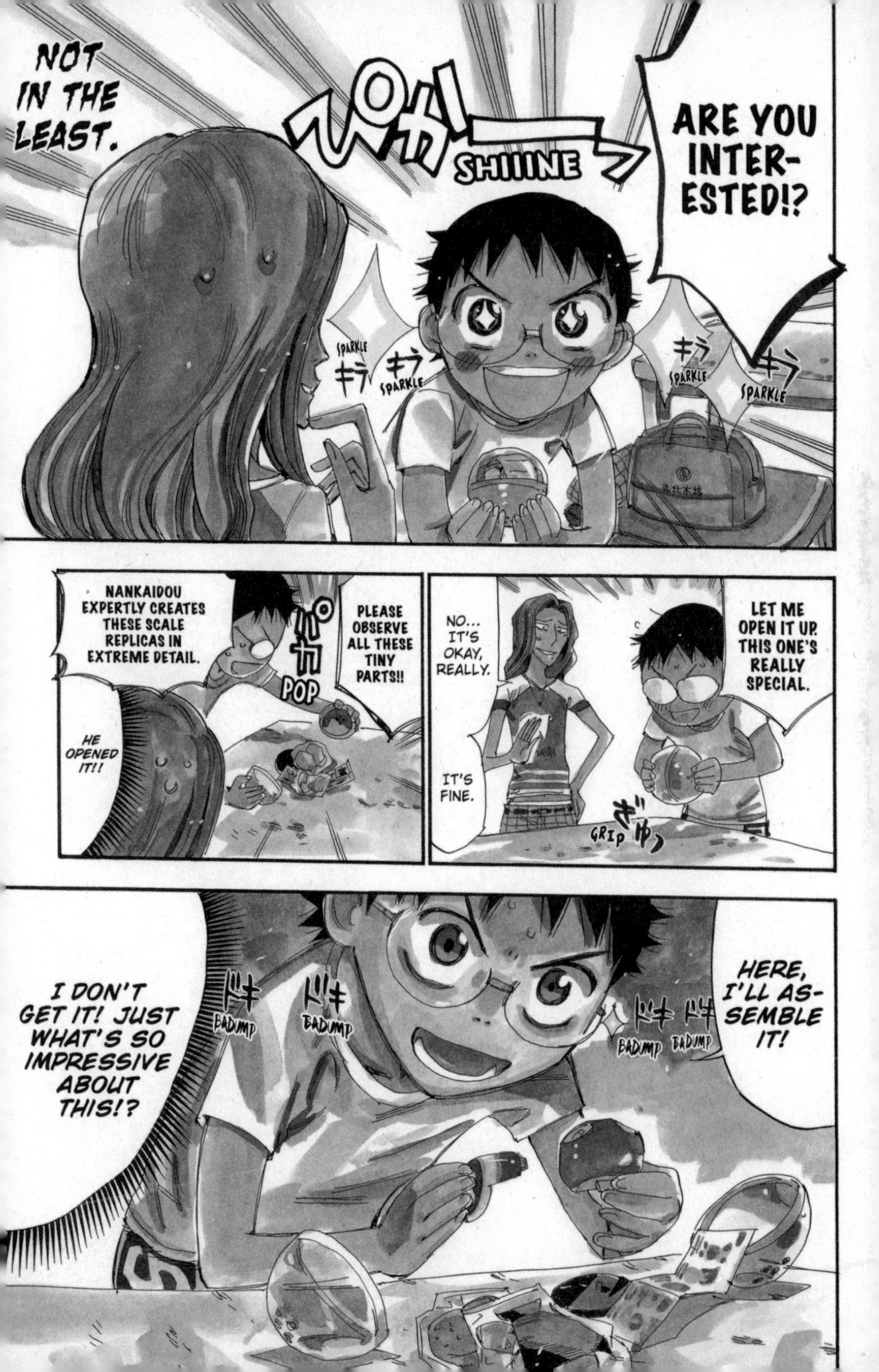
ARE YOU INTER-ESTED!?
SHIIINE
キラ SPARKLE
キラ SPARKLE
キラ SPARKLE
キラ SPARKLE
NOT IN THE LEAST.
LET ME OPEN IT UP. THIS ONE'S REALLY SPECIAL.
GRIP
NO... IT'S OKAY, REALLY.
IT'S FINE.
PLEASE OBSERVE ALL THESE TINY PARTS!!
POP
NANKAIDOU EXPERTLY CREATES THESE SCALE REPLICAS IN EXTREME DETAIL.
HE OPENED IT!!
HERE, I'LL AS-SEMBLE IT!
ドキ BADUMP
ドキ BADUMP
ドキ BADUMP
ドキ BADUMP
I DON'T GET IT! JUST WHAT'S SO IMPRESSIVE ABOUT THIS!?

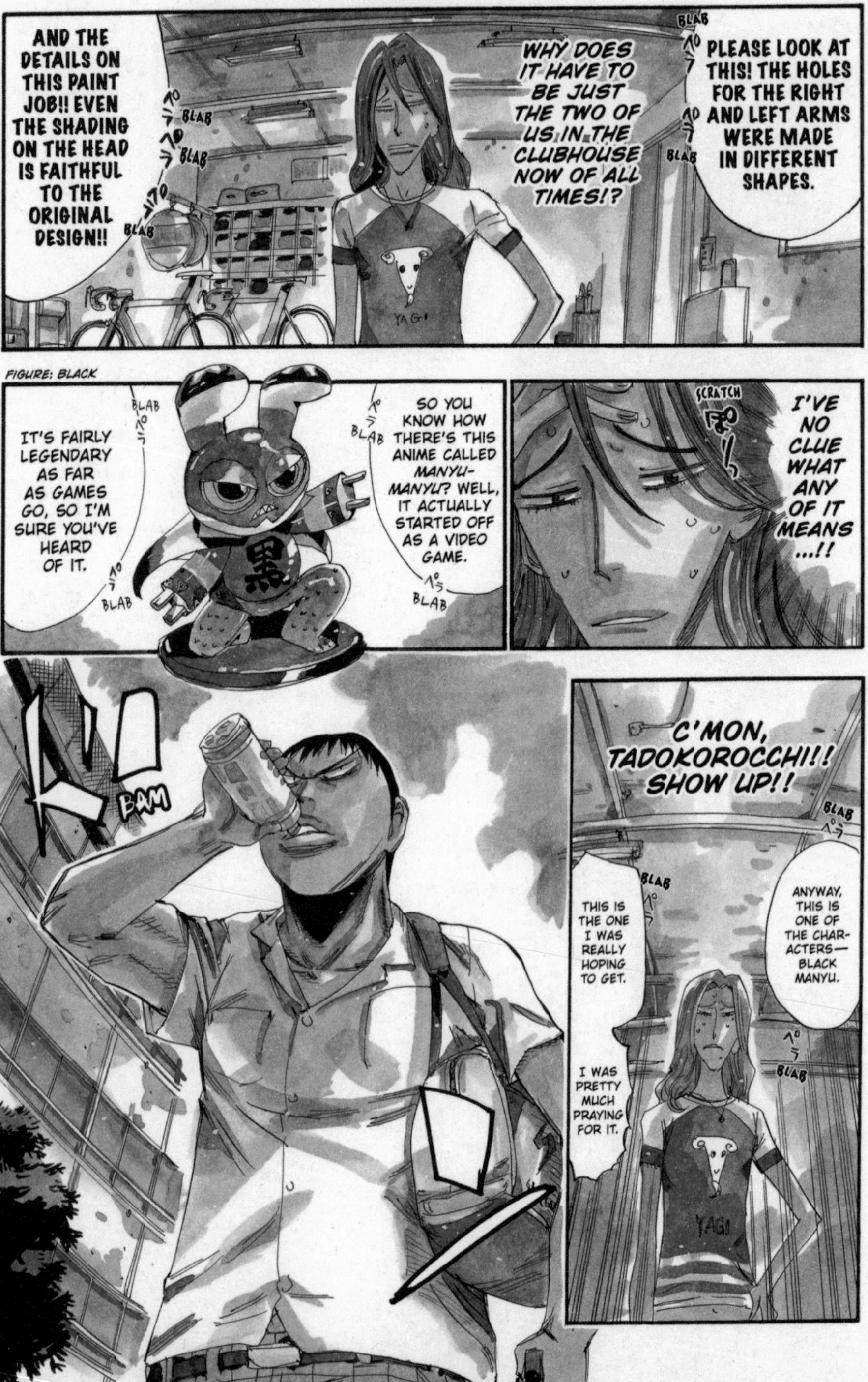BLAB
PLEASE LOOK AT THIS! THE HOLES FOR THE RIGHT AND LEFT ARMS WERE MADE IN DIFFERENT SHAPES.
BLAB
WHY DOES IT HAVE TO BE JUST THE TWO OF US IN THE CLUBHOUSE NOW OF ALL TIMES!?
BLAB
BLAB
AND THE DETAILS ON THIS PAINT JOB!! EVEN THE SHADING ON THE HEAD IS FAITHFUL TO THE ORIGINAL DESIGN!!
BLAB
FIGURE: BLACK
SCRATCH
I'VE NO CLUE WHAT ANY OF IT MEANS ...!!
BLAB
SO YOU KNOW HOW THERE'S THIS ANIME CALLED MANYU-MANYU? WELL, IT ACTUALLY STARTED OFF AS A VIDEO GAME.
BLAB
BLAB
IT'S FAIRLY LEGENDARY AS FAR AS GAMES GO, SO I'M SURE YOU'VE HEARD OF IT.
BLAB
C'MON, TADOKOROCCHI!! SHOW UP!!
BLAB
ANYWAY, THIS IS ONE OF THE CHARACTERS—BLACK MANYU.
BLAB
BLAB
THIS IS THE ONE I WAS REALLY HOPING TO GET.
I WAS PRETTY MUCH PRAYING FOR IT.
BAM

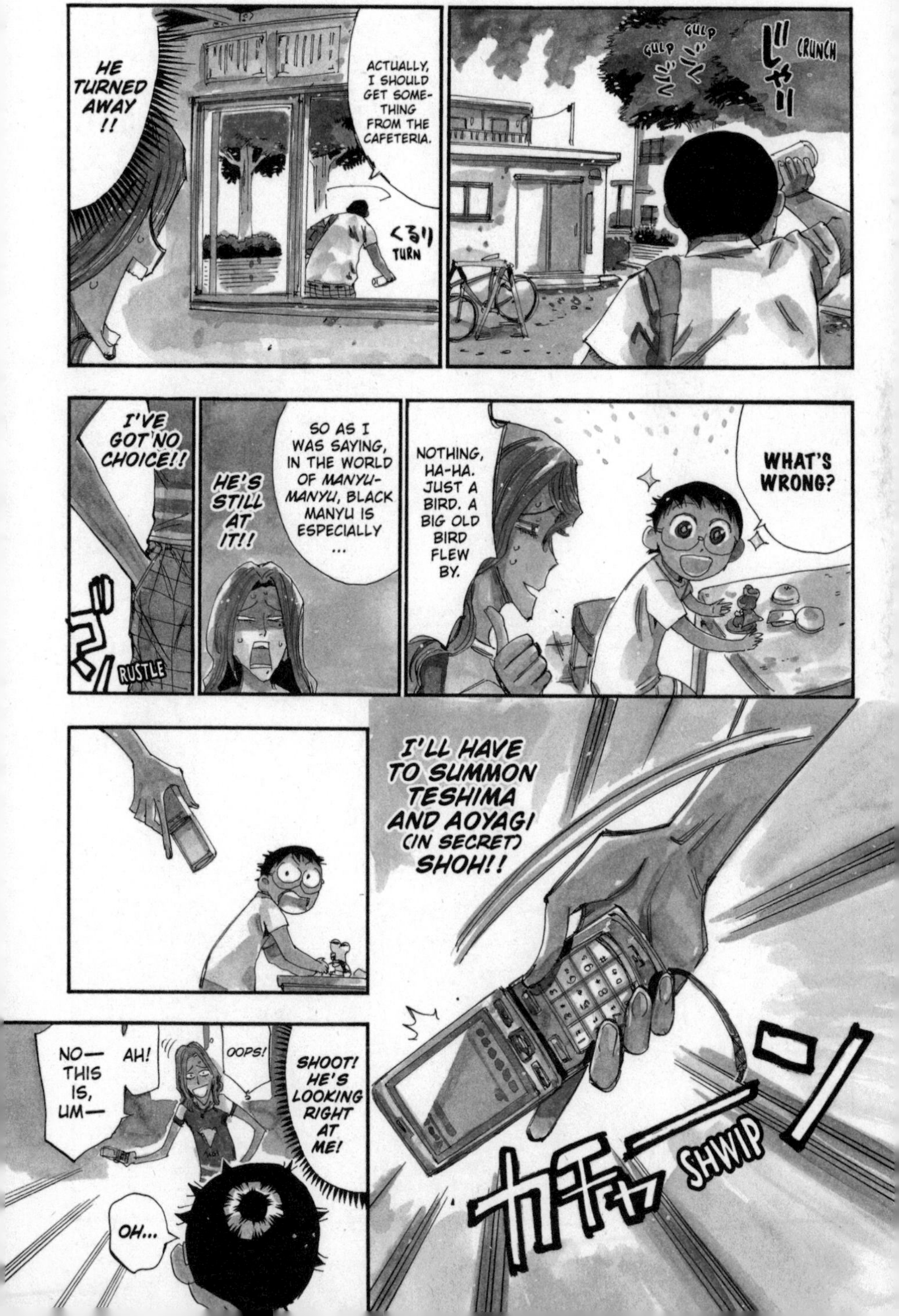
CRUNCH
GULP
GULP
ACTUALLY, I SHOULD GET SOMETHING FROM THE CAFETERIA.
くるり
TURN
HE TURNED AWAY!!
WHAT'S WRONG?
NOTHING, HA-HA. JUST A BIRD. A BIG OLD BIRD FLEW BY.
SO AS I WAS SAYING, IN THE WORLD OF MANYU-MANYU, BLACK MANYU IS ESPECIALLY ...
HE'S STILL AT IT!!
I'VE GOT NO CHOICE!!
RUSTLE
I'LL HAVE TO SUMMON TESHIMA AND AOYAGI (IN SECRET) SHOH!!
カチャ
SHWIP
SHOOT! HE'S LOOKING RIGHT AT ME!
OOPS!
AH!
NO— THIS IS, UM—
OH...

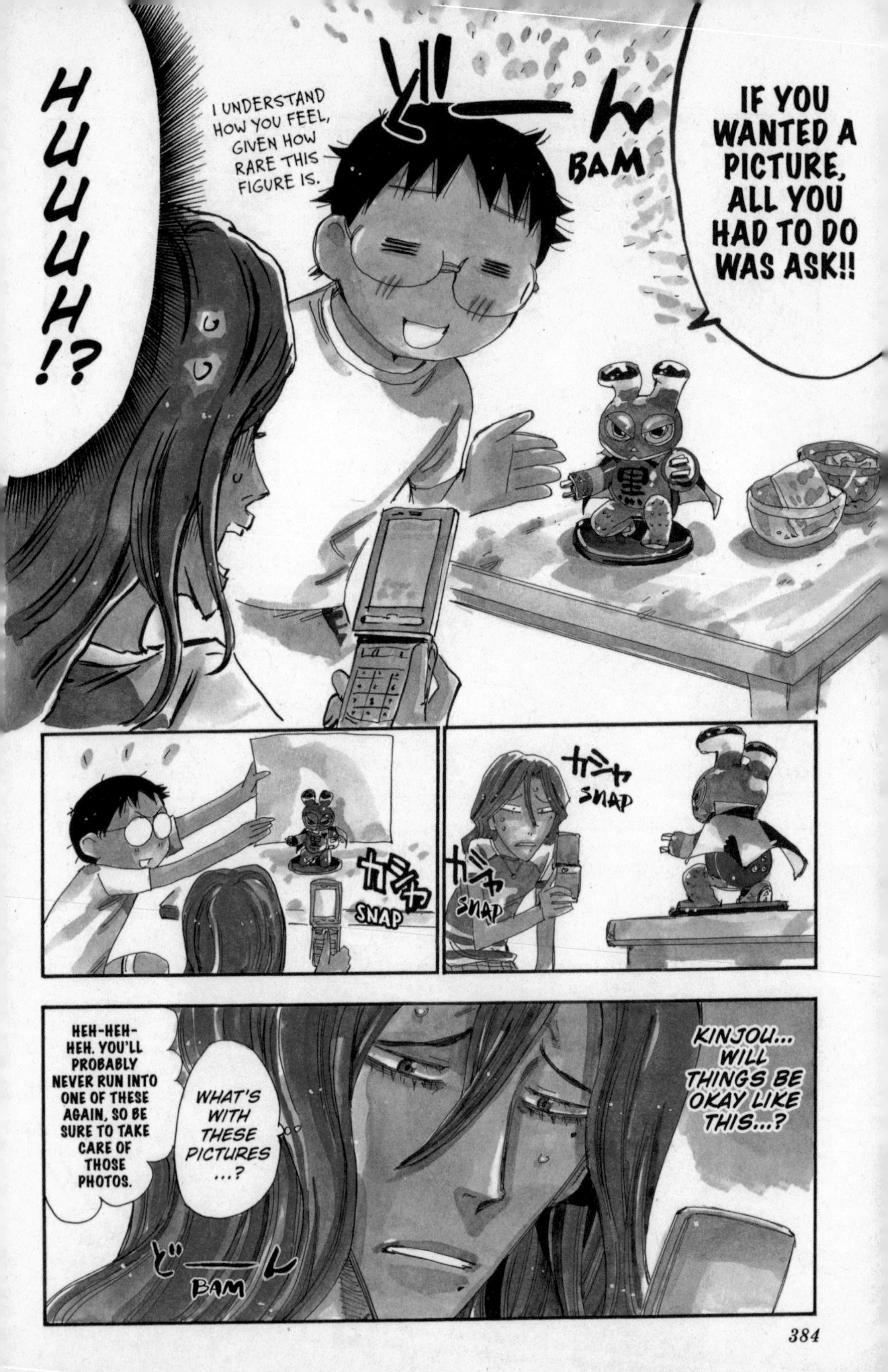

IF YOU WANTED A PICTURE, ALL YOU HAD TO DO WAS ASK!!
どーん
BAM
I UNDERSTAND HOW YOU FEEL, GIVEN HOW RARE THIS FIGURE IS.
HUUUH!?
カシャ
SNAP
カシャ
SNAP
カシャ
SNAP
KINJOU... WILL THINGS BE OKAY LIKE THIS...?
WHAT'S WITH THESE PICTURES ...?
HEH-HEH-HEH. YOU'LL PROBABLY NEVER RUN INTO ONE OF THESE AGAIN, SO BE SURE TO TAKE CARE OF THOSE PHOTOS.
どーん
BAM

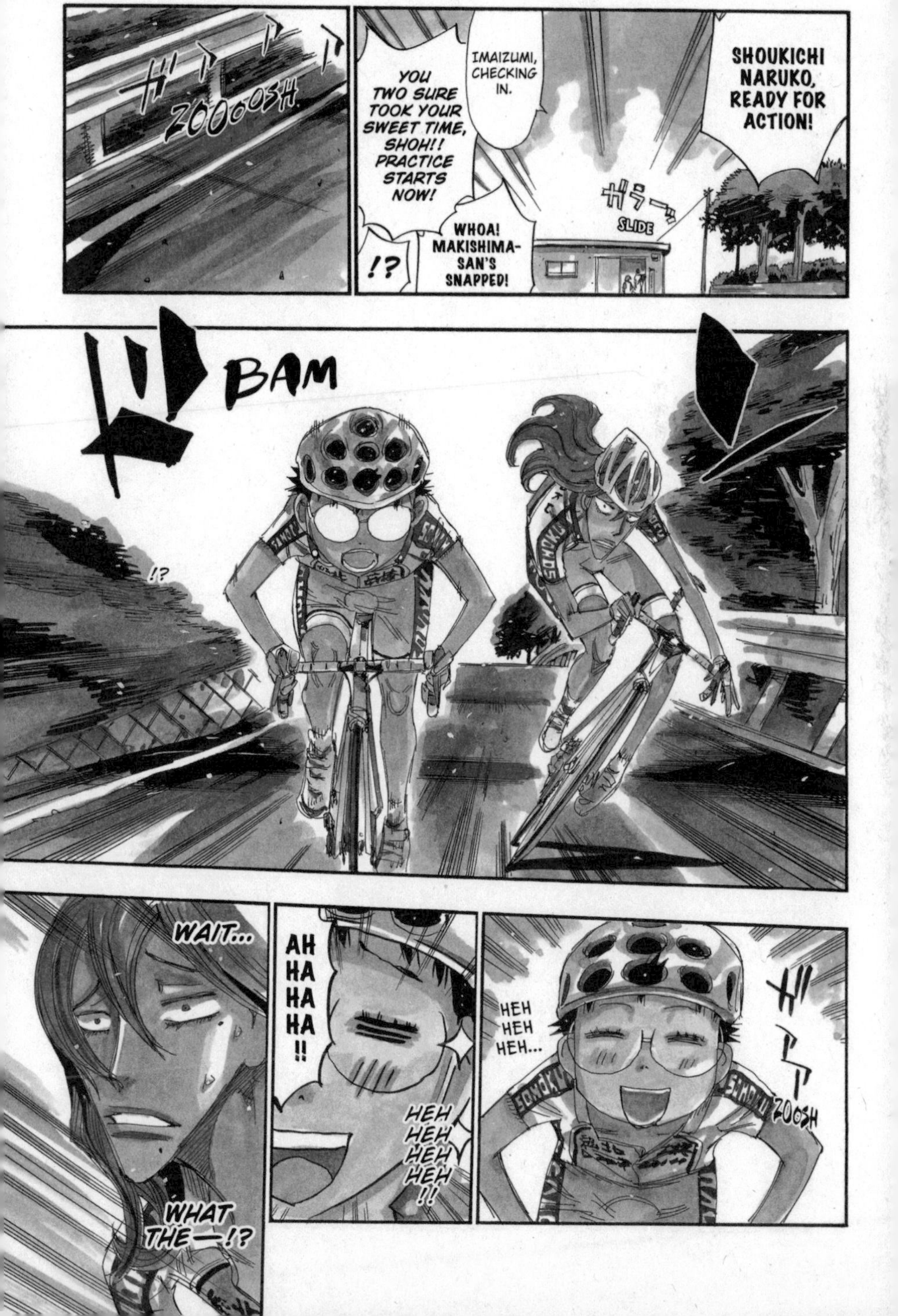
SHOUKICHI NARUKO, READY FOR ACTION!
IMAIZUMI, CHECKING IN.
YOU TWO SURE TOOK YOUR SWEET TIME, SHOH!! PRACTICE STARTS NOW!
SLIDE
WHOA! MAKISHIMA-SAN'S SNAPPED!
!?
ZOOOOSH
BAM
!?
HEH HEH HEH...
ZOOSH
AH HA HA HA!!
HEH HEH HEH HEH!!
WAIT...
WHAT THE—!?

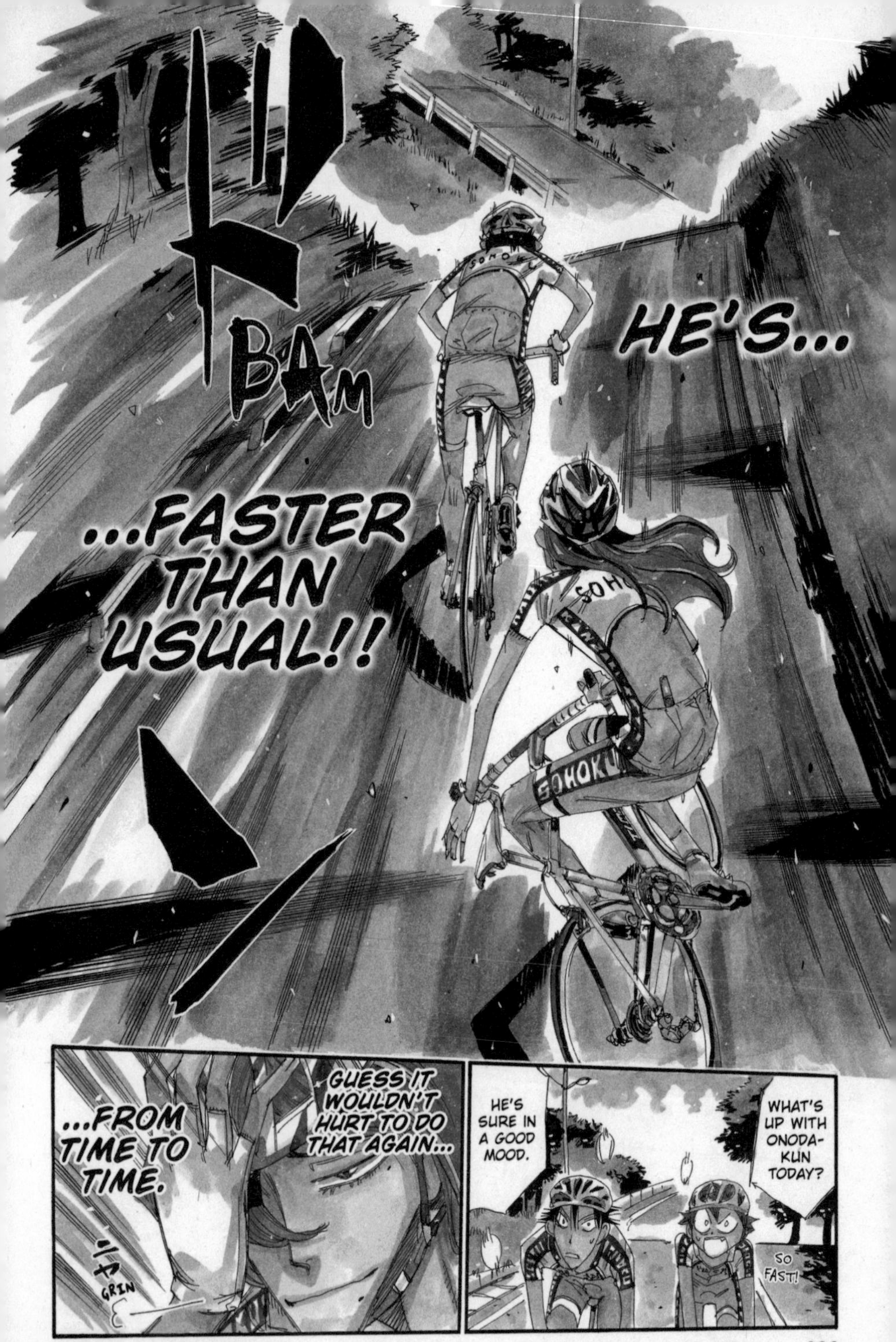
HE'S...
BAM
...FASTER THAN USUAL!!
WHAT'S UP WITH ONODA-KUN TODAY?
HE'S SURE IN A GOOD MOOD.
SO FAST!
GUESS IT WOULDN'T HURT TO DO THAT AGAIN...
...FROM TIME TO TIME.
GRIN

YOWAMUSHI PEDAL SIDESTORY/END

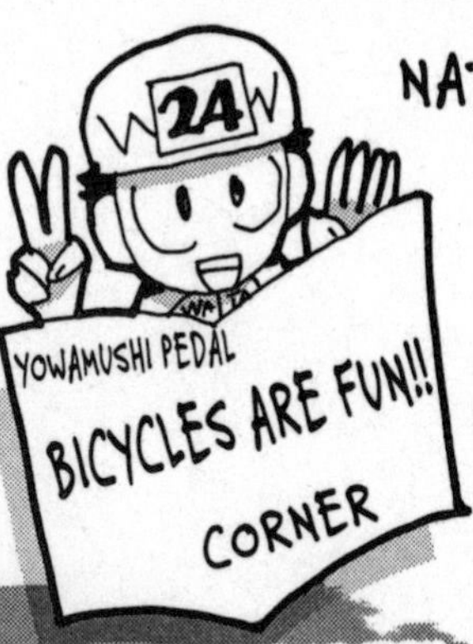
24
YOWAMUSHI PEDAL
BICYCLES ARE FUN!!
CORNER

NATURE! PERSONAL RESPONSIBILITY! PUSHING MYSELF TO MY LIMITS! THE MTB 100KM RACE GAVE ME ALL THAT AND MORE!

I RODE ANOTHER RACE THIS YEAR!! THIS TIME, IT WAS THE OTAKI SELF-DISCOVERY MTB 100KM RACE!! IT'S A BRUTAL RACE WITH A TIME LIMIT OF TEN HOURS ALONG FOREST ROADS WITH VIEWS OF CLIFFS AND SCREE SLOPES. THE ONLY SUPPORT IS AT EACH OF THE THREE CHECK-POINTS, SO YOU HAVE TO MAKE IT ON YOUR OWN STRENGTH. LITTLE DID I KNOW THAT THIS EXCITING RACE HAD ALL SORTS OF TROUBLE IN STORE FOR ME THIS YEAR...!

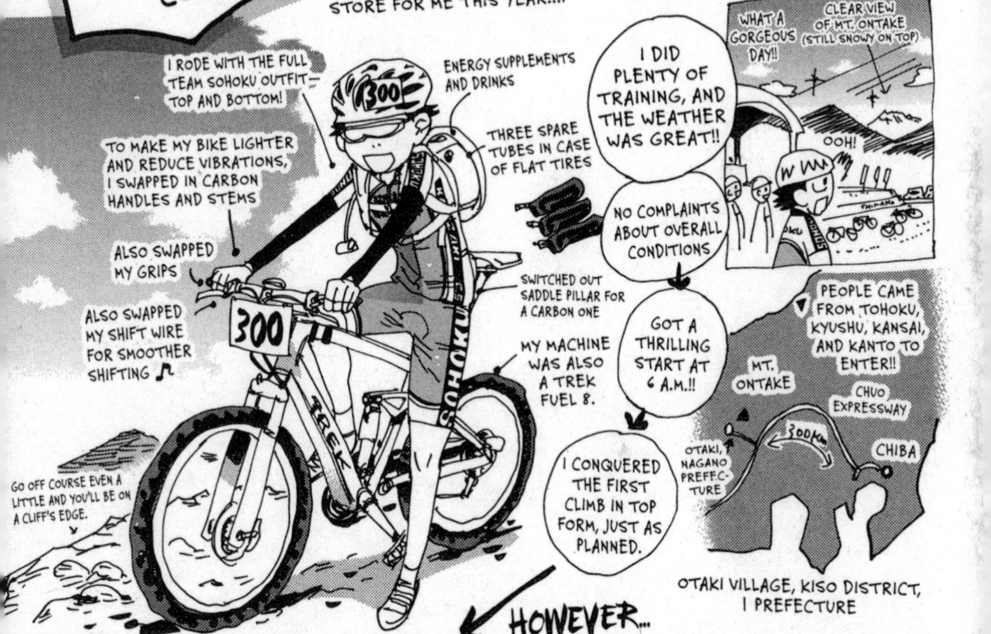
I RODE WITH THE FULL TEAM SOHOKU OUTFIT—TOP AND BOTTOM!
ENERGY SUPPLEMENTS AND DRINKS
THREE SPARE TUBES IN CASE OF FLAT TIRES
TO MAKE MY BIKE LIGHTER AND REDUCE VIBRATIONS, I SWAPPED IN CARBON HANDLES AND STEMS
ALSO SWAPPED MY GRIPS
SWITCHED OUT SADDLE PILLAR FOR A CARBON ONE
ALSO SWAPPED MY SHIFT WIRE FOR SMOOTHER SHIFTING ♫
300
MY MACHINE WAS ALSO A TREK FUEL 8.
GO OFF COURSE EVEN A LITTLE AND YOU'LL BE ON A CLIFF'S EDGE.
I DID PLENTY OF TRAINING, AND THE WEATHER WAS GREAT!!
WHAT A GORGEOUS DAY!!
CLEAR VIEW OF MT. ONTAKE (STILL SNOWY ON TOP)
OOH!
NO COMPLAINTS ABOUT OVERALL CONDITIONS
GOT A THRILLING START AT 6 A.M.!!
PEOPLE CAME FROM TOHOKU, KYUSHU, KANSAI, AND KANTO TO ENTER!!
MT. ONTAKE
CHUO EXPRESSWAY
300KM
CHIBA
OTAKI, NAGANO PREFECTURE
I CONQUERED THE FIRST CLIMB IN TOP FORM, JUST AS PLANNED.
OTAKI VILLAGE, KISO DISTRICT, I PREFECTURE
HOWEVER...

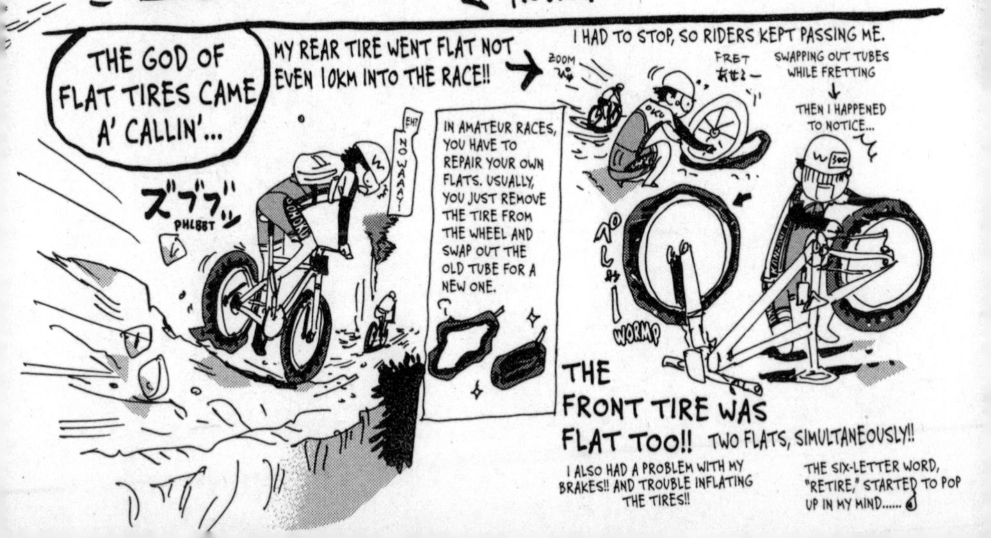
THE GOD OF FLAT TIRES CAME A' CALLIN'...
MY REAR TIRE WENT FLAT NOT EVEN 10KM INTO THE RACE!!
EH? NO WAAAY!
PHLBBT
IN AMATEUR RACES, YOU HAVE TO REPAIR YOUR OWN FLATS. USUALLY, YOU JUST REMOVE THE TIRE FROM THE WHEEL AND SWAP OUT THE OLD TUBE FOR A NEW ONE.
I HAD TO STOP, SO RIDERS KEPT PASSING ME.
ZOOM
FRET
SWAPPING OUT TUBES WHILE FRETTING
THEN I HAPPENED TO NOTICE...
WORMP
THE FRONT TIRE WAS FLAT TOO!! TWO FLATS, SIMULTANEOUSLY!!
I ALSO HAD A PROBLEM WITH MY BRAKES!! AND TROUBLE INFLATING THE TIRES!!
THE SIX-LETTER WORD, "RETIRE," STARTED TO POP UP IN MY MIND......

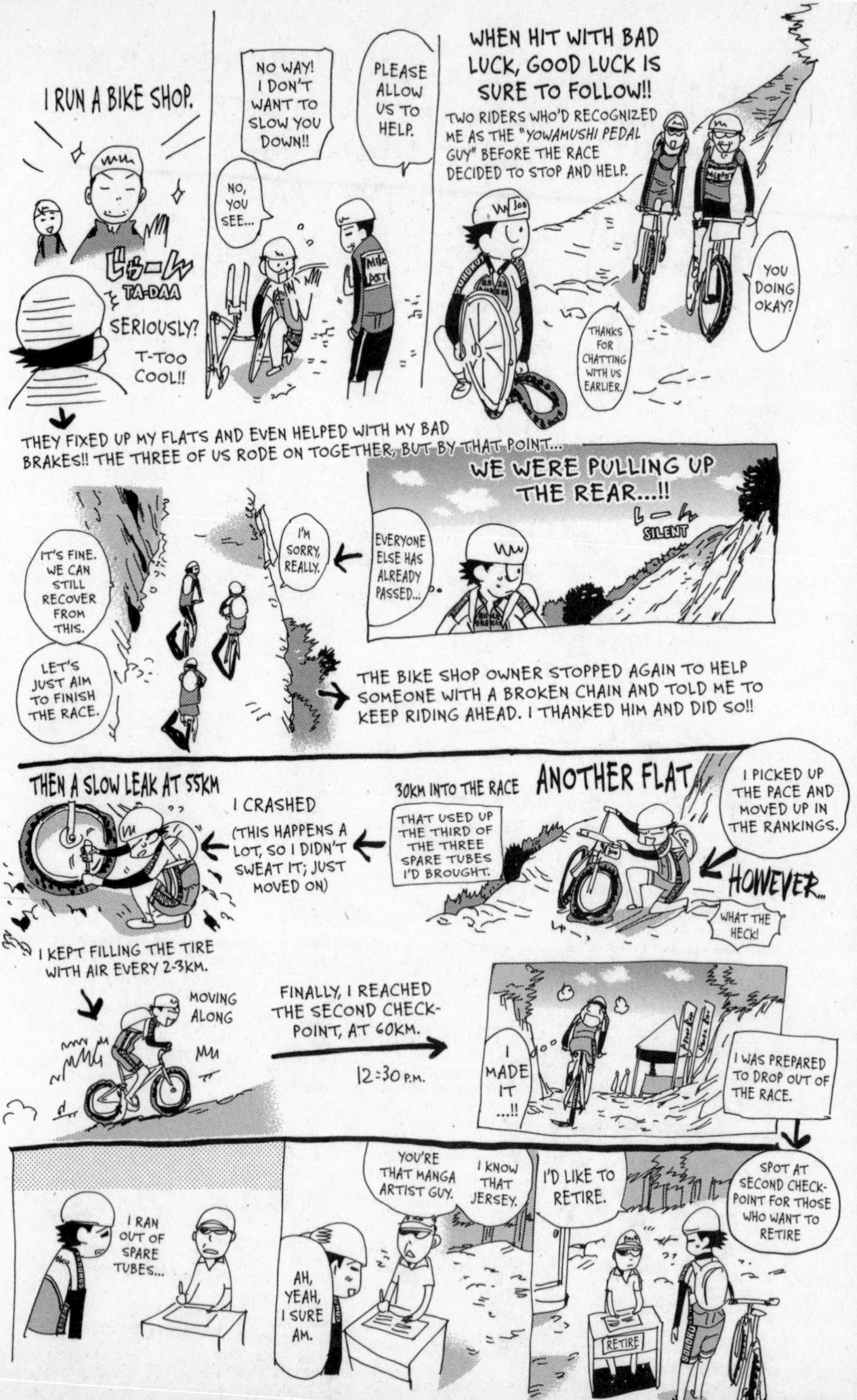
WHEN HIT WITH BAD LUCK, GOOD LUCK IS SURE TO FOLLOW!!
TWO RIDERS WHO'D RECOGNIZED ME AS THE "YOWAMUSHI PEDAL GUY" BEFORE THE RACE DECIDED TO STOP AND HELP.
YOU DOING OKAY?
THANKS FOR CHATTING WITH US EARLIER.
PLEASE ALLOW US TO HELP.
NO WAY! I DON'T WANT TO SLOW YOU DOWN!!
NO, YOU SEE...
I RUN A BIKE SHOP.
TA-DAA
SERIOUSLY?
T-TOO COOL!!
THEY FIXED UP MY FLATS AND EVEN HELPED WITH MY BAD BRAKES!! THE THREE OF US RODE ON TOGETHER, BUT BY THAT POINT...
WE WERE PULLING UP THE REAR...!!
SILENT
EVERYONE ELSE HAS ALREADY PASSED...
I'M SORRY, REALLY.
IT'S FINE. WE CAN STILL RECOVER FROM THIS.
LET'S JUST AIM TO FINISH THE RACE.
THE BIKE SHOP OWNER STOPPED AGAIN TO HELP SOMEONE WITH A BROKEN CHAIN AND TOLD ME TO KEEP RIDING AHEAD. I THANKED HIM AND DID SO!!
I PICKED UP THE PACE AND MOVED UP IN THE RANKINGS.
HOWEVER...
ANOTHER FLAT
30KM INTO THE RACE
WHAT THE HECK!
THAT USED UP THE THIRD OF THE THREE SPARE TUBES I'D BROUGHT.
I CRASHED
(THIS HAPPENS A LOT, SO I DIDN'T SWEAT IT; JUST MOVED ON)
THEN A SLOW LEAK AT 55KM
I KEPT FILLING THE TIRE WITH AIR EVERY 2-3KM.
MOVING ALONG
FINALLY, I REACHED THE SECOND CHECK-POINT, AT 60KM.
12:30 P.M.
I WAS PREPARED TO DROP OUT OF THE RACE.
I MADE IT ...!!
SPOT AT SECOND CHECK-POINT FOR THOSE WHO WANT TO RETIRE
I'D LIKE TO RETIRE.
RETIRE
I KNOW THAT JERSEY.
YOU'RE THAT MANGA ARTIST GUY.
AH, YEAH, I SURE AM.
I RAN OUT OF SPARE TUBES...

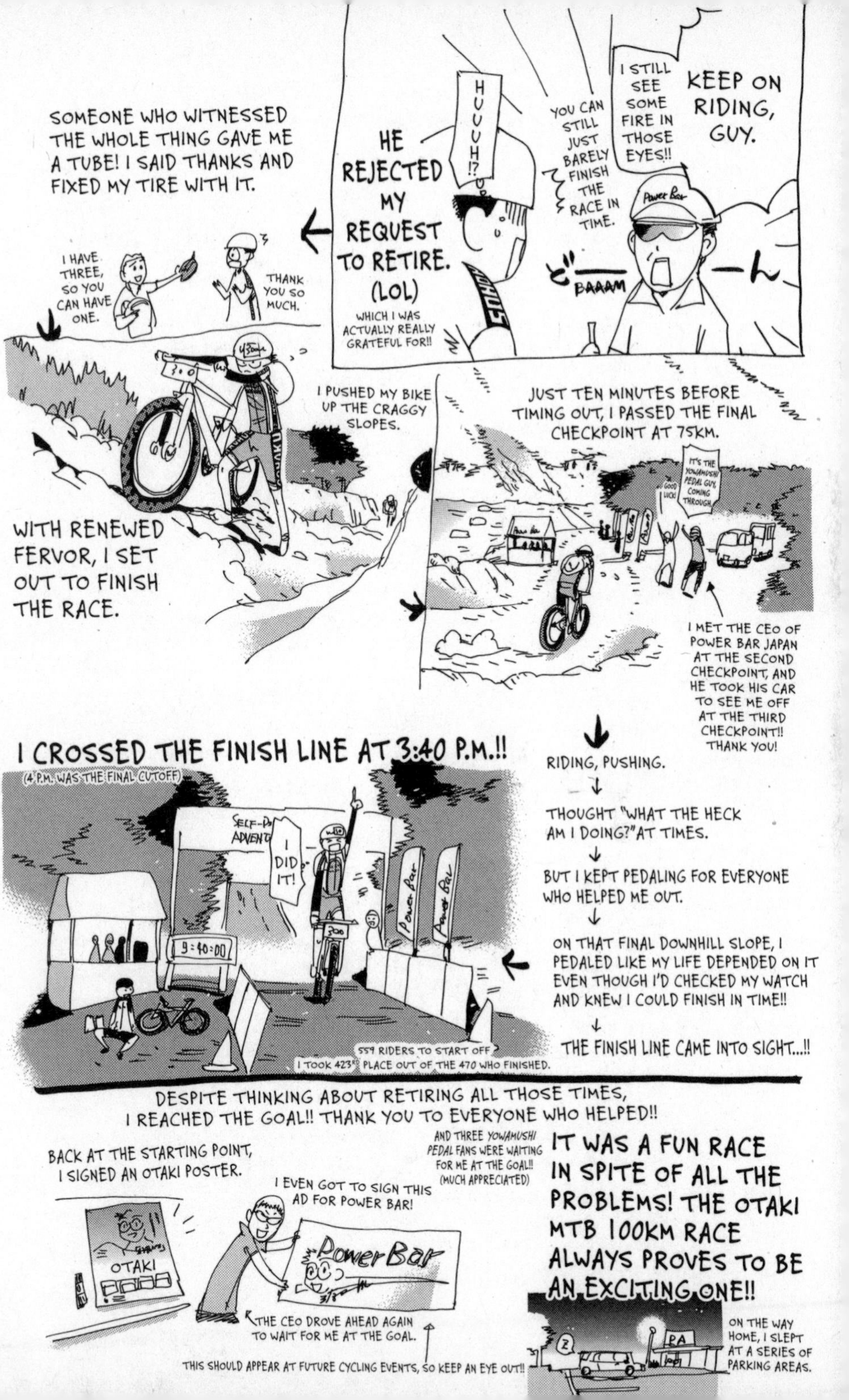
KEEP ON RIDING, GUY.
I STILL SEE SOME FIRE IN THOSE EYES!!
YOU CAN STILL JUST BARELY FINISH THE RACE IN TIME.
BAAAM
Power Bar
HUUUUH!?
HE REJECTED MY REQUEST TO RETIRE. (LOL)
WHICH I WAS ACTUALLY REALLY GRATEFUL FOR!!
SOMEONE WHO WITNESSED THE WHOLE THING GAVE ME A TUBE! I SAID THANKS AND FIXED MY TIRE WITH IT.
I HAVE THREE, SO YOU CAN HAVE ONE.
THANK YOU SO MUCH.
I PUSHED MY BIKE UP THE CRAGGY SLOPES.
WITH RENEWED FERVOR, I SET OUT TO FINISH THE RACE.
JUST TEN MINUTES BEFORE TIMING OUT, I PASSED THE FINAL CHECKPOINT AT 75KM.
IT'S THE YOWAMUSHI PEDAL GUY, COMING THROUGH.
GOOD LUCK!
I MET THE CEO OF POWER BAR JAPAN AT THE SECOND CHECKPOINT, AND HE TOOK HIS CAR TO SEE ME OFF AT THE THIRD CHECKPOINT!! THANK YOU!
RIDING, PUSHING.
THOUGHT "WHAT THE HECK AM I DOING?" AT TIMES.
BUT I KEPT PEDALING FOR EVERYONE WHO HELPED ME OUT.
ON THAT FINAL DOWNHILL SLOPE, I PEDALED LIKE MY LIFE DEPENDED ON IT EVEN THOUGH I'D CHECKED MY WATCH AND KNEW I COULD FINISH IN TIME!!
THE FINISH LINE CAME INTO SIGHT...!!
I CROSSED THE FINISH LINE AT 3:40 P.M.!!
(4 P.M. WAS THE FINAL CUTOFF)
I DID IT!
Power Bar
Power Bar
9:40:00
559 RIDERS TO START OFF
I TOOK 423RD PLACE OUT OF THE 470 WHO FINISHED.
DESPITE THINKING ABOUT RETIRING ALL THOSE TIMES, I REACHED THE GOAL!! THANK YOU TO EVERYONE WHO HELPED!!
IT WAS A FUN RACE IN SPITE OF ALL THE PROBLEMS! THE OTAKI MTB 100KM RACE ALWAYS PROVES TO BE AN EXCITING ONE!!
AND THREE YOWAMUSHI PEDAL FANS WERE WAITING FOR ME AT THE GOAL!! (MUCH APPRECIATED)
ON THE WAY HOME, I SLEPT AT A SERIES OF PARKING AREAS.
PA
Z
BACK AT THE STARTING POINT, I SIGNED AN OTAKI POSTER.
OTAKI
I EVEN GOT TO SIGN THIS AD FOR POWER BAR!
PowerBar
THE CEO DROVE AHEAD AGAIN TO WAIT FOR ME AT THE GOAL.
THIS SHOULD APPEAR AT FUTURE CYCLING EVENTS, SO KEEP AN EYE OUT!!

Translation Notes

Common Honorifics
-san: The Japanese equivalent of Mr./Mrs./Miss. If a situation calls for politeness, this is the fail-safe honorific.
-kun: Used most often when referring to boys, this indicates affection or familiarity. Occasionally used by older men among their peers, but it may also be used by anyone referring to a person of lower standing.
-chan: An affectionate honorific indicating familiarity used mostly in reference to girls; also used in reference to cute persons or animals of either gender.
-senpai: A suffix used to address upperclassmen or more experienced co-workers.
-shi: A more formal version of *san* common to written Japanese, it's the default honorific used in newspapers.
no honorific: Indicates familiarity or closeness; if used without permission or reason, addressing someone in this manner would constitute an insult.

A kilometer is approximately .6 of a mile.

PAGE 15
Hakone: A town located in a mountainous area of Kanagawa Prefecture, it's popular among tourists for its scenic views and hot springs.

PAGE 29
Naniwa: An archaic name for Osaka.

PAGE 172
Kyoto: Former capital of Japan located in the Kansai region. It's known for its plethora of traditional Japanese architecture, having come out of World War II relatively unscathed.

PAGE 173
Midosuji is referencing an old Japanese *warabeuta* (children's tune) called "Toryanse" that often accompanies a stop-and-go game much like London Bridge is Falling Down. The traditional lyrics refer to the narrow path to Tenjin Shrine, but Midousuji's destination is Mt. Fuji, of course.

PAGE 187
Domestique: A cyclist in a competitive team who focuses on helping the team and the ace over winning the race themselves.

PAGE 196
Goofs: Midousuji uses the term *zaku* in the Japanese version, which means "assorted vegetables for *sukiyaki* hot pot" but is also the name of the common enemy robot in the anime *Mobile Suit Gundam*. The former meaning refers to the rest of Kyoto-Fushimi being there to serve Midousuji, while the latter refers to how Midousuji treats his teammates as generic and interchangeable.

PAGE 213
Wussyzumi: In the Japanese version, Midousuji calls Imaizumi "Yowaizumi," playing off of the Japanese word for weak [*yowai*].

PAGE 297
Peloton: A cycling term for the "pack," or the main group of riders in a race.

PAGE 334
Chiba: A prefecture in the Kantou region of Japan. Chiba has both long stretches of mountains and large areas of flat plains, and is known for having mild summers and winters.

PAGE 380
Gachapon: Capsule toys that you can find in coin-operated toy vending machines around Japan.

PAGE 387
MTB: Acronym for "mountain bike."

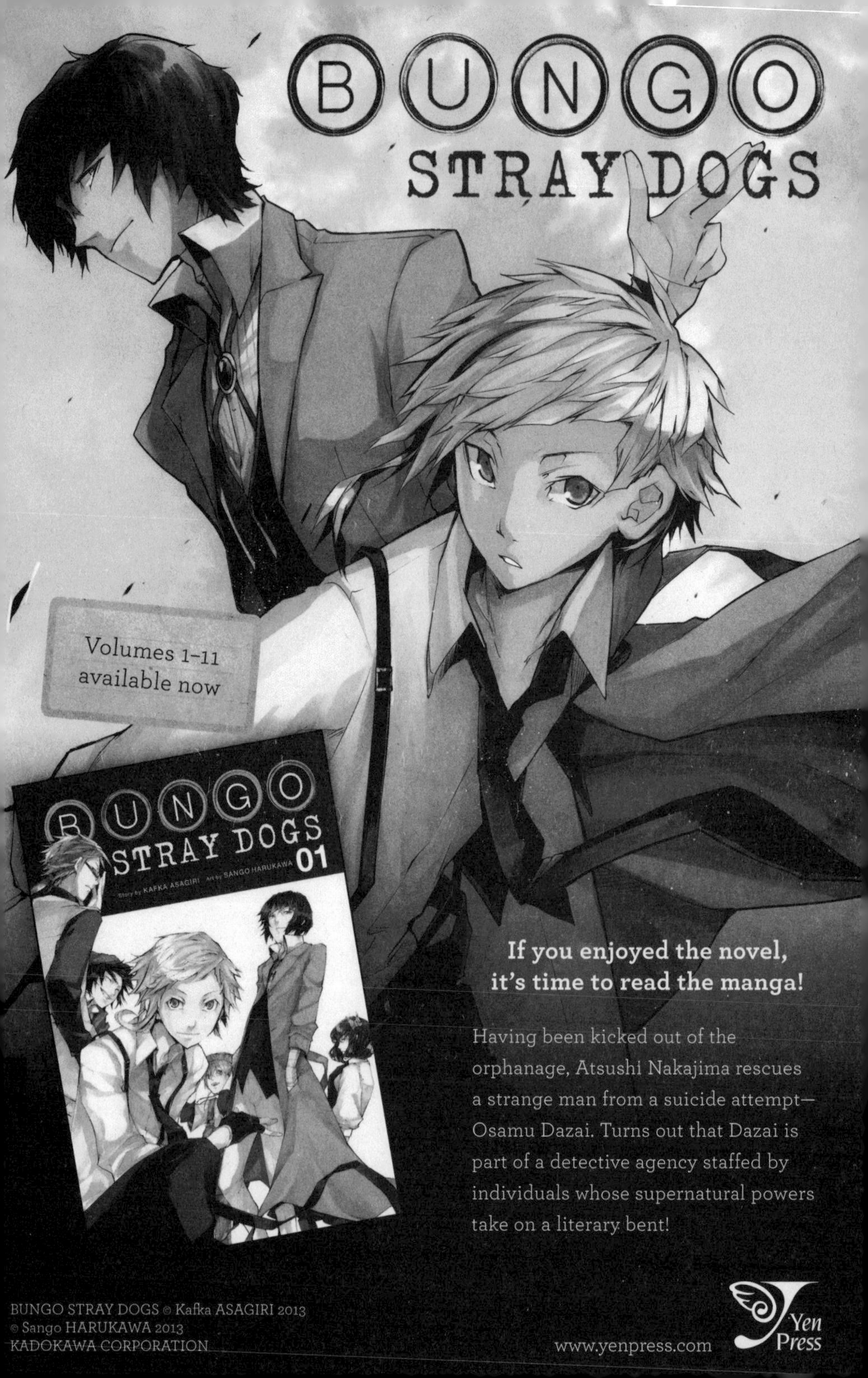
BUNGO
STRAY DOGS
Volumes 1–11
available now
BUNGO
STRAY DOGS
01
Story by KAFKA ASAGIRI Art by SANGO HARUKAWA
If you enjoyed the novel,
it's time to read the manga!
Having been kicked out of the orphanage, Atsushi Nakajima rescues a strange man from a suicide attempt—Osamu Dazai. Turns out that Dazai is part of a detective agency staffed by individuals whose supernatural powers take on a literary bent!
BUNGO STRAY DOGS © Kafka ASAGIRI 2013
© Sango HARUKAWA 2013
KADOKAWA CORPORATION
www.yenpress.com
Yen
Press

Two girls, a new school, and the beginning of a beautiful friendship.

Volumes 1-9
available now

CANNO

Kiss & White Lily for My Dearest Girl

In middle school, Ayaka Shiramine was the perfect
student: hard-working, with excellent grades and a great
personality to match. As Ayaka enters high school she
expects to still be on top, but one thing she didn't account
for is her new classmate, the lazy yet genuine genius
Yurine Kurosawa. What's in store for Ayaka and Yurine
as they go through high school...together?

Death doesn't stop a video game-loving shut-in from going on adventures and fighting monsters!

KONOSUBA: GOD'S BLESSING
ON THIS
WONDERFUL WORLD!

IN STORES NOW

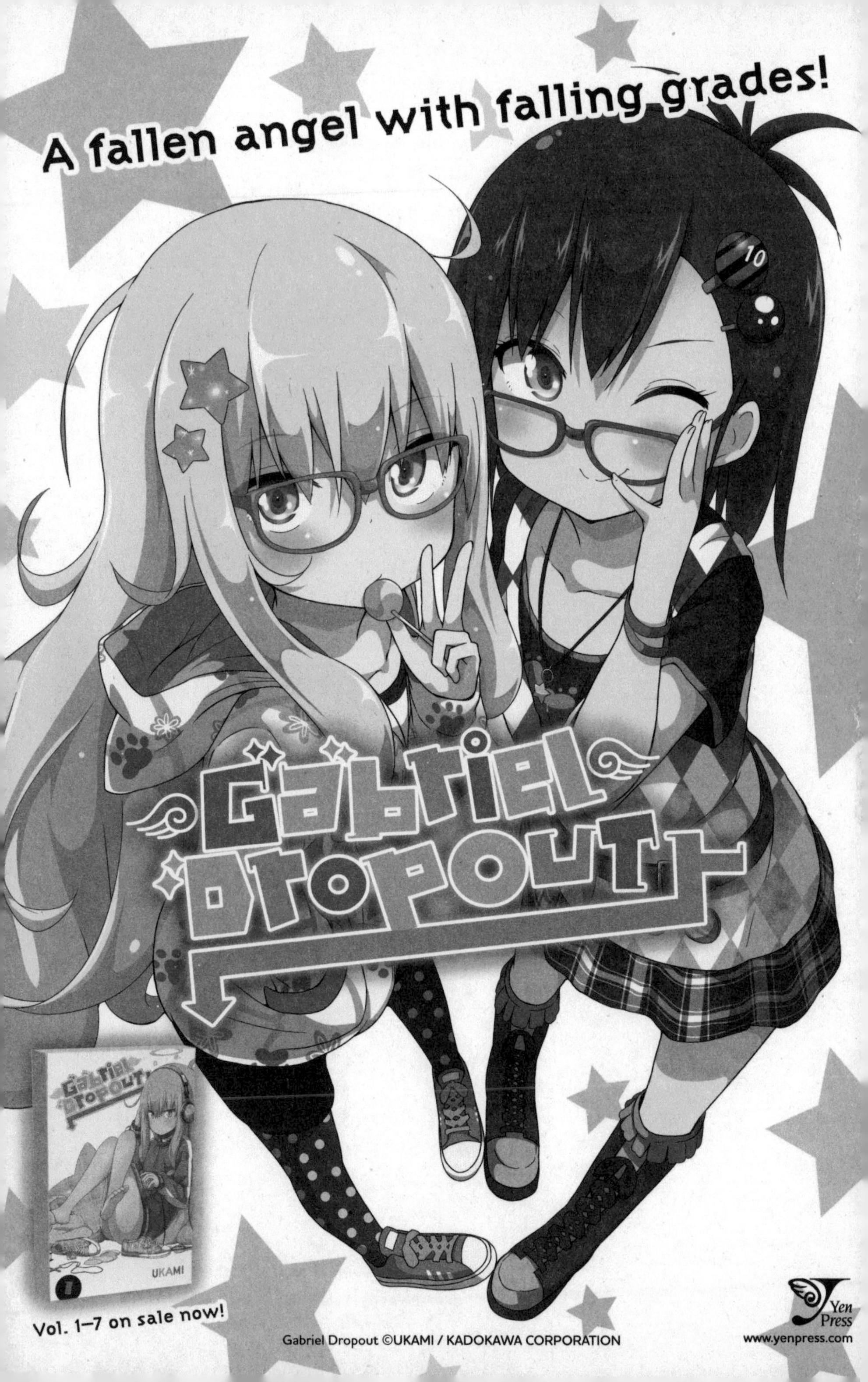
A fallen angel with falling grades!
Gabriel Dropout
Gabriel Dropout
UKAMI
1
Vol. 1–7 on sale now!
Gabriel Dropout ©UKAMI / KADOKAWA CORPORATION
Yen Press
www.yenpress.com

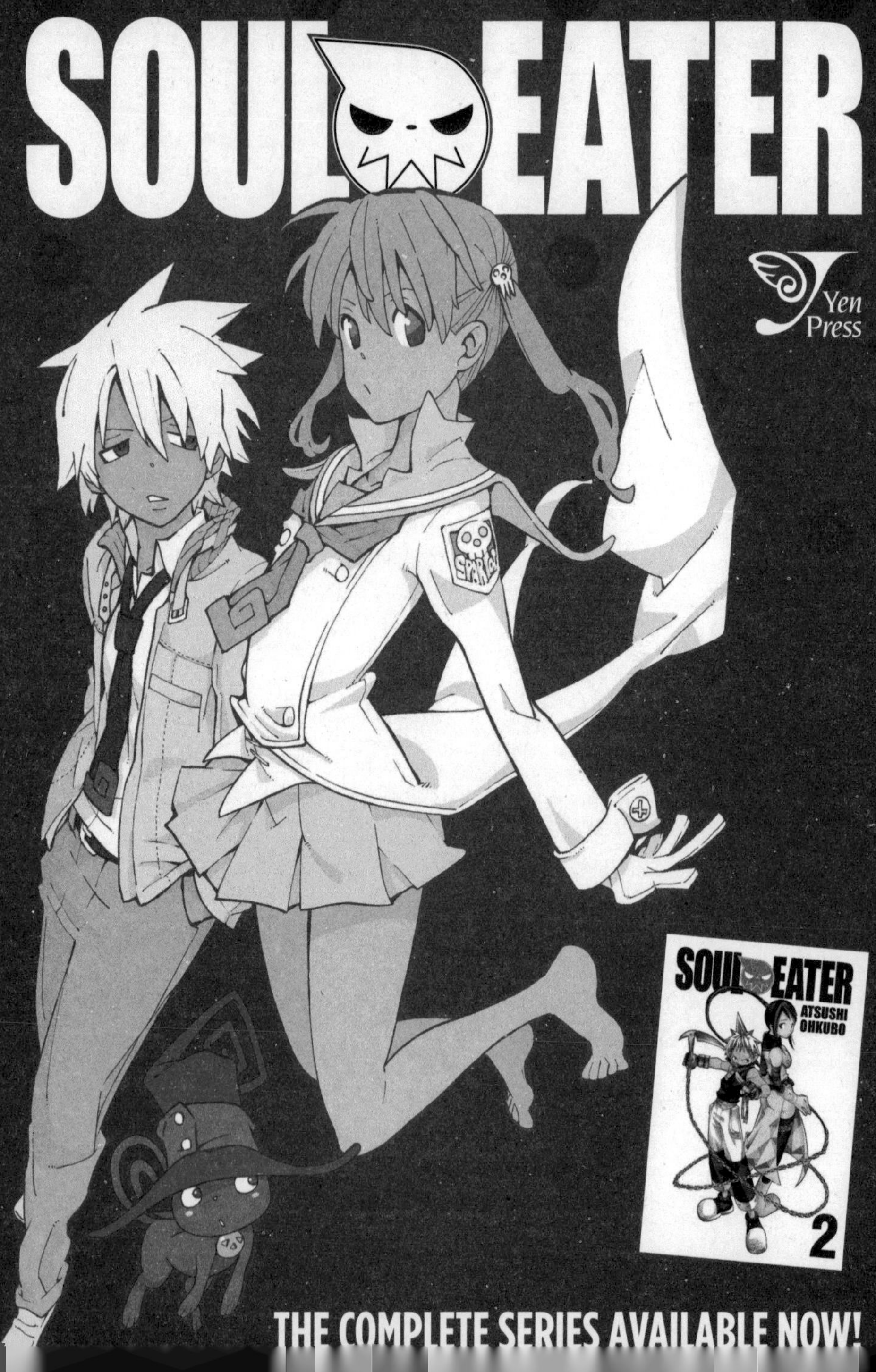
SOUL EATER
Yen Press
SOUL EATER
ATSUSHI OHKUBO
2
THE COMPLETE SERIES AVAILABLE NOW!

SOUL EATER NOT!

The
Phantomhive
family has a butler
who's almost too
good to be true...

...or maybe
he's just too
good to be
human.

Black Butler

YANA TOBOSO

VOLUMES 1-27 IN STORES NOW!

PRESENTING THE LATEST SERIES FROM

JUN MOCHIZUKI

THE CASE STUDY OF VANITAS

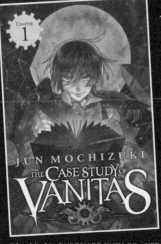

JUN MOCHIZUKI
THE CASE STUDY OF
VANITAS

**READ THE CHAPTERS AT
THE SAME TIME AS JAPAN!**

**AVAILABLE NOW WORLDWIDE
WHEREVER E-BOOKS ARE SOLD!**

www.yenpress.com

YOWAMUSHI PEDAL ⑫

WATARU WATANABE

Translation: Caleb D. Cook

Lettering: Lys Blakeslee, Rachel J. Pierce

YOWAMUSHI PEDAL Volume 23, 24
© 2012 Wataru Watanabe
All rights reserved.
First published in Japan in 2012 by Akita Publishing Co., Ltd., Tokyo.
English translation rights arranged with Akita Publishing Co., Ltd. through Tuttle-Mori Agency, Inc., Tokyo.

English translation © 2019 by Yen Press, LLC

Yen Press
150 West 30th Street, 19th Floor
New York, NY 10001

Visit us at yenpress.com
facebook.com/yenpress
twitter.com/yenpress
yenpress.tumblr.com

First Yen Press Edition: September 2019

Yen Press is an imprint of Yen Press, LLC.
The Yen Press name and logo are trademarks of Yen Press, LLC.

Library of Congress Control Number: 2015960124

ISBNs: 978-0-316-52099-7 (paperback)
       978-0-316-52101-7 (ebook)

10 9 8 7 6 5 4 3 2 1

WOR

Printed in the United States of America